Eleanor Roosevelt

BLANCHE WIESEN COOK

Eleanor Roosevelt

VOLUME TWO

1933–1938

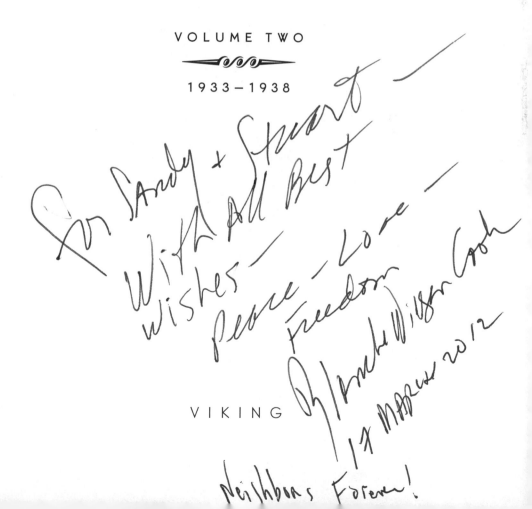

VIKING

For Sandy + Stuart With All Best Wishes — Peace — Love — Freedom

Blanche Wiesen Cook

17 March 2012

Neighbors Forever!

VIKING
Published by the Penguin Group
Penguin Putnam Inc., 375 Hudson Street, New York, New York 10014, U.S.A.
Penguin Books Ltd, 27 Wrights Lane, London W8 5TZ, England
Penguin Books Australia Ltd, Ringwood, Victoria, Australia
Penguin Books Canada Ltd, 10 Alcorn Avenue, Toronto, Ontario, Canada M4V 3B2
Penguin Books (N.Z.) Ltd, 182–190 Wairau Road, Auckland 10, New Zealand

Penguin Books Ltd, Registered Offices:
Harmondsworth, Middlesex, England

First published in 1999 by Viking Penguin,
a member of Penguin Putnam Inc.

1   3   5   7   9   10   8   6   4   2

PHOTOGRAPH CREDITS
In first photo section, pages 1 (top), 2 (top), 8 (top), 9 (below), 16 (below):
Corbis/Bettmann; 7 (top), 12 (top): AP/World Wide Photos; 12 (center): West Virginia & Regional History Collection, West Virginia University Libraries; 12 (below):
Arthurdale Heritage.
In second photo section, pages 3 (top and below), 4 (top and below), 5 (top),
7 (top), 8 (top), 9 (top), 11 (top), 12 (top and below), 15 (top and below):
Corbis/Bettmann; 5 (below), 6 (top), 8 (below), 14 (below): AP/World Wide Photos;
11 (below): Bachrach; 13: the Estate of Margaret Bourke-White.
All other photographs courtesy of the Franklin D. Roosevelt Library.

LIBRARY OF CONGRESS CATALOGING IN PUBLICATION DATA
Cook, Blanche Wiesen.
Eleanor Roosevelt, Volume One 1884–1933 / Blanche Wiesen Cook.
p.   cm.
Includes bibliographical references and index.
ISBN 0-670-80486-X (hc.)
ISBN 0 14 00.9460 1 (pbk.)
1. Roosevelt, Eleanor, 1884–1962.   2. Presidents—United States—Wives—
Biography.   I. Title.
E807.1.R48C66   1992
973.917'092—dc20
[B]   87-40632
ISBN 0-670-84498-5 (v. 2)

This book is printed on acid-free paper.
∞
Printed in the United States of America
Set in Minion
Designed by Francesca Belanger

TO MY MOTHER, SADONIA ECKER WIESEN

a constant inspiration

"Someone sent me a most amusing present of a goldfish bowl. I doubt if anyone living in the White House needs such a reminder . . . So, if I may offer a thought in consolation to others who for a time have to live in a goldfish bowl, it is: 'Don't worry because people know all that you do, for the really important things about anyone are what they are and what they think and feel, and the more you live in a "goldfish bowl" the less people really know about you!' "

(*My Day*, 7 January 1936)

"If you care for your own children, you must take an interest in all, for your children must go on living in the world made by all children."

—ER to the Southern Women's Democratic Union, New York; in the *New York Times*, 26 February 1933

"Peace time can be as exhilarating to the daredevil as wartime. There is nothing so exciting as creating a new social order."

—ER in the *New York Times*, 29 December 1933

"I think we had better begin to decide whether we wish to preserve our civilization or whether we think it of so little use that we might as well let it go. That is what war amounts to."

—ER, "Ways of Peace," 1936

"How men hate women in a position of real power!"

—ER to Lorena Hickok, concerning Frances Perkins, 1937

"What a nuisance hearts are, and yet without them life would hardly be worth while!"

—ER to Lorena Hickok, 20 February 1935

"How I hate doing these things and then they say someday I'll run for an office. Well, I'd have to be chloroformed first! [But if it improves these terrible] conditions even a little bit I suppose it is worth it. . . ."

—ER to Lorena Hickok, February 1935

"I think the day of selfishness is over; the day of really working together has come, and we must learn to work together all of us, regardless of race or creed or color. . . . We go ahead together or we go down together. . . .

—ER, 11 May 1934 Washington Conference on Negro Education

"Don't dry up by inaction but go out and do things. . . . Don't believe what somebody else tells you, but know things by your own contacts with life. If you do that you will be of great value to the community and the world."

—ER to Todhunter graduates, 3 June 1938

PREFACE AND ACKNOWLEDGMENTS

Everyone of a certain age, in every part of the United States, has an Eleanor Roosevelt story. Some say she was a good wife but a bad mother, a good friend but a bad wife, a bad woman with Communist friends, a good woman with Communist friends, a reckless and wicked activist with black friends, a good and visionary leader with black friends. Her life continues to illuminate our ongoing political and social divides. She is bellwether and key to the enduring controversies of the twentieth century.

To contemplate ER's life and times has been an exciting journey, a quest filled with discovery and surprise, agony and delight. ER wrote or dictated countless words many hours each day, every day. There are miles and mountains of ER's words, and those written by hand are often difficult to decipher. Even her great friend Lorena Hickok was occasionally perplexed. On 20 May 1937, Hick queried: "What is it you offer to send me, a Bible or a Girdle? . . . Since you mention it right after something about your riding and spell it with a small 'b'—it might be a bridle. On the other hand, I have no horse, so a Bible would make better sense. I'm very curious!"

Words ER dictated, and typed, are frequently connected to long reports, official papers, articles, columns, books—endless material to document many facts, especially the details and strategies of ER's influence and power.

My gratitude to the archivists and researchers who facilitated the search through the hundreds of manuscript boxes that comprise Series 70 at the FDR Library is profound. My former graduate student Paula Gardner coordinated a splendid team to look through each box. Without the excavations and photocopies made by Paula Gardner, Sue Murray, and Renah Feldman, this would have been a different book.

As with Volume I, this book could not have been written without the involvement of good friends, scholars and activists working for women's rights, peace, and justice.

Clare Coss was partner and companion throughout the research, writing, and editing process. As far as possible, we retraced ER's steps and met people who knew her in Greenwich Village, Washington, Detroit, Saint Louis, Chicago, and Campobello; at Arthurdale: in Warm Springs and Roswell, Georgia; in the high Sierra of Yosemite National Park; in San Francisco and Los Angeles.

We toured Arthurdale and the surrounding region with Women's International League for Peace and Freedom and environmental activists Regina Birchem and Dan Boleff. Their knowledge of Appalachia, the coal counties and devastated rust-belt areas so in need of another New Deal and other Arthurdales, dramatized all the information we gleaned as we visited Arthurdale, West Virginia, and Norvelt, Pennsylvania.

I am particularly grateful to Arthurdale Heritage Foundation's excellent staff—especially Bryan Ward, Deanna Hornyak, and historian Barbara Howe—and enthusiastic residents, including Marilee Hall and Annabell Meyer, for an unforgettable journey in time and community. As Bryan Ward noted, Arthurdale may have been dismissed as a wasteful failure, but the 165 homes on three to five acres never failed the people. Of the original homesteaders and their descendants, eighty-three percent are still there—private home owners, who were once given an opportunity to work and survive by their government.

For all the snickers about waste and losses, for ER and the people of Arthurdale, it represented security, and it remains a usable model to end homelessness and deprivation, urban crowding and rural waste. It is a program for national development and housing security urgently needed, yet to be seriously considered.

In Norvelt, Pennsylvania, Mary Wolk, then eighty-nine, took a day to tour us through the American Friends Service Committee model community for miners and steel workers, where Clarence Pickett and ER encouraged Doris Duke to consider privately funding model-home building, which she did. Mary Wolk thought the community should be called Brightness because everything "was so bright and airy and the future seemed so bright." But the town unanimously voted to name it after Eleanor Roosevelt, Norvelt, "and that was prefect."

The Atlanta Historical Society facilitated a marvelous March 1994 week that Clare and I spent contemplating ER's southern roots. From Atlanta to Bulloch Hall, the home of her paternal grandmother Mittie Bulloch, one takes a short drive to Roswell, Georgia, where administrator Pam Humphries and docent Deborah Gammon gave us a cordial tour through the home and grounds. From there, we drove to Warm Springs and benefited from the tour and materials given us by Beverly Bulloch, director of development, and Diane Blanks.

We are especially grateful to them, and to the residents of Warm Springs who opened their homes and shared their memories with us.

Hillary Rodham Clinton kindly arranged a tour through the family and private quarters of the White House. Curators Betty Monkman and Lydia Tederick generously prepared archival material and photographs to illustrate Roosevelt arrangements, including the seven-drawer highboy FDR at some point placed as barrier in front of his wife's connecting door.

In New York City, Dean Dresser thoughtfully arranged our visit to ER's private Greenwich Village retreat, rented from Esther Lape, at 20 East 11th Street; and Pat Paterline took time to tour us through ER's 1930's sanctuary.

For a delightful visit to Hick's Little House on the Dana estate at Mastic Beach in Center Moriches, I want to thank Doris Dana for her tour into the past with Hick and her father, Bill Dana; and the current owner, Anne Farr for her consideration and assistance.

Over the years, Clare and I visited Campobello several times. I am particularly grateful for the weekend seminar arranged by Linda Cross Godfrey, where we enjoyed the hospitality and warmth of that rugged island's local residents: Evelyn Bowden, Vera Calder, Elayne Gleason, Bette Lank, Cecille Matthews, Kathleen MacFeat, Lena Mills, Trudy Newman, Susan Plachy, and John McCarthy of the Lubec Light. I also want to thank the generous staff of the Roosevelt-Campobello International Park: Anne Newman, Carolyn Parker, and Jane Radcliffe.

A special joy of our location research was our effort to follow ER's trail to a remote lake in the High Sierra within the Yosemite National Park. We tried to get there on our own. One year, well on our way, we were turned back by a sudden electric storm, which we ignored until lightning bounced off our boots. Finally, we agreed to seek professional help. I called Elizabeth Stone O'Neill, the biographer of ranger-naturalist Carl Sharsmith and author of the beautiful *Meadow in the Sky: A History of Yosemite's Tuolumne Meadows Region*. We had never met, but I admired her books and was determined to get to Lake Roosevelt. She promised to find "the perfect guides," and introduced us to Ann Abbott.

Ann coordinated our trip to Lake Roosevelt, with intrepid Sierra Club guide Victoria Hoover, who forged the path to our goal. In July 1994, fifty years after ER and Hick camped at Lower Young Lake, we imagined ER's steps from there to the long, narrow mysterious lake named in her honor. We decided to go on foot, though ER rode on horseback. You cannot actually see this glacial lake until you are virtually upon it. Above the tree line, surrounded by meadows of tiny wildflowers, heather and snowbanks, it ripples with ice throughout the year. We presumed that after her journey, ER dove right in— and so did we. I am deeply grateful to Vicki Hoover, Ann Abbot, and Clare

Coss for this incomparable lifetime adventure; and to Betty and Carroll O'Neill for all we have subsequently experienced together in the High Sierra.

After our Yosemite trips, we visited in San Francisco with Agar and Diana Roosevelt Jaicks; Andy and Janet Roosevelt Katten, and Eleanor Roosevelt II. I am deeply grateful to ER's nieces for their family albums and many resources and I cherish their friendship and support for this project.

I am thankful to Jack Meyer, in Los Angeles, who arranged a most moving visit with ER's great friend Mayris (Tiny) Chaney and her daughter Michelle Martin.

Biographers and historians depend on archives and libraries, and I deeply value the important work done by the keepers of ER-related papers. The FDR Library is a congenial and helpful environment, enhanced by the concern and diligence of its professional staff, Frances Seeber, John Ferris, Mark Renovitch, Hallie Galligan, Susan Elter, Paul McLaughlin, and Ray Teichman, among others.

The Columbia University Oral History Project, under the superb direction of Ron Grele, is a unique resource for ER. I want to thank Tobias Markowitz for his research into the many interviews at Columbia, and Frances Madeson for her year as research assistant in New York's magnificent Public Library archives.

I want to acknowledge archivists at Harvard University Houghton Library, and the staff at the Schlesinger Library at Radcliffe. Until her untimely death, the hospitality of Schlesinger's director Pat King made every visit to Cambridge a delight. I particularly appreciate the kindnesses of Eva Mosely, Susan Van Sorlis, and Barbara Haber; and researcher Heidi Sander.

At the Walter Reuther Library at Wayne State University, I thank archivist Warner Pflug and research assistant Sandy Kimberly. I am, as always, grateful to David Wigdor, at the library of Congress, and at the State Department Historical office to David Patterson and William Slaney. For materials relating to Washington's Housing Commission, Dorothy Provine of the District of Columbia Archives is a treasured resource.

In Arizona, I am indebted to Harold Clarke and Bert Drucker for use of the Esther Lape collection in their possession; and to the archivists at the Arizona Historical Society, which houses the Isabella Greenway collection, notably Adelaide Elm and Rosemary Adeline Byrne. I am grateful to Isabella Greenway's son John Greenway for his memories and insights, and to Harold, Mary, and Bill Coss, Annette Kolodny and Dan Peters, for their hospitality in Tucson.

I appreciate the steady commitment of the overworked, efficient, and skilled editorial team at Viking: Barbara Grossman, Courtney Hodell, Reeve

Chace, Beena Kamlani, and Wendy Wolf. Deftly, and with good cheer, Beena and Wendy helped trim, shape, and shepherd a towering historical pile into a liftable volume. I hope readers will peruse the footnotes, the last refuge for exiled material.

Charlotte Sheedy, forever friend and agent, was always available for advice, encouragement, and comfort.

Many friends, students, and colleagues generously shared their research with me, pointed me to additional sources, sent books, articles, precious documents. I thank Mimi Abramovitz, Christie Balka, Maureen Beasley, Louise Bernikow, Allida Black, Adrienne Fried Block, Renate Bridenthal, Chris Brown, Joseph Ceretto, Anni Chamberlain, Sandi E. Cooper, Page Delano, Louise DeSalvo, Candace Falk, Abe Fenster, Joanne Grant, Bill Hannegan, Elizabeth Harlan, Alice Kessler-Harris, Susan Heske, June Hopkins, Glenn Horowitz, Mim Kelber, William Loren Katz, Susan Koppelman, Barbara Kraft, Brooke Kroger, Andy Lancet, Richard Lieberman, Deborah Ann Light, Thomas Litwack, John F. McHugh, Midge Mackenzie, Gerald Markowitz, Trudy Mason, Ted Morgan, David Nasaw, Marilyn Niemark, Ernest Nives, Eleanor Pam, Nancy Pinchot Pitman, Marjory Potts, David Rattray, Gerda Ray, Merle and Martin Rubin, Scott Sandage, Pierre Sauvage, Dagmar Schultz, Barbara Sicherman, Gloria Steinem, Alisa Solomon, Martha Swain, Amy Swerdlow, the late Patricia Spain Ward, David Wyman, and Larry Wittner. There were many others, and endless kindnesses; I apologize for those names momentarily missed.

I deeply appreciate Dr. Michael Brody's gift of the facts and documents of ER's relationship with the Brodsky family, and Eleanor Lund Zartman's memories of her aunt, ER's closest assistant, Malvina (Tommy) Thompson.

William P.T. Preston's many feats of friendship included rare books, and a deck upon which to relive the days of the Southern Conference on Human Welfare with Virginia Durr and Patricia Sullivan. I treasure these times, and those with Marge Frantz, concerning her father Joseph Gelders, and the SCHW; and with Abbott Simon and the late Vivian Cadden for their memories of the American Youth Congress.

Sandi E. Cooper and Alice Kessler-Harris took time out from their relentless schedules to read parts of what was initially a two-thousand-page manuscript. Gerald Markowitz read the entire manuscript, in its several incarnations, and helped transform a casual Luddite into a modern computer user. These were herculean acts of friendship and generosity, for which I am forever and profoundly grateful.

I am grateful to John Jay College's president, Gerald Lynch, and Provost Basil Wilson; to Frances Degen Horowitz at the Graduate Center; and to my generous colleagues and students. Throughout this process, I have depended on the spirit and vision of the women's biography seminar, and I thank you all.

This book, indeed my entire life, has been fueled and replenished on a regular basis by a network of love and support. In addition to those named above, a community of family and friends had sustained me; and I marvel at everybody's ability to put up with my nonsocial absorption in the past. For their forbearance and understanding, I thank my amazing mother, Sadonia Ecker Wiesen; my heroic sister, Marjorie D. W. Lessem; my nephews, Daniel Wayne and Douglas Jed Lessem; my nieces, Clare Ellen and Katie McGuire.

For hospitality and many nourishments in various locales, I am grateful to Marge Barton, Mary Frances Berry, Mindy Chateauvert, Frances Clayton, Rhonda Copelon, Marilyn Fitterman, Sharron Good, Jane and Jay Gould, Alvia Golden, Lucille Goodman, Gay Hemphill, Lyla Hoffman, Deborah Ann Light, Sandy Rapp, Claire and Jessie Reid, Patsy Rogers, Elizabeth Lorde-Rollins, Carroll Smith-Rosenberg, Lucius Ware, Leslie Weisman.

This book is in part dedicated to the memory of four women who supported and influenced this project in countless ways; their lives of example, love, and courage continue to advance ER's legacy: Bella Abzug, Diana Roosevelt Jaicks, Audre Lorde and Connie Murray.

Finally, this book would have been impossible without Clare Coss's keen discernment and galvanizing companionship. She emboldened and envigorated the entire quest.

CONTENTS

Sections of photographs follow pages 110 and 430.

Introduction

━━◖✦✦◗━━

$\mathcal{E}$leanor Roosevelt is the most controversial First Lady in United States history. Her journey to greatness, her voyage out beyond the confines of good wife and devoted mother, involved determination and amazing courage. It also involved one of history's most unique partnerships. Franklin Delano Roosevelt admired his wife, appreciated her strengths, and depended on her integrity.

ER and FDR had different priorities, occasionally competing goals, and often disagreed. Connected by trust, loyalty, and love, their partnership survived marital pain and affairs of the heart. They enjoyed different entertainments, and preferred different people. They offered different advice to their adult children whose personal lives were in turmoil. In the White House they ran two distinct and separate courts.

They were able to maintain a measure of privacy in their lives because a respectful press honored their privacy. Journalists accepted FDR's request to shield the public from his paralysis; and publishers accepted ER's intention to control information through her women-only press conferences. In 1934 when invasive reporters hounded ER on vacation with Lorena (Hick) Hickok, the First Lady responded with a high-speed auto chase that reverberates sixty years later in Princess Diana's tragic accident. ER's chase ended in a victory over unwanted publicity impossible today.

ER and FDR did not have a traditional, correct, or conventionally happy marriage; but it was one of Washington's most notably successful marriages. Fueled by power, they were each dedicated to making life better for most people. Together they did more than either could have done alone. ER served her husband's interests, and was his primary ambassador to neighborhood people, to poor and hardworking and hidden communities in the mountains and deltas of America. She brought folks who could not vote and, until the New Deal, did not count, into the mainstream of American public life. On divisive issues which he would have preferred to ignore, notably issues of race and racism, she was his conscience, proud to be on occasion his "hair shirt."

ER was forty-eight when she entered the White House. Her understanding of life and politics was informed and galvanized by love. She was surrounded by cherished friends, who rallied to her needs. Esther Lape and Elizabeth Read became closer than ever, and rented the First Lady a Greenwich Village apartment—a third floor walk-up that was her own private hideaway. Her former bodyguard and squire Earl Miller, and her friend and secretary Malvina (Tommy) Thompson, remained ER's most frequent confidantes and companions.

In 1933, ER was an accomplished woman who had achieved several of her life's goals. With her Val-Kill partners, Nancy Cook, Marion Dickerman, and Caroline O'Day, ER was a businesswoman who co-owned the Val-Kill crafts factory, a political leader who edited and copublished the *Women's Democratic News*, and an educator who co-owned and taught at a New York school for girls. Her literature and political affairs classes at the Todhunter School recalled her own education in England at Allenswood with her great teacher Marie Souvestre, who continued to inspire the paths ER chose as First Lady.

ER's friendship with Lorena Hickok was the most ardent and absorbing relationship of her middle years. Because Hick planned to write the First Lady's biography, ER sent ten- to fifteen-page daily letters to create a usable record. There was nothing simple about ER's friendship with Hick. Their times together were filled with excitement, turbulence, disappointment. Throughout her life, ER's emotions were stirred by correspondence. Beginning with her father, letters were her lifeline, the way in which she was best able to communicate her dreams, intimacies, desires.

Before she entered the White House, ER cast about for models to understand her new role and decide just what she might do from within the confines of the President's House. The record was grim, and every one of her predecessors sickened or died in the place. Washington was a lethal town for wives, with an odious history for women. Tough and resilient, ER set out to create another example. Surrounded by her own support network, she intended to survive the ordeal of First Wifery.

She was not a saint, and though often long-suffering, ER could be mean and cold and disagreeable. Initially she went everywhere with rambunctious dogs. They growled and snarled, barked and nipped, bolted and chased. Like her head housekeeper, Henrietta Nesbitt, who ruined the president's food on a regular basis, and was rude and unkind, ER's dogs represented an unacknowledged part of her character, and served various purposes. ER often admitted to feeling "low in my mind," discontented and depressed. She rarely expressed anger directly. But when she grew cold, she could freeze the stoutest heart. She never fired Henrietta Nesbitt, and she parted with her dogs only after they had lunged at several children, and bit at least one diplomat, one senator, and one friendly woman reporter.

As First Lady, Eleanor Roosevelt did things that had never been done before. She upset race traditions, championed a New Deal for women, and on certain issues actually ran a parallel administration. On housing and the creation of model communities, for example, ER made decisions and engineered policy.

At the center of a network of influential women who ran the Women's Committee of the Democratic Party led by Molly Dewson, ER worked closely with the women who had dominated the nation's social reform struggles for decades. With FDR's election, the goals of the great progressive pioneers, Jane Addams, Florence Kelley, and Lillian Wald, were at last at the forefront of the country's agenda. ER's mentors since 1903, they had battled on the margins of national politics since the 1880s for public health, universal education, community centers, sanitation programs, government responsibility for the welfare of the nation's poor and neglected people.

Now their views were brought directly into the White House. ER lobbied for them personally with her new administrative allies, in countless auditoriums, as a radio broadcaster, and in monthly, weekly, and, by 1936, daily columns. Called "Eleanor Everywhere," she was interested in everyone.

Once a shy and lonely child, a reserved and deferential young matron with five children, ER flourished in public life. During the 1930s she became a fierce warrior on the political battlefield. At the age of seventy-six, in 1960, Eleanor Roosevelt wrote *You Learn by Living*, and reflected on all she had learned at school; then as the wife of a democratic president in a time of despots. Competition and the thrill of the game of nations were at the core of her driving power. When she singled out the happiest day of her life, it was the day she made the first field hockey team at Allenswood. That sentence revealed a basic fact: ER was a very competitive woman, a team player who delighted in knockabout efforts on the muddy fields of play, and she hated to lose. She always advised her friends: "If you have to compromise, be sure to compromise UP!"

Competitive even as First Lady, she set herself the task of earning as much as FDR earned as president, $75,000.* At the end of the first year, as a result of her many lectures, articles, and commercial broadcasts, ER could write a friend: "I've done it! I've earned as much as Franklin." Today such commercially sponsored broadcasts would be considered an illegal or immoral conflict of interest, but ER rejected all criticism. She insisted that her work was useful, and she gave almost all her earnings to worthy causes.

The legacy of her childhood of tears and longing, her family grief and early abandonment, marked her life every day of her life. She was eight when her mother, Anna, died at the age of twenty-nine; and ten when her beloved father, Elliott, died of alcoholism at the age of thirty-four. From then on, she identified particularly with people in want, in need, in trouble, and devoted her time especially to those on the margins, or beyond its borders. After each visit to women's prisons, ER left haunted by the feeling that she could have been any one of the women on the inside.

There was no group beyond her concern, no people outside her imagination, no category of outsiders designated for abandonment. Every life was sacred and worthy, to be improved by education, employment, health care, affordable housing. Her goal was simple, a life of dignity and decency for all. She was uninterested in complex theories, and demanded action for betterment. She feared violent revolution, but was not afraid of socialism—and she courted radicals.

As fascism and communism triumphed in Europe and Asia, ER and FDR were certain that there was a middle way, what ER called an American "revolution without bloodshed." Her abiding conviction, however, was that nothing good would happen to promote the people's interest unless the people themselves organized to demand government responses. A people's movement required active citizen participation, and ER's self-appointed task was to agitate and inspire community action, encourage united democratic movements for change.

She forged new alliances with race radicals who began during the 1930s to challenge the entire structure of America's segregated political and cultural life. She was closest to NAACP leader Walter White, and educator Mary McLeod Bethune, founder of the National Council of Negro Women; and to white agitators Lucy Randolph Mason, Aubrey Williams, and Virginia Durr.

While FDR pursued a "Southern strategy" to keep peace with a congressional majority dominated by white supremacists who threatened mutiny with each effort to introduce a law against lynching, or economic justice for education, housing, relief, and rehabilitation, ER advocated for the biracial Southern Tenant Farmers Union created in 1934; championed the multiracial antisegregationist American Youth Congress in 1936; helped initiate—and integrate—the call for a second Reconstruction ignited by the Southern Conference on Human Welfare in Birmingham, Alabama, in 1938.

Between 1933 and 1938, while the Depression raged and the New Deal unfolded, ER worked with the popular front. Before the Soviets called for a united front alliance against Hitler in August 1935, ER called for alliances of activists to fight poverty and racism at home, and to oppose isolationism

---

* 1930s dollars are approximately ten times 1990s dollars.

internationally. She was among the first to make the connection: white supremacy, segregation, and lynching here; race violence and fascism there.

Active with the women's peace movement associated with Jane Addams, Lillian Wald, and Carrie Chapman Catt, ER spoke regularly at meetings of the Women's International League for Peace and Freedom, and Catt's Conference on the Cause and Cure of War. She departed, however, from pacifist and isolationist positions and encouraged military preparedness, collective security, and ever-widening alliances.

After the publication of *Eleanor Roosevelt, Volume I*, some people recoiled from the possibility that ER might have had passion and love in her life outside her marriage and apart from FDR. They were particularly disturbed by the presence of Earl Miller and Lorena Hickok at the heart of her story. One woman, a human rights worker, was aghast that ER had "lesbian friends, or was a lesbian, or some such thing." When asked if she read the book, she replied: "No, I wouldn't read it; I wouldn't touch it!" Such views, even on the part of those who claim to respect and admire Eleanor Roosevelt, reflect the kind of determined ignorance she worked so hard to uproot. After a lifetime of loving, with all the difficulties and contradictions love involves, it seems a peculiar and sad commentary that people who claim to know ER do not care to know about the relationships that most absorbed and concerned her.

There are still those who dismiss ER as naïve and uninformed. Books still appear that claim she knew nothing about sex or birth control. Even in 1998 a book appeared to explain: That was why she had six children and then ended relations with her husband. But ER was a lifelong member of the birth control league. She understood the facts of life, as well as where directions of the heart might lead. She actually considered love "a form of insanity." When in love one acted in unpredictable ways, often uncontrollably.

ER's life was about controversy and compromise; power and action. Between husband and wife, it was often about conflict and confrontation. On domestic issues FDR encouraged his wife to "warm up" unpopular subjects, and then he would proceed. On international issues, he discouraged ER's participation and demanded her silence as the fascist horror in Europe unfolded. These differences were the most bruising between them. ER could not remain silent over the London Economic Conference in 1933, the World Court in 1935, or the Spanish Civil War after 1936. She spoke out, and wrote articles to explain their differences.

Concerning Hitler's treatment of all those in his category of "lives not worth living," ER's silence was grievous and prolonged. Nevertheless, she struggled to remove barriers which limited hope for refugees, and she spoke to countless Jewish groups throughout the United States to demonstrate her conviction that bigotry must not be allowed to prevail here.

I contemplated ER's protracted five-year silence regarding Hitler's Europe curled in agony. As I struggled to understand it, three issues seemed significant:

Most Americans remained for so long unimpressed by Hitler's decrees against Germany's Jewish citizens because they were modeled on United States' laws against African-Americans. Humiliation, deprivation, segregation were staples of American life in the 1930s. The denial of citizen rights such as voting, access to schools, transportation, recreation facilities, park benches, swimming pools, movie houses were accepted features of life. White supremacy in the United States involved unpunished and frequent lynchings; instances of mob violence, public acts of torture and mayhem, defended as "states' rights" and somehow sacrosanct.

In that climate, to protest Hitler's atrocities would have invited world protest and condemnation of America's outrages. It was impossible. And then there was the Red Scare. From 1933 to 1938, the general feeling among democratic leaders in the United States and England, specifically among State Department officials and FDR's closest advisers, was that Hitler in Europe and Japan in Asia were forestalling communism. The Cold War was in full swing during the 1930s, and Hitler was preferable to popular front governments which included communists; and preferable to communist influence among youth, unionists, and antifascists.

As late as November 1938, British writer Vera Brittain wrote "Pacifism After Munich," in part her account of a visit to the United States, where she was "astonished by the violence of anti-German feelings amongst many peace workers . . . , for in England—except in terms of extremists who belong to the Left Book Club and the Communist Party—it is not felt with comparable vehemence."

After Kristallnacht, the mood in the United States hardened against Hitler, and it was precisely that antifascist vehemence that attracted ER to her new friends in the Southern Conference on Human Welfare and the American Youth Congress. Her alliance with the popular front began before the Spanish Civil War and lasted until it was destroyed by the Nazi-Soviet Pact in 1939.

Lastly, the 1930s was a time when human rights as a concept did not actually exist; and no nation was responsible to consider the domestic deeds of other nations. We live today in a different world. Fifty years after ER worked to place human rights on the international agenda, the Universal Declaration of Human Rights, adopted by the United Nations on 10 December 1948, every individual, citizen, committee, and nation is responsible and accountable—encouraged to protest human rights abuses, empowered to prevent ethnic cleansing, torture, lynchings, hate crimes, and genocide.

Every issue in this book is once again before us. With seven million homeless Americans, and a world nowhere at peace, it is still and again up to us—to understand, and to act on behalf of economic security, housing, health care, justice, peace. As ER's legacy continues to unfold it is fortified by national movements for civil rights, world movements devoted to human rights and the environment.

In *It's Up to the Women*, her first major book published as First Lady, ER told her 1933 readers that it was a national responsibility to educate healthy, socially engaged children who would work to preserve nature and prevent the extinction of "whole species." She foresaw desertification, and cautioned against the destruction of forests: "If one cuts down all the trees . . . the water supply will be dried up unless wherever a tree is cut another is planted. . . . One does not destroy what nature gives us to love and conserve."

Between 1933 and 1938 ER published countless articles and six books. She wrote in part for herself, to clear her mind and focus her thoughts. But she also wrote to disagree with her husband. From that time to this, no other First Lady has actually rushed for her pen to jab her husband's public decisions. But ER did so routinely, from her first condemnation of the misogynist clause in his 1933 Economy Act which resulted in the dismissal of federally employed wives, to her major 1938 essay *This Troubled World*, which was a point-by-point rejection of FDR's major international decisions.

Every event between them remains an issue before us. The experience of writing this biography between 1993 and 1998, sixty years after it all occurred, has been a painful but supremely hopeful experience. The world seemed ruined before the New Deal, and in so many places, faces ruin again. "Gloom" was a much-used word in Anglo-American circles during the 1930s. ER and her peers were forever being plunged in gloom. Now, the New Deal safety net, Social Security, public education face the wrecker; and we live through days of gloom.

To contemplate ER's life of example and responsibility is to forestall gloom. She understood, above all, that politics is not an isolated individualist adventure. She sought alliances, created community, worked with movements for justice and peace. Against great odds, and under terrific pressure, she refused to withdraw from controversy. She brought her network of agitators and activists into the White House, and never considered a political setback a permanent defeat. She enjoyed the game, and weathered the abuse. Energized by her friends and allies, she devoted some part of every day to the business of making life better for most people. To contemplate her life of action and determination is to reconsider the role of popular movements everywhere growing, reorganizing, still and again dedicated to a politics of care, love, and justice.

24 February 1999

1: Becoming First Lady

———◦/◦/◦———

*A*fter the election of November 1932, ER worried that her talents would not be used; that she would become a shut-in, a congenial hostess in the political shadows politically sidelined. In the months before FDR's inauguration on 4 March 1933, newspaper headlines broadcast the victories of fascism and tyranny in Europe and Asia as well as the intensifying agonies of America's worst economic depression. In that bitter climate, ER faced her return to Washington with a burst of activity that defied her sense of dread. Officially limited to social tasks, she felt at first burdened and defiant. Her great friend Lorena Hickok was so impressed by ER's initial distress that she titled her subsequent biography *Eleanor Roosevelt: Reluctant First Lady.*

ER wanted above all to be a player on the political team that worked to match FDR's campaign promises with significant deeds. To counter her fear that she would instead be forced into a life of political confinement somewhere in the shadows, a prisoner to the presidency, she plunged into the political fray. With the women activists of the Democratic Party, ER spent hours preparing lists of notable candidates for every level of government work. She wrote columns, stunned radio audiences, created endless controversy. The First Lady–elect was in the news almost every day—upsetting the complacent, encouraging people to imagine new liberal efforts to confront the Depression, which since October 1929 had plunged fifteen million unemployed and destitute Americans into despair.

It had been twelve years since ER's last sojourn in Washington, that small ungenerous town that had been for her filled with ragged memories. There as a child when her Uncle Theodore was president she had felt shy, lonely, outcast. There as a young matron when her husband was Woodrow Wilson's assistant secretary of the navy, she had felt humiliated, isolated. Betrayed by her husband's affair with Lucy Mercer, her friend and social secretary, she had suffered the loneliest time of her adult life.

She returned to that place that fed on gossip and power, a changed woman. Surrounded by loyal friends, she was devoted to her work, and felt secure in her life. During the 1920s, the Roosevelts had reconsecrated their partnership and created their own political bases. FDR refortified his polio-ravaged body, and ER repaired her heart; they both moved beyond the affair that had threatened their marriage.

While Eleanor and Franklin rebuilt their private lives, the world they had grown up in, the world they knew, disintegrated. The punitive Treaty of Versailles, which ended World War I and redrew the map of Europe, in addition to war debts and dizzying inflation, inflamed German nationalism and spurred popular movements dedicated to the demise of old ruling classes. Fascism and communism took hold as monarchies dissolved, empires collapsed, capitalism wobbled. While uncollected political and economic debts left over from the World War haunted and poisoned international relations, the wounds of Eleanor Roosevelt's earlier time in Washington marked her memories, and influenced her path.

After 1920, ER had carefully crafted a life that suited her needs. Like her Uncle Theodore, she was an activist—delighted to be on the move, among people, dealing directly with causes and crises. Never idle, she enjoyed many careers and was all in a day teacher, editor, columnist, and radio commentator. Her primary circle included her business and living partners Nancy Cook, Marion Dickerman, and Caroline O'Day. With Cook and Dickerman, ER shared a home two miles from the "big house" at Hyde Park along a small river called the Val-Kill. With O'Day, they co-owned the Todhunter School, the Val-Kill crafts factory, and the *Women's Democratic News (WDN)*, a monthly newsletter.

ER had resigned as editor and taken her name off the masthead as one of the four publishers when FDR was elected governor of New York in November 1928, but she had continued to write its unsigned editorials and attend policy meetings.

In February 1933, ER publicly returned to the *WDN* with a monthly column called "Passing Thoughts of Mrs. Franklin D. Roosevelt." She was to replace Elisabeth Marbury, who had regularly reported from Washington and had died suddenly of a heart attack on 22 January at the age of seventy-seven. Eager to be back in print for attribution, ER's first column was in part a tribute to Marbury, a Democratic Party stalwart and worldly raconteur.*

---

*Known as a generous hostess whose parties in partnership with her companion Elsie de Wolfe had highlighted the social season in Paris and New York before World War I, Bessie Marbury was a theater and literary agent with offices in New York, London, Paris, Berlin, and Madrid. Her clients included James M. Barrie, George Bernard Shaw, and Oscar Wilde.

Also in this first column, ER promised to provide "some pictures of the various activities that I imagine fall to the lot of every President's wife," and announced that she was free to disagree—even with her husband.

Like the country and his closest advisers, ER did not know actually what FDR intended to do as president. His priorities were unclear, since he had campaigned as both ardent liberal and fiscal conservative: He would balance the budget, and decrease taxes. Now, ER stated her own liberal goals for the administration: She disapproved of lowering taxes in the face of so many urgent social needs and wanted relief policies extended to provide work and new training for the unemployed.

In both her February column and her unsigned editorial, she emphasized the need for more public spending. She lamented recent talk about curtailing "some of these services." More services were needed, and "we will have to pay for [them] through taxes and our people might just as well face this fact. . . ."

Her views did not coincide with FDR's initial strategy, and he demanded space in the March issue to answer his wife and defend his first legislative acts. Between his mother and his wife, FDR was accustomed to outspoken opinionated women. But he did expect public unity on politically volatile issues. In the future ER would try to be more circumspect; this would be his only editorial rejoinder.

ER's views on international matters also departed from FDR's strategy. She deplored America's "isolationist" policies and considered economic nationalism dangerous. She wanted the United States to forgive the entire international debt, in order to end the worldwide depression and the rising tide of bitterness that threatened world peace. Her internationalism had become increasingly unpopular among politicians. ER worked most closely on these issues with her first feminist friends, Esther Lape and Elizabeth Read, who, through the American Foundation, campaigned for the World Court and now also promoted U.S. recognition of the Soviet Union.

ER's intimate circle also included Molly Dewson, who directed the Women's Committee of the Democratic Party; Earl Miller, her personal squire and champion; Louis Howe, the only close friend the Roosevelts shared; and Malvina (Tommy) Thompson, her hardworking secretary and personal assistant.

Born in the Bronx to an Irish mother and English father, Malvina Thompson was ER's mainstay from the time she spotted her in a Red Cross secretarial pool in 1917. She worked on every campaign after 1920, and became ER's personal secretary and administrator. Entirely loyal to ER, she was efficient, protective, and open-hearted. Tommy smoked cigarettes from morning to night, drank Scotch at day's end, and saw something funny in almost every situation. ER relied on her quick-witted support, and her fabulous sense of humor. Tommy's robust and hearty laugh lit up many tense situations, and she had a good time wherever she went.

Then, in 1932, Lorena (Hick) Hickok, a leading political reporter, was assigned by the Associated Press to cover ER during the campaign. Their friendship now eclipsed all others.

With her activist team ER contemplated the traditional fate of a First Lady. She was expected to give up her own life and stand by her man, affirming and silent.

She could not do it. Unlike her predecessors, ER claimed her right to a public role. Between Thanksgiving and Christmas 1932, she boldly broadcast her conviction that the tragic economic conditions which prevailed were due to the "blindness of a few people who perhaps do not really understand that, after all, the prosperity of the few is on a firmer foundation when it spreads to the many." She believed that everybody would soon realize there were only man-made reasons for so much deprivation in a land of overproduction. And now, because of her husband's election, she sensed a new spirit of giving all around her, and she hailed the renewed impulse toward generosity. "We are going through a time when I believe we may have, if we will, a new social and economic order."

Nevertheless, she was required by custom to give up her most public activities. She even resigned from the Todhunter School, although she loved teaching "best of all." She also agreed to end her radio broadcasts, with the hope that she might resume them.

On 3 March 1933, the eve of FDR's inauguration, she gave her last commercially sponsored broadcast in a series that had become increasingly controversial. On one occasion, she ignored prohibition and counseled women on moderate alcohol consumption. The Women's Christian Temperance Union (WCTU), and church groups attacked her as America's primary "Jezebel".

ER ended her last broadcast with a plea to her radio audience for their continued correspondence:

> The one great danger for a man in public life or for the woman who is that man's wife, is that they may be set apart from the stream of life affecting the rest of the country. It is easy in Washington to think that Washington is the country and forget that it is a small place and only becomes important as the people who live there truly represent the other parts of the country.
>
> I hope that my friends will feel as much my friends as they have always felt, and as free to talk to me and to tell me what they think as ever, and I want to know the whole country, not a little part of it.

FDR's election had imparted a vast sense of hope to a devastated nation, ER shared that sense of hope, and wanted to support him and be available to his needs.

For the inauguration, for example, ER initially announced that she intended to drive her own blue Buick convertible from New York to Washington, with her two dogs. But FDR had invited a party of cabinet members and special friends as his guests on the train, and ER told reporters that he wanted her with him, " 'so my place is there as hostess.' "

ER did not mention that she also planned to drive down with Lorena Hickok. According to Raymond Moley, then virtual leader of FDR's Brains Trust, she changed her mind after an emotional family drama. When ER announced that she "would load her roadster with belongings and drive down with a woman friend," FDR was stunned: It was the only time Moley heard him complain about his wife's independence; on this one occasion FDR wanted the entire family together.

ER consented. But then, early inauguration morning, she and Hick made a pilgrimage to the famous statue Henry Adams had erected to the memory of his wife, Clover. There, during ER's earlier years of solitude and sadness, she found strength in that holly grove while Washington gossiped about her gamboling husband and his well-known affair. Now she decided to begin her tenure as First Lady by meditating with her First Friend in the holly grove in Rock Creek Cemetery. As they sat in silence, Hick pondered ER's mood, and the power of Augustus Saint-Gaudens' statue, known as *Grief*:

> As I looked at it I felt that all the sorrow humanity had ever had to endure was expressed in that face. . . . Yet in that expression there was something almost triumphant. There was a woman who had experienced every kind of pain, every kind of suffering . . . and had come out of it serene— and compassionate. . . .

FDR's train party included his mother, Sara Delano Roosevelt; sons Elliott and James, with their wives, Betty Donner and Betsey Cushing; their two younger sons, Franklin and John, students at Groton; cabinet designates, Brains Trusters, Democratic stalwarts, and various intimates including Louis Howe, Marvin McIntyre, Missy LeHand, Grace Tully, Basil O'Connor, Henry and Elinor Morgenthau, and Dorothy and Samuel Rosenman.

While daughter Anna was already in Washington making arrangements, ER's train party included Lorena Hickok, Earl Miller, Nancy Cook and Marion Dickerman, and ER's longtime ally Agnes Brown Leach and her husband, *Forum* publisher Henry Goddard Leach.

Also aboard that special train was ER's new wardrobe, which she had collected during a shopping spree with Anna the week before. She replaced the schoolmarm look of the Albany years with a new stylish elegance, appropriate to Washington's social demands. For her inaugural gown she chose a hyacinth shade the press called "Eleanor Blue," and for her wrap a new shade of blue named "Anna Blue" (in compliment to her daughter). Both gown and wrap were of crystelle velvet, made by Arnold Constable. A "symphony in blue," ER's hat, "a Watteau type of crystal straw," in Anna Blue was covered with banded grosgrain ribbon "forming a small wing in the back," tilting down in the front. She carried a "large envelope bag" of Anna Blue antelope kid and wore white glacé kid gloves, "the smart eight-button length."

The press complimented ER's "elegant dignity" and the fact that her outfits were designed and made entirely in the United States, "so far as known." Her evening gowns especially were "of great beauty." For "very formal dinners," she ordered a gown of "misty blue satin, a new Lanvin shade," from Le Mouchoir of Madison Avenue, who described the effect as "regal." "The waist is draped in front. The back décolleté forms a deep V. . . ." Le Mouchoir also created daytime ensembles of various blues and "a rough tweed coat suit of mixed brown, beige and blue." Four hats to accompany the daytime costumes were made by Mme. Lilly Dache, also of Madison Avenue, and nine dresses were ordered from Milgrim's, including a "misty blue and silver brocade" gown with long sleeves and high neck that could be used for formal late-afternoon and evening affairs. In the evening the sleeves could be removed and the back unfastened to render it décolleté; unclipped "it falls in two wide revers, revealing a deep V. . . ."

ER was pleased by most of the initial press coverage: "Tall, slim and girlish, in a dark blue ensemble and hat . . . the next First Lady looked more nearly like an elder sister than the mother of Mrs. Curtis Dall, her daughter [Anna]. . . ."

Only Hick, whose campaign articles on ER had emphasized her routine thrift, her plain $5 and $10 street dresses bought off racks and on the run, seemed disturbed. She protested in a letter that ER had spent an unseemly amount of money on lavish and extravagant display, given America's grave fiscal situation. But ER believed that it was good for the economy to buy as much as possible and give work to many people.

While the press reported every detail of each outfit, ER referred to her buying spree in one sentence at the end of a long political letter to FDR: "I got a lot of clothes for myself & Anna in one afternoon last week as I imagine it is better to have plenty & not buy any new ones for quite a while!"

The point of her letter was an urgent appeal to FDR:

> Henry Morgenthau came to see me the other day & told me he felt he could serve really well only as Sec of Ag. & all the big farm organizations were for him. He had done well on all of your missions, he had made your

ag policy in this State a success & got the men who were helpful on your ag speeches. He did not feel he could be Asst. Sec. because he had been so near you he could not be under a chief & loyally work THROUGH him. He does not think [Henry] Wallace will be easy for you to manage or others to get on with and he is no administrator. He won't say he won't take . . . anything else but he does not feel he could serve you as well & he wants you to talk it over with him before you settle on Wallace. Please at least talk to him. —I have transmitted my message!

FDR appointed Wallace to Agriculture. ER was disappointed, as was Louis Howe. For decades Howe had been FDR's main adviser, closest friend, political confidant. But the presidency changed everything. Although Louis Howe remained first secretary, his influence was now rivalled by the young Columbia University professors around FDR, the new Brains Trust boys Howe despised.

Ray Moley, Rexford Guy Tugwell, and A. A. Berle were part of a new political landscape marked by intrigue and jealousy, stealth and duplicity. FDR enjoyed the political mix, the harrowing juggling that left everybody uncertain. It caused ER and Howe to forge an even tighter alliance. Regarded as outsiders among FDR's new insiders, they increasingly relied on each other.

ER and Howe ended each day with a drive and a meeting. They collaborated on big projects, and negotiated petty grievances. Howe was ER's greatest ally, and during the first administration, ER and Louis Howe were FDR's most honest and critical friends. With his health failing, no longer FDR's unchallenged lieutenant, Howe increasingly turned to ER for solace, support, and company. Together, they were a formidable team.

FDR's decision on Morgenthau intensified ER's efforts. With Louis Howe and Molly Dewson, she struggled for influence over FDR's appointments, and it was due to their insistence that he became the first president to appoint a woman to the cabinet: Frances Perkins as secretary of labor.*

ER was pleased to learn that her old school chums rallied behind her. They were not only delighted by her "lovely" new costumes, but they supported her goals. One of her six bridesmaids, Helen Cutting Wilmerding, a cousin and former Roser classmate, wrote with enthusiasm: "All the old tribe we grew up with in New York have turned towards you like sun flowers." ER

---

*In addition to Perkins and Wallace, FDR's original cabinet included Cordell Hull, secretary of state; William Woodin, secretary of the treasury; George Henry Dern, secretary of war; Homer S. Cummings, named attorney general after Thomas J. Walsh's sudden death; Harold Ickes, secretary of the interior; and Daniel Calhoun Roper, secretary of commerce.

was grateful for that information, "for I felt the old crowd might disapprove of many things which I did." And she was determined to challenge the women of her own class and culture. She asked Junior Leaguers, for example, to consider what they themselves might do, might contribute, might actually give up in order to make life better for those rendered homeless or impoverished during the Depression. She even suggested they convert space in their many-roomed apartments or country houses to provide temporary shelter for homeless families in distress. Privileged women and men, she repeatedly emphasized before the inauguration, had special obligations during these hard times: "Sooner or later we are going to realize that what touches one part of the human race touches all parts. Thus we are going to have to learn that the few must sacrifice for the good of the many if we are to preserve our present civilization."

The White House itself would be open to all her extended circle, even when they came to carp. ER's most violent detractors, including her increasingly reactionary cousins Alice Roosevelt Longworth and Corinne Robinson Alsop (mother of columnists Joseph and Stuart Alsop) were invited whenever they chose to attend. Despite nasty imitations of ER, Cousin Alice was not barred from White House functions until she publicly announced in 1940 that she would rather vote for Adolf Hitler than for her crippled cousin one more time.

As ER prepared herself for the Washington fray, she carefully considered and often repeated the dreary details of the lives of Washington wives, and her husband understood her discontent. Indeed, FDR's fiftieth birthday on 30 January 1933 was celebrated by a surprise party at Hyde Park orchestrated by ER and Louis Howe. It was a well-planned and hilarious affair; every guest played a role to evoke an event in Franklin's life. In the end, he responded with rhymes for all present. Regarding his wife, FDR recited:

> Did my Eleanor relate
> All the sad and awful fate
> Of the miserable lives
> Lived by politicians' wives?

ER derived little comfort from the examples of the First Ladies who preceded her. In her Uncle TR's Washington, she had met Ida Saxton McKinley, and she knew all her twentieth-century forebears. They all seemed to her hardworking earnest women whose lives were limited by invalidism, neurasthenia, depression. Many of ER's predecessors took to their beds, broken down by their efforts to cope with unending publicity, criticism, their husbands' wrath or neglect, the demanding but ill-appreciated responsibilities of political wifery.

Athletic, wealthy, and brilliant, Ida Saxton McKinley was raised by her father to take over his financial interests and run his bank. When she married attorney William McKinley, she was politically ambitious and extravagantly social. But during her husband's first years in Congress, which coincided with the sudden deaths of her mother and two daughters, Ida McKinley plunged into a mysterious invalidism that resembled epilepsy. She became pale and fragile. Grotesquely overwhelmed by her flamboyantly feathered and bejeweled costumes, she seemed bundled in satin swaddling offset by oversized diamonds. Generally carried to state dinners, she was confined to a wheelchair and propped high by overstuffed pillows. Her fainting spells and seizures were sudden and unpredictable. Whenever one occurred at table her husband simply placed a napkin upon her face until it subsided, whereupon she would remove it and continue the conversation as if nothing had happened.

Argumentative and bad tempered, Ida McKinley was called "the most demanding" invalid wife in political history. To "cure" her headaches and quiet her manner, she was dosed with "barbiturates, bromide sedatives, laudanum, and other powerful narcotics." She embarrassed her husband's friends, and they considered him a marvel of devotion: the "saint" of domesticity.

But when McKinley was assassinated in September 1901, she arranged his funeral and her return to private life without assistance. Upon her arrival home, Ida McKinley's era of total dependence mysteriously ended. Until her own death on 26 May 1907 she never had another seizure.

Although Ida McKinley's style was unique, even the women ER most admired seemed to suffer in the White House.

Helen (Nellie) Herron Taft trained as a teacher and thoroughly enjoyed politics. She was a daughter and granddaughter of congressmen, and many believed she badgered her reluctant husband to run for president and advised him on all appointments and issues. Most visibly her husband's partner, she was outspoken, progressive, creative. She was the skilled diplomat who arranged Japan's gift of three thousand cherry trees to adorn Potomac Drive and the Tidal Basin. But in May 1909, less than three months after Taft assumed office, she suffered a stroke that temporarily paralyzed her and left her speech permanently impaired.

ER was particularly informed and impressed by Ellen Axson Wilson, Woodrow Wilson's first wife. A career artist who continued to paint, she was widely recognized as a "Great and Good Lady." Renowned as an American Impressionist and associated with art communities in Old Lyme, Connecticut, and Cornish, New Hampshire, Ellen Axson Wilson participated in competitive exhibits and sold her paintings.

When her Cornish circle, which included Maxwell Parrish, met at her summer home in 1913 to consider the kind of national support for the arts France enjoyed, they imagined an official government bureau to encourage artists, award prizes, purchase works. Ellen Wilson replied that the congress-men who would endorse that view were "not yet born."

Ellen Wilson's efforts to build decent housing and abolish Washington's "alley slums" particularly captured ER's imagination as First Lady. Like Wilson, ER believed that adequate and healthy housing was the fundamental key to a more democratic future.

As Ellen Wilson prepared for her daughter's White House wedding, she wrote a relative: "Nobody who has not tried can have the least idea of the exactions of life here and of the constant nervous strain of it all."

Diagnosed with kidney tuberculosis, or Bright's disease, Ellen Wilson died on 6 August 1914, having been First Lady for only seventeen months. *The New York Times* concluded that her condition was aggravated "by a nervous breakdown, attributed to the exactions of social duties and her active interest in philanthropy and betterment work."

If ER had any particular feelings about the gossip concerning Woodrow Wilson's affair with Mary Hulbert Peck, during the time when ER's own marriage was in such disarray, she never referred to them. Evidently, Woodrow Wilson's advisers paid Mary Peck, an attractive divorcée, some still debatable sum of money for the intimate letters he had written to her over the years. The scandal surfaced between Ellen Wilson's death and the election of 1916, when some Wilson advisers hoped the mysterious Mrs. Peck would become the new First Lady.

It was the kind of gossip ER detested, and avoided. She never, for example, referred to Florence Kling Harding's much publicized marital strife, although she spent time with "the Duchess" during the war.

ER particularly admired two gifted and generous public citizens who became, for different reasons, silent as First Ladies. Her immediate predecessor, Lou Henry Hoover, chose silence; Grace Goodhue Coolidge's husband imposed it.

Unlike her husband, Grace Coolidge was witty, charming, and gregarious. She had been a dedicated and innovative teacher of the hearing-impaired. She believed all children could learn to speak, and she taught lip-reading as well as sign language. Calvin Coolidge, on the other hand, believed no woman could or should communicate in public life. He mandated his wife's silence on all political issues and also denied her many ordinary pleasures, including horse-back riding. Her friends complained on her behalf: "Calvin felt that woman's place was at the sink." Although Grace never protested, she confided to a friend that lives of political wives were "very confining."

ER's first official act as First Lady–elect was to attend Calvin Coolidge's funeral. On 7 January 1933, she journeyed to Northampton with her son James. ER's decision to attend was appreciated as "a sign of respect" for her Republican predecessors, Grace Coolidge and Lou Henry Hoover.

Geologist, linguist, and scholar, Stanford University graduate and outspoken feminist, Lou Henry Hoover had been for decades her husband's partner. They traveled together in search of mineral deposits and new speculative investment markets throughout Europe and Asia. In London and Washington during the war, she founded canteens, a war hospital, a knitting factory, a home for women war workers. She was an equal-rights feminist, headed the Girl Scouts, and as the only woman on the board of the National Amateur Athletic Association, led a campaign to introduce physical education for women "in every institution" in America.

Nobody believed Lou Henry Hoover when she announced that as First Lady she would be nothing but a pleasant "backdrop for Bertie." But she meant it. Except for occasional radio broadcasts, she ended her public role in American life. She hosted dinners and parties to entertain her husband, not to promote causes. Inexplicably, she refused interviews and banished the press. Controversy engulfed her only when she decided to invite Jessie DePriest to a tea for congressmen's wives.

In 1930, Chicago elected Republican Oscar DePriest, the first black member of Congress since Reconstruction. Despite their Quaker opposition to discrimination, the Hoovers did not decide immediately to open their White House. But it bothered Lou Henry that Jessie DePriest was not invited with other congressional wives her first year in Washington. Many meetings were held on the subject, and the president finally consented. Determined to avoid a rude incident, Lou Henry Hoover queried every congressional wife and found twelve who agreed to be cordial at a tea that would include the first black White House guest since TR invited Booker T. Washington and his wife for lunch.

On 12 June 1931, Jessie DePriest was received by the First Lady. Her visit in the company of twelve congenial women was brief and pleasant. But astonishing howls of protest followed. Virtually every Southern newspaper editorialized against this "arrogant insult to the South and to the nation." While several Northern newspapers celebrated the First Lady's effort to "put into practice the brotherhood of man," Southern editors and politicians predicted disaster, race intermingling, and Republican defeat in 1932. In response, Lou Henry Hoover went on a tour of Southern states, presumably to reassure white clubwomen.

Inevitably, as ER contemplated her new role, her thoughts lingered on her Aunt Edith's White House. With Edith Roosevelt, rules and ceremony dominated. Sumptuous feasts and formality were her legacy. Guests foregathered, and were greeted after a grand processional whereby the president and First Lady descended the White House's central staircase "to trumpets." "Not wanting to shake hands, she clutched a large bouquet."

Edith Roosevelt presided over a circle of scolds who collected information about Washington's "immorals." Those who "transgressed her code of upright conduct" were banished. Working women were not invited; adulterers were shunned. Aunt Edith detested the press and scorned "camera fiends." Her political sensibilities ran counter to everything her niece believed.

Noted for her ability to walk and talk as fast as her husband, some of TR's friends thought she controlled him; others believed she bullied him. Henry Adams always marveled at Edith's ability to silence TR: "He stands in abject terror of Edith. . . . What is man that he should have tusks and grin!" But for ER, Aunt Edith's assertive, imperious, even terrifying manner was eclipsed by her discontent. A prisoner to her "beloved shackles," she was plagued by headaches and assorted neuralgias.

Although never close, ER did not want to sever relations with her father's family. When Anna Roosevelt Cowles (Aunt Bye) died peacefully at her home in Farmington, Connecticut, during the night of 25 August 1931, ER's warmest link to her father's generation ended. Aunt Bye had been one of ER's great champions, the woman who most urgently insisted she be sent to school at Allenswood in England.

After Aunt Bye's death, ER made a special effort to reach out to her father's surviving sister, Aunt Corinne, a lifelong Republican who voted for Franklin because, she said, Eleanor was her niece, after all. But Corinne Roosevelt Robinson died suddenly of pneumonia on 17 February 1933 at the age of seventy-one. Her funeral, which both FDR and ER attended, was the last family gathering before FDR's inauguration. Now Aunt Edith was the last surviving member of her father's generation. And she never forgave ER for campaigning against her son Ted in that Teapot Dome car when he ran for governor in 1924.

Although Aunt Edith actively campaigned against FDR, ER nevertheless wrote from the White House—as if there were nothing but family tradition and warmth between them. Interested in her niece's initial tribulations as First Lady, Edith replied: "Your letter was an answer to prayer, full of things which I wanted to know. Much such conditions met me in the White House, and I am quite sure that I did not deal with them as efficiently as you have done."

ER's ability to invite her cousin Alice Roosevelt Longworth to inaugural events was even more extraordinary. Alice had, after all, declared war on Democrats and never missed an opportunity to deride Eleanor publicly. Her opposition to Franklin was shrill, often vulgar and cruel. She not only attacked his policies, she mocked his physical condition: "My poor cousin, he suffered from polio so he was put in a brace; and now he wants to put the entire U.S. into a brace, as if it were a crippled country—that is all the New Deal is about. . . ."

Alice seemed now to concentrate all her wit and flair into a private crusade to hurt her cousins. She had been the ruling Washington widow, the only important Roosevelt. Miserably married to Nicholas Longworth, the popular Speaker of the House who had rivaled Eleanor's father Elliott in his drinking and romantic escapades, Alice had nevertheless reveled in Washington society, and few knew the truth of her marriage.

After her husband's death in 1931, Alice devoted herself to ER's humiliation. She trotted out the old stories of FDR's wartime infidelities. She mocked and minced: "FDR is nine parts mush and one part Eleanor." She contrasted FDR's dependence with her father's robust self-reliance: TR's vigor; TR's brawn. ER's sons remembered that only Alice could bring their mother to the verge of tears.

Although ER never criticized Alice by name, she wrote an article in which she described her kind of malicious gossip and concluded that it reflected "not only a cruel but a despicable trait of human nature."

To fortify her spirits and armor herself against the animus of her closest kin, ER read and studied her father's letters—and decided to publish them. Indeed, ER wrote or edited three books between FDR's election and inauguration: one for children *(When You Grow Up to Vote)*, one for redemption (her father's letters), and one for the future *(It's Up to the Women)*. They enabled her to face her new position with a sense of personal liberation, and a clearly defined political program.

Moreover, while she abandoned her sponsored radio program and gave up teaching, she refused to give up editing *Babies—Just Babies*, a magazine she had started to help mothers avoid the kind of mistakes her parents had made and she had perpetuated with her own children. The magazine was filled with droll and informative stories, infant photographs, uplifting and curious advice, prizes, poetry, and whimsy. ER believed it offered young mothers a much-needed service. She personally guaranteed the reliability and quality of the magazine's advertisers; and called upon all her acquaintances—rich and famous, hardworking and unknown—to contribute baby lore. Daughter Anna detailed "24 Hours of a Baby's Life," not quite a celebration of her infant daughter's grueling, relentless schedule. Rosamond Pinchot wrote about "The Most Famous Baby in the World," Helen Hayes's daughter Mary MacArthur. "A Soviet Baby Is Born" featured extraordinary photos to illustrate healthful, contented infants and toddlers in factory nurseries.

The First Lady–elect wanted every young mother to have a less tormented and ignorant time than she had endured. She announced in the foreword to the first issue of *Babies*, printed in October 1932:

> There is an old Jesuit saying which—"Give me a child until he is seven and you may have him all the rest of his life." . . . You can decide in the first five years of a child's life whether that child is going to be nervous and

high-strung, unable to stand the hurry and excitement of modern life, or whether he is going to be given a foundation of calmness and sturdiness, a character, which in later life will enable him to gain that inner self-control which all of us strive for and only some of us attain. We can lay the foundations in those first five years of a healthy mind in a healthy body or we can lay the foundation for an undernourished, dyspeptic, uncontrolled and disagreeable man or woman.

Above all, ER sought to give advice to young parents she wished she had been given. She wrote of "tolerance," "patience," "forgiveness." She wrote of marital relations: Each parent "must want the other one to be happy. Then and then only will they be happy themselves."

ER's monthly editorials were filled with respect for children and encouragement for mothers. Anticipating the nurturing ideas of Dr. Benjamin Spock by over a decade, ER promoted demonstrations of warmth and affection. She advocated breast feeding because of its proven health benefits; and urged mothers to hug their children, hold them when they cried, rather than follow the advice of psychologist John B. Watson to allow them to cry for hours alone in a quiet room. Nevertheless, ER endorsed several prevailing notions concerning discipline and regularity: Character building depended on precise schedules for feeding and bodily functions.

ER's own confusion regarding the proper balance between affection, "democratic self-expression," and discipline lasted throughout her life. In the 1950s, she acknowledged that "too much belief in discipline when my children were young" was her greatest mistake as a mother: "I was so concerned with bringing up my children properly that I was not wise enough just to love them."

Her grandchildren benefited far more than her own children from her new emphasis on absolute respect for young people and their right to their own mistakes. But her youngest boys, Franklin and John (still at Groton), also benefited from her new perspective. She encouraged them to live boldly and self-reliantly and sought to protect them from the intrusive demands of Washington life.

As ER contemplated the White House, she turned for assistance to her great friend Isabella Selmes Greenway, whose place in Arizona still recalled the West her father and uncle knew. Could John be a hand there for the summer?

> He has had a little bit too much of Groton and his Grandmother and the things that money mean and I think standing on his own two feet is a very necessary experience for a time this summer.
> We would be quite willing to pay for him, only we would not want him to know. He does not want to be in the same place with Franklin, Jr., [who]

rather lords it over him so we are trying to do the same thing with Franklin, Jr. but somewhere else. . . .

Sixteen, two years younger than his brother, John was about to enter his junior year. In September, ER wrote Isabella: "John had such a good time & I am so glad you liked him. He's so different from F jr. but has capacities in his own way when certain things are either overcome or outgrown!"

Personally, ER's most momentous decision during these months of preparation and dread was to pay tribute to her father. Elliott Roosevelt had died of alcoholism at the age of thirty-four, when ER was only ten. *Hunting Big Game in the Eighties: The Letters of Elliott Roosevelt, Sportsman,* "Edited by His Daughter, Anna Eleanor Roosevelt," was filled with compassion for her father's struggle, and competitive family pride.

ER explained in her foreword that she had decided to issue his letters for personal reasons. Despite his "many shortcomings [he] was the one great love of my life as a child. . . ." Her children would "read much in many books of their uncles and aunts . . . but no less important in our daily lives are the things and the people who touch us only personally. . . ."

It was a brave book for America's First Lady to introduce to a judgmental society. Written to avenge her father as well as to establish her right to wear the Roosevelt mantle, ER wrote nothing of her parents' ordeal, of her mother's suffering and premature death at twenty-nine, when Eleanor was eight, or of her own longing. The cruel attacks hurled against her husband by her own relatives surely informed her decision to publish this book in 1933, and thereby redeem the family outcast.

It was an act of competitive retribution, in which ER emphasized her father's generosity, and youthful vigor—as opposed to her Uncle Ted, who "was delicate as a boy and shortsighted all his life."

Although it was not her intention, the book also established Elliott and his daughter in a social tradition of fabulous wealth and international privilege. Her father's life was one of global travel and big-game hunting that depended on an Anglo-American club of sportsmen and colonial rulership that seemed during the 1930s in rapid decline.

But ER ignored that aspect of her father's legacy and emphasized rather his "great love and tenderness" for his family and her impression of his sense of personal democracy: "He loved people for the fineness that was in them and his friends might be newsboys or millionaires. Their occupations, their *possessions,* meant nothing to him, only they themselves counted." However exaggerated her impression, that trait represented the core of her father's bequest to her.

As she prepared for the White House, ER made other tributes to her father's memory. She arranged to visit Abingdon, Virginia, her father's healing refuge, in order to meet the people who had meant so much to him during his long illness and exile. Also, she hung her paternal grandfather's portrait over the mantelpiece in the Monroe Room, where she later held press conferences for women journalists only. The room she chose was connected with power and influence: It had been used as TR's Cabinet Room and was known also as the Treaty Room. In 1899 William McKinley had there signed the treaty with Spain which ended the Spanish-American War and ceded Puerto Rico, Cuba, and the Philippines to the United States. FDR had suggested that ER take her grandfather's portrait to Washington. They intended to rent their New York City house, and FDR said, "You can't rent your grandfather."

Undoubtedly ER's most extraordinary tribute to her father was an impromptu speech she delivered one Saturday afternoon shortly before Christmas 1932. She astounded a New York Metropolitan Opera audience when she strode onstage between the first and second acts of *Simon Boccanegra* to appeal for money for Depression-ruined Americans: "When you come face to face with people in need, you simply have to try to do something about it."

ER told the comfortable matinee crowd how it felt to meet the "jobless face to face." She related the story of a man who came into her office saying he could not go home again without a job. He had been unemployed for months. "There was no heat at home, no food, and even the gas had been turned off. And there were five children." ER was moved by his story, and she hoped her audience would contribute all they could to the Emergency Unemployment Relief Committee. "After all, this is the richest country in the world. We cannot allow any one to want for the bare necessities of life."

ER's decision to address the opera audience that day was, in retrospect, no mere coincidence. Simon Boccanegra was the first popularly elected doge of Genoa. Generous, emotional, forgiving, he was a man of the people and a man of peace. Moreover, in Giuseppe Verdi's profoundly stirring tale of politics, love, and longing, Simon is also "the Good Father" accidentally reunited with his long-lost daughter Maria. ER appeared onstage after their astonishing reunion, and one of opera's most thrilling duets between father and daughter:

Simon Boccanegra meets Maria by chance during a bright morning stroll. She hears his lament for his country, its poverty and strife: "I weep over your fruitless Harvests / And I cry out for Peace / I cry out for Love."

As they speak, he discovers her lost history—and their matching pendants: "Figlia! a tal nome io palpito. . . ." ("Daughter! At that name I tremble / as if heaven had opened to me.")

It is the moment she has waited for all her life: "Father, you shall see /

your watchful daughter / always near you; / I will wipe away your tears. / We shall taste undiscovered joys . . . / I will be the dove of peace / of your royal palace."

ER remained a great fan of Lawrence Tibbett, who played Simon Boccanegra, and invited him to perform at the White House whenever possible. She never mentioned Ezio Pinza, who played the cruel grandfather. Simon's last gesture is to bless both Maria and her grandfather, whereupon Maria sings: "Oh Joy! Then the bitter hatreds are ended!" Finally, Simon Boccanegra places the mantle of leadership upon his daughter and her lover, Gabriele Adorno, named the new doge of Genoa.

ER's reconnection with her father and her childhood helped her to reach beyond fear: her fear of abandonment, betrayal, rejection; her fear of confinement and isolation. As she reconstituted her father's life, she embraced a powerful source of courage and vision that was her mysterious treasure. She ignored his neglect, his abusive self-indulgence, and celebrated instead her fantasy of his democratic generosity and her own commitment to all people regardless of class or station.

It enabled her to move on, beyond familial blandishments, and graciously invite seventy-two relatives to inaugural festivities. All the Delanos and Hyde Park Roosevelts, all the surviving Halls, and all the Oyster Bay Roosevelts who chose to attend, including her cousins—TR's children Alice Roosevelt Longworth and Kermit and Archibald Roosevelt, Aunt Bye's son Sheffield Cowles, and their families.

Still, despite her activities and emotional preparations, ER told reporters on the blustery, overcast day of FDR's inauguration, 4 March 1933, that she was certain about only one thing: "No woman entering the White House . . . can lightheartedly take up residence here."

According to Emma Bugbee, reporting for the *New York Herald-Tribune*, ER "stood motionless, with lowered eyes and folded hands, while her husband became President. . . . Her pale face and austere demeanor bore testimony to the solemnity with which she views Mr. Roosevelt's new position. . . . Many friends watched for an opportunity to wave to her, and strangers trained cameras upon her, but not once did she lift her eyes to the crowd or wave her hand or smile. . . ." One reporter noted that over "the vast throng" of 500,000 cheering spectators, "there hung a cloud of worry."

America was at a standstill. Men, women, and children begged on street corners, sold pencils, apples, old clothes. People spoke about gloom, despair, suicide, revolution. When farm prices fell to pennies, farm owners burned their crops, killed their livestock. Banks foreclosed mortgages and reclaimed farms and homes. There were riots at garbage dumps as people fought each other for scraps of food and kindling. Over two million people—called "hobos," "Okies," "tramps"—wandered the country searching for work.

The comfortable and the mean dismissed them as "bums." The comfortable and the mean luxuriated in bargains they did not need, and blamed the poor for littering their landscape. Giant "Hoovervilles" made of tin cans and frayed tires, scrap wood and debris, appeared along river shores and railroad sidings, in parks and woodlands. People were living in caves and culverts all over America.

The Depression never really touched the Roosevelts. Their properties were unmortgaged, their troubled holdings caused no particular hardship. No child needed to leave school. Sara Delano Roosevelt, the family's financial matriarch, was solvent, if occasionally grumpy. ER independently made ever-increasing sums from writing and speaking engagements. Her sole concern as First Lady was to improve conditions for those who suffered.

She blamed the war for the fiscal frenzy that had burst worldwide. By 1931, Germany, Austria, Italy, France, and England faced bankruptcy and ruin. All international agreements made during the 1920s crumbled. The gold standard, loan and tariff agreements, visions of free trade ended. By 1933, dictators swaggered across Europe and Asia. When Germany and then the Allies reneged on their war debts, Americans became increasingly isolationist. Germany, on the day of Franklin Delano Roosevelt's inaugural, witnessed a nationwide "blaze of bonfires and torchlight parades," in anticipation of a vote of confidence for the new Reich, the triumph of Adolf Hitler's National Socialist (Nazi) Party—already hailed as Germany's "last election." According to press reports, there were "no counter-demonstrations. . . . They were 'verboten.' "

Since anti-Nazis were imprisoned, opposition papers banned, and debate silenced by terrorist torture centers, Hitler was certain of victory. During the entire week of FDR's inaugural, the new U.S. administration shared front-page headlines with democracy's death in Germany.

Violence and poverty veiled the globe on that day FDR affirmed that "the only thing we have to fear is fear itself." With "solemn mien," the thirty-second president of the United States placed his hand upon his family's old Dutch Bible and turned to "Charity," 1 Corinthians 13, to repeat the oath of office after Chief Justice Charles Evans Hughes.*

In his dramatic Inaugural Address, FDR promised healing, bold action. ER was pleased; it was "a fighting speech."

"This is a day of national consecration. . . . Practices of the unscrupulous money changers stand indicted in the court of public opinion. . . .

---

*"And now abideth, faith, hope and charity, these three; but the greatest of these is charity."

"They have no vision, and when there is no vision the people perish."

FDR promised now to restore and build a New Deal with "social values more noble than mere monetary profit."

He would pursue that goal with all the fervor of a president at war. Initially the battleground was limited to domestic crises. International issues, though important, were "secondary to the establishment of a sound economic policy." The gravity of the domestic emergency eclipsed world trade and FDR's promise of a "good neighbor" policy that "resolutely respects the rights of others."

Immediately, he declared war on financial distress. "This nation asks for action, and action now." Therefore: "I shall ask the Congress for ... broad executive power to wage a war against the emergency as great as the power that would be given to me if we were in fact invaded by a foreign foe."

While the crowd stood to cheer those words, millions more listened for the first time to a presidential address broadcast by 180 radio stations and simultaneously "flashed around the earth by short-wave radio." Most Americans were thrilled to exuberance by FDR's words.

Caroline O'Day left Washington ecstatic: FDR, "within twenty-four hours, lifted our country out of a slough of despair." America had at last "found a leader and all would soon be right with the world." His address "will remain an inspiration for all time."

Eleanor Roosevelt was less sanguine. Words needed to be supported by bold actions. She feared the kind of desperation that had upended Germany, and she feared the random acts of violence and assassination aimed at her husband. As had been true throughout her life, occasions of joy and celebration were marked as well by sadness.

The Roosevelts' first days in the White House were framed by death. Hourly news bulletins discussed the decline of Chicago's Mayor Anton J. Cermak, who had been wounded in Miami on 15 February by bullets intended for FDR. Mayor Cermak and two women were shot by an assassin who attacked FDR's open car during a short victory parade. The president-elect was saved by a spectator, Lillian Cross, who grabbed the assailant's arm, while Gus Gennerich, FDR's bodyguard, pushed him down on the seat, and sat on him after he heard the first shot.

When Eleanor learned that her husband had held Mayor Tony Cermak in his arms on the way to the hospital, she wrote: The ride "must have been awfully hard on Franklin. He hates the sight of blood."

The assassin, Joseph Zangara, an unemployed thirty-three-year-old bricklayer, told the court: "I do not hate Mr. Roosevelt personally. I hate all Presidents, no matter from what country they come, and I hate all officials and everybody who is rich." Following Mayor Cermak's death on 6 March, Zangara was executed.

An additional note of gloom came with the sudden death of Senator Thomas J. Walsh, who was to have been FDR's attorney general. A vigorous and early Roosevelt supporter, the popular seventy-three-year-old senator from Montana had exposed and relentlessly pursued the Teapot Dome scandal. An aging widower, he secretly married the former Señora Mina Nieves Perez Chaumont de Truffin of Havana. Aboard the train to Washington from their honeymoon in Florida, he died of a heart attack. His wife of less than one week found him in their stateroom at dawn on 2 March, the day FDR and his entourage arrived in Washington.

Senator Walsh had chaired the almost-deadlocked Democratic convention in Chicago, and ER believed that "Franklin owed much to him for his skillful handling" of that unruly situation. Without him, FDR might have been denied the nomination. FDR considered Walsh "one of the three or four wisest men in the Democratic party," and he was stunned by his death.

At the inaugural, flags flew at half-staff in Walsh's honor, and ER initially canceled several social events and declined to attend the Inaugural Ball. But after countless protests, "the pleas of hundreds" demanding her presence, expressions of fear that all the money raised by the charity ball would be lost, and the disappointment of her own friends, she agreed to attend.

FDR did not attend this first ball, or any subsequent ones. Rarely seen in a wheelchair, he avoided public appearances that might reveal the full extent of his polio disability. Moreover, he was reportedly visiting with the woman he had promised never to see again, Lucy Mercer Rutherford.

The ball opened to a concert-reception during which the Army, Navy, and Marine Bands played, followed by the U.S. Indian Reserve Band, "composed of twenty full-blooded Indians, representing 18 tribes," many from Dakota and Oklahoma reservations. Chief Yowlache, a Cherokee leader and noted baritone, gave a concert in "full Indian regalia, including a $5,000 headdress of golden eagle feathers."

ER was resplendent. Her eyes sparkled with warmth and delight as she greeted everybody and was escorted through the vast throng to the platform by an enthusiastic floor committee. The fact is, ER loved to party, and to dance.

According to Cissy Patterson's *Washington Star*, "The new First Lady was a striking figure in a gown of blue and silver lamé." She greeted her friends in their boxes and mingled throughout the auditorium. Rosa Ponselle, "the Metropolitan Opera prima donna," sang "The Star-Spangled Banner." Given a prolonged ovation, she contributed "Dixie" for an encore. After the ceremonies, three dance orchestras presided: Rudy Vallee and "his famous Connecticut Yankees, Guy Lombardo and his Royal Canadians, and the Central Park Casino Orchestra."

ER's personal party included her mother-in-law, her brother Hall and his family, her children and their guests, Earl Miller and his wife, Louis Howe and his family, Nancy Cook and Marion Dickerman, Mary Dreier, and a full assortment of Roosevelts and Delanos. Although Lorena Hickok returned to New York after a supper reception but before the ball, ER's friends in attendance included publisher Eleanor (Cissy) Patterson, former member of Congress Ruth Bryan Owen "in a striking gown of black satin," and novelist Fannie Hurst, "perhaps the most picturesque figure at the reception."

Never again would ER be the wallflower at a Washington party, the silent partner off in a corner. The circumstances of 1933 demanded experiment and challenged all tradition, and ER was not the same woman who had been so blithely mistreated during those drear Wilson years. Nor was FDR the same man. However much Eleanor resented Franklin's presumptions, she admired his aplomb, fearlessness, vigor. However much Franklin resented Eleanor's goading, he admired her principles, honesty, loyalty.

If ER resented FDR's political wiles, his conniving and duplicity, she believed that his "desire was to make life happier for people." He faced life with a contagious courage. He gave people hope, and she trusted him generally to act on behalf of human betterment: "I have never known a man who gave one a greater sense of security. I never heard him say there was a problem that he thought it was impossible for human beings to solve. . . . I never knew him to face life or any problem that came up with fear."

In addition, she admired his mind, the range and intensity of his interests. He read voraciously, biography and history particularly, and remembered everything significant. ER was proud of her husband's "amazing ability to skim through any kind of book and get everything out of it." When she gave him *Gone With the Wind*, he returned it "in a very short time." She doubted he "read it so quickly." But he answered every question, and "I couldn't catch him out on a single point."

ER was happy when others recognized her husband's talents, and eagerly passed on compliments. A Swedish diplomat told her, for example, that when he met Calvin Coolidge, "he marvelled how any one could be president and know so little. But when he talked with you he marvelled how any one could know so much. . . ."

For all their differences, ER and FDR respected each other, depended on each other, understood each other. FDR never contemplated an uninvolved or silent First Lady. His wife was his adviser, partner, inspector general of choice. He relied on her advice, trusted her vision.

On 8 March 1933, when he asked his friend and mentor Felix Frankfurter to accept the post of solicitor general, the Harvard Law School professor was reluctant. FDR encouraged him, and said: "Well, there's no hurry about this. I tell you what I want you to do. I sometimes find it useful, and you might find it useful—I wish you would talk to your Mrs. about it." Frankfurter took the president's advice, consulted his wife Marion, who thought it was a bad idea and he declined.

Throughout the White House years, ER was to spend between sixteen and twenty hours a day running actually a parallel administration concerned with every aspect of national betterment. Domestically, nothing was beyond her range of interest, and she monitored every department through a friend or agreeable contact. FDR never credited ER with a job well done or publicly acknowledged her political influence. But little of significance was achieved without her input, and her vision shaped the best of his presidency.

2: Public and Private Domains

$\blacktriangleright$ᴏᴏᴏ$\blacktriangleleft$

ℰach night ER placed memos in her husband's bedside basket urging him to do what she believed needed most urgently to be done. Above all, she sought to extend her husband's efforts so that the New Deal would become at least in part a "square deal for women."

But no matter how many memos she wrote, no matter how much she influenced policy, the First Lady's official domain was the White House, where she presided over the domestic continuity of the nation's highest office. From 5 March until 15 June, while FDR worked on legislation to transform the country, ER had only one specific assignment: As first housewife she was to create a gracious and pleasant environment. The "President's House" was intended to be democratic and simple. ER was mindful that she now lived "in a house owned by all the American people." Within days, ER settled in and overhauled the entire place. It suited the moment—and the style of her own high-spirited and growing family. She rejected staff opposition, and insisted that the stately dignity of the old trees and the rolling greensward would survive her decision to install tree swings, slides, and a sandbox for her grandchildren. Such playthings were, after all, no less aesthetic than Pauline, the Tafts' executive cow, who grazed the White House lawns.

The election profoundly affected ER's children, and she sought to shield them from the dazzling new privileges, unrelenting demands, and public scrutiny heaped upon America's First Family. Privately, the first hundred days coincided with major family upheavals.

Her youngest sons, Franklin, Jr., and John, at school in Groton, were more protected from Washington's glare. But her daughter Anna and her children, Sistie and Buzzie, considered the place home. Anna was in love with John Boettiger, a political reporter for the *Chicago Tribune* whom she had met on the campaign train, and in the throes of a messy separation from her husband, Curtis Dall. ER was fond of Boettiger, but nothing was settled.

ER was particularly disturbed by her son Elliott's decision to leave his wife, Betty Donner, and their infant son, William. Elliott at twenty-two was still the family's most unpredictable child. He had refused to go to college and ended his formal education to marry as quickly as possible. Then, on 8 March, he left his wife and baby in the White House, announcing he would discover his true self on the Texas range. Betty, the daughter of an anti-Roosevelt family whose fortune in partnership with Andrew Mellon was associated with Pittsburgh's steel industry, was depressed and confused by Elliott's actions.

ER agonized over Elliott's decision to abandon his family, and soon realized that there was little she could do to control her children or protect them from relentless press attention and scandal. But she was determined to make the White House comfortable and welcoming for her family, their extended community, and the American people.

Her first day in residence she met her own guests at the door and ended the ritual of military aides and liveried ushers announcing visitors in "sepulchral tones." "My feeling about the White House is that it belongs to the people. Their taxes support it. It is really theirs. And as far as possible they should be made to feel welcome here. . . . And I want the visitors to be given every courtesy." By courtesy ER did not mean official correctness but personal attention: "Sometimes, when visitors are being shown through, I may be passing by, and if I can, I shall stop and talk with them and show them about. . . . I hate the idea that I might ever lose touch with people. . . ."

The new First Lady's public style as national hostess amazed even her closest friends and seasoned journalists. Bess Furman wrote: "The century-old White House wore a startled air today, as though listening to the sound of shattering precedents. . . . She had expected 1,000 guests for tea, but 3,000 came. . . ."

She kissed her guests as they arrived, and served tea in both the state dining room and East Room. Nothing so dramatic had occurred in the East Room since "Abigail Adams had hung her wash there to dry!"

Since FDR "was much too busy finding ways and means of meeting the financial crisis . . . to be bothered with anything else," ER reorganized "the household"—and practically everything she did "shocked the ushers." ER seemed rather proud to have distressed the man most noted for his exquisite knowledge of protocol, the longtime chief usher Irwin (Ike) Hoover, whom she had first met when her uncle, TR, was president: "My first act was to insist on running the elevator myself without waiting for one of the doormen to run it for me." Ike Hoover announced that "that just wasn't done by the president's wife." But she entered the elevator, closed the door, and replied: "Now it is."

Nancy Cook, her Val-Kill partner, known for her carpentry skills and love for detail, stayed on to help redecorate. Nan and ER concentrated first on the second-floor family quarters: They hung her pictures, and FDR's pictures and prints, and "much to the horror of the household staff" lugged and hauled furniture about. The long corridors, divided into East and West Wings, were remade into public sitting areas at the east end, a cozy breakfast nook and luncheon corner at the west end.

ER selected for herself Abraham Lincoln's bedroom suite, a spacious room with brick fireplace and a bank of windows, a smaller room with corner windows, and a bathroom at the southwest end of the house. Just above the large magnolia tree planted by Andrew Jackson, her windows faced south onto a lovely view of the Rose Garden and the Washington Monument. ER converted the larger space into her study/sitting room. "It took me so long to move from bed to dressing table to wardrobe [in that very large room] that I decided I was wasting good time, so I had my bed moved into the small adjoining dressing room."

The West Wing breakfast nook/luncheon space was just outside her doors, and across the corridor a small bedroom and study facing northwest was generally reserved for Hick. ER moved a Val-Kill daybed into her sitting room, and her closest friends slept there when the house was full, which it often was. Since no beds in the house were long enough for any of the extra-long Roosevelts, she ordered new Val-Kill beds made for the entire family.

ER often felt Lincoln's presence in her room. Especially when she was working late at night, the room would get cold, and there was always the knocking of old pipes. She felt chilled as odd changes of light and air occurred, and then she would get the "curious" but "distinct feeling" that there was somebody there. The image of Lincoln would come vividly to mind, standing by the window gazing thoughtfully out over Washington. If he ever spoke to her she never mentioned it. But she never doubted that his presence and the shades of others filled the house.

FDR's bedroom and study adjoined her rooms to the east. His bedroom faced out over the Washington Monument and the Jefferson Memorial; his study was a place of historic action, known over time as the Treaty Room, the Monroe Room, and TR's Cabinet Room. When seated at his desk, FDR faced a pastel portrait of his wife which hung above the hall door. A portrait of his mother was directly behind him. When he sat on the long leather couch, which he frequently did during meetings and in moments of relaxation, he faced his mother and had his wife behind him.

While the images of his mother and wife were always present in his study, at some point FDR decided to place a large seven-drawer highboy in front of the sliding doors that connected ER's study/sitting room with his bedroom. FDR's barrier to free and spontaneous access was no casual gesture. ER herself had placed a similar piece of furniture in front of shared doorways to end her mother-in-law's unannounced intrusions on the bedroom floor of their twin East 65th Street home.

ER's favorite space was the completely open and bright corner breakfast area in front of the large lunette window at the west end of the hallway. There she held her morning meetings with staff and relaxed with friends and family. Formerly Lou Henry Hoover's solarium, the West Hall sitting area had been filled with exotic birds, wicker furniture, and extraordinary California plantings. ER brought in large wooden screens, a Val-Kill walnut drop-leaf table, and old Grant-era leather furniture, which she covered in "cheerful" cretonne slipcovers. She had breakfast and lunch there, until the weather warmed and she could eat outdoors. From spring to first frost, ER preferred breakfast and tea on the South Veranda, just below her own windows under the magnificent magnolia tree.

The corridor area outside FDR's suite was known as the East Wing, and it served as a screening room after many dinner parties. Louis Howe's bedroom, once Lincoln's study, and corner sitting room were east of FDR's suite. The Emancipation Proclamation was signed on 1 January 1863 in Howe's bedroom. These rooms were among the largest in the house, and Howe initially complained they were too grand for him. But as his health deteriorated and he became bedridden, the space seemed a small comfort.

Across from Howe's rooms were guest suites, each consisting of bedroom, sitting room, and bath. Over the years the spacious northeast corner suite housed Winston Churchill, various visiting royals, and an endless stream of more intimate family and friends who happened by.

Like many women at midlife, ER at forty-eight experienced a new level of freedom, excitement, energy, robust health. She rarely slept more than four to six hours. She arose each morning at seven or seven-thirty, filled with anticipation and high purpose. After a glass of hot water and lemon, she did stretches and calisthenics; then rode her horse Dot, a gift from Earl Miller, in Rock Creek Park for an hour or more, usually between eight and ten.

After her ride she took a cold shower, then breakfasted. Her breakfasts tended to be hearty, with a large café au lait. She allowed nobody else to pour the steamed milk and coffee together into the oversized porcelain mugs and French coffee bowls she and FDR had collected on their travels.

FDR preferred breakfast in bed or in his large oval sitting room. Usually ER returned from her ride when her husband arose, about ten, and she went in to greet him after his tray was delivered. Occasionally he joined ER in the West Hall for coffee or lunch with special friends.

In late afternoons, after the day's work but before her teas and his cocktails, she went for a brisk walk and then swam in the new pool, often with FDR. According to ER, the White House's "fine pool" was built by public donations in response to an appeal made by the New York *Daily News.* New Yorkers responded generously to ensure the health of their former governor and favorite son.

Completed by May, it became FDR's main form of exercise and physical recreation. Hick recalled that FDR "was a wonderful swimmer" and could "beat any of his boys across the White House swimming pool. Once in a game of water polo . . . he knocked one of the newspaper correspondents out cold, dragged him out and revived him! With apologies."

Agnes Brown Leach and Henry Goddard Leach also joined the First Family in the swimming pool. Splashing "about with Franklin and Eleanor," Henry Leach wrote, was hilarious: "For Franklin's long arms were not affected by the infantile paralysis that handicapped his legs, and he sprayed and ducked his wife with shouts and deep-chested laughter. In a swimming pool the Roosevelts behaved like hippopotami."

According to ER, after FDR's pool time he "went to his room for a rub-down" from George Fox, "who went with him everywhere." After his massage, FDR read through at least six evening papers, "just as many as he read in the morning; then we all joined him in his study before dinner and enjoyed a short period of rest and informal conversation."

He then presided over evening cocktails, which he always mixed him-self, in his study. ER and her circle rarely joined FDR for cocktails. Generally, after pool time, ER presided over teas, "with a beautiful lace cloth on a small drop-leaf table, a small nosegay of flowers, cinnamon toast, tiny sandwiches, cookies, little cakes, candies. . . ." According to Henrietta Nesbitt, it was a cere-monial time, with Chinese tea sent by "Mrs. James . . . like the tea Mrs. James' father, Captain Delano, had imported a century before."

As chief White House authority, ER was efficient and executive. She gave or-ders with dispatch, often on the run, and expected them to be carried out cor-rectly, immediately. She never became, however, as formal or curt as Lou Henry Hoover, who evidently taught her staff a variety of hand signals for all manner of table and household activities, as subtle and specific as those she used with her horses in dressage.

Still, ER was often impatient with her staff. When she demanded a tele-phone installed on her desk, she expected it that day. When it failed to material-ize after two days, she was annoyed. Ike Hoover explained that she was in her room so often the workers could not get in; it was improper "to have men work-ing while the president's wife was in the room." ER was irritated: "Oh Spinach, [tell them] to get started!" Workmen were to ignore her presence. As owner of a factory she was, after all, "quite accustomed to having workmen around."

Ike Hoover, and his successors Howell G. Crim (even more formal than Ike Hoover) and, after 1941, J. B. West, were often startled by ER. West never got over his "first sight of Eleanor Roosevelt in her riding habit, jodhpurs and boots, striding into the Usher's office, calling for her horse. . . ." Despite his "protestations of neutrality," Crim rather "disapproved of Mrs. Roosevelt's breezy informality." According to West, Crim "never quite recovered from the shock of one of Eleanor Roosevelt's early-morning visits to the Usher's office," when she appeared in "a yellow bathing suit!" to deliver letters for him to mail, on her way to the pool. "Eight years later," West wrote, "Mr. Crim was still aghast."

While Crim was critical, West was more "in awe of this remarkable woman. She was formal and distant with her staff, yet kind and warm to people everywhere. And she accomplished so much. None of us had a tenth of her energy."

The Roosevelts were spontaneous, exuberant; their table conversation was intense, and argumentative. Sunday evenings especially were reserved for ER's scrambled-egg salons, when she whipped the eggs herself in her favorite silver chafing dish. Friends and advisers were invited to discuss specific issues or work out particular problems. The weekly event was known as "scrambled eggs with brains."

Most evenings were notable for the ongoing sparring that occurred between ER and FDR. Generally, she chided him and he baited her. She wanted him to act on behalf of this or that outrage; he wanted her to remember the limitations of partisan politics. He tended to smile and dissemble. She tended to scowl and insist. His friends tended to think her "strident." Her friends tended to think him "slippery."

Emma Bugbee recalled a typical Sunday-evening exchange. After hours of controversy, FDR provoked ER so that "she became furious and gave vent to her feelings heatedly, while he smilingly advanced contrary views. The next day [ER] was thunderstruck to hear him blandly quoting her remarks to the British ambassador as *his* views."

ER was so astonished by this event that she related it at length years later. Fully prepared to "listen in silence" and disagreement, she wrote, "I heard Franklin telling Ambassador Robert Bingham to act, not according to the arguments that he had given me, but according to the arguments that I had given him!"

> Without giving me a glance or the satisfaction of batting an eyelash in my direction, he calmly stated as his own the policies and beliefs he had argued against the night before! To this day I have no idea whether he had simply used me as a sounding board, as he so often did, with the idea of getting the reaction of the person on the outside, or whether my arguments had been needed to fortify his decision and to clarify his own mind.

Although FDR rarely acknowledged her influence, he encouraged her public stands. She served both as "sounding board" and front-runner. He knew he could restrain her, but he rarely tried. "Lady," he said after one evening's argument, "this is a free country. Say what you think. If you get me in Dutch, I'll manage to get myself out. Anyway, the whole world knows I can't control you."

Once, only once, Lorena Hickok "had dinner alone with the President and Mrs. Roosevelt. Just the three of us, in front of the fireplace in her sitting room." Since the Roosevelts were "exceedingly hospitable and liked to have company," they "rarely dined alone, or with a single guest." That night FDR gave Hick important advice: "Never get into an argument with the Missis. You can't win. You think you have her pinned down here (thumping the table with his forefinger) but she bobs up away over there somewhere! No use—you can't win."

Politically, ER was regarded by many as second-in-command. Some FDR advisers went to ER first, to get her advice on strategy. Others went to her afterward, for support in the struggle. Still others resented her presence at the table of decision.

Beyond politics, the Roosevelts increasingly lived separate lives. The White House was actually a divided home, not unlike a feudal manor house: allied in purpose, but with competing courts. There were distinct loyalties; and their boundaries grew more formalized over time.

Central to FDR's court was his secretary and closest companion since 1920, Marguerite "Missy" LeHand. Her suite of rooms was on the third floor, bright and comfortable though small. ER accepted Missy's presence and her role as second hostess with protective, even maternal, grace. They frequently rode together in the morning and walked arm in arm in the afternoon, two tall light-haired women who had much in common.

ER treated Missy as a junior partner, but not without criticism: "Missy was young and pretty and loved a good time, and occasionally her social contacts got mixed with her work and made it hard for her and others. To me she was always kind and helpful, and when I had to be away she took up without complaint the additional social responsibilities thrust upon her."

But ER was often excluded from a private space that Missy shared with FDR and his own circle. Since he was physically constrained, entertainment needed to be brought to him—movies, card games, cocktails, convivial people. Missy discovered and cultivated the people she believed FDR would relax with. ER understood that, but carped: "As Miss LeHand lived in the White House she very often, when I was not there, invited people she thought my husband would enjoy, or whom she personally wanted, but he never gave this type of social gathering a thought."

Actually it was the area of their greatest divide, since the cocktail parties and nightly entertainments Missy arranged frequently included moments of liquid hilarity ER could not enjoy. Several guests observed that when a party was going on in FDR's quarters, ER would occasionally stop by the door and ask if she and her friends were invited; when informed that they were not, she would wordlessly leave.

Theirs was a complex arrangement. In relation to Franklin, ER still occupied a lonely sphere which echoed the isolation of her childhood. Beyond the First Family's jolly facade, ER endured a lifelong sense of exclusion that represented for her an ongoing humiliation regarding FDR's domain.

Whatever she actually felt, ER's public attitude toward Missy LeHand was that of first wife to second wife in the culture of extended ruling families. Subsequently, when she contemplated the vagaries of love for the readers of *You Learn by Living*, ER accepted her occasional inability to "meet the need of someone whom I dearly love," and in a coded reference to Missy, advised others in her situation: "You must learn to allow someone else to meet the need, without bitterness or envy, and accept it; or somehow you must make yourself learn to meet it." For most women, ER concluded, there was yet another element to the maturation process "that is almost as painful as accepting your own limitation and the knowledge of what you are unable to give. That is learning to accept what other people are unable to give. You must learn not to demand the impossible or to be upset when you do not get it."

ER was proud of her executive staff and depended completely upon them. In addition to Tommy, ER was well protected by her social secretary Edith Benham Helm. Tommy Thompson was short and feisty, while Edith Helm was trim and elegant. Both were forceful women, devoted to their boss.

Tommy seemed to some staffers rather gruff, "with a look that said *no* before you asked." But she was invariably warm and friendly to the public and to journalists, who considered her a reflection of ER's open-hearted consideration. Tommy was ER's most important working partner, and they traveled everywhere together—except on private holidays. She worked endless hours every day, although she went home to her husband at night, usually after eleven.

Edith Benham Helm had been part of ER's Washington circle during World War I. The daughter and widow of admirals, Edith Helm understood the intricacies of Washington society and was associated with "all those formidable people" ER called "cave dwellers." Formerly the second Mrs. Woodrow Wilson's social secretary, she was a stickler for protocol and propriety.

Well served by her two formidable and trusted secretaries, ER was free to pursue her political and personal interests without devoting undue time to either the household or the endless details of formal Washington.

ER brought many of the women who had worked with her during the 1920s to the White House. Most of them had worked in the Women's Division of the Democratic State or National Committee. Her own former secretary Margaret Durand (called "Rabbit") was now Louis Howe's secretary. Louise Hackmeister, who had been chief telephone operator at Women's Division headquarters, where she handled ER's calls, became chief White House operator.

A much underrated White House presence, "Hacky" performed her duties with an efficiency that dazzled Washington: "If anyone is alive and on earth, Hacky will get them." A "character" and "a tall and tough gal," Hacky "had the affairs of the world at her fingertips." She was worldly and discreet; though nothing "escaped her," she protected all confidences. She traveled with the president, and ER considered her "remarkable": Hacky "recognized everyone's voice after once hearing it," and her own "cheerful voice and word of recognition" lent a "note of pleasure and real warmth of feeling" to the White House. On call twenty-four hours a day, she managed the presidential switchboard for twenty years; she knew and understood everything, including "who was in and who was out with the President." According to Lillian Rogers Parks, then a young upstairs maid whose mother Maggie Rogers was head White House maid, the staff "used to laugh" that the White House was "run by Hicky and Hacky."

Hacky shared an apartment with Mary Eben at the Wardman-Park Hotel. She was in charge of all the gifts sent to the president, and also influenced White House staff relations. Every week Lillian Rogers went to sew at their place, and she believed Eben helped change race relations: Despite Washington's rigid Jim Crow laws, "Mrs. Eben would have none of that," and arranged to have the doorman hand the young black seamstress the key as she entered "through the front door." Public defiance of back-door rituals by such Roosevelt staffers as Mary Eben, Lillian Rogers believed, helped pave the way for the civil rights movement that would "eventually open all front doors."

Mary Eben's racial views were in stark contrast to those expressed by the three dominant members of the president's intimate staff. FDR's secretariat, the men who controlled his access to the press and arranged his daily schedule, were "good old boys" of America's southland dedicated to all the trappings of "race etiquette," the customs and traditions of servility, segregation, and discrimination. Over time, ER collided with them regularly.

Press secretary Stephen T. Early of Virginia had covered the Navy for the Associated Press when FDR was assistant secretary and had been his press secretary during the 1920 vice presidential campaign. FDR wooed him back in 1932 from the motion picture industry. Appointments secretary Marvin McIntyre of Kentucky was also a longtime friend and former journalist who worked for a newsreel company. Originally detailed to the Navy,

McIntyre was also known as a poker genius. He had been with FDR's team since 1920.

ER had more cordial relations with members of FDR's staff who were responsible for her husband's physical comfort. Their presence in the White House relieved her mind, and she admired the men who met her husband's physical needs with consideration, sensitivity, and good humor, especially FDR's black valet Irvin (Mac) McDuffie, another staffer since 1920, who traveled everywhere with FDR. His wife, Lizzie McDuffie, was ER's long-time personal maid.

Former New York State trooper Augustus (Gus) Gennerich was, with McDuffie, responsible for FDR's physical well-being. A bachelor considered reclusive by some, Gus went about the White House with a frightful English pit bulldog who shared his third-floor room. With or near the president at virtually all times, Gus and Mac helped him get up and dress in the morning and put him to bed at night. But Gus, who, with Earl Miller, had been FDR's bodyguard during the Albany years, was invited for cards and evening frolics.

ER was particularly fond of Gus and subsequently wrote that during the Albany years he and Earl Miller brought great joy to the family when they played the piano "by the hour." "They were always finding kind things to do."

Earl Miller, who was closest to ER, remained in New York. One of FDR's last public acts as governor was to appoint Miller personnel director of the New York Department of Correction. In Washington, Gus was the president's most intimate aide. Devoted and charming, his rare combination of "great strength, gentle manners, and a gentle touch" impressed everyone.

However critical or aloof ER felt toward their nightly entertainments, FDR's staff relieved her of countless burdens, unmanageable responsibilities. Along with her own staff, they enabled her to perform the purely social duties of First Wifery with remarkable cheerfulness. Moreover, they enabled her to concentrate largely on the political and public goals that most interested her.

ER achieved her first notable White House success on 6 March with her press conference for women journalists only: "I was a little nervous at first, but the girls were so nice and so friendly that I got over it quickly."

The press conferences were Hick's idea: They would establish understanding and support for the First Lady's activities, and they would ensure jobs for women in Depression-weary newspapers and wire services. Both FDR and Louis Howe had agreed with Hick's suggestion and encouraged ER to do it.

That night, ER called Hick to report on the conference. Thirty-five journalists had met in the Red Room, "and there weren't enough chairs, so some of them had to sit on the floor." Male reporters made much of this, and wrote nasty commentary about docile newshens sitting at ER's feet. But

ER enjoyed herself: "It really wasn't bad. I think I'll continue with them." And, with the kind of competitive glee that had been part of her life since she made the first team at field hockey as a student at Allenswood, she concluded: "I really beat Franklin. He isn't holding his first press conference until Wednesday!"

Those first weeks, ER felt bludgeoned by family tensions aroused by the marital woes of her children. Her mother-in-law blamed her, and the children made conflicting emotional demands. It all left her "very weary." She turned increasingly to Hick for advice and encouragement. Surrounded by critics and pundits eager to pounce upon every mishap, she relied on Hick's refreshing directness and seasoned political savvy. Hick encouraged her to keep a diary, which she refused to do, but she agreed to write the details of each day in her daily letters. Ultimately, ER's letters to Hick became the fullest record of her political and emotional concerns. She confided her deepest secrets, most worrisome problems, mundane and significant moments.

ER spent hours at her desk at the end of the day, usually at one or two in the morning, writing to Hick—as she had written daily to those she loved all her life, beginning with her father. However busy she was, however many friends and allies surrounded her, she felt alone without Hick at her side. Each day their ten-, twelve-, fifteen-page letters were filled with diary details, political tidbits, expressions of love and longing:

> Hick darling/ Oh! how good it was to hear your voice. It was so inadequate to try to tell you what it meant. [Eldest son] Jimmy was near & I couldn't say Je t'aime et je t'adore as I longed to do but always remember I am saying it & that I go to sleep thinking of you & repeating our little saying.

ER called and wrote on Hick's fortieth birthday, 7 March, and they made plans to see each other the next week. "What shall we read Hick? You choose first. . . ." After she called again, and they spoke until two in the morning, ER added a postscript: "Hick Dearest I know how unhappy you are & I'm glad Jean [Dixon] will be with you tomorrow night. . . . My thoughts are around you!"

The next night when ER called after midnight, she was relieved: "Oh! it is good to hear your voice. When it sounds right no one can make me so happy!" And "Dearest, Your two letters this morning were such a joy."

That day Bess Furman told ER that Hick had agreed to come down on 20 March for the women's press party, which surprised and delighted her—"I miss you so much & I love you so much"—and they would have many good times together. It was late when ER wrote Hick: "I am going soon to find out if F is staying up all night or not! I think when things settle I'll have some privacy & leisure! . . . Perhaps we'll be almost human by the time you come! The one thing which reconciles me to do this job is the fact that I think I can give a great many people pleasure & I begin to think there may be ways in which I can be useful."

ER was almost completely settled by the end of the first week: "My pictures are nearly all up & I have you in my sitting room where I can look at you most of my waking hours! I can't kiss you so I kiss your picture good-night and good-morning. Dont laugh!"

ER's rooms were covered with photographs—on the walls, on her desk, on the mantelpiece above the fireplace. In her bedroom, on either end of her bureau were two large photographs, with a triptych in between. Earl Miller was on the right, Louis Howe on the left, and three smaller photos of a younger FDR and her brother Hall in the triptych frame. Hick shared ER's study wall above the fireplace with Nancy Cook, Esther Lape, Tommy, and several watercolors. A larger and contemporary photo of FDR was placed over her shoulder above her reading chair. Snapshots of children and grandchildren abounded.

Throughout her adult life, ER juggled countless relationships, but very few were emotionally absorbing. She craved company and rarely had a meal or even a walk by herself. She was restless and easily diverted. She tended to divide her day into fifteen-minute meetings. When the business was done, she stood to announce the meeting's end. For luncheons, teas, and dinners, she would combine the most unlikely people and trust to everybody's good manners.

Nobody else in ER's life filled the particular place in her heart now reserved for Hick:

> One more day marked off. . . . My dear, may I forget there are other reporters present or must I behave? I shall want to hug you to death. I can hardly wait! . . .
> The nicest time of the day is when I write to you. You have a stormier time than I do but I miss you as much I think. I couldn't bear to think of you crying yourself to sleep. *Oh!* How I wanted to put my arms about you in reality instead of in spirit. . . . Please keep most of your heart in Washington as long as I'm here for most of mine is with you!

But Hick worried about all the other people around ER, dreaded the time she spent with them, and feared the intensity of her other friendships. In response, ER wrote:

> Remember one thing always no one is just what you are to me. I'd rather be with you this minute than any one else and yet I love many other people and some of them can do things for me probably better than

you could, but I've never enjoyed being with anyone the way I enjoy being with you.

ER's nightly letters to Hick were filled with the often hilarious details of hectic days.

> Did I tell you that the first day in his office, at 5 pm FDR found himself with nothing to do. Horrors! Nothing like that had happened to him in years! So he reached under his desk & rang all five bells, & people ran in from every side to find him calmly demanding something to do! He had the start of a cold yesterday. I fed him a pill. At the conference in the evening he took a senatorial pill, a congressional pill, a treasury one, an attorney general one, & today he is cured! He is having such a good time that his mood is amusing most of the time!

Politically, ER felt effervescent. She was enthusiastic and filled with visions of usefulness. But her heart was divided. The day after she wrote Hick that she could not "bear to think of you crying yourself to sleep," they made plans to see each other. ER would not wait for Hick to attend the women's press party but would journey immediately to New York. There were political things to be done to bolster FDR's legislative activities, and they could spend two days together:

> We could lunch at the [East 65th Street] house Tuesday if Anna is out or if you don't mind having her with us but I thought you'd rather be alone in a crowd than have anyone else to talk to. It shall be just as you say dear. Stick to your diet . . . & you'll forget you are 40 and please go to the doctor next week.

On Monday, 13 March, ER took a late train to New York, "scorning a private compartment." She sat in "an ordinary Pullman seat" and dismissed Secret Service protection. Hick wrote the AP releases of the First Lady's visit.

The next day at the Women's Trade Union League meeting, where ER went to rally New York's women's network, she intended to be unobtrusive. But her very effort made headlines: "Mrs. Roosevelt Bars Police Guard." Upon her arrival the First Lady walked up to the uniformed policemen posted at the entrance and asked:

"What are you all doing here?"

"We're here to guard Mrs. Roosevelt."

"I don't want to be guarded; please go away. . . ."

"We can't do that, the captain placed us here."

ER entered the building and telephoned Louis Howe, who telephoned police headquarters, which sent the captain. ER met him at the front hall, pointed to the crowd that had gathered, drawn by all the uniforms, and said:

"Please take them all away. It's just an attraction. No one is going to hurt me." After the police were removed, ER "partook" of the WTUL luncheon, with young working women and members of ER's "committee on rest rooms [temporary shelters] for unemployed girls."

After the WTUL meeting, ER walked up Lexington Avenue to visit the New York League of Girls' Clubs canteen established "for girls looking for jobs" and the Unemployed Girls' Hostel maintained by the Salvation Army. These were ER's primary constituents, mostly single unemployed women whose needs New Deal legislation completely bypassed. Their very existence was ignored during the first hundred days.

ER returned to Washington by air on the 16th. *The New York Times* announced: "She Set Precedent as the First White House Lady to Travel in Plane." For ER the flight was noteworthy above all because she was not distressed by the ordeal of motion sickness, which had often plagued her, especially at sea. For some reason ER never became airsick, although her traveling companions Tommy and Emma Bugbee did: "Well, we had a very bumpy trip but I was fine. . . ."

The 17th of March was the Roosevelts' twenty-eighth anniversary. Seventeen guests were invited for dinner, which was festive in shades of green to honor St. Patrick's Day. Thoughtfully, Mrs. Nesbitt, head housekeeper, provided husband and wife with their favorite desserts: angel-food cake for ER, fruitcake for FDR.

ER was impressed by the after-dinner film *Gabriel Over the White House*. In the classic comedy starring Walter Huston, an insecure president is surrounded by tough-minded politicians who discourage his democratic faith in the people. Knocked out by a car accident and inspired by the Angel Gabriel, he awakens determined to be all he can be, do all he can do for the people of Depression America. The film's army of unemployed marchers who descended upon Washington from all over America caused ER to reflect upon her astonished dismay at Herbert Hoover's cruel response to the 1932 Bonus Marchers—and to argue with dinner guests who defended him.

She wrote Hick: Like Hoover, they would call "soldiers out if a million unemployed marched on Washington & I'd do what the President does in the picture!"

From May to June 1932, the Bonus Expeditionary Force, comprised of twenty thousand World War I veterans and their families, encamped along the marshy Anacostia flats across the bridge from the nation's capital in a sprawling "Hooverville." There to lobby Congress for the immediate release of their promised bonus, the veterans were optimistic as the Wright-Patman bill was debated. On 15 June the House passed the bill, but two days later it was defeated in the Senate, 62–18. As Congress prepared to adjourn and the sweltering heat of Washington's summer descended, they determined to stay until President Hoover addressed their plight. But Hoover refused even to meet with their representatives. He offered them train fare out of town, but they lingered and demonstrated. Convinced the Bonus Marchers were communist agitators, Red-controlled harbingers of an American insurrection, he decided to act. During the evening rush hour on 28 July 1932, one of the most photographed and widely witnessed moments of state terrorism in U.S. history occurred. "The Battle of Washington" was followed by a midnight attack on their campsite.

The burn-and-destroy mission was led by four units of cavalry wearing gas masks and steel helmets, with sabers drawn, backed by five tanks, followed by the infantry with fixed bayonets, all under the personal supervision of General Douglas MacArthur, with George Patton and Dwight David Eisenhower in minor roles. Over one thousand veterans and their families were tear-gassed and bayoneted. Although there was no resistance, more than 1,500 tear gas grenades and candles went off as the destitute army of unemployed and homeless Americans ran north into the night. Their campsites were burned, their meager possessions destroyed. As Washington watched the flames over Anacostia, Hoover's humanitarian reputation went up in smoke.

ER was stunned and wrote: "I shall never forget my feeling of horror when I learned that the Army had actually been ordered to evict the veterans. . . . Many people were injured, some of them seriously. This one incident shows what fear can make people do, for Mr. Hoover was a Quaker who abhorred violence, and General MacArthur, his Chief of Staff, must have known how many veterans would resent the order and never forget it. . . ."

When ER contemplated *Gabriel Over the White House*, which coincided with the news that Bonus Marchers prepared to return to Washington, she vowed to do whatever needed to be done "to prevent a similar tragedy."

In May, her opportunity arrived. Bonus Marchers returned not only to demand their bonus but also to protest FDR's Economy Act, which reduced their meager benefits by almost half. Although FDR promised nothing, he treated the veterans cordially. Administration officials met with them; they were given a clean campsite, with sanitation facilities at Fort Hood, Virginia, and three meals a day.

Louis Howe handled negotiations and met with them regularly in a government auditorium. But not until ER visited their campsite did they believe there was a dime's worth of difference between Hoover and Roosevelt.

Howe asked ER to drive him to the campsite. When they arrived, he announced he would sleep in the car while she toured the camp: "I got out and walked over to where I saw a line-up of men waiting for food. They looked at me curiously and one of them asked my name and what I wanted. When I said I just wanted to see how they were getting on, they asked me to join them."

ER spent over an hour with the veterans. They reminisced about the war and sang old Army songs: "There's a Long, Long Trail a-Winding," "Pack Up Your Troubles in Your Old Kit Bag." ER was introduced to a "Negro veteran whose breast bore many decorations" and who sang "Mother Machree." ER waded through ankle-deep mud to visit the marchers' living quarters and the new hospital. In the large convention tent, she addressed the group and apologized for the fact that she could tell them nothing about their bonus. But she had seen the war, toured the battlefields, and understood their anger. She had driven a truck through the railroad yards in the cold of night, and talked with the boys as they left. She had served coffee and prepared sandwiches for those young men, eager to go into the unknown. And she had seen them when they returned, hobbling on crutches or carried off the trains, and had visited them in hospitals.

Interrupted repeatedly by cheers, she concluded: "I never want to see another war. I would like to see fair consideration for everyone, and I shall always be grateful to those who served their country. I hope we will never have to ask such service again. . . ."

The entire group accompanied her to her car, and waved her off with songs and hope.

The veterans did not get their bonus. FDR urged them to join the Civilian Conservation Corps, which many did. Many also returned home galvanized politically. ER had helped to renew their faith. The First Lady would fight for their interests.

Many of FDR's advisers were horrified that his wife had shown courtesy to Red insurrectionists. Her visit, they protested, encouraged mob rule and raised expectations of support. Nonsense, she insisted: There was no reason for excitement. She had merely spent a decent moment with one of America's most deserving groups.

Although she could not persuade FDR of the wisdom of releasing the bonus, she was pleased with her first major diplomatic venture and hoped that it "had a good effect." ER told her press conference that there had been nothing to worry about: "It was as comfortable as a camp can be, remarkably clean and orderly, grand-looking boys, a fine spirit. There was no kind of disturbance, nothing but the most courteous behavior."

On 18 March, the day after the anniversary party, Hick arrived in Washington for a three-day visit, highlighted by the Women's National Press Club dinner. ER was the first First Lady to attend the annual frolic, and she broke all traditions when she agreed to take the "last word" of rebuttal at the end of the evening. There is no record of her remarks to the three hundred women in the grand ballroom of the Willard Hotel, since the "rule of no reporters present" prevailed during her talk. Nevertheless, she was triumphant, and Washington's most observant and critical women remembered her as "tall, vivacious, laughter-lit." ER's capacity to laugh at herself, spontaneously and robustly, was one of her most endearing qualities.

ER enjoyed these parties, and she soon introduced her own annual party for women of the press and other women in public life which alternated with the press club's. ER's annual Gridiron Widows party, for women only, given in the White House, was her indignant response to the fact that FDR and the men of the cabinet went off to the sacred and exclusive male journalists' annual Gridiron Club dinner, still closed to all women.

It became the highlight of her social season. For years the Gridiron Widows dinner was an occasion for unbridled merriment, political satire, serious costumes. All the women associated with the Roosevelt administration were invited: journalists and their guests, and "women distinguished in arts and letters." ER worked hard on her own skits for these parties, as she did for FDR's annual birthday frolic. Thus, at least twice a year, ER conceived and performed in rather wild theatrical routines, usually done with the help of her daughter Anna, Elinor Morgenthau, and Louis Howe.

Although Hick's first postinaugural visit to Washington was arranged around the women's press club party, and she was elegant in her new black gown, she did not even mention it in the fifteen-page article she wrote about her weekend. That omission underscored her pain and confusion as her career as a top political journalist clashed with her efforts to protect her First Friend, and began to unravel.

In her essay, Hick tried to reconcile her rough-and-tumble life with her new status as the First Lady's intimate friend. To protect ER and herself, she decided not to publish her story. But it provided significant insight into the tensions and dynamics of their efforts to confront and accommodate their new situation. ER was surprised when Hick hesitated upon entering her room. Hick explained:

> She looked taller than I had remembered, and stately. Her voice sounded the same—only far away. Perhaps it was the gown, which I had never seen before. Or the bigness of the room. . . . She reached over and laid her hand on my shoulder.
> "Don't be that way," she said.
> We sat on a sofa beside the fireplace. The room was blue—blue carpet, blue hangings, blue shadows outside the yellow circles of the lamps. . . .
> At length she said, "You must go in and say hello to Franklin."

She studied my face gravely for an instant. Then she laughed and held out her hand.

"Come on! You are a house guest, you know!"

Before the formal Saturday dinner Hick paused in discomfort as she confronted her actual situation as the First Lady's friend.

As I tiptoed out into the corridor, Mrs. Roosevelt came toward me—tall, cool, unhurried, in a white evening gown. Again that feeling that there was something different about her. I smiled uneasily.

"Franklin and the others are going down in the elevator," she said, taking my arm. "I'm going to take you down the grand stairway!"

My gown was new, and its hem swept the floor, the longest skirt I had ever worn. It seemed to me that black lace was wound round my ankles in great, heavy folds. Getting to the stairway required almost painful physical effort. . . .

Ahead of me, a reassuring stretch of crimson carpet. But my sense of relief was quickly invaded by new misgivings as my eyes picked out, away down at the end of the corridor, the black of dinner coats and the white gleam of bare shoulders. . . .

After dinner, Hick and ER joined FDR for drinks. "With amazing frankness we discussed public questions. . . . Seated on a sofa, smoking in an ivory cigarette holder the 15-cent brand of cigarettes he prefers, the President appeared to be enjoying himself thoroughly." ER knitted; calm returned. When ER took her dogs for their run, Hick and FDR agreed to "one more cigarette. . . ."

Over time the White House became in part Hick's own residence. It was during the Roosevelt era, much like a grand hotel, and Hick's shyness evaporated.

More immediately, on 12 April ER sailed down the Potomac aboard the *Sequoia* with FDR and Britain's prime minister, Ramsay MacDonald, as they discussed the London Economic Conference. But she was specifically exiled from the conversation, banished to the siderails while the men conferred beyond her hearing. As ER contemplated her isolated voyage, she wrote Hick: "Blue sky & sun, our first day on the river, and, tho I never think it is a very pretty river, still the remoteness is grand, and sun, even on muddy water, gleams and dances, and the trees are green." She paused to contemplate the men in deep and somber conversation, and wondered: "Is history being made? What road is the world going to take? And will this day count?" ER decried her lack of information: "I'd give something to know anything authentic on Germany or Russia."

Initially charmed by Labour Party leader Ramsay MacDonald, whose views of the World Court, disarmament, and international economic policies coincided with her own, she considered him "a great man." "What delightfully well-read, cultured people some Englishmen are!" His lunchtime stories fascinated her. "How do they read so much when they are so busy? I think they take more holidays." She was impressed by his daughter Ishbel, who was subsequently elected to Parliament, and they became friends.

A lifelong pacifist, one of the founders of Britain's Union of Democratic Control (UDC), which opposed World War I and called for democratic control of international affairs, Ramsay MacDonald was associated with America's leading pacifists and social reformers, including Lillian Wald, who had been president of the American Union Against Militarism, and Jane Addams, who was president of the Women's International League for Peace and Freedom.

In 1924, MacDonald became England's first Labour prime minister in a disastrous government that lasted less than a year. Now he headed a minority coalition government, sought to end imperial rule, and worked ardently for world peace and economic amity, particularly the reduction or erasure of wartime debts the Allies owed the United States. To right the wrongs of the Treaty of Versailles, his controversial "MacDonald Plan" emphasized military parity between Germany and France and voluntary British disarmament. Winston Churchill thought him mad, especially after Hitler achieved power.

The disarmament conference, which continued to meet irregularly in Geneva, had been stalled since 1931 and all MacDonald's other efforts collapsed during the worldwide Depression. Now he hoped to achieve an accord with FDR, to present Anglo-American unity at the London Economic Conference in June. FDR was delightful company, but vague and elusive. He seemed always to agree, but promised nothing.

ER feared that FDR's campaign deal with William Randolph Hearst, during which he promised to keep America aloof from Europe and its woes, remained his priority. She deplored isolationism and economic nationalism and doubted that her husband intended to agree to anything. On international issues he was vague and elusive with her as well, and it galled her. Ardent for peace, ER turned to her mentors for support, and astonishingly gave presidential correspondence to MacDonald's old ally, Lillian Wald.

The day before ER sailed on the *Sequoia*, Lillian Wald wrote to Mary Rozet Smith, Jane Addams's partner of forty years, promising to "send you and JA the correspondence between the Prime Minister and the President which brought about this visit."

Presumably, when ER visited Wald in April she had brought the letters with her, determined to pursue her convictions regarding this urgent meeting to secure economic stability and world peace. But FDR made it clear that international issues were not ER's business, and she was furious to be excluded from decisive conversations.

On 20 April 1933, ER addressed the annual meeting of the Travelers Aid Society, which had cared for over 2,600 homeless men and women during the year, over half under the age of twenty-one. The First Lady was irate that no relief was even contemplated for these young people, and spoke sharply about their neglect: "I think there has been so much emphasis on family relief work and family welfare that single men and women are having pretty much of a hard time. A basket of food does not do much good when the recipient has no place to cook or eat it."

ER was outraged that no New Deal legislation had even considered these facts, and she said so publicly. It was the beginning of her lifelong campaign for youth, affordable housing, and economic opportunity for all people.

That night, with advance press notice, ER flew over Washington with Amelia Earhart. Press secretary Steve Early's memo to photographers, "all right for movies and stills," enabled full documentation of the after-dinner party. According to *The New York Times*, "The First Lady of the Land and the first woman to fly the [Atlantic Ocean] went skylarking together tonight in a big Condor plane."

The flying party included ER's brother Hall; Amelia Earhart's husband, George Palmer Putnam; the plane's captain, E. H. Parker; and several reporters.

Amelia Earhart flew from Washington to Baltimore "without even removing her white evening gloves." ER told reporters: "It does mark an epoch, doesn't it, when a girl in evening dress and slippers can pilot a plane at night." Also in evening dress, ER flew part of the trip in the cockpit with Captain Parker.

She was delighted: "It was lovely. Out there in front with no obstructions to the view one could see everything and it felt like being on top of the world!"

When "the plane made a most peculiar serpentine side swing," Amelia Earhart laughed: "Oh, Mrs. Roosevelt's flying the plane!"

ER had taken flying lessons and this flight was in part a celebration for the Amateur Air Pilots Association, which she had joined. She was always disappointed that FDR specifically asked her not to fly herself, not to become a pilot. He had enough to worry about, and it was one of the few limitations he imposed, or asked her to make—for his sake. She complied, but she flew as a passenger whenever possible, and logged more miles in the air than many pilots.

ER rejoiced in the modern adventure. The world had changed so dramatically within her own lifetime: electric lights, long-distance telephone, radio, automobiles, movies, airplanes. A "new woman" in the 1920s, ER was a "modern" woman in the 1930s. Occasionally her modernity astounded the world, but she celebrated the best of the changes: "We can know and see many more people, we can do so much more in a day. . . . There is greater opportunity to develop." And all the new opportunities guaranteed a more "valuable and interesting" life than was previously available to women. "It is almost impossible to compare the girl of today with the girl of thirty or forty years ago."

For ER, even social obligations offered political compensation: Teas and receptions were the means by which the American people entered the White House and came face to face with the hearth that symbolized her husband's government. ER considered her job as First Lady important, even if "standing and shaking hands for an hour or so, two or three times a week," was "not exactly an inspiring occupation."

"At the first few receptions of each season, my arms ached, my shoulders ached, my back ached, and my knees and feet seemed to belong to someone else. However . . . I was lucky in having a supple hand which never ached." She was particularly grateful to the military aides who gave her wise advice about "how to stand and not grow weary." After an especially long reception line, when ER complained that she had become so stiff she could no longer bend her knees or actually move, a young Marine told her: "Oh, you should not stand so rigidly. Just bend your knees a little, frequently. No one will notice and you will be much less tired."

People noticed ER's warmth. One visitor wrote that she went through the line and then stood about to watch the First Lady's energetic greeting. She wondered: "Do you shake and think, or do you just stand and shake?" ER replied that she concentrated on faces,

> because being a little deaf I never really heard names. Of course, when you look at people carefully, you have various reactions: you think "what a pretty and intelligent face," or "what a kind face," and so on. However, when there are a great many people, toward the end faces become blurred. Once I walked into the dining room after the receiving was over and saw two old friends. "Where did you come from?" I said, and they told me they had gone through the line and that I had shaken hands with them warmly.

For all her public concerns, a peculiar flaw haunted ER's household administration: The food served at her table was notably dreadful, and each household decision was channeled through the routinely churlish acts of Henrietta Nesbitt, ER's stubborn choice for White House chef and head housekeeper.

3: ER's Revenge:
Henrietta Nesbitt, Head Housekeeper

———⟨ø⟩⟨ø⟩⟨ø⟩———

*E*R's careless attitude toward food during the White House years has long been dismissed as a reflection of her lack of interest in mundane matters. But ER was actually fussy, obsessed with details. She and FDR personally researched and designed the new White House dinner service of a thousand pieces of ivory china. Dirt and dust annoyed her to the point of conducting top sergeant equivalents "of a white glove inspection." She personally arranged fresh-cut flowers and centerpieces from the White House greenhouse and selected from a variety of silver and crystal decorations, always mindful of FDR's favorite, a silver boat sailing on a sea of glass. Flowers pleased ER. She attended flower shows and studied her friends' gardens. She took and gave cuttings; she was proud of her own garden at Val-Kill and fully appreciated the White House gardens and greenhouses. In light of her attention to detail, ER's determination to retain Henrietta Nesbitt, who exasperated FDR, reveals an aspect of ER's complex emotional reality.

Whatever the First Lady's conscious reasons, no household decision was better suited to dampen the president's pleasure. She could have had the services of the most accomplished chefs and household managers in North America. But she insisted on Henrietta Nesbitt, a political ally in the League of Women Voters and Hyde Park neighbor. She had operated a pleasant tea house, and ER liked her baked goods. Because her husband, Henry, was ill and out of work, she needed a job. ER also gave Henry Nesbitt a job on the White House staff. Moreover, ER transferred to Mrs. Nesbitt full responsibility for the White House. She supervised the kitchen, dominated the staff, controlled the food and the flavors.

White House meals served by "La Nesbitt" were noteworthy. The porridge was runny; the soups were watery; the salads were tossed with chunks of marshmallow and canned fruit. FDR complained. Guests commented. Gossips gossiped. The staff was embarrassed; friends and intimates were distressed. Some, like Harold Ickes, secretary of the interior, were discreet and relegated their thoughts to their private diaries:

The President and Mrs. Roosevelt gave their annual official dinner to the Cabinet last night. There were about eighty at table. I am bound to confess that the White House dinners are neither inspiring nor do they stand out as Lucullan repasts. I am not very fussy about my food . . . but it does seem a little out of proportion to use a solid-gold knife and fork on ordinary roast mutton.

It was not that ER did not herself care about food. When she traveled, she wrote home about new dishes, flavors, and spices that delighted her. She routinely took her friends to fine restaurants, and, in homage to her great mentor Marie Souvestre, preferred French cuisine. She regularly paused to compliment the creators of well-prepared dishes and sent praise to various chefs she considered exceptional. Nevertheless, tough meat and exhausted vegetables became expected White House fare.

Despite her genuine consideration for the needs and wants of her guests, ER allowed the food and drink served at her White House table to become a subject of derision. When wine was again served for the first time since Woodrow Wilson's administration, ER was quick to say the prewar custom of four to six dinner wines would not be revived. She would serve only "light American wines," and only two of them—a white and a red, "perhaps a sauterne and a burgundy."

According to Ickes, "Mrs. Roosevelt had announced that she would serve one glass each of two domestic wines and she kept her word. The sherry was passable, but the champagne was undrinkable. I hopefully took one drink and then set my glass down with a final gesture." Elizabeth Ann Farley, James Farley's wife, "almost made a face when she tasted the champagne. She was quite indignant. . . . She seems to be quite fussy about the quality and quantity of her wines, although Jim [the son of a saloonkeeper] never touches a drop. . . . It does seem to me that if decent champagne can't be made in the United States, it ought to be permissible, even for the White House, to serve imported champagne."

Days later, FDR "joked" about the dreadful drinks and explained that only minutes "before dinner he had asked Mrs. Roosevelt about the wine and she said she was going to serve domestic champagne from New York State, recommended by Rex Tugwell. The President told her that she ought not to serve domestic champagne, but she replied that it had been on the ice and that it was too late to change. The President said that he has been apologizing ever since."

ER's failure to consult a wine steward about what was possible or agreeable to serve after so many years of Prohibition was consistent with her refusal to employ anybody but Mrs. Nesbitt to preside over the kitchen. In anticipation of ghastly repasts, some White House guests routinely dined before they arrived.

ER was not unmindful of the complaints. She brought FDR's objections to Mrs. Nesbitt. But the head housekeeper always had an excuse: She was saving money, as she was told to do. But you said there would be thirty for dinner, and there were forty-two; of course the soup was watery.

Undoubtedly, some of the criticism heaped upon Mrs. Nesbitt actually belonged to ER. Gracious and generous, ER invited people to dinner throughout the day. House guests filled every room. Each had their own menus and needs; some were served separately on trays in their rooms. Teas and larger social affairs were attended by literally hundreds more than originally planned for.

Also, ER was interested in inexpensive and experimental foods that her nutritionist friends promoted for Depression-ravaged America. Enthusiastic about "new foods" Flora Rose and her team of nutritionists had developed at Cornell University, ER introduced them into the White House. For weeks, she served "economy meals" to illustrate the new range of inexpensive and healthful diets.

Until ER's efforts, the home economics movement in New York State was an under-funded educational Cinderella. ER championed it as a life-enhancing part of the struggle for women's rights and empowerment. One of ER's earliest trips as First Lady was to Cornell in March 1933. She and Hick were impressed with Flora Rose's inexpensive, "correctly balanced" meals. At a cost of 7½ cents for each adult and 9½ cents for each child (the difference between the 1933 costs of coffee and milk), the first 7½-cent White House lunch consisted of hot stuffed eggs with tomato sauce, whole wheat toast, mashed potatoes, prune pudding, and coffee or milk. ER assured the press that her low-cost menus would be limited to "occasions when there were no guests."

But neither household generosity nor her interest in 7½ cent meals explained ER's twelve-year defense of Henrietta Nesbitt, who was one of the greatest anomalies of the Roosevelt White House. Completely unprepared for her job, she was fifty-nine years old and had never worked for anybody else before. She told her husband: "It's just keeping house, and I've kept house all my life. Only, instead of seeing that you and boys are cared for, I'll have the President and his family to worry about. You'll see how simple it will be. I've been keeping house for six. Now I'll multiply by ten, and keep house for sixty!" She recognized that the "White House would be a big responsibility, but Mrs. Roosevelt had said I could do it, so I knew I could."

Politically, Mrs. Nesbitt was a fervent Democrat, and she credited ER for her views: She had studied "astrology, and the stars foretold that this was the start of the woman's era, that the man's world was coming to an end . . . Think of the progress women have made in the last eighty years! Before then a woman couldn't call her second-best bonnet her own."

However flamboyant Mrs. Nesbitt was politically, even ER was mystified by her culinary disasters. When confronted by the damage done to new peas she had herself bought from a woman's stand in the country, she complained: "Will you tell whoever cooked the peas tonight that they were just as hard as bullets, though they were small and should have been very nice."

Since Mrs. Nesbitt managed to ruin even salads and steamed vegetables (ER's favorite foods), ER proposed that Mrs. Nesbitt visit Schrafft's to learn how their chefs worked: "So I went to New York and spent a couple of days in Schrafft's kitchens, and . . . they showed me just how they managed to get every bit of vegetable from kitchen to plate, looking as if it were specially cooked." But all the "tricks" she learned were sabotaged by her discovery that she could cook "the vegetable water down to a broth" which she then used to smother the fresh steamed vegetables: That "was a trick of my own," and made everything "tastier."

Mrs. Nesbitt dismissed all criticism. When FDR said, "The vegetables are watery," he was bored by sweetbreads and brains, or "sick of liver and beans," she said, "these were figures of speech."

The White House food situation actually made national headlines in 1936: "FDR DEMANDS NEW DEAL—REFUSES SPINACH—CRISIS STRIKES." Mrs. Nesbitt "felt terrible. I was sensitive and overworked, and this was ridicule that curled up my very soul." And "I was doing my best. Keeping him content was my job. . . ."

But she failed, as did ER. He was merely given to "tizzy-wizzys" over food, she once told her head housekeeper. ER had persuaded herself that FDR, widely known for his epicurean tastes, really had no serious gourmet interests. Actually, before Henrietta Nesbitt entered the scene, ER told a reporter that if she served FDR "bacon and eggs three times a day he would be perfectly satisfied."

ER's curious disregard for her husband's tastes suggests an explanation for her persistent defense of Henrietta Nesbitt: The housekeeper was one expression of her passive-aggressive behavior in a marriage of remarkable and labyrinthine complexity.

Endlessly embattled but irrevocably united, Eleanor and Franklin had in their separate courts achieved a balance of power. ER only rarely but modestly complained about Missy; Franklin only rarely but quietly complained about Mrs. Nesbitt. Later, after Louis Howe's death in 1936, the balance between them was temporarily upended by the presence of Betsey, James's wife, in FDR's court. During that tense time, FDR bellowed rather loudly about Mrs. Nesbitt. ER reached for her pen, and seemed to jest at her husband's distaste and distress in her column. When his "tizzy-wizzy" over spinach made head-lines, he became furious, and it was a serious moment between them—not actually healed until ER took to her bed, after which FDR worked earnestly to restore his wife's good cheer.

ER's lifelong inability to reflect on the sources of her feelings resulted in headaches, sudden bursts of cold, unexpected and confusing acts of distance and derision. As a young matron she described her "Griselda" moods with impatience and dismay. She hated to acknowledge turbulence or depression. She once told a grandchild who was crying in the hallway, to go sit in the bathtub until the tears stopped. During the White House years she generally dealt with unwanted emotions by plunging into new and exciting work or mind-absorbing details. ER engineered her life. She assigned, perhaps even enjoyed, barriers and surrogates for her feelings. In addition to Henrietta Nesbitt and Lorena Hickok, to whom ER once wrote "your vehemence always makes me calm," there were her uncontrollable, rambunctious dogs.

Camouflaged by her considerate and gracious manner, ER's aggressive side was indirect. She initially went everywhere accompanied by two unruly dogs. At the end of each day, she walked Tommy to the gate for a final conversation, and to exercise her dogs. Unfettered, they barked and growled, leaped and frolicked. One night her little Scottie, Meggie, became "very obstreperous." ER wrote Hick: "barking loudly," she chased "a rather terrified woman with a little boy, who was peacefully walking home past the White House."

ER's Scottie and police dog, Major, were loyal to her and jealous of her attentions. Major was a present from Earl Miller, who trained him to protect his lady—to be suspicious of quick or sudden movements and to prevent anybody from getting too close. Once Major bit Hick on the elbow as she tried to loosen a stuck zipper for ER. Hick was amazed, since she considered herself one of Major's pals.

Though he was a large distracting presence, ER nevertheless brought her German shepherd to her first press conference. But Major barked at anybody who spoke, except ER. His behavior became so agitated that he was led away in disgrace. According to Bess Furman, Major preferred men in blue uniforms with brass buttons to the women of the press. Over time, both dogs nipped and growled without discrimination—friends, politicians, diplomats.

Major bit Arkansas Senator Hattie Caraway on the arm, during ER's first large Gridiron Widows party. ER was fond of Hattie Caraway, who, during the 1924 congressional hearings on the Bok Peace Prize and World Court, had protested the brutal questioning ER and Esther Lape endured. After Bess Furman wrote of Major's indiscretions, Meggie bit her on the face during a drive with ER, requiring several stitches. After other incidents, ER finally agreed to part company with her dogs. "That was a sad day for me and no one thought it wise to say too much to me about dogs for a long time."

One might argue that ER had an imperious temper, even a cruel streak. But saints and melancholy Griseldas are generally unconscious of such impulses, and tend to regret them when confronted by their impact.

Moreover, neither anguish nor spite settles the mystery of ER's support for Mrs. Nesbitt. A continual source of household unrest, she also contradicted many of ER's deepest convictions. Beyond FDR's state of general annoyance, her guests were discomforted, her friends insulted, her staff disturbed. Nobody was excluded from Nesbitt's sense of order. Upset by those who burned cigarette holes in the tablecloths, she asked ER: "Do you think the President can keep an eye on the tablecloths?"

That was too much for ER, who snapped "Of course not!"

Undaunted, Mrs. Nesbitt ordered a butler to keep his eyes peeled for offenders. He, alas, returned "grinning." FDR had burned "a hole himself, and when he saw it, he looked around guilty-like, and put his salt cellar over it quick."

ER's guests made demands, and Mrs. Nesbitt bristled at their presumptions, their manners, their clothes. "Some of the house guests behaved as if they were in a hotel." But ER "never complained." "With Mrs. Roosevelt it was intellect that mattered. I don't believe she noticed a person's color any more than she did their dress."

But the First Lady's efforts to democratize the White House bothered Henrietta Nesbitt. Imperious with the staff, she had contempt for "foreigners," and was rude to international dignitaries: "Usually for Orientals and South Americans we had a lot of sticky and colorful sweets."

According to Lillian Rogers Parks: "Getting around Mrs. Nesbitt became a way of life." One day in preparation for a visiting Latin American head of state and his family, she told the staff: "Don't bother to put the good linen sheets on the beds for these people." The maids "marched right into the guest room and put on the finest sheets we could find."

Mrs. Nesbitt's attitude resulted in tension and ill will, but ER ignored it. When ER entered the White House, she was told that she had to cut the household budget by 25 percent. To do so, she fired the resident staff, which was white, and replaced them with black staff, most of whom had been in service with her for many years. She explained that it was easier for white employees to find alternative jobs in Depression America.

Kathcrine Buckley, who had been chief cook for seven years, wrote a bitter letter to Jim Farley on behalf of the fired staff: "I consider it a disgrace to our [Democratic] party to place colored help in the positions that we now hold. Some form of preference should be given to those of us who serve with honor and efficiency. . . ."

Farley sent the correspondence on to ER, who replied to Buckley that she "grieved very much" over the need to let anybody go, but "government expenditures have to be curtailed . . .":

> I have had my own servants for a great many years. They happen to be colored, because I had colored servants when I lived in Washington, and have kept on with the same ones or their friends ever since; but the question of their being white or colored has nothing whatever to do with dismissal. . . .
>
> You will understand I know, that one does get attached to the people one is accustomed to, regardless of their race. . . ."

But then ER's black staff was supervised by Mrs. Nesbitt, who was outraged when ER extended her belief in workers' rights to the White House staff: The First Lady simply announced one day that "the eight-hour day had to be. It doubled our expenses, and also the help got the day and a half free every week." Despite ER's generous benefits, some still "grouched". In the beginning, "the girls had worked all day, and the butlers, too, and not a peep out of them." It left Mrs. Nesbitt exhausted.

She had expected to find support for her views from Franklin's mother. But when Sara Delano Roosevelt visited "during these troubles," she agreed with ER. "Mrs. James" and the First Lady "had more in common than the Republicans seemed to think. . . ."

Since ER fired servants when necessary, including several who drank or in any way caused trouble, one must pause to consider her unusual attitude toward Mrs. Nesbitt. Why did she protect the household's most continual source of discontent, who relentlessly distressed her husband's epicurean tastes?

Competitive and controlling, ER was politically direct, but emotionally evasive. Many of her intimates had reason to notice that when hurt or discontented, ER would withdraw, become detached. When her clear blue eyes turned to ice, warmth drained from the very walls of the room. Without a word of anger exchanged, ER could freeze the stoutest heart. ER's long-term loyalty to Mrs. Nesbitt might then be best understood in terms of her relationship to FDR.

According to Lillian Rogers Parks, Mrs. Nesbitt had a most determined "contempt for the desires of the President." If he ordered hot coffee, he might get cold tea. "If he ordered something special, she just ignored it." And every culinary thing she touched seemed to turn to gruel. While Mrs Nesbitt did not personally do the cooking, "she stood over the cooks, making sure that each dish was overcooked or undercooked or ruined one way or another."

But FDR could have demanded her removal. Although he side-stepped Mrs. Nesbitt's tyranny, he consented to her tenure. To do otherwise would have destroyed the first couple's hard-won balance of power. Over the years, "his" people sent gift baskets filled with delicacies from around the country and the world. Neighboring hotels increasingly received White House orders. Some believed he took such frequent trips home to Hyde Park because of his mother's exquisite chef. His friends were ever mindful of his favorite foods and from every trip hunters and fishermen sent their game—pheasants, turkeys, quail; and every sort of fish, smoked, broiled, baked. Generous offerings arrived well prepared, and ready to serve.

Domestic matters were never ER's favorite domain. She was convinced that women's energy, encouraged and unconfined, would change the world. It was the essence of her philosophy, her creed, and it enabled her to become the most loved, most controversial, most hated, and most effective First Lady in U.S. history. But as First Wife, her flaws were fabled. Eleanor Roosevelt was nobody's idea of a homebody.*

*Bess Truman finally replaced Henrietta Nesbitt—for insolence. During the summer of 1945, the new First Lady had been assigned to bring a stick of butter to her bridge club's pot luck luncheon. But Nesbitt refused: The White House was rationed like any other house, and no butter could be removed. "That was the last straw. All the weeks of unwanted brussels sprouts . . ." ended over that stick of butter.

4: Mobilizing the Women's Network: Friendship, Press Conferences, Patronage

———<small>∅∅∅</small>———

*D*errailed by the Great War, pounded by the virulence of the Red Scare, progressive values were in retreat during the 1920s. Leading artists and writers fled to Europe to escape the sense of crude materialism and political repression that had followed in the wake of wartime hysteria. Without an international war to justify their need to fight, political bullies turned their wrath upon liberals, feminists, and all innovative cultural expression or experimentation.

Hounded and harassed by Red Scare "patriots" and Ku Klux Klan excesses, some radicals and reformers lapsed into silence. Many, including FDR, joined the business boom parade. Others, like Frederic Howe, Woodrow Wilson's commissioner of immigration, now appointed to the Department of Agriculture, wrote bitter memoirs. Diplomats, like FDR's friend Bill Bullitt, left the disappointments of Versailles to party in exile—to "lie on the beach and watch the world go to hell." The tired and timid were overcome by a sense of political torpor.

But the women's social reform network remained steadfast. During the 1920s its organizations actually grew in strength and purpose—and became during the Depression America's most vital institutions of resistance to despair. Their settlement houses and community centers fed the hungry and continued to nourish hope. Internationally, while the United States retreated from its commitment to the League of Nations, only the women of the peace movement continued to agitate for mutual security policies and the World Court—led by Esther Lape, Elizabeth Read, and Eleanor Roosevelt.

During the first hundred days, from 9 March to 16 June 1933, Congress enacted fifteen laws and FDR created a new bureaucracy that rooted the New Deal. But at every level it bypassed women.

In the 1930s, with fifteen million Americans in a state of desperation and gloom, the women's social reform network received a new respect. While communists and fascists threatened revolution, the women's network had proposed only to humanize, democratize, socialize the capitalist economy.

While FDR resurrected the economy, ER mobilized the women's network to demand a New Deal for women. In 1933, that was revolutionary. Every woman appointed to a position of responsibility required a fight; every achievement for women involved a battle. ER confronted the task before her in a combative mood. She and her mentors, most notably Jane Addams and Lillian Wald, had been in this fight for a very long time.

Dismissed for decades as socialists, meddlers, misfits, the indefatigable women of social reform remained eager to offer their expertise and services to the government. They hoped that with capitalism on the verge of collapse, their progressive and internationalist themes would at last be given space on the national agenda.

Although FDR's Brains Trust failed to credit their work, the New Deal reflected their pioneering vision. Since the 1880s the great settlement house leaders had called for changes that would have guaranteed jobs and health care; housing, recreation, compulsory free education; decency in the workplace, security at home.

While Columbia University professor Rex Tugwell and other Brains Trusters were still schoolboys, ER's colleagues—Jane Addams, Florence Kelley, Alice Hamilton, Lillian Wald, Mary Elizabeth Dreier—championed industrial codes, safety and health standards, fair work practices, trade unionism, minimum wage, an end to child labor, consumer labels.

They introduced public playgrounds, neighborhood houses, free night classes, public health programs, and the Visiting Home Nurse Service. For a brief political moment, Progressive Party politicians sought their support. In 1912, both Theodore Roosevelt and Woodrow Wilson courted endorsements from Jane Addams and Lillian Wald.

In 1924, ER chaired the first presidential women's platform committee which presented the Democratic Party with the progressive women's agenda. Published on the front page of *The New York Times* on 25 June 1924, it established goals for economic security that predated the work of FDR's Brains Trusters by a decade: the right to bargain collectively; an eight-hour day; a federal employment agency to encourage full employment; abolition of child labor; equal pay for equal work for women and men; federal aid for maternal and child health; sex education and venereal disease prevention; public education for all; health care for all; an end to vigilante violence and the Ku Klux Klan.

The Red Scare and then the Depression unraveled their initial state and local successes, and by 1933 many of their achievements were undone. Sweatshop conditions reappeared. Eight- and ten-hour work laws passed state by state were scuttled. State and municipal industrial codes passed in dozens of progressive communities were ignored. Humanitarian programs were defunded.

Now ER and the women's network confronted the future with renewed determination. The First Lady was primarily an activist who considered the game of politics a team sport. FDR liked to boast that he was a "practical politician." He knew how to compromise, make deals, be duplicitous. ER understood the nature of the game, but wanted some assurance that it would be played for the right reasons, the most needful causes. During the 1920s she had written articles to demand real power for women and asserted that men played politics to win elections; women played politics because they sought to make things better for most people. FDR was the politician. ER was the agitator.

She was convinced that the federal government had a primary responsibility to confront basic and urgent social issues, and was most closely identified with two organizations that specifically anticipated the changes promised by the New Deal, the Women's Trade Union League (WTUL), and the National Consumers League (NCL).

The Consumers League movement began in 1888 when Leonora O'Reilly, a shirtmaker, called upon philanthropist Josephine Shaw Lowell (the first woman appointed to New York State's Board of Charities in 1876) to help recruit privileged women willing to meet with factory workers. O'Reilly's appeal for "help and sympathy from the wealthy and educated women of New York for their toiling and downtrodden sisters" resulted in the National Consumers League, founded in 1891.

Until her death, on 17 February 1932, attorney Florence Kelley led the NCL, and it had a mighty impact on America as consumers organized around her slogan to "investigate, agitate, legislate." Kelley, the daughter of Quakers and educated at Cornell University, was the divorced mother of three. Brilliant and determined, when she agreed to lead the NCL, she moved from Hull House in Chicago to Lillian Wald's Henry Street Settlement and became an energizing center of New York's progressive network, which included the leaders of the Women's Trade Union League, founded in 1903.

Kelley was the leader of the women's network which included ER, Molly Dewson, Frances Perkins, Rose Schneiderman, and Clara Beyer. They considered Kelley, in Perkins's words, "the mother of us all."

ER rejoiced when the network's first legislative success, the Sheppard-Towner Act, passed. Signed by President Warren Harding on 23 November 1921, it protected mothers and infants, provided health education, well baby clinics, childhood nutrition, and prenatal nursing care. Kelley and her circle were convinced a "new day had dawned." The act was opposed by the American Medical Association and Red Scare groups, including the Woman Patriots and the Sentinels of the Republic, which called it a conspiracy to "Sovietize" America. But the Supreme Court ruled it constitutional in 1923. The attacks continued, however, and in 1927 funding for the first federal act to protect mothers and infants ran out.

ER campaigned vigorously for the continuation of Sheppard-Towner. On 5 January 1927, she argued for its extension on behalf of the League of Women Voters, then an activist organization. She wrote to Senator Royal Copeland of New York, a physician:

> I hardly think it is necessary to urge [your support], as I know you as a doctor must appreciate the wonderful good [it] has accomplished, especially in the rural districts of our own State. . . .
>
> Of course, I realize that the old States rights cry might be raised, but then we might just as well give up any agricultural aid or any aid towards road building, and I do think mothers and babies are a fairly important asset to this country, and I feel sure that you feel the same.

Senator Copeland read ER's letter into the *Congressional Record*. But Sheppard-Towner was defunded, and not reconsidered until the New Deal. It was nonetheless so popular that forty-five states continued some form of infant and maternity care, without federal support.

ER and her colleagues also crusaded for a National Child Labor law to outlaw factory work for young children. In 1923 the Supreme Court declared unconstitutional both a federal child labor measure and a District of Columbia minimum wage law for women. Kelley was outraged: Why are "seals, bears, reindeer, fish, wild game in the national parks, buffalo, migratory birds, all found suitable for federal protection; but not the children of our race and their mothers?"

A child labor amendment to the Constitution was passed by Congress and signed by Calvin Coolidge in 1924, but state ratification was blocked by shrieks of Bolshevism: Various church groups and opponents of public health, public education, and all public improvements protested the amendment as a government intrusion into the "freedom" of family life. ER personally campaigned for it in 1928, and was attacked in the pages of *The Woman Patriot*. The amendment languished until 1933, when ER and her circle reignited interest in the outrages that faced "our toiling children." During the first months of the New Deal, several industries, including textiles, banned workers under the age of sixteen. But most industrialists preferred their economic traditions: Why hire a man for a dollar, or a woman for fifty cents, when you can hire a kid for a dime?

Even some of FDR's political allies squirmed away from the issue. In 1934 ER wrote Robert Bingham, publisher of the Louisville *Courier-Journal* and FDR's ambassador to the Court of St. James, to protest an editorial that branded Florence Kelley and other amendment supporters communists.

Actually ER's letter to the ambassador was a curiously diplomatic document, which revealed her ability to combine personal flattery with blunt political criticism:

It seems rather dreadful to make a complaint and ask a favor in the same letter, but that is what I am about to do.

A very old friend of mine, who worked very hard for the President in the campaign, has a daughter, Faith Whitney, who would like to be presented at court some time in the not too distant future. . . .

And now for my bitter complaint: I feel quite sure that you are not in sympathy with this editorial, but all the world has sent it to me and I wonder if you could say something, gently but firmly, to your editor about classing as communists these people who have worked for years for exactly what the administration has now done through its [National Recovery Administration] codes. Because of the code, great numbers of states are rapidly ratifying this amendment, and this would put the administration, and the President himself, in the class of communists.

With all good wishes and many apologies for being disagreeable. . . .

The real issue, ER wrote for publication, was the government's right to regulate, to intervene into the sacrosanct realm of private property, private enterprise, and the family: "It is said that this is no time to pass [the Child Labor Amendment] because many families are dependent upon the pennies which their children may pick up." ER did not argue with the right of children to make small amounts of money, but noted that the real objection was that this amendment "would be an entering wedge and would mean that Congress would tell the fathers and mothers of the country where they should send their children to school, and how they should educate them. I can only say that an entering wedge is already with us, for we already tell people that their children must be educated. We also tell people they must have their children vaccinated."

ER also intensified her commitment to the NCL's struggle against toxic wastes that imperiled the health of factory workers and people who lived near toxic dumps. During the 1920s, the NCL's first effort was to achieve a ban against industrial radium poisoning, especially among workers in watch and clock factories. ER joined that effort, along with the NCL's protests against untrue advertising practices, now reintroduced by Rex Tugwell.

Although Tugwell failed to credit her, Florence Kelley introduced the concept of ethical advertising and product labeling in a consumer campaign against advertising abuses as early as 1899: "What housewife can detect, alone and unaided, injurious chemicals in her supplies of milk, bread, meat, home remedies?" The NCL then published a "white list" of retail stores which met minimum standards of hygiene "and treated their employees fairly." The NCL's first white label campaign involved underwear—since every "lady," affluent or worker, purchased, for example, "drawers, chemises, petticoats, corsets," and "flannelette goods." To be awarded a white label, a manufacturer had to answer several questions: Were children employed? Were factory laws violated? Were decent work standards met?

The National Consumers League became the most influential consumer movement of the early twentieth century. By 1906 there were sixty-three leagues in twenty states; by 1913 there were thirty thousand members. When National Recovery Administration codes were introduced in 1933, the NCL's white label campaign became government policy.

Shortly after FDR's election, ER and her friend Lady Astor, the former Nancy Langhorne of Virginia, spoke at the thirtieth anniversary luncheon of the National Consumers League, which was also a memorial to Florence Kelley. The first woman to sit in Parliament, Nancy Astor's politics were complicated, but she admired ER and considered her Kelley's heir. "I came to pay tribute to two great women, Florence Kelley and Eleanor Roosevelt. . . . I was thrilled to think that you are to have a woman in the White House who doesn't deal with things at the top but with those at the bottom. I don't believe the world quite realizes what a wonderful asset it will be to have such a First Lady. . . ."

In response, ER's speech was uncommonly bold: "There is something fundamentally wrong with a civilization which tolerates conditions such as many of our people are facing today. We talk of a 'new deal' and we believe in it. But we will have no 'new deal' unless some of us are willing to sit down and think this situation out. It may require some drastic changes in our rather settled ideas and we must not be afraid of them."

Throughout the White House years, the NCL and the WTUL were the foundations upon which ER stood as she fought for a New Deal for women. To rally public support for the changes she championed, she also relied upon her weekly press conferences for women journalists only.

Every Monday morning, ER met with forty accredited "newsgirls," many of whom were hired because of her press conferences, and they tended to be loyal to the First Lady and to protect her from public criticism. They included outstanding reporters, representatives of both national press syndicates and small-town newspapers. Decades later, former Maine senator Margaret Chase Smith, during the 1930s wife of Maine congressman Clyde Smith, remained grateful that ER invited her to attend even though she wrote for one of America's smallest weeklies, in Skowhegan, Maine. During her first conference, ER created a relaxed atmosphere in the Red Room on the first floor, surrounded by roses and spring flowers. She passed around a box of candied fruit, and established the ground rules. She brought members of the women's network eager to address urgent issues; occasionally she brought visiting notables, women writers, performers, artists.

ER intended to manage the news. Her conferences were coordinated, carefully arranged. Louis Howe, Stephen Early, and Hick considered the participants and gave ER advice. FDR's advisers worried that she might get him "into trouble". "Louis Howe and my husband alone seemed unworried." She credited Howe with her "confidence" in journalists. "He had a very high regard for his own craft and insisted that newspaper people were the most honorable group in the world." ER shared his conviction, despite occasional tricksters who betrayed her trust. ER hated to be misquoted, and Tommy attended every conference to take her own notes.

However informal and charming, ER had a stern side. Her first announcement sounded fierce: The press conferences were "planned for your convenience," and everyone was to be guided by specific rules of conduct—no gossip, no leaks, no scoops. No kidding. She would take "no political questions whatever. Whoever does ask such a question never comes back."

Eventually, she changed her mind; and her press conferences became a vital source of news. But the women of the press respected ER's boundaries and acknowledged her threat: If she was displeased, they would be banished.

ER said that "all women in public life needed to develop skin as tough as rhinoceros hide." Focused on public policy, she ignored personal insults. Although attacks on her children upset her, she remained unruffled by criticism. When friends like Hick feared she would be wounded by a particularly vicious article, she was invariably unconcerned. During the first month in Washington, several male reporters trailed her everywhere, eager for a story. When her horse slipped in the mud, the press reported the mishap with a certain glee:

ER "was thrown into a mud puddle in Potomac Park." But, ER told reporters, the horse merely fell to its knees, and "I slid off very gracefully right into the mud. . . . It wasn't a real fall, I just slipped down to the ground." She remounted and continued her ride, and delighted in the cherry blossoms and Japanese magnolia trees just coming into full bloom.

On this occasion, ER sounded defensive. But generally the First Lady was resilient and tough regarding the press, and she used intrusive reporters, as she did her press conferences, to advance her political agenda. According to Bess Furman, at FDR's press conferences, "all the world is a stage"; at ER's press conferences, "all the world is a school." The fact is, both Roosevelts enjoyed "the bully pulpit."

Although she invited controversy, ER strictly limited discussion to those activities she considered newsworthy. She also rejected ghostwriters. When NBC asked her to read a script somebody had written for her, she replied with an official announcement issued by the White House press office: The First Lady would "never consent to have anyone write a broadcast or make one for her. She is sorry but has made this rule and has kept to it consistently."

Through her public activities, writings, and broadcasts, ER set a new pace, new goals, a new understanding of what was possible and acceptable for women to achieve. If her views represented heresy and radicalism to some, for ER and the women's progressive network they represented the substance and soul of America, the long-postponed American Dream.

Positions of influence and respect for women were central to that dream. As soon as FDR was elected president, Mary Williams Dewson (called Molly) and ER met to draw up a list of qualified women for federal appointment. Dewson arrived in Washington for the inauguration armed with the names of sixty women of achievement, all of them dedicated Democrats. By 1935 over fifty women had been appointed to ranking national positions and hundreds to leadership positions in various government agencies on the state and local level.

ER and Molly Dewson, officially chair of women's activities of the Democratic Party, actually controlled patronage for women directly. ER personally submitted their lists to Jim Farley, who as boss of the Democratic Party presided over patronage, or to Louis Howe or Frances Perkins, or an agency or cabinet official on whose goodwill she could rely. She could generally rely upon most cabinet members, except Harold Ickes.

Close to Jane Addams, Ickes had been legal counsel to Chicago's WTUL and was a board member of the National Association for the Advancement of Colored People. But he disliked ER, criticized her privately, and publicly disapproved of her "meddling." Some observers thought she reminded him of his wife, Anna Wilmarth Ickes, a forceful, independent woman of wealth whose published anthropological studies of Indians of the Southwest were highly regarded. Their difficult marriage was the subject of considerable Washington gossip.

The impact of Ickes's opposition to ER's influence was minimized by her alliance with Jim Farley. They had worked together since the Smith campaign of 1924. ER understood Farley, and respected his position. Her first words upon landing in Chicago during the 1932 convention were addressed to him: "A fine job, Mr. Farley." With FDR's entire party waiting on the tarmac, ER headed directly for Boss Farley, hands outstretched to thank him for his role in getting her husband nominated. Not everybody remembered to do that, and Jim Farley never forgot it. In return he accepted her judgments, which tended to be final, even though he often disagreed with her. "He trusted me as a person. . . ."

ER and Molly Dewson worked publicly and privately for every woman FDR appointed. Dewson recalled that she first went to Warm Springs, FDR's healing center in Georgia, in 1928 to lobby for Frances Perkins's appointment to New York's Industrial Commission, at ER's suggestion. Neither Dewson nor ER was personally close to Perkins. According to Dewson: "She is like Kipling's cat that walks alone. It was just that I admired her work for trade unionism and for better working conditions."

Patronage for ER involved two issues: She wanted to see progressive women Democrats in power to build momentum for a New Deal for women, and she wanted women who traditionally worked hard and long with no reward to receive tangible recognition. Occasionally ER sought to reward hardworking women with patronage jobs for their husbands, sons, nephews. "There is a young man . . . whose mother was a great help in the campaign. If he could get some kind of a job either in Seattle or in Idaho . . ."

ER was outraged when her preferred candidates were passed over for political reasons—such as competing patronage claims by male politicians.

ER's personal involvement in such matters was ongoing: "Dear Jim: I am horrified at the Donahue appointment! How could you do it before some of the other women had been considered? Is it McAdoo, and must we have terrible women who are opposed to us, just because McAdoo wishes it?" ER was rankled in part because she deplored "KuKu" McAdoo—Woodrow Wilson's son-in-law and a presidential aspirant who had accepted Klan support in 1924. By 1933, California Senator William Gibbs McAdoo was a regular stumbling block for progressive women.

While every achievement was arduous, Dewson and ER got notable women appointed to significant office. In addition to Frances Perkins, Mary Harriman Rumsey headed the Consumers' Advisory Board of NRA, Florence E. Allen was a judge of the U.S. Sixth Circuit Court of Appeals, Josephine Roche was assistant secretary of the treasury, Nellie Tayloe Ross was director of the Mint; and others.

ER celebrated every breakthrough women made. She hosted musical receptions in the East Room to honor Amy Beach, for fifty years America's most notable woman composer. Other women composers also gave concerts, including Iris Brussels, Charlotte Caldwell, Dorothy Radde Emery, Grace Boles Hedge, Mary Howe, and Florence Lowenberg.

ER worked hard to achieve a major appointment for her friend Ruth Bryan Owen. Daughter of Woodrow Wilson's first secretary of state, William Jennings Bryan, and attorney Mary Baird Bryan, Ruth Bryan Owen was appointed envoy to Denmark and Iceland. Elected to Congress in 1928 and 1930, representing Florida's fourth congressional district, from Jacksonville to Key West, she initiated legislation to protect the Everglades as national parkland; served on the Foreign Affairs Committee, fought for a Department of Education, and a better funded, enlarged Children's Bureau.

She hoped to be appointed secretary of the interior, and wrote her friend Fannie Hurst: FDR "thinks the time has come to put a woman in the cabinet," and Interior "having Education, Conservation for forests, care of Indians, National Parks & general safe-guarding of natural resources," appealed to her because of her congressional experience and environmental struggles.

However disappointed, when FDR named her "envoy extraordinary and minister plenipotentiary to Denmark," she became the first woman to hold a major diplomatic post. ER honored her with a festive dinner attended by eight hundred women and men, where Fannie Hurst toasted her great friend: Owen "was blazing a trail in diplomacy just as the women in covered-wagon days had blazed a trail in geography."

But for all ER's connections, Molly Dewson's vigor, and FDR's goodwill, opposition to women in public life continued. While Jim Farley considered ER's recommendations "with respect," Dewson realized "how much more clamorous the men are" about patronage. In April 1933 she wrote a seventeen-page letter to ER detailing Farley's reaction to the first hundred names they had submitted. There were delays and detours, they were unable to present more than one name at a time; it was agonizing. By June, Dewson reported, only seven women recommended by the Women's Division were appointed; six others were "pending." By July she was exasperated and wrote ER: "Heavens but the nicest of men are slippery as eels."

Throughout the 1930s, ER and Dewson worked every channel of influence to promote women to positions of respect, prestige, power. Only women in power, ER believed, would consider the needs of women without power; men in power rarely, if ever, did.

5: ER's New Deal for Women

———⟊⟊⟊———

ER's response to FDR's first hundred days was hopeful but also critical. After years of anxiety, drifting, waiting upon the "laissez-faire" or "natural" course of the economy to correct itself, the government acted. With amazing unity, Congress, the president, and business leaders agreed: The government had a role to play to save America from fiscal disaster. The president's first act in office was to call Congress into special session to deal with three problems: banking, the federal economy, and unemployment.

ER was impressed by the initial "spirit of cooperation." Business leaders "who ordinarily would have scorned government assistance were begging the government to find solutions for their problems, willingly accepting almost anything that was suggested."

But she considered it all merely a first step toward a far distant goal. Experimental and imaginative, the first New Deal still ignored the very foundations upon which, ER believed, democracy depended: housing, health care, and education. And virtually all of it discriminated against women.

Bankers and economic "royalists" were thrilled by FDR's first two pieces of emergency legislation: the Banking Act, which passed the first day with little opposition; and the more controversial Economy Act, which appealed exclusively to fiscal conservatives. It passed the House 266–138 only because sixty-nine Republicans voted for it, while ninety-two Democrats voted against it.

The Economy Act eliminated or downsized government agencies, reduced government salaries, cut veterans' pensions and medical support, and called for the firing of all federally employed women married to federally employed men. It made FDR seem "a states' rights, limited government, penny-pinching Democrat."

In the spring of 1933, FDR turned to the business community and focused on deflation, reduced government spending, and a balanced budget. In this phase of the New Deal he ignored the terrible impact state and municipal budget cuts were having, for example, on education. ER was particularly disheartened by America's neglect of its most precious resource, the nation's children. The U.S. commitment to education was paltry, and ER called rural education a total disgrace. Spending cuts in education diminished children's lives, and she joined New York's Episcopal bishop William T. Manning in opposing New York's "staggering and crippling cuts" in public education, including the layoff of eleven thousand teachers.

Bishop Manning (with whom FDR had worked closely during the 1920s to raise money to build New York's Cathedral of St. John the Divine) described the situation in a journal called *School:* Teacher layoffs resulted in greatly increased class size; evening schools, summer sessions, and continuation and adult education programs were abolished; athletic centers and school gardens were eliminated, repairs and replacements postponed, supplies and equipment reduced. Bishop Manning concluded that it was "not the time to weaken our schools, when the crumbling morale of many homes is only kept from breaking by the hope of opportunity for the children."

ER called for relief efforts that would employ teachers in community service. Voluntarily, teachers in New York City, she noted, were feeding hungry children in the schools at their own expense. "I think we should all give them thanks," but we should also investigate the dimensions of the need throughout the country "and make sure that no child suffers from malnutrition."

While FDR initially called for deflationary measures, cost-cutting that would balance the budget, ER called for increased expenditures. Their most public disagreement was clearly presented in competing columns of the *Women's Democratic News.* In response to her contrary views, FDR wrote his first and only editorial—to urge popular support for the Economy Act and for still further reductions in local taxes. The Economy Act, he insisted, would save the federal government "25% in its normal cost to the taxpayer." But federal expenditures were only 35 percent of the nation's total tax bill. Therefore, "the real meat in the coconut is the expenditures of local government which is over 50%. . . . The real saving, the big saving must be made in cutting the local governments. . . . It is the only practical way. It is their responsibility."

But that would dry up local spending for education and the public services that people needed most, ER had countered in her column. This was a time to expand government services. The real problem, ER wrote, was to levy taxes from "proper sources," from "people who are endowed richly with this world's goods, or such businesses as are making large profits."

ER urged more individual and community vigilance concerning "the way banking businesses are run." "Congressional investigations lately have given many people the feeling that they are a little too much like innocent lambs led to slaughter in the hand of our great financiers."

Contrary to FDR's initial legislation, ER called for a transformation in our "sense of values" so that we can "adequately help other human beings." She devoted several chapters of her book *It's Up to the Women* to those issues that required federal and local investment. Recreation—camping, hiking, sports—was basic to life. "We have been so busy making a living that we have had less time really to live. . . . I always feel that education should open as many avenues as possible to us so that we may have as many ways of obtaining recreation and enjoyment as possible."

Healthy family life required available, affordable health care, and ER called for medical security: Only "the very rich and the very poor" had real access to quality hospital care. For those of "average means" a serious accident or illness was a "calamity" that involved dreadful debts, preventable suffering, avoidable death.

She wrote that public health began with education, and included the construction of public health clinics, hospitals, and hands-on treatment: nutritional programs and agricultural experimentation to make healthful diets available to all. She called for family planning, now called sex education, for boys as well as girls: "To me it seems that one cannot lay too much emphasis on the necessity for planning family life in order that the health of the family may be kept on a high level." But it was years before the New Deal addressed education or health.

FDR at first ignored the fact that schools were closed or closing all over the country because local communities had run out of money as property taxes diminished. In Georgia, where at Warm Springs FDR enjoyed his "second home," 1,318 schools were shut down, and hundreds of thousands of students were locked out. In Akron, Ohio, schools remained open, as long as teachers agreed to work without pay. Chicago owed its teachers over $28 million; 85 percent of Alabama's schools were closed. Nationwide, over 100,000 teachers were unemployed.

Deflation, salary reductions, and cost-cuttings failed to address the magnitude of America's problem. Yet FDR's Economy Act was limited to such measures. It reduced all government salaries by 15 percent, and streamlined the federal bureaucracy. By June, dozens of agencies and commissions had been terminated. FDR cut aid to vocational education, agricultural colleges, and the Farm Bureau's experiment stations and extension programs by 25 percent.

An amazing document, contradicted by subsequent New Deal programs, the Economy Act represented the enthusiasms of his conservative budget director, Lewis Douglas. The tall, handsome, thirty-nine-year-old rugged individualist cowboy appealed to FDR. For a time this son of a great Arizona copper-mining fortune, whose father founded the Phelps-Dodge Company, was as close to the president as Louis Howe and Raymond Moley. A Social

Darwinist darling of Wall Street who "confused the principle of laissez-faire with the Word of God," Douglas gave FDR legitimacy among fiscal Tories but alarmed New Dealers, who watched in horror as he downsized or eliminated useful scientific, research, census, and survey programs—most of which were restored during the 1940s.

Although ER despised Douglas's methods, his cabinet presence gave her an ironic gift. To serve, Douglas resigned as Arizona's only representative to Congress. His decision enabled ER's closest girlhood friend, Isabella Selmes Ferguson Greenway, to join the Roosevelts in Washington. Elected in a landslide victory as Member of Congress at large, she served her 450,000 constituents (over 140,000 of whom were on relief) with vigor.

A warm and generous hostess, and a successful rancher, hotelier, and businesswoman, Isabella Greenway was devoted to the welfare of all Arizonans and successfully championed New Deal projects for her state. Unlike Douglas, she fought for the interests of workers and labor groups.

Greenway brought a welcome flamboyance to ER's circle. She cherished their biweekly "air our minds" luncheons, which featured good cheer and candid conversation with Frances Perkins, Mary Harriman Rumsey, and another of ER's girlhood companions, Elisabeth Cameron Lindsay, daughter of Henry Adams's friend Elizabeth Cameron. Married to Sir Ronald Lindsay, Britain's ambassador, ER appreciated Lady Lindsay's "keen," occasionally "wicked," sense of humor. "We looked at things from more or less the same point of view."

Of her core political group, nobody was closer to ER than Isabella Greenway. A woman of spontaneity and action, she was on a plane within thirty minutes when ER called her during the campaign to visit in California. When she arrived, ER asked about her baggage. She had her toothbrush in her briefcase, and knew she could depend on ER for a change of clothing and everything else.

Their first collaboration, begun even before Greenway was sworn in, was to protest FDR's Economy Act. While ER emphasized the cuts which affected women, Greenway condemned veterans' reductions. The founder of the Arizona Hut, a woodcraft factory to employ convalescent veterans, Greenway was outraged by the cuts which harmed them. She agreed with Louisiana Senator Huey Long: "Talk of balancing the budget! Let them balance the budget by scraping off a little of the profiteers' profits from the war."

ER was particularly outraged by the administration's decision to fire federally employed wives. Between 1929 and 1933 it had become customary for married women to be the first fired. Several states passed laws to fire and ban married schoolteachers, university professors, and hospital workers, regardless of their family situation or need. According to *The New York Times*, the First Lady insisted vehemently that it was a "very bad and very foolish thing" to establish marital status as a standard for dismissal. Why should hardworking, competent women whose work was useful be idled to offset other costs, or balance the budget?

ER also rejected FDR's idea that government workers were earning more than they needed. While he made a grand gesture of returning to the Treasury 15 percent of his own first salary check "as a symbol" of what government workers and others might do, ER declared that government salaries "in most cases are so small as to be hardly enough to support more than two persons, and certainly not enough on which to educate and rear a family."

Despite his wife's opposition, and an ever-growing storm of protest, FDR refused to address the hated marital status clause. Within two years, thousands of women were dismissed. Many had worked for over fifteen years, and they lost all right "to reappointment and to the pension, toward which they had been contributing." According to the Women's Bureau of the Department of Labor, "nine out of ten of those discharged were in real need of their jobs." Home mortgages were foreclosed; life savings were lost. The formerly working wives of Army and Navy personnel were now on relief. Some couples chose divorce to retain their family income; some men who earned less than their wives resigned instead. It was a bitter rule, and ER and her allies repeatedly spoke out against it.

It was astounding and unprecedented for a First Lady to protest her husband's legislation. But on this issue ER did so in many forums, in print and on the air, none more publicly than in *It's Up to the Women,* where her chapter "Women and Jobs" caused the most enduring controversy.

ER believed absolutely that individual happiness for women, married or single, required work outside the home. Without that, she insisted, there was no personal or economic independence.

ER specifically rejected the ancient tradition that "a woman's place was in the home. She must marry, and if she did not marry, she had no work in the world." The dreaded image of the spinster aunt, forced to become the family servant in exchange for food and lodging, might now be erased. The modern woman was a working woman, who wanted to be "able to do something which expresses her own personality even though she may be a wife and mother." ER refused to see a conflict between "a woman's career and a woman's home."

"A woman, just like a man, may have a great gift for some particular thing. That does not mean that she must give up the joy of marrying and having a home and children." In fact, she warned, "Mr. Man" might awake one morning "to find that you have a wife in your home who is an automaton— no longer a fulfilled and happy personality."

ER's political philosophy represented the radical end of New Deal thinking. It embraced the needs of unorganized workers, the marginalized, and dispossessed: landless and migrant farm workers in the Southwest; sharecroppers in the Southeast; urban "slum" dwellers; domestic workers; uprooted and unemployed industrial workers—women and men. It would be years before the New Deal addressed their needs, but ER was among the first to put them on the national agenda.

By publishing *It's Up to the Women* in November 1933, ER sought to go beyond the established network of women activists and reach out to all women in America to join her in a crusade for change and decency. The White House had never before been used as a platform from which the First Lady expressed dissenting political ideas.

Pioneering feminist scholar Mary Ritter Beard praised the book and celebrated "Mrs. Roosevelt as Guide and Philosopher" in the *New York Herald Tribune:* "For more than a century the Great White Father in the White House has been instructing his people in right conduct.... And during all those years the First Lady of the Land has remained in the background.... But now the Great White Mother emerges as a personality in her own right and starts an independent course of instruction on her own account."

It's Up to the Women lacked the verve and spice of ER's feminist articles published during the 1920s, and it was filled with homilies, home remedies, maternal advice. But for all the platitudes and evasions, ER's goal was subversive. As First Lady she meant to reach every woman in America: It was up to them to take charge, to organize and agitate on behalf of social progress. She challenged women to think for themselves; to consider their own lives; to take the battle for modernity into their own homes. ER criticized privileged women of her own class and culture who continued to live in luxury without a care for the world about them. She urged them to volunteer; to get out and about; to be satisfied with less material opulence. She addressed poor women of the cities, who always had to work outside the home to keep their families from starvation and who, without leisure or comfort of any kind, managed to feed and clothe their children and struggled to provide education.

ER addressed poor country women, who bore the additional burden of loneliness. One farm woman told her, "I haven't been outside my yard in nine months except to take the children to the doctor." There was "less opportunity on isolated farms to learn from each other and you will often find the farmer sending all the milk to town and feeding his children on condensed milk, sending the vegetables to the market or grocer and keeping none for the children."

In country and city, domestic workers suffered most. Domestic workers were generally disregarded and abused because of their "foreign" birth or African-American ancestry. Their pay was insignificant; their family and leisure needs were discounted. ER called on all women to consider the important work actually done by women in domestic service and to upgrade household work to "the plane of any other professional or industrial occupation."

ER's goal was long-range: to create a grassroots movement, led and informed by women, that would create a groundswell of support for the more essential changes New Deal rhetoric promised. FDR's goal was immediate: to achieve the possible from his political opponents. Their own needs dire, they momentarily supported government intervention.

The third bill introduced during FDR's deflationary binge was the low-alcohol content 3.2 Beer and Wine Act, a first step back from Prohibition. The sale of liquor would create a new source of taxable revenue, and the bill served as something of a diversion during the tense Senate debate over the Economy Act.

On 7 April 1933 "light" spirits were again sold legally throughout America. Although many expected the First Lady to condemn the legalization of liquor, ER was relieved. Prohibition never worked, and she deplored the bootleggers and gangsters it spawned. Like most Americans, ER considered it a welcome change, which helped transform the nation's mood.

However much America's spirits lifted, FDR himself acknowledged that his first three laws were not "constructive." They did nothing really to change the economy's direction. Nevertheless, they represented a useful political strategy: His deflationary, business-building steps ensured him the support of congressional conservatives, who were, at first, too grateful to oppose him. By April he changed course and pursued public works, unemployment relief, mortgage relief, and farm parity and began to transform government–business relations in America.

Several New Deal ideas sailed through, including the Home Owners' Loan Corporation, established to refinance mortgages and lend money to homeowners. Other acts were enormous, confusing, controversial. ER was particularly thrilled by the Tennessee Valley Authority (TVA), the Civilian Conservation Corps (CCC), and the National Industrial Recovery Act (NIRA)—which ER singled out for celebration in *It's Up to the Women.*

Workers in the past, ER wrote, had too little influence and made no decisions. The needy and the people most involved were never consulted. She believed NIRA was to change that. Through the National Recovery Administration (NRA) it sought to revive business by creating councils of business leaders, consumers, and workers; they would collectively introduce decent codes of industrial behavior.

She championed the new agency in every way, and she titled the last chapter of her book "Women and the NRA." NRA codes set wages and conditions of work industry by industry. The NRA's Blue Eagle became the first and most dramatic symbol of the New Deal, under the flamboyant administration of General Hugh Johnson. He had worked with Bernard Baruch during World War I in the War Industries Board, which served as the NRA's model.

The NRA championed "industrial self-government" and promised dramatic reforms, including occupational health and safety standards, unionism, and such workers' demands as minimum wages and maximum hours.

Conservatives considered Section 7A, which encouraged unionism, NIRA's most radical feature. It also established the Public Works Administration (PWA), which was to be administered by Secretary of the Interior Harold Ickes.

On 17 May 1933, FDR asked for $3.3 billion in PWA funds to construct roads, bridges, and other federal projects. It was America's first peacetime pubic works project, and FDR said that "history would probably record it as the most important and far-reaching legislation ever enacted by the American Congress."

For FR, Rose Schneiderman, Frances Perkins, and all their friends in the Consumers League and Women's Trade Union League, the NRA seemed the achievement of their lifelong goals. Perkins and Schneiderman had campaigned for industrial codes ever since the Triangle Shirtwaist Company fire of 1911, when 146 women perished. That tragedy resulted in New York's Factory Investigating Commission (FIC), which hired Perkins, Schneiderman, Mary Dreier, and Pauline Newman. In 1915, their work was supported by Al Smith and Robert Wagner, then New York legislators, and resulted in New York State's first Industrial Code. Perkins was the only woman appointed to New York's Industrial Commission in 1919, and FDR appointed her New York's industrial commissioner in 1928.

Now Perkins was secretary of labor and she appointed fiery, red-haired labor orator and former milliner Rose Schneiderman the only woman member on the National Recovery Administration's Labor Advisory Board. President of the WTUL, an expert on wages, hours, and industrial working conditions, Schneiderman was expected to submit ideal codes for those industries where women predominated. Schneiderman called her years in Washington "the most exhilarating and inspiring of my life."

They were also years of anguish. After her first month in office she denounced the NRA's imposition of lower minimum wages for women and demanded a single wage scale for men and women. ER, the National Consumers League, the National League of Women Voters, and the National Woman's Party joined her protest. It was one of the few times business and professional women who championed the Equal Rights Amendment joined hands with working women and their social feminist allies.

But their unity on behalf of a single wage scale was ignored. The act appeared with a "joker" clause: "When females do SUBSTANTIALLY the same work as males they shall receive the same pay." By 1935, pay differentials ranged from five to twenty-five cents an hour in over one-quarter of all codes—especially in businesses that employed large numbers of women. Despite all protests to Hugh Johnson and FDR, wage discrimination prevailed. Moreover, discriminatory NRA codes locked industrial practice into government policy.

Feminists compared NRA provisions with the plight of women in Italy and Germany: "Women are being forced back to the laundry tubs in Fascist Europe. Women are being paid lower wages than men under more than 100 of the NRA codes in effect in the United States today."

Although ER and such social feminists as Jane Addams, Alice Hamilton, and Rose Schneiderman argued for protective legislation for women workers and opposed the Equal Rights Amendment during the 1920s, ER believed in equal pay for equal work. She now publicly deplored wage scales that classed adult women with young boys and professional women with unskilled men, and that set minimum wages for women at half the wage rates for men, often in the same industry and at the same tasks.

She demanded a single minimum wage standard for NRA codes and repeatedly insisted that the New Deal should mean a "square deal for women": "There may be some special reason why they are doing these things at this time, and in any case I have no right to interfere, but I . . . hope that any such discrepencies may be only temporary. . . ." But pay differentials were permanent, and ER continued to speak out against them.

Schneiderman's efforts on behalf of African-American women were also blocked. Her only success was in the NRA code for the handkerchief industry, where she persuaded manufacturers to remove their ban on hiring black women for skilled positions. But she was unable to prevent a line in the laundry code that permitted employers to pay black women less than half the salary of white women, and she was unable to prevent the exclusion of domestic workers from all NRA consideration. Despite her protests, and ER's efforts to have domestic work valued as any other employment, they were denied NRA benefits.

Nevertheless, working women and men in various industries considered the NRA a great leap forward, and white women benefited especially by those codes that included mandatory minimum hourly wages and maximum-hour provisions. Moreover, Section 7A promised to end company unions and potentially encouraged labor's right to bargain collectively without restraint or coercion.

On 3 July 1933, Schneiderman wrote ER:

> I had a most thrilling time at the hearings on the cotton textile code where I sat in as a member of the Labor Advisory Board. The code, though not an ideal one, will go far toward making life and work for the tens of

thousands of textile workers more humane and secure. The fact that children under sixteen will now be outlawed from the industry will not only help make room for adult men and women but will also set a standard for other industries. General Johnson is a peach. . . .

For ER the NRA was only a first step. "It was up to the women" to end "sweatshop conditions" and buy only from merchants who sold Blue Eagle merchandise. She called for individual vigilance and consumer boycotts, and urged women to recognize that every act was a political act. Since women did almost 90 percent of all buying, how they spent their money profoundly influenced life for labor, industry, and agriculture. All personal decisions mattered. No woman should buy a dress or a pair of gloves made "under sweatshop conditions." "No matter what we can afford to buy, we cannot afford to buy at the expense of the health and strength of our fellow human beings."

An invigorated consumer movement was spearheaded by her friend Mary Harriman Rumsey, who was appointed director of the NRA's Consumers' Advisory Board in June 1933. Barnard graduate, key founder of the Junior League in 1901 (which ER joined as a charter member), and renowned horsewoman, the independent activist daughter of railroad financier E. H. Harriman was an imaginative crusader. Her father's generation emphasized competition, she told a reporter; his "was a building age." "Today the need is not for a competitive but for a cooperative economic system." Personally, Mary Harriman Rumsey created cooperative business ventures as well as community councils and neighborhood organizations.

Influenced by the works of Irish poet, mystic, and reformer George Russell (AE), she proclaimed consumers by right the third and equal partner in a cooperative commonwealth of business and labor. An ardent New Dealer, Mary Harriman Rumsey encouraged her younger brother Averell to leave his business interests, the excitement of Meadowbrook and his polo ponies, and join her in Washington, where all the "real excitement" was, she assured him, to be found.

ER supported every consumer and labor effort as the NRA developed. On Friday, 13 October 1933, two days after her forty-ninth birthday, ER was given a bouquet of red roses and the first labeled NRA garment, made under the Coat and Suit Code. Hailing a "new era" for labor, ER received Blue Eagle label 000001 and her daughter Anna received label 000002. As ER accepted her gifts, a new silver-fox-collared black cashmere-and-worsted coat, from the shop workers, she said that the code meant fair wages, decent hours, sanitary conditions, and regular work. It ended "the disadvantage of seasonal unemployment," and it ended the sweatshop.

When the millinery industry became NRA, ER attended an even more emotional ceremony. Using a gold thimble presented to her by Sarah Leichter of the Millinery Workers Union, the First Lady sewed the first label into her new dark-brimmed straw hat with white quills. ER was joined on the platform by New York's Mayor Fiorello La Guardia, who said: "Any industry that cannot pay a living wage is not worth saving."

ER's commitment to the NRA extended to her own small craft shop at Val-Kill, and to house servants: "One has no more right to expect sweat-shop hours and wages in one's own home than in a factory."

But the NRA was fatally flawed. Some considered it an industrialist's blessing. With no provision for price controls, manufacturers passed along increased wages to consumers. There was no government authority behind the NRA beyond its moral maxim: "We Do Our Part." And it was voluntary. There were mine owners, farm owners, countless companies without competition, with no need to join.

ER understood that the NRA was a limited first step. But she wanted it to succeed. After all, the War Industries Board had worked in wartime, and she hoped industrialists would be inspired by Hugh Johnson's enthusiastic leadership.

But Johnson's public style was wild and unpredictable. He was overworked, drank too much, offended too many. A missionary for capitalist self-control, he agreed to such labor demands as maximum hours and minimum wages, supported public works and full employment. Conservatives considered him a maniac: prolabor, pro-union. Radicals called him the Mussolini of the New Deal: a crusader for trusts, government-protected cartels. NRA's road was to be very bumpy.

ER worked to promote New Deal ideas that urged a truly mixed and planned economy. She championed public works and nationally owned industries and utilities to secure the income needed to pay for social services. If utilities were government-owned, rural America might be electrified, and everybody would have running water, indoor plumbing, access to public transportation. Utility profits could pay for a national health care program and for public education through high school. Depression conditions generated such dreams, and they seemed entirely feasible.

The Tennessee Valley Authority (TVA) was the first and last such experiment. TVA was a vast scheme that would electrify and develop one of the nation's poorest regions—the seven states of the Tennessee River basin: Virginia, North Carolina, Tennessee, Georgia, Alabama, Mississippi, and Kentucky. With this massive public works program, full employment would occur; poverty would disappear; the area's scourge of malaria, tuberculosis, pellagra would subside.

ER and FDR were united on every aspect of TVA, and she applauded his bold vision, which included local control, support for local crafts and culture, "and everything else" required for "a well-rounded civilization." Inevitably, controversy surrounded TVA. It was an amazing experiment in "public ownership" for an area almost the size of England, with a population of two million people.

Senator George Norris asked FDR how he would respond to all the charges of socialism, communism, fascism, and how he would define "the political philosophy behind TVA." FDR answered: "I'll tell them it's neither fish nor fowl. But whatever it is, it will taste awfully good to the people of the Tennessee Valley."

ER visited TVA often and considered it a model for the future: During the campaign of 1932 "my husband and I had gone through some of this TVA area" and were "deeply impressed by the great crowds," their hopefulness, and their poverty.

> Scarcely eight years later, after the housing and educational and agricultural experiments had had time to take effect, I went through the same area, and a more prosperous area would have been hard to find. I have always wished that those who oppose authorities to create similar benefits in the valleys of other great rivers could have seen the contrast as I saw it. I realise that such changes must come gradually, but I hate to see nothing done. . . .

Unlike TVA, ER considered the Agricultural Adjustment Act (AAA), a human disaster. It benefited only large farm owners and never "trickled down" to farm workers. The AAA raised farmers' prices, and promised farm owners parity with industrial prices. To ensure higher prices (farm parity), scarcity had to be created: The enormous annual surplus of produce—wheat, milk and milk products, tobacco, livestock, cotton—had to be eliminated. To achieve scarcity, Henry Wallace introduced a "federal allotment" plan, whereby the government would pay farmers to reduce their crop acreage. Payments would be supported by a processor's tax. In other words, not the farmer but the middleman would pay: Taxes on containers, boxes, and bottles were added to consumers prices.

Wallace's scheme was a disaster for the South, where plantation owners discharged and evicted their tenant farmers and sharecroppers once they were paid not to grow their usual harvest of rice, cotton, or tobacco. While the Farm Credit Administration relieved the farm mortgage crisis for farm owners and Wallace's allotment program guaranteed new profits to the largest landowners, the poorest and most devastated were now uprooted and torn from the land.

It led to unbearable misery and quickened the "great migration" from the rural South. To alleviate the most bitter consequences of AAA, more radical New Deal efforts were required, including the creation of the Farm Resettlement Administration of 1935—which ER heralded and championed from the beginning.

ER was appalled by the extraordinary waste involved in the AAA's first efforts to create scarcity: Over ten million acres of cotton were destroyed; over 300 million bushels of wheat and countless acres of corn were wasted; over six million pigs were slaughtered; over a quarter billion pounds of meat were buried or processed into fertilizer.

Ruby Black wrote in *Editor and Publisher* that the First Lady "raised unshirted Hell." But the First Lady denied it. Despite the fact that Black's source was one of ER's "best friends," Lorena Hickok, ER insisted that she made only one telephone call—and simply asked: Why do you destroy all this cotton when there are so many people shivering with cold? Why do you waste these pigs when thousands of people are starving?

That a decent and democratic nation caused such destruction without any distribution plan while Americans were ragged and hungry seemed to ER barbaric. Her complaints led to the creation of the Federal Surplus Commodities Corporation, which enabled Harry Hopkins's Federal Emergency Relief Administration to purchase farm surpluses and donate them directly to relief agencies. Later, the national food stamp program was created to enable poor consumers to purchase food surpluses in ordinary store transactions.

Although ER was annoyed with Hick for leaking a confidence, the women of the press were angry that ER was not credited for her achievement. In a column syndicated by Scripps-Howard, Ruth Finney wrote: "Of course all the male officials are convinced they would have thought of it themselves, but they had not done so up to the time she insisted it was the thing to do."

ER never forgave the secretary of agriculture. Her contempt for Wallace's initial activities and long disregard for the cruel conditions that confronted landless farm workers lingered. However liberal Wallace's views actually became, ER distrusted his judgment and was impatient with his statistical and scholarly approach to economic and human problems.

ER never relied upon Wallace as she pursued farm resettlement and the effort to create sustainable communities, which absorbed most of her personal time during the 1930s. She worked instead with Wallace's assistant secretary of agriculture, Rex Tugwell, who for a time was one of her primary allies. Handsome, erudite Columbia University professor of government, Rexford Guy Tugwell was known as FDR's most radical adviser. Called the Lenin of the New Deal, he was considered by FDR's opponents unacceptably Red, and by ER's friends unfortunately arrogant. He considered himself a genuine conservative determined to save capitalism through democratic planning and control.

Tugwell observed that mass production in advanced industrial societies guaranteed "permanent plenty" alongside widespread unemployment and poverty. He explained the Depression in terms of capitalism's short-sighted refusal to distribute the economy's inevitable surpluses. The problem was compounded by America's high isolationist tariff policies, which hobbled the export market. Like ER, Tugwell argued that society had a responsibility to achieve security for all its citizens through consumer protection, public works, and the creation of sustainable communities. Consequently, during the first years of the New Deal, ER was one of Tugwell's most abiding defenders. Their critics considered their views revolutionary and un-American.

Most controversial was Tugwell's consumer protection activities. He arranged an exhibit the press called Tugwell's "Chamber of Horrors" to dramatize the dangers consumers faced every day. He was amazed and bitter that his photographs of women disfigured, occasionally blinded, because they used various hair dyes, eyelash dyes, and dangerous chemicals for cosmetics failed to arouse a public outcry.

In March he issued an administrative order to lower the "maximum allowable" chemical spray residue (pesticide) on fruits and vegetables. Growers, especially apple producers, and politicians protested.

They howled even louder on 6 June 1933, when ER's old Sheppard-Towner ally, Senator Royal Copeland, introduced a new pure food and drug bill with a provision for precise labeling information for produce and canned goods. Industrialists went on a rampage: Tugwell sought to destroy confidence in American business.

Press attacks on Tugwell were unrelenting. Within the administration, he grew more isolated, and the consumer movement was increasingly ignored. Initially, FDR was pleased to be identified with an effort to upgrade Theodore Roosevelt's 1906 Pure Food and Drug Act, and he encouraged Tugwell. After FDR turned away from the controversy, ER persisted—as did Molly Dewson and Frances Perkins. ER spoke out: Women want to know what they are buying. What is hiding in that closed can? What are women putting on their skin? What are they feeding their children?

To ER's dismay, the press assaults rendered Tugwell's "charter of honesty and fair dealing" a complicated, marginal issue, easy to mock and dismiss. Leading food and drug lobbyists defended the "sacred right" to advertise as a fundamental freedom.

Subsequently, journalists acknowledged that they ignored or distorted the controversy "because of their publishers' intense opposition." Most publishers refused to "print such unmistakable news as Mrs. Roosevelt's endorsement of the bill."* Tugwell's consumer efforts came to naught, and the entire project was downgraded.

During the first years of the New Deal, ER's most dependable ally was Harry Hopkins. Only Louis Howe among FDR's extended staff was closer to ER.

Harry Lloyd Hopkins, a New York settlement house worker associated with Lillian Wald, was born in Sioux City, Iowa, and graduated from Grinnell College in 1912. During the Depression he conceived of a relief project that involved instant jobs for New York City's unemployed in parks and public facilities. As governor, FDR was impressed with Hopkins's effort and established New York State's Temporary Emergency Relief Administration (TERA) in 1931, which Hopkins chaired.

On 21 March 1933, FDR announced his decision "to launch the biggest relief program in history." Based on the work done in New York by Harry Hopkins and Frances Perkins and enhanced by the vision of Senators Robert Wagner, Robert La Follette, and Edward Costigan, the Emergency Relief Act created the Federal Emergency Relief Administration (FERA) to grant $500 million in aid to state and local governments.

It promised direct relief as well as the reemployment of millions of needy Americans. Hopkins's agency quickly became the most vital pillar of New Deal hope.

Within twenty-four hours after assuming office, Hopkins organized his staff, disbursed social workers to investigate the neediest situations, ordered state governors to establish state relief organizations, and spent $5 million of his half-billion-dollar budget.

Given such crying need, Hopkins insisted, there was no time to waste. One thousand homes were being foreclosed each month. Millions of real people were starving. There was little to investigate. Relief applicants were not "morally deficient." They were not responsible for their dreadful plight. Questions of "religion, race or party" were irrelevant.

FERA funds initially paid state relief agencies cash grants for food, clothing, shelter, and medical care. While Ickes's PWA funds moved slowly and involved big projects to get business moving, Hopkins wanted a Civil Works Administration (CWA) to provide immediate work for the relief of people in need. He hated the idea of the dole, and he believed in jobs: real jobs, at real wages.

*A Pure Food and Drug Act passed in 1938, but it was meaningless. Tugwell called "the Food, Drug and Cosmetic Bill," the Wheeler-Lea Act of 1938, "disgraceful." There were "no standards, no grades, no penalties for fraud, no restriction on patent medicines of however dangerous a nature." Congress had "truckled to every shabby interest." The issue was shelved until environmentalists persuaded Richard Nixon to reintroduce the issue.

Since there were no jobs, it was the job of government to create them. Within one month, Hopkins's new CWA found work for over four million men. When Southern members of Congress protested that the CWA wage level was too high, Hopkins replied: "Some people can't stand seeing other people make a decent living."

A reemployment program, CWA was not a "relief" project: There was no means test, just valuable work with decent wages. When General Hugh Johnson told a press conference that CWA wages were higher than NRA codes anticipated, a "perfectly absurd situation," Hopkins told the next press conference: "We are paying decent subsistence wages, nothing more."

The sparring administrators met face to face. Johnson wanted to know why Hopkins had not consulted him before he established his wage scales. Hopkins asked: "Why didn't you consult me before you approved your lousy codes?"

Johnson backed off. From ER's point of view, there was no contest. Hopkins had the best interests of the people of America uppermost in his mind: His work projects included manual and factory workers, teachers and nurses, artists and writers, professionals and service workers. He was highly regarded by ER, Frances Perkins, and Lillian Wald, and his vision seemed the triumph of their best efforts, finally established as national policy. Work replaced want. Jobs meant dignity. "A new standard of public decency was being set." Twenty million Americans benefited from federal relief funds during the dreadful winter of 1933–1934.

Inevitably, Hopkins had his detractors. He was high-strung and underweight, his eyes bulged and his energy bubbled. He chain-smoked and drank: endless cups of coffee by day, spirits by night. Disheveled and argumentative, he appeared as unkempt as Louis Howe. He liked to party with the rich and frolic in supper clubs. Divorced from Ethel Gross, a Jewish social worker, he left her and their four children in 1928. In 1929 he married Barbara Duncan, and their daughter, Diana, was born in 1932. His private life attracted gossip columnists.

Although Hopkins accepted sex segregation in employment and never included wage differentials in that large category he called "lousy," he was the first male administrator to acknowledge that the New Deal neglected women.

FDR's first hundred days did nothing for an estimated 140,000 homeless women and girls who wandered the streets and railroad sidings of America. Not one program acknowledged the needs of an estimated two to four million unemployed women, former workers in search of jobs. While married women were routinely fired, the plight of single, divorced, and widowed women was ignored.

On 20 April 1933 ER had addressed the annual meeting of New York's Travelers Aid Society, to portray the misery of thousands of homeless women. Like Meridel Le Sueur, who published a vivid description of their plight in her book *Women on the Breadlines*, ER understood that women suffered more quietly than men. They did not sell apples on street corners; they did not beg. They tended to disappear. They stared out the window, went to the library, sat on park benches, hid in the woods. They looked for work, sometimes solicited, and wandered about.

In January 1932, Le Sueur explained that her work was not fiction. "I did not write these stories, I recorded them. . . . A woman will shut herself up in a room until it is taken away from her, and eat a cracker a day and be as quiet as a mouse so there are no social statistics concerning her."

When Meridel Le Sueur's first story was published in *New Masses*, the editor advised women to avoid defeatism and consider "the unemployed councils . . . of the organized revolutionary movement. Fight for your class, read *The Working Woman*, join the Communist Party." ER insisted on a New Deal for Women, to alleviate widespread suffering, as well as to redirect such rapidly growing revolutionary sentiment.

Dismayed by official inaction, ER sponsored a White House Conference on the Emergency Needs of Women, on 20 November 1933. With Molly Dewson, the First Lady organized and planned the conference in less than a week. Fifty prominent women attended—social workers, clubwomen, private philanthropists, government administrators, and representatives of the WTUL, the Red Cross, the National Consumers League, and the League of Women Voters, among other groups.

ER presided at the November conference, and Harry Hopkins keynoted. He estimated that over 400,000 women required immediate help from FERA or CWA. Only fifty thousand women were actually on relief in the United States. Hopkins promised to increase that "eightfold" within "twenty-five days." But he needed help. He wanted imaginative advice about available work, tasks suitable for women. FERA projects could not compete with the private sector, and men had decided women could not work outdoors. They were deemed too weak to garden or to rake leaves. Construction projects were closed to women. Besides, women with families could not travel as men could and, ER noted, had to work in their own communities.

Ellen Sullivan Woodward, appointed to head the Women's Division of the Federal Emergency Relief Administration in September, acknowledged that it was harder to find 500,000 jobs for women than it was to find four million jobs for men.

ER and her circle pointed out that ten to fifteen hours at steamy washtubs doing tons of laundry, as well as birthing and lugging children, created women strong enough to rake leaves.

Within two months, under Ellen Sullivan Woodward's direction, more than 300,000 women were employed in various jobs. By January 1934, every state relief administrator was ordered to hire a Women's Division coordinator to get women of all races and backgrounds into the workforce, in professional, skilled, and unskilled areas. Projects were created in canning and gardening, and in public libraries and schools. Desperately needed social services were provided in private homes and public institutions; in state hospitals and prisons.

The wellborn daughter of Mississippi gentry, Ellen Sullivan Woodward headed the women's work divisions of various agencies as they were organized, beginning with the Civil Works Administration (CWA).

Skillful and ardent, Woodward was the only woman named to Mississippi's State Board of Public Welfare when it was created in November 1932, and she coordinated Mississippi for Roosevelt. In May 1933, Ellen Woodward left Mississippi for Washington, never to return.

At first Molly Dewson scoffed at her appointment. Woodward should be rewarded for her campaign efforts, but this job was too challenging for this "bit of southern fluff." Everyone who knew Woodward disagreed.

From the first, ER supported Ellen Woodward. The First Lady was chief adviser, "first sponsor, first critic, and first official friend." But for all their work, women's reemployment was slow, sporadic, inadequate. By 1938, 372,000 women had WPA jobs, but over three million women were still unemployed and almost two million women suffered the insufficiency of part-time work.

Over 25 percent of the women employed by FERA and WPA agencies were professionals: teachers, athletic directors, artists, librarians, nurses, performers, musicians, technicians, administrators. The vast majority were unskilled and were reemployed in domestic services, mattress and bedding projects, surplus cotton projects, and sewing and craft projects that appeared in every region. "In 1936, 56% of all women in the WPA worked in sewing rooms," which seemed to many the deplorable triumph of sex segregation: Unskilled men were given a shovel, a hammer, or a hoe, but unskilled women had "only the needle."

Both Woodward and ER were criticized for allowing such discriminatory practices, as well as wage differentials, to prevail. Civil Works Services (CWS), created specifically to provide jobs for white-collar women, paid its workers the prevailing local wage, often as little as the FERA allowable minimum: thirty cents an hour. CWA workers, mostly men, received a dollar an hour.

The effort to employ as many women as possible in the widest range of jobs allowable met the greatest wall of indifference. Nevertheless, many lives were improved by women's programs. In 1933, 60 percent of all nurses were unemployed. By 1934, CWA employed ten thousand nurses in schools, clinics, and hospitals, constituting 19 percent of professional women employed. FERA librarians delivered "books by packhorse in the Kentucky mountains, by flatboat in the Mississippi Delta, by snowshoe. . . ." Over one thousand libraries were opened in "log cabins, community houses, filling stations, country stores, barber shops."

Still, women's projects were continually demeaned. ER and Woodward had few, if any, real supporters among their male allies. Hopkins never endorsed the principle of equal work for equal pay, and despite ER's efforts, FDR never spoke out in favor of women's work.

The creation of the Civilian Conservation Corps dramatized women's struggle. ER was particularly enthusiastic about the CCC. Like FDR, she was thrilled by the concept that offered unemployed urban youth aged eighteen to twenty-five outdoor jobs through a program that combined wholesome education, a new respect for the environment, and country living.

On 31 March, FDR signed the Civilian Conservation Corps into law, with an antidiscrimination clause. Chicago's Oscar De Priest, the only African-American Member of Congress, had introduced an amendment to the CCC bill: "No discrimination shall be made on account of race, color, or creed. . . ." It was accepted by voice vote. Unfortunately, no provision to include women was considered.

Ultimately, three million men, including 250,000 veterans, planted two billion trees, stocked millions of waterways with fish, and built 52,000 public camp grounds and 123,000 miles of roads. They connected twelve thousand miles of telephone lines, protected grazing lands, drained mosquito-infested marshes, fought fires, battled crop disease, preserved wildlife habitats and historic sites, built hiking and horse trails in the national parks. They were responsible for so many magnificent deeds that Grand Canyon park rangers were asked if that great miracle of nature was a CCC project. According to Barbara Kraft: "At a total cost of $3 billion, the CCC was a bargain for the government and the country."

ER supported the CCC and helped establish lending libraries and book distribution centers for each camp. But she could not understand why women should be denied access to such a life-enhancing program.

She crusaded for a parallel corps, or a camp program, for needy young women that would combine education, recreation, and work in similarly wholesome surroundings. While FDR recruited 250,000 men, she demanded at least a hundred women in one camp by June. But her activities were scorned. Even in New Deal circles, the idea of "She She She" camps was ridiculed. Several state relief workers anticipated "serious discipline problems if women were brought together to live."

Frances Perkins supported ER's insistence on at least one camp for women, and their efforts resulted in Camp Tera. At first sponsored by New

York State's Temporary Emergency Relief Administration, it opened on 10 June 1933 on the shores of Lake Tiorati in Bear Mountain State Park.

When ER visited the camp the week after it opened, she was angry to find only thirty women there—when over one thousand had applied within days of its announcement. Hundreds of women had been registered, and ER wanted to know what knots in the red tape prevented them from being there.

The next day *The New York Times* headlined "RECRUITING SPEEDED FOR WOMEN'S CAMP." " 'Red Tape' Is Denied." "MRS. ROOSEVELT HOPEFUL." New York's State Conservation Department and the Temporary Emergency Relief Administration promised to expedite the number of women for admission to the camp, which had a capacity of 360. Sixty-five women would be admitted by the end of the week. The delay was explained by the necessity for "thorough investigations of each applicant." The women "must be without resources" and from age eighteen to thirty-five. ER denounced the requirements, and the age level was raised to forty. But nothing was done to alleviate the means test.

Louis Howe and FDR worked personally on every aspect of the CCC. Camp Tera at first had no radio, and the women wanted music. ER donated a radio, and over time contributed books and various amenities. To create camp programs for women that would be educational, appealing, healthful, and stimulating, she worked with Hilda Worthington Smith, chair of the New Deal's worker education project that was part of FERA's Emergency Education Program (EEP).

Created during the summer of 1933 by Harry Hopkins, EEP was intended to reduce adult illiteracy and provide a vast range of continuing educational opportunities for adults. "Illiterates are dangerous to a democracy ... easy prey to propaganda and exploitation," declared Hopkins. However patronizing EEP's statement of intent, it offered cultural and vocational education state by state and benefited millions of adults, including farm workers and sharecroppers, isolated mountain and urban youth, women and men. By 1937, 200,000 adults a year were enrolled in over twenty thousand classes, learning everything they wanted to learn: arithmetic, electrical wiring, ballroom dancing, Shakespeare, hygiene, and zoology.

The worker education program was one of the smallest components of EEP, but Hilda Smith infused it with energy and imagination throughout the thirty-five state programs she administered. As Bryn Mawr's dean, Smith had helped found the vital Bryn Mawr Summer School for Working Women in 1921, which annually provided one hundred industrial workers with scholarship assistance to attend college classes in literature, history, speech, hygiene, economics, astronomy, creative movement, and other "liberal subjects." ER and the WTUL supported this pioneering effort to provide working women "with complete freedom from economic anxiety and domestic care" while they studied. ER hailed Smith's goals to combine leadership training and academic skills to widen women's "influence in the industrial world and help in the coming social reconstruction."

During ER's November 1933 conference, Hilda Smith persuaded Hopkins to accept her idea of a nationwide program of residential worker schools and camps for jobless women. But little was achieved until ER called another conference on 30 April 1934: the White House Conference on Camps for Unemployed Women. Attended by seventy-five women and men, that conference resulted in a definite "plan of action." By 1936, ninety camps served over five thousand women; eventually 8,500 women benefited from some resident camp experience.

The educational camps varied region by region and reflected cultural differences. There was a camp on a Negro college campus for Arkansas sharecroppers' daughters, a camp in New Jersey for Eastern professional women, a college camp for Ozark mountain women, and a camp for Indian women of North Dakota who had never before left their reservations.

ER was disappointed in the judgment of relief administrators who refused to allow women "outside" work and prohibited them from reforestation and environmental projects. She remained bitter about discrimination in salaries and all benefits. Whereas young CCC men received a "wage" of one dollar a day, camp women received "an allowance" of fifty cents a week. Whereas men were generally recruited for a year, women were entitled to only two or three months in a camp program. Although the camps were not racially segregated, 90 percent of the campers were white; and arrangements to include widows and young married women with children were discussed but never materialized.

Whatever the limitations, campers were enthusiastic. Pauli Murray, who subsequently became an attorney, educator, minister, poet, civil rights activist, and one of ER's first African-American friends, believed Camp Jane Addams saved her life. A recent Hunter College graduate, she was unemployed and barely scraping by on the economic margins of Depression America. Exhausted and overworked, she was sent to the camp by her physician, Dr. Mae Chinn, because she was suffering from malnutrition and pleurisy. According to Pauli Murray:

> The camp was ideal for building up run-down bodies and renewing jaded spirits. . . . We slept in winterized barracks, two women in each room. . . . A staff of young, well-trained counselors planned a wide variety of recreational pursuits—dramatics, arts and crafts, hiking along marked trails, rowing, and, when winter set in, sledding, skiing and ice skating. The outdoor life gave me a tremendous appetite; I got over my cough and began to gain weight.

ER was never quite satisfied by the camp programs. She was displeased that the Army ran the men's camps in military style, and she regretted that more extensive opportunities were not offered for women. She wanted to see a more broadly defined program of two-year voluntary service and education that might create a national youth corps of women and men who would devote some time to the land and some time to the creation of schools, settlement houses, and health centers, and build the beginnings of an experiment in real utopian planning throughout America.

ER dedicated some part of every day to the achievement of the great promises introduced during the first hundred days, and she encouraged everybody to join her. She said in December 1933, "Peace time can be as exhilarating to the daredevil as war time. There is nothing more exciting than building a new social order."

6: Family Discord
and the London Economic Conference

———❦———

*I*n April and May, while FDR labored over New Deal legislation and the economy continued to sag, he addressed monetary issues with a suddenness that startled many—and had profound international implications.

On 19 April, FDR took the United States off the gold standard. Paper money would no longer be redeemable in gold; the dollar would fluctuate; U.S. prices would rise.

FDR considered it a boon for domestic market prices, whatever its consequences on international trade. But higher U.S. prices would further curtail foreign commerce, already diminished by the world Depression. FDR was unconcerned: After all, Britain went off the gold standard in 1931. Budget director Lewis Douglas, however, was horrified and threatened to quit. With images of runaway inflation raging in his mind, the kind of inflation that had devastated Germany in 1923, he wailed: "This is the end of Western Civilization."

ER was not convinced that "Western Civilization" was doomed; but international peace was threatened if Europe could not sell its products, correct its economy, and pay interest on the large wartime debt owed to the United States—a matter of grievous contention. ER worried about the impact FDR's decision would have, especially on England and France. She wrote a critical column for the *Women's Democratic News* to explain the situation and urge women to consider the grave international implications of her husband's decision:

> Great excitement is caused . . . by the President's announcement that no further gold exports will be permitted . . . until at least foreign countries now having a depreciated currency return to the gold standard. . . . This action . . . puts us practically on a parity with Great Britain and other countries that have gone off the gold standard. . . .
>
> While we may undertake many measures to improve our national conditions, those of us who are really thoughtful, know that the world is too closely bound together . . . ever to really prosper unless we all of us enjoy a certain amount of well being together. . . .

Also in April, FDR held meetings in Washington with representatives of eleven nations in preparation for the London Economic Conference. His sole priority was America's fiscal strength, but he sought also to be a world leader. He had no specific strategy, and was surrounded by advisers who disagreed completely. ER worried. He seemed to support each of the diplomats who left his office, smiling and satisfied. But, she knew, they disagreed with each other.

By May, ER felt exhausted, almost despondent. She craved a vacation, and went upstate with Nancy Cook, Earl Miller, and his wife, Ruth. "We all played pool," and since ER and Nan were "novices," they "furnished the hilarity of the evening." ER and Earl took a three-hour drive to visit a camp on Chazy Lake that he planned to rent for the summer. ER "promised to spend two weeks with" Earl and his party in September: "It will be very restful & yet plenty to do."

On her way home, ER had a curious experience, she wrote FDR, "with a young tramp." Unemployed, witty, and earnest, he approached ER for money as she sat in her car and waited for gas. She asked him why he didn't go into the CCC. He had tried, but the CCC required a home address. ER gave him $10 and her New York City card, with a specific invitation to call on her at five o'clock that Monday. He could pay her back when he got a job. Nancy Cook bet the First Lady that she would never see him or her money again.

He rather charmed ER, and she thought her husband should know that while she might "never see him again," he might in fact "turn up" at the White House, or in New York. If he did, she wanted her husband to do everything possible to "to get him in a reforestation camp," or onto some other suitable project. "He probably won't turn up but he might!"

Al Kresse did turn up. That Monday, as she pulled up to the East 65th Street house, a guard told her that "a bum had been hanging around saying Mrs. Roosevelt told him to meet her. . . . I don't know where he could have got that calling card of yours." She saw him on the corner, invited him for dinner, called a friend at Bear Mountain Park to take him into the CCC, and said, "You are going to work tomorrow. Where are you going to sleep tonight?"

She invited him to stay. Hick was horrified: "Sistie and Buzzie are sleeping in the nursery. There's nobody else here but you and me. How do you know he won't kidnap the children?"

ER had considered it all, and locked the elevator doors. But she trusted the young stranger. Al Kresse flourished in the CCC and became a supervisor. She entertained him and his parents at the White House; they corresponded for years, and she became godmother to his daughter.

People were not "tramps" or "bums" to ER. They were people with hopes, needs, unknown abilities. She trusted human nature, and believed in change. She opened her heart, took risks with caution, and was rarely disappointed— except by those who reviled the unemployed as if they were a different species.

The next week, for example, she enlivened a dull dinner for senators: "I threw bomb shells at them about federal control & setting minimum standards." She wanted homeless youth respected and decent wages ensured.

For all her enthusiastic work, in her most private life ER was disturbed. She did not know what her husband planned to do about the international issues which most concerned her, and her family life was diminished by her children's marital woes. She blamed herself, and wrote Hick:

> I don't seem to be able to shake the feeling of responsibility for Elliott and Anna. I guess I was a pretty unwise teacher as to how to go about living. Too late to do anything now, however, and I'm rather disgusted with myself. I feel soiled, but you won't understand that.

ER had been troubled by Elliott's behavior for over a year. In May 1932 she wrote FDR:

> I wish I knew what to do for Elliott and Betty. He is so utterly inconsiderate—and lacking in care and gentleness. I am writing to him today to try to make him understand certain things but I can't say that I feel very hopeful.

Then in March 1933, not quite twenty-three, Elliott abandoned his family. In April, after worrying about his whereabouts for weeks, Betty called with relief: Elliott had "reached Little Rock!"

"Well, my dear," ER wrote Hick, "there will be no misunderstandings between us."

The press was filled with details, and her mother-in-law became incensed and judgmental: "And so news of our family is out and about." SDR blamed ER for her grandchildren's troubles, and they released in her a tremendous surge of bitter memory. Hick sought to calm ER's spirits, and ER was grateful:

> Hick darling what a dear you are! Your letter warmed my heart and made me a little ashamed. What have I to be depressed about! I hate to see the kids suffer, but I know one has to, and I suspect they suffer less than I sometimes think. . . . I never talked to anyone. Perhaps that was why it all ate into my soul, and I look upon so many more emotions more seriously. . . . I was a morbid idiot for many years! Only in the last ten years or so have I made friends to whom I talked!

While FDR relied upon his wife to handle family crises, ER relied upon Hick for emotional advice concerning affairs of the heart. She sent a draft of a letter to Elliott, because "you see his side better than I do perhaps, and I do want to help him and not be too hard," "too preachy," or "austere."

ER considered Hick wise about emotional issues, in a way she herself wanted to be: "I love you on Elliott & you are just right." Her children's upheavals caused ER to reflect on the pain that accompanies human relations: "I'm feeling tonite that the greatest responsibility anyone can have is that of making someone else suffer, and I suppose we all do it. Lord, keep me from it ever again is going to be my daily prayer."

Ironically, ER had no idea how actually tormented Hick felt just then by her Associated Press colleagues, who pressured her to reveal what she knew about the Roosevelt family problems. She refused, and her emotional conflicts mounted as her position as star reporter unraveled. When Hick confided in Louis Howe, he told her that it was wrong for a reporter to get too close to her source. Throughout April and May, while ER leaned upon Hick and planned their summertime escape, Hick suffered in silence.

ER was aware of Hick's conflict, but minimized her agony. Protected by her own economic security, marital and class privilege, she encouraged Hick to consider other work, and future diversions: "I'm planning our trip." "FDR doesn't care which time I go off with you, so, having talked with him, I'm sure of being free and you can arrange for whichever two weeks you want. What fun we'll have just doing nothing—or doing anything. Some day we must see Europe!" In July, they would go north to Canada.

In May, Elliott announced his intention to divorce Betty and marry a woman he had just met. ER wrote Hick that her heart ached for Betty, who had "offered to give me back my pearls (which I did not take) & was swell" in many ways. ER agreed to meet Elliott in Los Angeles for a family conference. As she prepared to leave, her mother-in-law tormented her with accusations. Displeased by her grandchildren's divorces, unable to control their decisions, the family matriarch blamed her daughter-in-law privately, and publicly. Although their political alliance had strengthened as "Mama" increasingly supported ER's activities on behalf of poor and disenfranchised Americans, she continually goaded her concerning the children and relentlessly criticized her mothering.

Hamilton Fish Armstrong, founder of the Council on Foreign Relations and a "Hudson River" family friend, recalled one lunch shortly after the election, at the Big House presided over by SDR. Lord and Lady Astor and Amelia Earhart were among the guests, when a grandson needing money arrived "without notice." Miffed, though not discourteous, she told Armstrong: "I always like having the children, but don't like having extra vegetables picked just on the chance they may come. They never bother to telephone. . . . But of course they have had no bringing up."

In a moment of self-reflection, ER admitted that Sara Delano Roosevelt's taunts wore her down: "My zest in life is rather gone for the time being. If anyone looks at me, I want to weep, and the sooner this western trip is over, the better. . . . I get like this sometimes. It makes me feel like a dead weight and my mind goes round and round like a squirrel in a cage. I want to run, and I can't, and I despise myself. I can't get away from thinking about myself. Even though I know I'm a fool, I can't help it! . . . You are my rock, and I shall be so glad to see you Saturday night. I need you very much as a refuge just now."

While Father got all the credit for the good times, Mother carried the burdens on a daily basis, and always the blame. ER felt worst about Elliott, her father's namesake: Elliott was the baby she carried in 1909, when she was filled with grief after the death of the first baby Franklin. She believed everything her son did was somehow her fault; and nobody in her family discouraged that thought.

On 1 June, ER had an ordinary day: She rode in the morning with Elinor Morgenthau and Esther Lape, who had spent the night to discuss the international situation; held a press conference to express her dismay that work camps for women were insufficiently enrolled; met with the head of the art department of Howard University to discuss new programs for "teaching art to the Negroes." At five o'clock "all the world came to tea," and at six she "shook hands with a group of champion spellers." That evening, she received an honorary law degree and spoke at the commencement of the Washington College of Law.

But no matter what she did, she was distracted by her impending meeting with Elliott.

On the evening of 2 June, ER left for her first transcontinental flight—which, she wrote Hick, was perfect.

Deep in her thoughts as she flew to her son, ER was surprised to be bothered by the press at each refueling stop. "I must say that if all of us showed the same energy that the press photographers do there would be no stone left unturned anywhere in this country. I was even asked to get up and out of the plane at three and again at four o'clock in the morning so that pictures might be taken."

Although the details are lost, her meeting with Elliott was satisfactory, and ER liked his fiancée, Ruth Josephine Googins of Fort Worth, Texas. Charming, and determined, she wanted to marry Elliott "without delay."

Upon her return to New York, ER encountered two irritating letters from her mother-in-law and they had an unpleasant telephone conversation. When they met, ER confided to Hick, she had been "most agreeable superficially, but really horrid, so I am not proud of myself!"

ER wrote her husband in July:

Dearest Honey . . . I can't believe he's getting married for he has no job but I'm writing Anna to find out if he actually needs money. I think it is better to let him fend for himself but I don't want him to borrow from others or to give the impression to others that we won't give him anything. . . .

Upon her return from California, her family crises ongoing, ER turned her attention to the international situation. Closest to her heart was the fight for the World Court and cooperation with the League of Nations, which she continued to believe was the world's best hope against the devastations of war. While Senate opposition had kept the United States out of the League and in a diplomatic state of relative "isolation," Eleanor Roosevelt was in the leadership of a vigorous band of women and men who, since the 1920s, kept the World Court idea before the nation.

Although FDR publicly shied away from international controversy and said not one word in support of the World Court after 1932, ER never wavered from her conviction that "America, by some form of cooperation with the rest of the world, must make her voice count among the nations for peace."

As a board member of the bipartisan American Foundation, ER continued to agitate the cause with an unlikely team who disagreed on many issues but were longtime friends and fervent internationalists. It included Hoover's secretary of state Henry Stimson, Elihu Root—Taft's secretary of war, and most persistent champion of the World Court, and *New York Herald Tribune* publisher Helen Rogers Reid. It was led by ER's great friends Esther Lape and her partner, international lawyer Elizabeth Read, author of *International Law and International Relations*, a leading college text used in over 570 universities. Read was also ER's personal tax accountant and financial adviser.

ER's surprisingly close alliance with Helen Rogers Reid, later known as the heart of New York Republicanism, survived all differences during the White House years. Their friendship was rooted in old family loyalties, as well as in Reid's liberal and feminist vision. Born in Wisconsin, Helen Rogers was a Barnard graduate who became social secretary to Elisabeth Mills Reid, wife of Whitelaw Reid, owner of the *New York Tribune* and ambassador to the Court of St. James from 1905 to 1912. She continued to work as Mrs. Reid's social secretary, commuting between New York and London for eight years, until she married her boss's only son, Ogden Mills Reid, in 1911.

An ardent antifascist, Helen Reid was one of the first American publishers to give full attention to the German situation as it unfolded. On Sunday, 19 March 1933, the *New York Herald-Tribune Magazine* published a long and bitter analysis of "Hitler's War on Culture" by leading German intellectual Dr. Lion Feuchtwanger:

> In the land of Lessing and Goethe free scope is being given to man's destructive urge. School children are being taught prayers of hatred against other children. A concerted attack has been made upon the arts. . . .

The universities of Germany have been transformed into hotbeds of extreme nationalism. . . .

The apostles of Fascism . . . have made man's worst instincts their god and they have stirred senseless racial hatred to fever pitch. They declare that the Jews are to blame for everything. Hitler declares that "the Jews have conquered Europe and America," and are now embarked on an effort to conquer Asia. . . .

People ask, how could this great civilization have been brought to "the verge of ruin almost overnight? . . . Greatest is the amazement" of the world's ten million Jews "who have always looked up to Germany as the spiritual home of world culture. . . ."

Feuchtwanger believed Hitler's rise began with the war in 1914. "For more than four years nations worshiped force and exalted might. . . . The barbaric instincts and atavistic impulses . . . have taken deep roots. . . ."

Then came "the bitterness of defeat." "German Nationalists believed they could not have failed"; rather, they were betrayed by a "domestic foe," a "demoniac power . . . and they found this demoniac power in the Jew. . . .

"German super-nationalism" coupled with militarism now rules, and blames the Jews for everything: Hitler sees them reflected in every window, on every screen, responsible for the World War, its outbreak and its loss; for Bolshevism and capitalism.

As Hitler declares war on Jews, he decrees war on culture. He insists that Germany suffers "from too much education. . . . What we need is instinct and will . . . For our liberation we need more than an economic policy and industry; what we need is pride, spite, hatred, hatred, and once more hatred." He calls himself the *Trommler* (the drummer) and calls for agitation, nighttime torchlight parades, and random acts of brutality and violence to drum up hatred.

In ER's circle, Lion Feuchtwanger's article became the subject of intense discussion. Something frightful was happening that required international scrutiny. The World Court recognized the international conventions to protect racial, religious, and linguistic minorities. But in March, FDR decreed that national events within Germany and other nations were beyond the range of U.S. interests.

FDR's refusal seriously to consider them was tied to his election deal with William Randolph Hearst, the American Foundation's chief publishing enemy since 1924. Indeed, Helen Rogers Reid once wrote Lape that nothing could be done to "harness Hearst." He had the power to make and break leaders, to dictate policies.

In 1932, FDR's nomination was achieved because of Hearst's support, and FDR believed his future success depended on keeping that support.

Hearst explained his attitude clearly in a letter to his former wife, Millicent Hearst:

> I became alarmed at Gov. Roosevelt's internationalistic attitude. I feel very deeply and intensely on this subject. I cannot see that entangling ourselves in European affairs is going to do us any good in any way, while there are possibilities of such utter disaster as are terrifying to contemplate.
>
> The possibilities of being involved in a world war, and of being on the losing side, and of having our country subjected to crushing indemnity, and even deprived of some of its territory, is something that should make us hesitate at being overaltruistically interested in European complications.

Hearst decided to support FDR when he "came out with a very fine letter denying any desire to involve our nation in foreign entanglements. This was most reassuring and allayed my fears. . . ."

Hearst's support assured Roosevelt's nomination, and he concluded his letter: "I am glad to have had a hand in accomplishing it. . . . I will work everywhere for him, in our papers and over our radios and in the news reels. . . ."

After 1932, only ER, Lape, and their circle continued their World Court campaign for "ratification now." By the summer of 1933, "Delay" on the World Court was established bipartisan policy.

FDR's deal with Hearst—who delivered California and Texas—was faithfully kept. ER knew that it included FDR's agreement to turn his back on the World Court, all "entangling alliances," and multilateral efforts. Initially, when she learned of his convention promise, it had made her so furious she did not speak with her husband for days. FDR was so upset by his wife's stony silence that he called ER's friend and one of his champions, Agnes Brown Leach, to come for a visit and mollify her. Leach arrived, but supported ER.

For months it was unclear where FDR really stood regarding Europe's 1933 efforts for disarmament and international economic accord. He insisted only that his options were restrained by "pragmatic" politics: Hearst's support, Senate support. FDR would take no leadership risks concerning international relations that might threaten his domestic programs.

Daily, ER agonized over the dire headlines of aggression and betrayal out of Germany and Japan. Now her husband's policy seemed even to depart from Hoover's "nonrecognition" policy against aggressor states: FDR's new isolationist sentiments insisted upon absolute neutrality, and a refusal even to name the aggressor.*

---

*When Japan invaded Manchuria in 1931, Hoover and Secretary of State Henry Stimson issued a policy of nonrecognition: the Stimson Doctrine, which gave moral support to China and affirmed that Japan was an aggressor nation. But it called for no

In the spring of 1933, the US was silent as Japan moved deeper into China, stopping only thirteen miles from Peking before negotiating a truce on 31 May 1933.

Although FDR frequently recalled his family's close commercial ties with China, he did not suggest an arms embargo, or any other public response, even when Japan withdrew from the League of Nations in April. The western world was passive while the Soviets worried about their eastern territories, and Japanese militarists announced their "Imperial Destiny," which included East Asia, the South Seas, and the entire Western Pacific.

At the same time, all the news out of Germany was ghastly. Throughout April and May, ER clipped articles and filled FDR's basket with horror stories and urgent notes. Hitler made bellicose speeches, decried the punitive, vindictive Treaty of Versailles, and demanded full equality in armaments—either through French arms reduction or through German rearmament.

On 1 April, Nazis announced a national boycott of Jewish businesses and professions. Gangs of Nazis roamed the streets in Berlin and beat women and men seated at cafés and in parks; in other cities they brutalized Jews at random. On 7 April, Hitler obliterated the constitutional government, and henceforth he reigned supreme.

On 2 May, Nazis invaded and destroyed labor union offices, confiscated their funds, files, and property, arrested every union leader, and declared unions (active in Germany for over fifty years) dissolved. On 10 May, Nazi students at the University of Berlin ended a torchlight parade with a massive book burning that included the works of every notable German writer and scholar, including Albert Einstein, Erich Maria Remarque, Thomas Mann, and Stefan Zweig, as well as others, including H. G. Wells and Upton Sinclair.

Also in May, Franz von Papen announced that Germany had obliterated "the term pacifism." Before a vast Nazi rally, Papen, who as military attaché in Washington during the Great War had been accused of sabotaging U.S. transportation facilities, declared: "The battlefield is for a man what motherhood is for a woman!" Hitler was scheduled to address the Reichstag the next day, 17 May, and many feared he would officially repudiate Versailles and announce full rearmament at that time. England and France had unofficially agreed to declare sanctions if he did.

Finally, to ER's great relief, FDR ended a month of silence with an "Appeal to the Nations." Drafted with the help of Louis Howe and others, it echoed her sentiments for real disarmament and was sent to fifty-four nations and published throughout the world:

Despite "the lessons and tragedies of the World War," military weapons

---

action, neither economic sanctions nor arms embargo. FDR now called for stricter neutralism, which would not even designate the aggressor.

"are today a greater burden upon the people of the earth than ever before." The reason for such insanity was fear of "aggression" and "invasion." Modern technology changed everything. War planes and heavy tanks threatened civilians everywhere. Therefore, "the ultimate goal of The Disarmament Conference must be peace," which depended on the "complete elimination of all offensive weapons, and a solemn and definite pact of non-aggression."

FDR's speech was received jubilantly by citizens' groups around the world, and respectfully by national leaders. Hitler even recast his 17 May speech to respond to FDR's challenge: War represented "unlimited madness," destruction, the "collapse of the present social and political order." Confident that England and France were not serious about disarmament, Hitler rhetorically accepted the president's proposal:

> Germany is entirely ready to renounce all offensive weapons if the armed nations, on their side, will destroy their offensive weapons. . . . Germany would also be perfectly ready to disband her entire military establishment and destroy the small amount of arms remaining to her, if the neighboring countries will do the same. . . . Germany is prepared to agree to any solemn pact of nonaggression, because she does not think of attacking but only of acquiring security.

Then, on 22 May, Norman Davis, chair of the U.S. Geneva delegation, announced that the United States was willing to consult multilaterally "in case of a threat to peace with a view to averting conflict," and if in agreement with the determination, then to join in a "collective effort to restore peace."

ER and her friends were delighted by Davis's announcement and interpreted it as FDR's long-awaited commitment of involvement with the League in the interests of peace. For isolationists, it was a declaration of war.

Within days, however, FDR renounced both his own words and those of Norman Davis. He had meant to limit his promises to "consultation," not to extend them to a "collective effort." There could be no departure from "long-standing and existing policy."

For the moment world opinion hung suspended, confused by FDR's torrent of contradictory words throughout April and May. His "bland statements filled with pious nothings" caused some to believe FDR had no international policy at all. Isolationists were pleased; his internationalist friends were confused.

On 30 May the Disarmament Conference prepared to recess, after fifteen months of acrimony and hope. Attention shifted to the forthcoming London Economic Conference to open on 12 June.

The most immediate source of international tensions was the outstanding war debts virtually all Europe owed to the United States. England, France,

Germany, and Russia were broke. Germany could not pay its reparations to the Allies, and the Allies reneged on their payments to the United States. England agreed to make a "token payment." FDR abhorred the word "token," and Ramsay MacDonald agreed to dicker about the amount of partial payment. Only Finland fully paid its World War I debt in 1933.

America's Depression was part of a worldwide disaster. In 1931, Hoover had declared a one-year moratorium on debt payments. But he also signed the devastating Smoot-Hawley tariff law, which raised U.S. tariffs so high that European goods were no longer viable in the American market. Conditions worsened everywhere.

The London Economic Conference, which FDR also inherited from Hoover, was planned to end economic warfare, reduce tariffs, create a unified program to combat the global Depression, and begin the long journey toward international trade security and currency stabilization, which many believed would create a climate for peace through international commerce and fair market prices.

ER considered these among the most urgent issues on the world's agenda, and she wanted her husband to assume a leadership role at the London Conference. After all, both Roosevelts had long agreed that nothing happened in isolation: Economically and politically, European events profoundly affected the United States; and U.S. policies concerned Europe, where fear of unstoppable inflation and fiscal havoc predominated. Memories of Germany's 1923 inflation, when a wheelbarrow of worthless paper might buy milk or eggs, now haunted especially nations still on gold. Also, since 19 April, when FDR had taken the United States off gold and ended gold exports, America's cheap dollar had wiped out Britain's competitive advantage in the world trading market. France and Germany, still on gold, their currencies already devalued, faced fiscal disaster. In addition, there was wild speculation in money, stocks, and commodities as the dollar bounced about, in the hope that US prices might rise.

European leaders, both on and off gold, wanted to establish some new ratio, some international stabilization that would avoid wild swings in currency value and market prices. Currency stabilization was more important than the exact ratio or value of the dollar or pound, and FDR sent several delegates to the London Conference who agreed with that position.

In the *Women's Democratic News*, ER expressed her own concerns regarding these issues:

> Countries which have been impoverished by war are in debt to us. We have the major portion of all the gold in the world in this country. The only way in which other nations can pay their debts is by sending us goods. Our tariffs make this impracticable and in order to prevent our sending

them goods, they have begun to build up their tariffs and so our trade is growing less and less.

There were times, during the spring of 1933, when ER and FDR seemed to be two internationalists in total agreement. On occasion, FDR even sounded like a League-loving Wilsonian. In May he wrote Joseph Tumulty, who had been Woodrow Wilson's personal secretary: "I wonder if you realize how often I think of our old Chief when I go about my daily tasks. Perhaps what we are doing will go a little way toward the fulfillment of his ideals."

Then he took a firm stand against Hitlerism. On 8 June 1933, he telephoned sixty-three-year-old history professor William E. Dodd at his University of Chicago office: "This is Franklin Roosevelt. I want to know if you will render the government a distinct service. I want you to go to Germany as ambassador."

Southern and scholarly, Dodd was president-elect of the American Historical Association. Born in North Carolina, he received his Ph.D. from the University of Leipzig in 1900, and spoke German fluently. A liberal Democrat, he was best known for his histories of the old South, biographies of Nathaniel Macon and Jefferson Davis, and a celebratory biography of Woodrow Wilson. With Ray Stannard Baker he also edited *The Public Papers of Woodrow Wilson.*

FDR explained that he selected Dodd because of his reputation as "a liberal and as a scholar," and especially for his work on Woodrow Wilson: "I want an American liberal in Germany as a standing example." A dedicated antifascist, Dodd became one of FDR's most controversial appointments.

On 31 May, Secretary of State Cordell Hull embarked for London with enthusiasm, convinced that his mission was to achieve fiscal stabilization in a world of depression and economic chaos. He believed FDR fully supported his intention "to lower trade barriers and stabilize the currency exchange."

After all, FDR had publicly announced that the World Monetary and Economic Conference was of "vital importance to mankind." Failure at this conference would be, FDR declared, "a catastrophe amounting to a world tragedy." Ramsay MacDonald believed the "fate of generations" was involved: "We must not fail."*

At her 15 June press conference ER urged all women to realize they "have a special stake in watching national and international news. Every woman should have a knowledge of what is going on [in London]. It does affect the future amicable relations between the nations of the world. It has been stated that the debt question is not to be discussed. But whatever does come out will be vitally important to every woman in her own home."

Unknown to his wife, unknown to his secretary of state, throughout

---

*Unknown to Ramsay MacDonald, the pacifist Prime Minister, was FDR's executive order of 16 June 1933 to refurbish the U.S. Navy. See p. 132 and notes.

May FDR had encouraged Ray Moley to put the brakes on Hull's efforts. Appointed assistant secretary of state, responsible directly to FDR, Moley was an ardent economic nationalist who deplored free trade. Hull's State Department resented his presence, and his views. Unlike Hull, Moley argued that tariffs served useful domestic purposes. London must not be allowed to limit America's fiscal independence.

FDR's immediate goal in 1933 was to ensure higher prices for American farm products and manufactured goods. To limit cheap goods from abroad, he even raised certain tariffs, most notably on cotton, higher than Smoot-Hawley levels. Fiscal nationalists were delighted. But there was no agreement among FDR's international team, not among his six official delegates nor among his fifty advisers. FDR had sent them off with no instructions, and there was no clearly established policy. Each delegate sailed away with the illusion that the president supported his own particular interest.

But while they were at sea, FDR suddenly abandoned the reciprocal trade bill before Congress. He had simply decided to request "no action." Cordell Hull's hopes for international agreement based on reduced tariffs had depended on that bill. It would have provided clear evidence that the United States was sincere in its commitment to positive action. Hull was devastated: "I left for London with the highest of hopes but arrived with empty hands."

William Bullitt, appointed on 20 April special assistant to the secretary of state and executive officer of the U.S. delegation, was appalled. On 11 June he sent FDR an "ultra-confidential" cable to report Hull's complete collapse. Bullitt had "rarely seen a man more broken up, and his condition was reflected in that of Mrs. Hull, who literally wept all night." FDR sent a reassuring cable, which enabled Hull to remain and try to achieve something. After all, delegates from sixty-six nations had assembled to consider alternatives to fiscal chaos, economic despair. The need was great, and for the moment goodwill was in the air.

On 16 June, Congress adjourned, and ER and SDR traveled to Groton for young Franklin's graduation. In addition to his diploma, he received first prize from the Debating Society and another for combined excellence in scholarship and athletics. Several Roosevelt cousins also graduated, and three of TR's grandsons also won prizes. But if ER spoke to her relatives, she failed to mention it.

FDR was supposed to attend, but last-minute congressional details and lunch with Dodd prevented his leaving Washington until the next day in time for homecoming festivities. ER had already left for a week at Val-Kill while, from Groton, FDR and his sons embarked on a sailing adventure that would culminate in his first visit to Campobello since 1921—when he contracted polio.

James had chartered a forty-five-foot schooner, *Amberjack II.* Papa would be skipper; James, FDR, Jr., and John would be crew. FDR charted and piloted his own course. They would sail around Cape Cod and north-northeast to the Bay of Fundy, a total of 360 nautical miles.

The schooner was accompanied and protected by patrolling Navy planes overhead and Navy escorts including two destroyers and the cruiser *Indianapolis*, each with facilities for telegrams, information, and emergencies. A Coast Guard cutter with White House and Secret Service staff sailed behind, as did two press boats. One carried wire service and motion picture photographers. The other, the *Mary Alice*, carried four of FDR's favorite White House correspondents: Ernest Lindley of the *New York Herald Tribune*, Bill Murphy of the *New York World*, John Herrick of the *Chicago Tribune*, and Charles Hurd of *The New York Times*.

They all had strict orders to keep out of sight, except when invited. The *Mary Alice* revelers were, however, frequently invited—since they were well stocked with a case of bourbon. FDR's stores were dry, and the weather was cold and drear.

Hanging over them all, during long days of storm and relentless fog that kept the president's party idled and off-course, were the events unfolding at the London Economic Conference. FDR kept in touch through the communication facilities on the *Indianapolis*, both with his official delegation and with various experts he had called together for advice.

Baruch and Herbert Bayard Swope, Baruch's confidant and former editor of the old *New York World*, were the most ardent internationalists. One of FDR's last acts before he left Washington was to write Swope on 16 June:

> Would be delighted if you could accompany Raymond Moley for short visit to London. I am sending him soon and feel your presence would be exceedingly helpful to him in many ways. I should be personally grateful to have you do this, having confidence as I do in your judgment and your wide knowledge of international affairs. . . .

Evidently, FDR had second thoughts about Moley's economic nationalism, and wanted Swope to join the fray. But it is impossible to fathom FDR's motives, because he rejected every proposal both his London and New York teams, after days of argument and compromise, considered sound. He could not accept any monetary restraint that would adversely affect U.S. commodity prices. On 17 June, he cabled Hull: "We must retain full freedom of action . . . in order to hold up price level at home."

Then on 20 June, FDR sent what could only be regarded as an insult to his own banker team: "It is my personal view that far too much importance is being placed on existing and temporary fluctuations. Remember, that far too much influence is attached to exchange stability by banker-influenced cabinets."

Upon receipt of that cable, George Harrison packed his bags and left London. The others remained faithful and hopeful that some good, some agreement, could be achieved. Telegrams and telephone messages went back and forth during days of confusion as FDR sailed on.

While her husband sailed and dissembled, away from her questioning insistence and churning emotions, ER relied upon Baruch, who kept her informed. ER spent the week in the relative tranquillity of Val-Kill with Nancy Cook and Marion Dickerman, distracted and agitated.

Earl Miller visited, and had a calming effect. Occasionally she was able to write when Earl worked on his reports. But her letters to Hick were filled with discontent; she simply could not concentrate: "I wish I could work as you do, but I can't. . . ."

By the time she left with Marion Dickerman and Nancy Cook for their trip to Campobello to open the house and assemble the staff for FDR's much-anticipated homecoming, ER was distraught by the confusion in London.

Although the drive north was pleasant and their tour through northern New York, Vermont, and Maine was mostly "glorious," ER was in a sour mood.

When they arrived at Mary Dreier's home on Mount Desert Island in Maine, ER discovered that a large party was planned for the next afternoon, and she wrote with dismay: "I don't dare tell Nan, but this is not my idea of a holiday!"

The next morning ER awoke to discover that "FDR and the whole fleet" had anchored outside Mary Dreier's home in Southwest Harbor. ER worried that it was "rather overpowering for Mary Dreier, but she seemed pleased." ER's three sons went ashore for breakfast, and FDR invited ER and her party aboard the *Amberjack II* for lunch. By all accounts it was a "joyous reunion," and nobody discussed the London Economic Conference.

After FDR's detour to Mary Dreier, he continued his cruise while ER headed directly for Campobello to make the beds and prepare the great welcoming picnic to celebrate FDR's first visit in twelve years. Friends and neighbors gathered, including Louis Howe, Henry Morgenthau, the governor of Maine, and Norman Davis, who had returned with messages from the Geneva Disarmament Conference. Blanketed by fog, ER wrote Hick:

> I hope we have good weather . . . when Franklin and his fleet [arrive]. I love the place and like people I like to see it at its best. Fog is nice if you know a place and are with someone you like. It is like a winter storm. It

shuts you in and gives you a close & intimate feeling & adds to the joy of your fire. But you don't want to meet a new place in a fog any more than you want to be intimate with a new acquaintance.

ER loved Campobello in all weather: the brisk sea air, the pebbled beaches and extreme tides, the mysteries of the green-and-gray mists, the incomparably azure blue skies that followed the thickest fogs. Campo had been the first home ER furnished and arranged herself. Sara had purchased a rambling, comfortable twenty-four-room house in 1909 for her children's use. Her home was next door, separate and distinct. With no telephone and no electricity, for ER, Campo remained a refuge.

For a time on 27 June, the sun appeared and ER went sailing with Dickerman and Cook. She wrote Hick: "I'm sitting in the bottom of the boat, sniffing salt air & every now and then looking over the water to my green islands & grey rocky shores. I do think it is lovely, & I wonder if you will. . . . Do you like sailing? Or don't you?"

But FDR was fogbound and anchored off dreary Roque Island on Lakeman Bay, where he had been stilled for three nights and two days. During that time all the news from London was dreadful. The dollar soared to $4.30 in relation to the pound; the gold nations thought they would be wrecked if no agreement, no simple statement of intent, was made. France, Italy, Switzerland, Holland, Belgium, clamored for a sign of goodwill.

From New York the circle around Woodin's bed, including Baruch and Dean Acheson, urged FDR to make a positive statement concerning stabilization. Norman Davis sailed out to the *Amberjack II* with the same message—the future of the Geneva Conference depended on the success of the London Conference. Everything depended on economic trust, evidence of goodwill. Hull sent urgent telegrams. And for all the press reports about Hull's upset over Moley's arrival, Moley's private conferences with Ramsay MacDonald, Moley's usurpation of Hull's rightful role, there was now little disagreement over the need for FDR to agree to what was, after all, a most modest proposal. Moley's cables were now the most urgent of all, and his subsequent memory the most vivid: "On the day I landed at Plymouth, the dollar was at its greatest discount since our War between the States." Then on 28 June, the dollar went up to $4.43:

> France and the gold-standard countries were groveling in the dust, howling for something, anything, that might save them from being pushed off gold. . . .
> England and France weren't talking about stabilization at $4.00 any more. . . . They would have fainted with relief had they known that Roosevelt had indicated to me on the *Amberjack* on June 20th that he'd be

disposed to authorize stabilization with a high of $4.25 and a low of $4.05.

FDR's bargaining tactics had succeeded beyond his wildest imagining. . . . [Now they] asked only that he make some gesture—some small gesture—that would in no way limit his freedom of action on the dollar and that would, nevertheless, tend to discourage the mad exchange speculation of the preceding three weeks.

The gold countries had drawn up a "declaration," with England's agreement. Moley "was amazed as I examined it. It was brief, simple, and wholly innocuous." And it reflected one of FDR's own policy statements: "a statement that gold would ultimately be reestablished as a measure of international exchange value, but that each nation reserved the right to decide when it would return to a gold standard and undertake stabilization."

Moley believed FDR "would be overjoyed to learn that he had beaten the gold countries and England down to this." England's chancellor of the exchequer, Neville Chamberlain, visited Moley at the U.S. embassy to lobby this perfectly "harmless declaration" which would nevertheless "quiet the panic" of the continental nations.

Then Prime Minister Ramsay MacDonald, vastly "more emotional than Chamberlain," explained to Moley in "vivid terms" the origins of Europe's inflation phobia, the bitter suffering after the war due to uncontrolled inflation. They had seen it, lived it, it was not a banker's bad dream. "Fear of it, fear that the U.S. would push their currencies off the gold and into inflation, was sweeping over Holland and Switzerland and France. The consequences of fear, unchecked, might even be revolution in those countries. The moment was critical. It would cost Roosevelt only a meaningless gesture to dispel the psychoses threatening Europe."

Europe's inflation, the great inflation of 1921–23, now haunted all decisions regarding Europe's future. In 1921 the Allies decreed that Germany owed 132 billion gold marks in wartime reparations. Payment of Germany's reparations would enable Europe to pay its own debts to the United States. But Germany resisted with a "wheelbarrow" inflation that destroyed the economy. Personal security disappeared, savings evaporated, everything was rendered worthless as the mark, four to the dollar before 1914, seventy-five to the dollar after Versailles, went from 500:1 to 750:1, and then millions to one, up and up 20 percent higher each day during the 1923 inflation, until the government called a halt in 1924 when currency was pegged at four trillion marks to the dollar.

After dramatic changes in government, by a stroke of the pen the mark was restored: four to one. But the damage had been done. Germany would never be the same. For most Germans the inflation was Germany's revolution. Small businesses went bankrupt; millions of people were unemployed. For a time the madness was replaced by the appearance of stability and the hope of international reconciliation. But discontent and nationalist enmity seethed, ready to erupt during the renewed wave of international depression that followed 1929.

In 1928 the National Socialist Party received only 2.8 percent of the vote in a Reichstag election. But everything changed with the worldwide Depression. Financial insecurity impassioned Nazism. Few in Europe now doubted the force of Hitler's overwhelming power, or the dangers of unbridled economic inflation.

On Thursday, 29 June 1933, Moley's cable demanding a positive response reached FDR. Telephone conversations between Moley in London and Baruch, Woodin, Acheson, and also George Harrison, who joined them after he left London, revealed that all FDR's advisers were now in agreement. The hours passed. All day Friday and Friday night there was nothing but silence and delay. Saturday morning's silence was broken only by a telephone message: FDR's answer would be again delayed.

On Thursday, 29 June, FDR decided to defy the fog and after breakfast sail ashore. He lifted anchor at 8:30 A.M., determined to best the weather; he was calm and happy. The *Indianapolis* gave him a twenty-one-gun salute, and he was jubilantly greeted by the Coast Guard cutter *Cuyahoga*, the local herring fleet, and every yacht and rowboat in the area. FDR arrived precisely on schedule at 4:00 P.M., just as the fog lifted, "as if some giant, invisible hand had raised a curtain" to bear witness as FDR sailed his schooner through the dangerous Lubec Narrows and tacked across choppy Passamaquoddy Bay.

What might have been a triumphal dinner, filled with cheer and high spirits, was instead fraught with family tensions that erupted into unpleasant disagreement. Their friends were surprised by ER's vehemence after so much care and effort had gone into preparing her husband's return to his beloved island.

Although the records of that meal are sparse, Marion Dickerman and Henry Morgenthau remembered that ER believed it a mistake to send Moley to London. It humiliated and belittled Hull; "it weakened Hull's position." Moreover, the First Lady did not trust Moley's ambitions, and she warned FDR that he represented a "threat to the President's own power and prestige."

The next day, Friday, 30 June, ER invited the four reporters from the *Mary Alice* for lunch "and an afternoon of relaxation."

According to Charles Hurd, the First Lady "greeted us on the beach, and we walked up the path to the cottage." After lunch, the president "suggested a game of cut-in bridge." But they played "for only an hour or so" and then FDR said, "I think it might be more interesting to talk for a while."

The journalists had been "trapped." FDR's conversation "must have been conceived as spontaneously as a message to Congress." He talked bluntly about torpedoing the London Conference. It was off the record, not for attribution, a conversation among friends. But he suggested a Campobello byline. He wanted the story out, and he wanted it explained clearly.

Hurd wrote that the reporters "could see why Roosevelt was disturbed. . . . [He] might be an internationalist, something of an Anglophile through family and friends, a cosmopolitan; but at this stage he was determined that the U.S. was not to be pushed around" by international bankers, financiers, bullies. For the most part, Europeans wanted "concessions" from the United States—even though they all, except Finland, had defaulted on their "past debts." FDR noted that European bonds were held by private citizens; "American investors had trusted the debtor countries . . . and yet they had wound up with worthless and depreciated bonds. . . ." Their "resentment" was understandable, "and furthermore . . . he agreed with it."

FDR would accept no devaluation of the dollar "so that foreign governments could trade it at bargain prices in other markets." In fact, FDR would accept nothing from the London Conference.

Hurd's words are an ironic reminder of a letter FDR had written to Waldorf Astor in April. His mother would not be making her annual visit that summer: "I cannot let Mama go over because I am sure she would cancel all the debts!"

Each reporter left to write up the story, which hit the next day "like a bombshell." Hurd's *New York Times* story was reprinted throughout Europe, and wrecked the London Conference even before FDR sent the first of his own torpedoes directly to Moley, which finally arrived at three Saturday afternoon.

As Moley and Swope read FDR's words they burst into laughter. It was an argument against "rigid and arbitrary stabilization," which had nothing to do with the declaration at all. FDR pontificated that "so long as national budgets remained unbalanced currency would be unsound." Above all, FDR insisted, American prices and currency "must be free" of foreign entanglements, international pressures.

In the end, Moley and Herbert Swope believed they needed above all to protect FDR from his own errors. "The message must be seen by as few people as possible." As Bacon said, "kings cannot err." They decided to issue a statement that said only that FDR rejected the declaration in its present form. Also to protect FDR, Hull ordered the minutes "kept of the meetings of the American delegation" in London burned.

ER escorted the journalists down the steep wooden steps to the beach with their tension and their story palpable in the air. She learned from them the news her husband had failed to confide in her. Once again she had been shut

Eleanor Roosevelt arriving at the 1933 inaugural ball.

ER and FDR at the
Coronado Hotel,
California, 1934.

ABOVE: Sistie (Eleanor) and Buzzie (Curtis) playing on swings on the White House lawn.

ER and her mother-in-law, Sara Delano Roosevelt, at Campobello.

Head White House housekeeper, Henrietta Nesbitt, and ER.

BELOW: Edith Benham Helm (standing), ER's social secretary, and Malvina Thompson Sheider—"Tommy"—ER's private secretary.

ER and Marion
Dickerman at the
White House.

BELOW: Nancy Cook and
ER at Val-Kill.

The Women's Press Conference in the White House, 1933.

FDR greets British prime minister Ramsay MacDonald and his daughter, Ishbel, in Washington D.C., 21 April 1933.

FDR welcomes ER home from the Caribbean on their twenty-ninth anniversary, 17 March 1934.

RIGHT: Creating Arthurdale, 1933–36.

Typical Arthurdale homes.

On board the USS *Indianapolis*, 31 August 1934. *Left to right:* ER, Betsey Roosevelt, FDR, James Roosevelt, SDR.

ER at Lake Roosevelt, Yosemite National park, with Ranger Forrest Townsley, during her vacation with Hick, July 1934.

Relaxing at Chazy Lake, New York, with Earl Miller, August 1934.

ER the markswoman.

"I have to
be tied
and gagged,
they're
making their
movie, 'The
Lady and
the Pirate.'"

Later on this flight over Washington with Amelia Earhart on 20 April 1933, ER was at the controls.

Walter White, NAACP leader.

ER and her new friend, dancer Mayris "Tiny" Chaney.

out of a decision that mattered to her deeply, and she returned to the house in a state of fury and gloom.

She sat by herself in her blue-and-white room overlooking the bay and contemplated her husband's decision, while he hosted "a gay cocktail party" for his sons and the twenty-two houseguests that had arrived from all over to greet his return.

The party was prolonged, and dinner was delayed. ER waited two hours and then summoned the guests to the table. She was upset to find her teenage son no longer sober. That, compounded by her feelings about the doomed London Conference, unleashed a public scene: She "upbraided her husband . . . harshly, angrily, as if he were a naughty little boy." He became petulant: "You can't scold me this way. . . . It is not my fault and I didn't know what time supper was."

Curiously, several of FDR's biographers actually blamed his wife's anger for his truculent message to London. But FDR had already made his decision, and ER's bitter behavior signified her disappointment and distress. She felt personally betrayed. To the end of her life, ER referred to the international failures of 1933 with regret and wonderment:

> We once had a delegate [Norman Davis], a very fine man, a very valuable public servant, who used to go to the disarmament conferences in Geneva, and I used to wonder why no one took any interest in his going or the slightest interest when he returned. We didn't seem to care what he did or what happened. . . .

ER wrote that she learned one very important lesson during the summer of 1933:

> I came to the conclusion that . . . just having a few people in the government take an interest in trying to achieve peace is never going to achieve peace, that it has to be done by the interest of the people, and unless all the people—the men who work on the farms, the men who work in the factories, the scientists and teachers, and all the people who make up a nation—take an interest, we will fail. . . .

After FDR left the next day on the *Indianapolis*, ER, Nancy Cook, and Marion Dickerman drove Norman Davis to the train in Maine. His calming words and a magnificent sunset created a healing drive down, "and I recaptured a little serenity."

On her return, ER made plans to meet with the leaders of the international peace movement, including Carrie Chapman Catt, Jane Addams, Alice Hamilton, and Lillian Wald. More immediately, like Hull and Moley, she sought to protect the president. She did not discuss FDR's decision to wreck the London Conference. About her time at Campobello, she told her press conference only that there were a hundred people for a picnic, and she did women's work: "I made all the beds for 22 people." She did not add with anguish or wrath that men made momentous decisions, while women served in silence.

Sunday afternoon, 2 July, FDR returned on the *Indianapolis* to Washington, accompanied by his son Franklin, Henry Morgenthau, and Louis Howe. Homeward bound, FDR drafted yet another message to criticize the London Conference:

> The sound internal economic system of a nation is a greater factor in its well-being than the price of its currency, or currency exchange rates, or any of the issues debated in London:
> When the world works out concerted policies . . . to produce balanced budgets and living within their means, then we can properly discuss a better distribution of the world's gold and silver supply to act as a reserve base of national currencies. . . .

This was the specific "bombshell" that cashiered the London Conference. For many it was not only substantively shocking, it was arrogant and belligerent. Members of his own delegation were merely perplexed. They had no idea what it meant, or what kind of "jest" it was supposed to be. James Warburg resigned that week, because he could no longer interpret the president's vision.

It was over. Never again during the 1930s would the effort to achieve economic international accord be made. The British were astonished. Ramsay MacDonald felt personally assaulted. He told Moley: "This doesn't sound like the man I spent so many hours with in Washington. This sounds like a different man. I don't understand."

On 4 July 1933, *The New York Times* reported that the Nazi press praised FDR's action. German leaders regarded the "death agonies" of the London Conference with satisfaction, "because they see the end of any united front against Germany." They exulted that "the Americans merely turned the tables on the conference." Hitler was pleased, since FDR's policies confirmed his own: Economic nationalism ruled the day. One Nazi paper hailed "President Roosevelt's truths," because he "adopted an economic program which is the foundation of Chancellor Hitler's policy." One can only wonder what ER felt when she read those words.

FDR's decision was championed by an odd assortment of observers, including Louis Howe and Henry Morgenthau—who evidently encouraged him to write the final bombshell as they cruised south to Washington on the *Indianapolis*. Ultimately Moley was pleased:

The United States "had for once gone to an international conference without making ridiculous concessions. And I was gratified that the President's newly strengthened distrust of international 'cooperation' even in its mildest form had been, at last, unmistakably proclaimed."

Above all, Hearst was vindicated. His primary fear was that the United States would cave in on the European debt. The United States now only hardened its position. In 1934, the absolute isolationist Johnson Act forbade U.S. citizens to lend money to, or buy securities from, indebted governments in default to the United States. This was considered a great victory by a wide range of economic nationalists, even though it prevented credits that would have revived U.S. export trade and destroyed the rationale for the "token" payments some nations had been conscientiously making. But the Johnson Act was discriminately applied; and the debts were never repaid.

More than hope for international cooperation ended when the conference closed forever on 27 July 1933. European statesmen no longer trusted the United States. British leaders, from MacDonald to Neville Chamberlain, who had personally appealed to FDR in June, now despised the president. Throughout the 1930s, they simply dismissed FDR's sporadic diplomatic overtures as ridiculous and irrelevant. As ER feared most, a great opportunity for international leadership had been lost. Her husband had failed to take a risk for peace. Rearmament and economic nationalism would forevermore rule the day.

Surrounded by fascism, communism, and Europe's economic and imperial rivalries, FDR built a stronger navy and an economy unfettered by international accords with European leaders he judged untrustworthy.

For veteran peace activists allied with Addams and Wald, the conference was a bitter portent. Oswald Garrison Villard, *The Nation*'s longtime editor, returned from Europe "to admit a sense of almost complete hopelessness. . . . The London Conference dealt a deadly blow. . . ."

In London, Soviet Foreign Minister Maxim Litvinov, as in Geneva, where he made the only substantial proposal for general disarmament, made the only substantial suggestion for general prosperity: Litvinov offered a billion dollars' worth of business from Russia to prime business pumps in exchange for long-term credit.

Litvinov worked the room and walked away with stunning nonaggression treaties with neighboring states from Afghanistan to Estonia, and generous trade agreements with France, England, and the United States. Litvinov and Hull arranged for Russia to borrow $4 million with which to buy American cotton.

FDR, a man of endless imagination who enjoyed playing every angle, now considered alternatives to the specter of Japanese aggression in America's Pacific "sphere of influence" and Nazi Germany's rearmament without collective opposition. He decided to explore the possibilities for U.S. recognition of the Soviet Union. As if to make amends to his wife's disappointed circle, he turned to Esther Lape and her American Foundation to initiate a study of Soviet-American relations.

Indeed, on the same day London received FDR's bombshell, 3 July, the American Foundation issued a press release to announce the creation "of a Committee on Russian-American Relations." The committee would extend the work of Esther Lape's unofficial survey of national leaders and public opinion, conducted in June, which revealed "a genuine desire" for "trustworthy" information concerning our relations with the Soviet Union.

With her usual diligence and efficiency, Lape staffed her initial "Committee of Inquiry" with notable scholars, labor leaders, diplomats, and business leaders.

The purpose was to explore the terms "upon which other countries have recognized Soviet Russia; the collateral arrangements that have . . . accompanied or followed recognition; the extent to which there have been government guarantees of payments for goods sold to Russia; the facts as to the debts of the Czarist regime . . . ; the confiscation of property of citizens of other countries; . . . Russian trade with other countries and the U.S."

On 3 July, Lape wrote, FDR had read the initial report "personally, with obvious interest," and urged her new committee to work tirelessly all that summer, to be ready for his projected but as yet unscheduled autumnal meeting with Litvinov.

In addition, FDR wanted his wife to know that he appreciated her concerns, expressed so forcefully at Campobello, and cabled Hull on the eve of his return: "Before you sail, I want you to know once more of my affectionate regard for and confidence in you." He wrote nothing to Moley, nor did he say anything encouraging to Moley when they met. Moley knew that he had been personally "kicked in the face" and resigned as soon as possible without seeming to resign in protest.

FDR also encouraged ER's team not to abandon their fight for the World Court. He wanted now to mollify his wife. As ER knew, above all, he wanted to keep his options open. There were circles within circles. No decision was final.

7: Private Times
and Reports from Germany

$\mathcal{I}$n Washington, as ER and Hick prepared to leave for their holiday together, the First Lady made a momentous decision. She would transform her new column in the *Woman's Home Companion* into a correspondence with the American people. FDR had always told her that if she could promote popular support for a policy, he would pursue it.

Perhaps influenced by Lape's correspondence campaign on behalf of Russian recognition, perhaps influenced by Hick, who never underestimated the power of public opinion, and undoubtedly staggered by the failure at London, which elicited no particular public response, on Monday, 3 July, ER told her readers: "I want you to write to me."

ER hoped her column would become "a clearing house for millions." She urged everyone to write freely and without hesitation, "even if your views clash with what you believe to be my views." ER wanted to create a new climate of activity, controversy, and communication between the presidency and the public, and encouraged her readers to believe they had a friend in the White House, one who "is really a servant of the people."

ER's two-year contract with the *Woman's Home Companion* would pay her $1,000 a month, plus $325 provided for secretarial help. She used that to hire her daughter Anna to assist Tommy. Together, they kept up with the mail from her column—and kept it separate from her White House mail. A daunting task, since ER received more mail than any of her predecessors. After her invitation, within six months she received 301,000 letters; occasionally she received four hundred letters a day. She and her team answered every one, and referred most of them to the appropriate agency or individual concerned.

With ER's new column under way, she and Hick motored north from Washington early in the morning of 6 July. As promised, their vacation together was private, uninterrupted, and peaceful.

For Hick, the three months since FDR's inauguration had been agony. Her life as a reporter was completely disrupted by her friendship with the

First Lady. Daily, she had faced a cruel and unbearable decision: to report what she was told or overheard, or abandon the pretense that she was still one of America's best reporters. On one occasion she killed a story because ER asked her to, and suffered her first indignity as a valued AP star when her pay was slashed as a result of her discretion, and self-censorship.

Hick's work was an ongoing theme of their correspondence. She was tormented by a sense of pressure to change her life and abandon her career, which ER encouraged her to do. It would be easier for both of them, although the First Lady acknowledged Hick's anguish: "I do understand your joy and pride in your job, and I have a deep respect for it." But she added: "When you haven't the feeling of responsibility to the AP I know you have a happier time with me." There were, ER insisted, other even more rewarding alternatives: "I hope that whatever your decision, it may be the right one for you. I want you to be happy in your work, but I want you to be free from this worry over finances. . . ."

ER failed to appreciate that Hick's status as a national political reporter, one of the AP's highest-paid newshawks, was the very core of her identity. She suggested instead a series of articles for *McCall's*, and she introduced Hick to her literary agent Carl Brandt to discuss book and magazine possibilities. To Hick, these ideas seemed vague, remote, unexciting.

Finally, ER arranged an interview with Harry Hopkins, who offered Hick an interesting job as chief field investigator for the Federal Emergency Relief Administration. She would use her reporter's skills to explore real truths about life in New Deal America. Hick was grateful, and ER was relieved. She was sure Hick would make the best field reporter Hopkins could get, but noted incongruously: "It is so nice to do anything for you, &, Lord knows, you won't be spoiled by a little ease of life now."

ER evidently had no idea what it meant to Hick to lose her readers, and her byline. Moreover, her job at FERA involved endless travel, and long, hard hours.

To FDR, ER wrote: "Hick wanted me to tell you how much she appreciated your being so nice about her taking this job for Hopkins. I think she'll do it very well & she felt she must get out of the AP with all the Elliott & Anna troubles coming."

The turmoil and self-doubt Hick suffered as she abandoned her life's career is indicated by ER's note: "Some day you won't need me to tell you that you can write, and then I'll pat myself on the back."

In the weeks before their trip, ER repeatedly reassured Hick: Her new work, and their good times together, would soon replace all current anxieties.

ER had carefully planned an uninterrupted and secluded holiday. There would be no press, no fanfare, no intrusions. The Secret Service was aghast. ER planned to drive alone with Hick—unchauffeured, unprotected. Kidnappings were much in the news, though to Hick and ER "the idea of anybody trying to kidnap two women, one nearly six feet tall and the other weighing close to two hundred pounds, seemed funny."

"Where would they hide us?" ER asked. "They certainly couldn't cram us into the trunk of a car!"

FDR supported their effort at anonymity and privacy, and they had a joyous holiday. It was for each of them a time of self-discovery, and generosity. Neither had grown accustomed to being pampered. They each always tended to put others first. Now, spontaneous and carefree, they had no friends to meet, no obligations of any kind. They drove until dusk, and casually looked about for shelter.

Their first night was spent in a little house in the woods near the Adirondacks—drawn in by a little sign: A recently married young couple had decided to take in tourists. But the house was not quite finished, and there was sufficient hot water for only one bath. "Well—you're the First Lady, so you get the first bath," Hick told ER. But ER would not hear of it: She thrust "her long, slender fingers in my direction. I was so ticklish that all she had to do to reduce me to a quivering mass of pulp was to point her fingers at me." Finally, ER agreed to take the first bath. But she evidently took it cold, because there was plenty of hot water for Hick.

ER brought along one of her favorite books, Stephen Vincent Benét's *John Brown's Body*, and near Lake Placid they paused to make a pilgrimage to John Brown's grave. ER loved to read poetry aloud, and she particularly loved the rhythmic power of Benét's stirring evocation of the Civil War, America's most enduring crisis.

From Lake Placid they drove beyond Burlington, Vermont, to Mount Mansfield, where there was a small hotel about four thousand feet up a treacherous road. ER had always wanted to make that drive, and even though they arrived in the village at the foot of the mountain in darkness, "to the horror of the town's one policeman," who argued vehemently against it, ER announced that she would continue on. Hick was impressed:

> It was a narrow road, with steep grades and so many hairpin turns that I lost count of them. Very few women had ever driven up that mountain, and no woman had ever attempted it in the dark. . . . Not only did she drive up Mount Mansfield that night, but she did it in [high] gear.

Evidently ER sped up the mountain, which filled Hick with awe: Anybody else "would have put the car into low gear" and driven cautiously around those curves. But she was "a superb driver." Also, one suspects, reckless and stubborn—especially when she was entirely in control and with somebody who appreciated, even enjoyed her physical prowess rather than criticized or faulted her various efforts, as her husband and sons so routinely did.

For two weeks ER and Hick "wandered happily about" in Vermont, New Hampshire, and Maine. There were no reporters, and nobody noticed them. After several days Hick wondered about the mysterious anonymity. ER explained, "My dear, they're all Republicans up here."

Their time in Quebec and the Gaspé Peninsula was splendid; the provincial French food was perfect, and every accommodation satisfied them. ER later reported that the "trip around the Gaspé is I think as beautiful as any which I have taken anywhere."

After Quebec, they spent a week in Campobello. It was a vivid contrast to her various disappointments at the time of the London Economic Conference, and her letters to her husband while there with Hick were pleasant and jolly. The weather was good, and everyone, including SDR, was cordial.

ER wrote FDR from Campo that she decided to stay home alone "to sit on the balcony & watch the sunset over the water & listen to the waves a few feet away on the stones & catch up on mail. It has been a wonderful trip & Hick is grand to travel with. Nothing bothers her. She isn't afraid. She doesn't get tired & she's always interested! We've had plenty of interesting experiences!" ER reminded her husband "to swim every day, you need some exercise. I hope all goes well with you/ Love to Missy/ Love ER."

Hick accompanied ER to the Chautauqua Women's Club in New York, where her nationally broadcast speech created a profound stir. Prominent leaders of the International Congress of Women who had met in Chicago traveled to Chautauqua to meet ER, and she was inspired by the presence of international leaders including Dame Rachel Crowdy and Mme. Kraemer Bach.

The International Congress of Women was preoccupied with the cruel news out of Germany, led by Carrie Chapman Catt and her great suffragist friend Rosa Manus, among the first activist women to leave Germany. Manus created a center for Jewish refugees in Amsterdam, kept Catt fully informed, and visited regularly. In Chicago Catt launched the Protest Committee of Non-Jewish Women Against the Persecution of Jews in Germany.

In April Catt had attended a meeting called by several pacifist groups to hear the Foreign Policy Association's president James McDonald discuss his fact-finding trip to Germany. The next day, 25 April 1933, Catt wrote to Manus: "McDonald described the Hitlerite movement against the Jews 'as a revolution unlike any other revolution that has ever taken place." Catt was so troubled, her emotions "so stirred," that she could "not sleep last night." If the "world were not so poor, there might be a war immediately."

Catt worried that Austria would also "turn against the Jews," as would "other states of Europe, because that has been the case before." She believed that "Germans are a queer people for when they voted for the Hitlerites they must, in some degree, sympathise with their curious philosophy."

In Chicago, Catt's committee organized a petition drive to express "our horror over the mistake the German people have permitted to be made." From Chicago, the European delegates brought their protest petition to Chautauqua, which ER endorsed.

On 25 July 1933, before an audience of over seven thousand people, ER spoke dramatically about the need for a "new social order" and declared that women inspired all changes in human history. "If you go back a little bit and think of the old cave-dwelling days, I think you will agree with me that the first step probably to a little more comfort and a little better food came because the woman was not quite satisfied with the original cave. . . ." From epoch to epoch, ER assured her audience, women were in the vanguard of change.

In the shadow of London, and with women from the international congress talking about the triumph of the twisted cross, ER called for a spiritual revival, a return to real responsibility: "We must either cooperate together and rise as a whole or go down. . . . I feel that we should all enlist in the army of peace which is now trying to solve some of the biggest questions this country or any country has ever faced."

She hoped especially that women would "be the inspiration" to "set new values and give to us a new social justice, a wider mental and spiritual outlook, so that we can look back on this time and say that as women we helped to bring about a real advance in civilization."

ER was triumphant at Chautauqua, and Anna (Mrs. Percy) Pennybacker, whom ER regarded as one of her mentors, was ecstatic.* She told ER that her "masterly address" and "graciousness to each and every one in that never-to-be-forgotten reception" thrilled thousands of women from all over the world.

After Chautauqua, Hick began her new job. As she traveled for FERA, around the borders and into the heartland of Depression America, Hick reported directly to ER, as well as to her boss Harry Hopkins. Their new partnership helped expand and embolden New Deal activity.

---

*Known as the "Texas Cyclone," Pennybacker had been a friend of ER's since 1924. Leader of the General Federation of Women's Clubs, director of the Chautauqua Club since 1916, a devoted peace activist who worked closely with Carrie Chapman Catt and ER on World Court efforts, she was also a prominent Texas Democrat.

Hick's first trip went directly into one of the worst centers of poverty and deprivation—the depleted mining areas in Appalachia, particularly Pennsylvania and West Virginia. ER read parts of her vivid reports to FDR, who "was much interested." Hick's ability to bring the details of America's suffering directly into the White House also had an impact on ER's most personal crusade: the campaign for decent and affordable housing for all Americans.

At home, ER resumed her relentless schedule: She wrote articles, drafted speeches, answered letters, prepared for exciting autumn events to bolster her vision of a New Deal for women. Her work, she wrote, kept her occupied, which was "a good thing." Moreover it "keeps me away from Mama, which is also a good thing!" Best of all, ER wrote with enthusiasm, she bought Hick the car she needed for her travels—a used blue Chevrolet convertible. Hick loved her new car, and called it Bluette.

During the summer of 1933, ER took a series of short trips with almost everyone in her intimate circle. It was as if she intended to touch base with each part of her life as her tasks as First Lady increasingly absorbed her.

With Nancy Cook, Tommy, Bess Furman, and several other newspaperwomen, ER took a night train to Abingdon, Virginia, her father's last healing refuge. She had gone to that corner of southwestern Virginia to meet the people who had known her father and about whom she had been told many stories as a child. At the White Top Mountain Music Festival there was much interest in her trip because her father had lived in Abingdon "for two years when the Douglas Land Company owned most of White Top Mountain. They were trying to develop some mines and do some forestry work."

According to local legend, Indians held White Top sacred. "Too perfect to be lived upon, it was dedicated to the Great Spirit," until it was appropriated by settlers and speculators. ER's father represented the speculators, and the Douglas Land Company was owned entirely by her family. Largely because there was no coal in the mountain, it was spared and unspoiled.

At White Top, ER enjoyed the entertainment: Six-year-old Muriel Dockery played the mandolin; octogenarian S. F. Russell played the dulcimer. "One old man brought me his fiddle and told me it had been in his family two hundred years . . . originally brought over from Europe."

In that "most beautiful mountain setting," ER heard the tunes the community "kept alive in their mountain cabins." From a banjo recital of "Cluck Old Hen" to the medley of songs that began with "the Farmer's Curst Wife . . . ," ER was serenaded with a range of ballads and family hymns.

She enjoyed the square dances most of all. They "looked to me far more fun than much of the modern dancing of today." In fact, she decided to "take some lessons" and from then on promoted square dancing.

After a "delicious luncheon," ER and her party left reluctantly at four-thirty to catch the night train to Washington. It was for ER a thrilling twenty-four hours, packed with emotion and memory.

ER told the story of her childhood to her traveling companions during the train ride home. "Outside, at stations, people would be cheering, and she'd wave at them with one hand while she gestured to point up her story with the other."

ER then made her annual pilgrimage to Newport, for a weekend with her godmother, Cousin Susie Parrish:

> Newport depresses me, it is so smug. This is like another world. . . . At Hyde Park and in Washington I feel much closer to the grim realities of life, and all the rest of my life I feel a part of the life of the most insignificant citizen, but here I feel far away, like in a dream. —And they don't know it is a dream and that soon it will be over.

ER spent the second half of September at Chazy Lake with Earl Miller and his wife, Ruth, Nancy Cook, and a new friend who became important to ER that summer, Mayris Chaney. Blond and effervescent, she was called Tiny by ER, who always enjoyed her vital, warmhearted company.

In August, Earl Miller had brought "two little dancers" he met on vacation in Bermuda to Val-Kill, Mayris Chaney and her partner Eddie Fox. In April, on Earl's recommendation, they had performed at the White House after the state dinner for sixty in honor of Ramsay MacDonald. They "did some really charming dances" and were followed by "a young Indian girl, Princess Te Ata," who gave "interpretative recitations" which presented "some of the customs and thoughts of the Red Indians who are so rapidly being wiped out in this country." In June, ER invited Chaney and Fox to perform for the veterans' garden party on the White House lawn, which was "a very appreciative and enthusiastic audience."

That September, fun-loving Tiny Chaney joined ER's intimate circle. On 10 September ER wrote Hick: "This morning I rode with Earl at 7:30. From 11 to 12:30 I had a shooting lesson. I'm being taught like a prison guard. It is interesting, though, because there is so much more than I thought to learn. I did improve." Everybody enjoyed their carefree time at Chazy Lake, except Nancy Cook. While ER and her friends hiked, swam, rode, and played diverting games, Nancy Cook, who looked robust and athletic but was actually a heavy smoker and mostly sedentary, suffered: "I don't think Nan has ever been through such a test of friendship. She doesn't like to do any of the things we do. She's away from home, which she hates, and has to cook, which she used to like, but doesn't any more."

Earl was also under par. Often dispirited, and unhappily married, he had fallen in love with Tiny, who considered him a pal and rejected his affections.

ER evidently had no idea about Earl's state of mind and thought at the time that Tiny and Eddie were married. In any case she thoroughly enjoyed her own stay at the camp, and relaxed even as she learned to become "an expert dish washer and housemaid too." "The weather is fine, and I love it here."

During the summer of 1933, ER also took two trips that profoundly influenced the future course of her public life.

On 7 August she and Elinor Morgenthau drove to the little town of Saugatuck near Westport, Connecticut, to visit Lillian Wald, who was recovering slowly from cancer surgery at her country home, House-on-the-Pond. Wald had arranged for ER to be with Jane Addams and Dr. Alice Hamilton, who had just returned from a harrowing time in the new Germany. They talked all that afternoon and evening. After dinner, they went to see *Lady Godiva* at the Westport Country Playhouse, and they spent the next morning and afternoon in urgent, intense, far-ranging conversation.

With the pioneering veterans of social reform and the international women's peace movement, ER sat on a lawn chair in the garden above Lillian Wald's pond listening to the horror stories Alice Hamilton brought back from Germany. For three months she had witnessed the rise of Nazism with Clara Landsberg, who had directed evening classes at Hull House, taught German at the University School for Girls, and was the daughter of a rabbi. It was, Hamilton noted, "a rather dreadful experience" for Clara but she was "endlessly plucky."

Every woman they knew, everybody they cared about, was already in exile or in danger. Their personal friends, leaders of the Women's International League for Peace and Freedom, which Jane Addams and Lillian Wald had done so much to create, were in despair.

Peace leaders Anita Augspurg, Germany's first woman judge, and Lida Gustava Heymann were in Geneva, as was WILPF director Gertrude Baer. Life partners, Augspurg and Heymann had no plans "to return to Germany and seem to have grown much interested in astrology." Gertrude Baer was "restless" and insisted "she must go back but it would be useless. She would simply be sent to a concentration camp. . . ."

The "women of the old suffrage and reform groups" told Hamilton "they would never consent to turn Nazi." Every progressive women's organization refused to expel their Jewish members, and they were all dissolved, including the General German Women's Union, General Federation of Women's Clubs, International Association of University Women, Women Physicians, and the Union of Women Teachers of Germany. Hamilton considered this "really a proud record." But there was nothing to celebrate. Events had moved with shocking speed, and all women's work, all independent social work, was crushed. Within weeks the German women's movement "lost everything" it had achieved, and women "were set back, perhaps as much as 100 years."

All German women's groups were replaced by one organization for Nazi women, Deutsches Frauenwerk—German Women's Work—which had one definition: "To be a woman means to be a mother." Nazis declared war on "liberalistic-Marxistic democracy" and rejected women's emancipation as "contrary to woman's true nature," mired by "Jewish doctrines of sex equality and sex freedom, which render woman rootless."

Under Nazism, the state was everything, "and the state needs children, therefore the refusal to bear children is treason to the state." Family planning and birth control were condemned as Marxist, and un-German.

Unmarried women were redefined as "superfluous women." There was in Germany "a problem" of 1,900,000 single women. Eventually single infertile women were put into Hitler's category of "lives not worth living," "useless eaters." That category included Jews, Gypsies, homosexuals, political undesirables, the mentally impaired and physically imperfect.

ER, eager to have Hamilton present her dreadful testimony to FDR, invited her to Hyde Park. She also invited Carrie Chapman Catt, who spent the summer organizing the Committee of Christian Women to Protest Against German Cruelty and Injustice to Jews and corresponding on behalf of the petition she had introduced in Chicago.

Most women Catt appealed to responded with enthusiasm, including ER, Hamilton, and Jane Addams. She quickly gathered ten thousand signatures. Charlotte Perkins Gilman wrote: "Of course I am glad to add my name. . . . How could anyone refuse?"

Several notable leaders did, however, refuse. The chair of the Women's Foreign Missionary Society of the Methodist Episcopal Church, Evelyn Riley Nicholson, doubted the alleged atrocities, which were denied by her many German friends. Moreover, they seemed to her trivial when "compared with the military program which our government seems now to be quietly, but surely entering upon. What can we do to arouse the people in this country on that issue?"

Catt said that the campaign of denial was part of Hitler's astounding propaganda. She had received letters that cast doubt on the alleged atrocities, and they were all the same:

> As a matter of fact, there has never been anything in the modern world to compare with the scheme of the Hitlerites toward the Jews. It is their intention to push them back into the Ghetto, to rob them of their property and money, to deny them education in schools and universities, and starve them out by not permitting them a means of livelihood. We are well in-

formed about the situation there and I beg to assure you that it is worse than anything that has been told.

But Catt too was "shocked" by FDR's decision to build new battleships, and agreed that an effort to arouse public opinion against rearmament "should go forward." Catt thought that the naval buildup had snuck through in the relief bill because it provided "men employment and it gives the steel trust and many other enterprises a new business project with which to proceed . . . to put thousands on their feet."

Actually, on 16 June 1933, just as the London Economic Conference opened, FDR issued an executive order to allot $238 million of the NRA's funds for naval rearmament, including four new cruisers, two aircraft carriers, sixteen destroyers, four submarines, and several auxiliary vessels. According to William Neumann, FDR's decision kept the U.S. within its treaty limits but agitated a renewed arms race: "The American building program was the largest single construction undertaken by any nation since the end of World War I." Japanese militarists "used the American move as propaganda" to increase their own military budgets, which had been declining steadily since 1929, since the new ships "would upset the uneasy balance of power in the Pacific."

Perhaps those ships contributed to Catt's curious decision that she had nothing to discuss with FDR at Hyde Park, despite ER's urging. Her refusal to visit disturbed ER, who believed that FDR was eager for all information and was frequently moved to action by the last person he spoke with.

Worried because Hamilton had not yet replied to her invitation, ER wrote to Lillian Wald, who explained that Hamilton was traveling and was delighted that the president "will have an opportunity to hear about Germany that she knows so well. . . . *The Times,* last Sunday, August sixth, on the first page of the magazine section, had one story and other magazines are to have contributions from her.

"Having seen her, you will understand that she is acceptable even though a woman, to the faculty of man dominated Harvard. She's a wise woman. My very dear love to you."

Alice Hamilton was associate professor of industrial medicine at Harvard Medical School, the only woman member of the League of Nations' Health Committee during the 1920s, and Herbert Hoover's Research Committee on Social Trends. Her ten-week trip was documented by letters to family and friends. Hamilton took copious notes and wrote a series of articles, several of which were already in print by the time she accepted ER's invitation.

On 25 August, the great pioneer of occupational safety and industrial health arrived in the afternoon with her young cousin Russell Williams, whom she called her nephew and regarded as her son. They went directly for tea at the big house at Hyde Park. After her private meeting with FDR, the president drove Hamilton to Val-Kill for a festive family dinner, and the next morning she breakfasted alone with ER.

In an effort to understand the fearsome transformation that had so disfigured the land of her happy student days, Alice Hamilton was detailed and ardent in conversation with the president and First Lady. One can sense the urgency of her words from her articles and letters, which were filled with bitter observations, thoughtful analyses, grave foreboding.

Hamilton understood Nazi triumphs in terms of Hitler's simple strategy: At first communists and Nazis competed for Germany's attention. But Hitler's supreme genius was to provide Germans with a single scapegoat "for all their ills."

Hitler especially appealed to the young, who grew up during "the war when the food blockade kept them half starved." A settlement worker told Hamilton there were many "families in which the children . . . [never] realized the connection between work and food. They had never had work, and food had come scantily and grudgingly from some governmental agency."

> To these idle, hopeless youths two stirring calls to action came—one from the Communists, the other from Hitler; and to both German youth responded. But Hitler's propaganda was cleverer than the Communists', because his program is narrower, more concrete. . . . The Communist is taught to hate a class. . . . The Hitlerite is taught to hate each individual Jew. Many young Communists were brought under the banner of Hitler by appeals to national pride and race antagonism, but also by the ideal of a united Germany without class hatred.

> Hitler made each insignificant, poverty-stricken, jobless youth of the slums feel himself one of the great of the earth . . . a Nordic, far superior to the successful Jew. . . . Hitler told the young men that the fate of Germany was in their hands, that if they joined his army they would battle with the Communists for the streets, they would see Jewish blood flow in streams, they would . . . deliver Germany from the Versailles Treaty and then sweep triumphantly over the borders to reconquer Germany's lost land. He put them into uniforms, he taught them to march and sing together. . . .

> They really believe that Hitler will bring about a genuine socialism without class warfare. . . .

As a physician, Hamilton was particularly appalled by the movement against doctors "accused of being individualistic and treating their patients as individuals." "True German doctors" were now expected "to work only as part of the state," and "must concern themselves with the problem of race purity.

They must help decide which babies are to be killed at birth and which permitted to live, and which people are to be sterilized."

All spring, the most fantastic outrages occurred in formerly liberal Berlin. For Hamilton, the student assault against Magnus Hirschfield's Institute of the Science of Sex was stunning. The father of sexology, a Jewish physician, a homosexual, and a liberal activist, Hirschfield saw thirty years of research destroyed: "A procession of students in white shirts (for purity) drove to the institute in trucks . . . and at a blare of trumpets they entered the library of the institute, seized books and pamphlets, threw them into the trucks," and consigned all the papers and books to "purifying flames."

Students were "passionately behind the new movement . . . against all that the German universities had stood for. The burning of the books was their work and they were proud of it. . . ."

Hamilton did not understand why people were surprised by Hitler's methods and aims: Everything that happened in Germany since 30 January was clearly forecast in his 1923 book, *Mein Kampf:* "There is no mystery about him," and he was precise about "what he meant to do, all of it, from the prohibition of Cubism in art to the swallowing up of Austria, from the driving of Jews out of the singing societies to the abolition of the trades-unions. . . ."

Hamilton was particularly eager for people to understand Hitler's theory of propaganda, which was carefully explained, and she felt every leader of public opinion should take it seriously. Propaganda was to be aimed at "the most limited intelligence." The more people to be reached, the "lower it must go." It must be simple, direct, uncluttered. "It is a mistake to give one's followers too many adversaries to fight. That bewilders them and arouses doubt. One adversary only must be offered to their hate, and the same again and again." Hatred of the Jew is the glue that keeps it all together. It is the "subject he cannot keep away from. There are pages and pages that drip with hatred of the Jew in language too vile to reproduce."

Also to be destroyed are the "mischlinges," the mixed-bloods, responsible for "the loss of race purity, that has brought about the decline of all great nations." Not only Jews but Slavic and Alpine races are inferior, although on diplomatic grounds Magyars and Finns were deemed Aryans.

Hitler's foreign policy was written far into the future: The rule of the world now belongs to Aryan races. Germany needs land which is held by inferior peoples—land to the east: Poland, Ukraine, central and southern Russia. Some have advised an alliance with Russia, but that is impossible because the Jews are there—and the Jew is "only a ferment of decomposition." "Germany cannot ally with Jewry, which through Bolshevism seeks to rule the world."

Hamilton forecast Hitler's effort to ally with England, which would have happened earlier "had it not been for Germany's mistaken policy of trade rivalry and colonization."

Above all, Hamilton concluded, the world must see that "Hitler is a soldier. . . . Force is all he respects." "He loves rough, red-blooded words— 'relentless,' 'steely,' 'iron-hearted,' 'brutal'; his favorite phrase is 'ruthless brutality.' " He wants Germany turned entirely away from "modern life" and "achievements of the human mind, back to the days when physical force ruled the world."

During her last days in Germany, it began to feel "unreal, nightmarish." Hamilton wrote Jane Addams en route home:

> Do you remember [vertebrate paleontologist] Tilly Edinger, a spirited young thing we met [in Frankfurt] in 1919. Her mother [Anna] was the one who founded the "Air Baths" in the parks, where we saw those pitiful starved children. Tilly's father [Ludwig, a neurologist who had been Hamilton's professor] founded the Neurological Institute of the university. Tilly is a gifted young scientist who worked in the Neurological Institute. . . . When we saw her she had been formally expelled. . . . The night before a beloved old couple, her mother's uncle and his wife, had killed themselves. They had seen everything go, their grandchildren forced out of school, their sons deciding to go to Belgium . . . they themselves were told that they were not Germans but foreigners and a curse to the country and they decided death was better. He was a great benefactor to Frankfurt and founded the astronomical department, in recognition of which a little planet was named for him "Mauritius." . . .
>
> If only we could open our doors to these people, they are so fine, but of course we cannot.

Unlike Catt, who promoted James McDonald's work on behalf of refugees, Hamilton failed to promote changes in U.S. refugee policy. Although she knew that events continued to worsen with lightning speed, she did not believe that FDR could "make a formal protest any more than Germany could formally protest against the last Maryland lynching."

What was there then to do? Within five days of Hamilton's visit, FDR sent his first letter to Ramsay MacDonald since the London Economic Conference: "I am concerned by events in Germany." FDR feared the growing militarism throughout Europe and considered it "infinitely more dangerous than any number of squabbles over gold or stabilization or tariffs." Perhaps when the Geneva disarmament meetings resumed in September, some multilateral agreements might be achieved after all.

MacDonald replied vaguely, since he was in "a complete state of depression" and reported to be "inconsolable" after the crash of the London Conference. In any case, during the autumnal meetings Germany walked out of the Geneva Disarmament Conference, and quit the League of Nations on 14 October 1933.

ER remained in close touch with Alice Hamilton and Carrie Chapman Catt, and she spoke at events they arranged. Catt intensified her efforts that autumn: She traveled the country speaking to university and civic groups, and formed a committee to persuade FDR to ease immigration restrictions for Germany's desperate refugees.

Actually, America's immigration restrictions emboldened Hitler, and he said so publicly. In April 1933, he declared: "Through its immigration law America has inhibited the unwelcome influx of such races as it has been unable to tolerate." With no international expression of dismay or even concern, Hitler's policies hardened: On 15 July 1933, *The New York Times* quoted Hitler's *Volkischer Beobachter:*

> We merely wish to state that the United States possesses rigorous immigration laws while Germany has absolutely none thus far. We further point to American relations with Negroes—social and political. And finally, certain American universities have long since excluded Jews.

On 10 September 1933, Catt's efforts were supplemented by the American Civil Liberties Union (ACLU) committee of thirty-six members—including Jane Addams, Lillian Wald, Roger Baldwin, Reinhold Niebuhr, and FDR's own friend Felix Frankfurter—who appealed to the president to change immigration laws "to admit religious and political refugees, particularly from Germany, in harmony with the American tradition of asylum for refugees escaping from foreign tyrannies."

When, in October 1933, the League of Nations created an International Commission on Refugees, Catt, Henry Morgenthau, Sr., and others asked FDR to nominate James G. McDonald to chair the high commission. He agreed, the League of Nations ratified his appointment, and McDonald worked for two years to get the United States to liberalize its refugee policy and join an international agreement on refugees.

ER supported McDonald's efforts and joined Catt's activities to keep the refugee issue prominent. She continued to bring information and individuals like Hamilton directly to her husband, intensified her work for women's rights and international peace, and began to speak to Jewish groups as never before.

Above all, as racial and religious bigotry raged through Europe, ER turned her attention to the racial and religious bigotry that permeated U.S. relations, and to issues of poverty and despair—which, she said, fueled Europe's fascist fervor.

On 18 August 1933, ER sent her first letter of appeal for racial justice: She had been told by an African-American registrant that Camp Tera, the first CCC camp for women, "did not want colored girls."

W. H. Matthews, director of New York's Emergency Work Bureau, which presided over the camp, replied that "in the first small group . . . there were no colored girls." But now there were ten, and there was a no-discrimination policy. The objection reminded Matthews of other protests: Democrats say that we favor Republicans, Socialists that we favor both Republicans and Democrats, and Communists that we favor "everybody save them." In fact, "we go along doing the best we can for everybody, which just now is a poor best," because the budget was inadequate.

ER replied: "I know you are doing your best and I know how difficult it must be. I only sent you word about the colored girls because I thought it unfair. . . ."

In response to bigotry abroad, ER pursued fairness and justice in America. Because she failed for so long to mention specifically the crises Jews faced in Germany, it seemed as if she were on that subject actually muzzled: a prisoner of the administration's policy of absolute noninvolvement in the internal affairs of other nations. The situation in Germany, however, radicalized her views about what needed to be done in America.

After ER wrote her first letter concerning race, she drove to West Virginia, where she met Hick and Clarence Pickett, head of the American Friends Service Committee, for a tour of one of America's most impoverished areas. That day marked the beginning of ER's remarkable partnership with Pickett and the AFSC, which embraced both national and international concerns and spurred ER on to new levels of activism. After August 1933, ER dedicated herself to providing a life of dignity and decency for all Americans, first in an extraordinary experiment in sustainable community, or "subsistence homesteading," in a small West Virginia settlement called Arthurdale.

8: Creating a New Community

O n the morning of 18 August, ER drove alone to Morgantown, West Virginia, in response to Hick's plea that she see conditions in this area for herself. During Hick's first week at work she had gone to Philadelphia to meet Clarence Pickett, whose American Friends Service Committee had initiated several projects in the area. He told her that if she wanted to see the most serious ravages of the Depression she should visit the southwestern corner of Pennsylvania and go into West Virginia.

In Uniontown, Pennsylvania, where steel mills had been shut down for years, she found workers living in abandoned coke ovens. Stores were empty; nobody had any money. But not until Hick reached the Scott's Run area in Monongalia County, West Virginia, did she fully understand how horrible poverty could be.

Scott's "run" referred to the malodorous green, red, and yellow stream of mine and human waste that ran down the hillsides and through the valley into the Monongahela River. Hick was not the only visitor stunned by "the damndest cesspool of human misery . . . in America." In 1931 and 1932 when AFSC staffers began work throughout the thirty-eight coalfield counties in response to Hoover's relief efforts and an appeal by Grace Abbott of the Children's Bureau, they found 95 percent of the children in Monongalia County suffered from various curable but intense blights: malnutrition, defective vision, rickets, rotten teeth. The Friends introduced soap, toothbrushes, food programs, visiting nurses, social workers, garden and craft projects. But it was just a beginning, as Hick's report revealed:

> Morgantown was the worst place I'd ever seen. In a gutter, along the main street through the town, there was stagnant, filthy water, which the inhabitants used for drinking, cooking, washing, and everything else imaginable. On either side of the street were ramshackle houses, black with coal dust, which most Americans would not have considered fit for pigs. And in

those houses every night children went to sleep hungry, on piles of bug-infested rags, spread out on the floor.

The needs were monumental. There was no clinic, no free hospital bed, anywhere in West Virginia. In Logan, there was a diphtheria epidemic. A little girl needed to have a tube inserted into her throat to enable her to breathe. It was done in a garage.

Part of the problem was that most of the miners had been unionists who were blacklisted after a brutal series of strikes and lockouts between 1924 and 1931. Mining families were destitute, stranded; some companies were bankrupt; there was almost no work. Homeless and hungry, fifteen thousand people in the coal mining sections lived in tents and abandoned company hovels. By 1933 "the tents were so old and tattered that they provided practically no shelter at all." Some of the unionists were communists, and the mine owners had vowed they would never work again. Many had been idle for eight years.

In addition to strikes and antiunion violence, the coal industry had over-expanded, and prices had crashed; many of the mines were depleted, and technological changes, notably the diesel engine for locomotives, limited the need for the area's famous steam coal. The AFSC estimated that 200,000 miners were permanently out of work, while 300,000 "were employed only sporadically."

Hick's reports inspired ER: "What a power you have to feel and to describe. . . . How small one's worries seem in comparison to what so many human beings have been through. . . ."

When ER arrived in Morgantown, Clarence Pickett and Hick were there to meet her. Together they toured the area, visited families in the process of starving to death. Nobody knew who she was. Some, suspicious and fearful, turned away. But most were eager to talk, and many told her of their lives honestly, directly.

ER wrote a searing political column for the *Women's Democratic News* upon her return from West Virginia. She had personally heard of investigations in these "mining communities as far back as 1915." But "the reports were simply pigeonholed," and conditions continually worsened. What ER had now witnessed convinced her that the time for reports and timid talk were over: Workers in America had a right to "receive in return for their labor, at least a minimum of security and happiness in life. They must have enough to eat, warmth, adequate clothing, decent shelter and an opportunity for education." She continued:

> I do not believe if most of us knew the conditions under which some of our brothers and sisters were living that we would rest complacently un-

til we had registered the fact that in this country the day is past when we will continue to live under any governmental system which will produce conditions such as exist in certain industries and in certain parts of our country.

ER worried that if peaceful change were not agreed to, "because we recognize the justice of what should be done," the U.S. would suffer the revolutionary upheavals experienced by other nations, since "it is misery that drives people to the point where they are willing to overthrow anything simply because life as it is is not worth living any longer."

In one house, she witnessed six hungry children who had nothing to eat but scraps, "the kind that you or I might give to a dog." Two of the children "gathered enough courage to stand by the door," where their little brother held a white rabbit tightly to his chest.

> It was evident it was a most cherished pet. The little girl was thin and scrawny, and had a gleam in her eyes as she looked at her brother. Turning to me she said: "He thinks we are not going to eat it, but we are," and at that the small boy fled down the road clutching the rabbit closer than ever.

ER told that story frequently to raise money from her affluent friends and various White House guests for the community she worked to build for the desperate families of West Virginia. It even eased a $100 check out of William C. Bullitt, who said he hoped it might save that little rabbit.

To the First Lady, orphaned and uprooted from a home of her own, who for so long wanted a home that belonged to neither her mother-in-law nor the state, affordable housing became a lifelong crusade. During the first White House years she devoted some hours in almost every day to the creation of a model community to be located fifteen miles from Morgantown, just outside a little town called Reedsville.

ER was shameless about asking for donations, in time and money. And she wrote about it at every opportunity:

> I came to know very well a stream near Morgantown called Scott's Run, or Bloody Run because of the violent strikes . . . in the mines there. . . .
>
> I took many, many people to see this village of Jere, West Virginia, along Scott's Run, for it was a good example of what absentee ownership could do as far as human beings were concerned. . . . Some of the children were sub-normal, and I often wondered how any of them grew up. . . .
>
> It was quite usual to find all the older children sleeping on bags or rags on the floor and the mother and father and youngest children in the only bed, which might or might not have a mattress. Sometimes there was just a

blanket over the springs. The WPA mattress project helped considerably, as did the building of sanitary privies.

ER was especially impressed by Alice Davis, whose work with the AFSC the First Lady considered heroic. Davis had authorized the new privies, and was almost jailed because she had them built on private mine-owned property: She "had not known it was against the law to improve privately owned property." ER was outraged on Alice Davis's behalf:

> Breaking rules or even laws saved a good many lives. Every spring and every autumn . . . there had been an outbreak of typhoid fever; only after several people died would the company doctor appear to inoculate the rest of the population. No efforts were made to eliminate the cause of the disease. The Run in Jere, like all the others that ran down the gullies to the larger, main stream, was the only sewage disposal system that existed. At the bottom of the hill there was a spigot from which everyone drew water. The children played in the stream and the filth was indescribable.

ER intended to change all that, and worked closely with Alice Davis and her partner Nadia Danilevsky—the women who gave Hick her first tour of the area. College-educated, they were trained nurses and social workers who met during the eight years Alice Davis represented a Friends' project in Russia after the Revolution.

ER imagined a rural experiment in living that would be economically self-contained and agriculturally self-sufficient. She believed it was possible, as an experimental aspect of the New Deal, to build a community that promised democracy, dignity, education, work, and culture. All that was needed was a modest governmental contribution and earnest work by the homesteaders—who would themselves create the community and be in control.

Each home would be on two to five acres, and each family would have a cow, a pig, some chickens, and seed to plant a nutritious and attractive garden. There were plans to establish a manufacturing plant that would provide good work and guarantee economic security. Local crafts and music would be celebrated. People would eventually buy their own homes, reconstitute their lives. ER was committed to this chance to prove that America's poorest people could, with modest support, create the American dream of community and cooperation.

FDR completely supported ER's vision for Arthurdale. Convinced that country living offered more dignity and comfort to poor people than crowded anonymous cities, they both had long believed in creating community projects that would encourage people to remain in the country.

ER's own furniture factory at Val-Kill was built in 1925 with the hope that work brought into the declining farming community near Poughkeepsie would reduce rural flight to the frequently false promise of urban employment.

Their views were in keeping with a "back to the land" movement popular during the 1920s. England and France, Austria and Germany were noted for such experiments. But America had been reluctant to try them—until ER devoted herself to Arthurdale. When she returned from her first visit to Morgantown, she described to her husband the mean conditions mining families endured. FDR declared: They should be out of those caves and tents by Christmas.

When ER first discussed Arthurdale at her press conference in November, she said homesteading was her husband's idea: "It's a plan he has talked about ever since I can remember." Now, with ER at the helm, "the grand experiment" was under way.

Housing and community development were only vaguely on the national agenda when ER began her crusade. A Subsistence Homestead Division was part of the National Recovery Act (Section 208, Title II), and M. L. Wilson was named program director. Like the Roosevelts, Milburn Lincoln Wilson promoted a "back to the land" vision of community self-sufficiency. Transportation, electrification, modernization would make contented rural living possible nationwide.

Initially administered by Harold Ickes's Department of the Interior, the Subsistence Homestead program created by the National Industrial Recovery Act was granted $25 million for new construction. At ER's suggestion, Clarence Pickett was appointed Wilson's assistant, with "special responsibility" for the mining communities. Over time, there were to be fifty-two projects, and Arthurdale was the first, the flagship.

Wilson worked directly with ER and Pickett and they generally bypassed Ickes. Impatient with Ickes's methods, with governmental red tape and endless conferences, ER enlisted Louis Howe's support for immediate action. Together, they proceeded quickly to purchase the historic Arthur property in Preston County, fifteen miles from Morgantown. Once owned by Colonel John Fairfax of Virginia, it had been partly surveyed by his friend George Washington.

Now told it would take weeks for the necessary surveys, Howe called for an Army plane and achieved a Coast and Geodetic Survey for the topographical map within two days. Richard Arthur, a "gentleman farmer" reduced by hard times and about to lose his property for taxes, originally asked $60,000 for his land and estate, including his twenty-two-room mansion. Howe agreed to pay $45,000 for a total of 1,028 acres. The day after ER's birthday, 12 October 1933, Ickes publicly announced the Arthurdale project.

From the beginning, ER cautioned Howe not to be too stingy when it came to the new houses. At the first White House meeting of the project, Howe insisted on small Cape Cod prefabs—usually sold as summer vacation homes—because they could be erected with dispatch. At one point, ER snapped, "Louis, don't be absurd." Those houses would be impossible in an Appalachian winter.

The week before Thanksgiving 1933, ER journeyed to Arthurdale with Howe, M. L. Wilson, Clarence Pickett, Nancy Cook, and Eric Gugler, a New York architect and close friend, who became the project's chief engineer. The houses had been ordered; the fields were cleared, plowed, and planted; the foundations for the first fifty were ready. ER dined at the mansion, where the homesteaders were temporarily camped, and found them happy to have worked six days a week, arduously and energetically, preparing their homesites.

When the houses finally arrived in December, the homesteaders worked even harder putting them up in harsh cold weather. But once ten were up, Gugler stopped the work. They were a "fiasco." They failed to fit the foundations, plumbing lines had to be ripped out and new pipes installed, furnace units had to be relocated, virtually everything had to be redone. They were unacceptably small (ten by forty feet), flimsy, uninsulated, designed exclusively for summer use.

Louis Howe had stubbornly stuck to his initial ideas, and they represented nothing ER had in mind. They also caused endless derision in the conservative press; and cost overruns.

ER insisted that each new home include indoor plumbing, modern conveniences. Harold Ickes, long associated with Jane Addams and not notably mean-spirited, was outraged. ER and her friends were spending money "like drunken sailors." While over 80 percent of rural America had no modern conveniences, why should the rural poor have indoor privies? If everything ER suggested occurred, how would one be able to tell the rich from the poor? Actually, ER maintained, in matters of such simple dignity and decency one should not be able to tell the rich from the poor.

ER was perplexed by the grudging attitude that prevailed within her husband's own administration. She blamed Ickes, and considered him a callous bureaucrat. Unknown to ER, her husband agreed with Ickes.

In March 1934, the secretary of the interior complained to FDR that "the cost of the thing is shocking to me," and was astounded by the president's defense: We "could justify the cost, which will run in excess of $10,000 per family, by the fact that it is a model." Ickes asked "what it was a model of, since obviously it wasn't a model of low-cost housing for people on the very lowest rung of the economic order. . . . It worries me more than anything else in my whole Department."

FDR replied: "My Missus, unlike most women, hasn't any sense about money at all." And neither did Howe, asserted the president.

Subsequently, when Ickes complained yet again and told FDR he considered Arthurdale acceptable as "a demonstration of what could be done . . . for people with considerable incomes," but not for "people in the lowest income classes," Ickes noted that the president agreed, and he confided to his journal:

> I am very fond of Mrs. Roosevelt. She has a fine social sense and is utterly unselfish, but as the President has said to me on one or two occasions, she wants to build these homesteads on a scale that we can't afford because the people for whom they are intended cannot afford such houses. The President's idea is to build an adequate house and not even put in plumbing fixtures, leaving that sort of thing to be done later by the homesteader as he can afford them. He remarked yesterday that he had not yet dared say this to [Mrs. Roosevelt,] who wanted to build houses with all modern improvements.

Evidently, Ickes never told the First Lady her husband agreed with him, and FDR never confronted his wife about their differences.

Ultimately, the houses were built according to her specifications—with every modern convenience and decent amenity. There were bathtubs in bathrooms, enamel sinks and flush toilets. Sunshine passed through glass windows in every room; there were glass-enclosed sunporches, and rain porches. There were root cellars, smokehouses, barns; orchards and grape vines; apple trees and peach trees; laurel and rhododendron planted around each home.

However modest the first homes built, to the people of Scott's Run they were luxurious. There was central steam heat with a radiator in every room—even the bathroom. There were pantries, cutting boards, birchwood cabinets. All the electric fixtures were copper made at the forge. Everything engendered a sense of pride: pine or oak parquet floors; wood paneling beautifully crafted; "deep big closets"; built-in bookcases. There were electrical appliances, and refrigerators—which had been initially "forgotten," until Howe noticed and said ER would be disappointed and hurt: She had personally shopped for and selected the refrigerators. There were cement foundations, and coal rooms for the coal-burning furnace; there was a concrete laundry tub in the cellar, in a room with a window.

By June 1934, the first fifty houses were ready. ER and Nancy Cook personally presided over the interior needs of each house. ER had Cook appointed to the staff of the Subsistence Homestead Division "as a specialist." Cook worked with the craftsmen who studied with Bud Godlove and made the area's famous Godlove chair of native hickory and walnut. Temporarily, she administered the furniture and woodworking projects manufactured by the Mountaineer Craftsmen's Cooperative Association.

Supported by the Russell Sage Foundation, the popular crafts were exhibited and sold nationally by AFSC representatives. The association also did metalwork in pewter, copper, and iron; weaving and knitting. Cooperative craftsmen trained the homesteaders, and together they made all cabinets and cupboards and every piece of furniture for Arthurdale.*

In addition to tables and chairs, houses were furnished with one double bed, four single beds, occasional double-decker beds, two chests of drawers, and cribs if requested. Women employed by the Civil Works Administration made curtains, sheets, and pillowcases. Each home was also "supplied with blankets, quilts, bedspreads, twelve towels, and rag rugs." Expected to cost $2,000, ultimately each house cost over $8,000.

For ER, Arthurdale represented a future of dignity for every family. This was how people in America had a right to live. She was annoyed by petty accounting, mean-spirited trimming. This was an experiment in human development and community building.

The homesteaders would "all remain on public relief until the factory is opened and the first crops are harvested; but when a family makes its first payment the title to the land will pass to the individual homesteader. In twenty or thirty years the individual will own it free and clear of debt."

Arthurdale became identified with ER the way Warm Springs, Georgia, was associated with FDR: She confronted all the problems of creating a model community on raw land with the same verve her husband had devoted to his healing center. She fought critics and detractors who hurled endless assaults upon her judgment and vision. Determined to create proper homes for an estimated 125 families, a new school system, a health network, a new way of life, she returned again and again to oversee the work, to supervise every detail.

For ER, Arthurdale represented a "program of long time rehabilitation." While occasionally "charity may be necessary, our aim should be to get people back to a point where they can look after themselves. I have never felt that people should be grateful for charity. They should rightfully be resentful and so should we, at the circumstances which make charity a necessity." She was pleased to work with the AFSC on resettlement projects, because they represented her commitment to build up "people's own initiative and security." She saw Arthurdale as part of an ongoing experiment in the creation of "a new kind of community."

---

*The Arthurdale branch of the Mountaineer Craftsmen's Cooperative, which employed women and men, was a thriving concern. By 1936, it sold $43,000 worth of furniture—although the community's detractors added hourly labor costs, and complained that crafts always resulted in vast "losses."

Communities of this type presuppose that the people living in them are going to be interested in the welfare of the whole community and that they are going to be successful in bringing about certain changes in human nature. . . . [which will make people] less selfish and more willing to share their security with those around them. . . .

From the beginning, in August 1933, when ER first witnessed the mixed population of Scott's Run she had expected that Arthurdale would reflect the mixed population of the region.

The miners had represented many ancestries. According to a 1920 census, 60 percent of the population were foreign-born, 93 percent of whom were "southern or eastern European," Austrian, Bohemian, Croatian, Hungarian, Italian, Lithuanian, Polish, Greek, Romanian, Russian, Serbian, Slovenian, and Ukrainian predominating. There were also Canadians, Irish, Scottish, and Welsh. "Native" whites and blacks were almost equally divided, representing 20 percent each.

ER had been the nominal chair of the committee to select Arthurdale's families, to serve with Quaker and University of West Virginia social workers who knew the area's people. But she did not meet with the committee, which set up an elaborate screening process.

It became clear as soon as the first fifty families were chosen that the experiment would be restricted to white Christian "native" Americans. ER was displeased, because she felt Arthurdale's function as a "laboratory" depended on a random and diverse population. She said it was unwise "to hand pick the tenants because again I feel that it must be an experiment in ordinary life and an ordinary community contains people of every type of ability and character." The goal, she insisted, was to investigate the means to "bring out the best that was in any community" and to achieve "the highest level to which the family with an ordinary income can aspire."

But the committee insisted upon "congenial" residents. Every applicant was carefully scrutinized. There was an eight-page questionnaire, and intense interviews. "Moral character," "intelligence, perseverence and foresight," basic skills, demonstrated ambition, farm experience were prerequisites for consideration. Interviewers were to check physique, education, neatness, posture, agility, literacy, church affiliation, fraternal orders, garden club membership, debts, attitudes, defects. Although communists were not referred to, they were presumably unwelcome. Interviewers were to ask searching questions:

What particular farm jobs do you best like to do?
What particular farm jobs do you most dislike?
What games do you like to play with others?

[How] do you like best to spend your idle hours?

How much education would you like your children to get?

Indicate proper planting distance for rows of: beets/corn/potatoes/ cabbage/tomatoes/snap beans

Do you observe any rules in planting determined by the phases of the moon?

Specific questions were asked about the care and feeding of poultry, cows, hogs, and horses.

Among the first fifty families chosen, "native West Virginians" of northern European heritage predominated.* There had been protest meetings in nearby Reedsville against including blacks and foreign-born applicants, and they were excluded.

ER did not approve, and requested that the next group of applicants be diverse. The residents resisted, and the Homesteaders Club announced that Arthurdale was to be a "haven for whites only." On 11 February 1934, the First Lady asked them to reconsider, and to vote on the issue—which they agreed to do.

On 16 February, Claude Hitchcock, secretary of the Homesteaders Club, reported to ER that "after due deliberation by a fully attended meeting of the Club, we are not inclined to recede from our former position in regard to colored homesteaders on this Project."

The homesteaders enumerated their reasons:

1. The community in which we are located is thoroughly opposed to Negroes as residents, and we feel that we should not risk the loss of the respect we have gained in the community by admitting Negroes.

2. The admission of Negroes would necessitate the establishment of separate schools and churches, as our State laws forbid both races to attend the same schools.

3. Without prejudice to the race, and with the feeling that all races should have equal opportunity, we believe that those who are clamoring for admission are not Negroes, but are of mixed blood and far inferior to the real Negroes who refuse to mix with the white race.

---

*The first fifty families were selected from a pool of over six hundred applicants. Two hundred black families also applied, as ER had encouraged them to. It is unclear if there were any Jews among the miners of Scott's Run, but there was an area called Jew Hill. According to a Monongalia County social worker's survey during the 1920s, Jew Hill was a "settlement of twelve houses occupied by sixteen families" where six outhouses were shared by all the residents. Without hygienic waste disposal, the same "economic devastation" and "social chaos" existed in Jew Hill as in nearby "North American Hill."

Regretting that our views do not fully coincide with your own in this matter, and yet, bound in conscience to take this stand and hoping that our wishes may be respected, we beg to remain, Yours respectfully. . . .

Dismayed, ER sent Clarence Pickett the correspondence, and he replied: "I have read the enclosed. . . . I am not quite sure that we have yet exhausted that subject." But it was over. ER believed in majority rule and democracy was throughout so much of America restricted to whites. She accepted the home-steaders' wishes, and recommended the creation of another homestead for black miners in Monongalia County.*

Arthurdale was just the beginning: A model project was planned in Monmouth County, New Jersey, "for two hundred families of Jewish needle workers from nearby crowded manufacturing cities. A factory is to be built for their use. . . ." Subsequently called Roosevelt, it would also have acreage for "co-operative agriculture to serve solely" the homesteaders. Subsistence farm-ing would thereby, ER concluded, solve many difficulties of people "through-out our country who are now suffering from unemployment or . . . the poor standards of living imposed on them by slums and congested areas."

In June 1934, ER, Anna Ickes, Bernard Baruch, M. L. Wilson, and West Vir-ginia Congressman Jennings Randolph officially opened Arthurdale. At a re-ception at the Arthur mansion, ER spoke to the homesteaders and a gathering of "several thousand" who had come to celebrate the new pioneers:

> I want you to succeed, not only for yourselves, but for what it will mean to people everywhere, North, South, East and West, who are starting similar projects. You are the first, and your success will hearten [them].

Bernard Baruch's generosity to Arthurdale was stimulated by his first visit, when he witnessed the spirit of the people. The open warmth and glad-ness, the pride with which homesteaders presented ER with a basket of their first onions and radishes, moved Baruch: "You should have seen [their] faces. It was really the most remarkable thing I ever saw. . . . You felt their sense of responsibility."

ER announced she would take them home: "My husband adores onions."

---

*Although plans for fifteen Negro homesteads were proposed, and a tract of 350 acres in Monongalia County was optioned, it was allowed to expire. Despite many dis-cussions, no homestead for needy black miners was built.

Aberdeen Gardens, outside Newport News, Virginia, was America's only signifi-cant black homestead. Opened in November 1936, the site had 158 homes on 440 acres. Modest and pleasant, they were brick Colonial Revival homes, with indoor plumbing, amenities, warmth, and dignity.

For several years, ER continued to press her friends to support Arthurdale. Her girlhood chum Dorothy Payne Whitney Straight Elmhirst had, with her former husband Willard Straight, founded *The New Republic.* Now she too was engaged in the creation of an experimental school and community in Dartington, England. After her visit to Arthurdale, she wrote ER: "It is magnificent, the way you are directing this big undertaking. . . . I am going back to England so proud of my country at last."

Dorothy Elmhirst agreed to pay for medical services at Arthurdale and contributed to the first public health care unit in nearby Logan County, West Virginia.

Bernard Baruch consistently supported Arthurdale and virtually underwrote the community's innovative educational programs, from the nursery school to adult education. He also enlisted his friends the Guggenheims to build dental clinics.

Baruch contributed an initial sum of $20,000 to build the school, helped pay teachers' salaries over the years, and in 1934 paid to construct and outfit the fully equipped school gymnasium. ER wrote Hick: "I feel that Mr. Baruch is doing a swell thing in his interest in the homesteads. He's going to help with all the business end and he's going to give me the running expenses of the [school] for this year and the necessary equipment besides."

With private contributions from ER and Baruch, the school became a center of active creativity for the entire population. It was continually filled by meetings, music, square dances, festivals, craft shows; there were weekly canning, baking, and covered-dish parties.

For at least three years ER spent most of her own earned income to secure Arthurdale's success. Throughout the White House years, she deposited her money directly with the AFSC for use in various national and international projects. For 1934 the AFSC accountant reported that $56,000 had been deposited in "the ER Transit Fund," $36,000 by ER and $20,000 by Baruch. Of this $38,335.35 was expended. Most of the money was spent for teachers' salaries, school supplies and equipment ($13,000), Nancy Cook's Handicraft Educational Project ($16,000), Child Relief Health Work in Logan County ($6,000), and college scholarships for girls from Kentucky and West Virginia mining camps.

In 1935, ER wrote Pickett: "Mr. Baruch has given me 'carte blanche' and says that anything which I want I am to do with the money which he has given us, and that he will stand by for another year." He had contributed another $24,000—used mostly for the school.

Each Christmas ER sent boxes of presents to Arthurdale, as did tobacco heir Doris Duke. One homesteader recalled that there were always big boxes "of toys and goodies for each family, with their name on it." Once she received a doll from ER, which she still had fifty years later. Another year "there was a pair of roller skates in each box. What fun that was for the kids. . . ."

Within a year, Louis Howe's "lousy" prefabs, rebuilt by Eric Gugler's team, were followed by more agreeable structures. In December 1934, a group of seventy-five houses were begun, and these were completed in 1935. Finally, a group of forty houses, begun during the summer of 1936, were finished in 1937. After Gugler left to build the White House Executive Office Building, the remaining two groups were designed by architect Stuart Wagner, some of timber, some of stone locally quarried. Some were half timber, half stone. Some were in English Tudor style, others two-story colonials. Most included stone fireplaces. No two Arthurdale homes were the same.

The homesteaders decided themselves to buy an additional 450-acre dairy and poultry farm, which was run by the community association as a co-operative venture until the war. They also ran a cooperative store.

The community was intended to be self-sufficient and Baruch lobbied for industrial support with the business community and within the administration. He met with Ickes and other Interior Department representatives to argue that the homesteaders should not be charged more than $3,000 for their homes, whatever the cost overruns.

ER agreed and had earlier announced to her press conference that the government would absorb the errors made. But she worried about jobs and wrote Oscar Chapman: "Can you tell me when the factory will be started?

"I get panicky every now and then about these people having work."

With Baruch's help, ER negotiated with Gerard Bayard Swope for General Electric to open a factory to make electric vacuum cleaners, which worked for a short time. But it was insufficient, and nothing was really settled for years. Throughout the long ordeal to get suitable work into Arthurdale, ER monitored every grudging detail.

She even had to protest some administrators' decision to charge the homesteaders rent for use of a room in their own community center. "They want to use it for adult education and feel that they probably will not be able to produce anything worth while under two years, therefore, it would not be possible to have any money for rent. They are anxious to find out if this could be remitted for a period of two years. . . ."

ER's correspondence concerning Arthurdale was a running record of governmental complexity. She wrote regularly to dozens of officials in charge of various aspects of the project. On Arthurdale, she ran a parallel administration. She was concerned with personnel matters, broad policy issues, and she too considered every penny.

Several days after ER's letter to Chapman, FDR told Ickes he intended to remove the "Subsistence Homesteads Division and rural housing" from his domain and transfer them to Harry Hopkins. Ickes was relieved. ER too was relieved, and grateful that a stumbling block had been removed.

ER never doubted the rightness of Arthurdale, and considered it a success from every human point of view. The day after the first families moved in, she walked across the "newly planted grass to a small white painted house." It was one of the four-room houses, and on the living-room walls, "brilliant colored posters" had been tacked up, "and a prize for drawing which was framed together with some black and white sketches. It was evident that here was someone who liked to draw and so I asked her if she had had any teaching, and she answered, 'Never a lesson, but I liked to draw all my life.' " Her three little girls—six, eight, and ten—stood by her, and when ER marveled that all had been "settled quickly" and rendered "spick and span," she replied: "But I had to, because next week I must have more time for the garden."

ER wrote that there were those who believed "that a woman who has lived in two rooms without any windows, may not really be able to appreciate the four-room house." There were also those who argued that miners would only use bathtubs to store coal. But in each home ER saw individuals of value, with much to contribute, and they all wanted the opportunity to be clean, to shower and bathe.

In every home she entered, people told her virtually the same story: "We woke up one morning in hell, and went to bed the next night in heaven." It was that sudden, that complete. And for ER, it had nothing to do with charity.

Although ER regarded Arthurdale as an alternative to a "people's revolution," or "at least a people's party patterned after some of the previous parties born of bad economic conditions," many considered the rehabilitation and resettlement of destitute mining families unacceptable radicalism.

For all ER's enthusiasm, FDR's support, and the homesteaders' commitment, Arthurdale was relentlessly attacked. From the beginning, every indoor faucet, every shrub and tree was scrutinized and ridiculed in the press and vilified by an astounding array of hooters who opposed New Deal planning and called it socialism, communism.

Conservatives deplored the very idea of national economic planning and condemned federally subsidized work brought into an area previously plagued by unionists. Every effort to bring in work was blocked. By 1934 the Red Scare, seemingly suspended during FDR's first hundred days, was again under way to derail or diminish every suggestion actually to improve conditions.

For some, the New Deal had now become a "communist plot," led by ER and epitomized by Arthurdale. Gary, Indiana, school superintendent William A. Wirt claimed that ER was part of the communist "brain trust" that sought to weaken America: She headed a conspiracy to destroy West Virginia's tax and rent base by removing two hundred families to the new "communistic project."

The First Lady was amused by his charges: "I hardly think it would be found that people on relief were paying much, if any, rent." Furthermore, "I do not understand how he considers it Communistic to give people a chance to earn their own livings and to buy their own houses. It is a fact that the Government will provide the initial capital, but I hope that many private enterprises will do it . . . throughout the country in the future."

Arthurdale's abiding value, she concluded, was to suggest "to industry . . . that by decentralizing and moving out of large cities it may make it possible for great numbers of people to have more in their lives. . . ."

A startling spectrum of politicians and industrialists opposed ER's crusade. The Post Office Department originally agreed to open a plant to manufacture mailboxes and post office furniture. Then Congress defunded it. The war against Arthurdale's solvency was led by Democrats who deplored government competition with private business. Louis Ludlow represented a district in Indianapolis where a "Keyless Lock" factory employed hundreds of people. He claimed a similar one subsidized by the government would destroy profits, create destitution, introduce "state socialism," and ruin America. Funding for the factory was rejected 274–111. Congress had been "deluged" by protests from manufacturers and trade associations. Arthurdale, forever linked with socialism, was not meant to survive.

On 31 January 1934, Upton Sinclair telegrammed ER:

> Front page editorial in Los Angeles Examiner denounces your plan to have unemployed manufacture furniture in West Virginia factory using government relief funds. Examiner supports action of Congress forbidding United States Post Office to purchase furniture from this factory. Three hundred EPIC Clubs pledged to end poverty in California . . . are prepared to go to bat with reactionaries on this issue. . . .

Both ER and Upton Sinclair were stunned by the virulence of the Red Scare as it reemerged in 1934. In June and July, as ER presided over the opening of Arthurdale and then traveled through West Virginia and into the Tennessee Valley, the beauty of the region—the majestic mountains and tranquil valleys—which framed the cruelest poverty, seemed bitterly ironic. Now, as they struggled to improve the human condition and were confronted by such extreme opposition, ER exclaimed: "Man is vile but nature is glorious!"

As she drove those roads, ER longed for Hick—especially when the sunset was splendid or the moonlight extraordinary: "I think of you so much, and always wish you could enjoy everything nice with me!"

They would not be together until August. In the meantime, Hick was embarked on her own investigation of conditions in California's Imperial Valley, where the Red Scare was in full bloom: "This valley is the damnedest place I ever saw—except Southern West Virginia and Eastern Kentucky. There is the same suspicion and bitterness all through the place. An unreasoning, blind fear of 'Communist agitators.' If you don't agree with them, you are a Communist."

Hick was astounded by the intensity of California's "Red-baiting" crusade, which targeted all reform and unleashed a vicious smear campaign against Upton Sinclair.

The famed "muckraking" author, whose novel *The Jungle* (1906) engendered America's first Pure Food and Drug Act, was a renowned visionary who wrote *King Coal* (1917), *Oil!* (1927), and *The Profits of Religion* (1918), among many other works. In 1933 he upset his socialist allies by becoming a Democrat and creating a new movement, End Poverty in California (EPIC), heralded by his immediately successful seventy-page book *I, Governor of California, and How I Ended Poverty: A True Story of the Future.*

With one-fourth of the state on relief, or in desperate need (1.5 million people), there was every reason to believe the former socialist—who now named FDR his political leader—would be victorious, and breathe bolder life into the New Deal. But FDR was wary of political contamination by grassroots radicals, and struggled to ignore Sinclair. Nevertheless, ER invited him for tea at the White House in November 1933.

Charming, "boyish," and intense, Upton Sinclair appealed to ER, and they had much in common. Both were children of affluent and prestigious families; both their lives had been marked by an alcoholic, troubled father. Born in Baltimore to Southern aristocrats, Sinclair lived in poverty with his abandoned mother, except when he was sent down home to his rich relatives. As a child he asked his mother why some children were so poor and others so rich: "How can that be fair?" Like ER, as an adult he identified with outsiders, with people in trouble and need. Although there is no record of their conversation, he sent her his book—which she read.

His call for economic democracy matched many of her own convictions. But the president ordered ER more than once to "1) Say Nothing and 2) Do Nothing" regarding Upton Sinclair, and ER wrote him a letter to explain why she could endorse neither his book nor his candidacy. Marked "Private—not for Publication," her letter was not quite an apology:

> I have read your book and I have given it to my husband to read. Some
> of the things which you advocate I am heartily in favor of, others I do not

think are entirely practical, but then what is impractical today is sometimes practical tomorrow. I do not feel, however, that I am sufficiently in accord with your entire idea to make any public statement at present.

Sinclair's landslide victory in California's Democratic primary on 28 August 1934 astonished pundits and politicians throughout the country. He received more votes than his six opponents combined.

Some of FDR's advisers were disturbed by the president's persistent silence. Both Harry Hopkins and Henry Wallace publicly supported Upton Sinclair. Wallace declared his goals similar to "our present plan of subsistence home-steading." That, of course, was what the newly formed Liberty Leaguers who fought Arthurdale were afraid of.

Sinclair spoke of production for use, not production for profit. As governor, Upton Sinclair promised to rent California's idle farms and factories. The owners would be saved from debt and bankruptcy; the reemployed workers would own what they produced.

If EPIC was communism, declared Sinclair, "President Roosevelt's policies are also communism."

Sinclair's challenge was met with frantic opposition. FDR remained silent in the face of mounting pressure from the right, while a most amazing political creature was formed out of twisted words and propaganda: California's anticommunist crusade of 1934 introduced the all-media fright campaign.

For ER and the advocates of Arthurdale, it served as portent and warning. The anticommunist crusaders of California vividly illuminated the context for America's determined opposition to sustainable community, and all New Deal efforts really to provide decent, democratic, and humane alternatives to grinding poverty and neglect.

Hick's reports detailed the situation: The reactionary press was buttressed by "Vigilantes," who raided "Communist" headquarters. In San Francisco "they herded together and jailed a lot of poor devils who weren't Communists at all." For days, screaming headlines promised to rid "the state of Communists" and create "a peacetime death penalty for treason—i.e., 'Communism.'" Nobody was safe: Democrats were the primary targets.

According to Hick, except for Scripps-Howard, most of the newspapers in the area were anti-administration.

> The Chamber of Commerce crowd have been doing the most effective work. They are putting on a little under-cover campaign of their own. It's a whispering affair. They don't say much about the President. It's aimed mostly at Mrs. Roosevelt, Henry Wallace, Rex Tugwell, and . . . "the rest of the New Dealers." Mrs. Roosevelt especially is supposed to have strong Communistic sympathies and a tremendous and very bad influence on the President. . . .

Hollywood's brutal war against EPIC was played without rules, no holds barred. In one faked newsreel, trains chugged rapidly into California from all over the country, filled with "hoboes" and "bums" of all ages—dangerous, impoverished, and deadly—attracted by Upton Sinclair's promises of jobs and security. Now, Californians were warned, they would devour the state's remaining funds, and everybody would be impoverished. Besides, the studios would close and move to Florida. So would the citrus growers, so would the realtors, and of course the oil companies and utilities. California would become a ghost state if Republican Frank Merriam was not reelected.

Other films were made in which all EPIC supporters were gangsters, supported by ugly foreigners in dirty trench coats with beards, bombs, and accents. The maker of one "newsreel" boasted, "We hired the scum of the streets" to march through the cities with "Vote for Upton Sinclair" signs, and worried that the whole game could backfire if it lasted too long and all the people hired began to talk.

It was a $10 million campaign of misinformation and dirty tricks. EPIC telephones were tapped, offices were invaded; mail, stationery, and contributors' lists were stolen.

As 1934 campaign tensions mounted, ER was subjected to personal abuse. One particularly nasty moment occurred when Minnesota Senator Thomas Schall compared Arthurdale's furniture cooperative with her Val-Kill furniture factory and derided her as a price-gouging publicity hound: ER's name, he asserted, was autographed on furniture made in her shop—which cost five times the going rate for similar items.

ER understood during the 1930s that handcrafted work could never compete with factory-made items. Exquisite, individually rendered crafts had become luxuries. If "human resources" mattered, and workers were honored with a living wage, handcrafted goods would never again be "profitable." Still, she believed in their value—as made-to-order works of art.

She defended Arthurdale's cooperative fiercely, and her own shop:

> I would like to explain that our factory at Val-Kill was started [in 1925] as an experiment to see if one could run a very small factory in a rural community and make it pay and at the same time teach people—boys especially—a trade so that they would not drift out of the country community. . . . We have never since we began any of us who put the money into the factory, had one cent of interest on our investment.

All handicrafts and garden activities at Arthurdale were continually ridiculed. Every Godlove chair was counted a fiscal loss in time and pay. Every curtain, knitted sweater, woven rug became somehow a debit.

ER could not understand why so many politicians, including Democrats, who should be eager to invest in America's future were so niggling, especially since so many millions were spent on research for industrial profit, agricultural profit, and for businesses dependent on military profits. She asked M. L. Wilson to prepare a study of industrial research expenditures, which revealed that by 1925 over $200 million was spent annually for industrial and government research for companies such as American Telegraph and Telephone, General Electric, and Du Pont. ER never understood why human goals were not considered just as worthy. She brought the subject up repeatedly: "We spend a great deal of money every year" to improve "various crops and fruits and vegetables. . . . It seems to me that the time has arrived when a certain amount of money should be spent on an experimental station for improving social conditions. . . ."

Homesteaders wrote to ER about their mounting concerns and asked her to meet with their club to reconsider the fiscal limitations imposed upon them:

> We are to be limited to 30 hours per week at 45 cents per hour which gives us a wage of $54 per month and we will not be able to make very high monthly payments out of this wage on a homestead.
>
> [Consider also] that many jobs in the construction department on this project return a bigger monthly wage, jobs homesteaders could be doing, but which they are not permitted to do. We realize that we are not skilled in many trades but if we had received the cooperation of the construction department we could have by this time become good plumbers, bricklayers, stone masons, blacksmiths, mechanics, painters, electricians, and all the different trades on this job. The value of this would be not only that we could now be earning more, but that we could do many jobs of service in the community in the coming years.

ER and Baruch agreed with the homesteaders. Baruch in particular feared that unless the workers' community achieved responsibility and long-term employment to "carry themselves," the experiment was doomed, "no matter how good." ER considered the entire cost-accounting approach wrong. It was not just a question of housing and security, but education and human restoration. It was a process that would take time, and ER believed the government had a responsibility to support that process. "No community," she insisted, "should be expected to pay" the costs of what was in part a social "laboratory for the whole country."

Once Congress rejected government-supported work, ER turned to allies in private industry. Some of her contacts indicated interest, but felt hounded by federal requirements and withdrew.

Most notable was a plan for the National Home Library Foundation to build and operate a printing press at Arthurdale. ER was impressed by the foundation's goal to get good books into America's homes at low cost, and was close to many of the writers and progressives on its advisory board—which included Heywood Broun, Bennett Cerf, John Dewey, Albert Einstein, Dorothy Canfield Fisher, Felix Frankfurter, John Haynes Holmes, Frederic Howe, Eva Le Gallienne, Raymond Moley, George Russell (AE), and Hendrik van Loon, among many others.

After months of dickering, Sherman Mittell, the foundation's president, wrote Leroy Peterson, chief of the Economic Development Section of the Resettlement Administration, that he resented being hounded, and it was best "to forget" the idea. Mittell objected to being treated as a bad security risk, when he had been asked for a favor:

> We were originally interested because Mrs. Roosevelt liked the idea. It soon, however, developed into an inquisition, why I don't know. The information you ask for is available whenever you get down to telling us what's what. . . .
>
> I leave the whole matter up to her. She has but to ask and we shall carry out her wishes. I don't want to have any more scraps with you!

In a series of obnoxious queries, sent 12 August, 16 August, and again on 27 September, Peterson demanded detailed "definite information:" "Yearly production and sale of books." Names of "sales outlets," "principal buyers." Future prospects, inventories and location of inventories, titles, and future titles. What government agency seriously wanting to do business would begin negotiations with an inquisition of unnecessary demands? ER's allies began to believe the Washington boys were not serious: "There is around a growing acceptance of disaster for [homesteads]. They expect them to fail."

ER refused to let Arthurdale fail and turned repeatedly to Bernard Baruch. A deep friendship was forged as they worked together. ER grew to depend on Baruch and to trust his considerate judgment. Consistently, Baruch protected the First Lady. Even when they disagreed, he sought to defend and promote her interests. When a shirt manufacturer agreed to open a factory on a trial basis, Baruch wrote ER:

> I do not think you ought to be a party to starting anything in Arthurdale which does not offer those things you stand for—the right for collective bargaining, minimum wages and maximum hours. . . .
>
> I shall be available to you or anyone you suggest, when the contract is being made.

The Phillips-Jones Corporation, which made Van Deusen shirts, met all the requirements: It did not employ child labor, it established an eight-hour day with a minimum wage of $13 a week, and the plants' workers were affiliated with the American Federation of Labor. Baruch was satisfied, the Resettlement Administration was pleased, and after a further conference with Baruch, the deal was done.

ER increasingly relied on Baruch's judgment and generosity. On one occasion she wrote him:

> The enclosed is from a colored girl [Margaret Inniss of New York City] whose work came to my attention several years ago.
>
> If I check on the work that she is doing now and find it good, would you be willing to pay the rent for a year? My own money is all pledged.

Always an educator, ER was particularly interested in schools—which she considered the center of the entire experiment in community building. From the beginning, she worked closely with Elsie Ripley Clapp, who served as principal of the schools and director of community affairs.

A pioneering progressive educator with degrees from Vassar and Columbia, Clapp had worked with John Dewey and had previously taught at private schools in New York, South Carolina, Massachusetts, and Kentucky.

At Arthursdale, from nursery school, which began with toddlers of two, to adult education classes, girls and boys—women and men—were equal, and treated with respect. They learned history, geography, botany, by living, reading, and doing: They wrote and performed plays; crafted violins, guitars, and drums; hiked and studied rocks and soils. Girls took shop, and boys took cooking; and they all crafted amazing things: telephones, radios, costumes, pottery. There was an evening school with classes in child care, electricity, typewriting, accounting. There was no truancy at Arthurdale, and the entire family went to school.

Initially, ER and Elsie Clapp believed that through progressive education Arthurdale might light the way to an entirely new way of being:

> Men and women will finally learn how to live happily and securely together. . . . They will develop in an economy of peace and plenty rather than competition and want.

But the community wanted to be taught like other communities in the region, and it retreated from Clapp's innovations. By 1936, she moved on and the schools she created were turned over to the West Virginia school system. Some parents were disappointed, others relieved.

ER presided over the transition. On 12 July 1936, while Bernard Baruch was in a German spa seeking a cure for his gout, ER sent him five typed pages to explain her determination to "carry on the health work," and support the "nursery school. . . . I feel with the new families coming in, the health care and the nursery school are two vital things. . . ." She met with Rex Tugwell, who supported her efforts, and she returned to Arthurdale to explain to the Homesteaders the changes under way:

> They will run their own baby clinic, they can run their own music festivals, their athletics and many of the recreational activities through the Homesteaders Club. . . .
>
> I hope that you will feel I have acted wisely and have done what you would have done . . .

To the end of her life, ER visited Arthurdale regularly and felt a deep personal regard for the members of the community, who had changed so much from their broken-down years at Scott's Run and had caused so much change to seem nationally possible.

She was particularly moved by a visit to a homestead where a woman had just had a baby and her two other children were four and six. ER worried that she would have a difficult holiday season. But the woman assured her, "This will be a wonderful Christmas." Before they had nothing; and the children were too weak to cry. Until Arthurdale, "all we had for Christmas dinner was some raw carrots for them to chew on. This year they will each have a toy and we have a chicken, one of our own, that we are going to eat. It will be wonderful."

ER concluded:

> I don't know whether you think that is worth half a million dollars. But I do. The homestead projects were attacked in Congress, for the most part by men who had never seen for themselves the plight of the miners or what we were trying to do for them. . . . I have always felt that many human beings who might have cost us thousands of dollars in tuberculosis sanitariums, insane asylums, and jails were restored to usefulness and given confidence in themselves.

For sixty years, pundits and politicians judged Arthurdale a failure. But the homesteaders' descendants are still living on the land; their children and their children's children still enjoy the bright pleasant homes that have withstood all those bitter mountain winters, with temperatures twenty, thirty, forty degrees below zero, in warmth and comfort. For the people, Arthurdale was marvelous, and they called it "utopia."

ER had believed in it, fought for it, caused it to happen. From the point of view of the people of the community, everything about it worked: The school and sense of community endured, the residents flourished, and they continued to believe their own experiences might be, should be, put to future use. At their sixtieth anniversary celebration in 1994, they designed sweatshirts that read: "Arthurdale / The Dream Lives On."

Today, every family tells virtually the same story: We worked together, we danced together, and we learned together. Almost all the children went to college. They became teachers, doctors, lawyers, artists, musicians, accountants, librarians. Miraculously, all the boys who volunteered for war returned home. And everyone remembers every time ER visited, to encourage them, to sit with them on their porches, to dance (and to call the square dance), to give the Commencement address, to help develop their school programs, to bring a child a present.

ER learned a lot about respect and trust from her years working for Arthurdale. She also learned valuable lessons about the limits of influence and the conflicts of power. Ultimately, she concluded:

> Nothing we learn in this world is ever wasted and . . . practically nothing we do ever stands by itself. If it is good, it will serve some good purpose in the future. If it is evil, it may haunt and handicap our efforts in unimagined ways.

There was, concerning Arthurdale, one "evil," one issue that haunted ER, which she struggled to redress. In the process of building a model community, ER confronted the subject of race, the profound contradictions of America's peculiar barriers to democracy. She understood the range of bigotry from violent tradition to the determined silences of contempt, casual disregard, and honest confusion. She was surprised and dismayed when the residents of Scott's Run, who had worked together and unionized together, picketed and demonstrated to keep Arthurdale white.

Her plea for an end to discrimination failed. Arthurdale propelled the issue of race to the top of ER's agenda.

9: The Quest for Racial Justice

———∞∞∞———

*A*gitation against the inclusion of Negro homesteaders in West Virginia galvanized ER. Since blacks and whites lived and worked, suffered and struggled, side by side along Scott's Run and in the mines, ER was unprepared for the fierce opposition to the creation of a racially mixed model community. At that time ER decided to confront society's acceptance of segregation and long-neglected race policies.

ER called a White House meeting with Clarence Pickett and notable Negro leaders. After dinner on 26 January 1934, Mordecai Johnson, president of Howard University; John Hope, president of Atlanta University; Robert R. Moton, president of Tuskegee Institute; Charles S. Johnson, chair of social sciences at Fisk University; Charles C. Spaulding, president of the North Carolina Mutual Life Insurance Company; and Walter White of the NAACP met with the First Lady until after midnight—when FDR was wheeled in to greet his wife's guests.

Clarence Pickett recalled that the conversation was "unrestrained." For over four hours, the New Deal's failure to address urgent nationwide race problems was fully explored. According to Pickett, ER's determination to embark upon the long road ahead "set before all of us a new standard for understanding and cooperation in the field of race."

That White House meeting heralded a new moment in civil rights politics. Never before had black leaders been invited to discuss unemployment, lynching, unequal expenditures to educate children, the failure to provide housing, sanitation, running water. ER promised to make every effort to ensure black participation in all federal work and relief programs. She would fight for equal education funding and opportunity. ER assured the leaders that her door was always open, her heart with them.

ER's policy represented a new formation in America's racial geometry. Walter White and the NAACP had access to the White House, and a friend in residence. She circumvented the hostile and careless among FDR's team and cultivated those who shared her vision: Harry Hopkins and his assistant

Aubrey Williams at FERA particularly; Will Alexander and Rex Tugwell; Harold Ickes and various members of his racially diverse staff. From that meeting forward, ER regularly sent instructions, details, letters, suggestions to them, and expected a response. Over the years she relied increasingly on Aubrey Williams. Born in Alabama, Williams was a former social worker. Proud to call himself a "Southern Rebel," he was entirely dedicated to racial change.

ER asked Hopkins to pay special attention to the plight of America's most neglected people: "I wonder if you will watch the colored situation quite closely and let me know from time to time how things are going." In various capacities, as Hopkins's assistant at the Civil Works Administration (1933–35) and the Works Progress Administration (1936–38), Williams took on that task, and with ER and others attempted to right the wrongs.

ER was aware of the enormous challenge before her. Civil rights had never before been accorded national consideration, and now she introduced a commitment to action in a tense and divided administration.

The week before the meeting with national black leaders, ER flew down to Atlanta to meet Hick, and then they drove to Warm Springs. She had carefully prepared for their weekend reunion of 20–22 January and reserved one of the private cottages built in the woods for "three quiet evenings and breakfasts and I don't know if you realize how nice that sounds to me!"

It was their first visit after a long and trying separation, and afterward Hick wrote:

> Dearest, it was a lovely weekend. I shall have it to think about for a long, long time. Each time we have together that way—brings us closer, doesn't it? And I believe those days and long pleasant hours together each time make it perhaps a little less possible for us to hurt each other. They give us better understanding of each other, give us more faith, draw us closer. . . .

A curious location for one of their most intimate trips together, Warm Springs had never been a cordial haven for ER. FDR's polio healing center, it was more Missy's place. From 1924 when he, Missy, and various friends first visited, Warm Springs became FDR's retreat—where Missy presided. The bubbling 88-degree healing springs were the primary attraction. FDR and his friends created a country club atmosphere, with stables, golf course, swimming pools, a conference and community center, all in addition to the campus-like quadrangle dominated by Georgia Hall, the treatment center, physical therapy, and research areas. Comfortable cottages, mostly designed by Henry Toombs, were built for family and friends, including SDR. It was one of these that ER reserved.

FDR's own white clapboard cottage with green shutters stood high and faced west to overlook a deep stand of Georgia pine. It was a simple space, with nautical motif and Val-Kill furniture. Its center living-dining area separated two bedrooms—FDR's and Missy's, which opened onto a sunporch built to resemble the prow of a ship. Behind FDR's bedroom, through a connecting bathroom, was a tiny space called ER's bedroom. But when ER visited she usually stayed at the guest cottage behind FDR's home. She rarely visited without her own circle of friends, who stayed with her.

The kitchen was presided over by an extraordinary cook—Daisy Bonner, whose Southern feasts were legendary. When in residence, she and the other servants, FDR's valet Irvin McDuffie and his wife, Lizzie, a longtime Roosevelt maid, lived together in one unit (with sink and toilet) above the garage that housed FDR's favorite hand-controlled car. For bathing, the staff had an outdoor shower hose attached to the side of the garage.

While FDR did not intend to interfere with the local habits of the people, ER was always disturbed by the conditions blacks endured in Meriwether County and set out to improve them. Even sixty years later her efforts were remembered with scorn and resentment by longtime white residents, who said she was "intrusive" and "out of place." "We didn't like her a bit; she ruined every maid we ever had."

In conversation, one woman insisted that she always concerned herself with "business that was none of her business." When pressed, that turned out to be her interest in a school for Negro children. After FDR built a school for white children, she agitated for a school for black children. "And it was built; and it was built in brick too, the Eleanor Roosevelt School!"

When FDR was asked about facilities for black polio victims, he deferred to the prejudice of the area and helped build a treatment center at Tuskegee instead. According to local lore, ER was "much more interested in Tuskegee, than she was with what was going on here; and would spend more time with the polios there." "She was not liked or admired here; and she was never happy here. This was his place."

However accurate local memories may be, ER always made the best of her times at Warm Springs, enjoyed her rides, swam each day, and was proud of the good work FDR generated. She frequently brought her own friends to see the place, and she fully appreciated FDR's sense of it as a healing sanctuary.

Before white conquest, Warm Springs was an Indian healing refuge for wounded fighters of warring tribes: Cherokee, Creek, Choctaw, and others would travel to the springs, and as FDR frequently explained, honored the sacred healing space where "wars of the body and wars of the mind are absolutely taboo."

While at Warm Springs that January weekend, ER and Hick drove to visit Bulloch Hall, the familial home of ER's father's mother, Martha (Mittie) Bulloch, in Roswell, Georgia.

One can only imagine ER's conversation with Hick during their time in Roswell, so filled with complicated and lingering legacies. Always proud of her Southern heritage, ER had no romantic illusions about some peaceful, idyllic magnolia-and-mint-julep past. She deeply appreciated the power of race traditions—and she never doubted how hard it would be to change them.

On 27 January 1934, the day after her White House race meeting, ER spoke at the first National Public Housing Conference held in Washington, and denounced "slum owners." She declared: "Holders of property who exploit human beings must be made to feel that they are bad citizens. . . ." Outraged that poor people were charged exorbitant rents by greedy landlords for dreadful and meager spaces, she called for a public movement of protest and awareness, to "dramatize" what "thoughtless people will do in order to make a little more money."

Even before ER went to West Virginia in August 1933, she had toured Washington's "alley dwellings" or "alley slums," where twelve thousand blacks and a thousand whites lived in desperate circumstances.

Behind beautiful Georgian facades, high walls, and well-trimmed privets, Washington kept its long-neglected secrets: over two hundred ugly, crowded, festering hidden alleyways that had aroused protest for decades. As early as 1871, Washington's Board of Health declared them "injurious to health," and in 1874 it condemned 389 houses. But in 1878, Congress abolished the Board of Health and the program ended. In 1904, Theodore Roosevelt declared dilapidated housing a menace; in 1906, Congress created the Board for the Condemnation of Insanitary Buildings. But nothing happened.

Not until Charlotte Everett Hopkins, the "Grand Old Lady" of Washington who had known every president since Abraham Lincoln, persuaded Ellen Axson Wilson, the first Mrs. Woodrow Wilson, to protest this community scourge was there hope of real change. But Ellen Wilson's efforts to dismantle the alleys and convert them to parks or new roadways, which passed Congress on the day of her death, 6 August 1914, were suspended because of wartime priorities. Although the 1914 legislation had no provision for new housing, "Mrs. Archibald Hopkins" never gave up, and continued to imagine gardens and lovely homes someday where "alley dwellers hide now in Dickensian squalor."*

*Born in Cambridge, in June 1851, she was the granddaughter of Edward Everett, famed orator, statesman, and Harvard president. In 1878 she married Colonel Archibald Hopkins of the 37th Massachusetts Volunteers, son of Mark Hopkins, president of Williams College. From her famous home on DuPont Circle and Massachusetts Avenue, she organized her many voluntary projects for the dignity of all Washingtonians.

Within days of FDR's inauguration, she persuaded ER to accompany her on a tour of a hidden inner city.

On 20 March 1933, a cold and overcast day, they drove together in ER's open blue roadster. Hopkins told journalist Martha Strayer:

> We drove to North Capitol St. and I told her to drive back of Sibley Hospital. We turned into an alley. She said, "Where shall I go now?" I said, "Drive into that place that looks like a slit in the wall between two houses."
>
> We drove into Pierce Court. . . . It's 12 feet wide. On each side are three-story wooden tenements. There's no water in the buildings; it has to be carried from hydrants. . . . There are no toilet facilities except one for each building; outside, exposed, used by both sexes. In one room in that court, a social worker found 14 men and one woman sleeping. . . .

Unrecognized, they walked through other littered, crowded spaces where garbage was never collected by authorities paid to do so. They talked to the residents, learned of the suffering, disease, and infant deaths, the troubles and humiliations. They witnessed rats as big as cats. The alley death rate from tuberculosis was 50 percent higher than elsewhere.

Washington's leading civic activist had at last found another enthusiastic champion. ER determined to end the mean and vile conditions just behind the great and comfortable houses. The District's budget was completely controlled by Congress, and it was unwilling to address the needs of the disenfranchised residents of segregated Washington—so many of whom worked in service for their own families.

ER demanded immediate action: In Marshall Heights there was no running water, and women and children carried buckets very long distances. ER called for emergency water, new pipes and pumps. In many districts water pumps were next to outdoor toilets and sewage lines. ER pointed out that such conditions bred diseases that threatened the entire city. Emergency crews went to work.

ER's Washington campaign upset traditionalists even more than her commitment to Arthurdale. She introduced the untouchable issue of race and demanded that Negro residents receive respectful attention.

FDR had immediately endorsed Arthurdale, but he disfavored the alley dwelling bill in 1933, as "not in accord with the President's financial program."

During the winter and spring of 1934, John Ihlder and other members of the Washington Committee on Housing—which ER now served as "honorary chairman"—struggled to win administration support. The bill was changed "in accordance with Mrs. Roosevelt's suggestion" in order to remove "the objections of the Director of the Budget."

Unlike Ellen Wilson's legislation, the new bill included provisions for "a home construction program" as a "necessary complement" to alley demolition. Slum clearance was not to be another "Negro removal" project. Ihlder, a housing activist from Boston who had worked with Charlotte Hopkins for over a decade, saw the Washington project as a "demonstration" model for the nation and a key to FDR's economic recovery program: "The substitution of good housing for bad is a great task that will continue for several years and constantly create a tremendous demand for labor and materials that will stimulate nearly every line of industry and commerce."

ER and the Washington Committee on Housing worked continually to achieve results, but their campaign made slow progress.

On 29 January 1934, journalist Melvin Chisum, field secretary of the National Negro Press Association, wrote ER a letter about the Mobilization for Human Needs Campaign, which ER chaired. This national drive to raise private funds for all relief and social work needs that the New Deal proceeded "with almost no regard for the colored people in the more than two hundred cities where the work is advancing." Chisum continued: "You might not know that the Negro is being almost utterly disregarded and I submit that these too, with all their misfortunes and poverty are human beings and I feel quite sure that your Ladyship will agree."

Chisum had a specific suggestion that ER pursued for months: "A capable, intelligent Negro woman of fine training should be chosen to see to it that the Negro people . . . be not ignored and left out. . . ."

ER wrote Frances Perkins: "Is there anything in the idea of having a colored woman in the Women's Bureau, and would it be possible to get one appointed?"

Frances Perkins saw no reason for such an appointment at the time. Perkins feared it would only add to the "difficulty" of race relations and increase prejudice. Although the secretary of labor opposed wage differentials, and *The Crisis* referred to her as "kind, patient and unbiased," Perkins tended to flee from the race question.

ER might have turned to Ickes, who pioneered an antidiscrimination policy in his department, but she understood his well-known aversion to strong women with authority.

During the first years of the New Deal, Harold Ickes's Public Works Administration was the key agency for black employment in the construction and building trades. Ickes issued an order banning "discrimination on the basis of color or religion in employment for public works," and he backed it up with a quota system whereby black workers in each community were to be hired both as skilled and unskilled labor in proportion to their population in the occupation census of 1930. Although local overseers ignored his order throughout the South and elsewhere, in many urban communities PWA came to stand for "Poppa's Working Again."

Both officially and symbolically, Ickes uprooted generations of racial custom: He refused to have a staff member in the Department of the Interior who did not share his progressive views on race, and he single-handedly ended one area of federal segregation by integrating the department's cafeteria and serving some of the best food in town.

ER turned instead to Harry Hopkins, who rarely refused the First Lady's requests. When she asked about the appointment of a black woman, he immediately asked her to name a candidate. ER knew the perfect candidate for the first woman to advance Negro interests: outspoken and inspiring educator and organizer Mary Jane McLeod Bethune.

ER had met Bethune when she hosted a sit-down dinner at the East 65th Street home for leaders of the National Council of Women in 1927. The only black woman in attendance, and then president of the National Association of Colored Women, Mary McLeod Bethune entered ER's dining room, looked around at all the white women, so many of them from the South, and hesitated. Sara Delano Roosevelt noticed, and walked across the room:

> That grand old lady took my arm and seated me to the right of Eleanor Roosevelt in the seat of honor! I can remember, too, how the faces of the Negro servants lit up with pride when they saw me seated at the center of that imposing gathering. . . . From that moment my heart went out to Mrs. James Roosevelt. I visited her at her home many times subsequently, and our friendship became one of the most treasured relationships of my life. As a result of my affection for her mother-in-law, my friendship with Eleanor Roosevelt soon ripened into a close and understanding mutual feeling.

Born on 10 July 1875, near Mayesville, South Carolina, the fifteenth of seventeen children to former slaves and descended on her mother's side from "royal African blood," Mary McLeod grew up picking cotton and working hard. Brilliant and bold, she excelled in school and was even as a child an acknowledged leader. At ten she was enrolled in the Trinity Presbyterian Mission School, where she was mentored by a "loving and dynamic" teacher, Emma Jane Wilson, who encouraged her to go to boarding school and arranged a scholarship to the Scotia Seminary, a "missionary outpost" in North Carolina. She graduated with honors in 1894 and received a scholarship to the Moody Bible Institute in Chicago to prepare for a career as a missionary in Africa. But the Presbyterian Mission Board refused to send an African-American missionary to Africa, so Mary McLeod became a teacher and missionary in her own country.

With her husband, Albert Bethune, she moved to Florida in 1899 and started her own school for girls, the Daytona Normal and Industrial Institute at Daytona Beach in 1904. A singer and performer, she used her talents to raise money for her school. Because her husband resented her work, they separated. Alone with her young son, she toured the country telling and singing the story of her life.

Bethune's school grew from six students, five girls and her son, to an outstanding institution on twenty acres of land, with eight buildings, a farm, and a hospital that she established for the black people of Daytona in 1911. Hundreds of affluent and needy girls received an excellent education at Daytona Normal, a college preparatory and teacher-training school which emphasized "Self-control, Self-respect, Self-reliance and Race Pride." In 1929 she merged it with the Cookman Institute and became president of the coeducational Bethune-Cookman College.

Mary McLeod Bethune was also a suffragist committed to women's rights. In 1920 she organized a black women's voter-registration drive throughout Florida in the face of KKK terrorism. She worked closely with the National Association of Colored Women until 1935, when she helped found the National Council of Negro Women, an alliance of twenty-nine national organizations.

From their first meeting in 1927, ER was impressed by the vigor of Bethune's feminism, her race pride, and her compelling magnetism.

When ER suggested that she come to Washington in October 1934, Mary McLeod Bethune began a dazzling chapter in American politics. Originally one of thirty-five members of the National Advisory Committee of the new National Youth Administration created in 1935, she became director of Negro affairs for the NYA. The acknowledged leader of the unofficial Black Cabinet, which met each week in her home on Friday evenings to discuss priorities and strategies, she worked to forge the new activist civil rights movement.

Mary McLeod Bethune set the pace: She supported the effort to free the nine youths judged guilty of rape in the Scottsboro case even after their accuser had recanted her story, bolstered the reputation of the Southern Tenant Farmers Union organized in 1934, and dramatized the dreadful condition of sharecroppers throughout the South. She also created a grassroots organization in Washington, the New Negro Alliance, that boycotted discriminatory local stores, which she personally picketed, carrying "Don't Buy Where You Can't Work" posters. She supported the NAACP's efforts on behalf of anti-lynching legislation, protested the poll tax, fought for women's rights, and in every way sought to expand work and educational opportunities for black youth.

Called the "First Lady of the Struggle," Mary McLeod Bethune gained authority because of her ability to speak frankly with ER. They met regularly, traveled and attended conferences together, and became personally close. ER measured the reality of her own racism by the development of her friendship with Mary McLeod Bethune. At first she hesitated to embrace and kiss her on meeting, as she ordinarily did when she greeted other friends. ER was aware of that fact; it bothered her. Then, one day, her hesitation was simply gone.

ER devised a routine to greet Mary McLeod Bethune whenever she was scheduled to arrive at the White House. To avoid any disrespect by guards or an untoward incident, the First Lady waited inside the foyer door, so she could see the walkway, then ran down to embrace her and take her arm as they strolled up the hill. ER's public embrace was noticed and their friendship deemed a scandal by those who mourned any challenge to America's cruel race customs—which included a surprising assortment of Washington insiders, members of Congress, and members of FDR's personal staff.

In 1934, ER's behavior publicly announced that the private quarters of the White House had been integrated. She had tea for the Hampton Institute choir, dinner with Mary McLeod Bethune, lunch on the patio with Walter White. Although the indignities of segregation were not yet on the national political agenda, several ceremonies upon which America's "race etiquette" depended were defied at last.

Mary McLeod Bethune's first visit to the White House became a legendary Washington story. As she walked up the long front lawn to the main entrance, a gardener called to her: "Hey there, Auntie, where y'all think you're going?" Mrs. Bethune walked over to the gardener, looked directly and long into his face, and said slowly, wryly: "I don't recognize you. Which one of my sister's children are you?"

The early years of the New Deal were filled with little victories in a long and painful struggle. Beyond the big defeats, there were daily moments of pettiness, insults, little racial scratches that left open sores for later generations to heal. The magnitude of the challenge was revealed in a series of FERA reports Hick sent ER during her first two-month Southern tour.

A poor girl from Wisconsin, Hick had never been exposed to life in the heart of America's Southland. She had no Southern friends, white or black, and had never thought about slavery or peonage, or what daily suffering under a system of routine brutality might be like.

For Hick, a loose cannon politically, the rural South was an unparalleled odyssey of discovery, and self-discovery. Basically a populist committed to the underprivileged, Hick abhorred chiselers and cheats, hated snobs, and despised communists. Her sense of "the people" was largely limited to white Christian people. She had never thought about it much, but Hick identified with, and rambled on in, the language of white supremacy.

But bigotry and race violence were headline news in 1934. In Germany, Jews were never more than 1 percent of the population, and numbered less than 500,000 people throughout the entire country, but in the United States, African-Americans were over 10 percent of the population, and numbered over twenty million people, concentrated in small areas. There were entire cities, villages, rural areas in the "Black Belt" where Negroes were the vast majority of the population. If they had been allowed the benefits of full citizenship, they would have had influence, respect, power. But the poll tax, violence and threats of violence, the peculiar American habit of lynching—a depraved system that hid behind the rhetoric of "states' rights" and committed atrocities veiled under white sheets of Christian piety—defined a region swamped by cruelty and state terrorism.

When in 1934 the U.S. government recognized the existence of rural poverty as a national problem, most people who voted, and all the vested interests, opposed spending money on the rural poor. The cotton South and corporate North, agriculture and industry, opposed every dollar spent to rehabilitate or relocate America's rural poor. They did not vote, and they did not count.

Hick toured the South to assess the New Deal's first efforts to confront this bitter situation. A reporter with a keen eye for detail, she struggled to understand local customs. She was shocked by her first encounters with the mores of the Deep South, and her first instinct was to blame the victim. It took her almost a month to penetrate the tissue of lies and courtesy that camouflaged a quagmire of racial contempt, raw greed, and hatred.

In Savannah, she identified with the white opposition to the Civil Works Administration. In October 1933, Harry Hopkins wanted to put four million people to work immediately, at their own jobs—white-collar and professional workers, teachers, librarians, artists, entertainers; blue-collar and industrial workers, construction workers, miners, factory workers; lumberjacks and fishermen. He intended to pay close to the prevailing wage. FDR agreed; ER was enthusiastic about the grand scheme.

The CWA differed from FERA, which depended on local administrators whose attitudes varied widely from state to state. FERA was a state-operated relief agency, partly financed by the federal government. CWA was controlled and financed by the federal government. It was the most controversial New Deal agency to date, and in less than a year it achieved an amazing amount: 40,000 schools were built or improved; 469 airports were built; 255,000 miles of road were built or improved; 50,000 teachers were employed in adult education classes or rural schools; 3,700 playgrounds and athletic fields were built or improved. Of the 4,264,000 reemployed, 3,000 were writers and artists, a group that heralded the Federal Arts Program.

The CWA hired singers to bring grand opera to the Ozarks; musicians to give symphony concerts throughout the country; theater groups to perform in areas long denied any entertainment. Hopkins never understood why "great art" should be confined "to a few people." "If it is good for 20,000 people, it will be good for 20,000,000."

Every group was involved; 4,464 Indians were hired to repair their own homes on Indian reservations; another thousand were hired to excavate prehistoric Indian mounds for the Smithsonian Institution.

The CWA was widely condemned as wasteful and un-American. But only in the South was it actually despised—especially for the high wages paid on a nondiscriminatory basis. And Hick at first agreed with the white planters and business leaders who opposed those wages. Although she recognized their "racial prejudice," their "unconscious fear of Negroes," their fear that CWA funds would attract still more blacks to Savannah, she seemed at first even to sympathize with the economic roots of their opposition: Decent CWA salaries cut in on their traditional profits, based on their traditional labor customs—peonage, or virtual slavery.

Eventually, Hick criticized the South's economic aristocracy. But her first report out of Savannah featured pages of vivid, ugly dehumanizing rhetoric, followed by her conclusion:

> For these people to be getting $12 a week—at least twice as much as common labor has ever been paid down here—is an awfully bitter pill for Savannah people to swallow. . . . What makes it tougher . . . is that while these illiterate creatures, whom they regard as animals, are getting more money than they ever had in their lives before, hundreds of white working-men are unable to get CWA jobs, and their families are hungry. . . .
>
> Even people in our own show down here seem to think we are paying the Negroes too much. It spoils them. . . .

By the following week, Hick had a new perspective. She had met Georgia's FERA director, Gay Shepperson, "a grand human . . . and one of the most interesting women I ever met in my whole life." Shepperson had squired Hick around and helped her see beyond the whitewashed manners of Georgia's rulership. Now she understood that there was no labor shortage. On the contrary, over 200,000 women and men had enrolled for employment, and remained unemployed. Of that figure, CWA and PWA, with all their cooperative programs with private farmers and industrialists, had been able to place only 18,012: "What there is is a darned serious SURPLUS of farm labor in this state. And that's why the farmers get labor for almost nothing."

Hick then met other people, decent angry white citizens who wanted to see change in rural Georgia. One "prominent citizen," who wanted to be sure he would not be quoted, Mr. McConnell, assured her that there were "thousands and thousands of Niggers in this state living in slavery just as real as it ever was before the Civil War. . . . A farmer considers every Nigger living in a house—or the worst kind of shack you ever saw—on his place employed, whether he is paying him anything or not. . . ."

Another source took Hick into turpentine country to call on a producer who had a reputation for "a very hot temper."

> I wish I could make you see the place—away off in the woods, miles from everywhere, years away from civilization itself. A few unpainted, tumbledown shacks. A turpentine still. All hidden away in the pines, cut off from all the world by trees and swamp.
>
> In the course of our conversation, our host, who was complaining that his Negroes were dissatisfied because other Negroes, working for CWA, were getting $9 and $12 a week, remarked most of his men were "good Niggers" but that he occasionally had some trouble. And, with a grin, he held out his fist. There were several bruises on it. . . . As we drove away, the man who took me out there, said:
>
> "You have seen Simon Legree. That fellow has killed a couple of Niggers in his camps."
>
> "What do you mean?" I asked.
>
> I got no answer.
>
> The CWA administrator and the federal reemployment director in this country were telling me this afternoon about farmers . . . who take advantage of the fact that their sharecroppers cannot read or write, with the result that in many cases, at the end of the season, the sharecropper doesn't get a thing, and there isn't anything he can do about it. He just works for a shell of a house, a few sticks of wood to burn, a few grits and a little pork, that's all.
>
> Now all this, they point out, is due largely to one thing only—a surplus of labor in these rural areas. Blacks and Whites, who are hardly more than beasts.

Hick concluded that most of the labor force should be relocated and resettled into the kind of community that Arthurdale represented: "It seems fairly obvious that the only way out is to remove from the labor market enough poor Whites and Blacks so that members of both races who are left will have some sort of chance. . . ."

Hick emphasized the need for education and health care. Illiteracy flourished; schools were "a mess." Teachers were undereducated and rarely paid. Entire towns had one teacher, generally a young girl who had not completed high school. Hundreds of children had no clothes to attend school. Children could not read: "Why, some of them can barely talk!" Pellagra and tuberculosis were epidemic. "God, they're a wretched lot!" The people were called "lazy," and everywhere those who had too much blamed those who had nothing for their sorry state.

The more Hick saw the more she realized that she had accepted a pack of lies, the meanest lies imaginable—and told to her by folks who called themselves Democrats.

Hick was now outraged: "I just can't describe to you some of the things I've seen and heard down here these last few days. I shall never forget them—never as long as I live. . . ."

ER's responses to Hick's first letters concerning the South were restrained. Although she frequently disagreed, she was initially patient with Hick's passionate bigoted outbursts. In the letters that have survived, ER encouraged her to reread the life of John Brown and suggested she look harder and deeper into the causes and context of all that she saw.

ER gave Hick little lessons on the complexities of dignity. Even people on CWA wages had a right to "grumble." "People are never satisfied Hick dear, when things are done for them. . . . They like doing for themselves." "Human beings are poor things. Think how much discipline we need ourselves & don't get too discouraged."

By the time Hick reached Florida, she was incensed. Where only a month before she had attacked unionists and agitators, she now wrote Harry Hopkins:

> Now I'll tell you right off the bat for being mean-spirited, selfish, and irresponsible, I think Florida citrus growers have got the world licked. . . .
>
> Two weeks before Christmas the whole citrus industry just closed down for the holidays and turned everybody loose—without money or jobs. No wonder there's an "outlaw union" in the citrus belt and a strike. . . .

Hick's letters from Florida caused ER to recall her earlier years there during FDR's first battles with polio. A painful time of recovery and fear, they were combined with the permanent arrival of Missy and his jolly houseboat companions, and for ER endless months of loneliness and confusion. She had never wanted to return to that place again. But Hick's vivid descriptions of its natural wonders—flame-colored vines "covered with masses of brilliant orange flowers," camellias and lavender, orange and grapefruit trees "simply loaded down with fruit," the brilliant sky and warm waters—caused ER to reconsider: "I might like it with you, it may just be that I knew it best in my stormy years and the associations are not so pleasant."

Throughout the winter and spring of 1934, ER ended her days thinking of Hick. Their relationship deepened through letters of longing ER wrote in the quiet of the night, shortly before dawn when her day was done and the household slept. "Gee, what wouldn't I give to talk to you . . . to hear your voice now. . . . It is all the little things . . . the feel of your hair, your gestures. These are the things I think about."

While Hick toured the South, ER's days were full. There were guests all winter. Some stayed for days, others for weeks. There were lunches with Frances Perkins, long visits with Lady Lindsay, trips with Elinor Morgenthau, Earl Miller, and Nancy Cook, and an increasingly frail and demanding Louis Howe: "Quite a household when everyone has trays. Louis is in his room still all the time." And son John had to have his appendix removed. ER stayed with him, which eliminated her plan to meet Hick in Charleston, South Carolina. There were endless meetings on Arthurdale, and she struggled to keep the alley bill moving through Congress.

On 30 January, ER worked hard to make FDR's birthday galas successful. She attended three charity balls, and with Louis Howe (who rallied for the occasion) made FDR's traditional frolic with his closest political friends, members of his "Cuff Links Club," spectacular. In response to all those anti–New Dealers who attacked FDR as monarch, emperor, dictator, they celebrated "Dear Caesar." ER designed the costumes, decorations, and favors. With Louis Howe she wrote new lyrics to old hymns, skits, and "two stunts" of her own.

FDR was resplendent in purple tunic, adorned with a crown of laurel. Louis Howe headed the Praetorian Guard, with cloak and plumed helmet. The appealingly garlanded vestal virgins included Missy, Tommy, daughter Anna, Nancy Cook, and Marion Dickerman. ER was a thoroughly entertaining Delphic oracle, and, she wrote Hick, I "evidently answered to their satisfaction, at least they seemed amused!"

The snows of February rendered ER particularly romantic: A blizzard stalled Washington traffic, but ER was determined to drive to Williamsburg, which was very lovely "but very slippery." The day was beautiful "and I kept thinking about you. I love you dear one and I have wanted you all day."

On 4 February, ER and Hick had a long telephone conversation and discussed various possibilities for their future together. ER was philosophical:

> Dear, I often feel rebellious too and yet I know we get more joy when we are together than we would have if we lived apart in the same city and could only meet for short periods now and then. Someday perhaps fate will be kind and let us arrange a life more to our liking. For the time being we are lucky to have what we have. Dearest, we are happy together and strong relationships have to grow deep roots, we're growing them now, partly because we are separated, the foliage and the flowers will come, somehow, I'm sure of it.

ER was convinced that it would "all work out somehow." "Darling nothing is important except that I love you. . . ."

ER considered Hick's reports from the South vastly improved toward the end of her tour: "How I enjoy your mind: Its grasp of problems is so interesting and you do get so much out of people." Hick now believed CWA was an acceptable emergency measure. But the problems were long-term, permanent actually. The issue was not emergency relief, or even federally funded jobs, but rehabilitation and real development. And that required, Hick wrote, an expanded farm resettlement program—with meaningful educational programs, job training, gardening, and husbandry. An entirely new conception of life and community needed to be created.

By 14 February, Hick understood the politics of the Southern landscape:

> The truth is the rural South never has progressed beyond slave labor. The whole system has been built up on labor that could be obtained for nothing or next to nothing. . . .
>
> During the depression, the paternalistic landlord . . . was darned glad to have us take over the job. But now, finding that CWA has taken up some of this labor surplus . . . he is panicky, realizes that he may have to make better terms. . . .

Southern opposition to CWA intensified, and FDR was surrounded by conservative economic advisers who argued that if the government got into the business of full employment and real security, it would be paying the bills forever.

In that bitter climate, ER worked with no public support from FDR for the alley bill. While it passed the Senate and languished in the House, ER took the month of March to go with Hick to Puerto Rico and the U.S. Virgin Islands. ER arranged the trip to coincide with Hick's fortieth birthday on 7 March.

Unfortunately, *Time* magazine announced that fact in its 19 February 1934 feature article on relief, which was rather a friendly defense of CWA. Then, as an aside, and curled in a Timese smirk, there was a description of Hopkins's chief field investigator, Miss Lorena Hickok:

> She is a rotund lady with a husky voice, a peremptory manner, baggy clothes. In her day one of the country's best female newshawks, she was assigned to Albany to cover the New York Executive Mansion where she became fast friends with Mrs. Roosevelt. Since then she has gone around a lot with the First Lady, up to New Brunswick and down to Warm Springs. Last July Mr. Hopkins, who is a great admirer of Mrs. Roosevelt, hired Miss Hickok and now she travels all over the country using her nose for news to report on relief conditions. Last week when it was announced that Mrs. Roosevelt planned to visit Puerto Rico in March it became known that

Miss Hickok would also go along to look into Mr. Hopkins' relief work there.

Hick felt personally attacked. She wrote Hopkins's secretary, Kathryn Godwin:

> I suppose I am "a rotund lady with a husky voice" and "baggy clothes," but I honestly don't believe my manner is "peremptory." And I bitterly resent the implication that I got this job solely because I was a friend of Mrs. Roosevelt. I love Mrs. Roosevelt dearly—she is the best friend I have in the world—but sometimes I do wish, for my own sake, that she were Mrs. Joe Doaks of Oelwein, Iowa! I'm a bit sick, too, because it got out that I'm going to Puerto Rico with her. I had hoped it wouldn't—that I could sort of slide in, as part of the background, that she would get all the publicity, and that I could go fairly quietly about my business. Oh well—I'll do my best. . . .

ER tried to console Hick: "But why can't we do everything together? I always wish for you when things are good, and if they are bad you are the best companion I know." She encouraged Hick to focus only on their impending time together, "and then I'll hold you in my arms. . . ."

On the 12th, ER sent Hick a Valentine's card and enclosed a long letter:

> I love you dear one deeply, tenderly. . . . I can't tell you how precious every minute with you seems to me in retrospect and in prospect. I look at you long as I write—the photograph has an expression I love, so you and a bit whimsical, but then I adore every expression.

On the 14th, ER drove to Cornell with Louis Howe for her annual lecture. She spoke until 10:30, and wrote Hick: "I am very full of thoughts of you & I'd give a lot to talk to you. . . . I love you with all my heart & your picture is with me. . . . And will you be my Valentine?"

While ER was with Howe, Hick had three traffic accidents in North Carolina. In Fayetteville, a milk truck backed into her and "crumpled" her right fender "like a piece of cardboard." While standing still in a traffic jam in Durham, a bus backed into her. She honked on her two horns to no avail. The driver dented her fender, broke her horn, and "bent my temper." Then Hick scraped a fender in a narrow hotel entrance. Her beloved Bluette now resembled a battlefield relic.

The accidents combined with the *Time* article sent Hick into a frenzy. She wrote Kathryn Godwin: "Why the Hell CAN'T they leave me alone? . . . I'm so fed up with the publicity I want to kick every reporter I see. Which is a bad state for me to get into, since I'll probably be back in the business myself. . . ."

ER's efforts to comfort and soothe Hick's distress could not lessen the fact that she now felt dependent and insecure, whereas before she had felt robust and powerful behind her byline.

On 4 March they began their journey to Puerto Rico and the U.S. Virgin Islands. It was the first time the actual conditions of the people in the territories, their needs and wants, were seriously considered. ER's visit set in motion the beginnings of a New Deal for the islands.

There was no discussion, however, of radical, union, and nationalist movements that raged during her visit. She was kept from any chance to observe them or speak with their representatives.

ER and Hick were accompanied by a party of reporters who were also good friends, Emma Bugbee *(Herald Tribune)*, Bess Furman (AP), Ruby Black (United Press), Dorothy Ducas (International News), and one press photographer chosen from the photo pool, Sammy Shulman. They flew from Miami with Rexford Guy Tugwell, then assistant secretary of agriculture.

ER's first overseas flight landed in Cuba and then went on to Haiti. In Cuba, ER's visit was curtailed by a transportation and communications strike, which she was not allowed to see. Indeed, she evidently saw no Cubans at all, except the mayor of Havana and four soldiers. The mayor told her that a general strike was imminent, "a political strike that the communists are trying to cause."

Nor did she tour Haiti, where there was also unrest and no particular appreciation for the wife of FDR. ER and Hick dined privately with the governor and her party left at dawn. They stopped in the Dominican Republic for a formal reception with the island's president, General Rafael Leonidas Trujillo.

ER's first significant stopover was St. Thomas, where she was welcomed by a crowd that sang "John Brown's Body," protest and union songs.

On the first presidential-level fact-finding tour, ER scouted the situation for her husband, who was interested in the area's economic development. ER agreed with those who sought to establish a tourist industry in the U.S. Virgin Islands and in Puerto Rico. But she believed that all tourism discussions should be postponed until the wretched effects of poverty, starvation, and disease were overcome.

Wherever she went, ER had Sammy Shulman photograph the most outrageous sights—open sewers, vermin-infested courtyards and playing fields, tin-and-cardboard neighborhoods where makeshift shacks served as housing in areas destroyed by recent hurricanes.

In St. Thomas, ER and Hick were the guests of the first civilian governor of the Virgin Islands, Paul Pearson. Purchased from Denmark in 1917, the U.S. Virgin Islands were initially under Navy rule. Then in 1931, Herbert

Hoover transferred them to the Department of Interior and appointed Pearson to oversee America's "effective poorhouse." But Governor Pearson, the father of columnist Drew Pearson, was a controversial figure. A liberal Republican and a Quaker, he was stunned by the desperate poverty he encountered. Sympathetic to the native population, he was quickly opposed by Southern Democrats who feared that he intended to desegregate the islands. But ER liked him. On 10 March she wrote FDR: "My impression is the fundamental point of attack is housing. I like the Governor. I like his balance particularly, [and his] social viewpoint. . . ." In ER's honor, Pearson had "cut across the color line" and integrated the reception he held for the First Lady and her party. According to Bess Furman the evening "went off so well that we didn't know until the next day that it had been news—we had taken it to be an old island custom."

ER began her first day on St. Thomas by swimming with her press companions at Pearson's private beach. Furman and Dorothy Ducas "managed to steal a movie sequence of Mrs. Roosevelt coming up the beach toward us, in a bathing suit, skipping rope."

She dedicated the new Eleanor Roosevelt ward in the municipal hospital and met with local women at the new high school. It was the first public women's meeting on St. Thomas. The women of the Virgin Islands were still without the vote, as were the vast majority of men—who could not pay the exorbitant poll tax.

ER encouraged the women to organize a political club and become actively involved. Only if they organized, she said, could they expect to win the vote and end the hated poll tax. And then they would be free to pursue their own needs in their own way: "No matter how little you have done in the past, reach out for influence, and try to use it to make your government respond to what is best for your homes. . . ."

In St. Croix, ER inspected new government housing, new subsistence farms, CWA schools, a leprosarium, and the site of a proposed government rum distillery and made four speeches. She visited old slave quarters, the new federal hotel site, which she thought beautifully located, and new community centers.

Throughout her forty-mile tour, entire neighborhoods turned out to greet her. People seemed to her "happy and healthy," but there was so much more that needed to be done. When she suggested that flies be kept out of cooking pots, local officials assumed that she meant to insist that screens be made mandatory in the new housing. Virgin Islanders never forgot ER's brief visit and credited many new homesites, with windows and screens, to her expressions of dismay and concern.

In Puerto Rico, ER wanted her tour to be private. She wanted to travel only with her party of reporters and her friends currently resident on the island, Dorothy Bourne and Rose Schneiderman. She dismissed all police and military escorts; insisted that the governor's car in which she rode be stripped of all official insignia and that the license plate be changed. She even asked the driver to change out of his chauffeur's uniform into a white linen suit. Although many towns had prepared for her visit and the streets were lined with people to greet her, in other areas she visited factories, schools, and homes as an unknown stranger.

Again, ER was kept away from areas of tension and labor strikes, which in Puerto Rico were caused by CWA wage reductions. As in the South the local gentry had no intention of paying "relief" workers the CWA's minimum wage of 30 cents an hour; and as in the South, in some cases the wage was reduced to 10 cents or less an hour. ER avoided political issues and declined to comment on the growing movement for Puerto Rico's independence.

The economic situation in Puerto Rico was more obviously desperate than in the Virgin Islands, and ER was frankly alarmed by the level of official neglect. Despite a recent hurricane, in some rural areas no new construction was anticipated and chickens and children shared the earthen floor. Dozens of people crowded into one-room houses that had no windows, occasionally no roofs. In San Juan, shanties on stilts stood above malaria-ridden swamps. She explored the "swamp slums," where refugees of the 1932 hurricane still lived in huts of debris, and "swamp water and grasses showed through the cracks of the floor," and ordered Sammy Shulman to "Get this, to really show what it is like."

She was disgusted to learn that $1,200,000 in relief funds had been cut to $500,000 and limited to 522,000 of the neediest cases, and that the neediest families received between 50 cents and a $1 a week—to meet the needs of six, or eight, or fifteen people.

ER met with a group of sixty nurses who worked in a children's health program and heard of their battle against the island's four scourges—tuberculosis, malaria, hookworm, and enteritis. She promised to address their plight in Washington.

For two days ER motored through the hill country and rain forest, the mountain areas, where hurricanes had destroyed banana, coffee, pineapple, and grapefruit plantations, leaving only palm-thatched cottages where young girls and old women toiled over hand-embroidered lingerie and handkerchiefs for which they earned between 10 and 25 cents per dozen. It was an artful craft performed under cruel conditions. Relief workers assured ER that a garment code for Puerto Rico would be established, with minimum-wage provisions. It would abolish home work by creating municipal workrooms.

ER saw no reason for any such expectation, and nobody had asked the women if they would prefer municipal workrooms. While her expressions of concern pleased the liberal establishment, they sounded hollow to the rapidly growing nationalist opposition. To the Puerto Rican Nationalist Party, ER was merely the wife of "Puerto Rico's greatest oppressor." A local newspaper reported that after she visited impoverished needleworkers in the mountains, she dined on squab at the most sumptious mountaintop villa. Evidently only Puerto Rico's Senator Luis Muñoz Marín considered ER the "American conscience in Puerto Rico."

ER's last day in Puerto Rico included a visit to the university, a tour of the old Spanish town, and a private shopping spree with Hick. She returned laden with gifts, and suspected she had been recognized, but "everybody was very nice and polite."

When asked on her departure what her plans were for the reconstruction of Puerto Rico, she said: "I think the island is extraordinarily lovely. . . . It has wonderful possibilities for pleasure. . . ." When pressed on what might be done to combat malnutrition and malaria, she replied only that these matters were not her "province." Privately she made every effort to secure a measure of decency in a much-abused American colony.

Upon her return ER persuaded the president "to send down some labor people and industrialists" to see conditions for themselves. She also urged him to see the situation personally, which he did in July. After FDR toured the islands, he wrote "Dearest Babs" that the problems were as complex as she had described, and he did drive over to see "those vile slums in the water."

Hick's report to Harry Hopkins was stark: Puerto Rico was not a job for FERA. One hundred miles long and thirty-five miles wide, Puerto Rico was overpopulated and chronically undernourished. Except for the small class of colonial rulers, everybody was on minimal subsistence relief, or should have been. To curtail starvation, given the cut in funds that had already occurred, Hick recommended "more surplus commodities." Everything was needed, beginning with sanitation:

> No one could give you an adequate description of those slums. . . . Photographs won't do it, either. They don't give you the odors. Imagine a swamp, with stagnant, scum-covered, muddy water everywhere, in open ditches, pools, backed up around and under the houses. Flies swarming everywhere. Mosquitoes. Rats. . . . Put in some malaria and hookworm, and in about every other house someone with tuberculosis, coughing and spitting. . . . And remember, not a latrine in the place. No room for them. No place to dispose of garbage either. Everything dumped right out into the mud and stagnant water. . . .

In Ponce, for example, half the population of 87,000 lived in such conditions. In San Juan, the largest city (114,000), there were five such slums.

Housing was the primary problem. As on the mainland, money needed to be allotted for subsistence homesteads, farms, a resettlement program.

ER put into motion programs for new housing for the U.S. Virgin Islands and Puerto Rico—where the first new housing project was named Eleanor Roosevelt. She contacted allies in the Department of the Interior, especially Oscar Chapman, to discuss the political situation in the Virgin Islands and to promote suffrage, including women's suffrage. She also endorsed tourism and tax reduction.

According to Ruby Black, ER spent almost as much time on projects for Puerto Rico as she did on Arthurdale. She promoted ideas for reforestation, restoration, and reconstruction. The hurricanes of 1928 and 1932, which had ruined the citrus fruit, coffee, and pineapple industries, were only part of the problem. There were also chicanery and corruption. These were plantation economies, marked by race, class, and imperial violence.

Ickes convened a new Virgin Islands Advisory Council and at ER's suggestion invited Walter White to serve on it. The first meeting was held on 19 April 1934, and Chapman wrote ER that "our plans for the Islands are progressing favorably" and the housing program was under way. There would be "standard type" dwellings of two rooms and kitchen, "of concrete construction, at a cost of $525 each." By 1935 over fifty units of low-cost housing and several re-settlement homestead communities enabled small farming to flourish on the islands.

ER had traveled 6,638 miles and presented the United States with its first account of conditions in its closest island dependencies. But ER was shielded from many of the hardest political dilemmas. She never referred to the upheavals that coincided with her journey throughout the Caribbean and Central America—even though a strike had curtailed her own landing in Cuba, where a revolutionary movement had just been defeated and the liberal Grau government was replaced by the conservative rule of Carlos Mendieta, with the backing of Cuba's military chief Fulgencio Batista.

FDR had originally threatened to withhold recognition unless certain democratic conditions were met, but instead recognized the Mendieta government only five days after it had seized control. In March, while ER toured the islands, he approved a $4 million loan to the new repressive regime.

ER's visit to the Caribbean also shared headlines with the aftermath of the assassination of Nicaragua's hero General Augusto Sandino and his brother Socrates. Everybody knew that "General Somosa was primarily responsible for the killing," and still the assassins continued to enjoy "complete freedom and parade in the streets of Managua, boasting of their crime and displaying the pistol and gold teeth of Augusto and locks of Socrates' hair."

FDR supported Somosa. One of the most quoted presidential statements he ever made characterized Nicaragua's dictator: "He is a son of a bitch, but he's our son of a bitch." Every improvement ER considered regarding America's territories had to be filtered through FDR's international policies. The nature of the Good Neighbor Policy was complex and contradictory, and for many years it had nothing to do with a New Deal.

Over the years, ER persuaded friends and allies to visit the islands and see what could be done. Some invested in new industries, others promoted the tourist trade, still others found philanthropic organizations in Puerto Rico and the Virgin Islands. When Rexford Guy Tugwell was appointed governor of Puerto Rico in 1940 he introduced the reforestation programs she envisioned. But it was all sparsely funded, neocolonial.

After their trip, ER's first letter to Hick revealed that the pleasure of their time together and the excitement of shared work was frayed by Hick's growing discontent. Hick had actually been miserable in the company of her high-spirited colleagues; with them, she felt most keenly the loss of her professional life and status.

To console Hick, ER discussed the possibility of their living together and reassured her about the importance of her work with FERA:

> I believe it gets harder to let you go each time. . . . It seems as though you belonged near me, but even if we lived together we would have to separate sometimes and just now what you do is of such value to the country that we ought not complain only that doesn't make me miss you less or feel less lonely. . . . Darling, I ache for you. . . .

To a lost letter, the first of Hick's return trip south, ER replied:

> You are not childish only I get swallowed up by duties. . . . You give me so much more happiness than you realize dear for when we are together you are the "perfect companion." And I love to feel you love me just as you do & I do. . . .

In Washington, ER continued her round of daily doings; groups to see; luncheons, dinners, an occasional delight: She took several houseguests, as well as the Hopkinses, the Tugwells, and Anna and John to the opera. She sent Hick an amusing editorial by William Allen White: "Just in case you missed this choice bit!"

> These Roosevelts are born with ants in their pants and tacks in their chairs. They cannot sit still. Somewhere back of Franklin, Eleanor, and Teddy, back into the ancient line that runs past the golden age into the

realm of Mother Goose, some gay Roosevelt grandmother must have had an unfortunate but felicitous moonlight affair with a jumping jack.

ER and Hick would not see each other again until May. It seemed "so far away. . . . I wonder if always I'm not going to feel that a day is incomplete which we do not start and end together? Well, I do it on paper anyway."

Repeatedly, ER counseled Hick to discount people's emphasis on their friendship. But whenever colleagues referred to it, she felt assailed. ER noted: "I can just see how annoyed you were. . . . But it was natural. They probably think if they didn't know [then] you'd mind, if they only knew!"

Although ER courted good relations with the press, everybody in the extended Roosevelt family felt occasionally hounded and harassed. Hick hated to be named or noticed; all the Roosevelt children sought privacy and anonymity, to no avail. On 8 April, ER wrote, "F Jr has gone and done a fool thing." He had tripped a photographer, roughed him up, and broken his camera.

Most of Hick's letters from this time are lost, but on 9 April she wrote from her headquarters in New Orleans, the new and exquisite Hotel Monteleone in the French Quarter. For Hick, the real news about New Orleans was its fabulous food: She ended a long day of "gloomy conferences," for New Orleans is commercially "just a charming corpse,—with dinner at Arnaud's." It was a memorable feast with "two gin fizzes, some kind of a marvelous shrimp concoction known as shrimp Arnaud, pompano baked in a paper bag, potatoes soufflé, a pint of sauterne, crêpes suzette (I think I'll never order them anywhere else!) and black coffee. You never tasted such food! What a town for a glutton! . . ."

ER was happy in New York, but there more than anywhere her thoughts turned to a permanent situation with Hick:

> Someday we'll lead a leisurely life and write—so we can take our work with us & do all the things we want to do. Now and then we'll take Earl along because he seemed so lonely yesterday that my heart ached! Women do get along better alone than men. Even you dear, settle down to work and I drown my longings in routine but a man has something the quality of a lost animal!

While in Fort Worth, Hick lunched with Elliott and his new wife, Ruth Googins. She found Elliott more settled, more mature, "neither so hilarious nor so bitter." Ruth, she decided, was a good influence. Hick was interested that Elliott said that "the trouble with father (please don't repeat this to the President) is that he has too much of a tendency to compromise." Ruth told Hick that "Elliott adores" his mother.

While Hick toured the Southwest, ER returned to Washington in time for the final legislative battles over Washington's alley bill and emergency meetings with Walter White on the Wagner-Costigan antilynching bill. With Walter White and the NAACP, ER now turned her most urgent attention to the effort to end the race violence and lynching that had plagued the nation's history.

10: The Crusade to End Lynching

Of all the issues on ER's agenda, none was more bitter than the U.S. government's refusal to confront lynching. The ravages of the Depression and the rise of racial violence and fascism in Europe fortified white supremacists in the United States. Similarly, America's commitment to segregation and its ghastly habit of public lynching, unpunished and unopposed, emboldened Nazis in Europe. During the 1930s, the Klan regrouped, and a new generation of night riders appeared. Opposed to a New Deal for all, Southern leaders determined to retain their privileges which depended on humiliation and degradation, peonage and poverty.

There were twenty-eight lynchings in 1933, and it was clear to ER that the federal government had to take an official stance to oppose these atrocities. ER joined the NAACP's crusade to pass a federal antilynch law. Lynchings were not merely public hangings, they were community ceremonies witnessed by mobs of men, women, and children who worked themselves into bloodlust as torture and burning proceeded. They were a historically sanctioned tradition, protected by "states' rights," and local "law enforcement" agents and the "best people" in the area either participated in or condoned the event. Lynchings were as depraved a means of social control as any society had devised.

In 1934, ER joined a growing biracial movement of opposition to lynchings that called for a new day in the United States. Walter White's 2 April "Welcome Home!" letter concerning the Virgin Islands enclosed a lawyer's brief for the Wagner-Costigan bill which White hoped "you will find time in your busy life to read."

Introduced in January 1934, the bill (S.1978) called on the federal government to hold local officials accountable if they "failed to protect its citizens." Senator Robert Wagner of New York and Senator Edward Costigan of Colorado opposed America's long collaboration with mob rule. In response to the proliferation of lynchings in 1933, Wagner deplored the "shocking reversion to primitive brutality" and the community climate which "connived with mass murder."

The Wagner-Costigan bill promised "equal justice to every race, creed and individual" and would penalize the state or local government: If a lynching went unprosecuted for thirty days, federal law enforcement would intervene and charge local officials whose indifference or collusion made them responsible for the delay. They could receive a fine of up to $5,000 and/or a jail term of up to five years. In the original bill, the county in which the lynching occurred would be fined up to $10,000.

ER's alliance with Walter White intensified as they worked together to promote this legislation. Walter White, the NAACP's president, was white-skinned. With blond hair and blue eyes, he could easily have been a passing Negro rather than a Negro leader. His dedication to justice was forged during his college years at Atlanta University, when he began to investigate lynching for the NAACP. After graduation he continually risked his life by infiltrating lynch mobs on behalf of the Dyer antilynch bill of 1922. His researches resulted in his vivid book *Rope and Faggot.*

During the 1920s, a new liberal Southern movement stimulated by Will Alexander, a Methodist minister and social worker who founded the Commission on Interracial Cooperation, opposed race violence and promoted racial harmony. In May 1930, many people agreed with Will Alexander that lynching would soon become a "lost crime." But the day he made that prediction, at a Methodist church conference, another black man was hanged and burned, and in 1930 the lynching rate doubled. Alexander organized a Southern Commission on the Study of Lynching, which produced two monumental studies: Arthur Raper's *The Tragedy of Lynching* and James Chadbourn's *Lynching and the Law.* These books proved, Will Alexander declared, that lynchings "could have been prevented, and any honest, vigorous effort on the part of law enforcement officers could have found those who did the lynching."

The studies confirmed Ida B. Wells's 1892 analysis: Greed, not woman's honor, was behind most lynchings. Now, Alexander thought they "had stripped lynching of its last shred of respectability."

Insulted to be excluded from Will Alexander's Southern Commission on the Study of Lynching, Southern white women, led by Jessie Daniel Ames, a prominent Texas suffragist and director of Women's Work for the Commission on Interracial Cooperation, called a meeting on 1 November 1930 to repudiate the connection between lynching and the "honor" of Southern women.

Ames's new Association of Southern Women for the Prevention of Lynching resolved:

[Lynching] is an indefensible crime, destructive of all principles of government, hateful and hostile to every ideal of religion and humanity, debasing and degrading to every person involved. . . .

It brutalizes the community where it occurs, including the women and children who frequently witness its orgies. . . . It brings contempt upon America as the only country where such crimes occur, discredits our civilization, and discounts the Christian religion around the globe. . . .

Thousands of white Southern women joined the movement against lynching, which black women had pioneered since Ida B. Wells's lonely campaign generated the NAACP's activities in 1910 and the Women Anti-Lynch Crusaders of 1922.

Jessie Daniel Ames believed that Southern women needed to know their sheriffs and marshals. They needed to know the men under the pillowcases: She intended "to reach the . . . the wives and mothers of the men who lynched. . . ."

But she refused to participate in a congressional campaign. Ames told her biographer Jacquelyn Dowd Hall that she did not believe Southern women "would have gone along with us if we had endorsed a federal anti-lynching bill. They'd say we were following the Yankees and doors would have been closed to us."

ER admired Jessie Daniel Ames's commitment to education and protest; was impressed by her forceful publications. But in 1934 ER believed that federal legislation was needed, and she made several attempts to persuade Ames to join the effort.

After her first meeting with Ames, ER spoke with White, who was impatient with Ames's tired arguments. He agreed with her opposition to the $10,000 community fine because it would cause hardship and intensify opposition; it should be lowered. But he could not understand her "fear that anything done to stop lynching may increase lynching. The plight of the Negro in the areas where lynchings are most frequent is so terrible that it could hardly be worse." In addition, White concluded, violent groups were being refortified all over the country, including the Ku Klux Klan, "Nazi, Fascist, and other reactionary groups, who are so bitterly fighting the President's recovery program."

ER then invited Ames to lunch on 15 April. Ames had begun to realize she was increasingly isolated when state leaders of her own organization called for support of the legislation. Also, on 13 March 1934, 1,000 women representing 250,000 members voted unanimously at the Southern Methodist Woman's Missionary Council convention meeting in Birmingham, Alabama, to endorse Costigan-Wagner. Ames left uncertain, and ER wrote again on 20 April to persuade her to endorse the legislation.

The real urgency, White repeatedly wrote ER, was to get the president to speak out for the bill. Held up by a small group of Southern senators, it had popular support and a congressional majority. It could be brought up before adjournment—but only if FDR supported it. Every time he requested a meeting with the president, McIntyre told him the president was too busy.

FDR's refusal to speak out on lynching had been a matter of bitter observation even before the bill was introduced. In the autumn of 1933 he was asked at several press conferences to comment on three lynchings that occurred within weeks of each other. Each time, he replied only: No comment.

How, the *Philadelphia Tribune* editorialized in October 1933, could the president of the United States receive an honorary degree from Washington College in Chestertown, Maryland, without saying a word about the lynching that had occurred only hours before in Princess Anne County on Maryland's Eastern Shore?

The reference was to what *The New York Times* called "the wildest lynching orgy in history." On 18 October 1933, "a frenzied mob of 3,000 men, women, and children . . . overpowered 50 state troopers" to remove a prisoner from his cell. George Armwood, twenty-four, was accused of attacking an aged white woman. He was stripped naked, tortured, and hung. Then his body was dragged "half a mile on Main Street to a blazing pile in the centre of the thoroughfare." Although local officials made an effort to protect him, the mob "seemed crazed."

In November, during a concerted effort to get the state of Maryland to respond to Armwood's lynching, the NAACP called upon FDR to comment. Finally, after a California mob seized two white men out of a San Jose jail and hanged them, FDR publicly deplored "lynch law" as "a vile form of collective murder." On 6 December 1933 on a nationally broadcast radio address to commemorate the twenty-fifth anniversary of the Federal Council of Churches of Christ, FDR protested those in "high places or low who condone lynch law."

Walter White telegraphed that "12 million Negroes" applauded FDR's words. But the president would say nothing about the Costigan-Wagner anti-lynch bill, endorsed by long lists of mayors, governors, clergy, journalists, writers, artists, and college presidents as well as the National Council of Jewish Women, the YWCA, the Women's International League for Peace and Freedom, the ACLU, the Writer's League Against Lynching, and other organizations representing millions of Americans.

By April, White counted fifty-two Senate votes in favor and thirty opposed. He believed the bill would pass, if only it was brought out of committee and put to a vote. This time, White insisted, everything was in place: The bill's timing was perfect; Southerners who could not vote for it had indicated they would absent themselves. FDR had only to support it.

White feared that "failure to pass the bill will result in a serious increase in the number of lynchings." It was palpable in California, and across the South: A "mob spirit" was "now pent up not only against Negroes but against other minority groups."

ER wrote to White on 2 May:

> The President talked to me rather at length today about the lynching bill. As I do not think you will agree with everything that he thinks, I would like an opportunity of telling you about it, and I would also like you to talk to the President if you feel you want to.

She invited him to the White House for tea the following Sunday, 7 May. Sara Delano Roosevelt joined ER and White, and they had a long conversation. FDR had not yet returned from his afternoon's sail on the Potomac when White arrived. After the president finally joined them, he proceeded to banter until ER turned insistently to the subject at hand.

FDR was blunt: "Joe Robinson [Senate majority leader, from Arkansas] tells me the bill is unconstitutional." In addition, there was the threat of filibuster.

In rebuttal to each one of FDR's points, White presented dramatic and specific facts.

The president turned sharply: "Somebody's been priming you. Was it my wife?"

He turned to ER: Had she coached Mr. White?

ER suggested they continue the discussion.

FDR turned to his mother: "Well, at least I know you'll be on my side."

But SDR "shook her head." No, his mother agreed with Mr. White.

FDR "roared with laughter and confessed defeat." Walter White left the White House feeling optimistic.

But FDR still did nothing on behalf of the bill, and firmly stated he would not "challenge the Southern leadership of his party":

> I did not choose the tools with which I must work. . . . The Southerners by reason of the seniority rule . . . are chairmen or occupy strategic places on most of the Senate and House committees. If I come out for the anti-lynching bill now, they will block every bill [needed] to keep America from collapsing.

FDR did not exaggerate. The powerful opposition the administration faced was highlighted almost daily in long reports Hick sent Hopkins and ER from her second tour of the South, now into the Southwest—from Alabama and Louisiana into Texas, New Mexico, and Arizona. After FDR abruptly cancelled CWA because of Southern and conservative opposition on 1 April 1934, the relief situation worsened, and she was plunged into gloom. The

Depression intensified until federal work efforts were restored by WPA in 1935.

Hick wrote from North Carolina: "Sometimes I think the white people in the South would be perfectly happy if we'd take over the job of feeding all the Negroes just enough to keep them from starving in droves and cluttering up the streets and alleys with their dead bodies!"

On 11 April, Hick sent ER her report from Houston: "At no time previously, since taking this job, have I been quite so discouraged as I am tonight. Texas is a Godawful mess." Relief funds were exhausted, and the politics of the local administration and the state relief commission were scandalous: "God help the unemployed."

Relief in Houston "is just a joke. A case worker in charge of single women told me tonight that she had orders today to cut their weekly food allowance down to 39 CENTS! They've been getting less than 50 cents a week for some weeks. . . ."

Hick was particularly dismayed by the attitude of industrialists who dominated Texas's economy, especially oil drilling manufacturers. They told her at lunch their business was actually thriving, and they needed more workers. But they could not "take on any more untrained men. . . . 'It costs too much.' "

And that, Hick stormed, when "the relief load is 12,500 families with applications coming in at the rate of 1,100 a week. . . .

"Don't you see? Those babies are thinking in terms of 1929 profit. Why, they'll let orders go, dammit, before they'll permit their cost of production to go up and cut into their profit. Now, if that's following the spirit of the New Deal, I'll eat my hat. . . ."

Hick had no idea where it would all end. The prospects everywhere were tragic. She had dinner with several social workers who handled "unattached people, including single women." They told her that most of the young women "supplement their relief by having lovers or practicing prostitution." One night a male social worker put on old clothes and went through "the transient set-up, to see how the transients were treated. Several girls solicited him as he walked along the streets. To one of them he said:

'I can't. I have no money.'

'Oh, that's all right,' she said wearily, *'It only costs a dime.'* "

As Hick wandered about in search of some usable solutions, she slid back into her populist, racist views. She had met a "retired capitalist," the local chair of Houston's relief funds. He liked what he saw in his recent visit to Italy, "believes in Fascism," and concluded, "If Roosevelt were actually a dictator, we might get somewhere. . . ."

Hick was impressed. "Honestly," she decided, "If I were 20 years younger and weighed 75 pounds less, I think I'd start out to be the Joan of Arc of the Fascist movement in the United States."

Hick then had second thoughts; perhaps "Russia is better off."

> If we have to have a dictator, I personally would prefer Roosevelt. . . . I wonder if his best chance wouldn't be to go completely red and get it that way. Anyway, the 'fat boys' aren't going to play ball with him. Not on any voluntary basis.

Disturbed by Hick's ode to dictatorship, ER wrote that she would not show her "gloomy" report to FDR and hoped "somewhere you find things more cheerful."

A fervent democrat, ER was not amused by casual references to fascism and communism, and especially resented all discussion of FDR as a benevolent or potential dictator. ER was aggravated by Hick's reports from her second tour of the South. Renewed serenades to white supremacy, they reveal the depth of America's racial quagmire during the 1930s. While ER met and worked with Walter White in Washington, Hick sent reports from Alabama and Louisiana that contradicted everything ER believed in.

Unemployed professionals and white-collar workers failed to get the benefits due them while unionists were demanding more than their share and Negroes were devouring all available relief funds.

Hick had two suggestions: Create separate intake centers for white-collar workers so that they could get the benefits they needed and still retain their pride, and take most Negroes off relief. Hick's racialist conclusion was based on what she was told by caseworkers:

> In New Orleans, for instance, EIGHTY-FIVE PER CENT of the load is Negro! . . . There isn't much doubt in my own mind that thousands of those Negroes are living much better on relief than they ever did while they were working. You hear the same stories over and over again—Negroes quitting their jobs or refusing to work because they can get on relief. Perhaps only half the stories are true, but that's bad enough. And God knows the wages they receive are low, and that their standards of living ought to be raised. But God knows our money is limited, too. . . . If we were not carrying so many Negroes, I wonder if perhaps we couldn't solve the white collar problem . . .

White-collar workers needed to pay higher rents; their suits cost more than overalls. She was adamant; it was obvious: Whites needed money; blacks could do without. And "the more people we carry who really could manage to subsist . . . the less adequate will be our relief for the people who really have to have it."

Hick repeated that solution in her reports from Texas, Arizona, and New Mexico—where Indians and Mexicans dominated the relief rolls. In El Paso, 60 percent of the relief load was Mexican, and half were not U.S. citizens. Relief "is too attractive to thousands of Mexicans and Negroes who might be able to get along without it," while whites over forty-five would "*never* get their jobs back. They're our babies. And what are we going to do with them? . . . I'm talking about white people now." People like herself, stranded women and men, single or married, were in trouble.

Hick's screeds from the South galvanized ER. They coincided with her most vigorous efforts to build an antiracist movement, ensure relief equity, and achieve an antilynch law.

ER never allowed political differences to tear a relationship. But these differences pierced to the center of her political soul. One can only wonder why Hick sent ER messages so aggressively steeped in racialist bigotry, knowing how hard ER worked to change just such views and put issues of racial justice on the national agenda.

Since she knew it would aggrieve ER, perhaps her reports veiled other issues and emotions. When she told ER she wanted to return to her own work, become a foreign correspondent, and feared that ER was sorry they had ever met, ER replied: "No, I am *always* glad you were assigned to me in 1932," and she did not enjoy Hick's new career fantasy. "Europe and Peking" might well be "easier and pleasanter but you are seeing our own country in a unique way and . . . the rest of the world will perhaps come later!"

ER did not want their differences to end their relationship, and would more fully address Hick's attitudes when she had more time.

At the moment, she was preoccupied by Crystal Bird Fauset's new project. A member of the AFSC's Committee on Race Relations, Fauset returned to Philadelphia "deeply moved by our conversation." She thanked ER for giving "so generously of your time; and your interest, not only in the Institute but in the whole racial situation. . . ."

ER had promised to help finance and promote a summer seminar at the AFSC's Interracial Institute, and she quickly followed up with letters to friends. She wrote George Foster Peabody, president and treasurer of Yaddo, the writing colony, and a supporter of Warm Springs and other Roosevelt interests, for suggestions. She appealed to Vincent Astor, and sent a blunt request to Henry Morgenthau, Sr.:

> Dear Uncle Henry: Will you do me a favor and see Crystal Bird Fauset? She wants some help in getting up an interracial institute for the better understanding of the Negro problems. I do think it is important. . . .

Both Morgenthau and Vincent Astor offered to meet with Fauset; Peabody enlisted others and wrote ER: "I must say Bravo! You are splendid!"

ER presented her first forceful public speech against discrimination on Friday morning, 11 May 1934. She told the National Conference on Fundamental Problems in the Education of Negroes, meeting in Washington: "I noticed in the papers this morning the figures given of the cost in certain states per capita for the education of a colored child and of a white child, and I could not help but think ... how stupid we are. ..." Since democracy depends above all on an educated citizenry, a literate, informed, and concerned people, "we should really bend our energies ... to giving to children the opportunity to develop their gifts, whatever they may be, to the best that is in them. ..."

It was, for ER, a matter of self-interest and national preservation:

> There are many people in this country, many white people, who have not had the opportunity for education ... and there are also many Negro people who have not had the opportunity. ... Both these conditions should be remedied and the same opportunities should be accorded to every child regardless of race or creed. ...
>
> [You] can have no part of your population beaten down and expect the rest of the country not to feel the effects from the big groups that are underprivileged. ...

The federal government intended to help in the crisis; but this issue was chronic, because there were those who considered education "a menace." Some believed "it was better not to educate people to want more than they were getting."

In this speech, ER countered virtually every word Hick had sent to her over the past month:

> To deny any part of a population the opportunities for more enjoyment in life, for higher aspirations is a menace to the nation as a whole. There has been too much concentrating wealth, and even if it means that some of us have got to learn to be a little more unselfish about sharing what we have than we have been in the past, we must realize that it will profit us all in the long run.

ER was adamant, and optimistic:

> I think the day of selfishness is over; the day of really working together has come, and we must learn to work together, all of us, regardless of race or creed or color; we must wipe out, wherever we find it, any feeling ... of intolerance, of belief that any one group can go ahead alone. We go ahead together or we go down together. ...

ER's dramatic call for universal education and equality avoided the issue of segregation. But the group of educators, university scholars, and public school teachers she addressed that day came from every part of the country to demand a new deal for all children, and for the first time they officially condemned segregation.

Sponsored by the U. S. Office of Education, the conference resolved: "Enforced segregation, whether by law or local pressure in education as in the general life of the people is undemocratic."

According to Harvard Sitkoff, there was no opposition, and historian Howard K. Beale argued that separate schools were inimical to black students' "incentive, self-pride and esteem." They "stigmatize the Negro and give his children a sense of inferiority and the white man's children a feeling of superiority which can never be outgrown in later life."

ER's rallying cry "We go ahead together or we go down together," in the context of that national conference, encouraged the civil rights movement that began to blossom during the 1930s. Her May 1934 address was broadcast nationally over the NBC network, and published in the *Journal of Negro Education*. It inspired activists in Washington and throughout the country. "Certainly," Sitkoff concluded, "no individual did more to alter the relationship between the New Deal and the cause of civil rights."

On education, ER worked with John W. Studebaker, U.S. commissioner of education, Aubrey Williams and Hilda Smith, who shared ER's enthusiasm for the creation of a national youth program, adult education projects, equal opportunity from nursery schools to parent-education programs, and federal aid to education. But in the South, federal support for education was actually rejected by state and local officials. Nevertheless, in 1934, thirty-three states accepted federal funds to keep rural elementary and high schools open and to pay teachers work relief wages where all school funds and credits had been "exhausted."

In opposition to Hick's suggestion that blacks be eliminated from the relief effort, Aubrey Williams assured ER that all state relief administrators and school officers received an order which covered "the essential points referred to in Mrs. Roosevelt's memorandum" concerned with "complete equity."

> Since in proportion to population unemployment among Negroes is equal to, if not even greater than, unemployment among other groups, and since educational opportunities for Negroes are notably inadequate, equity demands that educational relief to Negroes be at least at the level of their percentage of the population in each state. . . .

Ironically, ER's 11 May address coincided with the start of Hick's two-week visit. ER wrote that she was to broadcast on Friday between ten-thirty and eleven-thirty, the day Hick was expected. Without mentioning the subject, she asked Hick to arrange her schedule with that hour in mind, "for I couldn't bear not meeting you."

There is no record of their conversations after Hick heard ER publicly repudiate everything she had written from Louisiana and the Southwest. But the day Hick left, ER wrote to apologize for their "bad times." ER's dismay and anger evidently exploded and she now promised "to try to keep on an even keel."

> Hick dearest, I know how you felt today, you couldn't let go for fear of losing control and being with me was hard. . . . Darling I love you dearly and I am sorry for letting my foolish temperament make you unhappy and sorry that your temperament does bad things to you too but we'll have years of happy times so bad times will be forgotten. . . .

During the two months until their reunion in July, Hick made a determined effort to be positive. There were improvements in the Midwest, and in Dayton, Ohio, successful subsistence homesteads were under way. ER was relieved that Hick sounded "so cheerful" and had finally found "this hopeful angle." "Dear for your sake as much as mine we must try to keep happy together and you simply must not get so emotionally tired and worn out. . . ."

But there was one more issue upon which ER wanted to take Hick "to task." More than once she had ignored "that phrase" Hick used so often to compliment intelligent women: "She had the mind of a man." Hick had used it once too often. Now, ER wrote, she never wanted to hear it again: "Why, can't a woman think, be practical and a good business woman and still have a mind of her own?"

During the last days of May, ER traveled to West Virginia with Elinor Morgenthau. They visited Alderson Prison for women, where the rehabilitation program seemed splendid, and Dr. Mary Harris "is a wonder." ER and Elinor Morgenthau visited Alderson annually, and supported the innovative programs that sought to return the women, many of whom had "not only a husband but a large number of children," to their families with both psychological and work skills.

Concerned about prison reform, ER visited them regularly. Once she left the White House very early in the morning and failed to tell FDR that she would be gone. When he asked Tommy where she was, ER's secretary replied: "She's in prison, Mr. President."

"I'm not surprised," FDR said, "but what for?"

ER's crusade to change America's stingy attitude toward the nation's neglected and rejected people increasingly met howls of protest. By 1934 every dollar spent, every schoolroom or new house contemplated, became part of the ongoing racial battle that drove and defined the twentieth century. But for ER and her allies, there was no turning back. There were many steps to take before people would no longer be condemned to suffer and wither. She was convinced that unless there was dignity for all, there would be security for none. White supremacy degraded the entire nation; a lynching diminished everybody's life.

In June 1934, while ER was at Arthurdale, White wrote urgent daily memos to the president to bring up the antilynching bill before adjournment. Disregard for the legislation, White lamented, "is obviously encouraging lynchers to begin their deadly work again." From South Carolina to California, lynchings had occurred; in South Carolina a grand jury had convened and every witness was sent threatening letters and crude drawings.

White was desperate: Representatives "of all races and residents of all sections . . . plead with you to act speedily and vigorously to save America from the horrors of more lynchings."

Congress adjourned on 18 June without bothering about the lynching bill. FDR had said nothing to push it along. It was a grievous loss, but ER, the NAACP, and all the bill's supporters regrouped to bring it up again in the autumn.

There was, however, one unexpected triumph: Congress finally passed the alley bill. On 6 June, ER told her press conference that she "suggested to the President" he invite Charlotte Everett Hopkins to the bill's signing, "and the pen used be given to her." On 12 June 1934, in the presence of her longtime colleagues, FDR complimented Mrs. Hopkins and celebrated a law that he hoped would make "Washington a model city" and serve "a great purpose." FDR also said the $500,000 revolving fund promised in the legislation "was by no means sufficient" and suggested the commissioners turn to Harold Ickes's PWA for additional support.

Charlotte Everett Hopkins said that the "worst thing we've had to fight has been indifference." Most people in Washington "don't know we have care." She hoped the new law would change that. It was her birthday month; she was eighty-three, grateful to see this day.

ER was at Arthurdale for the official opening ceremonies on 12 June, which coincided with the signing of the alley dwelling bill. Her two victories filled her with pride and renewed energy.

For all their difficulties over Arthurdale, ER and Ickes worked harmoniously on Washington housing—and Ickes asked ER not only to remain honorary chair of the Washington committee but also to become an official adviser.

ER was "very glad to accept" and for many years led that small group of Washington civic leaders initially led by Charlotte Hopkins, including FDR's

Uncle Frederic Delano and John Ihlder, who was named executive of the new Alley Dwelling Authority. The chief task of ER's Washington housing committee was to lobby for the construction of decent housing to replace the alleys, so as to prevent homelessness, displacement, Negro removal. It would be years before adequate housing was built and, as at Arthurdale, the purchase of every tree, kitchen amenity, and indoor toilet was embattled. ER participated in the ongoing fight item by item.

11: Private Friendship, Public Time

ER spent much of June at Hyde Park, in an unusually contemplative mood. As her train ran alongside the Hudson, ER reflected on the splendor of that wide rolling river and the countryside she knew so well. "I guess it is bred in me to love it." She had recently attended a conference on aging, which caused her to consider her own future, and wrote Hick: "It is sad to be helpless and poor or old, isn't it? I hope you and I together have enough to make it gracious and attractive!"

The key to ER's politics was her ability to empathize with the poorest, loneliest, most needful people in every circumstance. Her ethic was simple: She wanted to see the best she could imagine for herself and her loved ones made available to everyone. But ER was no longer certain what she wanted for herself.

As she worked in her garden at Val-Kill, the home she had shared with Nancy Cook and Marion Dickerman since 1925, it seemed no longer to serve her needs. Increasingly she felt confined, and she disliked the emotional tension between her old and new friends:

> I've been wondering the last few days what I really want for my declining years. I could completely take over the cottage at Campobello and make that the place to turn to when I want to be "at home" but it is far away not only for me but for my friends and quite out of the question for winter. Shall I build a cottage at Hyde Park? Perhaps I won't ever use it but I could lend it to people.

ER sent Hick a rose from Val-Kill, and wondered "if any of the sweetness of this little favorite rose of mine will linger by the time it reaches you? Everything at the cottage was a lovely sight in full bloom," and "I wanted you to see it with me."

In a pensive nostalgic mood, ER turned her thoughts to "Franklin's future." They had a lovely sunlit day: As she drove with her husband of almost thirty years along roads they both loved, ER hoped that "Franklin has a few years here, he would really enjoy it." Despite all the routine tensions he had with his mother, ER believed "he would enjoy it even with Mama here."

ER felt protective of FDR, but also angry and wistful:

> I kept thinking of the mess we had made of our young lives here and how strange it was that after all these years I came here as indifferent and uninterested as a stranger and I doubt if any child has any feeling about it because nothing has ever been his or her own here. It is a pity one cannot live one's life over again but at least one can try to keep one's children from making the same mistakes and if you cannot help them much financially one can at least leave them free!

ER did not give "vent to these thoughts so F doesn't have such a bad time!" They seemed in fact never to discuss the complicated emotions that often surfaced unexpectedly out of their past. ER's memories of bitter moments and profound hurt remained forever a veil between them.

The big house was crowded with Astors, Morgans, Molly Dewson, Nancy Cook, children and grandchildren. ER swam, relaxed; and spent an hour with Mama:

> She is unhappy & I see why and yet I feel so strongly she brought it all on herself but she can't help it for she just can't understand. She'll be 80 in September and I must make an effort to make it a happy day for her. I've been such an unsatisfactory daughter-in-law!

ER's uncharacteristic self-reproach was usually eclipsed by her deeper resentment of her mother-in-law, and her enduring dismay that her husband had never chosen to leave his mother's domain. She never understood her husband's refusal to build his own nest, to create for himself and his family his own space apart from his mother. There was, of course, Warm Springs, but that was his home apart from his family—into which she fit only on a slant. ER's feelings about her mother-in-law were bound up in her even more complicated feelings about her husband.

SDR had in fact changed profoundly to accommodate ER's public interests and her son's career. Always publicly loyal, on some issues she was one of ER's best allies. But ER never felt that room had actually been made for her at SDR's hearth, nor in her heart. SDR was contemptuous of ER's brother Hall and his children. She even treated his nine-year-old daughter, Eleanor, meanly: swirled her around, then pushed her away. "So this is Hall's daughter," and never said a word to the girl.*

---

*When asked if SDR had been treated too harshly by history, ER II said she was always cold to ER and her family, mean and cold. They never became kin.

SDR dominated her homes, and the family finances. Above all, she sought to control her grandchildren and direct their interests. Over the years she had bypassed ER's concerns, sabotaged her efforts at discipline, ignored her feelings. ER felt a transgressor at home—in homes that were always her mother-in-law's homes. Whenever anything went right, SDR took all the credit; whenever anything went wrong, she blamed ER.

Concerning the children's divorces, she was accusatory, judgmental, harsh. ER bore the brunt of her disapproval, and it made her feel an outsider in a land of strangers.

ER did not dwell long in that land; she had other spaces for escape, and friends for warm sustenance. But each family situation that concerned her husband, his mother, their children, pressed upon her heart, flattened her mind and spirit as she struggled to balance her feelings and be a good and helpful parent.

As ER contemplated her life and the future in June 1934, her thoughts turned to her increasingly unsettled relationship with Hick. She prepared for their July holiday with care, and considered her responsibility for their current tensions.

When Hick entered the swift currents of ER's social and private whirl, she anticipated private islands of time reserved for her alone. ER initially encouraged that expectation and gave Hick reason to believe that she was the First Lady's First Friend.

But their relationship had become an emotional roller-coaster. Because ER preserved their correspondence, we can follow the arc of love and longing, ardor and disappointment detailed by their letters, which wove a paper tapestry from September 1933 to the summer of 1934.

Unwilling to keep a diary, as Hick suggested, ER agreed to detail her day for the historical record—and for Hick who intended to write her biography. When Emma Bugbee asked about "doing a book on me," ER "was quite frank and told her I wouldn't want one now, and I had promised to work with you on it, and because I couldn't keep a diary, I was sending you daily doings for future reference. She was very nice about it and said she quite understood."

ER felt free to complain to Hick, to confide in her; and only in her surviving letters to Hick do we have a record of her moods alongside moments of vast historical import.

On 17 November 1933, for example, Russia was formally recognized and Henry Morgenthau was sworn in as Secretary of the Treasury, to replace the ailing William Woodin. But ER considered it a "fruitless day," because the festivities interfered with her ride: "I started to ride & then Litvinov was late & Henry Morgenthau wanted a ceremony," and by then it was noon "and too late to ride."

But "Russia is recognized," and William Bullitt was selected and soon "goes as Ambassador. I wonder if that is why FDR has been so content to let Missy play with him! She'll have another embassy to visit next summer anyway! I hope Henry will do well in the Treasury, it is a big responsibility."

On another occasion ER sent Hick a note about the surprising hurdles women faced, often in their own homes:

> I thought the enclosed might amuse you. It is a letter from Mama to FDR:
>
> "Dont let all the women pester you about their pet things and affairs in the north and west! I do think *some* things and ideas are over-done, and I would always consider a really good and intelligent *man's* opinion first. . . . Your father used to say: 'Most women go off half cocked and have neither *logic* nor justice.' *You* have *both*. Ever your —Mummy."

FDR was evidently also amused by his mother's letter, which he handed over to his wife

ER rarely acknowledged feeling hurt or insulted and fled from moments of solitude and reflection. She filled her time with mundane chores and details. They forestalled depression, and relaxed her mind. Each month she paid her own bills and balanced her own checkbooks. By 1934 she had five checkbooks, and she balanced each separate account, which gave her some semblance of regular control over her increasingly complicated life. ER confided her feat to Bess Furman, who considered it "incredible":

> 1. Washington house; 2. New York house; 3. Washington personal check book; 4. New York personal check book; 5. "The account of what I earn." She further differentiated these [accounts] by signing her name a different way in each. And they always all came out to the penny.

ER bragged to Hick that she balanced all her books on the train between New York and Baltimore. This was accomplished after a whirlwind day in New York, where she "bought Louis some clothes, started my [graduate Todhunter] class, spoke at the Junior League lunch, tried on two dresses at Milgrim's, was at my [Val-Kill] furniture sale for an hour . . . 5 to 6:30 spent with Cousin Susie. Then went and dined with Louis. Nan is happy because in two days we've sold $3,000 worth of stuff. . . ."

On return to Washington that night:

> [There were] six for tea and saw my chicks [grandchildren Sistie and Buzzie] to say good night . . . dressed, and had Molly Dewson to dine. She stayed till 10, and I longed to work, but since she left I've finished my checks, and signed all the mail. . . .

Missy has a head cold and went to bed before dinner, and Franklin is worried about her. We have had a little flurry with Gus [Gennerich, FDR's bodyguard]. His feelings were hurt but all is well again. I often wonder why people want to make each other unhappy. . . .

Hick, darling: FDR finds your reports most interesting. . . . I used your stories yesterday and shall again today.

Whenever Hick was despondent, and doubted the value of her work, ER reassured her:

What a picture you can paint! I nearly wept. If ever under any circumstances you give up writing, I'll flay you, whether I'm here in the flesh or flay you from some other world! You feel too much to live constantly in the midst of misery, and in the meantime nothing is going to happen to me, and, if you didn't follow me around a little, I'd have to start following you, and that would be much harder!

During the holiday season, ER resigned herself to public gossip about her children's marital crises. ER supported her daughter's divorce and Anna's new relationship with journalist John Boettiger. But she was unsettled when Louis Howe told her that during a meeting with a group of reporters one of them "casually mentioned . . . 'now that John B has his divorce I supposed we'll soon hear of Mrs. Dall's getting hers!' "

ER wrote Hick: "One cannot hide things in this world can one? How lucky you are not a man!"

No matter how much she longed for Hick, ER enjoyed her other friendships. She spent a weekend with Earl Miller and Tiny Chaney to help Earl move into his new house. "I love doing houses even someone else's." They worked until "one AM, but slept well. Tiny and I in the big double bed which was comfortable . . . only I wished it was you. Darling I'm beginning to be very impatient."

Hick too was impatient. She ended a sixteen-page report, lonely and gloomy in Iowa, with one triumphant thought: "Darling only 18 more days!"

ER promised to make time for a happy reunion in Washington. "There may be people staying here so I think one night anyway we'll stay away as otherwise we might have to be polite."

In the Midwest, Hick's letters were filled with worry that colleagues speculated about their friendship. But ER was sanguine: "Dear one, and so you think they gossip about us, well they must at least think we stand separations rather well! I am always so much more optimistic than you are. I suppose because I care so little what 'they' say! . . ."

On 28 November Hick wrote ER as she traveled for her Thanksgiving holiday to Minnesota. Her ten-page letter included the case of a seventy-year-old couple, a carpenter and his wife, who insisted that they would "rather starve than be on relief." And they were starving. "Now will you please tell me," Hick wrote, "what in the world one is going to do about cases like these."

It was for Hick a lonely Thanksgiving. "I suppose you arrived in Warm Springs today. Well I probably wouldn't be very happy there anyway. Oh—I guess I'm probably a little jealous. Forgive me. . . ." ER confided that she had a secret "little longing that FDR might think I'd like you to be here and insist on your coming to report to him. You know how one dreams? . . ."

They spoke several times on the telephone that weekend, and Hick continued to hear gossip about their friendship, but ER wrote: "Darling I know they bother you to death because you are my friend," but someday "I'll be back in obscurity again and then no one will care except ourselves!"

Despite her divided heart, ER enjoyed the communal Thanksgivings at Warm Springs. She presided with FDR at the festive dinner for children and adults with polio in the rehabilitation program. The amazing spirit and good cheer which radiated from FDR to the smallest child energized the entire community and made every challenge seem possible.

The weekend was relaxed and friend-filled. Nancy Cook busied herself taking photos; ER walked in the woods with Ruby Black and Marion Dickerman, and rode each day. Still, she missed Hick: "I love you tenderly and deeply and oh! I want you to have a happy life. To be sure I'm selfish enough to want it to be near me but we wouldn't either of us be happy otherwise would we?"

From somewhere in timber country, Minnesota, Hick wrote:

> Not a bad hotel and one day nearer you. Only 8 more days. 24 hours from now it will be only 7 more—just a week.
>
> I've been trying today to bring back your face to remember just *how* you look! Funny how even the dearest face will fade away in time. Most clearly I remember your eyes, with a kind of teasing smile in them, and the feeling of that soft spot just northeast of the corner of your mouth against my lips. I wonder what you will do when we meet, what we'll say. Well, I'm rather proud of us, aren't you? I think we've done rather well.

Hick felt better in Minnesota: The countryside was beautiful, people fascinating, and the Republicans "completely disorganized." She thought that "the President would have got a kick out of" the icy, slippery road she drove on that day through second-growth pines to observe a state reforestation program. "We drove for miles" sliding on "ice almost as bad as the time you and I drove down to New York from Hyde Park the Sunday before March 4th. Remember?" The president would have loved the dangerous ride, and the grand work the CCC boys had done in the area.

After her adventure, Hick relaxed in the hotel lobby before the president's speech and listened to the conversations all over the room, filled with high regard and the "popularity of FDR." As she considered the changes actually under way, Hick contemplated ER's role, and her own: "The Woman's Occupational Bureau, for instance. . . . We *do* things together don't we? & it's fun." Hick never got much credit for her ideas, relating to women especially, many of which ER popularized.

After FDR's speech, Hick added:

> Well, he came through marvelously and I think it was about the best speech I ever heard him make. You'd have got a kick, if you could have seen the crowd so quiet and attentive.
>
> You know—it is a rather thrilling experience to hear the president of the U.S. on the radio in the lobby of a hotel in Bemidji, Minnesota. Especially when he makes a speech like the one we just heard. . . . Please congratulate him for me.*
>
> Goodnight, dear one. I want to put my arms around you and kiss you at the corner of your mouth. And in a little more than a week now—I shall!

Hick's Minnesota rhapsody included an amusing encounter in Hibbing:

> My dear I'm feeling confused and indignant. An elevator boy just said to me: "Are you a girl scout leader?" "No," [I replied] but "why do you ask?" "Because of your uniform," he explained:
>
> I'm wearing that old dark grey skirt—the one you never liked—with a grey sweater and to soften the neckline a little, I wear the dark red Liberty scarf of mine knotted about the throat. That costume, topped off by a brimmed felt slouch hat and supported by low-heeled golf shoes, oh, Lord, I wonder how many people in the farm belt these last few weeks have thought I was a girl scout leader! My very soul withers in anguish. . . .

Throughout December, ER's letters to Hick grew more ardent, and she concluded her letter of 6 December with a stunning promise: "I love you and when this is over I'm going to think of nothing else!"

As Hick prepared for their reunion, she confessed: "You are going to be shocked when you see me. I should be returning to you wan and thin from having lived on a diabetic diet." That was, alas, not the case:

> Just you and Dr. McIntire try to live on green vegetables and fruit,

---

*FDR's 6 December, 1933 speech to the Federated Council of Churches, historic for its reference to lynching as a crime, was broadcast nationally: "From the bottom of my heart I believe that this beloved country of ours is entering upon a time of great gain. That gain can well include a greater material prosperity if we take care that it is a prosperity for a hundred and twenty million human beings and not a prosperity for the top of the pyramid alone. . . . It can be a prosperity built on spiritual and social values rather than on special privilege and special power. . . ."

without starch or sugar, in country hotels, where they have nothing but meat, bread, potatoes, pie and cake and see how far you'd go. . . . Besides I feel so perfectly well, and I'm living such an active life. . . . I have an appetite that would do justice to Paul Bunyan himself. . . . Ever hear of Paul Bunyan . . . he used to bite off the tops of Jack pines with his teeth! [After long days trudging through snow,] Lady, I get hungry!

To a lost letter concerning Hick's hangover ER replied: "Dear one, I never thought you were feeling badly from drinking. It never even crossed my mind. I never think of that unless it's obvious. I suppose, because it does not attract me, I never think of other women doing it!"

Hick's distressed letters and discontented outbursts had caused ER to worry about her health in general terms. She did not stop to think that a particularly unruly or upsetting letter might also be a drunken ramble. ER's level of denial was high, since even fleeting considerations of a drinking problem turned to thoughts of her childhood. Her father's erratic behavior imparted a painful emotional legacy. Especially when she was happy, in love, in a state of anticipation, fears of disappointment, betrayal, abandonment intruded. ER knew the pattern, and referred to it: "Dear one it is getting nearer and nearer and I am half afraid to be so happy. It is the way I felt as a child when I dreaded a disappointment! I love you dearly."

For all ER's promises for their reunion, she had not adjusted her unrelenting schedule. There were several stolen moments between endless rounds of obligations. The entire family and other friends had arrived for the holidays. Even times reserved exclusively for each other were preempted. Hick was on vacation, with nothing to do but wait. She spent hours alone in her West Wing room, tried to read a book, paced, gazed out over Lafayette Park.

It was puzzling: Had ER merely ignored White House demands in her nightly letters of romance and fantasy? Or was she unable to give time to herself, and so sabotaged her own good time? Had she acted like her father, and unconsciously treated lonely waiting Hick as she had been treated? Whatever the cause, ER's neglect created a stormy situation. With little she cared to do as she waited for ER's company, Hick felt like an intruder. Angry and hurt, she left for New York.

Subsequent letters reveal that ER had actually reserved only one evening for quiet time with Hick. Then, without warning, ER spent their one special evening with her distressed daughter.

After a week of telephone calls, their correspondence resumed on 23 December. Hick's abrupt departure jostled ER, who resolved to make amends:

Hick dearest. It was good to have a few minutes with you [on the phone] last night and I went to sleep saying a little prayer, 'God give me depth enough not to hurt Hick again.' Darling I know I'm not up to you in many ways but I love you dearly and I do learn sometimes. . . . Bless you and forgive me and believe me you've taught me more & meant more to me than you know and I will be thankful Christmas eve and Christmas day and every day for your well being in the world. . . .

Hick wrote Anna to explain her departure and ER wrote: "Anna read a part of your letter this morning and she said she hadn't been able to understand it and thought we must have had a fearful fight. But I told her no, you were just feeling very low." About their lost evening, ER explained the competing tugs that pulled at her heart: "Darling the love one has for one's children is different and not even Anna could be to me what you are. . . ."

Although ER regretted that Hick was not with them, the Roosevelts' first White House Christmas was filled with children and good cheer:

Dinner was jolly & then FDR read parts of the Christmas Carol & John B whispered to me it was the nicest day he ever had & he would never forget it! The young ones then went dancing. . . .

We drank a toast to absent friends whom we would like to have with us at dinner & I thought of you dear one as I proposed it. . . .

Determined to get Hick to return, ER called and then wrote:

It was good to hear your voice & you shall dine in bed & sleep all you want if you'll just stay here & be happy. Don't think I don't know what it is like to be jealous, or to want to be alone, because I know both emotions full well. . . .

No dear, you shouldn't make believe you are happy for me nor like things you don't like on my account.

ER assured Hick that once she arrived and settled in for the week everything would improve between them. And it did. Their pleasant week between Christmas and New Year's was followed by a new tone in their letters, and in their friendship. When ER no longer took Hick's presence for granted and altered her schedule, Hick became positively cheerful.

After that week together, ER had high hopes for their future: "Someday we will do lots of work together! I love you deeply, tenderly and my arms feel very empty. . . ."

The ardor of their winter correspondence lasted until their March Caribbean trip, after which Hick became depressed. Then in April and May Hick confused and rankled ER by her blustery diatribes against racial minorities on the dole. Their disagreeable May reunion, when harsh words were exchanged, was the worst time they spent together. Now, ER hoped to restore harmony with her plans for their July holiday.

FDR had declared 1934 "National Parks Year," and ER intended to take Hick to some of nature's most wondrous sights—places that had been part of her heritage since childhood, when her father and uncle spoke of their grandeur. While she kept the "itinerary" secret so there would be surprise adventures, she assured Hick that it would be an anonymous time, just the two of them far away from it all. "We must be careful this summer and keep it out of the papers when we are off together."

Hick's spirits lifted, and a playful tone reappeared in her letters:.

> And now I'm going to bed—to try to dream about you. I never do, but I always have hopes. The nearest I ever came was one night this week—I think it was the night I ate the Mexican dinner. My dream that night was that I was going to marry Earl, and your Mother-in-law was simply furious! Isn't that a honey?

Together, they planned visits with family and friends. Anna had found refuge from the press and a pleasant sanctuary for the children (Sistie and Buzzie) at the sprawling Nevada ranch home of her friends Bill and Ella Dana. There were horses to ride, and ER and Hick were welcome.

Then, Hick wanted ER to meet her former lover Ella Morse, with whom she had lived in San Francisco. Ella was the first woman who had encouraged Hick to give up her career. Worried about Hick's early diabetes, she had encouraged the thirty-two-year-old star reporter to leave her work at the *Minneapolis Tribune*, to live in comfort with her in San Francisco, travel to Europe—and write novels.

Hick loved San Francisco, and she wanted to write novels. But within several months Ella eloped with her childhood sweetheart, Roy Dickinson. Bereft, Hick journeyed to New York, where she resumed her career. Although they eventually corresponded regularly, Hick and Ella evidently had not seen each other since 1926. Now, once again in love and in a professional wilderness, Hick reconnected with Ella, and she wanted ER to meet her old friends, to know her past. ER replied with "dread" and uncertainty,

> but I know I've got to fit in gradually to your past, meet your friends and like them so there won't be closed doors between us later on. . . . Love is a queer thing, it hurts one but it gives one so much more in return!

ER was surprisingly direct about her jealous feelings. Frequently flirtatious, Hick met women in her travels who found her attractive, who squired her about, took her home for dinner, and for weekends. The names and details are lost, but ER's letters indicate that she was in no mood to entertain dalliances. When Hick confided that a new situation with yet another had emerged, ER wrote firmly: "How hard for you to have a lady who is in love in her mind with you. Well if she is in love you can tell her how to snap out of it!"

The lady was never again mentioned. Now ER was convinced their summer holiday of solitude and adventure would rekindle their relationship.

At Bill Dana's ranch near Lake Tahoe, Anna began the six-week residency required for a Nevada divorce. ER advised her daughter not to "take these days too hard. Remember even disagreeable things come to an end!"

ER was with her godmother, Cousin Susie, when newspapers headlined Anna's divorce: "This has been a long day and I am feeling very weary and so low in my mind—I could weep." Everything had gone wrong: She had car trouble, and an unpleasant visit with Elliott's former wife Betty—who was an hour late. Then Cousin Susie "made a scene and I became cold and calm." She apologized, but ER felt "somehow I never can thaw."

She missed Hick, "and would give the world to fly to you tonight."

Back in Washington for a day, ER found Hick's letters and her returned money order—which ER had sent as a gift for Hick's new car, a Plymouth convertible. ER was "glad about the car," but annoyed by the returned check: "I could spank you." ER now began to "count the days . . . what happy times we will have."

The last days of June were busy. FDR left for his tour of the Caribbean, the Panama Canal, and Hawaii, and ER completed several magazine articles, wrote radio speeches, and fulfilled an amazing array of responsibilities in order to be perfectly "free" with Hick until 26 August. In the meantime she was pleased and relieved that Hick was being comforted and cared for by her old friend Ella Morse: "I am so happy that Ellie met you and that the old companionship is there and I do hope she stays with you right along."

However delightful the visit, her time with Ella and Roy intensified Hick's insecurities. In response to a lost letter, which detailed those feelings, ER wrote:

> Yes, dear, I think you will remember that I once told you I wished you had been happy with a man or that it might still be. I rather think the lack of that relationship does create "emotional instability" but people do seem to weather it in time and who knows what the future holds. In the meantime Ellie and I will try to do a little stabilizing or at least help you to do it!

Nobody doubted in ER's circle that it was easier to be with a man in a man's world, even though her circle was composed of many women who chose a more difficult path. Women of privilege, status, and economic security, such as Esther Lape and Elizabeth Read, Nancy Cook and Marion Dickerman, were content in their individual lives and as couples. They had done better than "weather it in time." But Hick was now with Ella, who had found contentment with a man; and she felt alone, without work or status, or at least without the work that had given her an identity she was proud of. And she was in love with the First Lady, who was surrounded by her husband, her children and grandchildren, other friends, and endless obligations.

ER did not dismiss Hick's doubts and fears. It was hard to be an independent unmarried career woman without job security during the greatest depression in United States history, waiting to spend some private time with the First Lady. But ER assured her repeatedly that there was no cause for despair. They would have years of contentment in a relationship she believed would be enduring and lifelong. ER failed to appreciate the enormity of Hick's lost profession, which she minimized by assurances that she could always help find her useful work.

But Hick was apprehensive about their time together, despite ER's promise to "keep my itinerary quiet." ER became irritated, and insisted that there was nothing to worry about: "Things happen often enough, but for heaven's sake don't anticipate them!"

Hick's anxieties now extended even to ER: "Dear one, why should you feel shy and worried about seeing me, you don't feel that way about your old friends. I suppose it is just that you haven't known me long enough—well, try to feel you just saw me yesterday and we will pick up just where we left off!" Perhaps ER had dismissed from her mind how stormy and unpleasant their last meeting in May had been:

> I can't understand why you are so worried dear, why can't you just be natural? Of course we are going to have a good time together and neither of us is going to be upset.

One reason for Hick's increased worry was that ER had become during the spring of 1934 a controversial, well-known, easily recognized public figure. In the summer of 1933, ER might walk into a town and remain unknown. But her face was now seen by newspaper readers almost daily, and her voice heard in every home that had a radio. Not only had Arthurdale and her statements about race created a public stir, she had become a radio star.

In April 1934, she was approached with an offer she felt she could not refuse. It would help her advance all the causes she believed in, particularly Arthurdale: "I'm sorely tempted to take a radio contract for $3000 a week." The broadcasts would be "picked up wherever I am."

In May, ER decided to accept the controversial commercial contract for a regular six-minute broadcast offered by Johns Manville. She was criticized throughout the nation as a publicity hound who used her husband's office to make "large and easy earnings." One writer wondered how anybody might be worth $500 a minute. ER replied that indeed "no one is worth $500 a minute," but that she accepted the fee to give it away to the many people and the many causes that so desperately needed help. It was not paid to her directly, but to the American Friends Service Committee, which would spend it.

Her contract with Johns Manville was just the first among many. Selby shoes, a mattress company, even food and beverage concerns paid for her broadcasts. She was criticized but unrepentant. Her earnings financed worthy projects, and ER kept in closer touch with the American people.

In July, she began her vacation—and imagined that she might return to anonymity. From the Tennessee Valley she went to Chicago, where she toured the World's Fair with her brother Hall, and visited with John Boettiger, whose love for Anna seemed deeply genuine: "I loved seeing you in Chicago, John dear. I've grown to love you like one of my dear ones & I'm grateful beyond words for the happiness you've already given Anna & I trust you for the future."

Then she flew to Sacramento, dedicated to dodging the press and under another name—and believed she was invisible. But somebody leaked her presence on the plane, and she was greeted by an army of reporters and photographers. From the airport to the hotel, she was followed and hounded. Hick recorded the entire drama.

Having met the press corps in her hotel lobby the night before, Hick tried to outwit them. She later considered her effort "the silliest thing I ever did in my life." But she felt "really desperate" to get to Colfax and their hideaway at a friend's home without publicity. She appealed to the hotel staff for help. And they obliged:

> First they called the state police. I left my keys with the clerk, and during the night a state trooper drove my small gray convertible away and hid it.
>
> A Secret Service man accompanied him and removed my D.C. license plates, substituting California plates. He also had some Nevada and Oregon license plates, which he hid, along with mine, under the seat. Every time we crossed a state line on that trip, a Secret Service man would appear and change our license plates. Mrs. Roosevelt and I used to amuse ourselves by conjecturing what would happen to us if we were picked up for some traffic violation, and the police found four sets of license plates and a gun in our car!

Hick explained that ER had brought her gun in order to continue her target practice in the mountains. But on this trip the police remained their allies, against an invasive army of resourceful reporters.

Before they left the hotel, Hick pleaded with them, reporter to reporters: Wouldn't they give ER some private time to freshen up before their interviews? They agreed. "Looking as innocent as I could," she told them she did not know their first destination.

We left them in the lobby, took an elevator up, then another down to the rear entrance to the hotel, where we found my car, with a state trooper at the wheel. We threw our bags into the rumble seat, jumped in and started off, the state trooper driving.

Still in Sacramento, the trooper glanced into the rear-view mirror and announced:

"Sorry ladies, but they're right behind us, a whole carload of 'em."

The reporters had monitored every hotel exit. And they were hotter in pursuit after Hick's double-cross. The trooper made a dash for it, reaching speeds of seventy-seven miles an hour in Hick's new little coupe. Another trooper escorted them with his red lights flashing. But it was no use, and ER stopped the chase. They pulled off the road, and ER thanked the troopers: "You have been most kind, and we are very grateful, but I think you'd better leave us now. We'll have to find some other way out of this situation."

The press demanded ER's destination, the one question she would not answer: "I'm sorry, but I'm not going to tell you. This is my vacation, and I expect to be treated as any other tourist would be treated. I'll answer any other questions you want to ask." When they insisted, ER reached behind her seat for her knitting bag and calmly observed: "It's nice here in the shade, and I like to knit. I'm willing to sit here all day, if I have to, but I'm not going to tell you where we're going.' "

Eventually, ER persuaded the reporters to telephone their editors that there would be no story, or she would simply return East and relinquish her vacation. They drove to the next town, and ER invited them for breakfast while they put in their calls. Breakfast was pleasant, and the reporters were given permission to "lay off!"

Finally ER and Hick proceeded to Colfax, a small town north of Sacramento, where they were to spend a week near Ella and Roy in another friend's home, where nobody could find them.

ER and Hick had a "peaceful and enjoyable" time in Colfax. They dined occasionally with friends, occasionally alone; picnicked in the mountains; had "wonderful evenings," highlighted by ER's readings from the *Oxford Book of English Verse*. Hick had "never known anyone else who could read poetry as beautifully."

On 12 July ER wrote Anna the details of their "horrid" escape, and concluded with relief:

So far no one has found me here. We're in a house way off the road which belongs to a friend of Hick's who owns a T.B. sanitarium & they send us in our meals! It is up in the pines & lovely & we ought to . . . make our exit unnoticed. . . . Goodbye dear till Tuesday, I won't write again. Hick sends her best love.

After Colfax, they drove up through the Donner Pass in the High Sierras and down into Nevada to join Anna and the children at the Dana ranch. A green oasis in the desert, with its own electric plant and water pump, it bordered an Indian reservation and Pyramid Lake.

Bill and Ella Dana were fun-loving and worldly, and they became lifelong friends particularly close to Hick. ER described their home in the August issue of the *Women's Democratic News* as "a unique place on a very unique ranch ... with a most beautiful lake from which the Indians derived their livelihood as very large trout inhabit it." Called Pyramid Lake because "of the shape of some of the islands, it is also one of the three breeding places in the U.S. for penguins and I commend them to anyone as an amusing study. They are so tame on this lake that they come up to the children cavorting in the shallow water and their expressions remind me of ... an elderly wise old maid who wonders if the young are really quite sane in their gambols!"

In addition to daily swims in Pyramid Lake, ER rode Ella Dana's beautiful Palomino, Pal, while Hick rode a long-retired big gray, called Old Blue, who had to be kicked to keep awake. Hick had no desire to ride, but ER insisted that she would get very lame during the last part of their trip, which required horses, if she did not.

At some point during the week, ER finally revealed that part of their itinerary she had kept as a surprise:

They were to spend four days camping in one of nature's most magnificent cathedrals, Yosemite National Park. But Hick was amazed to read:

> "Miss Hickok will require a quiet, gentle horse, since she has not ridden for some time. ..."
> "How could you do this to me?" I asked her reproachfully.
> "Oh, you'll manage," she said comfortably.

Hick, who had actually never ridden, persevered, and put up cheerfully with ER's bullying notions of a good time. She got to enjoy Old Blue—well, at least sitting astride Old Blue while she listened to their guide, the Danas' horsetrainer, Bar Frances, a former Western "bad man" and sheriff, steeped in cowboy lore. Hick liked his company. They went out "just before sunset" and "always walked the horses, the reins hanging loose, while he taught me to roll cigarettes" and feel comfortable in a saddle.

Although ER made every effort to be unavailable, truly away on vacation, urgent business reached her. Clarence Pickett, for example, needed to transmit Arthurdale information: Elsie Clapp had arrived; there were school building delays; fifteen houses were almost ready, "and they are most attractive." All this sent on 18 July, when he knew she was on holiday.

He had tried to wire, but learned from White House receptionist Mary

Eben that ER was unreachable, hence he addressed her as "Mrs. Dana," as instructed, and sent his letter off to her hideaway at Arrowhead-D Ranch in Sutcliffe, Nevada—with a curious note: "The fact that this letter goes to you under an assumed name, I hope means that you are having complete isolation from the world and rest for a little while." Evidently, he saw nothing incongruous about his intrusion. For once ER did not reply until her trip was over, which Hick surely counted a little victory.*

From Nevada into California, ER wrote, "I drove over a very beautiful road past Mono Lake which is so highly mineralized that no fish can live in it. It may in time be somewhat changed because it is part of a development plan for the Los Angeles water supply."

Past Mono Lake, they drove over Tioga Pass into the Yosemite Park, where they left their car and met the park rangers who were to be their guides. They continued on horseback up beyond the Tuolumne Meadows "for two and a half hours, making camp at six o'clock in the evening on the edge of Young Lake in the High Sierras, 11,000 [feet] above sea level."

They set up camp at lower Young Lake, with snow-capped Ragged Peak glistening above. ER wrote: "Around the lake rose high white granite peaks and as we sat around a camp fire after our supper, the moon rose over the top of the mountain, a sight which I shall long remember for its beauty was breath taking."

Their days at Yosemite were exhilarating. They were accompanied by five "unobtrusive rangers," who served as guides and cooks, seven trail horses, and five pack mules, which carried their gear—which included a "canvas-concealed collapsible toilet and an umbrella tent." ER and Hick used the tent as a dressing room and spread their sleeping bags beyond the campsite, under the stars and pines. For ER "the first rays of morning light over the mountain peaks were almost as lovely as the moon light." From this base, "we spent several days climbing on foot and exploring on horseback and fishing for trout. . . ."

It was hot during the day, but freezing at night; "we simply could not get too many clothes and blankets." Although they had rejected a "VIP" tour, their guides were prepared for VIPs and they were made entirely comfortable. Ranger Billy Nelson was in charge of camp details, and he seemed to understand "celebrities." Famous for telling King Albert of Belgium, "You call me

*An even greater measure of her commitment to making this a perfect holiday was her stoical disregard of a painful physical ordeal: On 3 August, *The New York Times* reported that ER "underwent a surgical operation on an eye" while visiting her daughter at Pyramid Lake. Dr. Larue Robinson, an eye specialist, "removed an abscess." Called to see her on 17 July, he "performed the operation" on 21 July: "She took it like a Girl Scout, without a whimper, although it was very painful. . . ."

Billy and I'll call you King," Billy gave ER a hot-water bottle to put inside her sleeping bag. Subsequently, he rated her "first-rate like King Albert."

While ER enjoyed her vigorous day climbs, Hick found the nights "enchanting. . . . It's a wonderful experience to lie, warm and snug in a sleeping bag, high up in the mountains, and look at the stars." One of the rangers made fabulous flapjacks, and meals were memorable, especially the trout, which ER helped clean. But during the day, Hick had a grueling time. She was not an easy rider, could hardly breathe when she walked, and did not swim.

Each morning shortly after dawn she watched as ER dashed into the icy lake, which faced "a big bank of snow," and swam. She did not just plunge in and run out, she swam about. Hick jumped in only once—"and thought I'd never catch my breath again. It didn't bother her, though. Every morning those days she would take an ice cold shower or tub, as she had done since she was a child."

She continued, "Climbing mountains . . . didn't bother her either. One morning she and the Chief Forest Ranger climbed up to an elevation of some 13,000 feet. When they came down, I thought the Ranger was going to have a stroke. His face was purple." But as for ER, "You'd have thought she had come in from a stroll in Central Park!"

Hick referred to ER's fabulous day trip to a secretive, elusive lake near the base of Mount Conness which she helped stock with rainbow trout, now called Lake Roosevelt in her honor.

A scooped-out glacial basin, this long, lean, mysterious lake cannot actually be seen until virtually upon it. Above the tree line, surrounded by snow, it ripples with ice throughout the year, in an alpine world of red heather and purple lupin, mosses and magic.

It takes over three hours to reach this lake by foot from their base camp at Young Lake, up and down, fording winding Conness Creek which flows into the Tuolumne Meadows, across a forest of Larchpol pine and mountain hemlock.

With the exception of Lake Roosevelt, it is unclear precisely where ER went on her day trips out of Young Lake. One presumes she wanted to see as many of the sites John Muir introduced her Uncle Theodore to thirty years before.

After their sojourn in the high country, ER's caravan rode down to the ranger's station in the Tuolumne Meadows. They walked across the extraordinary "meadow in the sky," then motored to the Yosemite Valley, with its wondrous waterfalls: "and anything more beautiful than that valley by moonlight I have never seen."

Yosemite had special meaning for ER: She never forgot those bitter early days of her marriage, when so many of her efforts at physical activity were discouraged, or mocked—as they still were by some. Her physical stamina and courage at Yosemite were for ER a triumphant contrast to that drear day when she had so disappointed her father because she was afraid to ride her donkey down the hill in Sorrento; or the mean morning when she hesitated for just a moment and her new husband went off during their honeymoon to walk that relatively easy path up the four-thousand-foot Faloria in the Dolomites—with New York's fashionable hatmaker Kitty Gandy.

ER felt now a sense of victory over long-held taboos. She was free, unconfined, competent. A skilled horsewoman who exercised daily, she met the challenges of the High Sierra with ease, confidence, and surprising resources. Curiously, ER wrote nothing of the rough terrain, or the reality of her climbing feats across uncharted high-country mountains no CCC boys had pathed. Rather, she emphasized her failure to catch fish. But her high-seated horsemanship and long-legged gambols became the stuff of ranger legend; and Hick looked on with wonder and merely marveled.

Hick complained about nothing, and enjoyed herself as much as she could. Although bothered by the altitude, she learned to trust her gentle horse. The only "embarrassing" moment of Hick's wilderness adventure occurred on the long way down to the Tuolumne Meadows when her horse decided to play in the river: "I managed somehow to slide off and landed sitting down on the sand bar in water up to my chin, while my little friend went into the deep water and rolled!"

ER looked back to see her companion caught in the rapidly moving river, and the rangers quickly rushed to her aid. Long lectures on exercise and smoking followed.

Years later, ER wrote:

> [The days in Yosemite] were for me days of enchantment, but I was worried about Lorena Hickok. I learned that nobody who smokes a great deal and whose heart is not strong should try to camp above 10,000 feet. She more or less panted throughout the days we were there, while I climbed easily to 13,000 feet. . . .

After their camping trip, they spent a night at the luxurious Ahwanee Hotel in the valley. In the midst of dinner, Harold Ickes walked in and joined them.* Hick was undone. Her boss Hopkins and Ickes were then at the height of their feuds over New Deal projects and expenditures. Their differences were simple. Hopkins's projects were labor-intensive and intended to get the

---

*According to Ickes, ER had been with him at Hetch Hetchy (the dammed, once beautiful valley John Muir tried so hard to save, which ER never referred to) and invited Ickes to join them at dinner. "Later she went on a moonlight trip through the valley," and Ickes "went to bed early."

most possible people back to work. To build a road or housing development, Hopkins hired scores or hundreds of people with shovels and hand tools. Ickes "used what we in FERA derisively called 'the trickle-down method.'" Heavy machines built more efficiently and helped "heavy industry," which would then, presumably, rehire labor for its private needs. Nobody in Hopkins's shop believed in that method, and Hick had written reports lambasting Ickes. "It took us longer to build a road, but . . . it was just as good a road." FDR played them against each other and declared himself neutral. Everybody knew he gave Hick's reports to Ickes.

After dinner, ER was briefly called away. Hick and Ickes sat for a moment in silence on the terrace in the tranquil star-filled night. Ickes smoked his cigar, and Hick smoked her cigarette, and the cloud between them grew thick, until Ickes said: "I've been reading your reports. . . . Interestin'." Hick said, "Thank you, Mr Secretary," and prayed for ER's return.

Not another word was spoken, but Hick ranked that moment close to the worst of their trip. Another bad time was when hordes of tourists discovered them on a path to the lower Yosemite Falls, where they had paused to feed chipmunks. "We had just started to feed them when I realized that we were completely surrounded by tourists, all pointing cameras at us. Bending over to feed a chipmunk is not a very dignified position . . . and I lost my temper. We left hastily," ER all the while "trying to 'shush' me."

The absolute worst occurred on the way out of the park, when they stopped at the Mariposa Grove of giant redwoods. Awed by the majesty of the great sequoia trees, Hick felt "almost prayerful." But they were soon surrounded by tourists, and guides "who kept hurling statistics at us." "The final indignity" was when a guide named "one of those trees—which was probably a sapling when Christ walked this earth," General Sherman: "To me, it seemed positively sacrilegious. And I said so, right out loud. Of course I shouldn't have done that."

If ER was momentarily embarrassed by Hick's outburst, it evidently represented precisely her own feelings. She subsequently wrote:

> As we stood and looked at these giants of the forest and realized that they have been there from three to 4000 years and have withstood fires and storms and disease, we had a sense of time and of our own insignificance which is good for the soul and helps one to bear with fortitude the "bludgeonings of chance."

From Yosemite on 27 July, they began the long drive down to San Francisco. For Hick, that was "to be the high point" of their vacation, and she had prepared for it with as much consideration as ER had prepared for Yosemite. She chose a small, intimate hotel behind the St. Francis, where she had often stayed, "without telling the management who my companion was to be." The desk clerk and manager seemed startled when they entered. But they recovered quickly, and sent a bouquet of flowers to the room, with several letters for ER, addressed to Hick, that awaited them—including several from FDR, then anchored off Hawaii.

FDR had written regularly to keep ER informed during his cruise to Puerto Rico and the Virgin Islands, Haiti, Colombia, through the Panama Canal, and across the "broad Pacific." "The Lord knows when this will catch up with my Will o'the Wisp wife, but at least I am proceeding according to schedule."

FDR's party continued on to Colombia and the Panama Canal, where the "bitter feeling" against U.S. imperialism seemed to have waned. He was happy to be greeted by enthusiastic crowds and thrilling ceremony, "since in a sense this was a test visit to a South American Republic."

FDR signed these letters "Ever so much love, devotedly." Before he left for "that long 12 day trip to Honolulu," he added: "I so wish you were here with me."

Despite their eight-hour drive down to San Francisco, ER and Hick felt "rested and relaxed" as they went out to dine late in Hick's favorite restaurant. A quiet place, virtually unknown to tourists, it served "the best French food I'd ever eaten." It was exquisite and discreet, romantic and candle-lit, and nobody in the restaurant noticed them.

After dinner, they strolled, then took a cable car up to Russian Hill, where Hick pointed out the building she and Ella had lived in, "with its picture window that gave us a great sweeping view of the bay from our living room.

"Then we went over to a tiny park and sat in the moonlight, quietly talking and looking at the bay. . . .

"Around eleven o'clock we took the cable car back down the hill, stopped at a drugstore . . . for ice cream sodas and started to walk back to our hotel. It had been a perfect evening, we agreed. . . ."

But as they approached their hotel, the manager ran to meet them. He was "in a state of panic." The "lobby was filled with reporters." Presumably, with the eleven-week longshoremen's strike over on 27 July, America's journalists had nothing to do but hound the First Lady and her friend.*

*In June, a longshoremen's strike, led by Australian-born Harry Bridges, became a general strike that paralyzed San Francisco and moved up the West Coast. Some industrialists and politicians forecast civil war, revolution. In California, the press attacked Bridges as an alien subversive Red and condemned unionists as communists. But public opinion was on their side.

Secretary of State Cordell Hull and Attorney General Homer Cummings had

The manager insisted: "I didn't tell anyone . . . I didn't think you'd want to be bothered—if you had, you wouldn't have come to my hotel. You do believe me, don't you?"

Hick "believed him"; they were "good friends. I did suspect the hotel's one bellboy. . . .

"Through a barrage of exploding flashlights we walked through the lobby to the elevator. Mrs. Roosevelt shook her head as the reporters fired questions. . . .

" 'I'm here on vacation . . . I'd like to be left alone, if you don't mind.' "

In the morning the hotel seemed quiet, and they braved breakfast. But as they ate their cereal, a photographer walked up to them, kneeled before their table, and shot "flashlights right in our faces."

All that day they were followed by reporters, and tourists. From Fisherman's Wharf, to a ferry ride across to Sausalito, to the Fairmont Hotel for dinner, there was no peace, no privacy, no chance for a quiet or unphotographed word. They had managed shampoos at a beauty parlor unmolested, but it had all been too much. There is no record of their words to each other, except Hick's memory that as they locked the door to their room that night, ER "said quietly: 'I think we may as well leave tomorrow morning. Don't you?' "

As they drove away, Hick was hit by the final indignity: Tourists had stripped her car of all removable "souvenirs," including sunglasses, road maps, chocolate bars, a cigarette lighter. Nevertheless, their trip up the coast through the Muir Woods and along the Pacific "was leisurely and beautiful."

Their final evening together before they arrived in Portland, where ER was to join FDR and his party, was spent in a lovely hotel in Bend, Oregon. Windblown and road-weary, they arrived only to be told by the manager that the word was out, "and a lot of people would like to meet you."

ER asked to be excused, and they were allowed to freshen up and dine in peace. Shown to a table at a picture window "with one of the most breathtaking views," they relaxed. It was sunset, the mountains were snow-capped, and the food was perfect. ER and Hick left the dining room "very contented." But they walked into a lobby filled with people, reporters, and a reception line headed by the mayor.

Silently, ER handed Hick the keys. "I was apt not to behave well under such circumstances, she had learned." Almost an hour later, ER entered the

---

wanted to send the Army to crush the strike and restore "order." Others, including Frances Perkins and Harold Ickes, counseled calm. FDR appointed an Industrial Emergency Committee to investigate labor unrest and industrial violence. As FDR hoped, the strike ended peacefully, but with an intensified effort to crush the union and deport Bridges.

room, "slammed the door behind her—something I'd never known her to do before, nor did I ever know her to do it since that night—and sat down on my bed. On either cheek was a red spot. They used to appear that way when she was annoyed.

> "Franklin was right!" she said.
> "What do you mean?" I asked her.
> "Franklin said I'd never get away with it, . . . and I can't."
> She was silent for a moment. . . .
> "From now on I shall travel as I'm supposed to travel, as the President's wife, and try to do what is expected of me."
> Then she added defiantly:
> "But there's one thing I will not do. I will not have a Secret Service man following me about. NEVER!"

That was the last conversation recorded in Hick's book *Reluctant First Lady.*

Although ER did not refer to the evening in Bend at all, she noted that when they arrived in Portland, her room was filled to capacity with flowers. Hick, who had "a macabre humor at times, said: 'All you need is a corpse.' "

In fact there was a corpse to mourn: Anonymity and privacy had become historical fantasies. ER, the First Lady, belonged to the American people. There were no discreet hotels, no sacred groves, no secret passages. Their vacation was over. Hick returned to San Francisco, to resume her FERA reports, "and I returned to official life."

On 3 August 1934, ER joined FDR and his party for a reunion aboard the USS *Houston*. After lunch they drove east to the Bonneville Dam, and from there boarded the president's train for the five-day trip across the country, which served in part to launch the 1934 campaign.

They made many stops along the way, but saw nothing so amazing as the work under way for the Grand Coulee Dam, planned as "the largest dam on earth" and the source of cheap hydroelectric power. They drove fifty-seven miles through the Grand Coulee canyon, about two miles across, "bordered by rock walls rising 1,000 feet . . . which in past times was the bed of the Columbia River."

At the construction site, before an estimated forty thousand celebrants, FDR delivered "a militant defense of public works."

The Northwest was to prepare for "the probable migration of persons seeking . . . better opportunities of life than [are now possible] in worked-out or inhospitable areas, due to the vagaries of nature. . . ."

While the presidential train included five cars filled with reporters and officials, the private party included Tommy, Louis Howe, Steve Early, Harold

Ickes, Senator Burton Wheeler, other officials, and sons FDR, Jr., and John, now joined by James. Evidently their dinner reunion immediately burst into familial disagreement, when ER suggested "a more equitable distribution of income" between rich and poor, with a ceiling or "strict limitation" on income, which her sons dismissed as "subversive." To the amazement of observers unaccustomed to Roosevelt family table talk, a great shouting match ensued.

While "they were all going on at once," Ickes shouted to say he now knew how FDR learned "to manage Congress," whereupon Senator Wheeler observed: "Congress was never as bad." Ickes considered the evening "all very interesting and very amusing."

But ER worried: Ickes and the others "looked so horrified when they heard the boys arguing violently with Franklin . . . that I felt impelled to explain that in our family the boys had always been encouraged to express their opinions." She wrote nothing of her own role in the argument, which her views had precipitated.

ER's correspondence with Hick resumed that night:

> Darling, how I hated to have you go. It is still a pretty bad ache and I've thought of you all day especially as we drove along the road we had covered yesterday and which you drove over this morning— Well, dear one, I sent you a wire. . . . We have had happy moments and there will be more in the future but take care of yourself and remember I love you.

Although Hick had returned to her friends in San Francisco, she too felt forlorn: "There have been times when I've missed you so that it has been like a physical pain. . . ."

For ER, the only memorable stop during their long trip home was at Glacier National Park in Montana. There FDR, ER, and Harold Ickes were taken into the Blackfoot tribe in a ceremony attended by hundreds of the three thousand remaining members of the tribe. Ickes was named Big Bear, FDR named Lone Chief, and ER named Medicine Pipe Woman. FDR was given two other titles, Love Chief and Fearless Blue Eagle, and ER was also called Grand White Mother.

After the ceremonies, ER wrote, her sons "induced me" to join them for a swim in the lake. The woman who had just days before been swimming in the coldest waters shortly after dawn now paused:

> As I stood, hesitating and wondering whether I could bear the icy water, one of the boys gave me a push and I found myself gasping and swimming back as quickly as possible. The Indians stood watching us silently, as much as to say, "What fools these mortals be." . . . I decided the Indians were right and ran to the cabin. . . .

That unwelcome and unseemly push causes one to contemplate how vigorous ER was in the company of those who gave her courage and comfort, and how different she became with those who discredited or humiliated her. No longer the "reluctant first lady," she was determined to play an active political role in a country that needed her, among people who needed her; she faced her future with the hard-won knowledge that to act boldly or to pursue pleasure, whether in the high mountains or in the most frigid waters, she needed to feel free, to be cared about and considered, to be wanted and needed.

In the future, she arranged her life accordingly.

12: Negotiating the Political Rapids

During the summer of 1934 ER began to acknowledge, to herself at least, that she did not actually want an exclusive relationship. Once she realized she could not satisfy Hick's demands for exclusive time and their mutual expectation of private moments, ER understood that she had contributed to their problem by making promises she could not keep.

For years ER embraced a fantasy of her future retirement, in which she would be content to live a nonpublic existence. She encouraged Hick to join that romantic fantasy and consider where they might live, what remote country space they might build together. She spoke earnestly of a future life of privacy, shared work and travel. For now, public issues were her priority. Hick understood that, but still believed they had a right to exclusive time together. As their differences grew, ER sought to protect their changed relationship, convinced it would all work out, somehow.

After ER joined FDR, Hick returned to Bill and Ella Dana's ranch and Bill became Hick's boon companion. They enjoyed many of the same things—the peace of the countryside, roaring laughter, a good stiff drink, political conversation—and they enjoyed each other's company. Above all, Bill offered Hick a delightful cottage on the Dana estate on Long Island's South Shore. Hick was to live in the "little house" in Mastic for over twenty years.

Doris Dana, Bill's daughter, recalled that they went fishing in the morning, drove around much of the day, talked for hours. Around the place, they dressed alike, in corduroy knickerbockers or work pants, big hunting boots, checkered Western shirts, and great floppy hats in the rain; and they laughed alike—loudly, deeply, with gusto. But in August 1934, Hick seemed surprised that the Danas enjoyed her company—even without ER's presence. ER replied impatiently: "For heaven sake why shouldn't they like you for yourself? They are genuine people."

Hick was resourceful, and never wanted to be a burden or a bore. But there were days when she hated her life, days when she knew that she had made some seriously wrong choices.

After the summer of 1934, she tried to pull away from ER, to create a new life, restore aspects of her old life and professional successes. But ER always pulled her back.

On the road for FERA and alone in strange towns, Hick sent letters detailing her gourmand pleasures, accompanied by martinis and bourbon, wine and cigarettes. She knew she was wrecking her health. Her feet were swollen and sore; she had trouble breathing, disliked exercise, lacked stamina. She was stressed and depressed, and she ground her teeth in her sleep. Her gums bled, her teeth loosened. She needed dental care.

Hick was in fact unhappy in a romance she could neither control nor walk away from. It would be better, she occasionally assured ER, if they just did not see each other. But that was not Hick's first choice, and ER dismissed it as ridiculous. When Hick seemed most aloof or disappeared for a week, ER drew her back with renewed promises for the future; and her magic was compelling. The chemistry was forceful. And so their relationship continued, each trying to minimize the unpleasant moments, each trying to accommodate the other. Although they each made a generous effort, they moved from vastly unequal spaces, with very different expectations.

ER did not want to be free. But she wanted mobility, and spontaneity. She wanted to be able to move quickly and casually from the intimacy of a private conversation to the intensity of politics. She wanted, above all, to be unconfined.

Although she always denied it, her life was now driven by one simple fact: Her public life was her chosen life. She would always long for quiet moments with intimate friends, and she needed to be needed. Hick needed her; Earl Miller needed her; the people of America needed her. Increasingly, she embraced an ever-widening field of public activity, and an ever-growing community of new and cherished friends.

As ER scheduled her public life, routinely full eighteen-hour days— she also reserved some part of each day for joy.

Her morning rides through Rock Creek Park, afternoon swims in the pool with Franklin or alone, and long contemplative walks enabled her to concentrate and work effectively, often until three in the morning. But "joy" for ER depended upon her private friendships—especially when they advanced causes she cared about. As one considers the people ER toured around Arthurdale, for example, one appreciates her expanding network—and her ability to weave into each day work and pleasure.

Gertrude Ely, who became one of ER's closest friends, went to Arthurdale with her in 1934. "We drove there, just the two of us, [she] at the wheel of her open convertible. She was so happy, yet so busy. That's a good combination."

It was a good combination, for which she relied on women like Gertrude

Ely, a public-spirited philanthropist and activist. Like ER an organizer of the Junior League and League of Women Voters, she was an old friend who shared many of ER's interests, including birth control, world peace, racial justice, affordable housing, and social security. Fun-loving and adventurous, in 1931 Gertrude Ely was part of a merry but curious trio to tour the Soviet Union. Her companions were Nancy Astor and George Bernard Shaw.

ER spent significant time over the decades at Ely's home, especially when she sought privacy. Ely would casually tell other guests, often her young musical protégées, "I have a friend here for the weekend," and they would be astonished when ER came down to join them for dinner.

There was yet another side to ER that enjoyed spontaneous adventure, carefree companionship. She spent two weeks hidden in the Adirondack Mountains with Earl Miller, Nancy Cook, Marion Dickerman, and dancers Tiny Chaney and Eddie Fox.

ER's time at Miller's Camp Dannemora at Chazy Lake had been restful in 1933, and was even more fun in 1934. It was "absolutely quiet and peaceful and lovely," when ER wrote Hick that she hoped that she too was getting into "the right frame of mind to enjoy life."

Their turbulent vacation had marked their friendship: "I'm afraid you and I are always going to have times when we ache for each other and yet we are not always going to be happy when we are together. . . ." In contrast to their tensions, ER wrote effusively about her frolics at camp. Her day began at 7:30, when "we all, except Nan, did calisthenics in our bathing suits on the porch." They hiked mountain trails, played wild games, and somehow nobody intruded on her quest for quiet time, when she read, wrote letters, and contemplated the upcoming political campaign. ER proudly noted their various skills: As a straight shooter, Tiny was "about as good as Earl. She has the steadiest hand I ever saw." She wrote nothing of her own prowess with a pistol, although, when asked, she acknowledged she mostly hit the bull's-eye.

ER's hands were rarely still. When she did not read, she knitted, especially during long philosophical conversations on the porch in the evening. She wrote Hick that "your sweater is getting on, as I can knit without being rude."

One day ER sat unrecognized "with three elderly ladies and listened to their gossip: 'Uh! She is a dancer? I suppose that's her husband.' On my part blank indifference and apparent deafness! Three years ago I would have hated yesterday. I was amazed what a long way I have come in indifference to what people think!"

When Hick asked if she were really happy in that place with those people, ER answered: "Yes I am happy here and . . . I was analyzing [the reasons] today. Perhaps the real one is that I think I am needed and wanted . . . I suppose that is why I enjoy being with Anna and John, so often with the boys I feel tolerated! What curious creatures we are."

In 1934 Earl needed ER more than usual. On 24 June ER wrote Hick: "It is hard for me ever to believe in anyone having a nervous breakdown but I can see Earl has had one and is working hard to pull out." Evidently, Earl's unhappy marriage, which ER had encouraged, and his abiding sense of loneliness wore him down.

On 14 August, the anniversary of her father's death, ER visited Elinor Morgenthau, whose mother was failing, and who felt hurt and neglected by ER that summer. ER wrote Morgenthau:

> I can't think what I did to make you feel I didn't want to hear from you this summer. In fact, I did very much and missed having no letters and thought of you often. . . .
>
> I'm so sorry about your Mother and I know how you are feeling for it is much worse to watch someone you love suffer than suffer yourself. Poor darling, you have so many troubles and never seem to get a real rest. I'm going to try to plan in early Nov. to take you away for a long week end!
>
> Friendships are always important to me and please don't ever think the opposite no matter what stupid things I do which hurt your feelings. It is never intentional.

Hick evidently analyzed the reason ER's friends seemed disgruntled, and ER agreed:

> Yes, dear, you are right, I give everyone the feeling that you have that I've "taken them on" and don't need anything from them and then when they naturally resent it and don't like to accept from me, I wonder why! It is funny I know and I can't help it something locked me up and I can't unlock!

ER's reference to her inability to "unlock" has been used to "prove" an amazing variety of emotional and physical limitations. The wonder of her life is that despite all limitations, all childhood hurt and adult complexity, ER protected herself from further pain as best she could, while indulging her habit of emotional curiosity and commitment. The barriers she created to protect herself were not barriers to loving. She cherished Hick, and also Earl, because they had determinedly crashed through her protective barriers. Her aloof, seemingly cold demeanor, so forbidding to some, had represented a challenge to them. ER, in turn, responded to their persistence, trusted and felt secure with them. She felt needed by them, depended on their love, and intended to preserve it.

Actually many of ER's old friends were dismayed by how much of her heart she chose to unlock. They considered some of her new friendships, and activities, fraught with abandon. ER tended to ignore the tensions and endless jealousies that marked her many circles. When her friends were unavoidably thrown together, she trusted in everyone's good manners, and spent her time precisely with whom she pleased.

With her merry band at Chazy Lake, ER was mostly anonymous—until they made headlines: Their little motorboat grounded on a rock in the middle of the lake and ran out of gas. Neighbors saw their plight, rowed over with gas, and pulled them back into the water.

FDR sent a telegram glad that all were safe; but it was too embarrassing for a Roosevelt to run aground in a rowboat. Would his wife henceforth please remember to tank up, or manage to stay out of the papers. ER's summer frolic continued when her party joined FDR's at Hyde Park. By month's end, Hick felt ER was at peace with herself and her life. But ER assured her:

> F was amused by your comment. No dear, I am not at peace with God and man, not even at all times with myself so you need not be afraid of me. . . .
>
> Oh, dear one, what wouldn't I give to have you here with me tonight and . . . be able to take care of you. I always feel that you and Earl need me more than anyone when things go wrong for neither of you have anyone nearer to whom to turn and whom I must remember not to offend.

Harry Hopkins and his wife arrived at Hyde Park for Labor Day weekend, to discuss his European tour of relief work and housing. Although in Germany during Hitler's Nuremberg rally, which announced his "thousand-year Reich," he said nothing about it. Nor did he publicly refer to any of the fascist activities that made headlines and coincided with his tour through Germany, Italy, and England. But his visit reinvigorated the president's goals for the New Deal.

Hopkins's study of Europe's social insurance reconfirmed his commitment to public works programs and job security. Above all, Hopkins believed, a government program of economic or social security depended upon the creation of work: full employment.

Hopkins's weekend visit launched America's first national and permanent social security program. Current New Deal laws were limited state by state, needed to be refunded by Congress annually, and were regarded as emergency measures. New Dealers now believed the economy faced permanent conditions of unemployment and distress, and FDR appointed an Advisory Committee on Economic Security to begin work after the November elections.

As the 1934 campaign heated up at summer's end, fascist rumbles out of Europe and violent industrial reprisals against union activities within the United States encouraged New Dealers to be bold. ER argued repeatedly that the New Deal had so far "only bought time," that so much more needed to be done. Now, she wrote Hick with delight that FDR was in a "militant" mood. "He is very angry with [Budget Director] Lewis Douglas for choosing this moment to resign though he is glad to have him out." ER was interested that FDR was able to work "his rage out by having a good time" at the Morgenthaus' annual clambake.

Lew Douglas had opposed all public relief and public works measures. A conservative representative of the business community who wanted a balanced budget, he timed his resignation to the midterm elections without warning—which seemed to FDR a personal betrayal. Shortly thereafter, Douglas joined the Liberty League to attack the New Deal, and FDR personally. FDR called Morgenthau over to Hyde Park the morning of the clambake to announce: "Henry, in the words of John Paul Jones, we have just begun to fight!"

At the party that evening, FDR sang with vigor, and had the happiest time in recent memory. Since he became president, he had not seemed to his closest family and friends "so jolly as he was that night."

During this time of action within the Roosevelt household, a tone of tenderness toward Hick, rather missing in August, returned to ER's letters. She sent Hick a photograph that Tiny had taken of her—"I thought you might like to have it"—along with long letters that "take you worlds of love and I wish I could lie down beside you tonight and take you in my arms."

Hick worried that Lew Douglas's departure would hurt FDR, and the conservative press was bitter against alleged New Deal excesses. But ER was unbothered; "the papers don't worry me as much as they do you."

In the long minuet of their relationship, Hick now pulled back, and ER was mystified that Hick had failed to send her schedule. She went to Hopkins to learn Hick would return on the 15th. "I would die if you were that near and I didn't see you till the 23d."

In September, ER spent time with Earl, whose marriage was about to end in divorce—which evidently pleased him; and consoled Tommy, whose marriage was also about to end in divorce.

While at Val-Kill with Nan and Earl, ER awaited news of her son James, who had disappeared during a sailing regatta in a terrible storm. All the boats were in except his. ER and James's wife, Betsey, spent seven hours on the phone, "getting Coast Guard & naval boats out & we didn't want to tell Mama & at midnight he was reported in Portland & we just talked to him, 180 miles away from the place he was supposed to be! It's funny—how calm you are when . . . something serious is hanging over you. I felt queer in the pit of my tummy but perfectly fatalistic and numb."

On the 12th, ER wrote Hick from Newport, where she spent her obligatory annual weekend with Cousin Susie: "Well your photograph is on my desk and I will try to behave tonight." Dinners at Newport, surrounded by Republicans and her most social relatives, were always difficult. But this time much of Rhode Island was on strike, and "with Myron Taylor [president of U.S. Steel] on one side of me and [Rhode Island Governor Theodore Green] on the other," ER feared she would be indiscreet, or explode.

A national textile strike called by the United Textile Workers was under way, and virtually every factory along the East Coast from Rhode Island to Florida was engulfed by or threatened with violence. A Democrat, Governor Green told the Rhode Island legislature that the textile workers of Providence represented a "communist uprising." But unionists protested industry's failure to live up to their codes, including the abolition of child workers and minimum wage provisions.

FDR appointed John Winant, New Hampshire's liberal Republican governor, to chair a special board of inquiry when ten strikers were killed and scores wounded in the South. In Georgia, National Guardsmen rounded up 116 women and men, white union workers, and put them in what the press called a "concentration camp." Georgia Governor Eugene Talmadge loathed FDR and despised the New Deal, which encouraged unionism. He and other conservatives were determined to crush this strike. It was their declaration of war against communism, and against the New Deal.

Desperate for a settlement, Winant's committee and the union settled for a tragic compromise that left the union unrecognized, the strikers unprotected, and the deal a disgrace. FDR signed it, but no peace was thereby restored.

The textile strike highlighted America's new battlefields. After Winant's settlement, employers ridiculed the idea of national arbitration, and Southern industrialists vowed to rid the region of unionists. The vicious episode dramatized the urgency behind Senator Robert Wagner's independent labor bill, intended to protect against just such events, siderailed by the 1934 Congress. For ER, so long a WTUL activist, industrial violence against unionism was a dreadful development.

To fortify herself before her Newport dinner, ER had lunched with Esther Lape and Elizabeth Read at their Connecticut estate, Saltmeadow. They too deplored antiunion violence, and ER wrote Hick, "You would like them. . . . Darling I must dress. I love you and how I dread the next few hours. I hope someone is praying for me."

Ultimately the dinner was a courteous affair. FDR had once said that "Myron was a moron," but ER was surprised to find Myron Taylor interesting, and found she actually liked him. "The strikes are bad and I hate seeing soldiers and guns used, it makes me sick," but the violent situation kept the governor away from dinner.

Happy to leave Newport, ER drove with Louis Howe from his home in Horse Neck Beach near Fall River to Cape Cod, where she particularly enjoyed Provincetown. Optimistically, ER wrote Hick: "I think you'd like it—I've not been bothered at all on this trip by reporters so we might get away with it."

At Cousin Maude's in Portland, Maine, ER was joined by her daughter and John Boettiger. "They sat on my bed last night and talked and though you know that kind of happiness can't last, it is nice to have it for a time!" On her way home ER stopped in Cambridge to visit her sons.

ER and Hick arranged for their reunion to coincide with ER's fiftieth birthday in New York: "I'll be driving Anna down on Sunday as she takes the midnight to Washington—so don't be worried if she appears. . . . Tommy has a key and sleeps on the 4th floor but she won't bother us!" There was a hint of anxiety in her letters as she assured Hick that "we will have a peaceful time."

But they were interrupted by her daughter's medical emergency, and ER apologized: "I wish I had not had to leave you last night, tho of course I wanted to [visit Anna in the hospital]. You are a grand person dear, & don't ever think I don't appreciate what you are going thro for me."

Hick was again disappointed and ER felt in part a failure. Her solution was to persuade Hick to live in the White House whenever she was in Washington. But even as a live-in member of the household, she had very little time with ER.

That autumn for the first time a First Lady actively participated in a political campaign. ER campaigned vigorously for Caroline O'Day, who ran for member of Congress at large for New York State. A position that no longer exists, it was tantamount to senator—the "congressman-at-large" represented the entire state.

Supported in her decision to campaign by Louis Howe and FDR, and occasionally accompanied on the stump by her mother-in-law, ER dismissed newspaper attacks as "funny." Besides, she enjoyed every minute of it—the speeches, the "very big crowds," the partisan hoopla.

This one was for the women. ER's original political team, who had been "trooping for democracy" since 1920, now campaigned for one of their own. Caroline O'Day, Nancy Cook, Marion Dickerman, and ER were the Four Musketeers of New York State. Caroline O'Day ran for Congress with the men of the party behind her. FDR wanted her in Washington, and everything she and ER most cared about was on the agenda—women's rights and opportunities, labor rights, Negro rights, the World Court, international peace, social security—and she had a chance to win.

O'Day ran against a reactionary Republican attorney, Natalie Couch.

Blunt in the political fray, ER considered Couch dreary: "I'm sorry to say that I thought Miss Couch made a rather terrible speech and I shall be really sorry if she is elected."

ER was glad to be back "at my old work." "I like being in a campaign and with people I know again." She ignored all opposition, and served as Caroline O'Day's finance chair. She was delighted to support a remarkable friend who had given so many years of her life to the women's movement and to social service, she said almost every day, in her speeches to large audiences throughout the state:

> I think that Mrs. O'Day represents in herself the real reason why most women enter politics, which is in order to achieve changes in our social organization which they become convinced can be reached only through government.

That was a theme ER had consistently repeated since her 1928 article "Women Bosses," when she wrote that men go into politics to win elections and women go into politics to change the world: "The vast majority of women, I believe, turn to politics as the only means through which to accomplish the ends they seek."

ER's long friendship with O'Day served to contradict that false "theory that women cannot work together or for each other. . . . I never knew Mrs. O'Day to be jealous of anyone. . . . It has been a pleasure and privilege to work with her and under her."

In Buffalo on 25 October, over a thousand women attended ER's first debate against Couch, sponsored by the League of Women Voters. The audience was volatile. Although all speakers were warmly received at first, ER became crimson with outrage when Natalie Couch was booed. She was applauded when she attacked the Roosevelt administration for extravagance, but booed when she announced: "The people of the United States realize they no longer have a republic."

ER was the last speaker of the evening, and as reported in *The New York Times* began by scolding the booers. She admired "the League of Women Voters because we always listen to all points of view . . . because we know that all . . . opinions expressed . . . are truthful and are wholly worthy of our respect whether we agree with them or not."

Natalie Couch stood and bowed to ER, and the audience reunited in a round of applause. Then ER described the difference between Couch and O'Day, between traditional Democrats and Republicans: Couch wanted a balanced budget, and business incentives to the business community to lower the unemployment rate, which would reduce the relief rolls. But nobody sincerely believed that kind of trickle-down economics ever happened. How, ER asked, could a balanced budget be justified while so many remained unemployed, and suffered? "Are you going to stop feeding the hungry . . . ?"

Against all criticism, ER insisted: "I am acting as an individual. . . . I believe in certain things, and I think a person who does believe in certain things has the right to support them."

To charges that as First Lady she used her position unfairly, she replied: "As a citizen I too must live up to what I think is right."

It was ER's kind of political season, and she did not miss an opportunity. She attacked all those who attacked the New Deal, and she attacked especially her husband's enemies. "Hammering a fist into the palm of her hand and raising her voice," ER told twelve hundred women in Syracuse that the critics of her husband's administration were howling in the hollow. New Deal programs were "wasteful" only if the people helped were to be wasted:

> We have short memories. In the Spring of 1933 people came to Washington and said, "Take our business. Do anything with it to make it run."
>
> Now the sick man is better and doesn't like "regulation." He wants to get back and make as much profit as possible. He doesn't think about his neighbors. But the only good we care about is the good of the people.

ER emphasized that the NRA codes, under vicious attack, were "made by the industries themselves." "Now the industrialists try to pretend that they were imposed." As for government borrowing, ER considered it "a choice between two evils," debt or widespread misery.

Caroline O'Day was a lifelong pacifist, and her international views were absolute. In 1934, ER shared them: "The time is coming when we will discover that there are wars that are not worth having." In war there are no final victories, and "no question is permanently settled." ER believed in defense but wanted to take "every step toward peaceful solutions."

During the campaign, Hick lived most of the time in the White House, and ER's whirlwind schedule was unrelenting. There were also missed moments, and mixed signals:

> I am sorry you were hurt dear. But weren't you a bit hasty? I was back at 6:45 & lay on the sofa and read from 7:15–7:45 which was the time I had planned for you. I do plan times dear one to be with you but you have been here a good deal and the steady routine gets on your nerves. . . .
>
> I am sorry & cross with myself for not thinking ahead . . . but I wouldn't give up our times together and our happiness for these little troubles. You have been a brick and don't think that I don't know how hard it is.

Surely that note, and stingy half hour, added to their troubles.

On 1 November, ER delivered her last major speech for Caroline O'Day at a dinner attended by eight hundred notable Democrats and party leaders at the Hotel Biltmore. Independent third party candidate, who mostly ran against ER's presence in the campaign, attorney and Great War veteran Dorothy Frooks "crashed" the dinner, to confront ER. Daisy (Mrs. Caspar) Whitney, who chaired the meeting, refused to allow her to debate, although ER agreed to answer any questions she might have from the floor. But she failed to ask any questions. According to *The New York Times*, "Miss Frooks's presence was unknown to the large audience. Although Mrs. Roosevelt passed within arm's length of her as she left the dining room, Miss Frooks made no effort to interrogate her."

Hick worried about ER's image:

> Damn the newspapers! Here am I, keen to know what you said last night and how it went. And what do the papers carry? Complete and lurid accounts of Miss Frooks' presence. . . .
>
> And I hated the stories. They didn't say you ran out on it, but they certainly sounded as though Mrs. Whitney had placed you in the position of running out.

Hick was even more upset to read that ER wore "a blue velvet dinner gown," while Miss Frooks crashed the gate "in street clothes." Then, on leaving, ER was reported to have been "surrounded by a party of friends." "Damn it—I hated it. It made you sound like a rotten sport. Of course the stories may be inaccurate. . . ."

It all made Hick feel very radical, actually "red." Her "red" feelings that night were compounded by the fact that she had just spent two full days "with relief clients."

> God damn it—none of us ought to be wearing velvet dinner gowns these days! Not when, as the chief attendance officer in the Baltimore public schools said today, 4,000 Baltimore children couldn't go to school in September because they didn't have clothes. As she was saying that, the thought of that new dress of mine and of you in a blue velvet dinner gown—even though you *are* my friend, and I love you—irritated me profoundly.

Despite her ire, Hick signed off with a gentle note: "Darling—in a blue velvet dinner gown or out of it . . . I love you. . . ."

ER was at Hyde Park, in the process of writing Hick a long letter, when her protest arrived: "Miss Frooks borrowed a UP press pass to get into the dinner. Mrs. Whitney when she first saw her was unduly excited and insisted she must not speak." ER invited her to ask questions, however, and she "never asked one. She could have several times during my speech for I paused and spoke slowly." ER felt unjustly accused:

> I stood in the hall, right outside the door for 15 minutes waiting to find my coat and many people came to talk and she could have done so— She is crazy and I did not want to go on the radio with her . . . so I'm writing her to reach her after [the] election and not answering her wires. . . .

ER offered no apologies for her costume:

> Darling, if we all stopped wearing velvet dresses there would be worse times than there are. If you have money you must spend it—now, so I don't feel as guilty as you do. Of course if you could give it all where it would do the most good that would be grand but we can't always do that! Don't think me heartless but your vehemence always makes me calm!

Also, ER warned Hick not to let the wicked conditions she had witnessed in Baltimore swamp her emotionally. "If one feels too absolutely the misery around one, life becomes unbearable and one's ability to be useful is really impaired. . . ."

The elections of 1934 represented a great Democratic victory, and a mandate for the New Deal. Caroline O'Day won easily, and ER was credited with her success. New York's new congresswoman-at-large protested the mean-spirited press coverage: "The up-State papers said Mrs. Roosevelt spoke for me because I was too dumb to speak for myself. I resent very much the intimation that Mrs. Roosevelt would speak for a dumb-bell." Though clearly, O'Day said, "most people feel that 'what is good for Mrs. Roosevelt is good enough for me.' "

According to some newspapers, Caroline O'Day would merely be a Roosevelt yes-woman in Congress. O'Day admitted that possibility, except if it came to America's participation in war. In that event: "I think I would just kiss my children good-bye and start off for Leavenworth."

In Arizona, ER's great friend Isabella Greenway was reelected, but her various conservative friendships gave rise to rumors that worried FDR. ER wrote:

> Franklin wants to know if by any chance you really are a financial backer of an organization called America First? It is doing much the same type of thing that the Liberty League is doing and apparently is causing a great deal of trouble. Some one is spreading the report that you are the financial angel. Having heard a number of such reports . . . I doubt if this is accurate, but I would be glad to have my doubts confirmed.

Greenway replied:

> I never heard of "America First," but have a vague memory that Mrs. [Phoebe] Hearst started something in behalf of Franklin in October '32 called "America Incorporated" and we all contributed ten dollars. It's wonderful what we hear about ourselves, isn't it? . . .

Although Isabella was basically loyal to FDR's program in Congress, she departed publicly in 1933 and again in 1934 when she stood up for the veterans' bonus. Despite political disagreements, her friendship with ER was not diminished.

Initially, FDR sought to reassure and appease the corporate lobby that sought to destroy New Deal efforts and crush the burgeoning union movement. He tended to ignore growing discontent on the left, especially among workers and minorities.

Throughout the autumn, ER's correspondence with NAACP leaders revealed the profound dismay of organized black communities and voters. Efforts to renew the fight against lynching in the upcoming Congress intensified in the face of new and grisly violence. In September ER met with Walter White about "the very unsatisfactory way" Negroes were integrated into the Homestead Division's "subsistence colonies." She asked Clarence Pickett to give her the details of the Interior Department's efforts. Within weeks, Ickes's office compiled a report, "What Actually Is Being Done to Integrate Negroes into the Various Projects." Five projects were "under consideration," in Tuskegee, Alabama; Newport News, Virginia; Orangeburg, South Carolina; Philadelphia, Pennsylvania; and Dayton, Ohio. Tuskegee would consist of seventy-five homesteads, and land was "being purchased"; Philadelphia was to be a "bi-racial unit of 200 homesteads."

In November 1934, the New Deal scored a zero in the NAACP's *Crisis* magazine. In "The Plight of the Negro Voter," Oswald Garrison Villard—one of the NAACP's founders, long identified with reform causes, and *The Nation*'s publisher—wrote a particularly bitter assessment:

> Never before has the Negro voter in the North found himself in a worse quandary than today. Whatever the New Deal has done for the white workman it seems to have done less than nothing for the Negro. . . . Mr. Roosevelt is frankly not interested in the Negro problem; so far as I am aware a study of the Negro situation has not been one of Mrs. Roosevelt's multitudinous activities.

Villard more correctly observed that the power of the Democrats continued to reside in the hands of Southern congressional bullies, McAdoo, Pat Harrison, and Joseph Robinson of Arkansas particularly, all "typical anti-Negro southerners." Still, Villard admitted, the New Deal's effort to restore prosperity might trickle down and benefit "all Americans," while the Republicans "have absolutely nothing to offer anyone." This party of "big business, great capitalists, and tariff barons" exclusively represented, in Theodore Roosevelt's words, "the malefactors of great wealth."

ER was not unmindful of Villard's criticisms, and it engendered a correspondence with novelist Dorothy Canfield Fisher.

After Fisher sent her Villard's *Nation* editorial on federal aid to education, ER wrote: "there is much truth in what he says and it is always well said, but there are also some inaccuracies. . . . I always wish that he would be a little more temperate, because I think he would carry greater weight and not arouse antagonism, and at the moment we need all the influence we can get. . . ."

ER added:

> I have always been sorry that I did not have the courage to go and see you when you were living near Poughkeepsie. I wanted to so often, but felt I had no right to intrude upon you. I have so admired your books for so many years and have used your Hillsboro people—especially "Petunias, That's for Remembrance"—so often in my classes to emphasize [that] my girls should see a little more of the world than their own surroundings, with an understanding eye and heart, that it would have been the greatest pleasure for me to have had an opportunity to talk with you."

ER invited Fisher, then living in Vermont, to visit her at the White House. Fisher was delighted by ER's letter, "with its unexpected news that you know my work." She had also longed to meet, and had decided to make contact. "When I read what you said to the assembled DARs:

> I fairly bounded into the air with joy—and relief—and pride in you! And now I cannot resist writing you to tell you that the mental health of this big country is being infinitely improved by your courage in saying right out, on so many occasions, what intelligent good citizens think but had never dreamed could be said in public by someone in authority. Yes, you are "in authority" now, by virtue of the extraordinary prestige your personality gives you.

While Villard deplored the conservatism of New Dealers, Molly Dewson worried about radical challenges. As Dewson made plans to attend FDR's new advisory council assigned to develop Social Security legislation, she sent ER a letter filled with her concerns for the future—including evidence of growing radicalism in the youth movement, which she wanted ER to pass on to the president: "FDR likes his ear to the ground. He was talking to me about this difficulty of getting the young students on middle ground." She enclosed an appeal for money from a socialist college society associated with Norman Thomas, which showed how far from "middle ground" they were: Their letterhead called for "production for use and not for profit," and they actively recruited on college campuses:

> Joseph P. Lash, Editor of the Student Outlook, Monroe Sweetland and George Edwards—have been remarkably successful in building up vigorous and militant groups on almost every campus they have been able to reach. They have enrolled four times as many students this October than . . . a year ago. . . . They are building a strong student movement. . . .
>
> Side by side with this radical activity on the campus however, we are hearing of the formation of new and sinister types of college organizations. We have the spectacle of college officials in the East and West expelling students for their participation in the work of building a new social order. College presidents are organizing fraternities and athletic groups into vigilante organizations. This necessitates greater activity on our part than ever before.

Their activity was facilitated by successful publications: *Socialism's New Beginning, The Plight of the Sharecropper, Fascism, Traffic in Death, Campus Strikes Against War,* and *Italian Intellectuals Under Fascism.* New pamphlets, ready for the printer, included *The Negro in America* by Abram Harris, George Streator, and Norman Thomas, and *Labor Conflicts Under the NRA.*

By 1934 the issues of youth leaders were increasingly ER's issues.

Earlier Hick had also alerted ER to the radical path America's students had embarked upon. In May, Hick had met a young FERA colleague in Phoenix:

> [She is an] interesting and amusing little girl, three years out of Vassar, who now worked on a statistical survey on transients. . . . We spent the evening talking politics and economics. She is afraid there won't be a revolution, and I'm afraid there will be—so our argument was rather amusing. She admires the President greatly, but doesn't think he'll be able to put his reforms over because of Congress and the selfishness and stupidity of both Capital and Labor. She gnashes her teeth over what Congress is doing . . . and over the [conservative] tactics of the A.F. of L. . . . She feels very earnestly that there ought to be a change in the whole system and that, if the President can't swing it, we must have a revolution. What interested me most was that she said most young people she knows feel the same way! And she says the boys are for the most part dead set against war—that they say they'll go to jail first. Boys who were at Yale and Princeton when she was at Vassar! Interesting, isn't it? . . .

Unlike Dewson and Hick, ER was attracted by the causes that most engaged America's young radical students. She looked forward to fighting for them with the support of new allies in Congress, especially Caroline O'Day. A reconstructed southerner, born in Georgia and educated in Paris, O'Day had long campaigned against lynching, and all forms of discrimination. A member of the NAACP board, she was a fighter and bridge builder.

Shortly after the election, ER joined her husband for two weeks at Warm Springs. ER had invited Earl Miller and the Morgenthaus, but they had other plans. Still, Tommy, Marion Dickerman, and Nancy Cook arrived. Pleasant swims and strenuous rides through the countryside with Missy were diverting, and ER wrote several essays and columns with Tommy.

As ER and FDR drove together through the South, the impact of the New Deal was evident. Entire towns turned out for the president, "and everywhere they hang on his words." They "do look better Hick in spite of all your gloom." ER was pleased especially by all the "interesting things" being done by TVA "with cheap power."

ER wrote Hick daily, but their painful experiences together in groups, including gatherings of the extended family, rendered all longing senseless: "Dearest I don't wish you were here, you would hate it, but I miss you and think of you often and hope you are not too tired. My dear love and a tender kiss."

Hick was alone in the White House with Anna and John in November 1934, and they had a provocative conversation about the mercurial intensities of romantic love and unbridled jealousy. Although Hick's letters referred to are lost, ER replied:

> Hick dearest. Your letters of the 15th, 16th & 17th greeted me this morning. . . . You have been gay and I think on the whole you sound as tho life has been pleasant. . . . You poor dear with those two young things but just be comforted for Anna at least can't control her emotions & she knows it. They are sure of themselves for the moment just wait till their confidence is shaken. . . .
>
> You are right, there are only two ways to beat jealousy. One is not to love enough so as not to care if someone gives you less than you thought they might, the other is to love so much that you are happy in their happiness and have no more room for thoughts of yourself, but that is only possible to the old!

Then ER admitted her own discontent:

> I behaved very badly last night to Nan & this A.M. to FDR so I am not exactly "persona grata" to him or to myself & the sooner I can get away gracefully the happier I shall be. I'll tell you about it someday but it is too stupid to write about. Train quarters & this cottage are a bit cramped for me! . . . How discouraging it is that we must creep in this world. I wonder if we walk in the next, if there is one!

To Anna, ER explained her outburst in terms of one of FDR's habits she despised: He enjoyed mixing stiff drinks that rendered his company at first loose-tongued, then uncontrollably looped:

> I will probably fly home in a day or two. I'd like to leave at once but I injudiciously told Father I always felt like a spoil sport & policeman here & at times elsewhere, because I lost my temper last night. He's been giving Nan a cocktail every night & for two nights it went only a little to her head but it was so strong last night that she not only talked incessantly much to their amusement but couldn't talk straight & I felt he did it on purpose tho' he swears he didn't. Anyway he needn't make them so strong. . . . I just revolt physically from anyone in that condition & that makes her unhappy & yet I hate to be the one that keeps her from taking anything so I'd give the world and all to be out of the way quite aside from the fact that I'd like to be where I could have an eye on you young lady! Father says however if I leave before I have to he will feel hurt so! I'm an idiotic puritan & I wish I had the right kind of sense of humor & could enjoy certain things. At least, thank God, none of you children have inherited that streak in me, it is as well to have some of Father's ease & balance in these things. . . .

ER's upset in a situation that recalled those uncontrollable days at healing spas in Europe with her father released long letters of introspection. The situation was "disagreeable," but she noted, "I am behaving fairly well I think." She credited Hick for what she considered her new forbearance in such situations:

> Between your efforts and mine, two grown people who ought long ago to be past all such foolishness, may be achieving something for themselves at last! I am glad at least I can laugh at myself even in my worst moments and I think you can also.

Hick sought to bolster her spirits:

> Dearest: I don't know what you did to Nan and the President, but I don't believe you behaved *very* badly. Because it simply isn't in you to be-have *very* badly. The trouble is, dear, that most of us demand and expect too much of you—and this despite the fact that you really do give more of yourself to your friends than almost anyone else I ever knew. I suspect that at one time or another you've spoiled most of us. You did me. I say all this perfectly aware that I am the worst of the lot in the business of expecting and asking too much.
>
> But, darling, I'm trying not to be that way any more, and—*I'm going to succeed*. I only ask you to be a little patient. . . . Though, I don't think you'd be letting me down if you did lose patience with me. Anyway, we're, most

of us, pretty selfish—and you mustn't worry about behaving badly, because you don't, really.

ER replied: "Hick dearest, wouldn't you, like every one else, spoil me if you could! Tommy will tell you, however, just how disagreeable I was. Nobody was demanding anything of me. I was lacking in a sense of humor!"

Hick spent most of November touring pockets of poverty along the Mason-Dixon line. Everywhere the meanest sentiments prevailed. School-children starved while school lunches, which consisted of bread and soup, were reserved for those who had absolutely nothing at home. Also, the NRA was mostly ignored, and industry was planning to get it declared unconstitutional. A labor leader she respected told her that the NRA had "made about as much dent on industry as a sparrow's bill could make on an alligator's back!"

On 18 December, ER's holiday season was suspended and saddened by Mary Harriman Rumsey's death. One of ER's oldest friends, she was responsible for her first social activism in 1903, when she encouraged ER to join a small group of debutantes and college women who began to consider the poor. Mary Harriman founded the Junior League in 1901 and created the University Settlement House on Rivington Street where ER worked.

A fountain of magnetic enthusiasm, she was compared to "that youthful, winsome spirit with which Maude Adams endowed Barrie's Peter Pan—the boy who never grew up. She is volatile and effervescent. . . ."

An ardent patron of the arts, her life combined activism and sport. A member of one of the first women's polo teams, the Meadowlarks, Mary Harriman Rumsey was "one of the best horsewomen of her generation." She arose at dawn on her birthday, Saturday 17 November, to join the Piedmont fox hunt near Middleburg, Virginia. But shortly after noon, her horse stumbled after clearing a stone fence, and rolled over her. Riding sidesaddle, clamped to her mount, she broke four ribs and fractured her right thigh. It did not seem life-threatening, but fatal complications developed.

She died on 18 December with her three children, Frances Perkins, and her brother Averell at her bedside. FDR had just appointed Averell Harriman to replace Hugh Johnson as head of the NRA, and he always credited Mary for his career. She "lured him to Washington," where, she said, the New Deal marched with "humor and humanity to create a secure future" for consumers and workers, and "to put industry in its proper place."

ER canceled all engagements for the next two days and sat with Frances Perkins during the funeral services at St. Thomas's Church in Washington, then left with her that night for the burial at Arden.

Mary Harriman Rumsey's death was devastating to ER's small circle of confidantes. Their laughter-lit "air our minds" luncheons would never be the same. Isabella Greenway wrote: "The color seems to be wiped from the face of life with the going of Mary. I miss her a thousand ways over the hours. . . ."

At her memorial ER contemplated the political loss of her "daring drive" just when the fight for economic and social security was under way, and the personal loss of her longtime ally, who believed as she did that "the sole reason for the existence of any government is to improve the condition of its citizens."

13: 1935: Promises and Compromises

$\diamond\!\!\!\!\sim\!\!\!\!\diamond\!\!\!\!\diamond\!\!\!\!\diamond\!\!\!\!\sim\!\!\!\!\diamond$

The year 1935 opened with such promise that ER proclaimed it an "epochal" year. FDR's State of the Union address on 4 January was a fighting speech that radiated confidence and launched the second New Deal:

> Throughout the world, change is the order of the day. . . . In most nations social justice, no longer a distant ideal, has become a definite goal. . . . We seek it through tested liberal traditions. . . .
>
> We find our population suffering from old inequalities. . . . In spite of our efforts . . . we have not weeded out the overprivileged and we have not effectively lifted up the underprivileged. . . .
>
> We have, however, a clear mandate from the people, that Americans must forswear . . . the acquisition of wealth which, through excessive profits, creates undue private power over private affairs and, to our misfortune, over public affairs as well. . . .

FDR's powerful rhetoric was backed by specific plans to achieve "a proper security, a reasonable leisure, and a decent living throughout life," including "decent homes." And he repeated his June 1934 promise to "place the security of men, women and children of the nation first" on the national agenda. Specifically, he promised "a definite program for putting people to work" and a security package that included "unemployment insurance, old-age insurance, benefits for children, for mothers, for the handicapped, for maternity care, and for other aspects of dependency."

Work would replace the dole. "To dole out relief . . . is to administer a narcotic, a subtle destroyer of the human spirit. . . . Work must be found. . . ." But not made work, leaf raking, paper removal, junk work; real work to promote dignity and self-respect at real wages.

Initially social security legislation included work security, which was to be federally administered and not subject to the whims of state control where regional habits threatened race equity. The federal government would establish a vast program of public works, which would permanently improve "living conditions [and create] future new wealth for the nation."

These aspects of social security had long been demanded by the women's social reform movement—by Jane Addams, Lillian Wald, Florence Kelley. Frances Perkins and Harry Hopkins were part of that movement, and now Frances Perkins chaired FDR's cabinet-level Committee on Economic Security, which included Harry Hopkins.

All winter their plans progressed, and ER invited her mentors to the White House to contribute their thoughts. Lillian Wald wrote Jane Addams three weeks before FDR's address: "Most Beloved Lady . . . Mrs. R. acts truly as if she had been brought up in the Settlement. All the things we were wont to talk over in our conspiracies are important to her happiness." Wald also observed FDR carefully, and concluded:

> [The president is] a wizard in many ways. I swear he is absolutely sincere and wants to get across the best things possible for the least personality on our continent. . . . It's quite different of course than to have a great philosophy of economics or social fulfillment but he has the wish to have the country made a happy country for all who live therein. . . .
>
> Of course he sees too many people and they don't all advise alike and there are too many things that pull upon his attention but not much more than upon his wife's. They do team work. . . .

On 17 January, FDR presented his social security package, which included unemployment compensation, old-age benefits, federal aid to dependent children "through grants to states for the support of existing mothers' pension systems and for services for the protection and care of homeless, neglected, dependent, and crippled children," and federal aid to state and local public health agencies, with a strengthened Federal Public Health Service.

In this speech, FDR still included work security, as championed by ER, the social workers, and Harry Hopkins—which correlated unemployment insurance "with public employment so that a person who has exhausted his benefits may be eligible for some form of public work." The federal government was to assume half the cost of the old-age pension plan, "which ought ultimately to be supplanted by self-supporting annuity plans."

Only on health care did FDR waffle from the beginning. The medical profession, well organized and devoutly opposed to "health insurance," caused the president to withdraw that provision from the report submitted by his Committee on Economic Security. He announced simply: "I am not at this time recommending the adoption of so-called health insurance," although he said he intended to work with cooperating medical groups to find a compromise.

FDR wanted social security to be universal, simple, nondiscriminatory—as ER, Wald, Addams, and Harry Hopkins assumed it would be. According to Frances Perkins, FDR was adamant: "I see no reason why every child, from the day he is born, shouldn't be a member of the social security system." It could all be operated out of post offices, just "simple and natural—nothing elaborate or alarming about it." Every child at birth would receive a number; every unemployment claim and every old-age benefit would be delivered by the "rural free delivery carrier." Social security was sent to Congress with FDR's intentions clear: He did not intend to limit benefits to "just the industrial workers. . . . Everybody ought to be in on it. . . ." But Congress greeted the legislation with acrimony; fierce debates raged throughout the spring.

After FDR's speech, ER hosted the annual reception for the Supreme Court and then boarded the midnight train to New York to attend her daughter's marriage to John Boettiger. A private ceremony was held at nine o'clock in the morning in the second-floor library of the New York City home that Sara had built for ER, FDR, and herself. Boettiger had resigned from the anti-Roosevelt *Chicago Tribune* and temporarily became executive assistant to Will Hays, Hollywood's self-censorship officer. He and Anna rented a small apartment in New York, and Anna's children, Sistie and Buzzie, remained at the White House to complete the school year.

On the train, ER wrote John a letter that reflected her own experiences as a young wife and daughter-in-law:

> I won't get a chance to talk tomorrow so this is a last word of motherly advice. You know I shall always want to help you both to be happy but never let me interfere & remember that Anna is I think rather like me, she'd always rather have the truth even if it is painful & never let a doubt or a suspicion grow up between you two which honest facing can dispel. . . .

ER signed her letter "L.L."—for "Lovely Lady," John Boettiger's name for his mother-in-law. Charmed by the endearment, she always used it in her letters to him.

ER returned to Washington to participate in one of FDR's January initiatives, which the Senate took up immediately. For fifteen years, ER had been one of the lonely crusaders for the World Court. Despite his 1932 shabby convention deal with William Randolph Hearst, which was their most enduring public disagreement, finally, on 16 January 1935, FDR sent a message to the Senate:

> The movement to make international justice practicable and serviceable is not subject to partisan considerations. . . . At this period . . . when

every act is of moment to the future of world peace, the U.S. has an opportunity to throw its weight into the scale of peace.

That brief message represented the culmination of a long campaign ER and her immediate circle had led. To secure peace through mediation, negotiation, international law, seemed to ER and her friends Esther Lape and Elizabeth Read the last chance to avoid another round of world carnage.

Fascist terror and rearmament, war in Asia and Latin America heightened their sense of urgency. Should "outlaw" nations become dangerous, they would face a World Court with influence and authority, able to adjudicate differences and speak with a moral and united voice. They had championed America's entrance into the World Court since 1920, and in January 1935 their efforts seemed about to be rewarded by Senate ratification.

The World Court represented an ideal the United States had promoted and endorsed in 1899 at the International Peace Conference at the Hague, which established a court for international arbitration. In 1902, TR was the first national leader to submit a case to that court. It concerned a commercial land dispute with Mexico that had "dragged on almost fifty years." When the Hague ruling favored the United States, Jane Addams pointed out, Americans proudly championed international law.

But in the United States, "isolationism" swamped internationalism after the Great War. Except for international business ventures, any entanglement in Europe's woes or membership in international organizations seemed to self-styled "isolationists" dangerous, un-American, wicked.

In April 1933, FDR went out of his way to assure California Senator Hiram Johnson that he would not raise the World Court controversy during the "hundred days" special session devoted to domestic legislation. Then came the collapse of the London Economic Conference, and on 14 October 1933 Berlin announced its withdrawal from the Geneva Disarmament Conference and the League of Nations. The American Foundation resumed its campaign for U.S. adherence. But in December, FDR told ER to inform Esther Lape that "politically speaking . . . it would be unwise to do anything about the World Court."

In January 1934, following a conference with the president, Senator Joseph Robinson of Arkansas told the press that "the situation in Europe is so complex that this is not the opportune time to take up the World Court protocols."

Lape was furious. She and Curtis Bok went to Washington to meet with FDR and present the results of their independent poll, which revealed widespread popular and Senate support: sixty-five senators favored the Court, sixteen were opposed, fifteen were doubtful.

With fascism on the rise and German rearmament well under way, it seemed important for the United States to send a signal of support for international law. Never impolite to ER's closest friends, FDR told Lape he would consider action if the issue was "warmed up." Then, "when he judges the atmosphere to be propitious," he would, if he could, present it: "On this hope we rest."

Lape, ER, Carrie Chapman Catt, and countless others warmed the issue up, as FDR suggested. They wrote articles, gave speeches, lobbied senators. Hearst was furious, and Lape considered it a great victory when he editorialized against their "propaganda."

Congenial hearings were held in March 1934 before the Senate Foreign Relations Committee. Lape was pleased to have Catt and the women of the organized peace committees behind her. She wrote ER: "Everybody understands Franklin's feeling—that he cannot place his personal prestige with the Senate behind everything, and that the *whole* legislative picture must be taken into account." But the women were convinced: "If the Court comes up it will pass. Trouble is to get it up. . . ."

Lape asked ER to attend the 1934 hearings, but she could not: "I am terribly sorry, but Franklin thinks that I had better not go to any hearings. I never go to either the code hearings or to any of the others at the Capitol. . . ." She invited Esther and Elizabeth to stay at the White House. But Lape telegrammed her regrets: It "might on this particular occasion be embarrassing to you and even be interpreted as committing someone else to more aggressive line on court action than he wants to show at moment." Moreover, Hearst ran "cartoons three times during past week," and she was named among the "arch propagandists." Lape stayed at the Mayflower with Narcissa Vanderlip and Curtis Bok.

After the hearings, ER sent Lape the sad news that although they were a great success FDR's advisers were "all convinced" the World Court should not be brought up until after the 1934 congressional elections, since "it would just give Mr. Hearst another thing to pin his attack on. So I am afraid there is not much chance."

On 24 March, Senator Hiram Johnson confirmed ER's fears: If the Court was introduced, he warned, nothing else would get done. Johnson, who had voted against the Versailles Treaty, now announced that the World Court represented "the destruction of American sovereignty" and won an agreement to shelve the issue until Congress reconvened in January 1935.

The November 1934 elections had given the Democrats five more than the needed two-thirds majority, and a sufficient number of Republicans favored the Court to reassure ER's circle. The First Lady entered the January 1935 debates with essays and speeches that earned her a reputation as one of America's most vigorous peace advocates.

On 7 January, she wrote Hick about her "satisfactory day." There were morning meetings, lunch with Tommy, a drive with Louis. And from three to five, she locked her door and with Tommy wrote three radio speeches and one article. Nan arrived at five for tea; at six ER swam with FDR, then read for half an hour: Pearl Buck's latest novel, *A House Divided*, the final volume of her trilogy preceded by *The Good Earth* and *The Sons*, "and it is fascinating."

During that routinely hectic day, ER wrote one of her most provocative and enduring speeches for Carrie Chapman Catt's seventy-sixth birthday. Presented on 9 January 1935 at the tenth anniversary conference of the National Committee on the Cause and Cure of War and published in the book *Why Wars Must Cease*, ER's essay was in part a stirring rally for the World Court.

"Because the War Idea Is Obsolete" began with a headnote by George Washington: "My first wish is to see this plague of mankind [war] banished from the earth."

ER set out "to prove" that although we have not "as yet recognized it," in fact "the war idea is obsolete." There were many traditions which humans clung to until they simply gave them up, because they were obsolete—and eventually it was commonly recognized that they *were* obsolete. Killing witches, for example, was once the rage throughout Europe and America. When "people revert" to the killing and torture of old women somebody calls a witch, "we now say they are crazy."

But among nations "the war idea . . . hangs on . . . with outmoded and long-drawn-out cruelty." However, ER wrote, war "no longer worked," it no longer achieved its stated goals: During the American Revolution, "we desired separation from England and we achieved it." During the Civil War, fighting had "two objectives." Though "wasteful and costly" the Civil War "freed the slaves" and preserved a "unified nation." Therefore, the war idea was not yet obsolete.

But the "world conflagration" of 1914–18 "proved for the first time in our history that the war idea is obsolete. . . . It did not achieve its objectives." The United States fought, we were told, "to preserve democracy, to prevent the people of Europe from coming under the control of a despotic government which had no regard for treaties or the rights of neutral nations, and, above all, to end all future wars."

In terms of those objectives, "these four years were absolutely wasted." Then, at Versailles, the horror was compounded: Instead of "preventing future wars, the settlements arrived at have simply fostered hostilities. There is more talk of war today, not to mention wars actually going on in the Far East and in South America, than has been the case in many long years. The world over, countries are armed camps."

Civilization itself was threatened by modern warfare. There was no moral gain, and it was not good for the soul.

Private profit is made out of the dead bodies of men. The more we see of the munitions business, of the use of chemicals, of the traffic in [armaments], the more we realize that human cupidity is as universal as human heroism. . . . If we are to do away with the war idea, one of the first steps will be to do away with all possibility of private profit.

She defined war as quite simply a lose-lose situation: All families suffer the same when their sons are killed in battle. Moreover, "economic waste in one part of the world will have an economic effect in other parts of the world. We profited for a time commercially, but as the rest of the world suffers, so eventually do we."

ER rejected the widespread conviction that wars were inevitable; that human nature was warlike and thrilled especially to banners and cannons, trumpets and muskets. "That seems to me like saying that human nature is so made that we must destroy ourselves. After all, human nature has some intelligence," and is demonstrably capable of "good will," at least on an individual basis. Wars would end, therefore, when enough people worked to persuade "their government [to] find the way to stop war."

ER's speech was the clearest statement of her international views to date. She was proud to have it included in Catt's book with essays by women she so admired—including Alice Hamilton, Jane Addams, Dorothy Canfield Fisher, Mary Woolley, and Judge Florence Allen. *Why Wars Must Cease* represented an urgent appeal to prevent the next war, which seemed so imminent, and so preventable.

Although *Time*, generally in favor of internationalist solutions, considered the World Court "the deadest political issue in the land," the Senate debate was filled with fearful hyperbole. Isolationist "Bitter-Enders, the ragged remnant of 1919," including Hiram Johnson and William Edgar Borah, joined by Louisiana's Huey Long, did their rhetorical best to inflame fears about U.S. involvement in Europe's hideous disasters should the United States join the Court.

Huey Long, with dramatic frenzy, shouted that this meant the end of American sovereignty, the end of everything: "We are being rushed . . . into this World Court so that Señor Ab Jap or some other something . . . can pass upon our controversies."

Throughout the two-week debate, Hearst papers conducted an avalanche of opposition. From his retreat at San Simeon, Hearst "tossed his long, horsey head and charged." His editorialists "throughout the land shrilled and thundered with the threat of war. No attack on the Court was too preposterous to be splashed across the front pages of Hearstpapers." Moreover, his personal army of lobbyists descended on the Senate, met privately, made endless calls and unnamed deals.

Minnesota's Senator Thomas D. Schall not only attacked "37,000 foreign agents in the U.S. now working for passage of the so-called World Court," he roared: "To hell with Europe and the rest of those nations." He also attacked ER personally, until majority leader Robinson interrupted him: "I am not going to yield [to allow Minnesota's senator] to make one of his characteristic attacks on Mrs. Roosevelt."

Father Charles Coughlin, Detroit's radio priest, who broadcast nationally, led an incipient fascist movement that was crudely anti-Semitic, and his assault against the World Court included his charges that it would be dominated by Jewish money changers: America's "national sovereignty" was about to be sacrificed on the altar of the international bankers, that well-known crowd dominated by Rothschilds, Warburgs, Kuhns, and Loebs. Vote no. Vote against the World Court. "Today, tomorrow may be too late . . . whether you can afford it or not, send your Senators telegrams . . . vote NO! . . ."

ER broadcast to counter Father Coughlin's radio appeals against the godless, wicked World Court. She called for telegrams to illustrate the real "spirit of our country," which was unafraid "to join the World Court . . . I beg of you to let your [senators] know at once. . . ."

When the debate ended, on Friday afternoon, 25 January, prospects still looked favorable. But Senator Robinson agreed to a weekend recess. During that time, Hearst papers and Coughlin's broadcasts unleashed a propaganda carnival: It was the duty of every loyal American to save the country. Wire your senator. Keep America safe from foreign entanglements, foreign wars, foreign plunder.

Over forty thousand telegrams rolled into the Senate Monday morning. Individuals, churches, Sunday schools in little towns all over America sent wires. Western Union hired thirty-five extra clerks; the telegrams were delivered by wheelbarrow. It was unprecedented. When the vote was taken on Tuesday, 29 January, the Court lost by seven votes. Of ninety-six senators, fifty-two voted for, thirty-six against, the rest absented themselves.

After the tally, "jubilant Hearstlings tumbled over each other in their rush to telephone San Simeon. No less than 15 Senators telephoned congratulations to Detroit."

Privately, FDR thanked Senator Joe Robinson, and noted: "As to the 36 Senators who [opposed] I am inclined to think that if they ever get to Heaven they will be doing a great deal of apologizing for a very long time—that is if God is against war—and I think He is."

Publicly, however, FDR did little to block the drift away from the Court. He did not go on the radio, and he failed to throw any of the mighty weight of his office into the fray. *Time* wondered if the president had "really been heart & soul behind the Court? The wisest answer seemed to be: No."

When reporters trooped into his office the next day, FDR was dressed for his birthday "in a new grey homespun suit, a white rose and his best smile." When asked about the World Court vote he said only: "I am sending a note to Senator Robinson thanking him for a very able and very honorable fight."

ER, who had broadcast, trumpeted the Court at her press conference, and spoken at every available forum, including a great convention of Chautauquas that met at the White House, was devastated but did not criticize her husband.

Lape, who sat in the gallery throughout the World Court debate, was bitter about FDR's failure to prepare Senate leaders: "The votes were there . . . but there was nobody on the floor to deal with perfectly simple questions, nobody really handled it. Robinson was the leader, but inadequate and F should have realized that. . . ." It had been "a dreadful, dreadful experience," and she blamed FDR: "If the President wants something, the men know it." But even decades later, Lape was reluctant to criticize him: "The Court needed the President's leadership, but I don't think there is any point making that point."

Immediately after the vote, Lape canceled her expected visit to the White House—"I wasn't fit for anyone's dinner table"—and left Washington.

In her editorial for the *Women's Democratic News*, ER called the World Court defeat a "serious set back in our efforts to deal peacefully with the rest of the world. . . . We need a court of law to build up a body of international law." Now all the years of effort by genuine statesmen had been "brought to naught by a chain of newspapers and a limited number of broadcasts."

Unreconciled to the defeat, ER nevertheless defended her husband. She replied to a disappointed letter critical of her husband's public silence by a member of the National Committee on the Cause and Cure of War:

> I doubt if any public word by the President would have helped matters much. He sent for every Democrat and Independent Senator and talked to him personally, besides sending his message. I am afraid that the pressure must come from the people themselves and, until it does, we will never become a member of the World Court.

Actually, FDR had not rallied senatorial support, and on 30 January, ER confided her deeper feelings to Hick: "I rather expected the vote to go as it did. We are so prone to be led by the Hearsts and the Coughlins and the Longs and I am only really sorry that I pushed FDR to try to pass it." ER hoped especially that her efforts did not "imperil any of our other things!"

ER characteristically blamed herself, and was forever dismayed by the loss of what she considered the last hope for collective security in the struggle for democracy and peace. America's rejection of the World Court was for her a personal defeat, as well as a political tragedy which carried a cruel and bitter message to the future.

Unknown to ER, the U.S. ambassador to Germany, William Dodd, also considered it a major diplomatic disaster: If the Court had passed, "our Government's prestige in Europe would have been raised by about 50 percent." Like ER, Dodd rejected the international debt question as a fraudulent argument. Shortly after the Court vote he met with members of the Senate Foreign Relations Committee and explained why it was a chimera from a historical point of view: The United States had, from 1820 to 1850, repudiated over "200 million [dollars] of valid obligations and had failed to pay interest on nearly all obligations for a period of ten years."

Dodd did not understand why the senators were not better informed, and was convinced that if they had had such facts before them prior to the vote "we should have had a different result."

Other members of FDR's team did not agree. Harold Ickes was among those who censured ER's involvement. Ickes considered the vote a "decisive defeat" for the administration and blamed ER personally:

> [Senators] were bitter in their criticism of Mrs. Roosevelt. . . . It does seem to me that she is not doing the President any good. She is becoming altogether too active in public affairs and I think that she is harmful rather than helpful. After all, the people did not elect her President. . . .

A shocking aftermath of the World Court defeat was an administrative assault against Esther Lape's American Foundation: Federal tax authorities "served notice" that if the American Foundation continued its campaign for the World Court, it would lose its tax-exempt status. Lape blamed neither Morgenthau nor FDR, but that order silenced the American Foundation on international issues. World Court membership did not come up again until after World War II.

Lape never discussed the political decision to threaten the American Foundation's tax exemption. But tax investigations and similar fiscal harassments were a bit of political hardball FDR had used against such dangerous enemies as Huey Long.

Defeated, and punished, Lape transferred the American Foundation's "campaign of public education" to other issues of urgency, notably "public health, and medical care." Lape and her allies prepared a national health care proposal for the upcoming social security debates.

Whatever bitter feelings ER may have felt after the Court defeat, she and Louis Howe managed to be amusing and "worked up some things" for FDR's birthday dinner on 30 January. Then she joined Anna, Ruth, Elliott, Tommy, and Missy at the birthday balls, for "as short a time as I can manage!" But for weeks after what she realized was the final defeat for the World Court, she performed her obligations and chores within the grip of an unusually severe emotional depression. Until the spring, almost all her letters were despondent.

Her sense of personal loss and anguish was heightened by FDR's continued refusal to address the ongoing lynching issue. Walter White was distressed that it went unmentioned in his State of the Union speech—despite the autumn lynching of Claude Neal, advertised in fifteen newspapers and broadcasts over the radio. Men, women, and children were invited to one of the most savage lynchings in U.S. history on 26 October 1934.

Over one hundred men stormed a county jail at Brewston, Alabama, to seize Claude Neal, accused of the murder of a white woman in Marianna, Florida, where he was transported and tortured to death before a frenzied crowd of cheering participants. After an orgy of unspeakable violence and mutilation, the charred, disfigured remains of a man hung from a tree in the courthouse square, and photographs were sold for fifty cents each.

When FDR was asked by reporters if he would now support the Costigan-Wagner bill, he asked for time so that he might "check up and see what I did last year. I have forgotten."

Walter White sent ER the NAACP report that described the Marianna lynching and asked her if the Justice Department could not prosecute on the basis of the new Lindbergh law, since Neal had been taken across state lines. Attorney General Homer Cummings denied the law's relevance, since no ransom was involved. ER wrote White: "The Marianna lynching was a horrible thing. I wish very much that the Department of Justice might come to a different point of view and I think possibly they will."

Regretting that many people had "become more cynical regarding the attitude of the administration," White asked ER to appear at a protest meeting at Carnegie Hall. ER dropped a memo into her husband's bedside basket: "FDR I would like to do it, of course talking over the speech, but will do whatever you say." He said, through a memo sent by Missy: "This is dynamite." ER wrote White: "I do not feel it wise to speak . . . but I will talk to the President and see what can be done in some other way. . . ."

White encouraged his constituents to remain patient, "saying that perhaps the President will send a special message to Congress. He wrote ER: "I wonder if you could advise me if my optimism is well founded. It would help during this very trying period to know that our efforts have not been in vain. . . ."

ER replied:

> I talked to the President . . . this morning. He wants me to say that he was talking to the leaders on the lynching question and his sentence on

crime in his address to Congress touched on that because lynching is a crime. However he, himself, will write you more fully a little later on.

While FDR's Southern strategy kept him aloof, ER worked ever more closely with the NAACP. She welcomed James Weldon Johnson's invitation to attend a 12 February dinner to honor Arthur Spingarn's twenty-one years as chair of the National Legal Committee of the NAACP and looked forward to visiting a controversial art exhibit at a major New York gallery—the NAACP's "Art Commentary on Lynching." It featured works by Reginald Marsh, George Bellows, Thomas Benton, Julius Bloch, José Clemente Orozco, Harry Sternberg, Noguchi, William Gropper, and many others. Pearl S. Buck opened the exhibition, and there was vivid commentary written by Sherwood Anderson and Erskine Caldwell. The paintings and drawings were stark and blunt, including Reginald Marsh's award-winning *New Yorker* illustration of a mother holding her child on her shoulders to get a better view, captioned "This is her first lynching."

The New York Times called it a "macabre exhibition." The *New York World Telegram*'s art critic wrote: "It is an exhibition which tears the heart and chills the blood . . . this is not an exhibition for softies. It may upset your stomach. If it upsets your complacency . . . it will have been successful."

ER wanted FDR to support the Costigan-Wagner bill and did not intend to upset him with a political gesture he might deplore. She wrote Walter White:

> The more I think about going to the exhibition, the more troubled I am, so this morning I went in to talk to my husband. . . . [He] said it was quite all right for me to go, but if some reporter . . . [described] some horrible picture, it would cause more Southern opposition. They plan to bring the bill out quietly as soon as possible although two Southern Senators have said they would filibuster. . . . He thinks, however, they can get it through.

ER decided, therefore, that it would "be safer if I came without any publicity or did not come at all."

In the midst of negotiations regarding the lynching exhibit, an unfortunate incident confused ER's NAACP friends, and embarrassed the First Lady. Ellen Woodward received a picture of "three namesakes of the President," sent by Virginia's director of women's work, Ella Agnew. She thought the photograph "from the field" attractive and asked Woodward "to be sure that either Mr. or Mrs. Roosevelt sees it." Woodward wrote ER: "We know that you receive many foolish things but the pickaninnies are right cute! Also we note that it took three children to bear the one name, Franklin Delano Roosevelt."

ER replied: "Thank you so much for sending me the pictures of the little pickaninnies. They certainly are cunning and the President was very much amused."

On Sunday, 13 January, the *Richmond Times-Dispatch* ran a story about the "New Deal Triplets," thirteen-month-old Franklin, Delano, and Roosevelt Jones—Prince Edward County relief clients: "John and Mary Jones came on the relief rolls only a few weeks before the babies were born." To demonstrate their appreciation, "they decided to name their offsprings after their benefactor. . . ."

ER's letter was published as part of the story. Woodward had sent it on to Agnew, who said it was taken from her personal files. Many apologies went around, as did angry letters, including one from a Negro club:

> We wish to call your attention to the fact that the above term is highly resented by the Negro people. Feeling that your interest in this group would not willingly lead you to offer any offense, we respectfully bring this matter to your attention, confident in the belief that you will do whatever is necessary to correct the impression which its use has created.

ER replied: "I have your letter and assure you that no lack of respect was meant. . . . We always considered 'pickaninny' as a term of endearment and often use it for any child." Although she was in the vanguard of considerable change regarding race relations, for ER language changed last of all.

Throughout February and March, White trusted in FDR's good intentions, based on ER's encouragement. But the waiting game was hopeless, and embarrassing for White. His own reputation was jeopardized by FDR's continued silence. In February, former Missouri congressman Leonidas Dyer, who had introduced the famous Dyer antilynching bill of 1922, chided White for his faith in the Roosevelts. White had been "deceived."

> You and the CRISIS ought to tell the colored people the truth, which is that there is no chance whatever for this legislation [in a] Democratic Congress. . . . If the CRISIS is to continue in this deception I hope you will discontinue sending it to me.

Again White turned to ER: If he could only talk with the president; would she make one more appointment; they had the votes all lined up. ER tried, but McIntyre replied that FDR was too busy, and wrote a memo to Tommy: "Confidentially, this is a very delicate situation and it does not seem advisable to draw the President into it any more than we have to."

ER had penciled on White's letter to FDR: "I do think you could see him HERE and help him on tactics with advice. This ought to go through."

Two weeks later, Costigan brought his bill up—and the Southland arose.

Prepared to filibuster for months, the almost solid South would block every-thing on the Senate calendar, including the social security bill passed by the House. FDR was asked to call off the filibuster by an expression of righteous indignation. He refused to utter one public word of protest. Costigan caved in, and on 1 May withdrew the antilynch bill. *The New York Times* opined that the surrender looked like "Appomatox in reverse."

White thanked ER for her "deep personal interest" and resigned in protest from the Virgin Islands Advisory Council—which she had recommended him for. To FDR he wrote: "It is my belief that the utterly shameless filibuster could not have withstood the pressure of public opinion had you spoken out against it. In justice to the cause I serve I cannot continue to remain even a small part of your official family."

Fascist brutality and racialist rhetoric in Europe encouraged American lynchers. America's failure to demonstrate official opposition encouraged ra-cialist violence in Europe. The message seemed to be: Lynching was done; tor-ture was acceptable. ER committed herself to a long struggle. She wrote White: "I am so sorry about the bill. Of course all of us are going on fighting. . . ."

She sent FDR a scathing editorial White had sent her which condemned the president's silence, with a note: "Pretty bitter isn't it? I can't blame them though. . . ."*

FDR's silence and ER's interventions on behalf of the Costigan-Wagner bill revealed a deep level of political tension within the White House. Familial disagreements increasingly involved profound principles and ethical con-cerns. FDR insisted that practical politics, issues of strategy and tactics, were involved, and he expected ER to accept his wisdom on these matters. ER did not agree, and on this issue continued to write, network, and organize sup-port. But she spoke publicly only when and where FDR approved.

In May, Roy Wilkins invited ER to attend the closing session of the NAACP's twenty-sixth annual convention in St. Louis. This would be, Wilkins wrote, a "particularly significant Conference," which would address "the greatest crisis ever faced by the twelve million colored American citizens."

*ER's message was penned on an NAACP broadside that reproduced a 4 May editorial from *The Des Moines Register* sent to every senator. "Irony, Politics and The Negro" quoted FDR's 1932 campaign promise: Wherever the desperation of "the socially underprivileged" cannot be addressed by the states, " 'it becomes the positive duty of the federal government to step in to help.' " It concluded: "The si-lence of this same speaker boomed from the White House during debate on the Costigan-Wagner bill. . . . When the next mob dances in the light of flames about a stake in the south, that declaration of high duty and intent will be a ghostly wisp of smoke, drifting off toward the heavens."

There was, moreover, "great restlessness, doubt, and even some hostility among the colored people" toward the administration.

Wilkins cited the discriminatory practices of NRA, PWA, AAA, and FERA especially. Atop all the disappointments of 1933–34 was the recent failure of the antilynching bill even to get a hearing. Now, as the presidential campaign season approached, even the proposed work relief program, which was to become the Works Progress Administration (WPA), was met with "greater and greater cynicism." He believed "it would be good strategy from the Administration's standpoint, and good Americanism from the standpoint of the welfare of all our people, for some emissary to give a sincere word of reassurance. . . . We hope that you will consent to be that ambassador."

ER asked: "FDR should I go? or could you send someone really good & interested." Missy wrote Tommy to suggest that Oscar Chapman represent the First Lady, who should not go. ER acquiesced, but sent a public message of "deep regret that I was obliged to refuse to attend the conference."

The winter-spring congressional season of 1935 filled ER with despair. In addition to the collapse of the World Court and the Costigan-Wagner bill there were brutal negotiations over the social security bill. For months her letters were punctuated by unusual exhaustion, frustration, genuine confusion.

For over twenty years, Jane Addams, Lillian Wald, and others had publicly fought for mothers' pensions, widows' benefits, old-age security, workers' compensation, and unemployment insurance. From 1924 on ER championed universal protection, decent housing, and public health care for all Americans. The fight for economic security was not new, and it was wrong to credit Huey Long's Share Our Wealth Clubs and California's Dr. Francis E. Townsend with radicalizing FDR and driving the second New Deal into old-age pensions and steps toward real security.* ER and her circle had been agitating for these issues for decades.

FDR had introduced them to New York State when he was governor, and now they were about to become national policy. But something happened to social security between FDR's thrilling January speech, which so gratified ER, and the springtime compromises that devoured the universal aspect of his promise.

ER's papers contain an important file on social security, with FDR's heavily marked marginalia in an effort to explain changes in administrative

---

*Dr. Townsend called for the retirement of everyone over sixty; each retired person would receive a monthly pension of $200, paid for by a sales tax, to be spent each month, which would provide security and keep the economy pumped up. Many thought a Long-Townsend third party loomed for 1936.

policy. FDR instructed his wife to see especially pages 9 and 10 of "Statement of the Secretary of the Treasury on the Economic Security Bill." There one reads Henry Morgenthau's testimony to the House Ways and Means Committee opposing the president's stated intention that the federal government defray half the cost of old-age insurance and provide universal coverage:

> The national contributory old-age annuity system, as now proposed, includes every employee in the United States, other than those of governmental agencies or railways. . . . This means that every transient or casual laborer is included, that every domestic servant is covered, and that the large and shifting class of agricultural workers is covered.

Morgenthau proposed instead that they be excluded: "Under the income tax law, the Bureau of Internal Revenue last year handled something less than five million returns;* with the present nearly universal coverage of the Bill's provisions," he estimated 20 million people would be involved. That would require "minutely detailed, and very expensive enforcement efforts." Therefore, to avoid "the imposition of administrative burdens . . . that would threaten . . . the entire system," Morgenthau helped doom the promise of social security for all Americans.

Morgenthau's testimony astonished liberals. On 5 February 1935, he called for the exclusion of America's neediest and most insecure workers in what was to have been a universal system to abolish need and insecurity. The race factor was publicly ignored, but clearly FDR and his treasury secretary caved in to Southern opposition. Since the vast majority of Negro workers were in precisely the categories excluded, Morgenthau's proposal was part of FDR's Southern strategy and guaranteed a "Lily White Social Security System," which the NAACP immediately editorialized against.

Frances Perkins wrote that of the entire Committee on Economic Security, which she chaired, only Morgenthau "indicated his flat opposition" to the government "contribution out of general revenues" for old-age insurance. Instead he proposed a 1 percent tax by employers and employees, with no federal contribution at all. This created the regressive payroll tax for old-age security, which many considered reactionary. No security system in Europe, where social insurance was widespread,† was based on such a collection system, without governmental contribution.

According to Perkins, every member of her Committee on Economic Se-

---

*The low number of income tax returns reflects the very limited taxation system which prevailed until after World War II, when taxation was extended to cover virtually every income.

†Most of Europe had some form of social security before World War I. Pioneered in Bismarck's Germany (1870), it was achieved quickly in Austria (1881), Norway (1894), Finland (1895), Britain (1897), and France, Italy, and Denmark (1898).

curity was "startled" by Morgenthau's betrayal, since universal coverage "had been agreed upon" from the beginning. But: "There was nothing for me to do but accept, temporarily at least. . . ."

A truly liberal bill, introduced by Ernest Lundeen, Minnesota's Farmer-Labor Party representative, called for universal coverage and unemployment benefits for every unemployed worker to be paid for by federal funds and corporate taxes. But the administration bill, with Morgenthau's limitations, was happily accepted by the conservative and Southern-dominated House Ways and Means Committee, chaired by Robert Doughton of North Carolina, and the Senate's Finance Committee, chaired by Mississippi Senator Pat Harrison.

Everything ER had ever said on behalf of old-age security, work, and equity contradicted Morgenthau's proposals. What had happened to FDR's universal "cradle to the grave" security package? There is no paper trail to indicate the route to Morgenthau's decision. There is no evidence to indicate the discussions that must have dominated White House conversations. From her correspondence we know that ER was bewildered. Did her husband now really intend to curtail social security for the vast majority of working women and black men for reasons of administrative simplicity and ease?

On 5 January 1934, precisely one year before Morgenthau's great betrayal, ER had made a vivid and stirring address before the District of Columbia branch of the American Association for Social Security, which was broadcast nationally. She assumed Americans had already "accepted" the "merits of old age pensions," to replace the situation in most states where the poor and aged were treated in "a terrible way—through poorhouses."

She told of a family in her own village of Hyde Park: Annually, she drove this "old family—two old sisters and two old brothers—who had lived on a farm not far from us" to vote. Then one election day, she arrived to find one sister in tears because one brother had died, and the other "brother had been taken to the insane asylum"—undone by financial worry. There was no food, no money for taxes, and they were about to lose the family farm. She "was waiting to go to the poorhouse," where her sister "had already gone."

ER felt that she had been a dreadful neighbor, and also that the "whole community was to blame." They were a generous family, who gave "to the church and to the charities." They had always "done what good citizens should do and they simply had never been able to save. There had always been someone in the family who needed help; some young person to start. . . ."

Old people, ER argued, should be allowed to live in their own homes, with dignity and respect. "And I think it costs us less in the end."

How, ER wondered, could we be "happy knowing that throughout this country" countless people suffered so? That agricultural workers, domestic and service workers, teachers, seamen, nurses, and government workers might now remain uncovered by a social security law that excluded them was intolerable to ER.

On 27 February 1935, ER told her press conference the social security bill was just a "start." She was certain that changes would occur "year by year, in as big an undertaking as this." She hoped to see "a permanent ban on child labor, better unemployment insurance, better health care for the country as a whole, better care for mothers and children generally," and a New Deal for youth and labor. "Labor must share to a greater extent and receive a fairer return for its part in the world's work," and "capital [must] accept the fact of a more limited and reasonable return."

From February to May, Congress negotiated the social security bill onto the floor for debate. During that time there were many private meetings, painful negotiations, White House dinners where agreements were made, and lost. It was, judging from ER's letters to Hick, the winter and spring of her discontent. From the World Court to the antilynch bill to Morgenthau's message, ER was in an unusual state of gloom.

In January, Hick was alone in New York, where she had dental surgery. ER, in Washington, had "a good talk with your boss [Harry Hopkins] last night, who does seem to know what FDR wants him to do and to like it. He says he'll probably have work for you by the end of the week so I hope you will be healed and well." ER thought that if they had been together the hard days "might have been pleasant" despite Hick's "pain and discomfort."

> Here I hardly count anything in the way of personal contacts pleasant! Dear, I wish it could be a joy when we meet and are together and not such keen unhappiness but there is always the balance to everything until one gets to a certain kind of numbness. I saw my grandmother reach that after repeated blows and she retained her sweetness and ability to enjoy sun and flowers and children and whatever good things came to her. I suppose that is what we should all pray for.

Clearly depressed, she wrote Hick that she felt exhausted and found herself resting and napping. After she read ER's letter, Hick called to apologize for adding to her troubles by describing her surgical ordeal.

ER was glad for their talk:

> I don't know why you think it egoism to tell me about Saturday's pain. I would hate it if you didn't and [would] always wonder what really went on and what you hid! It is good advice not to fight things, that I'm sure about. It is what I do so much down here and what makes life hard for those around me! Don't worry over the [Arthurdale] Stories. I don't bother at all about them except in the fact that they will hurt the Homesteaders or Louis. It is more fun to help a few people and stick to a job and see results

but again life carries you and you must take what chances it gives you and not kick against the pricks! I do it all the time though I know it is futile!

Then, ER, who always wrote her own speeches and columns and never accepted anyone's offer to ghostwrite her words, revealed the depths of her anguish: She was to broadcast on "a day in the White House," and for the first time she asked Hick: "Would you like to write it?" Hick declined, and ER replied to her lost letter:

> I know how you feel about the White House and it is partly my fault because I have no enjoyment in my life here and you feel it and think I mind more than I really do. I've lived so much of my life "going thro" and being relieved when certain periods are over and yet I don't really mind. I'm just kind of cold about it and that makes me cold to those around! . . .

ER still hoped for greater happiness with Hick:

> If you and I work together someday, I think we'll have a swell time and if we steal a day or two away here and there and vacation in summer we'll be having more than our share of good times!

> I am perfectly well again and don't need rest anymore. . . .

FDR had contributed to ER's changed mood. Worried about his wife's depression, FDR made a point to present her with the first good news she had had in a long time: Congress would pass the $4 billion work relief appropriations bill within the next two weeks, and then he would "settle where [the] homesteaders go."

Although the bill did not actually pass until April, the Works Progress Administration (WPA) initiated a massive public works program that employed millions of Americans in exciting and useful projects. It was initially to have been the work security part of the social security bill, to guarantee jobs through federally supported public works as a supplement to unemployment insurance. WPA was actually FDR's compromise to Hopkins's vision of full employment as an entitlement in the social security package, which ER had supported. ER considered WPA a tangible victory, but only a "stop-gap," temporary and insufficient. She deplored especially the relief aspect of it, which continued the means test and social worker investigations that required destitution before consideration. But it was a beginning and would prevent many human tragedies.

Given ER's mostly sour mood throughout January, Hick decided to recuperate from her dental surgery at the Danas' place on Long Island. ER was pleased: "They are wise people and real people & it is nice to have them as friends." Besides, at the moment ER had little to offer:

Dear one, it is a gray and gloomy day! How I envied Elliott and Ruth, their youth and their dreams. . . . I have a curious feeling of being thru with dreams, old age really setting in. Old age is really nothing worse than that, having no more faith in the future, no dreams! I guess it is the day, for as you well know no one plans fuller into the future than I do and that does require faith!

These were hard times between ER and Hick. Hick was needy, and lonely. Her WPA assignment pending, there was nothing in particular she really cared to do. ER was also lonely, but preoccupied, and they were apart for weeks. Hick ruminated about her life's choices. She was only forty-two, but she felt very old, or at least worried about becoming old, and dependent. Like many single women, she had arranged her entire life to be self-sufficient. She believed in hard work, and she liked to work hard. Then, like many wives and women in love, with one dramatic flourish she had relinquished her hold on all she had achieved. She had done it for love, and out of a sense of loyalty. There was no way she could have pursued both her journalistic interest in the First Lady and her friendship with the First Lady.

ER had helped her find challenging, important jobs appropriate to her skills. But Hick never enjoyed her new work. The kind of respect and admiration she had had as a journalist now seemed filtered through her friendship with ER. Moreover, she no longer worked for people whom she understood completely. Although her work was often praised, and even influential, she never had a sense that it made a difference. Her words were neither published nor widely available. She had become anonymous. She was a newshawk without a newspaper, a writer without readers. A woman whose days were spent mostly alone, waiting for an hour or an evening, for a phone call or a letter from the only woman she cared to be with.

In the country, at the Danas' place, with time to reflect, she wondered about the rhythms of her life, her own chemistry and longings, her life's choices. Increasingly, thoughts of the future frightened her. As she had the year before, when she visited with Ella Morse and her husband, Roy Dickerson, Hick wondered if it might have been better to be a wife and mother. She confided her concerns to ER: Her professional life was in tatters; she faced a future of economic insecurity, in a climate that seemed to devalue or punish single women, alone and childless. Might not all anxieties evaporate, might not everything be transformed into comfort, if not luxury, were she to marry?

Whatever the actual words of Hick's fantasy, in a letter now lost, there were many benefits to be derived from such a solution. If she were to consent to be supported financially, she would also be protected by the mantle of society's approval. Many women not otherwise inclined, but without economic security, made that choice. There was much to be said for marital privilege, and ER replied:

> Of course you should have had a husband and children and it would have made you happy if you loved him and in any case it would have satisfied certain cravings and given you someone in whom to lavish the love and devotion you have to keep down all the time. Yours is a rich nature with so much to give that the outlets always seem meager. Dear one, I do love you and appreciate the fight you make not to make me unhappy, but there is no use trying to hide things from me because I know just how you feel!

ER's own feelings were just then ruffled by wild press criticism. Accused of personal ambitions, lust for power, and unseemly political interference, she patiently explained that she did whatever she did because it was right and just and fair, and had to be done: "How I hate doing these things and then they say someday I'll run for an office. Well, I'd have to be chloroformed first!" But if she could improve these terrible "conditions even a little bit I suppose it is worth it. . . ."

ER and Hick spent some part of the weekend before Valentine's Day together, and ER wrote: "Dear, it meant so much to have even that little time with you and it does give me so much more than you know in a sense of closeness and warmth. I love you very dearly."

From February to April, while social security and the $4 billion WPA bill languished in Congress, ER continually pressed FDR for a bold demonstration of leadership to fight the conservatives of his own party and traditional Southern trimmers. At dinner with Molly Dewson ER was fascinated to see that her husband "gets much less annoyed at her when she tells him things are wrong than he does at me!" That night, they both urged FDR to take a more active public role on the stalled legislation which was to define the second New Deal. He was determined to stay out of it but he wanted Hick to investigate the political climate, to "verify all the most glaring ward violations," and the people's real sentiments. Hick agreed to return to Washington for conferences: "Mabel [ER's upstairs maid] is so pleased you'll be here the 23d. She says she misses you so much. . . ."

That February, ER's letters were songs of duality. She yearned for Hick's company, yet was relieved when they were apart. ER frequently seemed unaware of the impact her words might have on Hick's already low spirits. From Cornell ER wrote: "Dear I wish you were with me, I was homesick for you in Ithaca. But you would hate the crowds and the telephones and the fawning. . . ."

With Earl the next day: "Dearest I have had a nice time and I love seeing Earl but I miss you too. One never seems to have everything at once! . . . Earl has a new girl, he is becoming or is in love with. . . . What a nuisance hearts are and yet without them life would hardly be worth while! . . . I love you dear, bless you sleep sweetly and won't it be grand to see you Friday."

ER's last February days at Hyde Park with FDR, his mother, several children, Nan, and Marion were highlighted by a "really big snow storm. . . . I love the country in winter! [and] F seems to be having a grand time." ER had such a pleasant conversation "with Mama for over an hour," she felt completely restored and persuaded Hick to spend most of March and April with her in Washington.

Hick had hesitated, which ER understood since "in Washington your sense of loneliness is intensified by having few old friends and being in a place you don't like with the only person you would like to see tied down to a very exacting job most of the time!" But ER could not leave Washington just then because Louis Howe seemed near death. FDR too had postponed his cruise because of Howe, and was now scheduled to leave on a ten-day Caribbean jaunt with Vincent Astor on 26 March.

While FDR sailed on the *Nourmahal*, ER and Hick spent the first two weeks of April together. Closer to congressional tension over social security and "the big bill," as WPA was known, ER found little comfort in FDR's notes from the *Nourmahal:*

> Dearest Babs . . . just fun—wonderful weather and smooth seas and I am already much tanned. . . .
>
> The news from Washington about the Big Bill is most confusing, and I get long contradictory appeals for all kinds of action by me! It is as well to let them try to work it out themselves, I think. . . .

ER was particularly mindful of the NAACP's opposition to "Lily-White Social Security." In March, NAACP's journal, *The Crisis,* published George Edmund Haynes's essay detailing his testimony before both the House Ways and Means Committee and the Senate Finance Committee. Except for old-age insurance, which was to be federally regulated, all management was to be left to the states—which, wrote Haynes, meant disaster for Negro citizens. The bill's purpose "is to alleviate the hazards of old age, unemployment, illness and dependency." But it was a defective insult, because "all domestic and personal servants are excluded from unemployment provisions," and it is "proposed to exempt farmers . . . thus eliminating tenant farmers. . . ." Ultimately, "about three-fifths of all Negroes gainfully employed will not be benefited at all."

To avoid the creation of social security for whites only, Haynes argued for "non-discrimination" clauses for certain titles: Title I, "dealing with old age [insurance]"; Title II, "dealing with allotments for dependent children"; Title III and IV, "dealing with unemployment and old age annuities [for poor people, not covered in Title I]"; Title VII, providing "maternal and child health"; and Title VIII, "providing for allotments to local and public health programs."

"This legislation is so vital to Negro men, women, and children and to peaceable race relations that every lover of fair play" needed to rally and support antidiscrimination provisions.

ER routinely distributed *Crisis* articles. In 1934, for example, she sent Donald Richberg, director of the NRA and the National Emergency Council, John Davis's charges of discrimination ("NRA Codifies Wage Slavery" and "TVA: Lily-White Reconstruction") and asked if they were true. After weeks of correspondence, she wrote Donald Richberg: "I hope you will try to see that justice is done. . . ." ER also expected justice to be done concerning social security.

But by mid-April, the only New Deal effort that seemed to move forward was Arthurdale. ER drove there with Nancy Cook, and was gratified to see the progress made by so many people who worked so hard. ER wanted everybody to appreciate how much ordinary people could do for themselves when they were given a chance and were not ridiculed, degraded, or belittled. ER's commitment to Arthurdale was heartfelt, and a genuine bond developed between her and the everyday people whose homes she walked into with so little pretense, and so much love. ER hated ceremony. The days she enjoyed most were those that had "very little 'first lady' about it, just simple and kindly hospitality and welcome."

But while entire communities such as Arthurdale might appreciate her support, Republican press attacks against her escalated. These rarely bothered her: "Every president and his family go through it and afterwards it is forgotten."

She was, however, sensitive to criticisms by her own family. On her return from Arthurdale, ER spent a "free" day in New York: She took Elizabeth Read to lunch; went with Elinor Morgenthau to the Neighborhood Playhouse to see a "very modern and moving" student dance company; visited with Cousin Susie, who had become a recluse and distrusted everybody; "took Tiny and Eddie to dinner." At some point, she spent a moment with her mother-in-law.

Their exchange added to ER's bitter spring. It began with an impulsive remark about the 1936 election. After a winter of relative peace between them, ER confided to "Mama that it would not break my heart if F were not elected." It was an act of simple trust about a fleeting feeling, and ER was horrified. But as she left the room, SDR turned to James and asked, "Do you think Mother will do anything to defeat Father? Is that why she stays in politics just to hurt his chances of reelection?"

ER indignantly wrote Hick, "Now I ask you, after all these years?" After thirty years, to be precise; and ER was devastated. Her old sense of being misunderstood, an outcast in the bosom of her own family, returned. It was incomprehensible that Sara Delano Roosevelt, who had worked so closely with ER on so many projects, from the WTUL to the Henry Street Settlement, to the Women's Division of the Democratic Party, to the Bethune-Cookman College, could still doubt ER's loyalty to her son—to his ambitions, his vision, his well-being.

Characteristically, ER blamed herself for letting down her guard and trusting her mother-in-law with her doubts and innermost feelings as she contemplated all the legislation she cared about stalled by FDR's Southern strategy. Filled with anguish and disappointment that he had refused to speak out more vigorously from January through April as she had urged him to do, she confided in her mother-in-law—who used it to attack her. ER never let it happen again. FDR's mother would always be his champion and defender; she would remain his primary goad, and conscience.

FDR always remained detached and above the fray when familial strife emerged, which only added to the tension. For days after SDR's remark, ER felt "ready to chew everyone's head off!"

Then Harlem exploded on 19 March 1935, when a young boy was caught stealing a 10-cent penknife and momentarily disappeared into the cellar of a Kress department store. Immediately, neighborhood women ran to the street and cried that he was to be beaten, lynched just as in the South. Police were called, not to placate the fearful, but to tyrannize them. Nobody knew that the boy, Lino Rivera, had been released and was on the subway headed home; nobody spoke to the people. Lynchings were much in mind. The Costigan-Wagner bill was in the headlines, and the death of Claude Neal lingered.

Residents assembled to protest and protect each other. An ambulance arrived, and a woman screamed: There is the hearse, to take him. The neighborhood exploded. All day and night, fires raged, windows were shattered, people were beaten. The toll was high: 100 wounded, shot or knifed; 125 arrested; 250 shop windows smashed; three dead, shot by the police.

A young assistant pastor of the Abyssinian Baptist Church, Dr. Adam Clayton Powell, Jr., explained: "Continued exploitation of the Negro is at the bottom of the trouble . . . as regards wages, jobs, working conditions." Everyone, businesses, utilities, even government assistance programs, "discriminated against Harlem's population. . . . And the people were finally fed up."

Mayor Fiorello La Guardia initiated a study, done by Negro sociologist E. Franklin Frazier. A monumental work, *The Negro in Harlem: A Report on*

Social and Economic Conditions Responsible for the Outbreak of 19 March 1935, revealed after twenty-five hearings what was widely known: A concerted effort to degrade the lives of Harlem's residents included everything from "the most vicious Negro hater" in charge of Harlem's relief bureau, to neglect and abuse in housing, health, education, and jobs; and a pattern of violence that "likened the New York Police Department to a racist army of occupation." La Guardia suppressed the report, but vowed to make changes, and did. Frazier's work stimulated consideration of America's ghettoes for years to come, and ER would participate on every level. But in 1935, there was little she could do, except cajole, request, argue—which she did.

Despite ER's confession of dread to SDR concerning four more years in the White House, as early as February 1935 ER and her circle had launched the women's campaign for FDR's reelection. Every state had a women's Reporter Plan committee, which published attractive pamphlets to highlight FDR's legislative achievements and future goals. Written and designed largely by Dewson and ER, they "put vitality into the party" and served as the major organizing effort of the entire 1936 campaign.

There was little resistance among ER's friends when asked to work for FDR's reelection. When various programs important to them failed, they dug in for the next battle. Agnes Brown Leach, a founder of the Woman's Peace Party, which became the Women's International League for Peace and Freedom, and an ardent internationalist who supported the World Court, was pleased to chair New York State's Reporter Plan committee. Leach once called her friend Frances Perkins "a half-loaf girl: take what you can now and try for more later," and that was generally the attitude of all the women in ER's network.

Ellen Woodward, for example, urged ER to speak to her husband about WPA—which until April seemed to limit work projects exclusively to men—and there was "much uneasiness felt by women all over the country." But there was no public criticism, as they closed ranks to support FDR's efforts.

Even Lucy Randolph Mason, a pioneering Southern rebel with proud Georgian roots, who was soon to spend the rest of her life campaigning for black representation, women's rights, and civil rights, said nothing about discrimination in social security in April 1935. Indeed, as head of the National Consumers League, Mason consented, and Dewson was proud that the NCL "swung into line with complete support" for social security: "I think we were the first organization to give support without criticism or further suggestion."

FDR's silence concerning these critical issues continued, and by the end of April ER was in a rare state. It was so bad she canceled a long-planned weekend with Hick, and told her to stay away for a few more weeks:

I'm too darn busy these days to be good to anyone and also too deeply upset I think. I'm glad I'm going to be away for a bit before you come home for I'm so on edge it is all I can do to hold myself together just now. That is not a good mood for you to return to, is it? . . .

ER "asked Tommy to have the [press] girls to supper [at her home] to-morrow night. I just had to get out of here and do something I enjoyed!" She hoped Hick would see Hall in Detroit and listen to FDR's speech. ER wanted Hick's reactions: "Mine are not reliable just now!"

ER's mood was transformed by FDR's 28 April 1935 Fireside Chat on the WPA and social security. As inclusive as ER had urged him to make it, when his resonant reassuring voice boomed across America's heartland to "My Friends," nobody was left out.

"The job of creating a program for the nation's welfare is . . . like the building of a ship," he said. You could not see it all as it was being built, and made seaworthy to sail "the high seas," but out of the many "detailed parts . . . the creation of a useful instrument for man ultimately comes."

FDR wanted it understood that he spoke this night to "the American people as a whole." There was no hint that he intended entire groups to be excluded from old-age pensions or unemployment insurance: At a certain age of retirement, people would "give up their jobs . . . to the younger generation," and "all, old and young alike," would have "a feeling of security as they look toward old age."

The work plan was the "most comprehensive" in U.S. history. WPA would "put to work three and one-half million employable persons, men and women. . . ." There it was: Woodward, Dewson, Perkins, and his wife had all urged him to say it, and he did:

> Our responsibility is to all of the people in this country. This is a great national crusade, a crusade to destroy enforced idleness which is an enemy of the human spirit. . . . Our attack upon these enemies must be without stint and without discrimination. No sectional, no political distinctions can be permitted.

ER was relieved, and had only one remaining cavil: FDR said nothing about one of the most important pending pieces of legislation, the Wagner labor relations bill, to promote democratic labor organizing and create a National Labor Relations Board to guarantee federal support for independent unionism.

ER supported Senator Wagner's comprehensive labor law, and her old friend Robert Wagner was impressed that she showed up unannounced and uninvited at several hearings and conferences to knit, listen, and demonstrate her approval. FDR supported it belatedly, after it was certain to pass.

Nevertheless, after FDR's speech, ER felt "much more cheerful." The next day she had a grand morning ride; spoke on the radio for child health care; saw congressional leaders, Helen Keller, several others; and received 2,800 guests at the garden party: "My calm has returned and my goat has ceased bleating. Why do I let myself go in that way?"

Now that peace was restored, Hick admitted she had been mightily worried that ER planned to leave her husband. The thought horrified Hick; it would be a national catastrophe. ER reassured her: "Hick darling. . . , I'm sorry I worried you so much. I know I've got to stick. I know I'll never make an open break and I never tell FDR how I feel. . . . I blow off to you, but never to F!"

Their correspondence emphasized ER's springtime upset for over a week, and ER explained: "Darling I do take happiness in many ways and I'm never likely to fight with F. I always 'shut up.' "

On 2 May, ER celebrated Jane Addams's seventy-fifth birthday and WILPF's twentieth anniversary with a White House reception and festive dinner at the Willard Hotel that had been planned for months by a committee chaired by Anna Wilmarth Ickes. In January, during the Cause and Cure of War Conference meetings, ER had suggested that a Congressional Medal of Honor be issued to Jane Addams—to acknowledge that military service was not the only honorable international work to be rewarded.

But Addams considered it a "wild" idea. She had been viciously attacked during 1935 by isolationists and Red-baiters who called her a communist; and the well-funded, widely distributed *Red Network* called her "the most dangerous woman in America." Since Congress was dominated by conservatives, Addams believed her entire career would be mired by controversy. WILPF reluctantly agreed, and the medal committee was disbanded.

At the "biggest dinner ever held at the Willard," Jane Addams's life and vision were celebrated by America's foremost reformers, activists, and New Dealers. Caroline O'Day was toastmaster and ER first speaker. She hailed Addams as one of America's "greatest living women." Broadcast nationally over NBC, the event also featured an international hookup that beamed from WILPF headquarters in Geneva. ER was, however, prevented from participating in that part of the festivities.

Silenced by the State Department on most international issues, ER evidently acceded without protest to a State Department memo: "It is the opinion of the State Department that Mrs. Roosevelt should not speak over the international broadcast. In foreign countries . . . it would be considered as official and as the equivalent of the royal family. . . ." As a result, ER's name disappeared from the final "Round-the-World Broadcast" list, which included Harold Ickes from Washington, Arthur Henderson from London, Madame

Krupskaya and Madame Litvinov from Moscow, and Prince Tokugawa from Tokyo, among others.

On 7 May, ER wrote Hick to continue their discussion of love and loyalty, relative and real happiness. She differed with Hick "on the thing which counts in the long run." For ER it was "never any one person's happiness, it is that of the greatest number of people." If one achieved happiness incidentally, "well and good, but remember always you are damned unimportant! No, dear, we [ER and FDR] won't have scenes. I made up my mind to that last time and I never have spoken to him about this but this burying things in your heart makes certain things look pretty odd in the future and I think a little plain talk then will be a violent shock. . . ."

Another source of ER's springtime upset involved FDR's insistence that eldest son James move to the White House to replace Louis Howe as his primary assistant. ER disapproved, foresaw press criticisms, and felt miserable when cruel articles about nepotism, favoritism, and scandal were printed. James, profoundly disappointed, withdrew—but only temporarily. Both her son and her husband were angered by ER's lack of support.

Dismayed to feel the culprit, ER looked forward to a serene week at Val-Kill with Earl. On a lighter note, she was delighted that Hick was now able "to touch the floor!"

The new pool at Val-Kill was lovely, and new pine trees were planted. When all the trees are in "we will be completely sheltered from the road and able to take sun baths in peace!" Earl had left for a guards meeting, "so Nan and I are getting our own supper and having it before the fire—That is the kind of thing I'd like to do with you. Perhaps we will on Long Island."

ER loved the peace of the cottage, and it was a "grand day," despite the "succession of notables" who visited the big house.

On her return from Val-Kill, three of Hick's lost letters and a wire awaited ER, and "made me think and try to formulate what I believe" about love and the meaning of happiness. Dealing with emotional issues was hard for ER. For years she simply avoided them, although her fundamental understanding about love remained constant from adolescence on, when Marie Souvestre sparked her feelings about romance with literature and poetry.

Her truest feeling about love survived hurts and disappointments. Elizabeth Barrett Browning's poem which she had sent FDR in 1903 reverberated through time and echoed in each loving relationship: "Unless you can swear, 'For life or death!' / Oh, fear to call it loving!"

ER's letter was labored, but carried a message of permanence. Yet it contained other messages about the vagaries of love and happiness. The wounds to her heart had left her wary and self-protective. She would not be hurt that way again. Not by FDR, not by Hick, not by anyone. Still, she did not retreat from love, or the pursuit of love:

> I think it is this way, to most of us happiness comes through the love we give and the return love we feel . . . from those we love. There does not have to be a balance however, we may love more or less since there is no measure of love. Over the years the type of love felt on either side may change but if the fundamental love is there I believe in the end the relationship adjusts to something deep and satisfying to both people. For instance I know you often have a feeling for me which for one reason or another I may not return in kind but I feel I love you just the same and so often we entirely satisfy each other that I feel there is a fundamental basis on which our relationship stands. . . .

ER grew up surrounded by people; she sought and found happiness in groups, juggled many relationships. Hick grew up isolated on the prairie; she often felt reclusive, craved solitude, and wanted an exclusive relationship. Wrenched from her profession, Hick now focused on one person to satisfy all her needs. But ER was increasingly preoccupied by affairs of state and the needs of all Americans. As a journalist, Hick had been secure, dashing, and independent. Now she had sacrificed her work and her selfhood, and was often irritable and needy. ER's role became increasingly maternal and care-taking, which satisfied neither of them. Still neither wanted their relationship to end, and she continued to pull Hick back when she moved away.

ER wanted Hick to find real satisfaction in her new WPA work, and she wrote hopefully: "It is a little like newspaper work again, isn't it?" For the first time in their correspondence, ER acknowledged that only when Hick was happy at work would there be contentment between them—which she promised to promote during their reunion the next week: They "must have happy times together always." And she encouraged Hick to see herself more clearly. Upon hearing that Hick's reunion with her friend and teacher Alicent Holt went well, ER noted: "You will never learn what a strong personality you have and how much people admire you but then I like that about you!"

The next day she wrote: "I love you dearly. Only four more days before I see you! A world of thoughts go to you daily and Mabel says 'sure be nice to have Miss Hickok home'!" And a day later: "Dearest I can hardly wait to hug you. There is no doubt about it part of one's joy in life is anticipation, if only one doesn't suffer as you do when fulfillment doesn't come up to the anticipation!"

On 20 May, ER held one of her most memorable press conferences. Ellen Woodward announced that women were to be integral to the new WPA program. She was again in charge of "women's work," only this time the projects were broadened to include "Recreation, Art, Music, Dramatics, Health and Research." There would be new adventures in publishing and theater, including state Guidebooks, historical records, book repair, and library work of all kinds. Artists, white-collar workers, and professionals would be included as never before. Delighted, ER introduced the "grand idea!" to America's journalists.

There would also be new programs for "Training Household Workers," which ER thought should be supplemented by programs for the housewife, "to set up standards for her household that would be decent and equitable to workers" and establish "a decent standard of living."

During the 1930s when so many working women served as household workers, ER's views were heretical and were condemned as subversive. Her support for WPA's servant training program and her insistence that servants deserved respect and equitable pay engendered rumors of "Eleanor Clubs," comprised of servants and malcontents who demanded minimum wages, maximum hours, and no longer acknowledged their servility or "their place." Eleanor Club rumors escalated over the years and included "pushing days" when Southern servants insisted on walking on the wrong (paved) side of the street and pushing whites off the sidewalk. After ER's press conference, she was routinely attacked for "ruining" America's servants.

On 21 May, ER made headline news: "First Lady Tours Coal Mine in Ohio." Invited to go down a coal mine with Clarence Pickett, ER had asked Hick to join them. It would be a two-hour trip "and we will get dirty. So wear suitable clothes, if you know what is suitable. I confess I am stumped."

They wore miner's caps and rode at the front of a mine train for two miles deep into the shaft, where they watched four hundred miners at work. *The New Yorker* commemorated the occasion with a cartoon of two coal miners looking up surprised, "Here comes Mrs. Roosevelt!" It became one of the most reproduced cartoons of the White House years.

Afterward, ER addressed the first graduates of "the People's University," in Bellaire, Ohio. A community-involved adult education miners' school that featured over forty courses, the university was initiated by local activists, teachers, unionists, and housewives, who taught two hundred students without salary. ER considered it an inspiring project and told her audience of 2,500: "We must educate ourselves to study changes and to meet these changes." Americans must begin to "know each other's problems." ER was told by a miner at the school that he had not only learned skills to earn more money, but ways to "lead a more satisfying life." That, ER insisted, was what all education must be about. She worked to see such schools emerge throughout the country, as part of WPA.

During the evening of 21 May, ER was informed that Jane Addams had died. She told reporters: "I'm dreadfully sorry, America has lost a great source of inspiration." The day before, she had heard of Addams's emergency cancer surgery and sent her a telegram: "Deeply distressed to hear of your illness. Good luck and best wishes to you." Her friends were unprepared for her sudden death, despite her long illness. Jane Addams told philanthropist Louise deKoven Bowen as they prepared to leave for the hospital: "I'm not afraid to die; I know I'll go on living, and I want to know what it's going to be like."

Bowen marveled at her serenity: "I went into her room and said, 'Jane, the ambulance will be here in an hour.' " She replied: " 'That's all right, for that will give me the time to finish this book I am reading.' " Jane Addams "was never known to be afraid of anything. . . ."

Jane Addams's obituary in *The New York Times* was detailed and generous: Known as the "greatest woman in the world," the "mother of social service," she also pioneered the activist peace movement.

For ER, who on 2 May had called her a "pioneer who still pioneered," Jane Addams's important legacy carried a new urgency—which was dramatized by the placement of her front-page obituary. In the next column *The New York Times* headlined Hitler's Reichstag speech on European affairs: In "a defiant and uncompromising speech," Hitler had announced German rearmament, the draft, and his intention to "achieve territorial revisions." All treaty agreements were ended, although Hitler asserted territorial changes would occur "only through peaceful understanding"—which was the only phrase of his speech "received in silence."

14: The Victories of Summer, 1935

——⟨𝒪𝒪𝒪⟩——

$\mathcal{E}$R returned from the coal mine in Ohio to a Washington in turmoil. Tensions mounted as opponents pressed the Supreme Court on the legality of the New Deal, and on 22 May FDR vetoed the veterans' bonus bill. It had passed by a large majority with liberal support, including ER's friends Caroline O'Day and Isabella Greenway. An issue since 1931, it had engendered two veterans' bonus marches—one repelled by Hoover, the other mollified by ER's visit. The issue would not go away, and seemed to ER's circle a matter of simple justice. Why not give the promised bonus now—to veterans who had risked life and limb and remained virtually everywhere marginal and underemployed? In her maiden speech to Congress in 1934, Greenway spoke on its behalf, and now she led the effort to override FDR's veto.

FDR appeared personally before Congress and broadcast his veto message. He condemned the Patman Bonus Bill as discriminatory, inflationary, and fiscally unsound. The effort to override passed the House, 322 to 98, but fell short of the needed two-thirds vote in the Senate.

ER stayed out of the dispute between her friends and her husband, but was relieved by FDR's appearance before Congress, which served another purpose: His determined, vital manner announced that he had resumed his leadership role. According to *Time*, his sulky "winter peeve" was over.

Then on 27 May 1935, the Supreme Court rejected the idea that the federal government had the right to protect the people economically and socially. In three unanimous decisions, it challenged executive authority and congressional legislation to enlarge administrative activities.

In the Humphreys case, FDR had "exceeded" his authority by removing William E. Humphreys, a belligerent Republican opponent, from his position on the Federal Trade Commission. This seemed a gratuitous slap at the president, since in a 1926 case the Court had ruled the executive had such removal power; FDR was astounded by the unanimous decision.

Then the Frazier-Lemke Amendment to the National Bankruptcy Act, which sought to protect farmers from mortgage foreclosures, was declared unconstitutional as a violation of "due process." Justice Brandeis opined that foreclosures were in the public interest of "eminent domain" and must be protected.

Finally, the National Industrial Recovery Act (NIRA), which created the National Recovery Administration (NRA), the fountainhead of New Deal activity, was toppled in the famous Schecter, or "sick chicken," case.

In Brooklyn, four Schecter brothers were found guilty on nineteen counts of filing false reports, ignoring wage, hour, and health inspection regulations, and selling chickens unfit for human consumption—all in violation of NRA's Live Poultry Code. The Supreme Court denied the federal government's right to regulate, since the chickens were not involved in interstate commerce. This decision ended the administration's right to set up codes regulating child labor, hours and wages, safety and sanitation conditions, and it doomed Section 7A, which encouraged labor unions. For all the cooperation between industry, government, and labor in the creation of these codes, NIRA was declared an unconstitutional delegation of legislative power to the executive.

The Court's charges of overcentralization, of excessive and illegitimate power, were a blow to the entire premise of the New Deal. Most states had been relieved to have the national government take over some responsibility for the care of the poor and unemployed. The South, anxious to preserve its race traditions of peonage and discrimination, hailed the decision as a triumph of states' rights.

ER regretted the decision that shot the Blue Eagle down. NRA had "seemed a simple way to keep bad employers doing what was right." She thought FDR would be devastated and told Marion Dickerman, who was at the White House that night, that she "dreaded" dinner. They were astonished to find him in a jolly mood, even more "zestful and buoyant" than usual, eager to renew the good fight.

On 31 May, FDR told his press conference that the Supreme Court sought to return America "to the horse and buggy definition of interstate commerce." He compared the Schecter case to the Dred Scott case in its grave implications. Since the Dred Scott case (1857) declared a slave not human but chattel property and helped engender the Civil War, it was a remarkable statement.

FDR asked: Did the U.S. government have the right to "control any national economic problem," or were America's most important issues in the separate hands of each state? Since virtually all commerce was now in some way interstate commerce, from sick chickens to raw materials to manufactured goods, all industrial and labor decisions impacted on everybody in every state. This was no time to abandon a nationally coherent recovery program.

The Supreme Court's challenge invigorated FDR. The only way to combat

the Court's reactionary sentiment was to press Congress on pending legislation to advance the New Deal, and go beyond industry-dominated NRA
codes. Until that moment, FDR had ignored Senator Wagner's national labor
relations bill, which guaranteed independent unionism, collective bargaining,
a balance of power between industry and labor, protected by a National Labor
Relations Board.

The Wagner Bill, supported by progressives, was opposed by Southern
leaders. FDR had opposed it in 1934, and as recently as 15 May had told reporters he gave it no "thought one way or the other." Now he called for its immediate passage. It had already passed the Senate, 63–12; it passed the House
in June by voice vote; and FDR signed the National Labor Relations Act on
5 July 1935.

American workers began to organize as never before—democratically,
militantly, multiracially. It was what ER and the Women's Trade Union League
had long hoped to see. In fact, as soon as NIRA was struck down, Rose
Schneiderman, Maude Swartz, and Pauline Newman consulted with Robert
Wagner. They had worked together ever since the Triangle Shirtwaist Company fire in 1911, when they all served on New York's Factory Investigation
Commission. Now they lobbied for a clause against the discrimination of
women workers (which was finally included in the 1938 Fair Labor Standards Act).

The women's labor movement was refortified by the Wagner Act, and its
passage revived several long-delayed WTUL initiatives. In Virginia, for example, as early as 1914 Lucy Randolph Mason became industrial secretary of
Richmond's YWCA to campaign for decent labor standards and workers'
compensation laws. For twenty years she combated "the lack of social control
in the development of southern industry." In 1931, the Southern Council on
Women and Children in Industry hired Mason to campaign for hour and
wage benefits for women and for a ban on child labor throughout the Southern textile industry. In 1932, when she replaced Florence Kelley as director of
the National Consumers League, she moved to New York. But shortly after the
Wagner bill passed, she decided to return to the Southern labor struggle.

The great-great-granddaughter of George Mason, who signed the Declaration of Independence and wrote the Virginia Bill of Rights, daughter and
granddaughter of Episcopal ministers, radical "Miss Lucy" became a force in
the multiracial union movement battling for a new South. She was fifty-five,
white-haired, and widely recognized as a Southern lady: "When Miss Lucy entered a union meeting, the men instinctively got to their feet." While Lucy
Randolph Mason organized Southern textile workers and was "roving ambassador" for the CIO, she became one of ER's key advisers on urgent labor and
race issues, civil rights, and civil liberties.

Also in May 1935, an excited Harry Hopkins escorted his Grinnell College friend Hallie Flanagan to a White House garden party to meet ER. The White House lawn was festive with hundreds of strolling guests, the Marine Band, and tables filled with refreshments and flowers. Uninvited, Flanagan was staggered by Hopkins's presumptions, but "learned that the busiest woman in the U.S. was never too occupied to give attention and understanding" to problems she considered important. And the idea of a national theater seemed to ER very important. Just returned from a European tour of government theaters, the director of Vassar College's Experimental Theatre was already known to the First Lady. She urged Flanagan to wait in the Blue Room, and they could meet after the party.

Flanagan waited a long time, "looking out on the broad white marble hallway with its stretch of red velvet carpet, its palms, and crystal chandeliers." Eventually, she was escorted to ER's "apartment, where she sat at her desk, looking as fresh and rested as if she had not just shaken the hands of some five hundred guests" in the mild-May sun.

ER asked specific questions about the costs and details of Vassar productions, and was interested in classical, experimental, modern plays. She wanted America to "consider the theater, as it was considered abroad, a part of education." She surprised Flanagan when she referred to "our heritage of Puritanism in its relation to the stage," which rendered the theater the "last of the arts to be accepted." With ER's enthusiasm and Flanagan's commitment, the new Federal Theatre became the core of WPA's most exciting arts projects.

Fully aware of Flanagan's radical vision, the First Lady became her chief adviser, defender, and most prominent booster. Pert, red-haired, dynamic, fiery Flanagan was controversial from the beginning. Her commitment to relevant theater, political drama, and mixed-media productions was nationally known years before she was appointed to the WPA. In 1931, *Can You Hear Their Voices*, for example, was hailed by the *New York Times* critic as "a play in which propaganda did not defeat drama." But make no mistake—"it was all propaganda—scaring, biting, smashing propaganda." And in the end a prison-bound father sends his sons off to communists to help "make a better world."*

With the directors of other WPA arts projects—Henry Alsberg, who planned a series of travel guides for every state; Nikolai Sokoloff who envi-

---

*Vassar's production of Whittaker Chambers's documentary of the Arkansas drought, which caused suffering and starvation while Congress "dilly-dallied on the dole," caused a sensation and toured nationally. According to Jane DeHart, Flanagan's biographer, *Can You Hear Their Voices* was a prelude to the Federal Theatre's popular "Living Newspapers."

sioned symphony orchestras in every community; Holger Cahill, who wanted to create community art centers in every neighborhood—Flanagan, and ER, thrilled to the possibilities of "a new people's art," with community theaters in every locale. The hills and hollows, valleys and deltas of America would be transformed by a shared popular culture.

Appointed on 27 August 1935, by 1936 Hallie Flanagan wrote ER that there were "3,654 theatrical people with 3,654 theatre temperaments, not only at work, but at peace."

ER encouraged Flanagan's goals of children's theaters, Negro, Yiddish, Spanish theaters, mixed ensembles, traditional and university theaters, straight revivals, classics done experimentally, regional theaters, touring companies, and dance, vaudeville, and marionette units. Plays were mounted quickly in all major cities that first year.

In Chicago, several vaudeville units played in parks, and two large theater companies offered a series of plays. A large vaudeville unit, including "a complete circus" of more than seventy performers, toured Boston. "50,000 persons weekly" attended Massachusetts theaters. The Negro Theatre in Harlem produced an "untitled play" by Zora Neale Hurston, *Macbeth*, and *St. Louis Woman*, by Countee Cullen and Arna Bontemps, directed by John Housman.

There were theaters in the Bronx, Brooklyn, and Manhattan, including the Popular Price Theatre, which boasted Lillian Wald's original theater team: Helen Arthur, business manager, and her partner director Agnes Morgan, along with Aline Bernstein and other notables who ran the Henry Street Settlement's Neighborhood Playhouse.

Soon the Federal Theatre Project employed 5,644 "professional theatre people, including actors, directors, designers, stage-hands . . . with many being added daily." Supported by Elmer Rice and Harry Hopkins, Flanagan wanted especially to produce adult, relevant, uncensored theater—which might also "throw a spotlight" on conditions of despair, on rootless rural poverty and "ramshackle tenements and unite an audience that something must be done."

ER relished Flanagan's political determination and quick wit; but Flanagan did not entertain everyone. When asked, for example, "Would you produce a play written by a Communist?" she replied: "If it was a good play, we would produce one written by a Republican."

After her long angry winter, ER won several victories—highlighted by the creation of the National Youth Administration, which represented a great personal triumph. Since 1933, ER had decried the neglect of youth, the discriminatory practices of the CCC, and the lack of training, jobs, and alternative education for young people suffering in every state. With schools everywhere in crisis, young women and men were just dumped into the stagnant economy without hope—entirely marginal to New Deal programs. Even WPA employment was limited to workers over twenty-four. ER had called repeatedly for a national youth program.

She spoke of a "stranded generation," compounded by the totally neglected factor of 200,000 "wandering women," who averaged twenty years old. ER asked Frances Perkins to investigate new programs for young women and suggested an alternative to CCC camps in "plant nurseries." But the secretary of labor dismissed the idea as seasonal and useless. ER then suggested "internships in public services"—libraries, government agencies, education departments, health centers.

She agitated for a specific youth program for over a year, and wanted it to include rural and urban youth, women and men. She held conferences with Education Commissioner John Studebaker, with WPA administrators Aubrey Williams (a Birmingham, Alabama, social worker and outspoken rebel son of the Confederacy) and Harry Hopkins. In June 1934, Studebaker called a national youth conference to address the calamity that faced almost four million "out of school employables," aged eighteen to twenty-three, who had nothing to do and nowhere to go. Studebaker wanted a youth division established in his department. Every time ER brought up the idea with FDR she was rebuffed.

Finally, in June 1935, Harry Hopkins and Aubrey Williams met again with ER. This time, ER returned to FDR determined to have the plight of America's youth addressed. All winter her suggestions, her concerns, her daily proddings had been discarded.

Hick continued to worry that ER would leave FDR; for months she feared fireworks. But ER only grew colder. And the White House became during the winter of 1935 an exceedingly frosty place. ER might have thought she was subtle, might have believed her husband failed to notice her prolonged silences, might even have imagined her blue tones of cold invisible. But he knew them as well as anyone. He had witnessed those icicles that might at any moment dart from behind her eyes, and linger unspoken as she pressed her lips. They were familiar, and dramatic—though he might choose to ignore them.

Now, in the summer of a bruising and disappointing year, her persistence was rewarded. As social security legislation continued its agonized trek through Congress, FDR accepted his wife's suggestion. In her memoir, ER described the conversation that launched the National Youth Administration, one of the New Deal's most useful agencies:

> I waited until my usual time for discussing questions with him and went into his room just before he went to sleep. I described the whole

idea . . . and then told him of the fears that Harry Hopkins and Aubrey Williams had. . . . He looked at me and said: "Do they think it is right to do this?" I said they thought it might be a great help to the young people, but they did not want him to forget that it might be unwise politically. They felt that a great many people who were worried by the fact that Germany had regimented its youth might feel we were trying to do the same thing. . . . Then Franklin said: "If it is the right thing to do for the young people, then it should be done. I guess we can stand the criticism, and I doubt if our youth can be regimented. . . .

On 26 June 1935, FDR announced the NYA, by executive order. Unlike other federal agencies and in contrast to social security's limitations, NYA was inclusive: It promoted fairness in all its programs for women and men and specifically rejected racial discrimination. Black and white workers were paid the same wages and received the same student benefits.

NYA provided aid to high school, college, and graduate students to continue their education and provided work projects to train out-of-school jobless youth, women and men. NYA's contributions to struggling students were generous: Over 200,000 high school students were supported "at a maximum of six dollars a month," 100,000 college students averaged $15 monthly, and 4,600 graduate students earned $25 to $30 monthly.

There were community and rural youth development, recreational leadership, public service, and research projects under way, for which $20 million had been allocated. Junior employment counselors were stationed at state employment offices in selected cities; a Negro office with Negro counselors was established in North Carolina; one hundred educational camps for five thousand women were planned; forty-five were opened by July.

In every state, African-Americans were fully represented. More than 120 Negro colleges participated in the student aid program. NYA employed white and black youths, women and men, in the arts and professions, in skilled and unskilled positions, and provided a full range of training programs in resident and non-resident projects.

ER remained NYA's "chief adviser, chief publicist, chief investigator." She worked more closely with NYA than with any other program except Arthurdale and conferred daily with Aubrey Williams, Mary McLeod Bethune, whose Office of Negro Affairs operated out of NYA, and Betty Lindley, who directed young women's projects. Little happened at NYA without her knowledge and input, and she "was very proud that the right thing was done regardless of political considerations." Actually, she noted, it was "politically popular and strengthened the administration greatly."

Of all ER's correspondence with administrators, her exchanges with

Aubrey Williams were marked by a unique candor and mutual trust. He sent ER federal analyses and state reports, and she sent him blunt policy recommendations:

If a group in Georgia developed "a clerical project for youth . . . why can it not be done in every state? . . ." "Was the Oregon library project accepted or not?"

NYA strengthened the burgeoning civil rights movement. Williams hired "Negro staff workers" "to insure full participation in Alabama, Arkansas, Mississippi, Oklahoma, Texas, Missouri, Michigan, and elsewhere."

ER was particularly interested in the women's camp program, headed by Hilda Smith. Although NYA was the least discriminating agency, women were still shortchanged. In many communities their very right to work was challenged, and pay differentials endured. ER resented it, and she wrote, broadcast, protested continually.

She urged Flora Rose and her friends at Cornell to do a survey of "occupations for girls," which Aubrey Williams agreed to sponsor. She urged Clarence Pickett to work with NYA projects for the "stranded coal areas" and wanted various training schools for girls, including "health and nutrition" schools, to supplement the subsistence homestead movement.

Ultimately, ER considered NYA a primary weapon in the war to achieve real security—which depended on education, job security, housing, and public health. She involved herself in every innovation, and her activities were appreciated by the workers in the field. Margaret Ordway, who headed a program in North Carolina, wrote ER a long letter of gratitude: "Out here we think of the NYA as your government child. Certainly no member of the alphabet family is more popular. This mountain district comprises seventeen counties," and Ordway wanted ER to know of their achievements—and their difficulties. NYA had funds for "pay-rolls." Ordway might employ "every eligible youth in Macon County," and had 114 enrolled. But in every county every supervisor had the same complaint: They had no tools, no materials, no way to train or teach. Without books, paper, crayons, it was hopeless. Still, "our mountain youth" were not idle:

> We have enclosed springs; piped water to a number of schools; erected drinking fountains; repaired windows . . . ; made passable some side roads to churches and schools. "Hit used to be what we had to tote the corpse, now we kin ride hit right up to the door."
>
> Eleven girls and women, living at distant places in the county (all I have found that possess the essential gift), are visiting pre-school children in the remotest coves and on barren mountain sides. They tramp miles and miles carrying their packs of scrapbook materials . . . and second hand

primers. . . . Some of these tots had never seen a book or heard a rhyme. *Suppose we had some real kindergarten materials?*

There were no fabrics for quilting, no wool for knitting. The girls had no skills, and there were no materials to teach them to weave or spin or basket. For each girl in the program, NYA funds were "a temporary blessing but it does nothing toward her bleak future."

NYA teachers like Ordway cared profoundly, and there were daily improvements in the quality of life. "When seeking to correct the girls whose appearance is rowdy, I suggest the First Lady should be their pattern, and it usually works." Ordway told one girl: "If you were to see Mrs. Roosevelt you would find that she does not . . . have gory fingernails, or smear paint on her cheeks."

Using the regional compliment, the girl replied, "with the most radiant smile: 'No, she wouldn't do nothin' like THAT, Mis' Roosevelt is *re-al common.*' "

ER passed this letter on to her husband, having penned across the top: "FDR, worth reading. Shall I see what Aubrey can do or is it hopeless?"

NYA represented a critical turning point in ER's independent role as First Lady and as her husband's partner in an increasingly difficult political climate. Robert Sherwood observed that she had become "the keeper of and constant spokesman for her husband's conscience." For months she had badgered, cajoled, and grown cold. She initiated and nurtured allies; joined and enhanced political movements. She refused to give up or give in. It was a woman's way of power. And as conservative opposition to the New Deal intensified, so too did her determination to achieve all that could be achieved— for all the people, including the most needy and still neglected.

She decided to write a series of articles during her summer vacation to address issues she wanted moved to the front of her husband's agenda. While FDR held Congress in session during Washington's steamiest summer months to deal with social security, a new banking bill to extend the Federal Reserve Bank's authority, and a controversial "soak the rich" tax law that increased inheritance and corporation taxes, ER left Washington for New York, and then Campobello.*

---

*FDR's 1935 Revenue Act, damned as a "soak the rich" law, boosted top personal and corporate income tax rates from 63 to 79 percent and raised estate taxes. But during the 1930s only 5 percent of the population paid federal taxes. Fewer than 10 percent of American families earned as much as $3,200; only 1 percent earned over $10,000. Only one individual, John D. Rockefeller, was subject to the highest tax rate. Not until World War II did income tax finally involve over 70 percent of the population. Before 1935 the people who could least afford to pay shouldered the heaviest tax

For ER, Campobello was always more than that Canadian island just across a narrow riptide from Maine's easternmost town of Lubec. At Campobello, weather was always memorable. Fond of quoting her mother-in-law's adage "All weather is good weather," ER was actually thrilled by stormy turbulence. For ER Campobello was the place where the power and endurance of love, friendship, commitment, overcame the pain of betrayal and fear.

At Campobello, ER and Louis Howe forged their permanent partnership on FDR's behalf in 1921; After FDR contracted polio, ER bested her mother-in-law who wanted her son to retire to Hyde Park as a country squire.

Now her first confidant and only intimate bridge to Franklin was often bedridden. All winter, Louis Howe had been close to death, in an oxygen tent, sometimes in a coma. Despite his advanced emphysema compounded by pneumonia, he rallied in March, and in June seemed on the road to renewed political activity. ER felt free to leave him for the first time all year, content to be back at Campobello to ponder the future—in a place filled with encouraging memory.

ER's guests might deplore endless days enveloped in fog and frost-filled summer nights, but with Tommy she churned out dozens of pages each day. The sprawling house was filled with guests and staff; and ER had a splendid time.

In addition to her working team, Tommy, Earl Miller, Nancy Cook, and Marion Dickerman, there were visits with Molly Dewson and Polly Porter in Castine, Maine. Rose Schneiderman, Jo Coffin, Helen Keller, and the Clarence Picketts, with several relief workers, spent their holiday at Campo, including "a Miss May from Kentucky and a young girl Mary [Davis] has taken in the whole summer. Quite a household, isn't it?"

Characteristically, ER wrote Hick: "Oh, I wish you were here. I ache for you when things are so lovely but you wouldn't be happy so let's just hope it will be equally lovely whenever we are together later on."

Content herself, ER was dismayed that Hick was again disgruntled with her work. She had helped Hick secure her WPA job, because she dreaded Hick's idea of going to Europe or Asia as an international correspondent, and apologized:

> I realize that it would be easier for you to go where new sights and duties offered distraction. I blame myself much for putting you through all

---

burdens—through excise taxes on cars, gasoline, liquor—which accounted for 55 percent of federal taxes collected. Only 27 percent was collected through individual corporate taxes. The Social Security Act added another regressive tax, the payroll tax. Nevertheless, taxes exacerbated tensions between FDR and business conservatives—who stepped up their war on the New Deal.

this and offering you so little when I hoped to really help. You need not fear however that my love is less or that your suffering will alter my feelings it just makes me very sorry.

But ER was now the journalist, and at Campo she wrote two syndicated newspaper articles, a long piece on women in politics not yet placed, and a column for *Cosmopolitan*. ER did not pause to consider how Hick might feel—even as she discouraged Hick's hopes to resume her own career.

ER's days were also filled with robust physical diversions. She walked Tommy and Nan along the rocky precipices above the shoreline: They "are stiff and wary but we are sticking to it daily!" She took the tiller and sailed herself; and although "Marion has had the curse, tomorrow we are going to start playing tennis." ER was interested that Earl played tennis "naturally, although he knew nothing in fact of the game." And she had time to read: Louis MacLeod's "The Divine Adventure," an Irish allegory, which was charming; and *Elizabeth of Russia*, which "I enjoyed." ER and her company read aloud *Rebel Saints*, a book of radical Quaker history, which "proved so interesting we didn't go to bed till 10:30, which is very dissipated for us!"

Hick replied to ER's notion of a "quiet" and "tranquil" summer with her own fantasy:

> It was nice to think that you wished I were there. You're probably right, though when you say I'd not be very happy. I'd probably feel like a fifth wheel. Well—never mind, darling! The time will come when it won't matter to me that there are so many others who have priority rights to your interest and affection. Then I daresay we'll be one nice big happy family (!?). You must admit, though . . . it's sometimes rather tough to be the most recent of the people who have any claims on you! I have no seniority rating at all! I am so very much an outsider. But when the time comes when I don't care so much—or at least not in the *way* I care now—it will be easier. Anyway, I'm glad you're up there & enjoying it. And we'll have our time together later on.

ER "had to laugh! No dear, we won't ever be a happy family party here! We might spend a night or even a weekend in close proximity now and then but never more, somebody's feelings would be hurt and I'm too old to live under a strain. You and I will always want to have some time alone together. . . ."

Politically, Hick was disturbed by the economic situation throughout the Northeast and confused by her interviews with certain work relief administrators:

> Saw Mr. Herzog, the WPA man, this afternoon. He's certainly hard boiled enough. Maybe he's right. I don't know. But it *does* strike me that

we're slightly inconsistent in our attitudes toward—and treatment of—the unemployed.

We start out, in 1933, by working ourselves up into a sort of frenzy of sympathy for them. We do everything we can to make the acceptance of relief "respectable." We put in a CWA program with wages away above those paid in private industry.

And now, in the state of New York in 1935, we turn 'em over to a man like [Lester] Herzog, who seems to think, rightly or wrongly, that they *are* bums and chiselers, goes at his job with this attitude.

"By God, we'll quit coddling these babies and get 'em off relief!"

Hick was especially incensed about Herzog's plans for women:

[He thought they] ought to be working as domestics. God damn it—I just wish some of these people who think all unemployed women ought to be delighted to hire themselves out as maids or scrubwomen had to take a whack at it themselves. Believe me, Madame, I've been a servant—a maid-of-all-work, a slavey in a boarding house! I know what it's *like*. People make me sick. . . .

ER and Ellen Woodward struggled to diversify women's work, and Woodward wrote ER that by October more than sixty thousand women were "actually at work on WPA projects" in thirty-four states. There had been notable successes regarding training and reemployment in private industry, and new programs included bookkeepers in New York City, public health nurses in Mississippi, and library projects throughout the country.

During 1935 there were almost one thousand library projects in forty-two states, which employed ten thousand women in work relief. Books were cleaned, fumigated, mended, rebound; newspapers were clipped for research projects, scrapbooks, displays; library books were classified, catalogued, indexed; books were transcribed into braille using blind workers; professional librarians ran countless reading and community programs.

In Leslie County, Kentucky, women on horseback carried books into remote areas accessible only to packhorses. One group of the "Packhorse Library Project" comprised four women with books in their saddlebags who began the day at "Hell-for-Startin Creek," then followed "a tortuous, twisting stream with a rocky bed and brush-tangled banks" to "Devil's Jump Branch," where they separated, each following a different tributary to reach fifty-seven mountain communities.

But for all the exciting and innovative projects in libraries, museums, laboratories, recreation centers, and schools, more than 50 percent of women at work in the WPA were still in sewing rooms, and a great many worked as domestics. During much of 1935, Woodward's letters to ER concerned their shared enthusiasm for "training courses for household workers." By 1936 there were training programs "for every branch of household service" in twenty-one states, with more than 7,600 women enrolled.

ER sought economic justice for women in WPA, and Woodward wrote: "For the first time in the history of industry, women were accepted on an equal basis with men." WPA employed married, widowed, and single women with dependents, as well as single "unattached women" without dependents.

Virtually all unemployed nurses were employed on WPA,public health projects, resulting in a massive public health crusade. Thousands were immunized against diphtheria, smallpox, typhoid. Antituberculosis campaigns were generated, and schools and camps for tubercular children created; treatment for long-ignored regional scourges of pellagra, malaria, hookworm became commonplace. Child care and maternity clinics mushroomed; first aid, hygiene, and home care instruction proliferated.

Sewing rooms, which were so offensive to Hick and others, were surprisingly diverse places that frequently included nursery schools, staffed by "a teacher, a registered nurse, a nutritionist, and a janitor." Everything manufactured, from clothing, to dolls and toys, to household supplies, was "released to needy people or institutions." Regional handicrafts were encouraged: "the patch-work quilts of the Carolinas; the leather works of New Mexico and Arizona; the spinning of raw wool in Missouri; the weaving of blankets in Kansas; the knitting of Siwash Socks [a traditional Indian pattern, dyed with the juice of native trees] in Tennessee." Moreover, the sewing rooms "gave unskilled women workers . . . a chance to hold up their heads and earn a fair week's wage," wrote one former critic who visited a New York State sewing project.

At the end of July, ER sent Hick her just-completed article "Can a Woman Be Elected President" for comment:

> I hope it will interest you, I put a lot of work in it but I know it is controversial and will cause violent differences of opinion. Marion, for instance disagrees with a lot of it! Tommy didn't think I'd handle it in this way and is interested but I don't think is entirely in agreement either!

Although her closest friends were disappointed, ER insisted on publishing her long turgid article, which concluded that women were not yet ready to run for high political office. The essay was stimulated by negative publicity heaped upon ER after several June graduation addresses. ER had been criticized for her views and unseemly ambitions, and several Republican papers suggested her presidential aspirations were linked to FDR's fragile health.

In response, ER wrote a rhapsody to the kind of man a president needed to be, and used the opportunity to warn, even scold, women in politics. Sometime between suffrage and the Depression, women stopped marching for women. They seemed to ER no longer sufficiently interested in public affairs to demonstrate on behalf of their own needs or to advance social policy. They joined fascist and communist movements which were making deep inroads; but women who had once stood up for social justice as a group seemed now to ER uninformed and disorganized, their interests diffused and unfocused.

If women were, "as a rule," somewhat "more sensitive" than men, it was partly because they had had to adjust to their environment more completely. "It has been their job to live with men as peacefully and as pleasantly as possible and to bring up children and help them to adjust to their environment." Women had "not been physically dominant, therefore they have used their wits to make life more pleasant and agreeable, and to achieve their own ends with as little friction as possible."

Ultimately, ER discounted the stereotypic myths attributed to women. "My own experience leads me to believe that men are as temperamental as women and as apt to be personal and lose the objective point of view as most women." Still, in 1935 men were unready for a woman president, and ER concluded that the women's movement, in disarray, was also unready.

ER wanted women to prepare themselves, to build networks of women's support and action.

ER presented a formula for leadership:

> [Women] should come up from the bottom and learn their jobs in public life, step by step, and above all, they must learn to take other women with them and not to hang onto a job because they feel they will never get another one and therefore be unwilling to let another woman profit by their experience. . . .

ER's views on women in politics had changed little since her 1928 *Redbook* article "Women Bosses," which argued that "women must play the game as men do." Not until there existed a strong, aware, united women's movement would it be possible for a woman to succeed or survive in the vicious vortex of power politics.

But once women did organize and achieve leadership positions, ER was convinced "the advance of the human race toward the new goal of human happiness will be more rapid than it has ever been in the past."

ER wrote that article while many grievous compromises to limit social security were being debated in Congress. She was disappointed and angry that organized women, who had since the 1880s fought for aspects of the social security package, including Sheppard-Towner and aid to dependent children, did not vigorously oppose the race and gender restrictions that degraded the bill.

She was dismayed that when urgent public activity was needed to achieve full employment and real social security, the women's movement seemed moribund and quiescent.

ER had written *It's Up to the Women,* convinced that women were then America's most interested and organized group. She never changed her mind about the potential of women with power, and once told her radio audience that only women could adequately lead a peace crusade. When enough women organized for peace, wars would end, because "a woman's will is the strongest thing in the world."

But during the summer of 1935, ER turned to youth—the newly reorganized American Youth Congress, which now addressed precisely those issues of discrimination, housing, and jobs that she considered most urgent. Always on the lookout for any hint of public activity, the kind of grassroots activism that she considered the engine of democracy, she was thrilled to learn of the AYC's second meeting in Detroit during the Fourth of July weekend, which included groups as diverse as the Southern Tenant Farmers Union, and the NAACP, along with traditional church, Y, university, and student groups. ER had been displeased by the first meeting of the AYC in 1934, which she considered undemocratic. But the events surrounding the second conference caused ER to change her mind.

Determined to hold an integrated meeting in Detroit, the AYC had signed a contract with the Fort Wayne Hotel to prevent discrimination in meeting rooms and guest rooms. But when black delegates arrived, the hotel refused to register them. When white delegates threatened to leave, the manager capitulated. All went smoothly until Saturday night while some delegates attended a dance and others met at a local drugstore—which charged Negro patrons double what white patrons were charged. A spontaneous demonstration ensued, with pickets and placards, young people in both formal dance attire and casual dress marching and singing and creating a stir.

When ER subsequently met with AYC leaders in January she was already one of their most ardent champions.

ER was also gratified by the NYA's first conference on the problems of black youth, which she considered a stirring success. On 8 August 1935, Aubrey Williams and Mary McLeod Bethune held a conference of Negro leaders and New Dealers committed to racial justice.*

*Among America's notable black leaders in attendance were Channing Tobias, director of New York City's YMCA; Robert Weaver, Department of the Interior; Eugene Kinckle Jones, Department of Commerce; Howard University law professor William Hastie; Elizabeth Perry Cannon, Spelman College; A. A. Taylor, Fisk University; Ira Reid and Mordecai Johnson, Howard University; Marion Cuthbert, YWCA; and Walter White.

It resulted in a permanent committee that fought for equity in education, training for leadership, inclusion in all NYA programs. For ER, the New Deal's future was increasingly up to the youth—now organizing to confront the intense bigotry that everywhere limited progress.

Throughout the summer, ER corresponded with Walter White, whose many suggestions were sidelined in Washington. Although WPA salary differentials were prohibited, the NAACP lobbied for "a qualified Negro appointed as a Deputy Administrator in every state," and Negro administrators responsible for the "proportional integration of Negroes in each project."

While ER sent White's suggestions on to Aubrey Williams and others, on 5 August 1935, Stephen Early sent a "personal and confidential" memo addressed to "Dear Malvina" at Campobello: "I have been asked to send you a memorandum containing information for Mrs. Roosevelt concerning Walter White. . . . The memorandum is sent at this time because Walter White has been bombarding the President with telegrams and letters." White wanted Costigan-Wagner brought up again, before Congress adjourned at the end of August; he complained about the War Department's policy regarding the assignment of "Negro reserve officers in CCC camps"; he complained about many things. "Frankly, some of his messages to the President have been decidedly insulting. . . ."

Early was irate:

> I am advised by those familiar with White's actions at the Capitol that it was he who some time ago went into the restaurant within the Capitol Building and demanded that he be served, apparently deliberately creating a troublesome scene, compelling his eviction from the restaurant and giving rise to an issue, made much of in the press at the time. The belief in some quarters is that he did this for publicity purposes and to arouse negroes throughout the country through press accounts of his eviction. . . .
>
> Mr. [Rudolph] Forster [the executive clerk] advises that Walter White, before President Roosevelt came to the White House . . . has been one of the worst and most continuous of troublemakers.

Grandson of Confederate General Jubal A. Early, Steve Early celebrated the mythical magnolia South, and resented all efforts to change the patterns of his homeland. ER usually ignored Early's contempt for her allies and sought to maintain cordial relations with her husband's most important public relations aide. But this time she replied directly to his protest against Walter White:

> I realize perfectly that he has an obsession on the lynching question and I do not doubt that he has been a great nuisance with his telegrams

and letters, both now and in previous administrations. . . . I do not think he means to be rude or insulting. It is the same complex which a great many people belonging to minority groups have, particularly martyrs. . . . It is worse with Walter White because he is almost white. If you ever talked to him, and knew him, I think you would feel as I do. He really is a very fine person with the sorrows of his people close to his heart.

As ER considered Early's challenge, her spirits were bolstered by her sense of new movements, and new alliances. Throughout America there had been student strikes for peace in April 1935; a new American Student Union led by Joseph Lash and Molly Yard was organized for activism against fascism, war, and race bigotry, and its earnest activities were displayed during the July AYC meetings. Not irrelevantly, ER wrote her letter to Early the day Aubrey Williams and Mary McLeod Bethune opened their exciting NYA conference. ER was profoundly encouraged by these new radical movements for democracy and change.

As ER prepared to leave Campo, she wrote Hick: "We have Marion to thank for a really lovely day [of sailing]. . . . You would have loved the wind and the big waves today, and the white foam on the dark rocks."

Although she hated the thought of leaving, she looked forward to their reunion, and had second thoughts about their decision to spend the summer apart. ER now felt apologetic about their difficult time together in 1934:

> After all dear, . . . last summer was really the longest time I've ever been with one person but I stupidly didn't realize how weary you were and did the wrong things for you. I think now if we have chances to be together I won't be so stupid or so selfish.

As ER's productive and idyllic days at Campo ended, Hick completed her New York tour and was surprised by the upsurge in opposition to FDR among businessmen. The Depression had taught them nothing:

> Not one damned thing! And more and more I'm sure that Harry Hopkins was dead right when he said, "Don't forget it—this is a war between the 'haves' and the 'have-nots.'" I think the President needs to get out around the country. Only even then—everybody will "yes" him. When even Isabella Greenway—whether she's right, or whether she's wrong—doesn't feel she can come right out to his face and argue with him, what can you expect of the rest of the country. I certainly do not think she was much impressed by what he was saying at dinner that night. But she never said a word. In my own small way, I'm as bad as any of the others. He'll turn to me and say, "Am I right Hick?" I don't always think he is, but I haven't the nerve to say so. . . .

Well—you don't mind my raving on, anyway. Or *do* you?

If you got a laugh out of my idea of the possibility of a "happy family" at Campo—I was equally amused at your idea that I could get a newspaper job, telling them I never saw you and didn't know what was going on. They'd never believe it, dear—unless I actually did quit seeing you. And that would be expecting a good deal of me. . . . I'm not prepared to give you up *entirely!* (And I don't believe you would want that, either). . . .

With all my heart I love you.

ER did not blame Hick "for being gloomy" and wondered, actually, how anyone could hear all she heard and "keep your balance and keep calm." "If you are doing nothing you are preparing FDR" for the difficulties of the coming election campaign: "And I think you are going to make him concentrate on administration which seems to me very necessary."

With a new Red Scare bubbling up, ER relied on Hick's reports and more routinely passed them on to FDR.

In Buffalo, Hick was escorted by an old reporter friend who said that "FDR had slipped, badly—and among the middle class and relief groups. . . ."

"A year ago," he said, "most of these people would knock your block off if you said a word against Roosevelt. But now—you can walk into any saloon in East Buffalo and pan the hide off him—without ever getting an argument. . . ."

[There were no jobs, and a] Republican "whispering campaign" [was] circulated among the unemployed and . . . lower salaried group. People who have jobs are being made to feel that the President's program may cost them their jobs—"because it interferes with business." . . . They are being told: "You don't owe your job to Roosevelt. You got it back in spite of him, and, if he keeps on the way he's going, you'll lose it. . . ."

On 14 August 1935, one day after Hick wrote that worrisome letter, FDR signed social security into law. For all its defects, the Social Security Act created a groundswell of enthusiasm for the New Deal among working people who voted. It also constructed a "safety net" that saved millions of Americans from neglect and despair.

FDR considered 14 August 1935 the most significant day of his administration. Though the act was flawed and insufficient, it was a momentous beginning: The U.S. government had tried to "give some measure of protection to the average citizen and his family against the loss of a job and against poverty-ridden old age."

Far from being "universal," social security was virtually segregated racially, and women were discriminated against. Agricultural and domestic workers, the self-employed, workers in small businesses with less than ten

employees, "casual labor" or transient, part-time, seasonal, and service workers (such as laundry and restaurant workers), maritime workers, workers in
nonprofit organizations, including hospital, charity, and religious workers,
and local, state, and federal government employees, including teachers, were
excluded from the only "entitlements," old-age and unemployment insurance.
As a result, 80 percent of black women were excluded; 60 percent of black
men were excluded, and 60 percent of white women were excluded. Only half
the workforce was included.

Only old-age insurance was the direct responsibility of the federal government, paid for by payroll taxes shared by employer and employee. By
1 January 1937, "Social Security" numbers were assigned to 38 million workers, now entitled to a secure old age. All other programs, including old-age assistance (for those not insured), unemployment insurance, aid to crippled,
disabled, and dependent children, aid to the blind, and maternal and child
health services and vocational rehabilitation were to be jointly administered
by state and federal governments.

Despite an excellent Social Security Board, headed by progressive Republican John Winant, each state determined social security benefits. Residents of
the Southeastern states received the lowest benefits in every category, and traditional discriminations prevailed.

After months of debate, haggling, and compromise, the Social Security
Act introduced a two-tier welfare system, one for mostly white male industrial
workers in interstate commerce who were entitled to insurance, and another
for the truly needy, who generally remained truly needy. They depended on
meager benefits cruelly limited by "means tests." If a family was not destitute,
had any property, a car or even a shack, they could receive no aid—until they
gave up whatever they had. "Aid to Dependent Children" was quickly marked
by local custom, and various levels of discrimination emerged state by state.
Welfare for children did not include their mothers, who were reduced to a nationally sanctioned state-by-state form of beggary, "pitied but not entitled."

ER considered the Social Security Act a first step, that gave America time
to think: What was needed to avoid permanent poverty, she declared, was an
entirely new way of thinking.

Actually to achieve a New Deal, ER worked ever more vigorously with
youth and the most radical members of FDR's expanding administration—
notably Aubrey Williams and Mary McLeod Bethune, Will Alexander at FSA,
and Hilda Smith, who headed the WPA's worker education programs. The
First Lady's influence on them was noted by Hilda Smith, who inscribed her
1935 book of poetry, *Frontiers*, to ER, "who has helped us all to push on to
new frontiers, and has always led the way—."

15: Mobilizing for New Action

*O*n 27 August 1935, ER responded to Elinor Morgenthau's worries regarding Europe:

> German news is horrible and I don't wonder you feel as you do for I feel much the same. The Italian news too is dreadful and I feel keenly that if we were in the League we might stop this conflagration and if it starts even if we remain neutral we will suffer in the end. It makes me sick.

Italy's intention to absorb Ethiopia was announced in February 1935. For months the United States barely took notice of the situation. During her time in Campobello, before a cabinet-level discussion occurred concerning Italy, ER wrote one of her most important essays, "In Defense of Curiosity." She hoped Morgenthau would read it in the *Saturday Evening Post* of August 24th.

It was an earnest statement of her political philosophy, which emphasized America's international responsibilities. "In Defense of Curiosity" called upon Americans to realize the connectedness of all life, the many and mysterious paths which joined each individual home to every part of the larger world. An unsubtle protest against the folly of isolation and the defeat of the World Court, it was also a vivid protest against the bigotry, ignorance, and apathy that still hobbled New Deal relief efforts.

She began by confronting the many criticisms hurled her way because of her own interests beyond the "home"—that area so many still believed the only legitimate space for women:

> A short time ago a cartoon appeared depicting two miners looking up in surprise and saying with undisguised horror, "Here comes Mrs. Roosevelt!"
>
> In strange and subtle ways, it was indicated to me that I should feel somewhat ashamed of that cartoon, and there certainly was something the matter with a woman who wanted to see so much and to know so much.

The concept of home, ER argued, needed to be expanded: It "is the primary outpost and link to the rest of the world." Only "a kind of blindness" limited the home to "the four walls of the house" in which one lived. "No home is an isolated object . . . All of us buy food, and food costs vary with conditions throughout the country and the world." Trouble with sheep in Australia affected the cost of woolens in Detroit. Wars anywhere touched the lives of our own children in countless ways. But unless each family was aware and curious about world conditions, public opinion would be nothing "but a reaction to propaganda."

ER considered curiosity "a fault" only when limited to "idle gossip" used to demean and undermine people. She believed in privacy, and the right of even the most public figure to live a private life: "Every human soul has its own secrets and its own right to keep them buried if it wishes."

But every human contact depended on curiosity, an open and free exploratory mind. There were rich people, ER wrote, who could not imagine how poor people lived, and did not care to know: When she took her own students to see tenements in order to inform them about the need for public health, some of their parents worried about contagious diseases. They failed to realize that residents of these communities visited their own Park Avenue homes every day, as messengers, servants, and workers.

Her own curiosity led her to contemplate the night sky:

> I often wonder, as I look at the stars . . . if someday we will find a way to communicate and travel from one to the other. I am told that the stars are millions and millions of miles away, though sometimes they look so near, but it seems to me, at times, to be almost as hard for people who have no curiosity to bridge the gap from one human being to another. . . .

ER's goal was to create a groundswell of interest in world events among ordinary people who would seek to influence policy, who would pressure FDR and his State Department advisers.

The U.S. response to Mussolini had been at first benign, if not supportive. FDR appointed his friend Breckenridge Long, an affluent Democratic Party loyalist, ambassador to Italy. Long initially rhapsodized about the achievements of Mussolini's new "corporate state." His dispatches from Rome compared fascism favorably with the New Deal: "Italy today is the most interesting experiment in government to come above the horizon since the formulation of the Constitution 150 years ago." Mussolini "is one of the most remarkable persons . . . And they are doing a unique work in an original manner, so I am enjoying it all."

A son of the old South (the Longs of North Carolina, the Breckenridges of Kentucky), Long was dazzled by Italy's new "sanitary conditions":

The cities have changed. . . . The streets are clean. The people are well dressed. . . . The country roads are well paved and clean. The farms are all teeming with people, just now reaping wheat by hand. The country seems as if it had been manicured every morning. The whole temper and attitude of the people have changed. They all seem happy. They all seem busy. . . . They are spending large sums on public works. . . . Roads have not only been built but they are being carefully attended to and swept clean. . . . Many men are in uniform. The Fascisti in their black shirts are apparent in every community. They are dapper and well dressed and stand up straight and lend an atmosphere of individuality and importance to their sur- roundings. . . . The trains are punctual, well-equipped, and fast. . . .

During the summer of 1933, Italy had moved to devour Albania—and Long counseled neutrality: "I think we are entirely justified in playing the game with Italy in Albania."

But when Italy moved into Ethiopia in February 1935, Long regarded Mussolini's militarism with concern and urged FDR to pay more attention to international matters: "I think we must contemplate that Europe will be at war within two years," and make "our plans for the future."

FDR called Long a pessimist, but Long insisted he was merely a realist. By September 1935, Long condemned the Fascisti: They were "deliberate, deter- mined, obdurate, ruthless, and vicious."

According to Ickes's secret diary, FDR's cabinet began to recognize the se- riousness of the situation on 27 August 1935, the same day ER wrote to Elinor Morgenthau. According to Ickes, FDR introduced the subject with levity:

Some interest is being shown at Cabinet meetings these days in the Italian-Ethiopian situation. The President said recently that the Italian army of occupation places most of its orders for supplies in the British colony of Kenya and that recently the first item on a large order that went to the suppliers in Kenya was for five hundred women of easy virtue. War is certainly a great civilizing influence.

ER was disturbed by America's inaction concerning Italy's aggression and now joined Hick's fantasy of new work as a war correspondent: "I think the war idea is a good one . . . I'll be tempted to join you if war comes in some ca- pacity," provided FDR did not get reelected, "but I think he will by a small margin."

On 31 August, ER wrote Hick: "That Ethiopian development does put some questions up to us, doesn't it?" By the 20th of September she noted that FDR "thinks war in Europe is very near but I still hope Mussolini will come to his senses."

On 3 October 1935, without a declaration of war, Mussolini's tanks invaded Ethiopia. The League of Nations condemned the invasion, and on 11 October "economic sanctions" were imposed. But steel, iron, coal, petroleum, gasoline were unmentioned; trade continued and the League's rhetorical sanctions were meaningless.

Breckenridge Long counseled absolute neutrality for the United States. Covertly, England and France supported Mussolini's drive into Ethiopia, abandoning the principles of the League. Ethiopia, a League member, had formally appealed for protection of its sovereignty as early as 3 January 1935, and then again on 17 March. "Watchful waiting" involved the League's permission for Italy's use of the Suez Canal to transport arms, supplies, and troops. Italy mobilized, and was ready to advance from its colony in Eritrea as soon as the rainy season ended. England and France conducted secret negotiations that doomed the principle of collective security.

Perhaps ER slipped George Padmore's *Crisis* editorial into FDR's basket: "Where profits are concerned there is no morality among imperialists." And then there was the race factor: Who disagreed with Mussolini's expression of contempt over Ethiopia's membership in the League? What official spoke up when Mussolini asked a French interviewer: "Has the League of Nations become the tribunal before which all the Negroes and uncivilised peoples, all the world's savages, can bring the great nations which have revolutionised and transformed humanity?"

Even Winston Churchill, who alone among English leaders had opposed the Anglo-German naval treaty, who alone warned against German rearmament and the Nazi menace throughout 1935, was uncertain about Ethiopia: "a wild land of tyranny, slavery, and tribal war," an unequal, unworthy "member of a league of civilized nations." Moreover, in "the fearful struggle against rearming Nazi Germany ... I was most reluctant to see Italy estranged." Nevertheless, Churchill feared that if the League collapsed, there would be no deterrent "to German aggression," and urged England to defend the sanctity of the League covenant "even to the point of war." But he was, again, virtually alone.

England and France were concerned about their own African imperial interests, which Mussolini promised not to disturb. Since England and France, as members of the League, were pledged to defend Ethiopia, their failure to act signaled the death of collective security, the death of the League. When the United States considered its own boycott, but also excluded oil, Italy was given the means to pursue its war to victory—entirely unimpeded.

On 18 June, England had signed a naval pact with Germany in response to France's 2 May 1935 pact with the Soviet Union. The world seemed now to teeter on the brink of disaster. Competitive nationalism ruled the waves, and washed ashore to swamp the last independent African nation.

After seven months of brutal warfare, of poison gases, and aerial bombardment, Emperor Haile Selassie made his final appeal to the League:

> Do the peoples of the world not yet realise that by fighting on until the bitter end I am not only performing my sacred duty to my people, but standing guard in the last citadel of collective security? Are they too blind to see that I have my responsibilities to the whole of humanity to face? I must hold on until my tardy allies appear. And if they never come, then I say prophetically and without bitterness, "the West will perish."

England's appeasement policy was self-interested: To counter Mussolini in Africa would be to encourage the growing anti-imperialist movements underway in Asia and Africa, and to bolster as well antifascist groups that were perceived as overwhelmingly radical or communist. England, the Soviet Union, and the United States continued to sell oil to Italy throughout the war.

Few diplomatic betrayals were as crude as the Hoare-Laval agreement, whereby Britain and France acceded to Italy's conquest of Ethiopia, gracing it with the mantle of "territorial concessions" agreed to by statesmen in concert united, rather than condemned as the first major war of fascist aggression.*

It was a bitter time for peace advocates. On 2 May 1936, after months of atrocities and the use of weapons forbidden by Geneva agreements, Haile Selassie left Addis Ababa. Subsequently, ER received an urgent letter from a regular correspondent in London:

> May I draw your attention to the terrible state of things in Abyssinia. The cruel Italian occupation goes on with the help of poison gas and bombs used on a defenseless people. But the worst feature of all is the vile treatment of women by the bestial Italian soldiery. Reports have filtered through to the Ethiopian Legation in London that no woman is safe in her house & that any Italian soldier has the right to enter any house & abuse the wife, mother or daughter & the husband, if he resists, is put in gaol.
>
> I think the women of the world should rise in protest against this vile treatment of their Ethiopian sisters. You, as the wife of the President, could do much. I beg you to raise your voice on their behalf. . . .

*On 7 December 1935, Sir Samuel Hoare and Pierre Laval ceded two-thirds of Ethiopia to Italy, including vast territories impossible to conquer. They left a corridor through Italian territory to the Red Sea for Haile Selassie. The cynical secret pact, signed in Paris, was immediately scooped by the press, and it created a sensation. Laval's government fell, and Hoare was forced to resign (though he was later appointed home secretary, ambassador to Spain, and air secretary). Prime Minister Stanley Baldwin's government survived.

Given FDR's isolationist policy, there was nothing ER could do. She wrote her daughter prophetically: Even if the Italians won, they would be unable to colonize the area.

Haile Selassie was also prophetic: Ethiopia was a prelude. And America remained, in Churchill's words, "remote and indifferent." In the United States, the most consistent coverage of Ethiopia appeared in *The Crisis*, which editorialized in September 1936:

> When the League failed Ethiopia it failed the world. . . . A weak country like Ethiopia should not have appealed in vain to the rest of the civilized world when she had been subjected to wanton aggression.

The betrayal of Ethiopia, the growing threat of fascist militarism, segregated social security, the future of WPA and NYA, consistently derided as wasteful and communist, created a vast sense of disappointment in the Negro community. Walter White feared the growing bitterness among Negro leaders because of "the generally wretched conditions in which so many Negroes find themselves."

In September, White appealed to the First Lady to help arrange an urgent conference with "a small and carefully selected committee to discuss confidentially and frankly the situation with regard to the Negro." The NAACP board promised "no publicity . . . either before or after . . . in order that there might be frank discussion" between the president, White, Joel Spingarn, James Weldon Johnson, and several others on immediate matters of national and international concern.

ER promised to try to arrange a conference after FDR returned from his Pacific cruise at the end of October. Before that, she was told, the president "has every minute taken." FDR's upcoming Western tour and Pacific cruise were to be in part a healing conference between the feuding titans of his work relief programs, Harold Ickes and Harry Hopkins. Also FDR hoped the fishing and relaxation would benefit Ickes, recently widowed and much distressed.

ER and Ickes were the two people close to FDR who cared profoundly about race issues, but they were only occasionally allied. Part of the problem between them was ER's friendship with his wife Anna Wilmarth Ickes and Ickes's feelings about outspoken women—who reminded him of his wife. According to Ickes's biographer, Jeanne Nienaber Clarke, Harold and Anna were in "a power struggle" throughout their twenty-five-year marriage. Moreover, until his appointment to FDR's cabinet, Anna was the one with the power.

Harold was a poor boy married to a rich and domineering woman. T. H. Watkins described their marriage as "an emotional charnel house," marked by uncontrolled tempers, jealousy, and cruelty. He was a womanizer;

she was a scold. She was cold; he was colder. "More than once she broke my glasses." He denied he ever struck her; he just did whatever he needed to do to subdue her, whereupon "her hysterics" subsided and she lapsed into a prolonged "semi-cataleptic" state. By the 1930s they lived apart, but kept up appearances.

On the night of 17 November 1933, Anna Ickes attended her first White House dinner for the cabinet and returned with Harold, contented. He used the warmth in the room to announce he loved another. Harold wrote in his journal that he "really felt sorry for Anna that night. It was a blow between the eyes." She tried to kill herself with pills, but changed her mind and called the doctor. Their scenes worsened. Publicly a dutiful and devoted wife, she lived mostly in Illinois, where she served in the state legislature from 1928 to 1934, and New Mexico, where she continued her studies of the Pueblo, Taos, and Navajo peoples.

Then, on Saturday night, 31 August 1935, Ickes, alone in his office, was surprised to see one of his staff walk in looking grim and upset. Anna had been in a car accident in Santa Fe, returning from a tour of the Taos Pueblo with journalist Genevieve (Genno) Forbes Herrick, with whom Anna had spent the month of August; a member of the Turkish embassy, Ibrahim Seyfullah; and her driver, Frank Allen. Their car was hit and overturned. Anna was dead; the others were expected to recover.

ER and several cabinet members attended Anna's funeral in Winnetka on Tuesday, 3 September. Ickes wrote that he felt nothing; "my feelings were absolutely dead."

We can only imagine ER's own feelings during that funeral, as she considered yet another Washington wife who suffered grief. Since Ickes had confided in Louis Howe when his affair was about to create a public scandal, there is no doubt that ER knew many of the details of their last turbulent years. It had become a subject of considerable gossip, because Harold's lover and her fiancé were both on his payroll and the fiancé, an irate fellow who sought revenge, sent anonymous letters threatening to go to the press. In dread, Harold turned to Louis Howe, who initiated a Secret Service investigation. Moreover, Harold, in love with a much younger woman, behaved with adolescent indiscretion and admitted: "It's funny what sex can do to a man."

As ER contemplated the passing of a public-spirited reformer and scholar whose private life was marked by pain and misery, she worried too about her friend Genno Herrick, who remained in critical condition in the hospital. One of the newspaperwomen with whom ER was closest, Herrick was now a popular syndicated columnist who had quit her job as a "front page girl" for the *Chicago Tribune* because she did not want to write anti-Roosevelt stories for her Republican publisher.

Three years later, when Ickes decided to marry Anna's friend Jane Dahlman, ER wrote her daughter: "I'm glad you like Jane Ickes, but I am sorry for her." In another letter ER noted: "I don't find Harold Ickes attractive, but I think he is honest in his belief in the New Deal. . . ."

ER left Winnetka for Hyde Park and signed a contract for another series of articles with her new agent, George Bye. She wrote Hick: "Will I ever have any leisure I wonder? I haven't since I was married!" ER continued to use her relentless schedule to guard against hurt or upset feelings: "Mama is probably furious with me but I'm so busy I don't care!"

ER also agreed to write a daily column to be syndicated six days a week to scores of newspapers nationally. Hick had initially suggested that every woman in America would be interested in the details of ER's life. ER's new column, "My Day," would begin in January 1936.

Although ER had edited and written monthly columns for the *Women's Democratic News* since 1925, and also a range of random articles for various publications, she decided now to become a professional writer and a syndicated columnist. She wanted, and received, Hick's advice and editorial commentary. Their daily September correspondence was dominated by notes for the revision of ER's work and letters of gratitude for Hick's help. Hick read and rewrote patiently and generously, but their role reversal made her weary and grumpy. She destroyed most of her letters written during this period. ER wrote:

> I think I know what you mean about structure, it comes from not [thinking] through from the start and building up step by step and I think I can do that better. It is muddy thinking. I'll be glad to have your analysis but I hate you to do it when you are so tired.

ER never paused to consider that her great friend was depressed about this turnaround in their lives.

Hick and Louis Howe together helped ER develop a more journalistic style, and her writing gave her a new sense of confidence.

> Dearest, you can be as tough as you like in your criticisms. . . . I want to do good work and I want the help which you can give me, no one else is half as good as a critic and I'm very grateful to you. And don't mind at all!

On 8 September 1935, Huey Long was shot. Hick, on the road in Indiana, wrote ER:

> Well, Madame, what do you make of the Long business? I've been thinking today about all the people who must be secretly hoping he'll die,

but who would hate to admit it even to themselves! Boy, it creates an interesting situation! . . . But if Huey dies, he'll be a martyr.

Thirty hours later, at 4:06 A.M., Tuesday, 10 September, Huey Long died—forever a martyr to the lost cause of "Every Man a King." FDR's potentially most formidable opponent in the 1936 campaign—the man Jim Farley predicted would take millions of popular votes away from Roosevelt—was gone.

Hick also sent good news from Indiana: Everyone supported FDR. "Farmers. Prosperous as Hell. And, on the whole, strong for the President. Sentiment out here much, much better than in the East." A fabulous sunset made Hick feel wistful: "I wonder if the time will ever come when I'll not long for you when I see a beautiful sunset, or hear music that stirs me."

ER was in Detroit the day Huey Long died. She had agreed to launch the Brewster Community slum clearance project, the first of Ickes's national public works housing developments. Accompanied by her brother Hall, with whom she had lunched and toured the city earlier that morning, ER addressed a crowd of four thousand at City Hall, who cheered her words: "You see, housing is one of the things nearest my heart," the key to every problem; it included education and health, crime prevention, and every possible social issue.

ER agreed with PWA housing authority director Dwight Hoopingarner, who defined a slum as "an inhabited uninhabitable habitation."

The Brewster project comprised fifteen blocks of slums, to be replaced by "modern, low-cost apartments." After her City Hall speech, "10,000 children and adults, the majority of whom were Negroes, awaited the ceremonies" at the site, where ER announced that $6 million was allocated for Detroit's program, and then waved her handkerchief—whereupon a dynamite explosion caused dilapidated buildings to collapse "in a cloud of dust."

ER and Hall then toured the neighborhood, where "mounted police kept back thousands [who] pressed in to applaud." ER paused in an alley slum and "stood beside a refuse heap" to give a radio interview. "I sometimes wonder whether heat or cold is more terrifying in these sections. . . . We must see these eyesores are wiped out. . . ."

Detroit's newspapers were impressed by her gracious manner, her "characteristic" familial energy, and her costume, which honored the grateful, hopeful people of Detroit. ER dressed smartly for this gala event and the press detailed her ensemble: an attractive print silk suit, in soft shades of blue, green, and white on a background of dull rose, with bands of blue fox at the jacket sleeves, accompanied by gloves and shoes of dark blue kid, and a stylish blue hat. ER had received a large bouquet of roses and a corsage of gardenias at City Hall, which she carried with her to the ceremony, where a program of songs by Negro children preceded the demolition—the first ER had actually witnessed.

Following that notable day, ER spent a quiet dinner hour with her brother, and they took the seven-o'clock train for Hyde Park. The many flowers given ER were sent to local hospitals and the German Protestant Orphans Home, at her request.

But that was not the end of the story. A photographer had filmed ER smiling and leaning over to receive a bouquet of roses from a five-year-old Negro girl, Geraldine Walker, whose home was among those to be "rehabilitated." There was another photograph of ER handing a single rose from her bouquet back to Geraldine Walker.

Those photographs were twisted into hate propaganda for the 1936 election campaign. During the autumn of 1935, *Georgia Woman's World* began an anti-administration campaign that emphasized and exaggerated ER's relations with Negroes. It was a lurid campaign, that implied ER was un-American, actively Red. The photographs of ER and little Geraldine Walker were used to represent a crime against America's most honored traditions. Indeed, the 1934 tactics employed against Upton Sinclair and EPIC were increasingly directed against ER personally and the New Deal generally during the 1935–36 campaign season.

When asked about the photographs at her press conference, ER replied that they were taken with her permission and that she had no objection to their publication and distribution. She was proud to say that she and the young girl exchanged flowers during a reception for a Detroit housing project; and the two fine men in uniform who had accompanied her to her car were students at Howard University, where she had spoken.

The crime was not that ER gave a flower to a child, or was polite to student escorts. The First Lady had crossed the color bar. Hers were irrevocable acts of defiance against the symbols of a national heritage no longer shared nor certain, but riven to the core.

Felix Frankfurter wrote that he felt nothing but pride "that the First Lady of the nation" replied "in such a simple, straightforward, humane way. . . . I know it's the very law of your being so to act—and that makes it all the more a source of pride for the Nation. 'They know not what they do,' these race-baiters and exploiters of unreason. And you render deep service to the enduring values of civilization by serving the nation as a historic example of simple humanity . . . in the highest places."

It is amazing how radical simple decency seems in a mean-spirited and bigoted time, when the rule of the Klan was more acceptable than handing a flower to a child. ER insisted on her right even as First Lady during the campaign season, to act spontaneously with grace and good manners and to do as much as possible to transform America's most bitter customs. ER was among that small minority of antiracists during the 1930s who helped move America along a new, uncharted path.

The week after Detroit, Walter White sent ER W.E.B. Du Bois's recently published *Black Reconstruction*. White hoped she would read this "depiction of the background" of so many Southern and race problems. He also hoped she would invite "Roland Hayes, the great Negro tenor," to the White House before he embarked on his tour of "France, Spain, Egypt and Italy."

ER promised to read Du Bois's book "as soon as I can, and I will also try to get the President to read it." She would arrange to invite Roland Hayes, and since "we usually have two artists at an entertainment," hoped he would agree to sing with "the Hampton [Institute chorus] or some other group."

That week ER also decided to invite a black woman journalist to her press conferences. But Steve Early told her she must not: FDR had no black journalists at his press conferences, and she would create a terrible precedent that would "just make the President more vulnerable." ER acquiesced, but the subject came up again, and again.

Racism delayed, derailed, or minimized every effort toward decent housing ER championed. In Detroit, for example, in the spring of 1937, she received a note from her brother: "This is what happens when you withdraw your valuable interest—just nothing." The Brewster project had been abandoned for a year. Some foundations were laid, but funding had dried up. It resembled a cemetery, a memorial "of a grand idea," and was used as a playground. ER sent Ickes Hall's note and asked: "Would you be good enough to tell me what has happened to the Detroit Slum Clearance Project. . . ."

Ickes's staff explained: All work had stopped when the Washington PWA office rejected contractors' bids as too high. There was some hope that work would resume by summer. But in the meantime the slum dwellers whose shacks had been rendered dust now lived in ever-worsening conditions. Detroit's housing shortage had become "intolerable," as everyone waited patiently upon Washington politicians who competed for dollars and counted dignity in dimes. ER was sickened that the hopeful citizens of Detroit, cast out by the wave of her fluttering handkerchief that had demolished their homes, were now in a worse situation.

To stimulate a popular movement, ER again joined forces with New York's most vigorous housing advocates, led by Robert Wagner and Mary Simkhovitch. In December 1935, ER helped launch the national campaign for slum clearance and affordable housing. She spoke at the National Public Housing Conference to celebrate the completion of "First Houses," the first federal project actually built for 120 families on New York's Lower East Side.

Senator Wagner declared that more than 500,000 families "in this rich city barely lived in substandard homes, and one-third of the population of the country is housed in homes injurious to their health."

ER, Wagner, and other American "housers" now demanded that the United States join enlightened European nations and recognize housing as an aspect of public security. Mayor La Guardia referred to the opening of the Rikers Island penitentiary the same week, and emphasized the clear preference for government investment in "low-cost housing instead of high-cost prisons."

ER's Arthurdale ally Herbert Bayard Swope presided at the conference and introduced ER as a "rugged individualist." She "rejoiced in this beginning" of a nationwide effort to provide "decent living quarters," presented greetings from the president, and said:

> I hope the day is dawning when private capital will devote itself to better and cheaper housing, but we know that the government will have to continue to build for the low-income groups. That is a departure for us, but other governments have done it.

PWA representative A. R. Clas, responsible for New York's project, assured the conference that the U.S. government was in the process of doing it: Fifty-seven projects to house 130,000 persons were under way. But everybody agreed new national legislation was needed. ER's old friend University Settlement director Mary Simkhovitch was now president of the National Housing Conference and considered their meeting the beginning of a national crusade to ensure pleasant, affordable housing for every American.

Everyone deserved his or her own home, ER had long advocated, and in a bold, unprecedented gesture the First Lady secured a home exclusively for herself in New York's Greenwich Village.

ER rented an apartment from Esther Lape and Elizabeth Read in their house at 20 East 11th Street, one block east of Fifth Avenue. On a quiet tree-lined street, it was a comfortable third-floor walkup in a typical brownstone building. One entered through a wood-frame door with an opaque glass etching of a Grecian-style woman bathing. It was her own hiding house away from her mother-in-law, the Secret Service, and official Washington duties.

Unlike other First Ladies who broke down under the relentless pressure of their days, ER created a sanctuary where she had privacy and could entertain her very own company, in her own style, with her own things.

Anna, excited by her mother's New York City adventure, which she considered a major declaration of independence, asked Hick to join her in a new set of cocktail glasses for Christmas:

> Ma is really getting quite a kick out of her apartment and having people come there who will sit around and feel at home—and have a drink—on her. In a funny way I think she has always wanted to feel in-

cluded in such parties, and so many old inhibitions have kept her from it until now.

ER's new apartment also seemed a declaration of independence from Hick, and their autumnal correspondence became even more strained. But when Hick canceled one of their few dates, ER was unusually annoyed:

> I could shake you for your letter of [19 September]. I've never even thought of being in Washington [without] you. . . . I know you felt badly & are tired, but I'd give an awful lot if you weren't so sensitive. You are worse than Elinor Morgenthau & haven't her reason!

At the very end of a nine-page letter devoted to political matters, Hick replied:

> Dear, I don't think I *quite* deserve that shaking you say you'd like to give me. I was only trying not to be selfish   to treat you as I would Jean, Howard, or any of my other friends! . . .
>
> Goodnight, and please don't be cross with me. I'm not in *most* of my relationships with people, "worse than Elinor Morgenthau." And sometime you may find that to be true in my relationship with you.

ER had a very special relationship with Elinor Morgenthau. She was the First Lady's riding companion; ER wrote to her as she did to Hick and Earl, regularly and intimately; they exchanged significant gifts, shared books of mutual interest, traveled together, worked together—particularly on skits for various parties, which were often dramatic and hilarious. They had fun together, and ER missed her when they were apart: "I wish you were here to ride with me. Missy tried it for three days and can't stand the exercise and though I like the army groom he isn't much company!"

Although she was one of ER's cherished friends and primary confidantes, Elinor Morgenthau always felt just outside the magic circle. She was not one of the four Val-Kill partners, and her relations with Nancy Cook and Marion Dickerman were particularly strained because she felt their anti-Semitic bias. She had little to do with Esther Lape and Elizabeth Read, but even during their brief encounters must have felt their disdain. Even years later, Esther Lape's references to Elinor Morgenthau were unkind. She was "very insistent" on her friendship with ER, Lape recalled, and was a clumsy rider: "You had to feed Elinor M into her saddle like a bag." Once she "dropped her riding crop, and ER asked, 'Esther won't you get it for her?' "

As a result, Elinor Morgenthau often felt lonely and unwelcome among ER's other friends. When Hick felt the same way, ER urged her to believe she did not have Morgenthau's reasons for such sensitivity.

From Cleveland, trying hard not to feel isolated, and determined not to sound like Elinor Morgenthau, Hick wrote a peppery political report. It was the kind of "long and explosive" letter that pleased ER and had attracted her to Hick in the first place:

> Well, the Cardinal is in town. And Al Smith. And, I suppose, Jim Farley, who is, according to the dope I hear, having a confab with Governor Davey between masses. They are all here for the Eucharistic Congress, in case you don't know. . . .
>
> God, but that sap, [Governor] Davey, has made a mess of things! Buzzie could run for Governor of this state and give him the trimming of his life.

Hick's letter detailed evidence of corruption and sleazy politics, worth a grand jury investigation. Hick was told by an AP reporter friend: "Just seeing Davey in Washington a few weeks ago apparently did the President a lot of harm. . . ."

In addition to the corruption, Hick found WPA "a mess." Whereas 200,000 men were supposed to be working, only 26,000 were in fact working.

> In the meantime relief has been cut so that in October in Cleveland food allowances will be 25 percent below what they were in August, no rents will be paid, no clothing issued—and teachers are reporting that children are showing up at school without any underwear—and there'll be fuel only for cooking. Tonight, September 23d, it's so cold in Cleveland that I have the heat on in my room. They are expecting riots in Cleveland next month, Madame. . . .

Hick now identified with the people on relief, struggling and starving as they confronted New Deal inefficiencies:

> For, damn it dear, that's just what we are—and *damned* inefficient. Mr. Hopkins and Mr. Ickes fighting for power, Mr. Hopkins' lieutenants, ambitious to make careers out of relief. . . . Delay. Confusion. No organized, workable plan. . . . I rather hope they *do* riot!

The situation in Toledo was even worse:

> Men coming around to the WPA office actually weeping and begging—"For God's sake, when are you going to put me to work?" Everybody terribly worried. Darling, it *is* so hard even for me not to feel a little bitter at the "big shots" these days. The President, Ickes, Harry Hopkins, all well fed, well clothed, warm, and comfortable, complacently starting off on a vacation. While out here in places like Cleveland and Toledo thousands of people *aren't* getting enough to eat, are facing eviction, begging for little jobs at a "security wage" that none of us could live on. . . . Oh, I know it's

just human nature, and that it happens all the time in private industry. . . . But, dear lady, *we* are dealing with the welfare of millions of helpless people. . . .

Well, there isn't any use in my raving on any more.

Goodnight, dear, wherever you are. I feel a good deal as though I were shouting into space!

ER and Tommy were with FDR, Hopkins, and Ickes to tour the West transformed forever by New Deal projects. From the Boulder Dam site, ER wrote: "The first glimpse of the newly created lake which will eventually be one hundred and fifteen miles long, surrounded by colorful hills, was a sight never to be forgotten." Her Western sojourn gave her a new "appreciation of the size and majesty of these United States": "We crossed the Colorado River to look from both sides at this marvelous dam," so filled with the promise of water, flood control, and the creation of unlimited and inexpensive power.

ER and Hopkins were taken to the base of the dam in a bucket, to "get even a better realization of its heights." They walked about and examined the area "where the giant turbines" were to be installed. It was a thrilling sight, and ER left Colorado convinced that the New Deal permanently contributed to the well-being of America: new resources, national parks and hiking trails, waterways and hydroelectric power. The changes were profound, and majestic.

The presidential train went on to California, where FDR had "a marvelous reception." As did ER, who spoke at the Hollywood Bowl for the Mobilization of Human Needs. The stadium was packed and enthusiastic, although her "voice behaved badly."

ER wrote Hick that FDR "finished in a blaze of glory" and "got off happily and safely" for his fishing cruise with Ickes and Hopkins. She questioned FDR's wisdom in bringing the two warring New Dealers together in such a tight space: "I don't think anything will be accomplished and I doubt if anyone except FDR has a good time but this is not my trip!"

Actually the cruise was remarkably healing. Ickes enjoyed his companions, and ended his resignation fantasies. He was particularly awed by FDR's courage, especially when he was "transhipped" from the *Houston* to his little fishing boat in rough weather: "Never once did he act self-conscious; on no occasion did he seem to be nervous or irritated. Cheerfully he submitted to being wheeled up and down the special ramps . . . to being carried up and down like a helpless child when he went fishing." And with his powerful arms and shoulder muscles, he brought in huge fish—after hours of determined battle.

Ickes especially appreciated FDR's military aide, Colonel Edwin Martin (Pa) Watson, the man who ensured FDR's good cheer: Watson "simply bubbles with good humor and one cannot feel grouchy or dispirited" in his company. But the real surprise was companionable Harry Hopkins, "with his easy manners and keen wit."

As they departed, ER's party flew over and circled FDR's cruiser "to say goodbye again." It had been a splendid Western trip, and it vigorously launched the campaign season.

While FDR cruised, ER spent most of October settling into her new apartment. She was euphoric. The simple joy and complex excitement that occurs when one claims a new space for the first time was enhanced by the fact that this move was long overdue. ER claimed her first private space during the week of her fifty-first birthday. Undoubtedly protected by her women's press corps, her privacy was preserved. She and Hick spent one happy day together before Hick resumed her travels for WPA.

From the beginning, 11th Street was for ER a working space, and the front guestroom doubled as Tommy's office and bedroom. Esther and Elizabeth lived below ER on the first two floors. As at Val-Kill, ER enjoyed especially the screened sunporch outside her bedroom window and above Esther's garden, where she slept until the first frost.

After her birthday, ER returned to Washington and "a dreadful story" about John Boettiger's momentary decision to work for the TVA. The article also "dragged" ER in, and she was enraged by the relentless price paid by an entire family when a parent agreed "to serve his country! . . . I'm beginning to think obscurity the greatest boon we can ask for in this world!"

Her brother Hall was with ER at the White House, where she was "back at the old routine." The house was "upside down," and there was an interesting discussion about the invective and criticism recently heaped upon the children. ER wrote: "I am a bit sorry for James and John, even for F Jr. It is funny you can't be as indifferent when your children or your friends are concerned as you are about yourself!" She wrote: "Gee! If FDR could get out this year!"

From West Virginia, Hick sent ER "the pages for your engagement book for January and February" and presents for her apartment, including an iron ashtray, and wicker basketry which ER collected in great quantity. Hick's report from this return trip to West Virginia was as vivid as her earlier ones, and she remained amazed by the daunting poverty amid the state's natural beauty:

> One scene, about fifty miles from Charleston, I'll never forget—out across a valley, with a wide, foamy river down below. The colors on the mountains are beyond description. . . . Even the mean little houses are lost in this splendour!

And here in this place of breathtaking loveliness, people were so poor, an appalling and heartbreaking apathy triumphed:

Today I drove by a house that was burning down. A little grey, unpainted cabin in a little grey unpainted town. And silently watching the
flames as they shot up through the roof, a little group of people. They
weren't trying to save the house. . . . And in that silent apathetic group
must have been the people who had lived in that house that was burning
down! Driving on through the town, I observed that hardly anyone appeared to be interested in the fire, although the flames and smoke were
plainly visible from the main street.

During her second day in the rural south, Hick saw WPA projects which
cheered her and wrote ER the reason she felt so good was that she revisited an
"awful tent colony" that had two years before gotten FDR "all worked up."

[Now] those tents are gone, darling! Every last horrible one of them! And
only 15 of the 63 families remain there—living, not in tents, but in wooden
houses they built for themselves, with the aid of the relief people. Gardens
around them. Even flowers. . . . *And all but 15 of those blacklisted coal
miners are back at work—and in the mine that blacklisted them!* Isn't that
simply swell?

Hick credited Mrs. Kimberling, the social worker, who with amazing concern and activity had rehabilitated the entire community. In 1933, rebellion
and homicide were in the air. Now the area was transformed. Hick was ecstatic: What Mrs. Kimberling had achieved with "the mine bosses is almost beyond belief. Gosh, what a great job. . . ."
Major Turner, West Virginia's state director of public welfare, particularly
moved her. He removed children from a local reform school. The children,
eleven and younger, were paroled to him personally. He placed them in a
camp he established for three months, where he " 'de-louses them, physically
and morally'—cleans them up, builds them up, and tries to give them a better
outlook and break them of the bad habits they've acquired in reform school.
Finally he places them in carefully selected homes," which he monitored for
abuses and irregularities.
Hick identified with those children: "When I was a kid there was no one
to give me that much protection. But even what I went through was better
than a reform school." Hick believed that she would never have had a chance,
had she "landed in one of those places. . . ."

ER asked Hick to revisit Red House, a West Virginia resettlement community
she cared about almost as much as Arthurdale. The First Lady was troubled by
reports of widespread dissatisfaction. Hick confirmed ER's suspicions:

First of all, you'd hardly recognize Red House now. . . . The houses are
finished. The homesteaders are living in them. There are curtains at the

windows. Gardens were raised this summer. The brilliant colors of autumn flowers are most effective against the greyish walls of the houses.

The place was attractive, but community morale was low:

> The air is full of rumors. . . . They are unhappy because they have no work except that given them around the homestead. They don't want that. They want jobs. . . . They are beginning to quarrel among themselves. The women's club . . . has pretty much gone to pot. . . . There [was upset about] the houses. The lack of closet space, for instance—as you predicted!

The walls cracked as the houses settled. "You can see daylight around some of the pipes, up under the roofs, around the windows. . . ." While fixable, and basically comfortable, they were cheaply made, and it showed. Still, for those women who had to carry water every day two miles up into the mountains, running water meant a lot.

Without ER's supervision and regular oversight, many more corners were cut at Red House than at Arthurdale, and indignities occurred. Hick was furious:

> One thing that burns me up so is that they don't ever think of these people as individuals, but as units in a project. I don't think you can deal with these people that way. . . . They need a Miss Clapp at Red House. Or a Mrs. Kimberling. She didn't think of those 63 miners as units. . . . There are 120 families at Red House. And I think the heads of those families should be treated as 120 individuals, not units. . . . (I'll bet Rex and Grace [Tugwell] wouldn't agree with me!)

The women of the community wanted a library and a nursery school. Everybody wanted to pitch in, but everybody was discouraged. And Hick doubted that the bureaucrats in Washington would really understand. Hick was reminded of "the idea you had last spring, for someone to come and live for a few weeks in every one of these homesteads to watch the morale and mental adjustment" of the people of Arthurdale, Red House, Crossville, Tennessee. People wanted respect and control over their own lives and communities. But no study of their needs, skills, and interests was made.

ER was grateful for Hick's description of Red House: "You confirmed just the things I've been feeling. These people can't make a go alone until they get on their feet and work is the most important factor in real rehabilitation."

ER knew "things were bad for some time. If only human beings could be different!" She sent Bernard Baruch to Red House. "And I imagine that he will have much to tell [the Tugwells]. . . ."

Subsequently, Baruch met with FDR who was "eager for progress"; and Red House was "thoroughly investigated." ER wrote Hick, "If something doesn't get done I'll eat my hat."

ER used Hick's reports in a variety of ways, and assured her they were important: "F may say I don't know but he can't say that of you."

In November, ER and Hick spent ten days together, and ER faced the holiday season in a cheerful mood. Part of the reason was that she was pleased by her husband's recent speeches. It was noteworthy, really, the extent to which ER's moods lifted when FDR's words reflected her views.

ER cherished the holidays, and all year long selected gifts for her family, household staffs, their families, and the widest variety of political and personal friends. Annually she arranged individual evenings for Hick, Louis Howe, Earl Miller, Esther Lape and Elizabeth Read, Nancy Cook and Marion Dickerman.

On 2 December, ER wrote Hick from Val-Kill, where she was spending a vacation week with Earl Miller, Marion Dickerman, Nancy Cook, and her brother. Hall's increasingly distressful alcoholic condition eroded ER's long-held hope that he would someday get himself under control: "Hall blew in this morning and we had a hectic talk as he was trying to telephone every one in the world."

On that cold December night, ER longed for Hick's warmth: "Darling. I had a good night's sleep on the porch but I missed you and used my sleeping bag and a hot water bottle!"

On 12 December 1935, ER celebrated the twenty-fifth anniversary of the Urban League with a call for racial justice. Her address was nationally broadcast over NBC's Blue Network at 10:45 P.M., and subsequently published:

> We have a great responsibility here in the U.S. because we offer the best example that exists perhaps today throughout the world, of the fact that if different races know each other they may live peacefully together.

But peace would be possible only if discrimination ended, "inequalities," and "many grave injustices" ceased.

She understood that "the Government in its new efforts and programs was not always fair to the Negro race." But this "is not the intention of those at the top, and as far as possible I hope that we may work together to eliminate any real injustice." She hoped for national unity to "stomp out" lynching and racial violence, so that we be able to face the other nations of the world and to uphold our real ideals here and abroad, [as an] example to the world of "peace on earth [and] goodwill. . . ."

While ER emphasized race as 1936 dawned, Hick emphasized the ongoing injustices women faced:

Oh. God damn this women's work anyway! It seems that up here in Houghton [Michigan] they have a practice house, for training maids, a project dear to the heart of the state director of women's work. The only trouble is . . . they apparently reached the saturation point of placing the trained maids they turned out. . . . So . . . they began shipping them to Detroit and Chicago.

Hick was particularly outraged that they were paid only $10 a month:

Why, damn it, the houses of prostitution in Chicago are full of country girls who went to the big city for less than a living wage. It's been that way since the beginning of time. Now *should* I tell that damned fool of a woman down in housing, when I see her in Detroit next week, a few of the facts of life? or shouldn't I? . . . .

ER shared Hick's outrage "about the maids—I hope you went in and told the lady!"

On 19 December ER was disquieted by Mary Harriman Rumsey's memorial service, held on the first anniversary of her death. ER hated funerals and deplored memorial services:

Darling, don't let anyone hold memorial meetings for me after I leave you. It is cruel to those who really love you and miss you and means nothing to the others except an obligation fulfilled and certainly it can mean nothing to the spirit in another sphere if it is there at all! I'd like to be remembered happily if that is possible, if that can't be I'd rather be forgotten.

On 20 December 1935, ER formally signed her contract with United Features for her new daily syndicated column, "My Day." ER's column would give her a regular forum to express her most heartfelt concerns. It was a fitting end to 1935, a year of defeats and progress. The Social Security Act, however flawed, had changed the nation's views about governmental responsibility, and housing and race were on the national agenda as never before. ER's public statements had everywhere created a stir. Although all their political enemies were lined up and strident, the campaign was enhanced by a new civil rights movement everywhere unfolding. There is no way to measure the impact of ER's public words and activities on other people, the courage her acts of simple courtesy may have imparted. On the air, and in speeches around the country, the First Lady set a pace, took a step, indicated what was imaginable, possible, done.

One of the South's most significant activists for race justice noticed. Lillian Smith, from her home atop Old Screamer Mountain in the northern

Georgia foothills of the Blue Ridge, wrote her first words against racism and began to publish a magazine that became *The North Georgia Review*, and then *The South Today*. She called 1935 "a mean bad year," but considered Eleanor Roosevelt "a symbol of the future" where people might all "live as integrated personalities, free to grow, to believe as they wish, to say aloud what they believe, free not to bow to any great power or authority whether of state or church or economic power."

But there was one subject ER avoided. Even in her letter to Elinor Morgenthau she failed to refer specifically to the pitiless facts that confronted Hitler's victims, and worsened daily.

On 14 September 1935, German Jews were stripped of citizenship, and denied all political or civil rights. In two Nuremberg laws, the "Law for the Protection of German Blood" and the "Reich Citizenship Law," Hitler's anti-Jewish crusade was legalized. The law had nothing to do with religion, only ancestry. There were full Jews and mongrels *(Mischlinges)*, or part Jews. Fundamentally, a Jew was anyone with one Jewish grandparent, including Roman Catholic converts, priests and nuns.

On 27 December, at the last cabinet meeting of 1935, FDR told of a recent letter from Ambassador Dodd in Berlin: According to Ickes, FDR "said it was the most pessimistic letter he has ever read." William Dodd "thinks that nothing can restrain Hitler. The President remarked that, of course, some allowance should be made for Dodd's intense prejudice against Hitler, but there seems to be no question that the international situation is very grave indeed."

Neither FDR nor any member of the State Department protested, or referred to the Nuremberg laws, although Dodd warned that they represented "complete subordination for the Jews" and foreshadowed their "complete separation" from the German community. Dodd had wanted the United States, Britain, and France to boycott the Nuremberg rally, the Nazi Party's annual spectacle, but the State Department rejected his proposal. Among the diplomats, only Dodd refused to attend.

On this issue, ER remained silent for five years.

16: A Silence Beyond Repair

—◦◦◦—

*E*R's silence concerning the increasing violence against Germany's Jews, radicals, and dissenters has traditionally been ascribed to her lack of information. But ER had full and immediate knowledge. During the summer of 1933, Jane Addams, Lillian Wald, Carrie Chapman Catt, and especially Alice Hamilton provided details about events in Nazi Germany. Even after ER arranged a meeting with Hamilton and FDR, and despite all the information that arrived on his desk from his own friends, most notably Felix Frankfurter, a policy of administrative and State Department silence prevailed.

While FDR encouraged ER to speak out on certain domestic issues and did not prevent her from addressing others, a firm policy of public silence was imposed on her concerning most international issues. On this issue her response, however, is unique—her silence extends even to her private correspondence.

On 16 December 1933, ER received a desperate and haunting letter from a German refugee residing in London. An affluent, educated Jewish woman, Maria Meyer Wachman typed her letter in English from her refuge in the Park Lane Hotel:

> Dear Mrs. Roosevelt,
>   Will you please forgive a foreigner, who dares to write to you. I do it simply as one woman to another, and my reason for my writing must be my excuse at the same time. I have no other to offer you.
>   Having the fullest confidence in your kind understanding for the matter, I have so very much at heart, I herewith beg you to help us, us Jewish people from Germany. If you would tell the American women and men the crime that is done by not helping us, I do believe—in spite of all—they will hear and listen and—finally admit this fact, if you tell them and challenge their conscience.

Maria Meyer Wachman was one of Germany's first refugees. She lived in London for almost a year, hoping that the world would notice and protest Hitler's atrocities.

But nothing has been done so far . . . Besides the psychological suffering, we are not allowed to take any job in a foreign country, that means that our children have nothing to expect than starvation. I say every child is a present from heaven and its first right is to expect [to live] in peace. There is no political wrong, no civil crime, simply born a Jew, the same race, the Christ was . . .

As a poor human being, I appeal to you as an American woman and mother, high placed in life, I appeal to the world-wide American sense of justice . . . Can you really stand by and watch this? Can you stand and see us more or less all gassed?

I should like to have your word, you will do something . . .

ER responded to this appeal with a terse note: "My dear Miss Wachman: Unfortunately, in my present position I am obliged to leave all contacts with foreign governments in the hands of my husband and his advisers."

There is no comparably curt reply on any domestic subject in her entire correspondence. Since silence is the ultimate collusion, how can it be explained? There are of course many possibilities.

FDR insisted that diplomatic affairs be left to specialists, and ER's letters relating to international relations, even personal letters sent abroad, were drafted or approved by Sumner Welles or another member of the State Department. One can only imagine the conversations between ER and FDR that resulted in such full compliance with State Department policy.

FDR relied upon and required the enormous German and Catholic vote; and the support of the Southern Democrats who dominated Congress. Anti-Semitism was virulent throughout the United States, and was agitated and fortified by Nazi propaganda, Nazi triumphs. Eleanor relied on her Jewish friends, including Elinor Morgenthau and Bernard Baruch, who feared that domestic Jew-hatred would be intensified by protests against Germany's official anti-Jewish decrees—and they too wanted America to remain aloof from Germany's agony.

Finally, there was the widespread conviction that Hitler, and Fascist successes in Europe and Asia, represented a useful force to stop the growing Communist movement.

Whatever the reason, the United States' determined silence of 1933–38, combined with Britain's appeasement and collaboration, allowed Hitler to believe he had no serious opponents. In that period, he moved slowly, step by step, assessing the danger. Unchallenged, he moved on.

While ER's silence reflected her husband's official noninvolvement policy, it stands alone. She wrote several columns concerning the London Economic Conference of June 1933, and opposed her husband's decision to end multilateral efforts in favor of economic nationalism. She publicly endorsed a strong position at the disarmament conference, agitated for U.S. membership in the World Court, and continued to call for collective security in the interests of world peace.

A measure of FDR's curious policy regarding Germany is his contrary position concerning the Soviet Union. When he met with Maxim Litvinov in November 1933 to reestablish diplomatic relations, FDR insisted that religious freedom in Russia was basic to their negotiations.

Russia had been unrecognized since the Bolshevik revolution of 1917, but there was now a sense of urgency to normalize relations. In addition to Hitler's renewed militarization and announced intention to move east beyond the confines of Versailles, the Soviet Union was eager for alliances in the face of an alarming threat of war from Japan.

On 7 November 1933, at 5:45 P.M., ER welcomed the Soviet commissar of foreign affairs, Maxim Litvinov. Committed to collective security, urbane and cosmopolitan, married to British writer and literary scholar Ivy Low Litvinov (considered by many an "Eleanor type"), he had many supporters among antifascists who trusted his integrity.

Churchill called him "that eminent Jew," and appreciated his western orientation. After Russia was admitted to the League of Nations on 18 September 1934, Churchill wrote, Litvinov "spoke its moral language with so much success that he soon became an outstanding figure."

Recognition of Russia was FDR's first positive international act. ER called it, along with the Good Neighbor Policy, one of his "first points of attack in our foreign policy." In addition to the strategic and security concerns behind his new diplomacy, he was prompted to recognize the Soviet Union because business interests were eager to reestablish trade with the powerful, resource-rich nation, which then covered one-sixth of the earth's landmass.

With complete freedom to determine the rules for recognition, FDR emphasized religious freedom and the settlement of World War I debts, which became the chief snag, although Russia owed the United States far less than Britain and France did.* In the end, Russia agreed on a sum that ranged between $75 and $150 million, which represented Litvinov's assessment of the Soviets' real debt for their part of the war against Germany.

*In the autumn of 1933, debts owed to the United States, in principal and not counting interest payments (which FDR insisted the Soviets pay at 7 percent), included: France, $3.9 billion; Great Britain, $4.5 billion; Italy, $2 billion; Russia, $337 million. Because of the worldwide Depression and Germany's initial default, Allied payments were not made (except by Finland), and each country sought an official reduction of their war debt. Britain, for example, demanded an 80 percent reduction. ER believed all wartime debts should be forgiven, and wrote a column for the *Women's Democratic News* to explain her conviction. After 1934 no serious effort to collect the debts was made, although the issue continued to encourage U.S. isolationism.

Prior to Litvinov's visit, Esther Lape chaired a year-long study on the "Relations of Record" between the United States and and the USSR. Lape's report concerning Russia's eagerness to negotiate and settle differences was persuasive. Thomas Lamont wrote Lape that Litvinov should erect an icon to her for her influential work.

FDR personally handled all negotiations with Litvinov, and he felt that everything went smoothly—especially concerning freedom of religion. According to ER, he "used to speak often" of his success on that issue, and he proudly repeated his conversations with Litvinov, which lasted into the early morning of 17 November. They met in FDR's study after the cabinet dinner, with Henry Morgenthau, William Woodin, William Bullitt, and William Phillips. Ted Morgan described the scene:

> 'Well now, Max, you know the difference between the religious and the irreligious person. Why, you must know, Max. You were brought up by pious parents. Look here, some time you are going to die, and when you come to die, Max, you are going to remember your old father and mother—good, pious Jewish people who believed in God, and always said their prayers. I know they must have taught you to say your prayers . . .'
>
> By this time, FDR noted, Max was as red as a beet and FDR said, 'Now you may think you're an atheist. . . . But I tell you, Max, you had a religious bringing up, and when you come to die, Max, that's what you are going to think about, what your father and mother taught you . . . ' According to FDR, Litvinov hesitated, squirmed, grew uncomfortable . . . but I had him. . . .

Litvinov explained that church attendance was "discouraged." But it was permitted. Technically, therefore, Russia had freedom of worship. He agreed to FDR's only specific proposal: Church services would be available and protected, especially for U.S. citizens who visited Russia.

FDR also demanded assurances that Russia would cease communist propaganda within the United States. When his meetings with Litvinov were discussed by the cabinet, Frances Perkins pointed out that Nazi propaganda flourished within the United States. According to Ickes, Perkins presented evidence that "Germany is exceedingly active here building up German sentiment . . . [for] anti-Jewish, pro-Nordic, and extremely nationalistic" views. FDR had at the time no policy concerning Nazi propaganda.

FDR told ER that Litvinov was cordial, spoke perfect English, and was a surprisingly adept negotiator. She wrote Hick that FDR believed he had achieved more than "two-thirds of the essentials," but "every session" was "like pulling teeth."

The White House recognition ceremony included the first telephone conversation between the United States and the USSR. ER noted there "was considerable excitement" when Litvinov phoned his wife and son in Moscow, and the two countries formally resumed diplomatic relations.

On a personal level, the new alliance was launched with a feeling of warmth and hope. But opposition to the Soviet Union and widespread fear of communism hobbled every diplomatic step. One day, FDR's mother called upon her son to advise him formally that his decision troubled her. According to ER, "she felt this would be a disastrous move" and would be "widely misunderstood by the great majority of their old friends." ER wrote:

> My husband told me this with great amusement, adding that he thought his mother was entirely correct and that probably many of his old friends were going to have to put up with a number of shocks in the years to come.

For some, the shocks began with FDR's decision to send William Bullitt as America's first ambassador to Moscow. Anticommunists were horrified. But FDR wanted somebody in Moscow acceptable to the Russians, and able to advance this new alliance, as a countervailing power to fascism. The U.S. policy of nonrecognition, from 1917 to 1933, represented in part Woodrow Wilson's betrayal of Bullitt's first secret mission to Moscow—to end the total blockade and counterrevolutionary intervention which involved U.S. troops. In February 1919, Wilson had appointed Bullitt to lead a fact finding commission, with a view "to negotiate peace." Bullitt toured Russia with radical journalist Lincoln Steffens, friendly to the Soviets, and was impressed by Lenin—and Russia's plight.

Because of the U.S. and Allied blockade, "every man, woman and child in Moscow and Petrograd is suffering from slow starvation."

Bullitt believed peace could not occur "until peace is made with the revolution," and he was convinced he had negotiated a genuine peace proposal. Lenin had pledged to give up noncommunist areas of its vast empire, including Siberia, the Urals, the Caucasus, Finland, Murmansk, and the Baltic states. And he agreed to assume a share of Russia's war debts. In return, Russia sought an armistice, a peace conference, termination of the economic blockade, and withdrawal of occupying forces.

On 25 March, Steffens and Bullitt returned to Paris, where Steffens met with Bernard Baruch, whom Lenin wanted to develop industry and natural resources. It was originally to Baruch that Steffens said: "I have been over into the future, and it works."

The next day, 26 March, Wilson rejected Bullitt's work. He expected counterrevolutionary forces to topple Bolshevism. Bullitt resigned "as noisily as possible." Out of that "cave of winds" came the disastrous Treaty of Versailles, in which Bullitt could see "at least eleven wars."

That was when Bullitt decided "to lie on the sand and watch the world go to hell." Humanity seemed doomed. Steffens wrote that nobody wanted war, but "we will not give up the things that cause war."

Now, FDR assigned Bullitt to redeem his failed 1919 mission. He arrived in Moscow on 11 December 1933, and immediately went to lay a wreath on journalist John Reed's grave, "in tribute to the faith and passion of the revolution."

But the nation of the future was locked in the grip of Stalinist insanity. Only Litvinov really ever talked with Bullitt, and he found himself a virtual prisoner in the embassy. Betrayed again, he resigned his Moscow post with unending bitterness in 1936.

Bullitt's hatred of Stalin's Russia dominated all other considerations. Subsequently, as ambassador to France, he campaigned for a Franco-German rapprochement: a new economic and territorial understanding that would undo the wrongs of Versailles. Hitler's domestic policies did not concern him, and he despised William Dodd for his foolish preoccupation with Nazi brutality.*

Although Bullitt's detractors dismissed him as a "big Jew from Yale," and Ernest Hemingway, who hated Bullitt, called him a "half-kike," Bullitt always denied Jewish roots. Like other members of FDR's State Department and inner circle who had Jewish relatives, or were thought to have Jewish relatives, Bullitt wanted nothing to do with the "Jewish question," and never spoke of it.

For Bullitt and the careerists in FDR's State Department, Germany was not the enemy. At this time, only a small group of ER's friends were distressed by the human realities in Germany.

In the spring of 1934, Clarence Pickett and his wife, Lilly, visited England and Europe for the AFSC "to explore whether we could do anything to prevent the barbaric treatment of Jews and to assist the immigration of those who were so fortunate" as to get out. Pickett also studied housing and "resettlement schemes, for in this matter Germany and Austria especially were far ahead of the U.S." After their five-week tour, the Picketts typed a lengthy "confidential" report for their friends, including ER. Their vivid, stirring observations updated what she had learned from Alice Hamilton the year before.

In Paris, the Picketts confronted the "deep human tragedy of the refugees from Hitler Germany." More than four thousand families awaited relocation. Little was being done officially, although some individuals initiated private

---

*William Dodd's opposition to Nazism disturbed his State Department colleagues. They considered his reports excessive, and useless. Moreover, he had been told by FDR upon leaving for Berlin that the Jewish issue "was not a government affair" and the United States could "do nothing" about it. Bullitt waged a relentless campaign to have Dodd replaced by someone who could get along with Hitler.

colonization programs. For example, "Joseph Rosen, an American Jew, . . . colonized 100,000 Jewish families in Russia and is now in charge of a large farm in France where he is training fifty Jewish boys from Germany to farm with the plan to send them on to Palestine next year."

France seemed "very weak," "ultra conservative," and unstable. The government appeared "paralyzed with fear" because of "Hitler Germany." Fascists and communists seemed to dominate; some talked of a "preventive war" against Germany, while pacifism grew rapidly.

England was disturbing: The government was "inactive and conservative." Hostility toward the United States prevailed, marked by "ignorance, antagonism and aloofness." Despite a left and pacifist movement, "Fascism grows stronger. Two leading papers are supporting Sir Oswald Mosley. . . ."

In Geneva, they wondered if "the beautiful new" League of Nations building would be "completed in time to entertain the funeral of the League," since it seemed doomed in the current climate.

Vienna was filled with music and discord. "Austria makes one weep and laugh." Economically paralyzed since war's end, it was academically brilliant. Vienna featured "some of the best housing work anywhere in Europe." But much of it was demolished in the battles of February 1934. To crush his opposition in Vienna, Engelbert Dollfuss, Austria's Catholic fascist chancellor, destroyed entire neighborhoods of workers' apartment houses built by socialists. Models of community living, they were blasted by howitzers and bulldozed. Thousands of workers, social democrats, socialists, and radicals were seized, killed in random shootings, executed.

Although Dollfuss rejected "Anschluss," unity with Hitler and absorption by Germany, his triumph was nevertheless a defeat for democracy. Driven "by German Nazis on one side and Italian Fascists on the other," Dollfuss, the Picketts judged, was a brutal nationalist "religious fanatic." "And now the Pope really rules Austria, with Mussolini a strong ally. . . . No one can predict the future. But the Nazis grow in strength and are obviously hopeful of finally attaining power."

Within months of the Picketts' visit, Hitler-supported Nazis attempted a putsch on 25 July 1934 and assassinated Dollfuss. But the Austrian military remained loyal, members of his cabinet rallied, and Minister of Justice Kurt von Schuschnigg assumed power. Bavarian Nazis crossed the frontier in large numbers, but were stopped by Mussolini, who dispatched three Italian divisions to the Brenner Pass. Hitler retreated. The Anschluss required further preparation. Hitler appointed Franz von Papen minister to Vienna—assigned to expand the Austrian Nazi Party, with "a monthly subsidy of 200,000 marks."

From Vienna, the Picketts went to Prague, where they found Czechoslovakia "a relief." Thomas Masaryk, president for fifteen years, had "kept his eye . . . on the needs of his people for land and homes, and freedom to live un-fettered lives. Democracy is a strong tradition and freedom of thought, press, assembly and worship is sacred." But there were "jitters now," because the Nazis banned "Germans living in Czecho-Slovakia," and the country was filled with German refugees. Masaryk, eighty-four, had been reelected for another seven years; but the Picketts doubted Central Europe's most democratic na-tion's ability to survive.

Finally, the Picketts arrived in Berlin. They did not "feel dogmatic" about Germany. Behind "the rule of the roughnecks," there seemed "great human motives at work." Above all, Germany needed to "recover" from the legacy of Versailles.

Writing much as Alice Hamilton had, the Picketts detailed Germany's woes. Without employment or hope, youth put its faith in Nazism. "Unem-ployment has decreased, but by evicting Jews, throwing women out of jobs, trying to force people to employ more servants, etc. . . ."

Fiscally Germany remained a nightmare, but economic worries were di-verted "by Jew persecution and violence to all complainers or non-cooperators. We feel that the situation is so difficult that concentration camps, and exile and persecution are likely to continue for a long time."

"As to the Jew, he is again to suffer long and hard for his race and reli-gion." Berlin's Rabbi Dr. Leo Baeck, "one of the finest religious leaders I have ever met," told Clarence Pickett that his congregation had expanded from sixty or seventy people to hundreds in search now of spiritual understanding and community. There were "two, three or four services each Saturday" to ac-commodate the large crowds: Rabbi Baeck said that always "my message is the same—let no drop of bitterness enter your hearts no matter what comes."

Dr. Baeck spoke of a recent celebration in Worms to mark the syna-gogue's "900th year of consecutive service. Jews were in Germany before Christ's time. They love Germany. Most Jews will remain in Germany, will be driven in on themselves, but will suffer through." To accommodate children dismissed from Germany's public schools, Jews "established 400 small private schools and maintain them by voluntary contributions." They also retrained physicians, lawyers, and other professional people now barred from their work as carpenters, locksmiths, repairmen.

The Picketts left Europe with a sense of dread. Poverty, political torpor, repression prevailed. "We are really in a period like the Thirty Years War." They were convinced that Germany was "a menace to world peace." One of their closest English associates planned "to move to the country to avoid the impending destruction of his city in the war air raid. We are seeing the prelude—to what?"

Whatever ER felt as she read the Picketts' report, however much her thoughts must have turned to her Jewish friends, like Bernard Baruch, who continued to go to Austria and Germany each year for the curative waters of Central Europe's spas, or the Morgenthaus, who traveled abroad annually, she wrote nothing about the agonizing information presented to her.

In her June 1934 column for the *Women's Democratic News*, ER referred to the Picketts' report only vaguely, and on a slant. She wrote nothing of the political situation or the atrocities, not even about Vienna's destroyed housing. Her words regarding Europe were bland. Her column was personal. It heralded the end of Washington's social season and the end of a familial era: Her youngest son graduated from Groton, "and now we have no boys in school—next year we will have two at Harvard."

Concerning Europe and Asia, ER wrote:

> Though formal entertainment . . . has come to an end, [guests con-tinued to arrive, including] a Japanese Prince . . . the Sultan of Johore . . . and Anne O'Hare McCormick writer of articles and traveller during the last year in thirteen different countries. Mrs. McCormick's account of conditions in Europe are most interesting as was that of Mr. Pickett of the Friends Service Committee who has just returned from a study of the Friends' work in certain parts of Europe and at the same time of the differ-ent methods which have been used in Germany, France and England in their subsistence homestead ventures. It is a help to us to have the knowl-edge gained by other countries to guide us a little in what after all are new experiences.

How does one understand ER's failure to impart the Picketts' message to her readers? How did she decide to neglect their presentation of fascist vio-lence and repression, omit entirely the situation confronting Jews and refu-gees, ignore indeed the gravamen and substance of their observations?

ER's silence, despite all the information sent to her, remains in retrospect thunderous. She was frequently advised by her husband or State Department officials to remain discreet and uninvolved, and diplomatic silence was occa-sionally ordered for no apparent reason in relation to the most banal and seemingly uncontroversial issues, such as the April 1935 international broad-cast to celebrate Jane Addams's birthday and the WILPF's twentieth year.

In May 1935, an extraordinary exchange of memos concerned the deci-sion of an international flower show in the Netherlands to name "a new tulip" for the First Lady. Press reports were blocked after discussions between Steve Early, ER's staff, and William Phillips, then undersecretary of state. Early wrote Tommy: "I think it would be a mistake if we gave publicity to this very complimentary message from Amsterdam." He suggested a note to express "Mrs. Roosevelt's appreciation" of "this very complimentary message" be sent by the State Department to the U.S. embassy. To censor news about a flower show surely indicates the depth of America's isolationism.

The State Department opposed all public expressions of protest against Hitler's activities. On 8 January 1934, Senator Millard Tydings of Maryland submitted a resolution (SR 154) requesting the president "to communicate . . . an unequivocal statement of the profound feeling of surprise and pain experienced by the people of the United States upon learning of the discriminations and oppressions imposed by the Reich upon its Jewish citizens . . ." Further, the resolution called upon FDR "to express the earnest hope of the people of the U.S. that the German Reich will speedily alter its policy, restore to its Jewish nationals the civil and political rights of which they have been deprived, and undo so far as may be the wrongs that have been done them."

The State Department strangled the resolution. Hull argued it would impinge on FDR's "constitutional initiative." Although State Department counsel R. Walton Moore acknowledged historic precedent, such as Congress's 1867 resolution to protest Turkish dominion over the people of Crete, he advised against it nevertheless because it "might lead to embarrassing recriminations about the Negro problem in America."

Sam Rosenman urged FDR to support it, after it was modified to express Senate opinion solely. A significant rally for the Tydings resolution ensued. Isabella Greenway was urged to support it by her Phoenix constituents, one of whom wrote: "I assure you that such action on your part will be deeply appreciated by every citizen of Arizona of the Jewish faith, and those who . . . believe in equal rights and religious freedom."

She replied: "I recognize the importance of this Resolution and can assure you that it will receive my careful attention when it comes before the House of Representatives." But it remained buried in the Senate Foreign Relations Committee, because of State Department opposition.

Greenway's correspondence is significant, since she and ER met regularly for an "air our minds" lunch. The lunches were important to ER, and she referred to them in a "My Day" column:

Four of us, all intimately connected with public life for many years—two through our husbands, and two through their own efforts—get together every few weeks at luncheon to unburden our souls. Each time we do it, I think what a safeguard it is to have anyone anywhere in the world whom you feel you can talk to with absolute sincerity and with no danger of having the rest of the world knowing anything about it, or of any misunderstanding arising between you individually. . . .

We laugh together a great deal, but I often come away with the feeling that back of the laughter something serious was really on our minds and all the better for being off our minds.

The State Department considered the suppression of another protest during the spring of 1934: On 7 March a broad spectrum of public citizens organized a "mock trial" at Madison Square Garden. Sponsored by the American Federation of Labor and the American Jewish Congress, "The Case of Civilization Against Hitlerism" attracted twenty thousand people. Several of FDR's former colleagues participated, including Al Smith and Raymond Moley. Academics and politicians abounded, including New York's Mayor Fiorello La Guardia, Senator Robert Wagner, and Woodrow Wilson's last secretary of state, Bainbridge Colby, who presided. According to Arnold Offner, German officials protested immediately upon seeing advertisements for the event.

Although his wife was Jewish, Secretary of State Cordell Hull wanted no protests against Germany. He was "disappointed" that he could not stop the Garden event. Hull assured Germany's ambassador it was no reflection of U.S. policy, and he "frowned on the American Jewish Congress' invitation to the German embassy to provide counsel for the defendant." Germany's ambassador Hans Luther was persuaded that American diplomats had tried to prevent the rally and it was all the work of "liberal, pacifistic, Jewish, Socialist, and Communist circles." Hitler was furious, and he threatened William Dodd in a meeting on 7 March: The cursed Jews would be "eliminated" in Germany "if outside agitation did not stop."

Silenced on the situation in Europe, ER sought to limit the rise of anti-Semitism and race bigotry within the United States. Her work with the NAACP intensified during this period, and she responded with clarity and outrage whenever Jewish groups or individuals were attacked in the United States.

Given the deeply pervasive bigotry in the country, her every gesture toward Jews was guaranteed to achieve publicity. Aware that even her presence at a Jewish gathering was controversial, ER appeared regularly before Jewish groups. In April 1933, she attended a Jewish Federation luncheon at the Hotel Commodore, which elicited profound gratitude:

> In view of the many unkind discriminations and in some instances ruthless persecutions to which my co-religionists, at present, are subjected in other lands, your gracious [presence] . . . was a very heartening evidence of the liberal feelings entertained by the First Family of our Land.
>
> May our glorious land ever be blessed with leaders of enlightenment. . . .

ER replied: "I was very glad indeed to attend the Jewish Federation Luncheon and I am very gratified to know that you feel it was helpful. Both my husband and I deeply appreciate your good wishes." Before she actually spoke before a Jewish group, however, she carefully considered which organization to address. As usual, in such matters she relied upon Elinor Morgenthau's advice.

Elinor Morgenthau was ER's closest Jewish woman friend. Although she and her husband were secular "assimilationist" Jews who tended to turn away from Jewish issues during the 1930s, she was extremely sensitive to the Jew-hating world surrounding her. A most extraordinary and revealing description of Elinor Morgenthau, only slightly disguised, was captured by South African writer Sarah Gertrude Millin, who spent several days with ER in New York City and at the Executive Mansion in Albany in 1929.

Being Jewish in a hostile world, Millin observed, was akin to suffering a chronic disease. Some suffered in secret, while others "cannot stop discussing it, so there are Jews who keep their Jewish pain to themselves and others who speak of it. . . ."

After a long talk with Elinor Morgenthau over lunch, Millin wrote:

> This woman was of the kind who had, all the time, to be speaking of Jews. She did so in a frightened, determined manner, out of a courage invoked to overcome fear.
>
> She passed from the position of Jews in America to the position of Jews in Palestine. She told me how odd she thought it that when the Arabs murdered the Jews the British Mandatory should sympathize, not with the Jews, but the Arabs.
>
> Having said this, however, it struck her that, as a South African and therefore British, I might be offended. . . .

But Millin reassured her:

> "Oh, no" . . . "you're quite right . . . and it makes my Jewish blood boil too."
>
> There was a momentary standstill at the table, and then the talk went on.

After the luncheon, while strolling with ER, Millin probed her about the Jewish situation in America, and ER was frank to impart her own understanding. Concerning her friend specifically, ER explained:

> "Mrs. X belongs to a distinguished family and she has married into another distinguished family. They're among our best citizens—wealthy and cultured. I like them tremendously. Nevertheless, they're not socially accepted."
>
> "Simply because they're Jews?"
>
> "Yes. . . ."

"It's never over in America."

"Like the last drop of Negro blood. . . ."

ER acknowledged that there "are schools which won't admit the children of the greatest Jewish families in the land, and clubs and hotels which won't admit [even men and women] . . . in the highest official positions. . . ."

On one occasion ER intervened to advocate for the admission of a Jewish friend's child to a school that claimed "there was no vacancy":

> [But] immediately afterwards, another child was accepted.
>
> "It was a really serious affront. . . . The mother cried when she told me about it. It was unbearable, she said, for her to meet people officially who, in effect, would not let her child associate with their children.". . .
>
> "And what can one do?" went on Mrs. Roosevelt. "The will of the people is a difficult thing. . . ."

Millin asked about ER's own school, Todhunter:

> "Jews are not excluded. . . . In fact, at this moment, the heads of both the upper and lower schools are Jewish girls."
>
> "Because they're the top of their forms?"
>
> "No. It goes by election. They've been chosen by the girls themselves. That shows a good spirit, don't you think?"
>
> "Are there many Jewish children in the school?"
>
> "Quite a number."
>
> "As many as you would like to come?"
>
> Mrs. Roosevelt's honest grey eyes looked down into mine.
>
> "No."
>
> "You mean, there's a limit?"
>
> "Not technically."
>
> "But it works out that way?"
>
> "I'm sorry—I'm very sorry—but I'm afraid there's a feeling—even, I think, among the Jews themselves—that the spirit of the school, and the school itself, would be different if we had too large a proportion of Jewish children."
>
> I knew it was so: that the Gentiles resented the idea of too many Jews; and that the Jews, dreading this resentment, equally resented it.
>
> I asked her if she thought it would ever be possible for Americans to consider all their fellow citizens—Jews too—as simply Americans.
>
> [ER replied:]
>
> "That is the American tradition. . . . the difficulty is that the country is still full of immigrant Jews, very unlike ourselves. I don't blame them for being as they are. I know what they've been through in other lands, and I'm glad they have freedom at last, and I hope they'll have the chance, among us, to develop all there is in them. But it takes a little time for Americans to

be made. And, meanwhile, the old stock can't feel they're Americans, and unfortunately they also class real Americans who are Jews together with them. Well, one day, I hope, we'll all be Americans together."

In ER's culture and family of origin, Jews were regarded as different, though not necessarily inferior. Even Jews of "old stock" were tinged with a vague sense of otherness.

Henry Morgenthau III recalled that despite all the apparent closeness between the Roosevelts and the Morgenthaus, "there was a certain distance. . . . For example, in those days I could not have gone nor would they even have thought of my going to the same schools that the Roosevelt children went to."

In turn, old-stock German Jewish families regarded Central and Eastern European Jews as "the other kind"—folks who refused or failed to assimilate, and were to be shunned. While individual Jews occasionally entered America's mainstream, they were discouraged from leadership circles. Those invited in were exceptions, made to feel exceptional.

Bernard Baruch was a rare exception, ultimately a remarkable bridge between FDR and Winston Churchill. Baruch's friendship with ER grew slowly, awkwardly, surprisingly. He was not of her class, and not of her kind, but they actually enjoyed each other's company. That seemed to many of ER's other friends incomprehensible. Some thought he merely used her—to get closer to FDR. Others thought she merely used him—for his material generosity to causes she cared about.

Actually the closer Baruch grew to ER, the more FDR withdrew. FDR's inner circle and "Brains Trust" dismissed Baruch as "obnoxious," the "wolf of Wall Street." Evidently Sam Rosenman particularly advised the president to avoid him.

But ER increasingly relied upon him. When they first met in January 1918, ER was candidly, though privately, anti-Semitic—especially in correspondence with her mother-in-law. When, as wife of the assistant secretary of the navy, she was obliged to attend a party given by the Admiralty to honor Bernard Baruch, then chair of the War Industries Board, ER wrote her mother-in-law that it was a party "I'd rather be hung than seen at." It promised to be "mostly Jews." After the party, ER reported: "The Jew party was appalling. I never wish to hear money, jewels, and sables mentioned again."

Within months of that party, FDR invited Felix Frankfurter home for dinner. ER found her husband's friend unpleasant. The Harvard professor and public servant was, she wrote SDR: "an interesting little man, but very Jew."

ER's caustic comments concerning Jews remained a routine part of her social observation for many years, diminishing as her friendship with Baruch and other Jews flourished. In November 1918, ER and Baruch sailed for Europe aboard the same ship and evidently waltzed together and spent long hours in comfortable conversation. ER loved to dance, and Baruch at six feet four—as tall as her brother—was strikingly handsome in formal attire. She, at six feet, was as tall as his wife, Annie Griffen—with whom he never traveled. In Paris, Baruch presented ER with "a lot of roses." He thought her gracious, interesting, and charming. She thought him gallant, interesting, and unusual.

Throughout the 1920s he supported her new concerns, especially the Todhunter School, and their friendship solidified during Al Smith's 1928 presidential campaign. Together they witnessed "the horror prejudice could make" in a nation's political life as they encountered in city after city burning crosses, and various demonstrations of violent religious bigotry against Smith, against Catholics, against immigrants and "others."

During the 1930s, ER called Baruch "one of the wisest and most generous people I have ever known." Like Earl Miller, Baruch always "defended" ER. He stood at her side whenever she needed him or seemed to be in trouble, and he usually arrived before the trouble began. On one occasion ER wrote Baruch an intimate letter of gratitude: "There are few people one trusts without reservation in life and I am deeply grateful to call you that kind of a friend." For publication, she noted that she appreciated his respect for her views and values: Bernard Baruch "looks on me as a mind, not as a woman."

Among the reasons ER considered Baruch a wise and splendid friend was his 1929 dealings with Churchill, which engendered Baruch's status as Churchill's "favorite American."

Shortly after the stock market crash, Churchill, an enthusiastic gambler, visited New York and decided to play the exchange as if he were in Monte Carlo. He appeared at Baruch's office to do so. William Manchester described the scene: "At the end of the day he confronted Baruch in tears. He was, he said, a ruined man. Chartwell and everything else he possessed must be sold; he would have to leave the House of Commons. . . ."

Baruch calmed him. He had lost nothing: "Baruch had left instructions to buy every time Churchill sold and sell whenever Churchill bought. Winston had come out exactly even because, he later learned, Baruch even paid the commissions."

An ardent sportsman, trained as a boxer, courtly and vital, Bernard Baruch was defined by social contradictions. Committed to his marriage, he was a renowned though somewhat esoteric womanizer. According to Helen Lawrenson, although "a philanderer, Baruch was not a passionate man." There was a pattern to his interests: He preferred political women, "with spunk and talent," women "who could make a keynote speech at a political convention," and then fancied himself a "mentor to their careers." He encouraged them to work, to succeed, to triumph.

Although there were others, Helen Lawrenson, Clare Boothe Luce, and ER were his most frequent and notable women companions. According to Lawrenson, Baruch always treated his wife with courtesy and respect, but she was not interested in politics and travel and "seemed content to let him go his own way." Throughout the 1930s, whenever Baruch returned from Europe, he "brought back gifts for various women friends, including Mrs. Roosevelt and me, but Clare had first pick."

Associated with New York and financial success, he considered himself above all a Southern gentleman. In 1905 he purchased a twenty-four-thousand-acre estate, Hobcaw Barony, in South Carolina, a string of former plantations and "nine Negro villages."

Bound to South Carolina, the state of his birth, "by ties of blood and love," Baruch transcended customary and partisan boundaries in his friendships but never challenged the South's traditional "race etiquette." Baruch always saw himself as a Southerner first, then as an American. According to Margaret Coit, Baruch never identified himself as a Jew, and when he said "my people," he referred primarily to Americans, Southerners, or even more specifically to South Carolinians.

He felt Jewish entirely by accident and irrelevantly. His father was an immigrant from Poland who was educated and became a physician in South Carolina. A Confederate officer and pioneering healer who introduced public baths and the appendectomy to America, Dr. Baruch, ironically, also became a member of the Ku Klux Klan. Baruch's mother's family arrived in the colonies in 1695. His mother's forebear Captain Isaac Rodriguez Marques, an affluent Sephardic Jew, sailed out of Amsterdam with three ships. Baruch liked to think he was a pirate.

The Marques family fought in the Revolution and before the War of 1812 moved to South Carolina. Bernard Baruch's mother, Belle Wolfe Baruch, was a member of both the Daughters of the American Revolution and the Daughters of the Confederacy. Bernie was eleven when his family moved to New York, and his mother became regent of the Knickerbocker Chapter of the DAR and president of the Washington Headquarters Club and the Southland Club of New York. Still, Baruch understood that his Jewish heritage limited his opportunities. He might have been president, he told Coit, if he had not been a Jew—and had not Jew hatred become again a major political theme after World War I.

The twisted history of race and racism, of passing and power, causes one to pause long enough to consider the concept of Dr. Simon Baruch's membership in the Ku Klux Klan. Margaret Coit explained the "terrible secret" his sons unfolded proudly after his death by dismissing the 1870s Klan as a redemptive order "created to free the South from the Reign of Terror of Reconstruction, where order was nonexistent." Simon Baruch's Klan rode against "carpetbaggers and scalawags," not against blacks, Jews, or Catholics. It "bore no resemblance," she argued, "to that mongrel outfit of the 20th century, which burned a fiery cross" to express its contempt of that Jew Baruch.

During the 1920s, when Henry Ford launched his "paper pogrom," Baruch was his chief target. Ford's newspaper, *The Dearborn Independent*, printed as truth the "Protocols of the Elders of Zion," a vicious hoax that purported to prove that an international capitalist Jewish conspiracy ran the world's business. Ford's lurid Jew-hating campaign lasted until 1927. But his popular articles were published in a four-volume work, *The International Jew*, reprinted in several languages, and quoted extensively by Hitler in *Mein Kampf.* *

According to Ford, Jews in America controlled banks, cotton, sugar, industry—especially the fashion and film industries. They were the most dangerous people on earth. And the worst, in Ford's fantasia, was Bernard Baruch. Banner headlines vilified him as a munitions profiteer, chief of the "Jewish Copper Kings," "the most powerful man in the world."

Baruch read the headlines in his office, and left for home. His wife and children, astounded, were in tears. Neither Baruch nor his wife, Annie Griffen, ever recovered emotionally.

Nevertheless, as Ford's violent rhetoric became Hitler's brutal policy, Baruch remained mysteriously silent, and managed to ignore the refugee issue entirely. On the other hand, Baruch in America and Churchill in England were virtually alone in the early years of Hitler's remilitarization when they called for urgent defense spending, concerted opposition, mobilization.

Each was reviled for his efforts; Churchill was out of step with Britain's "appeasement," and Baruch with America's "isolationism." In addition, Baruch received letters labeling him a meddlesome, dangerous "dirty Jew." Headlines during the 1930s again screamed "International Banker," "Jewish Warmonger."

Baruch never understood why he was so widely regarded as a Jew first. He never understood society's rejection of his Episcopalian wife, Annie Griffen Baruch, and their children, raised in her church. But he believed in assimilation, and scorned group identification.

Like Baruch, the Morgenthaus were assimilationists by custom and family tradition. In 1917, Woodrow Wilson appointed Henry Morgenthau, Sr., ambassador to the Ottoman Empire. Faced with the future of Turkey's crumbling interests in Palestine and Britain's mandate over the area, Morgenthau re-

---

*In 1927 Ford repudiated his campaign, and ceased his publications. On 7 January 1942 he publicly apologized to "my fellow citizens of Jewish faith," and condemned "hate-mongering."

jected Zionism as "wrong in principle and impossible of realization." He considered it an "East European proposal," which would hurt "the Jews of America."

As FDR's secretary of the treasury, Henry, Jr., shared his father's views. According to Henry Morgenthau III, "there was a very strong drive for total Americanization." Zionism suggested a "dual alliance." The Morgenthaus, and most Jewish friends in the Roosevelt orbit, "certainly, until Hitler, were really moving away from Jewish things." And they all "would have told Mrs Roosevelt, 'You don't want to have anything to do with these Zionists.' She accepted the Jewishness of her Jewish friends, and certainly when it came to Jewish matters probably would have accepted whatever they had to say."

Unfortunately, during the early years of the Nazi era, they had virtually nothing to say.

When ER proposed her for membership to the Colony Club in 1937, Elinor Morgenthau was blackballed: Jews were not members. ER, who with Mary Harriman had been one of the founders of the Colony Club, resigned in silent protest. Months after, when the press asked about her resignation, she said only that she had no time for membership. Elinor Morgenthau did not want the First Lady to make a fuss. Every slight was an agony, and she did not want to embarrass or hurt ER.

Whatever Elinor Morgenthau privately thought about Hitler's intentions, throughout the 1930s she publicly ignored them. An outsider with no sense of privilege or expectation of justice, Elinor Morgenthau was determined to protect her friend the First Lady from suffering any political abuse on her account. When, therefore, ER asked which Jewish group to address, Elinor Morgenthau was eager that she limit her appearance to the least controversial, the most secular and philanthropic federation.

Louise Wise, wife of Rabbi Stephen S. Wise, had invited ER to address the Women's Association of the American Jewish Congress, which had grown significantly from 200 member organizations. It was, Mrs. Wise wrote, "eminently now worth your while to address this group." She assured ER that the "theme could be one of your own choosing, but your coming would strengthen our movement and would make us feel that even if you do not wish to discuss the subject which engrosses us now, that your mere presence would hearten us in the very difficult crisis we are facing."

Because the American Jewish Congress, and the Wises, were identified with public protest, including the growing German boycott movement, Elinor Morgenthau urged ER to speak instead to the Federation of Jewish Women's Organizations. She drafted a letter for ER to send to Louise Wise, along with a note to Tommy that she needed to explain "the matter to her personally." In her draft Elinor Morgenthau "purposefully" omitted the name of the organization "I think Mrs. R should address," leaving it to Mrs. Wise "to do that, or if she doesn't want to do so, to turn down Mrs. R—rather than have Mrs. R turn her down."

ER sent Morgenthau's draft exactly as she wrote it:

> I am sure you realize that I must limit myself in regard to the number of addresses that I can give, particularly outside of Washington. On the other hand, I would very much like to address a large group of Jewish women. Is there no one organization which embraces, so far as possible, all Jewish women's clubs or organizations? If there were such a group or Federation, it seems to me that it would be most fitting for me to make my first address to Jewish women, since I have been in the White House, to an organization of this type.

Louise Wise deliberately misread the implied message and replied: "I need hardly tell you how glad I am to have your acceptance of my invitation to speak to Jewish women in New York. Acting upon your suggestion and in glad compliance," she invited "other large Jewish women's groups in order that we may have the widest possible hearing for your valued word. . . ."

According to the press, ER's speech, before three thousand members and guests of the Women's Association of the American Jewish Congress, "crowded into the grand ballroom of the Hotel Commodore," was a great success.*

Although ER did not wish, in Mrs. Wise's words, "to discuss the subject which engrosses us now," she was not criticized for her failure to do so. According to Florence Rothschild in *The Wisconsin Jewish Chronicle*, as ER stood "in that huge room decorated with the Stars and Stripes and with the blue-and-white banner that bears the Shield of David," every woman in the room felt honored:

---

*The week of ER's correspondence with Louise Wise, on 23 November, she presented the American Hebrew Medal to Carrie Chapman Catt for the promotion of better understanding between Christians and Jews in the United States. ER was proud to present the medal to her mentor, the first woman to receive the award. But she did not mention Catt's petition of nine thousand Christian women to protest "the shocking German program against the Jews," celebrated by other speakers. Nor, during her 28 February address at the Commodore did ER refer to Catt's committee of appeal to FDR to ease immigration restrictions to allow sanctuary for those suffering persecution. According to *The New York Times:* "The appeal pointed out that the legal German immigration quota was 25,957, but that fewer than 600 had been admitted since last July." U.S. consulates were rigidly enforcing a 1930 order that required definite proof an alien would not become a "public charge" and add to unemployment. Catt's appeal was supported by Jane Addams, Mary Dreier, Lillian Wald, Mabel Walker Willebrandt, and many others close to ER.

Some of the First Lady's listeners may have felt disappointed that . . . she avoided making any statements on specifically Jewish questions. Personally, however, we regard it only as an additional instance of her tact that at the very beginning of her address she emphasized that she was speaking not as a non-Jewess to Jewish woman but as an American to fellow Americans.

ER spoke about the New Deal, and urged her audience to consider the desperate plight of the "40 [to] 60 percent of the population . . . living on relief, or starving." She urged women to be "even ahead of the men, in their attitude toward recovery."

ER's very presence at the Hotel Commodore was interpreted by other speakers as a "repudiation of propagandists' attempts to set up racial, religious, political and class divisions in this nation."

Whenever ER spoke to Jewish groups she was greeted both by fervent gratitude and an avalanche of protest filled with race hatred, anti-Semitism, and occasionally personal threats. Stunned by the depths of the problem in America, by 1935 she spoke out against anti-Semitism and race hatred wherever she found it in the United States.

She wrote letters to recommend Jewish students to various colleges and supported a wide variety of causes, including Jewish orphanages, philanthropies, and aid societies. On one occasion, she wrote the president of Wheaton College:

> I understand you take a certain number of Jewish girls and I am wondering if there is a chance of your taking Ruth Liberman. I have met the child and she impresses me as a thoroughly nice person. Of course, I would not think of asking you to do anything you do not feel you would do ordinarily.

Since ER's private acts of domestic concern contrasted with her public international silence, it is important to consider FDR's policy, and his own silence. In addition to regular diplomatic correspondence, FDR received vivid descriptions of events and personalities from Felix Frankfurter, who was visiting professor at Oxford in 1933 and 1934. He had close friends throughout Europe, and relatives in Vienna.

Frankfurter's letters to FDR from Oxford were filled with information, clippings, suggestions for specific things to do. Forever the teacher, in his letters he was instructive and pertinent. On 17 October 1933 he sent clippings from the London *Observer*.

> [They contained] illuminating glimpses into the violence and madness now dominating in Germany. Developments make it abundantly clear

that the significance of Hitlerism far transcends ferocious anti-Semitism and fanatical racism. Dr. Alice Hamilton is right in insisting that the attack against the Jew is merely an index to the gospel of force and materialism that explains the present rulers. . . .

Frankfurter suggested FDR broadcast in German to say "some plain things that need to be said." Because of strict propaganda controls, German citizens were completely "barred from knowledge of the outside world. . . . No other voice in the world would carry such weight as yours. . . . By such an act you would become the rallying center of the world's sanity."

FDR did not answer that part of Frankfurter's letter. A month later, on 23 November 1933, Frankfurter sent FDR an urgent appeal from James McDonald, the League's high commissioner for German refugees: McDonald had received evidence that Germany intended to issue a formal decree establishing "a second-class citizenship for German Jews:"

> Such action once taken would not only further humiliate and degrade 100s of 1000s of men and women; it would make much more difficult any softening in the German government's attitude later. Such retrogression to the inhumane and unChristian practise of an earlier age should, I think, be forestalled if there is any conceivable way of doing so.

McDonald considered the situation dire. Refugee problems were already "too large to be handled satisfactorily." If conditions worsened there was "grave danger that something like an exodus—panic in practice and proportions—may be precipitated. This would create a situation in the bordering countries beyond the possibility of ordered control. You will at once sense the tragedy of such a situation. . . ."

On 22 December 1933, FDR wrote a long chatty letter in which he answered virtually every point his friend and mentor had raised in several letters, except those dealing with Europe and refugees.

Perhaps they spoke on the telephone. In any case, Frankfurter continued to send FDR urgent European information. On 20 February 1934, he telegrammed:

> London advises from Vienna indicate serious danger of excesses particularly anti-Jewish. Deeply hope it will commend itself to you to make appropriate representations to Austria if indeed you have not already done so. International usage and our own precedents amply support such action. We joined in protest to Roumania in 1872. In 1891 President Harrison declared "suggestions of humanity" warranted protest to Russia. In 1902 TR invited Powers to make representations to Russia. None in better position than you to make such appeal. Time of essence. . . .

For all the historical precedents to condemn anti-Jewish pogroms, FDR made no such appeal. Two days later, Frankfurter sent him a clipping from the *Manchester Guardian* concerning events in Vienna, and a long historical lecture:

> I need not tell you that Austria is really the football between the rivalries of Hitler and Mussolini. . . . The victimization which the Germans have made so familiar is proceeding and will continue to proceed in Austria. . . .

In March, to Frankfurter's relief, FDR appointed George Messersmith, a known antifascist, to the embassy in Vienna.

After a month of correspondence from Frankfurter, FDR wrote another long gossipy letter. Again he answered every one of Frankfurter's points, paragraph by paragraph, except those which referred to the situation in Germany or the plight of Jews.

The spring and summer of 1934 were seen by many observers as a turning point. Hitler now bellowed his determination to rearm, solidify his forces, pursue his expansionist goals, eliminate his opponents. On 30 June he initiated a massacre of his earliest supporters, the Brownshirts of the SA. During the "Night of the Long Knives," Hitler's new storm troopers brutally murdered five thousand to seven thousand of his former political allies.

Winston Churchill wrote in *The Gathering Storm* that it showed beyond doubt "that conditions in Germany bore no resemblance to those of a civilised state." He continued:

> A dictatorship based upon terror and reeking with blood had confronted the world. Anti-Semitism was ferocious and brazen, and the concentration-camp system was already in full operation for all obnoxious or politically dissident classes. I was deeply affected by the episode, and the whole process of German rearmament, of which there was now overwhelming evidence, seemed to me invested with a ruthless, lurid tinge. It glittered and it glared.

Then, on 5 September 1934, the annual Nazi Party rally at Nuremberg turned into another ominous show—as Leni Riefenstahl and her crew of hundreds worked to immortalize Hitler's "Triumph of the Will."

In that overheated and tense climate, with Klanners and Nazis organizing in the United States, FDR decided to send a letter of greeting to a well-publicized Nazi rally in New York's Madison Square Garden. Ignored by his biographers, associates, and staff, that decision created for history a profound sense of confusion. Although fully reported, it was quickly forgotten and failed to become an abiding controversy.

On 7 October 1934, *The New York Times* ran a four-tiered headline: "Germans Here Ask Place in Politics / 20,000 at Madison Square Garden Hear Pleas for Greater Recognition / GATHER IN NAZI SETTING / Flags and Uniforms Abound—Message from Roosevelt and Hitler's Name Cheered."

According to the *Times*, swastikas and Nazi bunting mingled with U.S. flags at a mass meeting attended by thousands of cheering "Friends of the New Germany."

Outside, six hundred police officers guarded Madison Square Garden for fear of disturbances, which "did not materialize." "Several hundred" protesters, "mostly" men and women of the Young People's Socialist League, marched up and down Eighth Avenue with placards. They were kept far from the event, and there were no "outbreaks, no arrests."

Inside, the scene "resembled the news photographs of a rally somewhere in Germany. At one end of the arena a huge platform had been erected. At each side of the platform stood pylons, fifteen feet high," one topped by a Nazi swastika, the other bearing black, white, and red German pennants. Atop each pylon were illuminated red papers symbolizing Germany's "eternal flame." Signs in German and English ordered: "Germans of America, Awake."

Over a thousand ushers, men and women in Nazi costumes and adornments, served with military precision.

Various speeches and a chorus of two hundred men electrified the crowd—as did FDR's greeting, sent, Dr. Griebl explained, because the president was unable to attend. Before he read FDR's words, Griebl urged Germans to "help our President in carrying out his program of reconstruction and recovery." He also warned: "Those who fight us must perish—socially as well as economically—because of our determination to destroy our enemies completely and without any consideration whatever."

Dated 27 September, FDR's letter was a nonpolitical celebration of the contribution made by "persons of German blood to the upbuilding of this country."

> The arrival in Philadelphia of the first company of German settlers on Oct. 6 1683 [marked] the beginning of the great German immigration movement to this country. . . . soon spread to the South & West. . . .
>
> By their quiet courage, their great industry, and their knowledge and skills in the arts and crafts, these German settlers contributed greatly to the wealth and prosperity of the country. Dr. Benjamin Rush . . . recorded the excellent qualities of the German farmers, [and they] "produced in their children not only the habits of labor but a love for it! . . ." [Their contributions and qualities] have become a valued part of the common heritage of the American people.

Received with great swells of cheering enthusiasm, Dr. Griebl "called for three 'heils' for 'The Leader, Adolf Hitler,' and also for the President of the United States." That ceremony was followed by "The Star-Spangled Banner" and other speeches, several emphatically anti-Semitic.

One of FDR's loyal constituents, Mrs. S. Miller of East Orange, New Jersey, sent ER a clipping from *The Jewish Examiner*. Because she considered the First Lady "one of the most understanding and tolerant persons we have in this country today," Mrs. Miller considered it urgent to send the enclosed information:

> There is no doubt in my mind that under President Roosevelt's administration the security of the Jewish people is protected. However, it is equally important that for future peace and safety the present day hatred and propaganda against the Jewish people should not be encouraged.
>
> I am enclosing a report I just read to explain my writing this letter.

The Jewish Examiner emphasized the participation of self-styled U.S. patriots, including "branches of the American Legion and the Veterans of Foreign Wars" who joined forces with the "Friends of New Germany, as the American branch of the German Nazi Party prefers to be known." The meeting was dedicated to a " 'hate the Jew' program," and speakers "promised" a Nazi candidate in the next presidential election.

Between Heil Hitlers and the Horst Wessel anthem, greetings "from President Roosevelt were read to the assemblage," to wild applause.

ER replied: "I read your letter with interest and will make every effort to see that the Nazi movement is discouraged."

The week after FDR sent his letter of greeting to Madison Square Garden, ER spoke to fifteen hundred women gathered to support Hadassah, the women's Zionist organization of America, at their 16 October convention dinner in Washington. Accompanied by Elinor Morgenthau, ER praised Hadassah's achievements in Palestine, and presented " 'a word of greeting' from the president, which was received with applause."

The featured speaker of the evening, Rabbi Milton Steinberg of New York's Park Avenue Synagogue, emphasized European Jewry's "completely impossible" situation and the need to "build a social order which shall be an expression of Jewish idealism" in Palestine. In her brief remarks, ER emphasized "the tasks to be done in this country by American women, Jews and Gentiles," working together "side by side." "We must not let barriers grow up between us, but with good-will . . . [disregard] pettiness, unkindness and injustices for the things we want to see accomplished."

Elinor Morgenthau tailored her remarks to honor her friendship with the First Lady and spoke of women's unity. She urged delegates to remember that "in America discrimination against the Jew is the exception and not the rule." She urged Hadassah women to be stalwart. "Don't live in fear of false accusation. In spite of criticism, don't trim your sails. Be true to yourselves and walk the world with dignity."

ER's silence concerning what Louise Wise had called that "subject which engrosses us now" grew louder. In November, she turned aside an amazingly stark appeal by a woman who wrote from Oregon:

> Dear Mrs. Roosevelt: Will you please read the enclosed. . . . Is there nothing to do about this, wouldn't a protest of prominent people of this country have any effect? . . .
> Can you do anything?

With her letter, Alice Youngbar sent a copy of "Prisoner of the Nazis," condensed from *The New Republic* by *The Reader's Digest*. Written anonymously, and first published on 8 August 1934 with an editorial confirming its veracity and "the fact that the conditions described are continuing to the present day," the article vividly detailed conditions at Dachau, Germany's first major concentration camp:

> At present it harbors about 1700 prisoners, mostly Communists or members of organizations known as sympathetic. . . . There are only about 40 Jews, mostly manual workers or clerks; some few . . . business men from small villages who had been arrested from motives of personal rancor or envy. . . .

The Nazi commandant of the camp announced the camp's policy: "Always remember that no human beings are here, only swine. . . . No one who does harm to a prisoner need fear reprimand. . . ."

Impossibly unhealthy food rations, hard labor, and dispiriting abuse faced every inmate. "The cells are provided with a noose in case the prisoner wants to hang himself." The filthy, cold, harrowing conditions people endured within Dachau were vividly detailed. Communist and Jewish prisoners were tortured for hours, beaten and mutilated:

> [Communist parliamentarian] Deputy Fritz Dressel . . . tried to cut his wrist with a piece of glass, but he was discovered while he still showed some signs of life and was transferred to a first-aid station. A few hours later he was again "discovered," lying in a pool of blood, his arms pulled out of their sockets. Schloss, a businessman from Nuremberg, was killed in less than three days by blows on the testicles. An attorney named Strauss, from Munich . . . was transformed into a quivering white-haired old man. They compelled him to swim in ice-cold water while they lashed him with oxtails. After four days of torture he was shot. . . .
> Other Jews were forced to scrub especially befouled toilets with their

bare hands. . . . Despite the fact that the Commander promised that any prisoner who harmed a Jew would be released, the Jews received every kindness from the other prisoners. . . .

The great majority of the Storm Troopers did not take part in the torturing. Some of the guards even had the courage openly to oppose it. They were placed in "protective custody." Several of the Special Police sympathized with the prisoners, so that every third week the guard had to be changed, and only the most brutal were kept permanently at the camp.

With that article in her hands, an article thousands of Americans read in *The Reader's Digest*, one can only imagine ER's inner turmoil as she composed one formal sentence in reply to Alice Youngbar's plea: "My dear Miss Youngbar: Unfortunately, what you have read is something which happens in Germany over which we have no control."

ER's understanding of "no control" short-circuited protest, even inquiry. She volunteered no private or public response to reported atrocities as they intensified between 1933 and 1938. As one searches the record for a hint of activity, a glimmer of concern, regarding the situation in Germany, one finds instead her many and amazing acts of personal generosity toward individual Jews in need or in trouble within the United States; her increased efforts against discrimination and racial violence domestically, where her influence might have some impact on public policy; and an intensified campaign to promote collective security.

ER at first sought to make a difference to one individual, one heart, at a time. Privately, throughout the 1930s, beginning with the Brodsky family, the First Lady contributed in countless ways to Jewish individuals and families she met in her travels and through correspondence.

Desperate to get help for his fourteen-year-old sister, Bertha, Frank Brodsky, then twenty-one, appealed to the First Lady: His sister needed an operation for scoliosis, the spinal disease suffered by ER's Aunt Bye, which the family could not afford. His mother was unemployed, and his disabled father, who had lost an arm to a sawmill, had only a meager paper route. Moved by young Frank's cry for help, ER traveled to Brooklyn to meet the family and arranged to have Bertha receive medical care at the Orthopedic Hospital on 59th Street, founded by her grandfather "Greatheart" Theodore Roosevelt.

Bertha spent ten months in the hospital, and the surgery was successful. On 7 February, ER visited and signed her diploma from the Straus Junior High School in Brooklyn. Subsequently, ER sent her cherries, candies, flowers, and books—with a request for secrecy since she could not send gifts to all the children there: "I do not like to have anyone's feelings hurt, so I think the less we say about it the kinder it will be."

Over the years they visited regularly, corresponded often. ER tried to find Frank a job first as a messenger at Milgrim's and then in the Housing Division. She wrote Rexford Guy Tugwell:

> I am interested in a Jewish family in Brooklyn, New York, and I am very anxious to get them settled on a homestead. There is a boy who is pretty well trained and who could do some clerical work. He is interested in housing.
>
> Will you let me know if there is any chance in the future of getting a homestead for them?

In subsequent letters ER wrote insistently, though stereotypically, on Frank's behalf: "This boy is particularly anxious to get some kind of a position in the housing division and would probably work as the Jews do when they work to improve themselves constantly."

In scores of letters, ER worried about their mother's declining health, Frank's changing job prospects, their new and better flat. In 1936, ER sent Bertha to camp for two weeks. "I hope you will have a grand time and that it will do you lots of good." Both Bertha and Frank visited the White House, and a lifelong friendship developed.

For all her enforced silence concerning Hitler's policies, ER was outspoken about the scourge of war. From 1933 on she met with activists at the White House; gave galvanizing speeches; and earned a reputation as "the First Lady of the Peace Movement."

She wanted the world to demilitarize in spirit as well as in actuality, and urged an end to war toys. In December 1933 she wrote a column for the *Woman's Home Companion* to argue "that the glamour of the gorgeously dressed soldiers" created in children a memory of excitement, which might just as well be replaced by "armies of foresters and farmers."

When members of the National Student Federation, representing college leaders of America, converged with the more radical students of the National Student League and the League for Industrial Democracy, she insisted they meet together. After her address, in which she emphasized the need to find "goals to replace the war impulse," she answered a question by "a Negro student:"

> It is natural to look upon war as glamorous, as showing supreme love and sacrifice for patriotic reasons. But it is just as patriotic and just as self-sacrificing to live for one's country in a way to make it a help to the world and all the people in it. . . .

ER acknowledged that it was "conceivable" that America might be "forced into war." But every effort should be made to settle differences by "legal means." There were always "warring interests and warring classes—people fighting for themselves." But selfish interests and greed served no big interests: "We have believed in the individualistic thing. We can't go on that way. We must work together on big things."

Although ER supported the Nye Committee investigations and spoke out against military profiteering, she wrote nothing about the renewed military commerce under way. In May 1934, Hick reported from Ajo, Arizona, that a copper mine had opened, "putting 400 men to work, on *orders for munitions plants in Europe and Japan.*" Hick also wrote Harry Hopkins that another mine over one hundred miles from Ajo was reemploying workers, and the superintendent of the New Cornelia mine, near Tucson, "is telling his friends it's all foreign munitions business."

ER's information that U.S. mining interests supplied Germany and Japan predated by six months FDR's information from Dodd that war preparations in Germany were in high gear. In November 1934, Dodd and his son toured Bitterfeld, Leipzig, Nuremberg, Stuttgart, Erfurt, and other places: "Every smokestack showed great activity. . . . [and] great preparation for war." Consular reports indicated that "poison gas and explosives" were being produced; factories operated day and night; in Dresden a thousand new planes were reported.

There were many protests against U.S. trade with Germany and Italy in copper, steel, arms, oil, and munitions, and ER was convinced that only a blockade, real collective action, would prevent another war. Yet no serious boycott that included oil and other resources was even contemplated.

Despite Ethiopia's fierce, unexpected, and costly resistance, Mussolini won. Afterward, he acknowledged that he could not have done so had it not been for the fact that both the United States and Britain continued to supply him with oil.

Instead of the development of a united front against aggression in Ethiopia, the League was diminished and Europe remilitarized. The Franco-Soviet Pact of May 1935 was followed almost immediately by the Anglo-German Naval Agreement in June. WILPF's efforts to keep disarmament on the world's agenda, which ER supported, were eclipsed by the League's failure to respond to the war in Ethiopia—followed on 7 March 1936 by Germany's occupation of the demilitarized Rhineland.

On 2 May 1936, Haile Selassie left Addis Ababa, and Italy's African empire was now Italian East Africa and Italian Somaliland.

Then, on 18 July 1936, the Spanish Civil War exploded. Francisco Franco's forces, hiding out in Africa, were transported in Italian and German planes and ships to crush Spain's democratically elected Popular Front government. The Spanish Civil War claimed a significant part of ER's attention for the next three years. But it was not the big international story that summer.

The Nazi Olympics of 1936 dominated the world's attention. Fifty-three nations participated in the Berlin Games. Anguished at Nazi prohibitions against non-Aryan athletes and the exclusion of 35,000 Jewish athletes who were no longer citizens and whose clubs could not participate in training or tryouts, various athletic groups and veteran Olympic officials in the United States called for a boycott.

U.S. artists and writers also demanded a boycott of the Olympics art exhibition. George Biddle introduced a resolution at the First American Artists' Congress that was unanimously adopted: American artists would have nothing to do with "a government which sponsors the destruction of all freedom in art, . . . which sponsors racial discrimination, the censorship of free speech and free expression, and the glorification of war, hatred and sadism."

Both ER and FDR ignored the boycott effort. Neither Spain nor Russia sent athletes. Ironically, alternative games were planned for Spain, but were canceled by Franco's Nazi-fascist invasion. Several colleges, including New York University, Notre Dame, Ohio Wesleyan, Purdue, and Long Island University refused to compete. The U.S. branch of WILPF called for a boycott, and *The Crisis* editorialized, "Stay Out of the Olympics":

> *The Crisis* joins other publications in opposition to American athletes taking part. . . . Upon the grounds of poor sportsmanship and discrimination, America, of course, cannot raise a very sincere howl. . . .

Segregation in the United States had resulted in discrimination against Negro athletes during the 1932 Los Angeles Olympic Games. "We should address ourselves to the color line in our own backyard," *The Crisis* concluded, and withdraw the U.S. team from the Nazi Olympics.

> [The German] government is founded officially upon suppression of religious, political and social liberty, and upon terror and brutality. We ought not contribute anything, either in money or prestige to such a government. . . .

An "Olympic Committee on Fair Play in Sports," led by Judge Jeremiah T. Mahoney, campaigned for nonparticipation. He and all boycotters were dismissed by Olympic officials as "extremists," communists, and Jews. When on 15 July the U.S. team of over 385 athletes, the largest to date, left for Berlin, anti-Nazi protest was "conspicuous by its absence."

The Nazi Olympics represented a gigantic propaganda victory, a feast of

Nazi pageantry. Hitler officially suspended anti-Jewish activities during the games. Anti-Jewish posters and wall signs were removed; most anti-Jewish publications were suspended. Every German was called upon to participate in the propaganda effort to end "all prejudices against the German nation": "We must be more charming than the Parisians, more easy-going than the Viennese, more vivacious than the Romans, more cosmopolitan than London, and more practical than New York." Courses were given in the "fine art of hospitality," and western visitors who arrived by train noticed "a quite astounding" display of eager service.

Not everybody was fooled by such camouflage. On 12 January 1936, *The New York Times* explained the context: "For the Olympics the War Against Jews Is to Be Waged with Less Publicity." The "cold pogrom" now focused on a pay-as-you-leave plan to eliminate the Jewish population of Germany, which resulted in a movement to "buy exile." The fiscal "project for a Jewish mass exodus" was supported by Germany's finance minister, Dr. Hjalmar Schacht. If it helped Germany "get gold, foreign exchange or raw materials," if European and American Jews raised the capital and created an "International Liquidation Bank," with headquarters in London, it served several purposes.

The Nazi Olympics cast a floodlight upon the complicated issues of race and racism in the United States and Germany. When Hitler failed to greet Negro athletes, magazine and newspaper articles concerning U.S. racial attitudes appeared. To avoid Nazi disfavor, U.S. Olympic coaches benched Jewish athletes, notably Sam Stoller and Martin Glickman.

Germany won the most medals, but black U.S. track star Jesse Owens, who won four gold medals, was the enduring hero of the games. *The Crisis* editorialized: There was "one good thing Little Hitler did for Negro Americans." He demonstrated the "meaning of fascism, about which we have been hearing so much. . . . The masses have been indifferent. But Hitler has changed all that . . . Fascism is the last thing American Negroes want. . . . [It] is a system where a white man who runs third is better than a Negro who runs first, breaks a world record, and gets a gold medal. That is as bad as Mississippi. . . ."

Hitler did not invent the biomythology of Anglo-Saxon superiority. His assertion "The Nordic race is entitled to dominate the world" was an echo, not an innovation. Throughout the United States, during the 1930s, major newspapers carried paid advertisements that announced: "No Jews or Catholics need apply!" Hitlerites understood the nature of race relations in the United States and were greatly encouraged. Nothing was done or said by public officials in the Anglo-American world to cause Hitler to think he did not have support for racialist outrages.

During the first three years of Hitler's regime there were many opportunities for protest. But they passed in silence. As propaganda, no event had more approval overtones than participation in the 1936 Olympic Games orchestrated to celebrate Nazi virtue, Nazi solidarity, Nazi strength.

For the Roosevelts in 1936, all international events were eclipsed by the U.S. election campaign—which mandated even more silence.

17: Red Scare
and Campaign Strategies, 1936

───◦/◦/◦───

*E*very decision ER made in 1936 was related to her husband's campaign for reelection. With the New Deal barely under way, the nation was bitterly divided. In the South, voting remained limited by poll taxes and tradition to propertied white men. Conservative businessmen joined with Southern racialists and a group of Democrats who personally hated FDR to stop the democratization of America. In August 1934 they chartered the Liberty League to end "Red" rule and kill the burgeoning labor and civil rights movements.

Fueled by rhetorical vitriol led by Hearst, who promised to excommunicate the "imported, autocratic, Asiatic Socialist party of Karl Marx and Franklin Delano Roosevelt," Liberty Leaguers represented a peculiar bipartisan spectrum. Various du Ponts, major industrialists, and oil barons were joined by former Democrat luminaries—including FDR's 1924 running mate, John W. Davis; John J. Raskob, once Democratic Committee chair; and Al Smith, now FDR's most bitter enemy. In January, they declared war.

With unlimited campaign funds for 1936, their new Red Scare collected steam and threatened everything ER most cared about. A Democratic future depended on her husband's reelection. She would do nothing to tempt one vote away from him. She was convinced, however, that victory depended on exciting the interests of African-Americans, women, and labor unionists.

Politically, the first crisis ER confronted in 1936 involved another kind of silence—censorship in the federal arts program. Hallie Flanagan and Elmer Rice, director of New York's theater project, had created "the Living Newspaper"—a brilliant form employing scores of actors and dramatizing the news without expensive scenery, just "light, music, movement." Their first New York production was to be *Ethiopia*, chosen in part because an operatic company from Africa was stranded in the United States and on relief. Flanagan decided to use the members of the company as drummers and chorus "in the courtyard of Haile Selassie." The Newspaper Guild participated in the show, and the facts were accurate. "There was no caricature; the characterizations and quotations were as literal as we could make them."

To dramatize Mussolini's invasion, Haile Selassie's resistance, and the League of Nations' sacrifice of the struggling African country was radical enough. But then they requested permission to use one of FDR's broadcasts, and unleashed "a crisis which threatened to end the whole idea of the living newspaper." Joseph Baker at WPA and Steve Early objected to a government production entering dangerous international waters. On 18 January, Baker wrote Flanagan: "No issue of the living newspaper shall contain" any reference to international officials or issues without prior approval "in advance by the Department of State." Since prior approval hampered "timeliness," essential to the Living Newspaper, *Ethiopia* was not to go up "with the present script."

Flanagan appealed to ER: "I have the gravest fears as to the storm of criticism which will result if this is closed. Schools, universities and newspapers will read it as a political move. . . . Mr. Rice will probably resign and this also is very serious. . . ."

ER appealed to FDR, spoke with Early, and wrote to Baker: The president "feels that [*Ethiopia*] should not be given up, but that some adjustment should be made. No one impersonating a ruler or a cabinet officer should actually appear on the stage. The words could be quoted. . . ."

FDR's compromise was not enough. The WPA banned *Ethiopia*. Elmer Rice cried censorship, and told Baker if it was banned he would resign. Baker thereupon took out a typed letter of resignation ready for Rice's signature. Flanagan was furious, and sent Rice's press statement to ER: He would not remain "the servant of a government which plays the shabby game of partisan politics at the expense of freedom and the principles of democracy."

Ethiopia was banned largely for political reasons. The decision occurred after Rice announced the Living Newspaper's future productions, including plays on "the handling of relief, and conditions in the South." ER demanded an explanation from Aubrey Williams—who wrote ER that Rice and Flanagan planned to produce works on "Soviet Russia, the Scottsboro Case, Sharecroppers, etc. . . . only those things which are highly controversial and which immediately bring to the fore opponents . . . of this sort of activity on the part of the Federal Government." Harry Hopkins had decided to terminate this project, and understood that Rice would resign.

In this election year, Baker assured Southern congressmen, no federal funds would support the Living Newspaper on sharecroppers. Only "standard plays the public wants" would be performed. Immediately, a "traveling company" went South "with a play called *Jefferson Davis.*"

Flanagan remained convinced that Hopkins still supported uncensored theater, and she hired Rice's assistant Philip Barber to head the New York project, and the next Living Newspaper controversy: *Triple-A*, a play to protest the Supreme Court's January decision that the Agricultural Adjustment Administration was unconstitutional.

Although the play went beyond the Supreme Court's attacks against the New Deal and included farmer-worker unity to combat excessive profits, it was not censored. It was powerful and emotional; audiences filled the theater night after night. Poverty and corruption, politics and struggle were in the air. Hearst and Republicans condemned "U.S. Dollars for Pink Plays."

ER supported Flanagan, and WPA pressure momentarily eased. The theater thrived, twenty plays were in rehearsal, and Flanagan was grateful for the First Lady's interventions: "Everything is clearing up so splendidly: Mr. Baker is giving me an administrative assistant, sorely needed; and in many other ways I notice a release from tensions which is, I am sure, due to your good offices."

But in 1936, ER set theatrical limits. The Chicago revue *O' Say Can You Sing* planned to include a sketch of the First Lady. Flanagan asked for ER's approval, and assured her it was done in a spirit of "great admiration." A minute-by-minute account of her typical day, it recalled *Time*'s rendition of Eleanor Everywhere:

Flash! The wife of the President was an unexpected visitor at one of the Federal Theatre Productions in Chicago last night. Although she claimed she was traveling incognito, the audience recognized her the minute she got up on her seat in the *middle of a number* and started making a speech on the plight of our coal miners. . . .

We take you now to the White House boudoir where we see her in the act of preparing her daily [column]. . . .

The scene is set between Mrs. President and her secretary, "Miss Givens."

Mrs. President: . . . At 7:30 A.M.—Arose/ 7:31—Bathed/ 7:32—breakfasted/ 7:33—Received a delegation of coal miners from Scranton and shook hands with each one personally/ 7:34—Took another bath/ 7:35—Received a long distance call from the senior class president at Vassar, inviting me to lead the annual daisy chain/ 7:36—Received miners from Albuquerque and shook hands with each miner/ 7:37—Took another bath/ 7:38—Relaxed for 60 seconds puttering in the White House garden. . . .

That takes us to 7:42 and a quarter—found myself with three-quarters of a minute to spare so I caught up with contemporary literature by reading *Anthony Adverse*! . . . 7:43 Finished *Anthony Adverse* and realized that I had spent eleven minutes in the White House. Too long! I felt hemmed in! . . . My Vanderlust gripped me—I went to Alaska!

Secretary: By Plane?

Mrs. President: No, Dog Sled! I arrived at the mines all covered with slush. . . . At 12:01 I shook hands with all the miners. . . . at 12:03—I felt homesick so I took a rocket back to the United States/ 12:04— . . . My, how good it was to see . . . our wonderful land with its mountains, rivers, lakes and those quaint little Republicans dotting the countryside. . . .

At 12:05—I was catapulted to a CCC Camp in Bear Mountain and spent two minutes preserving our forests with the boys. . . . At 12:07— Back in Washington—Miss Givens, how did I get back to Washington?

Secretary: I believe you were shot from a cannon. Then you read your fan mail.

Mrs. President: Oh yes! . . . Quite amusing! . . . I received an offer from the Olympic Committee to represent America in the hop, skip, and jump/ At 12:08—I felt a speech coming on concerning the hard coal problem. So I rounded up some miners and made it/ At 12:09—I took a bath, didn't I?

Secretary: No, Mrs. President, you had yourself dry-cleaned!

Mrs. President: Oh yes! No water! The Drought! / Between 12:10 and 7:00 P.M. I amused myself by laying four corner-stones, founding two day nurseries—and one night school. And . . .

It went on into the night, even into her busy dreams. ER returned the play with her two-word rejection scrawled atop the page: "Refused Permission!"

Although ER censored this play for political reasons, she remained enthusiastic about the arts program. Indeed, her detailed involvement was almost on a par with her commitment to Arthurdale and affordable housing. On 19 February, for example, she wrote Baker:

When in New York . . . I heard there was much complaint because the money for wages for the actors and actresses . . . was not coming through. Will you check on it? Also, there is a great deal of comment [that] rehearsals were taking so long. . . .

By the end of February 1936, WPA employed 4,300 artists. Schools, hospitals, museums, armories, airports, public buildings had received paintings, murals, sculptures, prints. In the South, "experimental demonstration galleries" became the area's first public galleries and regional museums; thousands of community centers provided leisure programs, including art classes for children and adults. There were musical groups, chorales, bands, and orchestras founded across the country. ER considered it all thrilling, heartening, the essence of New Deal community-building.

During the 1930s, an alarming movement to get women out of the workplace, to limit them to marriage and motherhood, to brand them responsible for unemployment, family tensions, and all wickedness intensified. Distressed by the persistent attacks against women, which a surprising spectrum of Democrats participated in during the campaign season, ER became increasingly forceful in her defense of every woman's right to choose her life's direction.

When John Studebaker invited ER to select any topic for a Washington Town Hall Forum, which he chaired, she quickly suggested women and work, and named her panel: Fannie Hurst, George Creel, Josephine Roche. For ninety minutes on Sunday, 2 February, ER spoke candidly to an overflow audience of fifteen hundred:

> There is something inherently good for every human being in work. Only through work can a woman fulfill her obligation to herself and to the world and justify her existence. . . .
> It is the right of any woman who wants to work to do so.

Her speech lasted forty minutes; then, "skillfully and good-naturedly," she responded to a challenging, though largely agreeable, panel and audience:

> Isn't it a fact that women have always worked, often very hard; did anybody make a fuss about it until they began to be paid for their work?
> Since widows and spinsters are now regarded as America's greatest menace, should not they be allowed to fight our future wars? In such case, of course, men should not insist upon the sole right to declare war. . . .

ER received countless letters of protest on this issue, which she patiently answered: "I am afraid that your attitude towards women is completely foreign to my more modern ideas. . . ."

Issues of women and work remained high on ER's agenda. In meetings with the General Federation of Women's Clubs and other organizations of business and professional women, ER championed equal protection laws for women and men, eight-hour days for women and men, and equal pay for equal work.

Working women made many contributions, and ER used every opportunity to celebrate them. She introduced Mary Breckenridge at a White House reception for women, on 6 February: Breckenridge directed the "Frontier Nursing Service in Kentucky, which is carried on by nurses on horseback [who presided over] small clinics dotted here and there in the mountains."

On 18 March, ER broadcast with Charl Ormond Williams for the ninth annual celebration of "National Business Women's Week" as "the first business and professional woman to be mistress" of the White House. There were sixty thousand members of the Federation of Business and Professional Women, and eleven million working women in the United States. ER called upon that vast constituency to promote the idea of an important new agency the nation needed: a federal department of "education, the arts, social welfare, and health." Charl Williams reminded the broadcast audience that ER had called for such a department, and federal aid to education, as early as 1924—when she chaired the Democratic Party's first women's platform committee.

The year 1936 opened with significant upset in ER's private life. Louis Howe was dying, and her relationship with Lorena Hickok became ever more uneasy. Although she still relied on Hick for advice on both public and family matters, she had now virtually no leisure time to offer her.

As the New Year celebrations wound down, ER confided in Hick that she was "very sad" to see her children go off to their own homes and would especially miss the comings and goings of her grandchildren. She had no intention of growing "too dependent" on them, "for as you have so often said, I must let go!"—but they did create a jolly atmosphere.

Time with Hick was now rarely jolly. She arrived on 7 January for a week, and ER wrote the day she left: "Darling, you were low and I know that in some way I hurt and I am sorry and I wish I had not but all I can say is, I really love you."

Unlike Tommy or Louis Howe, Hick could not simply fold herself into ER's life, or White House activities. For years Hick had kept her own social life to a minimum to be available to ER, whenever she had a minute or an evening to spare. Now Hick returned to the company of her New York friends. Although ER would have been pleased to join Hick and her friends, mostly newspaper people and writers, Hick discouraged her presence.

ER seemed, at first, confused:

> Hick darling. It was nice to get your letter and hear your voice last night, but I hardly know what to do. Would you rather I did not try to see you this week-end since you have friends and other plans? I'll call you anyway and you know I won't feel hurt if it complicates life or if it makes it harder just to have to see me in a crowd. If it does I'll just write and telephone and we'll forget I'm in New York!

Hick was torn, and their visit was awkward. ER wrote: "It was good to see you this morning being leisurely with Newky [Helen Newcomb] and I do hope the next few weeks bring you many happy times dear."

Each time Hick drew away, determined to regain some independence, ER responded by pulling her back. For years, ER had kept Hick's bank books and occasionally paid her bills. When Hick decided to reclaim control of her finances, ER insisted she continue as caretaker of her accounts so that Hick would not overspend or bounce checks. Their lives remained interwoven, and ER was pleased to report: "You have in the savings $255.43."

As January unfolded, Hick became more aggressive about her own needs.

> I rather hope that, if you are going to call, you will call tonight. Since I'll be out both tomorrow and Saturday evenings. I could call you, I suppose, but I MUST keep my hotel—I mean, my PHONE—bill down. What

with Prinz in the hospital, a new car in the offing, and Aunt Ella coming to visit me. Finances aren't so bad, though.

She was "not broke," just living rather high and on the edge.

But independence was a relative thing. ER encouraged Hick to take advantage of the efficient White House laundry service. Hick did: "Yes, I mailed my laundry to Mabel today. . . . Goodnight, and much love."

On 20 January, news came of King George's death, which caused ER to reflect: "No, one can't be sorry for people who are dead unless one believes in a hell after death which I do not, but it is bad for those who live on here and don't know what the future holds beyond the barrier."

On 24 January ER's cousin Corinne Alsop arrived to stay at the White House, although she was in Washington to participate in the anti-FDR Liberty League festivities, which were to feature New York's former governor Al Smith. Unprepared for the profound change in the once liberal Democrat whose presidential campaign she ran in 1928, ER had even invited Al Smith to stay at the White House.

One of ER's contributions to FDR's 1936 campaign was her lecture tour, "Ways of Peace," which reinforced in part the administration's strict neutrality policy. The new weaponry already used against Ethiopia by Italy and against China by Japan escalated war's devastation. Everywhere she spoke, she emphasized one theme: Military defenses "would be of comparatively little value in the next war," which would be an air war against civilians and destructive beyond imagining. "I think we had better begin to decide whether we wish to preserve our civilization or whether we think it of so little use that we might as well let it go. That is what war amounts to."

ER wanted to keep the United States "out of war," and remained convinced that only collective security, united action, would prevent war. If war erupted, it would swamp every nation. ER disagreed with peace advocates who counseled unilateral disarmament. She wrote Jeannette Rankin, pacifist and former member of Congress, that armaments caused distrust between nations, but that disarmament must be international so that no one country leaves itself open to attack or invasion."

On 1 February, she addressed the American Youth Congress and criticized its commitment to absolute pacifism. While she agreed that military training in schools "should never be compulsory," it should be offered for "those students who desire it." Above all, she criticized supporters of Youth Against War and Fascism who endorsed "anti-war strikes," and the Oxford pledge, which affirmed that under "no circumstances" would this generation fight in any future war.

On 9 February 1933, students in the Oxford Union initiated the pledge, as a protest against empire, militarism, and conservative rule. By 1936, radical students throughout the United States took it. But ER feared for the future, and understood the pacifist's dilemma: Peace required collective security, which meant resistance against aggression. To defend a small nation attacked by a militarized power required preparedness and confrontation, an economic blockade at least. Nations must be willing to cut off oil, copper, steel, basic trade with the aggressor. Unilateral disarmament in a militarized world with Hitler and Mussolini at the helm seemed to her madness, as insane as war itself. She told her student audience that they had not "thought through all its implications." ER lamented both her husband's official non-involvement which led to the sacrifice of Ethiopia, and the students' absolute pacifism.

As ER contemplated the demands of the presidential campaign and the daunting international situation, she began to draw on new friends and allies. She asked Fannie Hurst to keynote the Women's Press Party: "I do like her." Mount Holyoke's president, Dr. Mary Woolley, the only woman delegate to the Geneva Disarmament Conference, arrived for tea and evidently stayed for dinner with Anna Louise Strong. It was a scintillating evening.

Lillian Wald initially asked ER to meet with Anna Louise Strong in 1935: "You may remember her as the girl who went to Russia thirteen years ago and who . . . has been back numerous times to lecture and to try to have us see Russia as she sees it." Wald wrote ER that Strong's "numerous books have been well received" and "she knows Russia now better than anybody else."

Best known as the woman who launched the Seattle general strike of 1919, Strong first went to Russia for the Quakers; she worked there mostly as a journalist, and taught Trotsky English. Her controversial autobiography, *I Change Worlds*, was published in 1935, and now, Wald wrote ER, she planned to return with a mission:

> It is whispered . . . that the rich Jews in Europe and America are negotiating for 10,000 German émigrés to go to Buro Bidgin [as a safe haven for Jews]. Anyway Anna Louise Strong is going to visit the place in Siberia.
>
> If it means anything at all to you let me know. . . . She is an attractive creature and fair. . . .

ER replied immediately:

> I would love to see Anna Louise Strong. Do you think she would care to come to lunch with me . . . ? If so, I will try to get Franklin here or arrange for her to have a chat with him afterwards. Thank you so much for thinking of it.

ER was eager for more information about Russia since Maxim Litvinov was the only foreign minister who consistently called for collective security against fascism, and ER distrusted U.S. ambassador Bill Bullitt. But it was bold indeed for the First Lady to invite the first lady of U.S. radicalism to the White House.

A persuasive, action-oriented woman, Anna Louise Strong impressed those who met her as formidable, the kind of woman who "commanded everyone to drop what [he or she was] doing and concentrate on what Anna Louise was doing." Ella Winter, married to Strong's mentor Lincoln Steffens, described Strong as "a huge woman with cropped gray hair, china-blue eyes, and a manner so impersonal that I wondered if she would go on talking if one went out of the room."

ER was not bothered by her manner; they shared an ethic, but differed about how to achieve it. Strong championed socialism, then communism. ER believed capitalism could be transformed into something humane that included economic democracy as well as political justice. They were fascinated by each other, and a cordial friendship and lasting correspondence developed between the First Lady and one of America's most notorious heretics.

After their February 1936 dinner, ER wrote Hick: "Anna Louise Strong evidently thinks we are beaten." But Strong wrote ER:

> I am glad for your sake that you are much more optimistic than I am. . . . To a person as sincere as you I felt that I owed the most sincere and thoughtful analysis I could make.
>
> But wisdom did not begin and will not end with me, and you have thousands of wise people helping you as well as millions who trust your leadership. So perhaps you may succeed either in repairing the capitalist system to fit human needs or in making a more or less painless transition to some system that will. If anyone can, I think you can.
>
> In any case, if there is ever any time when anything I know can be of use to you, please call on me. This applies not only to your term or terms in the White House, but to . . . whatever future awaits us.

Preoccupied by publishing deadlines and the demands of the campaign, ER impulsively sent Hick a telegram asking her, "if free," to meet her train at Grand Central on 17 February. But Tommy accompanied her to the city. When Hick saw them descend the train steps, she stormed away. ER wrote the next morning:

> Hick darling. I am so very, very sorry. I ought to know it must be alone or not at all and you probably felt I brought you down under false pretenses but I didn't mean to even though I did. You were sweet to telephone this morning and I am grateful.

For ER the trip up and back to Washington was not wasted: "Tommy and I worked all the way down on the train."

Upset by opposition to her efforts to protect immigrants and refugees, Frances Perkins met with ER "to talk over her troubles on the Jewish question." For over a year, Perkins sought to find a way to "relieve the strain on terrorized people" by removing some of the restrictions against immigration. Herbert Hoover's Depression-era executive order against economically dependent immigrants without American relatives to vouch for them was still rigidly interpreted so as to prevent even the allowable immigration quotas from being filled. Perkins wanted FDR to issue a new executive order. But he refused, and anti-immigration contempt swelled in Congress.

Over half Germany's Jews were already in exile by 1936. While most had fled to neighboring countries, those with friends or relatives in the United States sought sanctuary with them. A growing population of immigrants on tourist visas and immigrants with no papers at all created a grievous situation of harassment and deportation. Concerned about rising anti-alien sentiment, ER and Perkins were allied with Caroline O'Day, who wanted to introduce legislation to prevent the deportation of illegal aliens—many of whom had been in the country for years, were employed, and had young children born here. ER believed that a more liberal Labor Department interpretation might facilitate their becoming citizens.

Perkins assured her that was impossible. Nobody "who is in this country illegally can become a citizen, under existing statutes." Deportation remained a possibility—even "for persons of good character," although there were individual Jewish cases over which Perkins had jurisdiction that she tried to resolve happily, with visa extensions; others were denied.

Charles Milgram, for example, appealed to ER for an extension of a "temporary visitors stay for two worthy Rabbis," Salamon Horowitz and Szmul Elia Epstein. They were well known and highly respected. ER wrote: "Send at once to Frances Perkins and ask if it can be done." Their visit was extended, for six months. Perkins was embattled over each case, and confronted a mostly hostile Congress and State Department. Although ER responded to each letter sent her by needful refugees and forwarded most of them to Perkins, unless FDR issued a new executive order there was no hope for a policy change.

At the end of March, the Women's Democratic Committee veterans, ER's core team, arrived in Washington to spend several days with her to strategize the 1936 campaign. Nancy Cook, Marion Dickerman, Molly Dewson, and Agnes Brown Leach, along with Caroline O'Day, met regularly, and were particularly annoyed that the men seemed so confident while their enemies got off to a vigorous start.

Only several days after Al Smith damned FDR at the Liberty League banquet in January, 3,500 Southern Democrats met in Macon, Georgia, to denounce the New Deal and repudiate FDR. Led by Georgia Governor Eugene Talmadge and funded largely by Liberty Leaguers, Dixiecrats blasted "Russocrats" and made dire warnings about Negro influence and the loss of states' rights.

At the Macon meeting, ER was the primary target: She had encouraged Southern Negroes "to embrace" collectivism; and was determined to destroy white supremacy. The *Georgia Woman's World* magazine with photographs of ER receiving flowers from a black child in Detroit, and the First Lady escorted by two black youths in uniform, Howard University students, was on every seat. Thomas Dixon, author of *The Klansman*, filmed as "The Birth of a Nation," received the loudest cheers when he called the NAACP the "worst communist organization" in America.

The NAACP defended the New Deal. *The Crisis* editorialized that ER and FDR were attacked for "forcing social equality on the South" because they "received a handful of Negroes at the White House with ordinary courtesy" and because FDR appointed several Negroes "to richly deserved positions. They forget that Blacks of northern and western states voted for FDR. . . ."

The creation of a Southern opposition party with Talmadge as its nominee must have jolted FDR, who had compromised so much in order to maintain Democratic unity. Walter White, for example, wrote ER an indignant letter during the 1934 campaign when FDR agreed to end the national work relief minimum wage after his meeting with Talmadge: "I most certainly do feel [abolishing the minimum wage] was aimed at the Negro. It is significant that this ruling came immediately after Governor Talmadge of Georgia had visited the President at Warm Springs. . . ." For Talmadge, every New Deal program that failed to discriminate was odious. White was stunned that the administration would do anything "to conciliate him," since it was known that Talmadge planned "one of the dirtiest anti-Negro campaigns that has been promoted in recent years in the South."

Now, Talmadge initiated a campaign dedicated to FDR's defeat. All the President's prior efforts to conciliate the diehard South seemed wasted, and bitter.

ER was never sanguine about elections. Tricks and traps might derail any "sure" victory. She was disturbed that the Democratic campaign was slow to start. The racist South was in the enemy's camp, the working South doubtful, and she was troubled that Alf Landon, a progressive Republican, courted the traditional black vote. He tried to distance himself from the Liberty League and the Macon Democrats, who were nevertheless in his camp. ER wanted this fully understood, and was impatient for the campaign to begin.

Moreover, Democratic women were irate: They needed to be reconciled, their enthusiasm reignited. For months, as Molly Dewson prepared work for the women's committee, she complained to ER about the haphazard men's team, headed by FDR:

> I was disappointed that Franklin could not see me but not surprised because I marvel night and day at what he does. Yet sometimes to be perfectly frank with you I wonder whether some of the persons the papers say he sees are more important to see than I am. . . .

Dewson was particularly disappointed that her effort to get her rainbow flyers filled with New Deal information into every neighborhood was slighted. Like ER, Dewson wanted no votes taken for granted. Their literature was first-rate and their speakers were ready; but spring conferences were not yet planned, and they lacked "some human wonder like the President to go into the states and make the women forget their disappointment over patronage, to draw out the stored up venom." An "emotional orator" was needed to go around the country and ready "women leaders" for the battle. Apathy reigned; there were "rotten situations" in several states; Dewson felt "powerless," and signed her letter "Your gloomy Gus, Molly."

By April, ER was puzzled and miffed that the men continued to do virtually nothing and had not even begun their campaign. On 18 April 1936, she wrote Jim Farley: She wanted at least "one really good woman's speech" made at the convention in June. ER was eager to go over details with Farley and sent personnel and patronage suggestions:

"Senator and Mrs. Costigan are very hard up." Despondent over the failure of his antilynch bill, the senator was ailing and ER wanted Mrs. Costigan to "have a job on some commission. . . .

"Don't forget that Molly wants a job either on the Social Security Board or as an assistant secretary doing [something] she is fitted for.

"I forgot to say that Phoebe Omlie should be given consideration. Is there any chance of moving [Eugene] Vidal? If so she might be assistant secretary in charge of aviation and considering all the fighting she might be rather acceptable to all concerned. . . ."*

Farley assured ER that he would discuss all her suggestions "and be governed by your wishes on anything I do relative to the activity of the women."

---

*ER's reference to tensions between Gene Vidal, director of air commerce, and other Department of Commerce officials, including its secretary, Daniel Roper, is one example of her endless ability to involve herself in every aspect of FDR's administration. In September, Vidal (Gore Vidal's father) was removed. Amelia Earhart (his champion and lover) was furious and threatened to abandon her promise to ER to campaign. She wrote ER, who appealed to FDR, and Vidal was temporarily restored. After that Earhart made twenty-eight speeches for FDR throughout the country.

ER also pursued major political alliances and policy issues. The Women's Trade Union League was scheduled to have its first national convention in seven years in Washington. Close to the working women's group she had supported for so long, ER invited a delegation to stay at the White House. Rose Schneiderman was "overwhelmed": "You are a perfect saint. . . . It will be something they will remember all their lives."

The press made much of the White House's week-long house party for fifteen union women, including "seven Alabama textile workers, six New York garment workers, a waitress and a stenographer." When a reporter asked Nell Morris how she felt about her proposed visit, she said: "I think it's the most wonderful thing that ever happened to a Southern girl. It's an honor to the state of Alabama."

FDR greeted the delegation on their arrival, and made them welcome. ER promised to keep the kitchen icebox unlocked and looked forward to breakfast at seven.

New York dressmaker Feige Shapiro was awed to be assigned Lincoln's bed, where for the first time her "toes didn't touch the end." She awoke the first night, and exclaimed aloud: "Imagine me, Feigele Shapiro, sleeping in Lincoln's bed!"

Forty years later, Pauline Newman noted that it was the first time working women had been White House guests. Annelise Orleck considered that fact key to their enthusiasm for FDR: For all the wage differentials and Democratic opposition to working women, he "treated them with respect."

That respect was extended as well to an amazing gathering of six thousand country women from every state in the union and twenty-four nations, representing Africa, Asia, Europe, and the Americas. The Associated Country Women of the World triennial convened in Washington in June. The women were hosted at a White House garden party, where FDR announced that their meeting proved farmers and farmers' wives and daughters could learn from each other and cooperate to achieve conservation as well as bountiful crops.

FDR emphasized the need to undo "past mistakes," restore "the former gifts of nature to their former value," and see that "harmful practices of the old days shall not be repeated." It was a diplomatic event as well as an environmental one, and peace and international trade were part of the agenda.

At an evening reception ER celebrated country women as leaders and "full partners" in building the future. Radio gave rural women access to the "outside world;" better transport enabled easier travel; the telephone "banished loneliness." It was an extraordinary convention that heralded a concept later called sustainable development and the movement toward women's emancipation in rural communities throughout the world.

Also in April, ER met with pioneer journalist Ishbel Ross, who had completed her 1936 classic book on women reporters, *Ladies of the Press*, which celebrated both ER and Hick. ER was pleased, and wrote: "I do like Ishbel Ross and she likes you."

Although the First Lady had only just started her work as syndicated columnist, she was a hero: "Never was there such a gift from heaven for the working press." ER's greatest contribution was her women-only press conferences. America's newswomen now had unprecedented "access" to information, and could get a "straightforward answer" to any question. Above all, ER believed the "public has a right to know. . . ."

When unavailable, she telephoned stories in, kept one reporter from "scooping another," tried not to scoop them in her own writings, encouraged them to call her. "She took an interest in their families, their ambitions, their work, their clothes."

ER's relations with the women of the press engendered a protective situation. Ross marveled that she was such "an experienced politician [she] rarely says anything she needs to regret. She is candid without being indiscreet. . . ." But when she overstepped into public controversy a reporter was bound to say: "That is off the record, isn't it?"

During FDR's first administration, ER's energy and stamina became her most legendary traits. Ishbel Ross's story about one of ER's Arthurdale trips was often repeated. She and the reporters took a night train from Washington, arrived at 6:00 A.M., and motored over three hundred miles around the region. The reporters "heard her make fourteen speeches. At the end of the day they were desperately tired, but she wanted to chat" for hours on the train. Shortly before midnight, ER arose to retire. They indicated approval that she was "to get some rest at last." But she said she was not at all ready for bed. "Malvina and I will do a magazine piece. . . .' "

ER's most controversial action during the political season occurred on 18 April 1936. As chair of the Washington Committee on Housing, she had helped plan a day-long conference on "Better Housing Among Negroes." Southern Democrats were outraged by her participation in the fully integrated conference, and it received very little publicity in the national press, although 513 people representing 169 organizations attended. Robert Weaver, administrative adviser on Negro affairs in Ickes's Department of the Interior, keynoted the opening session, "The Significance of Housing."

ER concluded the conference with an address that evening. Because she spent most of that week at the bedside of Louis Howe, whose every last breath seemed a miracle of effort, she spoke without notes. Nevertheless, her words resounded, and Washington Housing Committee secretary Florence Stewart reported that everybody heard only "very enthusiastic comments on [her] inspiring and instructive address. . . . I was told this morning that a Negro who had been working for some time in racial relations had to retire in tears because she was so touched by the understanding and sympathy for her race that was expressed by Mrs. Roosevelt's manner as well as her speech."

As if in direct retaliation for the success of this biracial conference, Congress declared war on the Alley Dwelling Authority, and the House Appropriations Committee eliminated its appropriations. At an emergency meeting, ER demanded the restoration of $300,000 for one of the District's most important civic efforts.

While the ADA battled for its life, several District "Citizens' Committees" petitioned the Washington Committee on Housing to rent the Langston Project "to white families instead of to colored families." Built by Hilyard Robinson, with all modern conveniences, the Langston Project was Washington's first decent project for black residents of Washington. ER was incensed, and her committee refused "to advise the Housing Division to rent these dwellings to white families."

The Langston Project was saved for African-Americans. Moreover, after many memos between ER and Ihlder, and ER's determined activities, FDR sent a message to Senator Carter Glass: "I would like very much to have the item for Alley Clearance restored." ER, and FDR, considered housing initiatives basic to the democratic effort; and they needed to disprove Alf Landon's contention that only the Republican Party was the same party in all sections of the country.

When ER returned to the White House after midnight from her triumphant speech and the festivities that closed the 18 April Conference on Better Housing Among Negroes, she received a call that Louis Howe had died in his sleep at 11:10 P.M. at the Naval Hospital. She wrote Hick: "They just noticed his breathing was changing, called the doctor who did what he could but he never responded and was never conscious. A merciful way for him. We got Franklin as soon as the Gridiron dinner was over. . . ." ER spent hours getting Howe's wife, Grace, and son Hartley "on the telephone but finally succeeded and they took it okay, thank Heavens!"

Although Louis Howe had been in the hospital since 21 August 1935, ER was unprepared for his death:

> I think I felt Louis would always be an invalid but still always there. Although for a long time the real person has been gone I shall miss some of the things that made one at times almost resentful. He was like a pitiful, querulous child but even when I complained I loved him and no one will ever be more loyal and devoted than he was.

Howe's death plunged ER into gloom. Funeral arrangements "always recall previous experiences and depress me unreasonably. I hate funeral parlors. I hope I get put rapidly in the ground in the least expensive of coffins. It all seems so unimportant when 'you' no longer exist."

ER arranged every detail of Louis Howe's funeral. "There have been endless questions all day, seating, flowers, etc." ER comforted his family, arose early to meet his daughter, Mary Baker, and others at the train, and considered the services, held in the East Room, just as Louis "would have wanted them to be"—filled with his family, friends, allies—and his most significant enemies and detractors. The journey to Fall River for Louis Howe's burial "was a trying trip," but the cemetery service "was lovely and the place itself is beautiful." According to newspapers, FDR seemed dazed, and "appeared oblivious to everything around him. . . ."

For eight hours on the train back to Washington, ER contemplated Louis Howe, who since 1911 had been her husband's chief advocate and adviser, and since 1920, her own confidant, mentor, and jolly chum.

He painted; had a wild sense of humor, a pleasing and trained tenor voice. They both loved the theater, and they enjoyed creating theater together. Since FDR never went out, much of their time together was spent inventing entertainments for his amusement. They worked on sets, lyrics, spoofs.

Howe was considerate of her foibles. ER marveled that he once sat at a restaurant table he did not like, eating food he found disagreeable, without a complaint—because he knew a complaint would embarrass her. Very little embarrassed him. Called a medieval gnome in the press, he answered the phone: "This is the Medieval Gnome speaking." He had cards printed: "Colonel Louis Rasputin Voltaire Talleyrand Simon Legree Howe."

Their relationship was intimate and unique. She shopped for his clothes; he bought her extraordinary gifts. Wherever he went he thought about what she would like. When his great friend Fannie Hurst served him cognac in a "tiny ruby glass," one of a Venetian set of mixed and vivid colors he thought exquisite, he said: "How Eleanor would love these." Fannie Hurst offered them for her as a gift. But Louis never accepted gifts, as a political rule. Hurst—flamboyant and generous—was stunned and hurt. When he realized she was offended, he accepted them for ER—which pleased everyone.

ER worried especially about his devoted assistant Margaret Durand. "A merry freckle-faced girl" he called "Rabbit," Durand joined the Roosevelt team in 1928. According to Howe's secretary and biographer Lella Styles, Rabbit "devoted her life to him . . . as he devoted his to Franklin Roosevelt and no tribute paid her would do her justice."

That night, ER wrote Hick: "Rabbit is the one I am most sorry for just as if I should outlive FDR I know Missy would be the one I should worry about!

I rather hope however that I will be the one to go, before I go through this again. . . ."

ER learned lifelong lessons from Howe: "Never admit you're licked." She added: "If you have to compromise, be sure to compromise up!"

She pondered Howe's death in terms of FDR's loss. Howe was older than FDR, deeply trusted and respected: "Louis Howe's death left a great gap in my husband's life. . . . For one reason and another, no one quite filled the void." Each new adviser "disappeared from the scene, occasionally with a bitterness which I understood but always regretted. There are not many men in this world whose personal ambition is to accomplish things for someone else, and it was some time before a friendship with Harry Hopkins, somewhat different but similar in certain ways, again brought Franklin some of the satisfaction he had known with Louis Howe."

Personally, Louis Howe had never disappointed ER. Above all, they shared a sense of why the game of politics was actually played. One built places like Arthurdale, with dispatch and despite all opposition, because it was right to do so. They shared a vision of public responsibility, which was for each of them in entirely selfless ways what the quest for public power was all about. At the time of Louis Howe's death, ER wrote in her column:

> There never was a more gentle, kindly spirit. He hated sham and cow-ardice, but he had a great pity for the weak and helpless in this world, and responded to any appeal with warmth and sympathy. His courage, loyalty and devotion to his family and friends will be an inspiration to all of them as long as they live.

Over the years, ER wrote about Howe's impact on her own life, her political evolution, and her public style. But ER rejected his conviction that she could serve in any elective or public office she chose. Specifically, Howe wanted ER to contemplate the presidency.

In a letter to Hick, ER explained his vision of the future: "He always wanted to 'make' me President when FDR was through, and insisted he could do it."

One of Howe's last legacies was an eleven-page essay, "Women's Ways in Politics," a celebration of women's activities. Howe wrote it for Molly Dewson to use in the 1936 presidential campaign: "Forty years ago . . . a woman inter-ested in politics was as scarce as an Irish snake." Public interest among women was "regarded with raised eyebrows as denoting a perverted and plebeian taste which raised grave suspicions as to the social standing of her ancestors." Even after women achieved the vote, "male political leaders" regarded women "with an indifference that to me was incomprehensible." But women's demands for social reform "rudely awakened" men from their "peaceful sloth," and they be-gan to concede power to women in local party organizations.

Since 1928, Howe concluded, women had actually transformed the political game. He credited ER and her circle with introducing a new sense of determined independence: "Our women once tasting a sense of political power, have made in this short time many sweeping changes in the men's organizations . . . and now are rapidly approaching an equal power with the men."

Howe listed women's attributes: They wanted and demanded facts. They wanted their facts free of rhetoric and confusion. They understood how to write leaflets free of cant and artifice. They were always skeptical, and unlike men who were willing to accept "their leader's statements" without evidence or investigation, women demanded real arguments. Howe believed his female coworkers "revolutionized the character of campaign literature."

Howe also considered "women very much superior to the men" in their "actual work among the voters." The women's division of the Democratic Party "organized a flying corps of women." Without any compensation, they went door to door, in every community, "armed with literature and prepared to debate any question with intelligence. We called them at headquarters the 'Grass Trampers' and to their devotion, to their intelligence, to their tireless activities I cannot pay too high a tribute."

Howe concluded his essay "with a prophecy which will be violently disputed by almost every man." If women continued to progress in politics during the next decade as they had in the past, they would run for every possible office and there was "not only the possibility but the advisability, of electing a woman as President of the United States." He continued:

> And if the issues continue to be as they are now—humanitarian, educational, and all the other features of the so-called "New Deal," it is not without the bounds of possibility that a woman might not only be nominated but elected to that office on the ground that they better understand such questions than the men.

Howe died firmly convinced that ER could be that candidate.

18: The Roosevelt Hearth, After Howe

*t the height of the campaign season, ER and FDR had to contend with the loss of the bridge between them. Louis Howe was the one friend who had consistently served their partnership: With wit and discernment, he helped adjust moments of confusion, disagreement, stubbornness, coldness. After Howe died, no one else spoke the kind of blunt truth to power they had both relied upon.

FDR had lost the one man he could turn to for selfless advice, offered always in his best interest. ER had lost the one man who understood them equally, and who considered ER essential to FDR's success. Frances Perkins believed ER had "loved him the way you love a person who has stood by you in the midst of the valley of the shadow and not been afraid of anything, a person who has stuck it out with you in physically, mentally and emotionally impossible situations."

For as long as Howe lived, ER had an ally whose views mattered to FDR. Once on their own, ER and FDR began to fly apart. Communication grew harder for each of them, and for their work together. Almost immediately, FDR made a series of political decisions ER opposed and argued fervently against. In the past, Howe would have joined her. He would shout and stamp, bang his fists: "Idiot"; "damned fool." Invectives and warnings would fly: This is too dangerous; positively stupid. Now FDR was surrounded by people who increasingly told him whatever he most wanted to hear. Several of them regarded ER as that difficult woman in their way. In the past, Howe had protected her from those who wanted "to get the pants off Eleanor and on to Franklin." ER was now alone when she entered FDR's court, and tensions increased between them.

FDR's first decision was to call upon his eldest son, James, to replace Howe as secretary, companion, chief adviser. No president after John Adams had done that, and there was a democratic tradition that condemned, or at least disfavored, nepotism. ER worried about her husband's reputation, and she worried about her son, not yet thirty. She argued and cajoled; she argued and grew cold, as was her way. FDR explained that he had a right to have his clever, strong, trusted son beside him.

The delicate balance between ER's court and FDR's court tilted dramatically when James and his wife, Betsey Cushing Roosevelt, joined the White House family. Forever sensitive to the plight of a daughter-in-law, ER sought to maintain warm, noninterfering, generous relations with her sons' wives. In most cases, she succeeded. But Betsey Cushing Roosevelt, beautiful and efficient, was utterly charmed by FDR, and completely disinterested in ER.

Betsey blamed ER's public interests for FDR's loneliness, and she set out to make up for his wife's neglect. She would amuse and entertain him, protect and pamper him. Her attentions pleased FDR, made James jealous, and infuriated ER—who now felt herself disdained and diminished by two Mrs. James Roosevelts who acted as if she were irrelevant or, worse, an interloper in her own home.

ER was astonished to find that Betsey interfered with household matters, invited guests for dinner, reordered the table, countermanded orders, menus, and plans, even when she was in residence. Critical and rude, Betsey seemed to despise her mother-in-law. On one campaign trip, Betsey sounded as if she resented ER's very presence: Awakened by an excited voice in the adjoining stateroom at 3:30 A.M., Betsey heard ER tell FDR about her unexpected meeting with her brother Hall. Betsey complained to the president about his interrupted sleep over inconsequential news. But FDR defended his wife: "Bets, you don't understand her at all—she has no concept of time."

During a particularly festive White House party, ER invited Betsey to dance—which resulted in a spiteful confrontation when ER noted that Betsey was reported to be a splendid dancer, but she stepped on ER's feet twice. No, smiled Betsey, Missy was the good dancer. Subsequently, Betsey concluded that ER did not so much like to dance "as to lead."

Although FDR defended his wife from direct assault, he insisted on Betsey's continued place at the table. According to James, "Father approved because Betsey delighted him. She was pretty, playful, a teaser. She flattered him, and he adored her." Ultimately, there was nothing but bitterness between ER and Betsey, who subsequently became a fountain of reliably mean stories about her once and former mother-in-law.

Many people stepped momentarily into the cavernous gap Howe left. Felix Frankfurter sent letters of advice and proposed an army of young men to serve, many of whom did so. But nobody took Howe's place, and nobody cared to bridge the widening space that developed between America's First Couple.

Immediately after Howe's funeral, ER set about to refurbish her own court. She increasingly relied on Tommy for companionship. After touring Todhunter students through the Williamsburg restoration, she wrote Hick: "I was in the state when one doesn't want to do anything more, but now I'm glad I came for we had a glorious drive down and Tommy is a nice comfortable person for I never feel she expects attention or entertainment, and by lunch time I felt smoothed out. . . ."

ER's closest allies were Harry Hopkins and others in WPA and NYA; also Rex Tugwell, now at the Resettlement Administration, which had authority over Arthurdale and other communities.

ER was relieved to write Hick that she spent part of the afternoon with Rex Tugwell, "and I do feel he is doing a better and better job and I wish the public knew it." She worried, however, about Harry Hopkins and his wife, Barbara, who was diagnosed with cancer: "I would like to help them, , , ."

ER looked forward to Hick's spring visit:

> The tennis court is now in order and I think it would do us good to play a little! You sounded cheerful about the job too! Isn't it nice when things turn out better than you feared? It rarely happens however. . . .

On 23 April, ER replied to a lost letter from Hick reminding her that however lonesome and troubled she felt, she was loved "above everyone else":

> Dearest one. It was grand to find your letter when I came in tonight and I was amused at your soliloquy on consoling unhappy husbands and wives! Darling, you are lonely but you granted that the experience of loving and being loved above everyone else or to the exclusion of everyone else is one worth having. There is no guarantee that you won't be more unhappy in the long run and you who don't accept change easily would find it harder than most people. No, I rather think that tho you suffer now you might have suffered more the other [married] way. You are a sympathetic sweet person tho the way you put up with everybody's confidences and by jinks I'm going to try to be happy with you! . . .

Hick's April visit to Washington, where she agreed to medical tests, revealed that she had a diabetes flare-up and required a strict regimen of rest, exercise, and diet. It helped explain her fatigue and her irritable moods. She returned to New York to spend time with her Minnesota librarian friend Jeannette Bryce, and ER wrote that she was glad Jenny was there to monitor her new dietary regimen. But whenever Hick was with another or had a good time without ER, Hick's letters were filled with words of agony and complaint. It was as if she was afraid to admit she was happy or in any way satisfied in

the company of others. Perhaps she hoped to reassure ER, or forestall jealousy. While ER only rarely expressed jealousy, she could not hide her true
feelings—which leaked out, however disguised:

> I am glad that Jenny is an attractive companion but gosh I should
> think she might just spend Sunday reading and taking a walk, what will
> happen when you work on your report for two days? You've certainly taken
> on a responsibility!

When Jenny and Hick traveled through the countryside, ER felt wistful: "I
miss you dear and often wish I were Jenny. . . ."

ER hated to be alone and managed to have virtually no time in that condition. Surrounded by people, she generally managed to do two or more
things at once. At meetings, listening to speeches, traveling, even watching
films in the dark, her hands were always busy—writing or knitting.

There were meetings with union women; an "air our minds" lunch with
Lady Stella Reading, Frances Perkins, and Isabella Greenway; several important speeches; and a fascinating dinner with Earl Miller to meet his new date,
Roberta Jonay, a dancer whom ER liked immediately. After dinner, she met
with Baruch to discuss WPA, Arthurdale, and the election. ER had a most
"amusing time" another evening as she discussed adult education with various "big wigs." ER thought she did "a good turn" when she explained "why I
thought worker's education important and oh! boy some of these men are
naive!"

In the spring of 1936, workers' education was assaulted. Hilda Smith was accused of supporting communism, and ER was accused of supporting Smith.
One correspondent considered it "odious" that ER contributed $4,000 from
her radio speeches to support Hilda Smith's "communistic" work.*

ER declared that she actually could not give money to the WPA's Workers'
Education Division, since "the Government can accept no money from private individuals." She did contribute to a school for "union and non-union
girls," for which Smith had donated her own home. ER also gave $25 a year to
Bryn Mawr's summer school for working women, which was not "communistic." She observed:

> Of course, if you do not approve of unions nor of allowing workers to
> become educated you might disapprove. They do discuss communism, but

*Hilda Smith and her sister donated their familial home, Vineyard Shore, and
thirty-six acres to New York State for the Vineyard Shore School, with ER's advice and
support.

I have always believed ignorance was a sure way to fall a victim to propaganda. I do not believe in communism, because I do believe in freedom and in our form of government, but I did not attain that loyalty through repression.

But the renewed Red Scare targeted ER's activities and closest allies. At one of its first sessions, in February 1935, Martin Dies's House Un-American Activities Committee (HUAC), charged that "communists" captured and controlled workers' education. Republicans and Southern Democrats escalated those charges for the campaign season, and emphasized that some programs for working women were actually biracial. ER did not consider workers' education communistic in the land of opportunity, and publicly defended its importance, as well as the controversial books used.

ER was unbothered by the ongoing controversy Louise McLaren, director of the Southern Summer School for Workers, engendered. In her report, McLaren proudly listed the authors found in the school's library and curriculum, including such radicals as Mother Bloor, Myra Page, Grace Lumpkin, Fielding Burke, Leo Huberman, Agnes Smedley, and Langston Hughes. HUAC charged: "REDS RULE FERA SCHOOLS." ER defended the freedom to read, dissent, learn; the need for public controversy in a democracy.

As a result of her persistent support, Hilda Smith noted, workers' education was actually expanded.

By the summer of 1936, the National Youth Administration had conducted more than two thousand classes taken by 65,000 workers in thirty-four states. Over eleven hundred teachers were employed, and there were winter follow-up classes for their ninety camp and resident school programs.

Still, many snags and discriminatory aspects concerning women's camps and opportunities persisted, when compared to the CCC program. Although the puny women's "allowance" of 50 cents a week was scrapped for a $22.50 monthly wage, to be sent home to "dependents," that represented about half the wage CCC youth received. Also, "single, unattached" women were discouraged by the WPA program, since they were "not part of family groups." Above all, the issue of appropriate work was still unresolved. "Landscaping" remained "unsuitable" for women, although ER argued that many women were landscapers. Clerical work, sewing projects for toy and recreational products, and the manufacture of braille books seemed the safest, though land "beautification" projects, gardening, and canning became possible.

Despite all opposition, from Vermont to Mississippi and west to Utah and Montana, local enthusiasm and widespread support flourished for workers' education and the women's programs. Smith was endlessly grateful to ER for the program's triumphs:

I know we have you, the President and Harry Hopkins to thank—an invincible trio! You have given Workers' education a chance to demonstrate what could be done. To see all the new young people, teachers and workers, throughout the country, who have identified themselves with the movement makes me very happy.

Throughout the spring and summer of 1936, ER also defended Camp Jane Addams at Bear Mountain, now routinely called a Red citadel. With Tommy and Mark McCloskey, regional director of the NYA, ER spent three hours at the camp and spoke personally with the 126 campers. ER upheld the right to disagree in America: "You can't take human beings and put them into molds and say I want you to believe this. . . . You have got to let things come to them through their own experience. . . ."

While the conservative war against workers' education and ER's views raged, the left also mobilized to protect and expand WPA programs. In that campaign, ER stood with radical workers, who annoyed Mark McCloskey. ER saw no contradiction between capitalism and programs to ensure workers' education and opportunity. Some, including McCloskey, thought that made her a dupe of communist propaganda.

ER had responded favorably to a radical worker, Sarah Rosenberg of the Workers' Alliance, who had complained that Camp Jane Addams did nothing to prepare women for their future: They had no real training, left without jobs, and faced ongoing misery. Some therefore considered "suicide or tramping on the roads." McCloskey assured ER:

> No one in NYC knows the resources of the Relief Agencies better than the Workers' Alliance. It is one of the "leftist" groups that have been camping on the doorstep of every federal and local agency . . . and undoubtedly every girl who attends Camp Jane Addams is advised of all private and public relief agencies. . . .

It seemed that everything ER did to make life for America's most neglected people better, sweeter, and more hopeful was assailed in 1936. She was particularly criticized for hosting an integrated White House garden party for sixty delinquent girls, aged thirteen to twenty, residents at the National Training School for Girls. Eleven of the inmates were white, fifty were Negroes; and ER dared to unlock their doors, invite them from behind their "ten foot brick walls," for an afternoon of cake and ice cream. That seemed unbearable to her many critics. But ER considered her party a simple, human thing to do. She had been so "appalled" when she visited the reform school, which was "not a school at all, having no teachers" and no educational programs, she invited them to the White House "to have a good time." After the party, she demanded a completely new rehabilitation program that would train and educate the young women to return to their communities as useful citizens: "It seems to me that complete segregation in gloomy surroundings is hardly the way to achieve this objective."

It remained a source of amazement to ER that so many people could disregard people in need, ignore their hurt, dismiss their humanity, from outcast girls in distress to the unemployed. ER urged comfortable Americans to consider all individuals "human beings with all the tastes, likes, dislikes, and passions we have ourselves." She wondered:

> how we can make the more fortunate in this country fully aware of the fact that the problem of the unemployed is not a mechanical one. It is a problem alive and throbbing with human pain.

New Deal programs had done little actually to lessen unemployment, which remained a growing problem. Mechanization in both agriculture and industry rendered "labor" idle, perhaps permanently.

On 4 May, Hick wrote a long letter about conditions in the Ohio steel industry:

> Youngstown is terribly depressing. The steel mills are running full blast, 80 percent of capacity, as good as 1929. They never get up to 100 percent except in war time. And yet—
>
> In the last three years they've spent Ten Million Dollars modernizing these plants, and the result is that in 1936, with the mills operating at 1929 production, they are employing *10,000* fewer men than in 1929!
>
> I obtained these figures, Madame, from the Chamber of Commerce. They are probably *very* conservative. And this year $2,000,000 more is to be put into modernization. That means *more* men laid off. . . .
>
> The whole population is worried. . . . Ninety percent of the men employed by WPA used to work in steel. They run all the way from roustabouts, in the majority . . . to skilled and semi-skilled workers, such as rollers, shear-men, catchers, and so on. The gloom you hear in the coal country . . . is nothing compared with this. These people are afraid—and getting desperate. . . . They see their jobs slipping right out from under them—snatched away by the machine that was supposed to make life an easier, more gracious thing, but which is really taking away their bread and butter.
>
> To run these modernized plants, the steel companies are going out after college and high school youngsters. . . . The process of turning a steel ingot into a sheet of [metal] that can be bent into the body of an automobile can now be performed by three or four bright young men in white shirts, who stand in a little nook away up in a gallery and—press buttons.

The same process under the old system . . . involved the hard, sweaty labor of a hundred men or more! . . .

ER read Hick's report to FDR, who encouraged her to write a "My Day" column, using Hick's words. ER wrote:

If you mind I'm terribly sorry, I wanted to wire for your consent but F wouldn't let me. I think he wants me to be the whipping boy and though he can't bring the question out he wants it out. . . . A week from tomorrow you will be here. Bless you and all my love.

If Hick did in fact mind that her words were now grist for another reporter's column, there is no evidence that she complained to ER. Clearly, ER's priority was to advance FDR's goal, regardless of the inevitable corporate protest—which soon occurred.

While Hick traveled, ER prepared for the Democratic convention and spent time with SDR, who had broken her hip. ER was relieved by her mother-in-law's high spirits while confined to her bedroom: She seemed positively "cheerful," and insisted that she was comfortable; she "has her lovely trees to look at, and an oriole, which came twice yesterday. . . ." For all their conflicts, ER admired her tenacious independence and resilient outlook. ER enjoyed her mother-in-law's favorite maxims: "All weather is good weather," and, when one complained of insufficient time: "You had all the time there was."

By 1936, ER's expanded interests eclipsed her friendship with Nancy Cook and Marion Dickerman. While Cook worked with ER on various resettlement projects, a palpable strain had intruded into their once harmonious partnership. Also, Marion Dickerman complained that most of Todhunter's parents were Republicans, and its reputation as "ER's school" was a handicap.

The first tangible evidence of their frayed bond was the decision to abandon Val-Kill Industries. They agreed to disband the furniture and pewter shop and to give the tools, machinery, and stock to their workers. ER was eager to let it go, and wrote Hick: "Dearest a glorious day. . . . Nan's lawn is lovely and we had a grand, quiet time. . . . Tons of work . . . moving the shop out."

Nan and Marion would remain in the cottage; ER would take over the factory building, reconstruct it as a home for herself, and build an apartment for Tommy. Everybody would have more privacy. Until then, ER had had to negotiate with Cook and Dickerman whenever she had houseguests for the night, an arrangement that had become exceedingly annoying. Although Hick refused to visit ER at Val-Kill, regular visits by relatives and grandchildren and Earl Miller's frequent presence, alone or with his ever-changing young women and their relatives, had increasingly disturbed Nancy Cook and Marion Dickerman.

ER believed the new situation was mutually agreeable. She wrote Hick that the move was "really a great relief to [Nan] and will mean a more peaceful life." But she was deluded. Marion Dickerman condemned as cold and detached ER's public announcement regarding the shop:

> [The furniture machinery] will be taken over and operated by one of the expert craftsmen, Otto Berge. . . . The weaving will continue under the direction of Nellie Johannesen. During the winter months she will teach the art of weaving to any women who wish to learn. . . . Miss Nancy Cook, President of Val-Kill, who has conducted the shop since its founding, finds the various craft projects have grown to such an extent that she can no longer give them her personal attention. . . .

Dickerman lamented that these "dry, matter-of-fact words told nothing of the heartache this meant to Nancy Cook, who had invented the enterprise and for whom it had been the center, the essence of creative self-expression." Cook and Dickerman felt abandoned, rejected.

ER sought to rely on Hick, but she was mostly unavailable—and in Michigan with Alicent (Alix) Holt, ER endured several days without a note, and on the 28th wrote Hick with some irritation: "I shall be glad to get some letters from you tonight! I'm not accustomed to being so long without news and I don't like it."

At Cornell, while she was on her annual visit with Flora Rose, ER and Elinor Morgenthau received a disturbing call from Henry Morgenthau, who reported that FDR was "upset and taking it out on his friends; he had been horrid all week." ER supposed part of the reason for FDR's mood involved the Supreme Court's ongoing opposition to the New Deal, the rapidly deteriorating international situation, "and I can imagine some other things!"

Actually FDR's ordinarily buoyant spirits had been unraveling ever since Louis Howe died. He had postponed his entire campaign effort until September, and he acted as if the impending Democratic convention in June had nothing to do with him. Although Howe had been bedridden since January 1935, FDR wrote Ambassador Robert W. Bingham in London on 4 May 1936: "It was sad, indeed, to have Louis taken from us and the end was very unexpected and sudden."

With Howe's death, all associations at the Roosevelt hearth were transformed. The circle was broken. New friendships were created; old ones were terminated; every relationship was jostled in some way. During the spring and summer of 1936, while ER worked and campaigned, Hick took long vacations with others.

At Val-Kill, Tommy and Henry Osthagen helped design ER's new cottage. Earl was there with Roberta Jonay. ER had seen her perform at the Copacabana and other nightclubs, thought her talented, and wanted her seriously to study dance: "She is a sweet child!" But Roberta was torn between wanting to be an artist and her love for Earl. "Roberta fears that 'to be hurt again would be too much for him' and I entirely agree!"

ER enjoyed the plans for her new home: "I'll have definite estimates this week. It is fun to build or change things over." ER's decision to remodel her private space, to alter both the business and living arrangement of Val-Kill, occurred within weeks of Howe's death. It was as if without her most trusted champion and reliable political mentor, ER needed to fortify her own domain. Her decision to renovate the factory for herself where she would be fully in charge, where her time and space would be fully protected, reflected major changes in her intimate circle. She now had an apartment in the city and a home of her own at Val-Kill over which she presided with complete independence and control.

Still, she longed to hear from Hick: "I wonder where you are, I hate not knowing—A world of love." The next day, ER wrote with relief: "It was just grand to have your wire this morning and know where you were. . . ."

During the summer of 1936, they were very far apart.

19: The Election of 1936

ER dreaded the first campaign season since 1911 without the emotional support of Louis Howe. Fully aware that the people now around FDR wanted her to recede into the background, to say little or nothing on the campaign trail, she tried to abide by their idea of a winning strategy. As early as February she told her press conference, "I am not making any campaign speeches." Firmly, she rejected political questions about the future, and announced that during the campaign all her public or paid lectures would be "made on a non-partisan basis."

But she could not do it. Every word, every column, carried political messages. Reaching out, acting on her sense of responsibility in hard times, was for her a basic instinct and an emotional need. She might forever deny that she was "political," but she was determined to fight for her goals.

No matter how embattled she became, ER always paused to notice and give thanks for the splendors of the natural world. Each sunrise was a miracle, each sunset a mystery. From the roll of the fog off the sea in Campobello to the curl of her favorite apricot-colored roses, the wonders of earth's changes in each season were at the core of her political ethic. Her anguish at the ravages of poverty, the cruelties of dictators, was in direct proportion to her spiritual sense of gratitude while riding through the woods or walking along the shore.

Often her columns reflected the unity of her vision. During the first days of summer, for example, she wrote of a visit to Elinor Morgenthau's farm. They went into the field to see "four of the most enchanting colts." ER recognized "something appealing in all young animals, but a colt with its long legs and confiding ways, is somehow particularly attractive."

When ER saw "a very large bull lying on the ground," she asked Morgenthau if it was "well-behaved."

"No, it is extremely vicious," she replied. But it had fought with another bull, and now could hardly move.

That reference to vicious uncontrollable behavior led ER to discuss Dorothy Thompson's powerful column exploring the hate-filled, mendacious political climate that defined the campaign season in 1936. Thompson had asked: "Who is to blame? You and I are to blame." There are so many "things we tolerate and know are untrue." ER wished Thompson's "message could get across to thousands of citizens. She is right—we are to blame for much of the bigotry, ignorance and vice in this country because so few of us think it necessary to do more than keep quiet."

ER had long understood that activism helped her forestall depression, and now she was urged to keep quiet. In the summer of 1936, ER felt vulnerable, lonely, and alone. Howe was gone, Cook and Dickerman were no longer friends, and it was the first summer since 1932 that she spent entirely without Lorena Hickok. Although they corresponded, Hick remained in the Middle West with various friends, Jeannette Bryce, Adel Enright, and especially Alix Holt.

ER wrote often, as she did on 1 June: "I miss you badly, and love you much." But Hick refused to alter her plans, even when ER asked her to. She was mystified that in Chicago, with Hick so nearby at a Minnesota lake, they would not see each other.

While Hick was with Jeanette touring the Minnesota lake country and then with Alix in Michigan, ER was on the campaign trail in the South. Despite the Talmadges and bigots, the South seemed vigorous for Roosevelt. FDR "purrs like a cat under the enthusiasm and friendly welcomes. . . ." But ER wearied "of cheering crowds" and wrote that she would "like them less if they booed but I'd be more interested!"

Her agreement to stand beside her husband, circumspect and speechless, combined with the unrelenting pace of the campaign train and a stunning heat wave, drained ER's spirits. She spent hours on the train "fantasizing about the peace and quiet" she would have when the campaign ended. Initially, she boasted: "I can stand this pace but the others break down." Tommy was "really exhausted." Eventually, even ER's "head [felt] odd with the heat!"

ER dismissed the Republican platform as "the same old bunk." She hoped theirs would not be "so long," although she knew it was "foolish to hope it will be any less 'bunk-ish.'" She sent Hick an article by Bruce Barton about ER and the Dionne quintuplets, which "will amuse you!" But she rejected its premise: "Won't it be a surprise to them all when I sink into peace and obscurity!"

According to Barton:

The quintuplets should be kept together, carefully nurtured, and educated in writing for the newspapers, traveling around the country and talking on the radio. At the age of sixteen they should be brought to the United States [from Canada] and put in training to become the wife of a future President of the U.S. No *one* woman ever can stand the pace that has been set by Eleanor Roosevelt.

Future Presidents will have to have five wives at least. It will be an advantage to have them all look alike; four can be recuperating while the fifth is out doing her stuff. Even for five, it will be a tough assignment.

On ER's return to New York on the 18th she found several letters from Hick, and a wire—all now lost. In reply, ER was aggravated by Hick's "decision not to come home till September. Are you taking the absent treatment because it helps? If so I won't say a word—Otherwise, I should say sometimes too much conscience is an unpleasant thing! Well, dear it is for you to decide for you are the one who suffers and I just enjoy what I can have and learned long ago to accept what had to be—."

Hick evidently dealt with her own disappointment about having no journalist's role during a presidential campaign by becoming involved with two other women who were in competition for her affections. Although most of Hick's correspondence is lost, Alix Holt's 14 June letter to Hick sheds light on the situation:

> Carissima, what did I say that made you imagine I think you quite perfect and love you for that reason? Truly, you flatter yourself! Aren't we a bit absurd, thinking about the why and wherefore and how of this friendship of ours? And I'm afraid I started it. Anyway, in spite of your being "hollow" and my being "stupid," we still seem to be fond of each other, and probably shall continue to be. I suspect I shall love you as long as you do me, at least, and perhaps a little bit longer. When do you suppose we shall begin to take each other for granted, as we do our other friends? I think we had better try, don't you? But, darling, I'm glad to know you really need me. And I do you.

ER had no intention of losing this particular battle. And she did not lose it. After Hick's June week with her, Alicent Holt virtually disappeared from the game of hearts. With stoic patience, ER waded through the moment—which lasted all summer.

As always, she sent Hick daily letters, and detailed the doings at Val-Kill, which began to resemble a three-ring circus. Earl and Roberta and Tommy and Henry and many grandchildren were in ER's new home. They played croquet, sat around the garden, swam in the pool, prepared hot dogs at the still-shared fireplace, all of which upset Nan and Marion. Val-Kill, once an idyllic retreat, was now under a growing cloud of tension, threatening and unpleasant. In the midst of all her company ER longed for Hick, her only trusted confidante when it came to Democratic politics and her personal feelings about FDR.

On 22 June, ER went to White Sulphur Springs, West Virginia, to honor Alice Hamilton for her pioneering work on industrial health and occupational diseases. The evening gave ER perspective about her own private anguish:

> [Dr. Hamilton] is such a dear. So gentle and unassuming and yet look what she's done! A lesson to most of us who think we have to assert ourselves to be useful and particularly good for me as I was feeling rather annoyed with FDR. Nothing unusual just a little feeling on his part that he was abused because I didn't cooperate with his plans about Hyde Park when I wasn't asked at the time to sit in or express an idea! Then my pride was injured at his perfect forgetfulness of part of a political suggestion I had made on the train and I was annoyed until I realized tonight how small it all was sitting by the sweet-faced woman who has probably given the impetus to workman's compensation and research into industrial disease and saved countless lives and heartbreaks!

On the way home, ER stopped at Alderson Prison for Women "and saw two faces which haunt me. Gosh! We might any one of us be there." She noted, "Tommy is weary in body, and I'm weary in mind."

ER listened on the radio to the Democratic convention in Philadelphia. The platform was being debated, and it seemed "to be going smoothly," although at dinner FDR seemed worried and tired. In another room, Sam Rosenman, Stanley High, Ray Moley, and Tom Cochran all worked on FDR's acceptance speech. ER concluded her letter with an ambiguous promise:

> Goodnight dear, and bless you. Do what you think is right this summer and I'll meet you wherever you wish whenever I can but remember I am going to do a paid speaking tour beginning November 9th till I have to go for Thanksgiving to Warm Springs. Part of October I may be on a trip with FDR and part of September I'll be helping Earl settle his house. . . .

During the June convention, while her closest political friends set off for Philadelphia, ER sat at home with nothing to do. Dewson invited ER to speak at one of the daily women's breakfasts where all the steam for the campaign of 1936 was being generated. Each morning women from every region introduced their needs, and new strategies were forged. Molly Dewson planned these big breakfast rallies to guarantee an enthusiastic campaign—only the women could provide Democratic unity.

ER was sorry to write Dewson that while she "would love to be at a breakfast," it was her political obligation to stay away from the preliminaries and arrive with FDR for his acceptance speech. "Otherwise, I might get myself into trouble!" She wrote about the preliminary festivities from a great distance:

> The magnolias out of my window are in bloom and they look beautiful at night. I listened [to the convention] to the bitter end last night and wondered if in 1783 they whooped it up so much. It seems undignified and meaningless but perhaps we need it!

The Democratic women considered ER their leader. Even Frances Perkins, who was closer to the president, considered ER the heart of the Democratic women's movement. At one breakfast, "the loudest cheers" arose when Perkins departed from her prepared speech to pay tribute to the First Lady. According to *The New York Times*, Perkins celebrated ER with "deep feeling":

> I want to speak of a prominent woman Democrat who is not here. She is kept away by convention—not political, but social convention, although she is not a woman to be bound by convention.
>
> Her genius is the capacity to love the human race and to hear and understand the misery and wants and aspirations of people. . . .
>
> If ever there was a gallant and courageous and intelligent and wise woman, she is one.
>
> I know that many women . . . when they go to vote in November for Franklin Roosevelt will be thinking with a choke in their throats of Eleanor Roosevelt.

Upon Perkins's last words, a spontaneous demonstration of prolonged enthusiasm erupted throughout the ballroom.

Although male politicians ignored the vigorous and important work done by the Women's Committee, ER and Dewson had organized many aspects of the convention, and the women's famous "rainbow flyers" explaining and celebrating New Deal achievements were on every seat.

Bess Furman reported the convention was a "dull dish," predictable and routine from the "masculine viewpoint." But in terms of the women, "Philadelphia made history." More women were in attendance than ever, and Molly Dewson's committee demonstrated a "New Deal woman's movement of impressive proprtions." However dramatic and inspiring the women's movement, "it was so ignored by [male] politicians that it might as well have been underground."

Four years of patient organizing by Molly Dewson and the other stalwarts of ER's inner circle had resulted in a convention represented by 219 women delegates and 302 women alternates. More than five hundred women "surged through Molly's huge mezzanine-floor headquarters."

Women, led by ER, had long understood that space was symbolic. At Philadelphia, the Women's Division headquarters were as large as Jim Farley's "big reception room" combined with vice president Garner's headquarters and Charley Michelson's publicity room. It was, Dewson promised, only the beginning. M. W. ("More Women") Dewson would not rest "until women permeate the party on a 50-50 basis."

Daisy Harriman was "enchanted." There were three times more Democratic women in Philadelphia than there were Republican women in Ohio. "I must dash right over and tell Alice Longworth!" When Furman asked Harriman how she managed her lifelong friendship with Alice Roosevelt Longworth, the future minister to Norway replied: "Oh, we've had the most interesting time. We never fight."

Harriman cited a recent dinner where she had been the lone Democrat among Republican leaders, all of whom attacked FDR and the New Deal the entire evening. As Daisy Harriman left, Alice Longworth said: "You can't have had such a nice time."

"Quite the contrary" Harriman replied: "I thought I was right back in 1907. It was just the way Wall Street talked about your father."

For ER the campaign was in the details. As chair of the first women's platform committee in 1924, ER had been insulted, excluded from final policy meetings. Her progressive platform, worked up with the advice of her social work mentors, had been discarded. In contrast to that bleak time when ER, Caroline O'Day, and Elinor Morgenthau patiently sat outside the closed platform committee door, shunned and snubbed by the party leaders, who never allowed them to present the platform they had been asked to prepare, Dewson's team of fourteen platform writers was given time and consideration. And it resembled, almost plank by plank, the platform ER and her associates had prepared in 1924: the eight-hour day, conservation of public lands, labor's right to bargain collectively, a federal employment agency, equal pay for equal work, federal aid for maternal and child health, child welfare, education to eliminate venereal disease, an end to vigilante violence.

In 1924, "vigilante violence" referred to the reemergence of Ku Klux Klan and Red Scare terror that followed World War I. In 1936 it was again a political factor, with lynchings and anti-union violence everywhere on the rise.

Caroline O'Day presented the women's platform, and proposals to change the convention rules to provide two representatives from each state (a man and a woman) on the platform committee. But real party equity remained elusive. Despite the unprecedented number of women delegates and Dewson's many triumphs, their male allies treated women shabbily.*

Dewson had expected to be appointed vice-chair of the Democratic National Committee. She assumed she had the support of Farley, Flynn, and

---

*Still, the 1936 convention was the beginning of the long march toward the Democratic Party's fifty-fifty rule, which Bella Abzug achieved in ER's honor in 1978.

FDR. But at the last moment she was betrayed and Farley supported her archrival, Emma Guffey Miller. Astounded, Dewson wrote Farley: "I go to your defense with loyalty and ardor practically every day. . . . The few times I have disagreed with you I have told you and no one else except Mrs. Roosevelt to whom I feel primarily responsible."

Sister of Pennsylvania's Senator Joe Guffey, Emma Guffey Miller was an ardent Democrat with clout. Jim Farley replied: "Molly, I can't help it. Senator Guffey is using such pressure on me." Dewson gave Farley an alternative: Appoint as many women vice-chairs as there were men, and Guffey could be one of them. He agreed, but men clung to their dominance: Farley appointed eight women, then added two men.

Although women were used to get out the vote, they continued to be excluded from policy meetings, and were generally ignored by FDR's inner circle. In the past, Louis Howe was their bridge to power, and he made sure FDR complimented their work. That task was now left to ER, even while she herself was made to feel less and less part of the campaign. If some of the men listened to her views out of courtesy or consideration, many others merely gazed in her direction when she offered a suggestion and, without the dignity of a reply of any kind, continued their conversation as if she had not even spoken. It was an old and lingering trick; women got used to it. When they persevered, as ER did, they were called strident.

On Saturday, 27 June, ER accompanied FDR to Philadelphia for his acceptance speech. The huge outdoor stadium was filled with anticipation and ebullience. Eager Democrats had waited five days for this moment. Over 100,000 people had assembled by seven o'clock, and it had rained all evening. Their feet muddy, their clothes wet, they cheered and sang through warm evening mists, and one significant downpour.

It was the largest political rally in U.S. history. The waiting crowd had been roused by soprano Lily Pons, several bands, Eddie Peabody's banjo, and Tchaikovsky played by the Philadelphia Symphony conducted by Leopold Stokowski. Most reporters, including Bess Furman, assembled at five o'clock, were soaked to the skin, and took bets on whether FDR's fabled weather magic would be repeated on this unlikely night. Then, just as he appeared, the rains stopped; a half-full moon glowed brightly, and the wind grew still.

FDR's car arrived at ten o'clock, as vice president John Garner completed his lackluster acceptance speech. The orchestra played "Hail to the Chief" as FDR walked on his son James's arm to the rostrum. But he was interrupted by the "most frightful five minutes of my life." It was a moment which demonstrated the complexities and triumphs of FDR's character.

Arthur M. Schlesinger reported the scene: In "the blur of faces," FDR rec-

ognized illustrious poet Edward Markham, and waved. As the eighty-four-
year-old poet went to shake FDR's hand, the crowd surged forward and the
president was jostled. "Under the pressure," his right steel brace "snapped out
of position," and FDR toppled over. "Mike Reilly of the Secret Service dived
and caught him . . . just before he hit the ground."

But pages of his speech fell into the mud. While Jim Farley and "other tall
men clustered around to hide the scene," Gus Gennerich knelt and snapped
the brace back. "Reilly, fearing that some Secret Service man might shoot
down the white-bearded stranger in the confusion, shouted frantically to
Markham, 'Don't move!'

"Roosevelt was pale and shaken. . . . 'Clean me up,' he ordered"; and keep
your "feet off 'those damned sheets.' " But then he noticed Markham, "close
to tears, a look of agony on his face." FDR, paused, turned, smiled, "took
the poet's hand in his." All was well. When the president reached the platform, he seemed "tranquil and unperturbed, while he quietly reassembled the
smudged and crumpled pages."

The campaign of 1936 was dedicated to the extension of the New Deal, to
the demise of those who would inflict despair and permanent poverty on
working Americans. Accused by his enemies of communism and fascism,
FDR introduced a new way—a democratic way—to economic security. He attacked "economic royalists" who controlled America's material life, built kingdoms of concentrated wealth which dominated industry. "These tyrants of
our technology" thought they could forever control the "railroads, steam and
electricity; the telegraph and the radio."

The twentieth century ushered in an age of giant "corporations, banks
and securities; new machinery of industry and agriculture, of labor and capital." Modern civilization changed everything, created new power centers and
new problems, disempowered "many thousands of small-businessmen and
merchants" who "were no more free than the worker or the farmer."

The "privileged princes of these new economic dynasties, thirsting for
power, reached out for control over Government itself. They created a new
despotism and wrapped it in the robes of legal sanction. . . ." They erected a
"new industrial dictatorship" which controlled the "hours men and women
worked, the wages they received, the conditions of their labor. . . ."

> For too many of us the political equality we once had won was mean-
> ingless in the face of economic inequality. A small group had concentrated
> into their own hands an almost complete control over other people's prop-
> erty, other people's money, other people's labor—other people's lives. For
> too many of us life was no longer free; liberty no longer real. . . .
>
> Against economic tyranny such as this, the American citizen could ap-
> peal only to the organized power of Government. The collapse of 1929

showed up the despotism for what it was. The election of 1932 was the people's mandate to end it. Under that mandate it is being ended. . . .

And now, FDR promised, democracy's march would enlarge democracy's scope:

> The royalists of the economic order have conceded that political freedom was the business of the Government, but they have maintained that economic slavery was nobody's business. . . .
>
> Today we stand committed to the proposition that freedom is [indivisible]. If the average citizen is guaranteed equal opportunity in the polling place, he must have equal opportunity in the market place.
>
> These economic royalists complain that we seek to overthrow the institutions of America. What they really complain of is that we seek to take away their power. . . .

Domestically, FDR's speech was revolutionary. He hoped it would have international consequences: All was not "well with the world: Clouds of suspicion, tides of ill-will and intolerance gather darkly in many places." America's domestic success might rekindle hope among those in other lands who had grown "too weary to carry on the fight" for freedom and had "yielded their democracy" for illusions.

In America, FDR declared, "we are waging a great and successful war. It is not alone a war against want and destitution and economic demoralization. It . . . is a war for the survival of democracy. We are fighting to save a great and precious form of government for ourselves and for the world."

Though he never mentioned fascism or communism, FDR's speech resounded throughout the world, and reverberated for decades with the conviction that there was another way, a democratic way: "There is a mysterious cycle in human events. To some generations much is given. Of other generations much is expected. This generation of Americans has a rendezvous with destiny. . . ."

When she first read FDR's speech, ER hesitated: She considered his rhetoric vividly crafted, but "not specific enough for me." After he presented it at Franklin Field, she was enthusiastic. She wrote: "I think F *felt* every word of his speech." His delivery was powerful and dramatic; "it was a wonderful sight."

Afterward, his wife and mother beside him, his children and grandchildren close by, the cheering went on and on. The band played "Auld Lang Syne." When it was done, FDR asked that it be repeated, and he and the entire audience joined in song. Then in an open car, to the horror of the Secret Service, ER and FDR drove around the stadium surrounded by a wild display of hope and trust, as the roaring cheers continued into the night.

Harold Ickes considered it "the greatest political speech I have ever heard":

> [FDR presented] the fundamental issue that must be decided in this country . . . whether to have real freedom for the mass of people, not only political but economic, or whether we are to be governed by a group of economic overlords. It is clear that the President's speech created a profound impression in the country.

ER wanted her husband's splendid words transformed into real action, actual legislation, democratic citizen movements committed to change. She worried, as she always worried during campaigns, that platforms and promises would dissolve into nothing after the election. In her subsequent article for *The Democratic Digest* she wrote about that star-filled, rhetorically galvanizing night:

> You could not feel anything but solemn, for no man faces such a great crowd . . . without recognizing the fearful responsibility that rests upon him and how many of his fellow citizens depend on his sincerity and ability. . . .

ER also had a message for political women in 1936. To all women in public life she offered specific advice and encouragement, based on her own experiences—and especially relevant, she noted, to this campaign:

> You cannot take anything personally.
> You cannot bear grudges.
> You must finish the day's work when the day's work is done.
> You cannot get discouraged too easily.
> You have to take defeat over and over again and pick up and go on.
> Be sure of your facts.
> Argue the other side with a friend until you have found the answer to every point which might be brought up against you.
> Women who are willing to be leaders must stand out and be shot at. More and more they are going to do it, and more and more they should do it.

ER subsequently added: "Every woman in public life needs to develop skin as tough as rhinoceros hide," which seemed particularly appropriate after FDR's triumph in Philadelphia. Upon their return to Washington, FDR complied even more fully with his advisers who wanted ER kept as quiet and as invisible as possible. With nothing to do, ER wrote Hick glum letters, and berated herself for her sense of detachment: "It has always been so [somber] a business for me (living I mean). . . . Gee! I wish I could even be excited about all this, I can't and I hate myself!"

Despite her feelings, she carried on, and called women's meetings to plan strategy. ER's core group of state and national leaders were the worker bees of the campaign effort, block by block; they prepared the literature; they rang the doorbells.

In New York, the entire campaign organization was built around ER's veteran network and remained under the much-concealed direction of ER herself. Caroline O'Day was associate state chair; Nancy Cook ran O'Day's office; Agnes Brown Leach was in charge of all organization work; Bessie Beatty ran the publicity department; Grace Greene ran the speakers' bureau; *New York Post* publisher Dorothy Schiff Backer was radio chair, assisted by Elinor Morgenthau; Mary Dreier conducted literature distribution; and Mrs. N. Taylor Phillips was in charge of voter registration.

State activities were coordinated weekly with Dewson's national efforts. It was an amazing and complex apparatus—which worked. With one caveat: It was up to the men to call upon and use their efforts.

But the new group around FDR was not interested in their contributions. Moreover, the press was vicious, and ER was routinely the target. Even a friendly article declared her a debit, or at least a mixed blessing. In July a *New York Times Magazine* article by Kathleen McLaughlin profiled ER. Her political views were favorably presented, but her role in electoral politics was dubious:

> There is no middle ground with regard to Eleanor Roosevelt. . . . She is undeniably both an asset and a liability. . . . It is possible that no woman before her will have swung so many votes both for and against. . . .

For all ER's disclaimers about silence during the campaign, McLaughlin wrote, everyone knew about her "private post office" to FDR, the "small basket" by his bedside she filled at the close of each day with observations, analyses, and reports. Nobody doubted that the busiest First Lady remained busy. She received over "105,000 letters in a single year" and traveled "38,000 miles in 1933, 42,000 miles in 1934, and 35,000 in 1935." Her own personal goal was still to "go everywhere and see everything." ER remained Eleanor Everywhere, with endless influence.

The article hardened the Democratic strategy to keep her under wraps. FDR's new advisers emphasized opposition to ER's column, her controversial pronouncements, and especially her paid lectures and broadcasts. The Republican campaign glorified the traditional concept of First Lady: Mrs. Landon was depicted as the perfect prairie wife—hardworking, silent, at home. FDR's inner circle was envious.

Her feelings in turmoil, ER was unusually alone. Hick, still with others, sent letters of encouragement, pep talks on paper to raise ER's spirits. ER replied to a letter now lost concerning Philadelphia: "You sound happy and you are right, when I write you stupid, sorry-for-myself letters, I would deny all my sentiments six months hence. I know at the time I say it I'm an idiot!"

Hick's own attitude during June and July seemed carefree. No longer a journalist on the campaign trail, she seemed almost disinterested. Her new commitment to having fun was no possible source of comfort for ER, although Hick tried to entertain the First Lady. During the summer of 1936, Hick wrote a series of uncharacteristic letters filled with follies and risqué jokes; her usual political observations were replaced with vivid descriptions of pastoral places, and visits to burlesque and drag shows.

From a resort hotel on the shore of Lake Superior, Hick wrote:

> Dearest: At last I've found the perfect place, in all the world, to spend a weekend. This is it. A simple, quiet, scrupulously clean little hotel away up on the northernmost tip of the Upper Peninsula of Michigan. Inexpensive. Alicent and I have a lovely room, with water lapping against the rocks right outside our window. . . . Very good food. Nice, simple, friendly people. And all this in a setting beautiful beyond description.

They had driven over a magnificent road built by the WPA: "Really dear, that road is one of the most beautiful WPA jobs I've ever seen, anywhere." And the scenery reminded her of the Gaspé Peninsula. The lake was azure, the hills lush, "beautiful forests all along the way. Lots of virgin pine. (One of the Old Man's best remarks while I was there recently: 'Will you please tell me of what earthly use is a virgin pine?')." She continued:

> I wish so much that you were here tonight, dear. It's away after 9 o'clock, but still light. . . . This is a beautiful little bay, so deeply blue in the day time, but now all orchid and pink and gold in the sunset. Scattered about it are rocky little islands covered with scrubby, hardy little pines. They suggest Chinese screens—or Japanese prints. And it's so quiet. So very, very restful. . . .

But there was no radio, and no newspaper. She could not even read FDR's speech. "Goodnight, dear. I wish I could bring you here sometime. . . ."

They had no plans to see each other until the end of September, which was such "a long way off," and ER assured Hick, "I can meet you anywhere you wish."

After her Michigan vacation with Alicent, Hick went to Chicago, where she spent most of her time with a male friend named Kruger:

> Kruger complicates the situation in that I have to dress every night and dine out with him. But he amuses himself daytimes, and I do like having

him around. I'm gradually making a liberal out of him, and it's fun. Tonight we dined at Colsino's, one of the less lurid night clubs which is famous chiefly for its Capone connections. For the most part, we found it depressing. The inanities of sin! There was one funny thing. They had billed one June St. Clair "America's most alluring woman." After waiting all evening, we finally saw her. She was fat, forty, very much bleached. Her hair looked like cotton. She bustled about the floor for a few seconds, looking for all the world like a worried, frowsy housewife. Then she stopped in front of the curtain, dropped her dress, which was all she had on, and stood there for a split second—naked and very UN-lovely. . . .

Came back and found several dozen flat-chested gals and anemic young men, delegates to a Baptist young people's convention singing "Old Black Joe" in the lobby! In the Continental Room, just off the lobby— air cooled and very expensive—there's a dancer who calls herself Countess Something-or-Other. She wears a very sheer jade green chiffon gown with nothing under it save a very tiny "jock strap" and an ineffectual brassiere. . . . Isn't Chicago funny! Tomorrow morning we're going to the zoo. . . .

While Hick tried to cheer up the depressed First Lady with accounts of nightlife in the heartland, ER struggled to enjoy diversions. During the July Fourth weekend she joined FDR's party aboard the *Potomac* for a cruise down the James River. Hardly an assemblage of her preferred mates, it included Ickes, Missy LeHand, Farley, several politicians, and FDR's Harvard friends, courtly Virginians who impressed Ickes: Even "the abolition of slavery has not served to destroy this distinctive . . . culture."

ER wrote Hick:

Dearest, how I wish you were here tonight. . . . It was nice on deck but I hated making polite conversation and you would have hated it even more, wouldn't you? I think I envy you off with one person and when the day's work is done you don't have to be with a crowd. Oh! well, most of the time I'd rather have the crowd than be alone with any of them but I'd like a few hours with you now and then!

While ER felt refreshed by a visit with England's outspoken social work leader and wife of the new ambassador, Lady Stella Reading, Esther Lape, and Elizabeth Read, FDR enjoyed an unusual private party at Harold Ickes's place. Missy LeHand had told Ickes that the president "wished he knew some place in the country where he could go and have a quiet and undisturbed evening" with friends. Ickes offered his home, but since FDR had not been to the home of any other cabinet member "the White House wanted the thing kept as quiet as possible."

It was a small group, with Missy LeHand, Grace Tully, Tom Corcoran, and several others; an evening made notable by splendid food and drink. Ickes wrote:

> I served Chateau Yquem, a good claret, and a good vintage champagne. We had liqueurs afterward and when the dining table had been removed, the butlers brought out and put on a table, with a supply of cracked ice, Scotch, rye and bourbon whiskey, gin and Bacardi rum. . . .
>
> The party was a great success. . . . Tom Corcoran had brought his accordion . . . and sang practically the whole evening. . . . The President seemed to enjoy himself hugely and he entered into the fun very naturally and spontaneously. . . .
>
> [FDR carried] his liquor well. He must have had five highballs after dinner. He drank gin and ginger ale but he never showed the slightest effect. . . . He must have had a good time because he didn't leave until half past twelve and then only after Miss LeHand prodded him two or three times and insisted that he must go home and to bed.

It was precisely the kind of drinking party that ER would have hated. During the summer of 1936, her world and his seemed to grow ever more separate and distinct.

On 14 July, ER saw FDR and her sons off for a leisurely sail on a chartered yacht, the *Sewanee*, to arrive at Campobello at month's end, when he would be joined by ER and her party. Until then ER spent time at Val-Kill, to work on political strategy with the Women's Democratic Committee. She wrote Hick: "I feel fine and very cheerful but I'd like to feel I was going to have you in Hyde Park in August."

FDR's political advisers were either puzzled or enraged by his nonchalance regarding the election, and his decision to take a vacation at such a critical time. Steve Early and Stanley High were in touch with ER, who agreed to wire FDR regarding urgent decisions for speeches that needed to be made before Alf Landon's campaign dominated the news.

FDR refused to take Alf Landon seriously; and he paid no attention to the third-party candidacy of William Lemke, whose Union Party was comprised of radicals and fascists. It was led by Dr. Frank Townsend, whose old-age insurance scheme competed with Democratic alternatives, and brutal racists and anti-Semites, including Huey Long's successor Gerald L. K. Smith and Detroit's radio priest Father Charles Coughlin. Coughlin astounded observers when he pulled off his coat and collar at the Union Party convention to call FDR a traitor and liar. With little hope of victory, Unionists fronted for Landon; and prominent conservative Democrats defected to him all spring.

Several summer polls indicated Landon had a significant lead. FDR's team was actually in disarray, with nobody clearly in charge, engulfed by disagreements and rivalries. ER looked on aghast and angry. Ickes was also aroused: The Landon camp has gone into high gear, and "we have continued to sit by. . . ."

> [While FDR] smiles and fishes and the rest of us worry and fume. . . .
> With even our own private polls showing an alarming falling off in the President's vote, the whole situation is incomprehensible to me. It was loudly proclaimed that Louie Howe had supplied most of the political strategy . . . and I am beginning to believe that this must have been true. I do know that Howe was the only one who dared to talk to him frankly and fearlessly. . . . He could reach him not only directly but through Mrs. Roosevelt. Jim Farley tries to please the President. . . . I do not think that he takes advice from anybody. . . .

As late as 20 July, Steve Early told Ickes that "there were no campaign plans and no budget." Ickes despaired: "We are in bad shape and in grave danger." Stanley High told him:

> Mrs. Roosevelt is worried and so is Farley, but the President himself seems to be up in the clouds. . . .

Because the women were so completely organized, the situation was not really dire. They had assembled a series of appealing speakers, highlighted by stars and heroes, including Ruth Bryan Owen, who agreed to leave her diplomatic post in Denmark to tour the country for FDR. Dewson wrote:

> I am all for your having an airplane. And I do wish that you would look with favor on having Phoebe Omlie of the U.S. Department of Aeronautics to pilot you. She is a superb pilot and in the early days won cross country races from the men. She is one of the few recognized and licensed airplane mechanics. Better than all, she is a very calm and easy person to get along with.

Ruth Bryan Owen agreed:

> I would be a poor sort of feminist if I had any inhibitions about a woman pilot. I am delighted to join up with Miss Omlie.

Ruth Bryan Owen's plans were only slightly upended in June when she unexpectedly announced: "Now I would suggest that you get seated and hold on to the arms of the chair before you read the following paragraph!" She had fallen in love with "one Kammerjunker Kaptjan Borge Rohde, of the Danish

King's Life Guards and Gentleman in Attendance on the King at the Danish Court." They would be married as soon as possible, after reaching the United States. A university scholar, Captain Rohde was a linguist who impressed everyone with his vast charm and wit. On 10 July, the Roosevelts hosted their wedding party at Hyde Park. It was a memorable occasion, jolly and glamorous. Fannie Hurst was the bride's attendant, and the party stimulated political activity. Ruth Bryan Owen Rohde resigned from the diplomatic corps, and made more than fifty speeches around the country for FDR, accompanied by her new husband.

But as July unfolded, the Women's Committee seemed to be working in a vacuum, and ER considered the situation alarming. Even in Campobello the inaction galled her. As she read the newspapers and polls, she could not remain silent or inactive. She considered what Louis Howe would do and fired off a rigorous memo, which covered all the issues Howe, supported by his pool of six hundred workers, had fully coordinated in the past.

ER cast her memo widely—to the president, Jim Farley, Charley Michelson, Stanley High, Steve Early, and Mollie Dewson—and she wanted immediate action: Landon's people had hired advertisers and radio scriptwriters, "and the whole spirit is the spirit of a crusade." Now "we have got to get going and going quickly." She wanted it understood that her letter was "a matter of record" and expected "to get the answers in black and white":

> 1. At the meeting in Washington, the President said that Mr. Michelson, Steve Early, Stanley High and Henry Suydam would constitute the publicity steering committee, and I take it this must include radio, speeches, movies, pamphlets, fliers, news releases and trucks. . . .
> I hope a meeting will be held immediately for organizing and defining the duties of the members and that you will have the minutes kept at every meeting in order that a copy may go to the President and if the committee is willing, one to me as well so that I may know just what is done each time also.
> 2. Who is responsible for studying news reports and suggesting answers to charges, etc.?
> 3. Who is responsible for . . . the radio campaign, getting the speakers through the speakers' bureau, making the arrangements in the states for people to listen and getting in touch with Chester Davis, for instance on agriculture . . . ? In other words, who is making decisions under your committee . . . ?
> 4. Who is in charge of research? Have we . . . complete information concerning all activities of the New Deal . . . ?
> Who is to check on all inconsistencies in Landon's pronouncements . . . ?
> 5. What definite plans have we made for tying in the other public-

ity organizations, both of men and women with the national publicity organization? . . .

    6. Have you mapped out continuous publicity steps which will be taken between now and November? Is there any way at least of charting a tentative plan of strategy for the whole campaign . . . ?

    7. In the doubtful and Republican states what special attention do you plan to give . . . ?

    8. Who is handling news reels . . . ?

ER went on for several more points, and she had specific suggestions: "I think it would be well to start some Negro speakers, like [Mary McLeod] Bethune to speak at church meetings and that type of Negro organization."

Her formidable memo reflected her years as Howe's closest colleague in building a successful political organization. ER demanded answers to her questions, "mailed to reach us" at Campobello no later than 27 July, when FDR was scheduled to arrive.

ER wrote her daughter on 24 July that the Democratic National Committee's "publicity was a disgrace to their organization! Steve has answered my memo with explanations and excuses and I await the others. . . ."

Jim Farley sent a ten-page, single-spaced reply, which reassured her. Farley had a long talk with Will Alexander, "who is very active in the Negro movement, and he would create a Negro division." Sidney Hillman's labor party movement promised to bring in "many thousands" of people who had not previously voted.

ER was relieved by Farley's full reply. She had feared his opposition to FDR's purge campaign would limit Farley's activities. Farley had opposed FDR's public rebuke of powerful Southern Democratic leaders. Farley was stunned when, with Georgia's Senator Walter George beside him on a campaign platform, FDR announced: There "is little difference between the feudal system and the fascist system. If you believe in the one you lean to the other."

Farley had not been among those who advised a dramatic convention courtship for the Negro vote. But ER was delighted. She had first crossed the Democratic Party's color bar in 1924—when she invited Mary White Ovington of the NAACP to send a plank to her women's platform committee. Ovington had replied: The NAACP intended to secure "legal and civil rights for colored men and women," and wanted ER's committee to include a plank that guaranteed the protection of voting rights for colored women in every "part of the country."

In 1936, for the first time, that seemed the official position of the Democratic Party—and it upset congressional diehards of the formerly solid South. Twelve states, including Kentucky and West Virginia, sent black delegates to the Philadelphia convention. According to William Leuchtenberg: "The convention was the first to seat a black woman as a regular delegate and the first to provide for a black press conference and to seat blacks in the regular press box." When an African-American minister gave the opening prayer at one session, "Cotton Ed" Smith stormed out shouting, " 'My God, he's black as melted midnight." When Chicago member of congress Arthur W. Mitchell, elected in 1934, "became the first black ever to address a Democratic convention," Smith left for South Carolina, announcing: " 'I cannot and will not be a party to the recognition of the Fourteenth and Fifteenth Amendments."

ER was convinced that her husband's success depended on the votes of blacks, Southern race radicals, youth, and the left-labor coalition, and wrote immediately to Will Alexander.

ER was no replacement for Louis Howe, but she did move the campaign forward. Moreover, she promoted radical biracial youth and labor movements, including the Southern Tenant Farmers movement, for which she was most specifically attacked by Liberty Leaguers, breakaway Southern Democrats, and Lemkeites. This hurt Landon, not FDR. Nineteen thirty-six was a year of radical unity, and ER represented the power of the popular front.

The haters of 1936 declared the Roosevelt administration dedicated to a mulatto America: Negroes were invited to White House banquets and slept in White House beds. ER and her friends supported the antilynching bill "for the purpose of permissive ravishment."

A foul and widely reprinted ditty purportedly represented the First Couple's theme song:

> You Kiss the Niggers / And I'll Kiss the Jews
> And We'll Stay in the White House
> As long as We Choose

In 1936, Liberty Leaguers and Lemkeites fell into a political void. Landon and the Republican Party pleaded with them to take their support elsewhere.

In August, Ickes addressed the annual convention of the NAACP and boasted that the Roosevelt administration had made the "greatest advance since the Civil War toward assuring the Negro that degree of justice to which he is entitled and that equality of opportunity under the law which is implicit in his American citizenship." In October, Mary McLeod Bethune told a radio audience: "Never before in the history of America has Negro youth been offered such opportunities."

While FDR sailed with his sons, ER contemplated her own life. With her friends scattered, she mostly brooded through the most exciting campaign of her life, with time on her hands and nothing she needed to do. In a reflective mood, she felt again a need to reconnect with her past and tell her own story. During FDR's first campaign she had decided to edit and publish her father's letters, to write *It's Up to the Women*, and to write a children's book. Now she decided to write her memoirs. ER wrote to calm and fortify herself under duress. From July to November, around the edges of her husband's campaign, she worked on a book to be called *This Is My Story*.

Almost nonchalantly, she wrote Hick: "I rather think I'll write up my childhood for the kids." There was, she wrote, no other way her grandchildren would ever know all those "people no one else can remember." Everything was so different, and living conditions were so changed, "I could almost feel I was writing about another person it all seems so far away."

In mid-August, ER spent part of the week at Democratic Party headquarters in New York City. She met with all the groups to mediate their competing interests, edited the literature, and did whatever came to hand. Once campaign chair, she was now administrator without portfolio, and she hated it. Nobody in FDR's circle asked her to do anything at all.

She disliked her situation so entirely that she wrote about it in "My Day"—in an attempt to be philosophical:

> Since I am no longer responsible to anyone else for the accomplishment of any specific piece of work, I have had a great opportunity to observe the work of other people. . . .
>
> I hope that if I am ever back in some kind of executive position, my present opportunities for observation will prove fruitful. . . .

ER concluded her column with hopes for youth, a future generation of activists eager for responsibility: Those who "can think up new ways of giving service, different ways of doing things . . . those who have imagination and originality will get somewhere. There is always room at the top. . . ."

While ER felt keenly the leadership gap at Democratic Party headquarters, she put her faith in the possibilities of the burgeoning youth movement, so refreshing, outspoken, and exciting.

She was cheered by evidence of a new people's coalition that emerged at summer's end, with a vigor that surprised forecasters. In addition to the new power of organized labor, led by John L. Lewis, a former Republican, who contributed a vast sum of CIO money to FDR, nonpartisan progressives and humanitarians forged a new FDR coalition—based partly on loyalty to ER.

The *Women's Democratic News* was particularly pleased when Lillian Wald, founder of the Visiting Nurse Service and Henry Street Settlement, the "first lady in social work," agreed to write an article, "Why I Am for Roosevelt."

Having listened to both conventions with earnest hope, she was "discouraged" that "nothing significant" was said by Republicans: "It was sad that in probably the worst crisis that the country has ever known . . . hate was the most obvious sentiment. . . ."

Wald despised their abusive carping, their petty lack of gratitude for all New Deal achievements: "I kept thinking of a valorous neighbor who at great risk and discomfort plunged through the broken ice to rescue [a] small boy. . . . When the rescuer carried the child to his father, he was rewarded with: 'Where's his hat?' "

Wald firmly believed FDR would "go further" in social security and "correct past mistakes" concerning all issues that involved human betterment.

In conclusion, Wald wrote personally:

> May I say that Franklin Delano Roosevelt and Eleanor Roosevelt have given themselves in great ways. . . . They have set an example of great power and unselfishness to us and to the world, and . . . have earned our love and gratitude and loyalty and support.

Wald's support was important to ER. After she and Elinor Morgenthau visited her in August, ER wrote a column to celebrate her mentor:

> I always fall under the spell of her personality and wonder what quality it is which makes an individual able to sway others by the sheer force of her own sympathy and understanding of human beings. . . .

But no moments of pleasure or diversion satisfied ER. To be idled and mute within the political blizzard wore on her nerves. During the autumnal phase of the campaign, the imposed silence sickened her. In September, she took to her bed with aches everywhere and a raging fever. She had never before been felled by illness, and her condition frightened everybody who loved her.

FDR, who had never seen his wife take to her bed so completely, canceled appointments and rushed to her bedside. *The New York Times* explained that he left for Washington from a rain-soaked day at Harvard, where he delivered "a plea for tolerance before an international audience" assembled to celebrate Harvard's three hundredth anniversary. Originally scheduled to go to Hyde Park to celebrate his mother's eighty-third birthday, he changed his plans "at the last minute."

ER was touched by everyone's attention, and noted in a "My Day" column:

> It is so unusual for me to be in bed that each new person arriving looks at me with a more concerned expression than the last. Even my brother, who is very much the way I am and who thinks things are better downed afoot than abed, comes in to give me a worried once-over twice a day.

Frances Perkins sent "beautiful red roses," with an unusually warm note: "Dear Eleanor—My dearest love & good wishes. Take care of your precious self for once!!"

Lillian Wald wrote: "Beloved Lady and Friend . . . [this is to remind you] you are not the 'forgotten woman' and that the 'flying buttress' [FDR's term for Wald] to the Administration is active and primarily laments your separation from your beloved tasks."

Hilda Smith and Aubrey Williams detailed the progress of ER's special interests. Williams's account of WPA's first fourteen months cheered ER and pierced through her fever to remind her what they were fighting for. To "avoid the development of a permanent class of chronic dependents," and to provide decent work at real wages: "No larger, more complicated, or more difficult task was ever attempted by a government in peace or in war."

WPA's contributions were tangible for workers, and for the nation:

> In place of bitterness, gnawing and growing discontent, and wasted skills of hand and brain, we have . . . :
>
> 109,000 public buildings . . . including 83,000 schools
>
> 400,000 miles of road improved, 121,000 miles made new. . . .
>
> 5,000 water control works . . . 1100 new swimming pools, 5000 tennis courts, and 25,000 playgrounds built. . . .
>
> 1,000,000 children immunized against typhoid and diphtheria
>
> 500,000 people taught to write the English language. . . .

For all the concerned and cheerful notes that flooded into her bedroom, ER's illness was not quickly diagnosed, nor corrected. She was mystified: "Everyone who is sent in to make a test . . . goes away saying that as far as his particular branch of medicine is concerned I am a perfect specimen." Yet her fever lingered, and she could barely move.

Through it all, ER dictated her daily column to Tommy and studied the morning papers:

> [The newspapers] are rather terrifying reading these days, with Japan taking over Shanghai and the ever-growing tenseness in Europe. I have a curious kind of resentment about the physical damage done to age-old monuments in Spain.
>
> It seems as though a generation that had gone mad was wiping out things which are really not their heritage alone, but the heritage of the world at large. We have looked upon these things so long as sources of education and culture and pleasure, that to think of them being destroyed in the course of a few weeks is a very depressing sensation.

ER could not abide the devastation of Spain and repeatedly wrote anguished columns against fascist bombings and atrocities. She did not understand why there were not howls of protest everywhere against the dreadful situations people faced:

> We read daily about people being killed in Spain, not only soldiers, but women and children. We know that in this country many people do not have enough to eat, or proper medical attention, or an opportunity to lead a normal life, but none of these situations evokes the same passionate interest as a [fictional romance or] story. . . .

ER's physical collapse, with echoes and reverberations of her youthful Griselda crises, frightened FDR. At the prospect of actually losing his wife's presence and support, FDR showed a new level of consideration, and took her less for granted. After September 1936, he personally planned special events and birthday parties for ER, as she had always done for him. Her illness drew ER and FDR closer together, and she reentered the campaign. Although she remained in the background, except when crowds called for her to speak, ER was not the only woman aboard the campaign train; she was not alone; and she was not bored.

Bess Furman described the scene as "victory rode the rails." Amid all the noise of a presidential special, ER sat serene, read, knitted, wrote: "Cram and jam and crush and rush and jostle. Bands, bouquets, noted names, significant speeches." And there ER sat "calmly in the midst of turmoil knitting sweaters, dictating her column to Tommy, even writing her memoirs." When she read some of the pages aloud, they "sounded as though they had come from the depths of silence, instead of right out of bedlam. . . ."

On the campaign train of 1936, ER recalled the emotional turmoil she felt during the 1920 campaign train when her friendship with Louis Howe really took root, and she realized that her life with Franklin would always be in part a public life. In 1920 FDR was nominated for the vice presidency, and ER wrote in 1936:

> I am sure I was glad for my husband, but it never occurred to me to be much excited. I had come to accept the fact that public service was my husband's great interest and I always tried to make the necessary family adjustments easy. I carried on the children's lives and my own as calmly as could be, and while I was always a part of the public aspect of our lives, still I felt detached and objective, as though I were looking at someone else's life. This seems to have remained with me down to the present day. . . . It is as though you lived two lives, one of your own and the other which belonged to the circumstances that surround you.

It was ER's habit to tell her story, particularly the story of her childhood, to her closest friends and confidantes. But to share her life with the people of America was a brave and extraordinary expression of trust, and community.

She wanted certain things known, and she believed her experiences and struggles would be helpful to other women. But it was also as if she now needed to reconnect with those moments in her life which had given her strength. Because she wrote her memoirs so shortly after Howe's death, in an environment she shared particularly with him, her brief references to her great friend, particularly on the 1920 train, are evocative. It was on that trip that ER learned "a certain adaptability to circumstances," and she credited Louis Howe for her education.

> He knew that I was somewhat bewildered by some of the things that were expected of me as a candidate's wife. I never before had spent my days going on and off platforms, listening apparently with rapt attention to much the same speech. . . .
>
> Louis Howe began to break down my antagonism by occasionally knocking at my stateroom door and asking if he might discuss a speech with me. I was flattered and before long I found myself discussing a wide range of subjects . . .

While ER told many emotional truths in *This Is My Story*, she carefully avoided many others. She wrote nothing of her intimate life, gave no hint of marital tension, and intended to be discreet about the controversial issues which divided America. Starkly, however, her passage on servants and race illuminated the great chasm still to cross over in order to reach beyond disrespect and diminishing stereotypes.

On Sunday, 11 October, as the train procceded into Cheyenne, Wyoming, ER was unusually feted for her birthday. While she always made a great fuss over FDR's birthday, she had tended to ignore her own and FDR had often been away at sea on that day.

ER wrote her daughter:

> Many many thanks for my gloves and birthday letters. . . . I wish I could have been with you and not had quite such a public birthday. Father even mentioned it in his speech to the crowd and I told him afterwards I could cheerfully have wrung his neck!

Tiny Chaney joined the train at Omaha and, with Earl Miller, added a special glow to her birthday. There were countless letters, and a very nice party; and Mark McCloskey added an Irish toast: "May the best day you ever had be the worst one you'll ever see."

In October, ER felt compelled to break her political silence—for family reasons. Her cousin Alice Longworth, in her own vigorous campaign for Landon, attacked FDR as a "Mollycoddle," with a "Mollycoddle Philosophy."

ER was outraged, and she leaped for her pen. There she was one cold and blustery morning, as she read that headline, sitting beside her husband "without a coat," while the rest of us "had pulled our coats around ourselves closely." FDR was no mollycoddle, which implied "dependency and an easy life." She compared his dedication despite all physical odds to her Uncle Theodore's commitment to a "strenuous life." Nobody, she insisted, "who really knew both men" could call her husband such a name. TR always insisted on the "security of the home" first. "Naturally, that means an easy and dependent life for the youth in that home."

FDR had "brought himself back from what might have been an entire life of invalidism, to physical, mental and spiritual strength and activity." He could not be accused of either "preaching or exemplifying" a mollycoddle philosophy. He did not seek "greater security and ease of life" for mollycoddles, but for hardworking people. Mollycoddles were not the maids and workers, but those who have had "too much ease, too much dependency, too much luxury of every kind."

ER explained the difference:

> [I knew a woman who] complained sadly to her maid that she must close up one of her five estates and give up the support of a hospital she had subsidized, because of her increased taxes. The maid reflected . . . that out of her reduced wages she had to support five people during the depression instead of her customary two.
>
> I wonder which of the two, the maid or the mistress, was in danger of acquiring a mollycoddle philosophy? Which of the two needed a little help and concern to make life easier?

By the end of October, ER discovered that even her silence made headlines. In Providence, for example, the *Journal* announced: "First Lady Does Unexpected Here." Arriving on the night train from New York, ER, her secretary, and an unidentified newspaperwoman bypassed a waiting crowd and the Secret Service ready to take her to the Biltmore Hotel. Instead she "walked briskly" into the Union Station restaurant for a quiet, leisurely breakfast. "The First Lady checked her own five bags at the check room, tipped her own porters, and then proceeded to the telephone booths. . . . Attired in a pinstriped navy blue tailleur, a silver fox scarf and a wine-colored velour hat," ER and her "two women escorts" were unbothered, "practically unnoticed," in the station, although she consented to a reporter's questions.

She had "no idea" about her future plans: "My dear, I don't know. I go where the President goes." Told the president's special train had arrived and awaited her "in the siding beyond the station," she ran off to meet him— assuring a local police official she knew the way. As she dashed down several streets, the large crowd began to recognize her, and "the clapping increased to a loud crescendo."

In October, according to newspaper polls, the election was very close—with Alf Landon running slightly ahead. But huge and enthusiastic crowds throughout the country convinced FDR that there was no contest. In September, when he began his formal campaign with a speech in Syracuse, he dismissed the Popular Front support. As if to answer charges of communism daily hurled at him by Hearst, the Liberty Leaguers, and Father Coughlin, he announced: "I have not sought, I do not seek, I repudiate the support of any advocate of Communism or of any other alien 'ism' which would by fair means or foul change our American democracy." New Deal liberalism was American conservatism: "Reform if you would preserve."

Then, on 31 October, FDR's campaign tour culminated with a rousing radical speech at Madison Square Garden in New York City, which thrilled the Popular Front and most liberals, while it caused others to sputter with horror. He rejected the Republican doctrine that that government "is best which is most indifferent." The enemies of fiscal hope and social peace were now well known:

> [B]usiness and financial monopoly, speculation, reckless banking, class antagonism, sectionalism, war profiteering. *They* had begun to consider the government of the United States as a mere appendage to their own affairs. And we know now that Government by organized *money* is just as dangerous as Government by organized *mob.*
>
> Never before in all our history have these forces been so united against one candidate as they stand today. They are unanimous in their *hate of me—and I welcome their hatred.*
>
> I should like to have it said of my first Administration that in it the forces of selfishness and of lust for power met their *match.* I should like to have it said of my second Administration that in it *these forces met their master.*

For some, that speech ended an era. FDR's former friend Raymond Moley despaired: "Thoughtful citizens were stunned by the violence, the bombast, the naked demagoguery of these sentences." For others that speech represented a new time, a truly New Deal.

Not as certain as her husband that the polls were wrong, and eager to ensure his victory, ER sprinted to the finish line. She spoke to dozens of organizations and personally went door to door. Two days before the election, ER spoke at four major events, including a Women's Democratic Club luncheon for six hundred at the Hotel Commodore, where she praised the impact women had on politics: "As a rule women join political parties and organizations because they have certain things which they want to see accomplished." Now more than ever the "spirit" of women and their tremendous influence could be seen throughout the government. She also spoke at teas and luncheons, where she continued to claim she did not "talk politics," only FDR did that. She received tumultuous applause everywhere, especially at the Essex House luncheon of the National Pro-Roosevelt Association of Women Lawyers, where she addressed eight hundred women attorneys and judges.

On 3 November, the family voted at Hyde Park at eleven in the morning. FDR and his mother arrived in the first car; ER, who drove her own car with Nancy Cook, was the third to vote, and she drove off with her son Franklin, Jr. SDR was "enveloped in a royal purple cape resembling an Inverness" and wore "her usual" black velvet hat. ER wore a blue tweed suit with a white scarf, and "a sport hat." Anna and John then voted. As she left the polls, ER promised reporters a buffet supper when they arrived to monitor the returns with the family.

On 3 November 1936, FDR won an unprecedented landslide victory. Over 44 million Americans, representing 83 percent of eligible voters, voted. FDR received 27,476,673 votes, Landon received 16,679,583. His victory was the largest in presidential history. He lost only Maine and Vermont, to achieve an electoral college victory of 523 to 8. There were great victories in each house of Congress as well. The 75th Congress would be over 75 percent Democratic.

FDR now had a mandate to fulfill the promise of the New Deal, the promise of economic and political democracy for all.

The week after the election, ER's imposed silence officially ended. While FDR embarked on a cruise to South America, ER proceeded on a lecture tour. She told reporters who asked why she was not with her husband that she chose the lectures "instead of the cruise because her husband never had approved of women on battleships. . . ." They would be reunited after Thanksgiving.

ER was joyous and eager to plunge into the most controversial issues before the nation. Her month-long tour took her west from Pennsylvania to Michigan. On 8 November in Philadelphia, she addressed an audience of two thousand at Temple University, where she made a rousing speech on the need for democratic action and community activism.

The most dramatic moment of the evening occurred during the question period, when she called for changes in the Social Security Act to include domestic and agricultural workers. "The act is not static. . . . In England where they have had social security legislation for nearly 25 years, there have been revisions nearly every year." The fight for the future had just begun: "We must not think that our leaders can do what we wish done unless we do our share." Elated to be unmuzzled, ER hit the lecture circuit with vigor and publicly criticized her husband's compromises. She called upon every citizen to demand more from their government—to demand real social security.

20: Postelection Missions

$\mathcal{E}$R was profoundly moved by the "glorious day" of triumph FDR's vote of confidence represented. The people had voted with thunderous clarity, "in the privacy of a voting booth. In the end the will of the majority is carried out peacefully." For all the name calling and crude misinformation, American democracy worked. But only individual involvement, grassroots activism, would result in the actual changes needed to fulfill her husband's promises.

In column after column, in every public lecture, she urged citizens to realize "that true democracy is the effort of the people individually to carry their share of the burden of government." People, acting on behalf of their own needs and wants, must hold government accountable.

ER wondered what her husband really meant to do now, actually do. She wrote her daughter as she toured the Middle West:

> I've just written Pa to say goodbye. . . . Darling, if he wanted to be King or dictator they [would] *fight* for him! It is terrifying & yet it must thrill him to know how many people he has put on their feet. A rather grand, gaunt looking detective who was with us last night [in Kansas City] said to me "I was lost in '33, didn't believe in the country or in anything. I'm 53, I've worked for the public all my life & never been late to work once & I've been a [Republican] didn't vote for Mr. R in '32 but in two years he had me. He gave me back my courage & I've got back all I thought I'd lost & this year I *worked* for him!"

ER devoted her lecture tour to the need for ardent citizen action. Everywhere she spoke, from River Forest, Minnesota, to Far Rockaway, New York, large audiences responded with enthusiasm. She even managed to keep her unruly voice low, aided, she wrote Hick, by "this catarrh which is a pest."

Eventually, even she was satisfied with her own performance. To FDR she wrote that all went "well but very hectically. It would be easy to be a lecturer or the wife of the President but both. Oh! My."

ER was relieved to be back in public life on her own terms, and her depression lifted entirely. She was also cheered that her protracted separation from Hick was over. She had not returned even when ER took to her bed in September. Rather, she considered removing herself completely from ER. After Spain was torn by civil war, Hick decided to become a foreign correspondent. ER discouraged her, and wrote in September: "I'd hate to go to Europe & see a war" but "if you really want it I'll speak to Roy Howard," owner of the Scripps-Howard newspaper syndicate. With more enthusiasm, she noted that Tommy thought Grover Whelan "would give you the NY Fair publicity job." Unable to break away, Hick again abandoned her reporter's dream, and agreed to the World's Fair job. ER was relieved.

Before ER left for her tour, she and Hick had a pleasant reunion. The only tension of the evening involved Hick's Minneapolis friends, whom ER looked forward to meeting. But Hick worried they might be treated casually, or coldly. ER was stunned by Hick's lack of trust. Hick was stunned that ER did not appreciate how torn she felt, both hesitant and eager for her old best friends to meet her new best friend. Tommy had compounded Hick's agony when she tried to protect ER's time, and said ER was booked many hours each day. Evidently Hick exploded; then she apologized profusely, for weeks.

Ultimately she sent ER a long letter filled with information about each friend, practically dossiers. She ranked them in importance to her and explained who might want to meet ER, with personal time, who might merely attend her lecture and shake her hand: "Well, if any of these people *should* show up, will you please be extra nice to them? For my sake?"

The prospect of ER's meeting her great friends sent Hick into a frenzy. Perhaps she feared that ER would not like or appreciate her down-home, unpretentious, hard-drinking, mostly journalist buddies, women and men. Perhaps she feared that they would tell her too much, repeat hilarious stories, reveal old secrets. Perhaps she merely felt guilty, since she hated to be with ER's friends. Whatever the reason, for days her letters were filled with apologies and insecurity.

ER knitted Hick a sweater while she traveled; it "is growing rapidly and looks lovely." Hick sent the monthly calendars she hand-created, which ER used for her appointments. She also sent ER clippings and assorted correspondence to entertain her on the road. Hick was glad to see that three thousand people filled the hall in Philadelphia—"pretty darned good wasn't it?" She particularly liked "what you said about the people with greatest opportunities sometimes being in greatest need for education in civic matters."

In New York, Hick concluded her WPA job with a festive social whirl. She dined out often and well, went to special places for special cocktails, took out-of-towners sight-seeing; she thanked ER for arranging her interview with Grover Whelan.

Hick wanted ER especially to enjoy Milwaukee:

> How I used to love Milwaukee—years ago when I was a cub reporter there . . . ! a little German coffee shop, made famous by Edna Ferber—that's where I started to put on weight—and that beautiful, beautiful [Lake Michigan]! And I was young then and full of hope and bright dreams. No money. I lived at the YWCA. Sometimes mostly on beans. But those were brave days!

ER replied that she did have a magnificent view of the lake, and in fact had made a pilgrimage to Edna Ferber's coffee shop for Hick's sake, but it was gone!

In Milwaukee ER was told she would have no audience "because the old lady running the show has a communist introducing me who tried last year on Armistice Day to tear down the flag and so all patriots [would] stay away." And her talk was scheduled for the big auditorium "which at best only FDR would fill! I dread it! Why will they take these huge places which no woman can fill—I think I'll go out for $200 per and have a smaller audience, what think you?"

Hick rejected it as a terrible idea: ER would always be able to pack the largest possible auditorium. Just wait and see. Actually, thousands showed up to hear ER, as Hick anticipated. "I'm keen to know what the papers say about your speeches. Have you tried out the anti-lynch stuff? Of course you wouldn't get much reaction on that in the North." Hick also thought that the introducer in Milwaukee might not be a "Communist after all, dear. So many people are labelled Communist these days!"

ER did not speak for the antilynch law during her November trip. Her tour coincided with Armistice Day, and she focused on international peace. She tended to close her meetings with poetry. One verse expressed "the futile feeling" among peace advocates as they contemplated "this world where force is still rampant," where "the madness / That pulses in the kingdoms of men" presages the "hopelessness, horror and sadness" of the "world slaughter again. . . ."

On Armistice Day, ER concluded with a vivid protest by Richard Le Gallienne, "The Illusion of War," which "expresses so well something we all should remember on this day":

> War
> I do abhor;
> And yet how sweet

> The sound along the marching
> street
> Of drum and fife, and I forget
> Broken old mothers and the whole
> dark butchering without a
> soul.

ER ended with the startling suggestion that Americans remove all glamour from war, end "the strutting of the living" that did little to memorialize the dead during Armistice Day observances. As slaughter once again appeared in Asia, Ethiopia, and Spain, ER suggested that rather than look back "to the world's greatest mistake, why can't we train our energies on what is to come? Even by a display of sincere respect for the war dead we somehow dignify what should be a matter of gravest shame."

As she toured, ER thoroughly enjoyed meeting Hick's friends: "Darling, how you do castigate yourself! Do learn to be a little simple, free and natural and do what you want to do! I have such a bad time teaching all of you that I don't need to be protected! . . . Next time you want me to see someone say so!"

Concerning her World's Fair interview, Hick reported that Grover Whelan "didn't swoon exactly. But he was courteous, and I'm to see him again." ER was encouraged: "I hope and pray you get it." ER anticipated that they could work together on a publicity job, and "we'll have some fun planning your campaign. I think I can help."

Hick was grateful for ER's ease with her friends:

> You were a dear to send the wire and a very *great* dear about my friends. Oh, you always do the nice thing—and I always blunder. How you can even *like* me is beyond me. . . . I can't for the life of me understand why a person like you would care anything about a person like me, and therefore it has been hard for me to have any confidence in you. . . . Torn as I was between loyalty to you and loyalty to some of my old friends I had worried about it for months. . . .

Hick hoped that Tommy was not hurt by her outburst:

> I think a lot of Tommy. She and I were good friends long before I knew you, and, as a matter of fact, I'd never have known you had it not been for Tommy. Anyway, she is a much better friend than I am—much less selfish. . . .

Hick wrote one final letter, which revealed her ultimate fear:

You and Tommy were probably bored stiff. Tell Tommy . . . I'll try not to pull anything like that on you again. . . . I guess I'll drop that subject now. I acted like a damned fool, and I'm ashamed of myself.

ER responded with letters of reassurance, and love:

Darling, will you never learn that love can't be pigeon-holed and perhaps we love people more for their weaknesses than for their best qualities of which you have a lot though you forget them when you are down. . . .

ER also appreciated Hick's need to return to her career as a writer, and she sent Hick to her agent George Bye. He encouraged Hick to write a book about Depression America based on her FERA reports. Bye's enthusiasm and confidence thrilled Hick: "So—with George Bye leading me by the hand, and with you pushing from behind, I MAY write a book!" She acknowledged her hesitance, however, which "amused him, a little. 'Good Lord,' he said, 'are you always so humble and so unsure of yourself in anything you do?' 'No,' I assured him. 'I was a damned good reporter and knew I was.' "

Despite the crowds, the ovations, the generous press coverage, ER wrote Bye that she was "a bit discouraged." Her tour had been scheduled too soon after the election, and she feared that her resounding success was merely a reflection of FDR's popularity. But she was wrong: Every hall was filled with people who came to hear her and left entirely satisfied. Both Bye and her lecture agent Colston Leigh were ecstatic. Hick reported that Leigh told Bye that "you were a grand success, and that he already had your March dates just about filled!"

In Detroit, ER's brother Hall took ER and Tommy to lunch "and made me choose a car but I begged not to have it till next Spring and I'll turn in my Buick. . . . I don't really want it but what am I to do?"

Hick was perplexed: "Darling. I think it's nice that Hall is giving you a car. Lord knows you give enough to other people! Why shouldn't someone give you something now and then? Is it a convertible? I hope so. When you start driving a closed car I'll think you are really getting old."

Hick wrote to ER from the White House, which in everybody's absence was a "gloomy" place. It was conducive to writing though, Hick noted, and being good to oneself—which was a comfort just then, while she mourned her friend the great diva Ernestine Schumann-Heink, who died in Hollywood on 17 November, at the age of eighty-three.

I wonder if, at the end, she wasn't very weary. It was an eventful life, filled with glory, but I think she had her bad times. I wonder what will become of all the people she supported. The last time I saw her I believe she told me there were some seventy of them! Well—I hope "Erda" will be happy in Valhalla!

ER replied: "I thought of you when Mme Schumann-Heink died. Would you like to wear her ring now or put it into safe-keeping? I am careful of it but I never want you to feel you can't do what you want with it!"

Hick, of course, wanted ER to wear the sapphire-and-diamond pinky ring Schumann-Heink had given her in Milwaukee so many years before, and which she gave ER in 1932. ER wore it until her death, and the subject was not referred to again.

ER was pleased that Hick was already at work rereading her correspondence for a book on the hopes and needs of the American people and the government's responsibility to ensure those needs. ER wrote Martha Gellhorn, who had spent time with Hick in New York, to ignore Hick's complaints: She was not "at all frantic. . . . She grouses a great deal, but I think she really is much interested and I am sure she will do a good job."

As Hick read their daily correspondence in Louis Howe's spacious rooms, her spirits lifted. When she returned to New York, she accepted the World's Fair job and looked forward to earning $5,200 a year. Her publicity department would be under Joseph Clark Baldwin, whom she liked. Hick was pleased by the upswing of her life: "I came on home and celebrated, before my simple home-cooked meal, with a whiskey and soda, all by myself. And now, with that off my mind, I turn to my book."

ER thought that "$100 a week ought to be OK in New York and I hope you will enjoy it besides feeling confidence in yourself again!"

With the security of her new job, which was to begin in January, Hick decided to spend her remaining money on Christmas presents. ER wrote, "I don't approve of spending *all* your money on Xmas. Suppose you put one fourth in the savings account!"

Happy that Hick would remain nearby, ER learned that Anna and John Boettiger were moving to Seattle. Her daughter and son-in-law had accepted an offer to edit and publish a Hearst paper, the *Seattle Post-Intelligencer*. Politically curious, there was evidently no familial discussion concerning Hearst's proposal. Although FDR had mostly followed Hearst's isolationist prescription demanded for his 1932 support, the publisher had turned viciously against the president after the 1934 strikes, and the Boettiger appointment was part of the newspaper's strike settlement with the Newspaper Guild.

ER and FDR were furious about Hearst's 1936 campaign excesses, his brutal Red-baiting assaults. At a cabinet meeting before FDR left for his cruise, Tom Corcoran reported that, stunned by the landslide, the Hearsts and Liberty League boys had decided to promote a new "era of good feelings." Ickes hoped that FDR would not be fooled by such opportunism, where-upon the president gestured "thumbs down" on all future relations with the publisher.

ER never forgave William Randolph Hearst for the role he played to keep America out of the World Court, and Hearst's relentless crusade against the Democratic Party, transformed in his words into a foreign crossbreed of "Karl Marx and Franklin Delano Roosevelt," filled her with revulsion. After he had orchestrated one of the filthiest campaigns in U.S. history, ER considered Hearst's apparent fondness for her children manipulative. He hired son Elliott to run his radio stations in Texas, and now offered Anna and John a sweetheart deal they accepted: $30,000 for him, $10,000 for Anna, who agreed to do the women's page.

However dismayed by her daughter's move, ER made no effort to dissuade or influence her adult children. She wrote Hick, that "of course John and Anna are blissful." Although she dreaded the "complete separation . . . I'll get used to it and I wouldn't spoil their joy by ever saying a word about it, W.R. seems to like employing the Roosevelt family, odd isn't it?"

To FDR, ER wrote twice: "I shall miss them badly but it does seem a grand opportunity and they will love it and so life is life, not always very pleasant!" A week later, she sighed: "I can hardly bear to have Anna & John go but they are so happy that I wouldn't let them know for worlds & it is better than Europe. . . ."

Hearst's stunning deal gave John and Anna absolute control over the editorial page; and if the struggling paper became financially solvent, they would get 5 percent of the profits as a bonus above their salaries. While neither ER nor FDR expressed an opinion, various intimates were chagrined.

Hearst's effort at reconciliation began on election night. FDR told Farley, who told Ickes, that while his sons answered telephone calls at Hyde Park, one of them overheard Marion Davies, Hearst's companion, speaking with John Boettiger: "Hello, John, this is Marion Davies. I just wanted to tell you that I love you. We know that a steam roller has flattened us out, but there are no hard feelings at this end." Then Hearst got on the phone to repeat Davies's message. Several days later, Hearst papers ran a signed editorial in which Hearst, noted Ickes, "slobbered all over the President." Ickes and others hoped FDR would have nothing more to do with Hearst.

Hick, however, was not so rigid. She had a reporter's conviction that a paper was as good as its editors and writers. After all, her friend Tom Dillon had been managing editor of the paper before Hearst bought it, and another friend, Hazel Reavis, worked on it:

> It's an old paper and used to have a fine reputation before Hearst got hold of it. Of course, I'm thrilled, as you must be, for them. That's a pile of money, dear! And it takes John back into the kind of work he really loves.

And I think Anna will love editing the woman's page, learn a lot at it, and be darned good at it. Gosh, it's a magnificent opportunity for her to acquire professional experience, "on her own," so to speak. Also—I think Seattle is a beautiful city—a grand place to live. . . . It will be good for Sisty and Buzzie. Outdoor life the year around. . . . in the country, with horses and dogs.

As for you—dear, it *will* be tough. . . . I hate to think how much you are going to miss Anna. . . . You *are* one of those people who "can take it." *Aren't* you? . . .

While ER was stoic about personal disappointments, and could "take" such setbacks, she was painfully thrown when her husband announced the first policy decision of his second administration: He would cut spending and pursue a balanced budget. Given the desperate situation of continued, actually unrelieved, unemployment, still at least 20 percent, it seemed precisely the wrong thing to do. Moreover, he called for cuts in agencies ER had hoped would be expanded, including WPA. Only Henry Morgenthau was enthusiastic about this decision; others feared it would abort the entire recovery program. Given FDR's unprecedented victory, and his radical campaign rhetoric, this was a staggering, baffling decision.

Hick's reaction was mixed. She was glad she had had the good sense to leave Hopkins's team before the cuts: "Harry is slashing his staff unmercifully" in Washington's central office, as well as throughout the states. "Eighty were let out of one department. . . ." Yet she considered the cuts "the right thing to do." ER disagreed. She agonized over WPA cuts for weeks, and wrote her daughter: "This WPA cut is being badly done and I am worried. . . ."

While Hick waited for her World's Fair job to begin, she worked on her book, which was harder to write than she had expected. Still, reading her correspondence rekindled her ardor, and a tone of romance reappeared in her letters to ER: "I'm awfully grateful to you, for all kinds of things. And I love you a very great deal." Between them, carping ceased and gruff self-abasements diminished; they spent satisfying times together.

ER wrote Anna, rather proudly, that Hick's dramatic history of America, gathered by "her four years of investigations," was under way. Although Hick complained to one and all, and called ER "an ogre because I'm insisting she write now while the story is fresh . . . !"

ER went to Hyde Park for Thanksgiving while Hick stayed in New York with her sister, Ruby. But FDR, Jr., was stricken in Cambridge with what at first seemed a "sinus" attack. Then he began to hemorrhage dangerously at the slightest turn of his head, and a streptococcus infection resulted in a very high temperature. It lasted for almost a month, into the Christmas season.

ER rushed to be with her son, in the Massachusetts General Hospital in Boston, and wrote FDR, then cruising the Pacific: "Poor Mama was disappointed about Thanksgiving but [Anna & John] and the children and Johnny and Betty were with her. . . . You sound very jolly & I hope James is fine. . . ."

FDR, Jr.'s, physical battle coincided with the announcement of his engagement to Ethel du Pont, who joined ER for the holiday-hospital vigil. The irony of a Roosevelt–du Pont engagement, combined with Hearst's employment policies, seemed peculiar in 1936 and entangled the family in unruly personal thickets: The du Ponts had financed the Liberty League, championed by Hearst, and were FDR's most determined political enemies. ER wrote her husband:

> Of course I told FJr the drawbacks but I never opposed Ethel or the duPonts as a family just the money and his position—I've always dreaded those grand affairs but I did not refuse to go to the wedding—I guess we'll survive all that gossip.

On hospital duty Thanksgiving day, ER, feeling forlorn as she went back and forth from her empty hotel room to her suffering son, wrote Hick: "I'm rather weary, but I'm thankful for you dear today and all those whom I love, Bless you and a world of love."

ER left FJr to attend the Army-Navy football game, a rare event in the First Lady's life. She had surprised and delighted Hick and Howard Haycraft when she sent their tickets, although Hick understood that ER did not "really give a darn about seeing the game. Darling, if you don't want to go, don't." But ER knew that it meant something to her friends, and her son John.

ER confided the true feelings of her divided heart in her Thanksgiving letter to Elinor Morgenthau. "Never was I more reluctant to start out [for Boston] than last night. . . . Ethel comes in the morning and I return to New York." She would "go to the game Sat so Johnny can sit in the box." As for Anna and John's move, ER wrote, "I might as well confess to being depressed. . . ."

ER's presence at the historic game at West Point, which Navy won 7–0, created headlines. Accompanied by four companions, including her son John, and "Lorena Hickok, an aide," ER was seen to "munch" an egg-and-lettuce sandwich before the game and bundle into a "seal coat," which she added to her green wool coat with mink collar, in a desperate effort to keep out the blustery wind; and she was observed alone at the train station before the game ended.

ER denied that she left the game out of boredom. She needed to dash down to Washington from West Point to "collect some clothes." She wrote FDR that her dash to Washington was urgent: Having toured "half the nation," everything was "dirty," and she had nothing left to wear.

ER kept the worst hospital news from her husband, and was glad to read in the newspapers that he and James were having "a grand time." Happy at sea, FDR reported fully to both his mother and his wife. His first letter, just out from Charleston, went to "Dearest Mama: Just an au revoir note," and a promise: "I will send you a line from Trinidad and will think of one day there 32 years ago!" He referred to the trip his mother had arranged when she tried to lure him away from his engagement with ER.

He sent "Dearest Babs" a full description of the customarily wild cross-dressing naval tradition, which featured drink and drag, at the equator: "Great fun 'Crossing the line'—Marvellous costumes in which King Neptune and Queen Aphrodite and their court appeared. The Pollywogs were given an intensive initiation lasting two days, but we have all survived and are now fullfledged Shellbacks."

The USS *Indianapolis*, he wrote, was an especially "happy ship." His companions were "jolly," and the ship was "steady" at the great speed of twenty-five knots with "no vibration." He was relaxed, and the fish were fabulous.

Uninformed about his son's worrisome condition, FDR wrote that he hoped "it will clear up quickly and think it will if he will go to bed early for a week. . . . Jimmy is in fine form, and works daily at his ship and [Marine] Corps duties."

FDR had commissioned his son a lieutenant colonel in the Marine Corps Reserve, a rank he considered appropriate for his personal aide. ER disapproved, and wrote a censorious letter inquiring if James was now "a 2nd Lieut. or a Lieut. Col." It might have seemed a joke, but James wrote that "Father kidded me for days about that one," and he was hardly amused: "Frankly, I felt like an impostor in that starched white uniform with silver leaves on the shoulders." And then came Mother's letter, "inquiring in that disingenuous way of hers. . . ."

FDR concluded his letter to his wife with "Loads and loads of love—and try to get lots of sleep preparatory to that — Social Season. Another year let's cut it out and take a trip to Samoa and Hawaii instead! / Devotedly F."

FDR's fantasy trip together to Samoa and Hawaii was particularly welcome just then as ER prepared not only for Christmas but the "Social Season" compounded by the demands of the Twentieth Amendment, which ended the "lame duck" term and for the first time moved the president's traditional March inauguration to 20 January.

While FDR sailed, ER and Hick enjoyed an increasingly rare week together, mostly anonymous and happy. After several days in Washington, they drove to Arthurdale, then visited Alice Davis and other friends in Virginia.

After the holiday part of his cruise, FDR had a triumphant reception in Rio de Janeiro. The enthusiasm of the crowds for the hero of the New Deal and the Good Neighbor Policy was unprecedented, and heartening. ER would have been pleased, her husband wrote:

> I do wish you could see Rio. The harbor—the colors and the *orchids*— common as sweet peas! . . . YOU have been given a *huge* silver tea set by the

Brazilian government, very old Brazilian hammered silver! and a great rarity and not at all bad looking.

There was real enthusiasm in the streets. I really begin to think the moral effect of the Good Neighbor Policy is making itself definitely felt.

FDR's speech to the congress of Brazil made a strong impression worldwide: The fact of international "understanding and good will," of friendship within this hemisphere as a model of true amity, was the "best answer to those pessimists who scoff at the idea" and all possibilities of peace.

Although Brazil's President Getulio Vargas was a fascist-allied dictator, everywhere FDR went, crowds cheered, "Viva la democracia! Viva Roosevelt!" Along the beautiful streets of Rio that day everything seemed possible, negotiable. FDR felt ebullient. Vargas even whispered into his ear as they drove through the tightly packed, wildly cheering crowds: "Perhaps you've heard that I am a dictator?" FDR smiled as he continued to wave and replied, "Perhaps you've heard that I am one, too."

When FDR addressed a huge gathering in Montevideo, James proved himself a protective and quick-witted aide. His father removed from his pocket a blue-and-white handkerchief to mop his brow. Suddenly the crowd cheered wildly, and James realized that they were responding to the Uruguayan national colors in FDR's hand. Instantly, James leaned over and "whispered ferociously" in his father's ear: "For God's sake, don't blow your nose in that handkerchief." Immediately, FDR waved it vigorously at the crowd.

In Buenos Aires, FDR was greeted by two million Argentines, who showered him with flowers. According to one eyewitness, his reception "exceeded in warmth and spontaneity anything that has ever occurred in Argentina."

On 1 December, FDR opened the first Inter-American Conference for the Maintenance of Peace with a stirring address to "members of a family [who represent twenty-one republics of the Americas] and meet together for their common good":

> I am profoundly convinced that the plain people everywhere in the civilized world today wish to live in peace. . . . And still leaders and Governments resort to war. Truly, if the genius of mankind that has invented the weapons of death cannot discover the means of preserving peace, civilization as we know it lives in an evil day. . . .
>
> The madness of a great war in other parts of the world would affect us and threaten our good in a hundred ways. And the economic collapse of any Nation . . . must of necessity harm our own prosperity.
>
> Can we, the Republics of the New World, help the Old World to avert the catastrophe which impends? Yes; I am confident that we can. . . .

FDR's prescription for hemispheric peace included strengthened democratic movements, more freedom and security, greater trade and commerce through reciprocal agreements, frontier and territorial mediation, cultural and educational exchanges.

Ongoing border controversies within South America required adjustments, FDR declared, which "may appear to involve material sacrifice." But, he concluded, there "is no profit in war. Sacrifices in the cause of peace are infinitesimal compared with the holocaust of war. . . . Democracy is still the hope of the world. . . ."

FDR was impressed, even pleased, that his Buenos Aires speech was banned in both Germany and Italy. But his words concerning democracy and peace puzzled various Latin American delegates to this Buenos Aires conference. Concerned about investments, material interests, and the future of U.S. commerce, the United States supported new hemispheric dictators Trujillo, Somoza, and Batista. The bitter factor of regional control was still alive. U.S. activities in the Americas since the Monroe Doctrine had been domineering, acquisitive, violent. The Colossus of the North, El Pulpo—the octopus—was distrusted despite FDR's personal appeal.

Any extension of U.S. power in the region was resisted. Argentina particularly warned against any further encroachment on Latin American sovereignty. Indeed, the Argentine foreign minister, Dr. Carlos Saavedra Lamas, who had just returned from Geneva, where he presided over the League of Nations Assembly, insisted that only the League should be called in for arbitration, negotiation, and general peace-keeping.

FDR, in his speech, had honored Saavedra, the recipient of the 1936 Nobel Prize for Peace. He had great influence, and his commitment to the primacy of the League was supported by the five Central American nations as well as Uruguay, Bolivia, and Chile.

There were many achievements at Buenos Aires, but there was no mutual accord: Each nation remained free to define its position, as well as its commercial and military relations, independently. There was only unanimous support for the principle of nonintervention: A treaty was signed that banned direct or indirect intervention in the internal or external affairs of any Central or South American nation. Ultimately this first of many conferences laid the foundation for a regional organization, the Organization of American States (OAS), and for improved hemispheric relations.

FDR left the conference with the cheering citizens of Brazil, Argentina, and Uruguay uppermost in his thoughts. Millions of people had appeared on the streets to rally and chant, "Democracy! Democracy!" FDR perceived their enthusiasm as a repudiation of both the fascist and communist challenges. He told Ickes that he believed his trip "strengthened the democratic sentiment throughout the world and has had favorable repercussions among the peoples of Europe."

But in Latin America, as Franco, Mussolini, and Hitler ravaged the Spanish countryside and bombed civilians, there was little enthusiasm for FDR's policy of strict neutrality. Many in the Spanish-speaking republics identified with and supported Spain's Popular Front government.

Modern unrestricted warfare had been under way since fascist rebels declared war on the democratically elected government of Spain on 17 July 1936. In response, the great nonfascist powers led by Britain, France, and the United States declared absolute neutrality. Franco was armed and supported by Rome and Berlin. Neutrality created a fantasy of containment: FDR joined that fantasy and gambled that war and fascism might thereby be limited to Italy, Spain, and Germany, while communism and threats from the left would be crushed in Spain, as in Germany and Italy.

Fear dominated the situation. France's Popular Front Socialist prime minister, Léon Blum, feared that French aid to Republican Spain might cause Britain's conservative prime minister, Stanley Baldwin, to aid Germany. Blum also feared that France's aggressive right would topple his government if he aided Spain. The Conservative rulership of Britain considered fascism an acceptable barrier to Popular Front, radical, and dangerous democratic movements. Nobody doubted that uninvolvement, or neutrality, in Spain was an aggressive act of support for fascist forces.

FDR joined that policy with unnecessary enthusiasm. His policy of noninvolvement went so far as to call for an end to private commerce and airplane sales to Spain—despite conventional international law, which specifically allowed commerce, including arms sales, with legitimate, recognized governments and nations in a state of civil war. For many, including peace advocates and Senator Gerald P. Nye, strict neutrality and an embargo against Loyalist Spain was an act of war. Nevertheless, that was what FDR called for.

ER disagreed completely with her husband's policy on Spain. It was the first international issue she refused to be silent about. ER spoke and wrote about Spain continually.

The situation worsened on 26 November when Germany and Japan sealed a pact of mutual accord, which threatened to isolate Russia—Spain's only ally. ER and her circle of peace advocates had hoped that FDR's Latin American tour would strengthen the League of Nations response against fascist aggression in Spain. But no serious discussions about Spain were held, and FDR left Buenos Aires with a display of triumphant achievement.

Personally, FDR's trip was plunged into gloom by the sudden death of his closest and most trusted personal aide, Gus Gennerich. A former New York City police officer, first assigned to the governor in 1928, Gennerich had been closer to FDR than any man besides Louis Howe.

Fifty at the time of his death, August Gennerich was six feet tall, muscular, agile, and efficient. He traveled everywhere with "the Boss," listened to his speeches, made useful suggestions. FDR called him "my humanizer," his dependable "ambassador to the man in the street."

Gennerich had guaranteed FDR's physical dignity, from his morning rituals to his nighttime needs. He helped the Boss bathe, dress, and move; he carried him with assurance and aplomb. He locked his braces, wheeled his chair, got him in and out of cars and fishing boats, up and down stairs, onto stages.

In less than six months, FDR had lost the two men who had ensured him both emotional and physical support. More than most, they had pierced FDR's facade of endless cordiality and determined good cheer—which served also as a notable barrier to intimacy, even to knowing. Gennerich was one of very few companions with whom FDR could enjoy moments of carefree relaxation, or abandon. It was Gus Gennerich who accompanied FDR to such intimate parties as Ickes hosted; and it was Gus Gennerich who participated, with a watchful eye, in the liquid revelries at Warm Springs and elsewhere that ER disliked so much.

FDR was devastated by Gennerich's death, and he wrote ER full details as soon as the ship left Buenos Aires on 2 December: "Dearest Babs: The tragedy of poor Gus hangs over all of us. . . ." It was "a real shock and a real loss for as you know good old Gus was the kind of a loyal friend who simply cannot be replaced."

ER wrote:

> Dearest Franklin, I am so sorry your trip had to be saddened and I'm deeply grieved that you have lost Gus who was so loyal and devoted. I'll miss him a great deal for I really loved him but for you the loss is very hard in so many, many ways. I've had his room locked [as FDR had requested] and asked . . . to keep everything intact until you return.

ER was particularly thankful that "Jimmy was with his father on this trip" that went so quickly from cheer to grief, which ER felt was the sorrowful pattern of life.

Hick wrote: "Gus was an amazing person, wasn't he?" At the White House, two administrative assistants who were friends of hers, Johnny and Wade, were bereft:

> It seemed they had some mutual friend, a man who had known Gus for years, and Gus used to go out to their house a lot and play the piano for them! I never knew until last night that they knew him. They used to go to his birthday parties, at the Mayflower. Marvelous parties, they said, with one of the White House servants—it sounded like Mingo—to wait on his guests. All kinds of people used to be there, they said—high and low. And they said Gus was a gorgeous host. . . . They are coming to his funeral if it's

permissible. I told them I thought it was. . . . I judge by what they said that, if his friends all come [to the White House funeral] there will be some crowd!

FDR asked ER to prepare the funeral service in the East Room, which she arranged. And everybody was aggrieved to think about Gus's plans for retirement; he had bought a farm near Hyde Park that FDR helped him furnish. It accentuated the tragedy, FDR wrote ER: "Gus was really living for that farm—he thought about it day and night," and bought things for it at every stop. "Ever so much love. I've missed you a lot and it will be good to be back Tues. Eve. / Devotedly F."

As FDR sailed home, King Edward abdicated his throne. FDR was bemused, and wondered about diplomatic protocol at dinner with British officers in Trinidad: "Do I or do I not propose the 'health of the King'? Awful dilemma. It is however to be solved by good manners and not by State Dept diplomatic protocol."

Presumably the president toasted the king, although Ickes noted that FDR was "disgusted" by the abdication, and thought that Edward "could have forced this situation." He could have been crowned and then announced that Mrs. Simpson was now "the Duchess of Cornwall." The president and everybody aboard had "guessed wrong" and bet King Edward would keep his throne.

Hick also wrote of the abdication, which became something of an emotional litmus test in ER's circle: "Poor little King! , , , I wonder what he will do. Lord, but living is such hard business, for so many people!"

Hick could not have known Edward's politics, and her enthusiasm for the "great little guy," who was also an ardent friend of new Germany, related to her identification with the king's loss of throne—and career—for the woman he loved:

> Poor fellow. I do hope he'll never be sorry—disappointed or disillusioned. I'm sorry for Mrs. Simpson. She will have an awful job on her hands. What will he do with himself all these years that are left? He's only in his early 40's. They can't go sailing around on yachts forever. I wonder if he won't be very bored and restless and unhappy . . . —and if she can keep him happy. He probably doesn't know it now—but I'm afraid he is in for some very bad times. . . .

ER too considered it rather a shame. Like FDR, she was surprised that Edward had decided to abdicate: "Well, and so—all is lost for love. Too bad he couldn't have served his people and had his love too!"

It was, for many, a dismal holiday season. Spain cast a grim shadow, and within the White House, one loss followed another. Shortly before Christmas, Marshall Haley, the twenty-year-old son of ER's personal White House maid Mabel Haley, died. Tommy called to notify ER in New York, and she was grateful that Hick, who was in Washington, wanted to go to Virginia for his funeral service. "The world has seemed so full of sorrows these past weeks."

Hick was the only white mourner at Marshall Haley's funeral, and the staff was impressed by her consideration for the family and the young man, who had been studying to become a minister and was president of his class. She wrote ER the details of the day:

> They buried [Marshall] down by the railroad tracks. It just looked like an unkempt field to me. . . . I didn't think it was a cemetery—there isn't even a fence around it. . . . Then it occurred to me . . . very few colored people can afford to have tombstones. . . .

Hick drove down with Lizzie McDuffie, the White House maid:

> Mrs. MacDuffie is a fascinating person! She was a most diverting companion. . . . She recited a lot of poetry to me—Paul Laurence Dunbar, some deliciously funny things in dialect, one about a Welsh clergyman that she said was the President's favorite, and a very stirring thing, called "Hagar's Farewell to Abraham." My God, what feeling she puts into those lines! One was Paul Laurence Dunbar's "Abandoned Plantation" . . . or "Deserted Plantation," and she told me that every now and then the President's mother sends for her and has her recite it to her. "I guess," said Mrs. Mac-Duffie, "she feels it might happen to Hyde Park some day, that the young folks don't care so much for it, and she's seen all those other places along the Hudson, deserted after the old folks have died." . . .
>
> My dear, I think you must do a novel about your mother-in-law sometime! She also told me all about "Gone With the Wind," which she borrowed from a Secret Service man and read last summer and liked a lot. She said she understood they were going to dramatize it, and that she would dearly love to play the Negro mammy in it! "She's exactly like my own grandmother was," she said. And that led to a discussion of slavery. . . . She told me about her grandparents—all slaves, and her mother was born in slavery—and what they did after the Civil War. . . . Fascinating stories.*

Between hospital visits to Boston where her son Franklin was still in serious condition, ER spent several days with Earl Miller, who uncharacteristi-

---

*ER wrote the producers to suggest Mrs. McDuffie for the role eventually played by Hattie MacDaniel.

cally asked her for a favor. Earl loved to cook and bake almost as much as he loved to ride and shoot, and now requested ER to do something "I know nothing about! Earl wants me to try and watch John make a cake to find out what he does wrong! Then I'm to show him about ironing shirts! In the meantime," ER wrote Hick, "Earl's nerves are about like yours for different reasons so it is probably a good thing I'm here!"

Earl "is another person like you in whose soul there is no peace. He has to attain it himself but I think it is harder for him than for you because he has no intellectual resources which he has developed."

Hick replied: "I'm sorry Earl was so upset. Poor dear, you just jump right from the frying pan into the fire, don't you? . . ."

ER now worked harder than ever; saw more people in a day; took on new projects. At first her relentless schedule was her lifeline; increasingly, it was what made her happy. She dined with Bernard Baruch, and he stayed until after midnight. She wrote Anna: "Baruch dined with me alone . . . and he is a stimulating guest. He wants something and I rather hope Pa gives it to him for I think he'll make something out of it."

The next night Molly Dewson spent three hours with ER to discuss the future of the second administration, and she too "wants something." Then she met with Monty High about the NAACP's antilynching plans, with a delegation from Arthurdale, and with several other groups. She wrote Anna: "For one and all I must *do* things, so my work is cut out for me after Pa gets back."

In December, Hick spent many days rereading their vast correspondence in Louis Howe's room:

> Today I stumbled into a lot of the early letters, written while I was still with the AP. Dear, whatever may have happened since—whatever may happen in the future—I was certainly happy those days, much happier, I believe, than many people ever are in all their lives. You gave me that, and I'm deeply grateful. There were other times, too—many, many of them.

It was painful for Hick to read those early letters and confront so much passion spent. Now their relationship was neither routine nor tumultuous; moments of longing and loneliness were largely passed. Those hectic romantic times when they abandoned discretion in order to spend a week or weekend with each other in some secluded inn were over.

Hick wondered what to do with the letters when she was finished. "Throw them away? In a way, I'd like to keep them, or have them kept somewhere. They constitute a sort of diary, as yours to me probably do, too. They might be of some use when I get around to that biography. What do you think?"

ER's interests, priorities, emotional needs had changed. Her political commitments now eclipsed all private considerations. But she valued their correspondence, expected Hick to write her biography, and never considered discarding the letters.

Hick was happy to report that she did not really mind "reading them so much today, although some of them make me feel a little wistful. I don't suppose anyone can ever stay so happy as I was that first year or so, though. Do you? . . .

"Goodnight, dear. You have been swell to me these last four years, and I love you—now and always."

21: Second Chance for the New Deal

FDR returned from his cruise on 15 December. At dinner that very night ER showed him a letter Hilda Smith had sent about her conversation with a Washington taxi driver, who said: "It is nice to know, isn't it, that the American people have so much intelligence. Moreover, they have a long memory."

The driver had been a glass-bottle blower in Pennsylvania whose employer committed suicide when the banks failed. His company's workers, three hundred men, were dismissed. He was on the road for two years; he stood on breadlines, slept in parks. In 1933 he arrived in FDR's Washington, worked hard, got a taxi, and moved to Virginia to be able to vote: "I never cared before who was President. . . . It takes a hungry man to appreciate Roosevelt."

This election was about the working people of America. FDR's promises could not be achieved by cutting the budget, or downsizing WPA. ER was disturbed by her husband's first postelection decision to trim and cut. The election mandate, she insisted, was to push for the larger goals in housing, work security, and racial justice. They were the themes ER emphasized in her busy correspondence between the election and inauguration. Also, she introduced a subject we would now call "affirmative action."

She wrote Jim Farley about her visit with black Philadelphia activist and writer Crystal Bird Fauset, who reported that black women WPA administrators were disproportionately fired:

> There are 500 more colored women relief cases . . . than white. . . . But in the supervisory capacity, there have always been a great many more white than colored. So in cutting down [Fauset and her allies] have tried to bring it a little more into line. However, they have left in every case the two to one ratio, meaning two white women to one colored woman in a supervisory capacity. This seems entirely fair as . . . there are more colored women in actual need of work to support their children. . . . This is going to happen all over the country. . . .

ER urged Farley to speak directly with Senator Guffey, who "has a big colored constituency and I think he would perhaps want to consider it." She concluded: "There is one other point that I should like to emphasize—we did make a tremendous play for the colored vote, and we got it, but we got it because they thought on the whole we were fairer. . . ." The Negro vote went to FDR ten to one, and ER wanted that trust honored by Democrats—especially by her husband.

He had agreed to an article placed in *The Crisis* by the Democratic National Committee, "Roosevelt the Humanitarian," which celebrated him as a pioneer in race relations "who spread true Democracy" and ended government rule exclusively "by and for the few powerful, rich men." PWA, WPA, NYA, and CCC benefited hundreds of thousands of Negroes, and the Home Owners' Loan Corporation saved homes and farms. "FDR is America's second emancipator." ER now wanted those words written by his publicists translated into new action.

ER believed that FDR could now be "independent" of Southern Democrats, since the South had voted out the most vigorous "bigots," including South Carolina's Ed Smith and Georgia's Eugene Talmadge. However much the race question seemed to FDR too hot to handle, the very fact that the First Lady spoke so publicly and earnestly served to change the nature of the political landscape. During the campaign, race became a political factor in unprecedented ways. While FDR's advisers continued to worry about the impact of ER's racial concerns on Southern Democrats, they were the significant losers of 1936.

For the first time, hundreds of thousands of blacks who were able to vote left the party of Lincoln and voted Democrat. For the first time black Americans were actually involved in the national democratic process. There was reason to believe that Roosevelt's reelection might begin to end, even in the South, the worst aspects of an economy that kept black Americans landless and economically marginal.

ER was in New York on Friday, 18 December, when FDR held his cabinet meeting, and was cheered when she heard of a "surprising" turn of events. Vice president Garner "suddenly, out of a clear sky," bowed to each Southern cabinet member and said: "With all due respect to you . . . and although I live in Texas and all my ancestors came from [the South], I am in favor of an antilynching law." The cabinet seemed to agree, and Ickes noted: "It begins to look as if real justice and opportunity for the Negro at long last might begin to come . . . at the hands of the Democratic Party. . . ."

It was, for ER, a very hopeful sign. Uncertain of her husband's plans, particularly on matters of race and relief, she had confided to Elinor Morgenthau immediately after the election: "As you know I rather dread the future, but they may . . . manage better than I dare hope!"

But when she pressed her husband for his response and urged him again to make a public statement on the antilynch issue, he refused. FDR had returned exhausted from his trip, and depressed by Gus's death. He had little patience for ER's agenda. His first order of business was to achieve an embargo around Spain in the name of "complete neutrality" and a campaign to get the Nobel Peace Prize for Cordell Hull. FDR believed "no one deserves it more than Cordell and he should have had it this year instead of Saavedra Lama."

Spain was to be an agonizing issue between ER and FDR, and incomprehensible to his more liberal advisers. Not only did FDR seek an absolute embargo against the democratic government of Spain, his State Department in August announced that American exporters and American ships had the right to land supplies in Spanish ports held by Franco's rebels. This despite U.S. Ambassador Claude Bowers's report that Franco's forces were "the same element as that opposing your administration." Like Dodd in Germany, Bowers was an historian who did his own research. He believed the fascists were hated, and doomed to fail. He wrote FDR on 26 August 1936, "the thing will be over soon." But that was before FDR's "neutrality" blockaded and strangled Republican Spain, while his State Department allowed oil and supplies to Franco's troops.

Given the Supreme Court's ongoing opposition to the New Deal, there was a bitter irony in the fact that the Court actually gave FDR executive authority over foreign affairs. To support either side of a conflict, the Court ruled, FDR had freedom of action "in this vast external realm" of international relations. The Supreme Court's decision involved an embargo against Bolivia and Paraguay, at war in the Chaco jungles during 1934. Curtiss-Wright Export Corporation sued for the right to sell machine guns to Bolivia. The Court held that international powers did not derive from the states, but resided in the nation, and the "important, complicated, delicate and manifold problems" of international negotiation required the president to have "a degree of discretion and freedom . . . which would not be admissible were domestic affairs alone involved." FDR did not actually need congressional authority for an embargo, nor for the right to supply the legitimate elected Popular Front government. Those decisions were entirely his.

Although FDR's sympathies were thought to be with the democratically elected government, his aggressive embargo policy devoured its ability to survive. In September he wrote Bowers: "What an unfortunate and terrible catastrophe in Spain!" FDR agreed with Claude Bowers's report that the press falsified news from Spain:

> You are right about the distortion of the news. . . . Over here the Hearst papers and most of the conservative editors are playing up all kinds

of atrocities on the part of what they call the Communist government in Madrid—nothing about atrocities on the part of [the Franco] rebels.

Determined to ignore German and Italian military support for Franco, FDR insisted on "our complete neutrality in regard to Spain's own internal affairs."

Actually, he agreed with William Bullitt, who saw Spain as a key battlefield in the competition between expanding communist influence and expanding fascist influence. Bullitt preferred the latter. Horrified by his months in Moscow, Bullitt was now the U.S. ambassador to France, eager to achieve a Franco-German alliance. On 8 November 1936, he wrote FDR: "The war in Spain, as you know, has become an incognito war between the Soviet Union and Italy."

The Spanish Civil War persuaded Europeans "that there is such a thing as European civilization . . . [which] may be destroyed by war or Bolshevism." To unite Europe against communism, Bullitt now urged FDR to "assist diplomatically" in a reconciliation between France and Nazi Germany. Bullitt did not want a "grand gesture"—just some quiet work to "prepare the ground" and the prompt removal of William Dodd from Berlin. Bullitt wanted America's most outspoken anti-Nazi ambassador replaced by career diplomat Hugh Wilson. Bullitt was blunt: "Dodd has many admirable and likable qualities, but . . . he hates the Nazis too much to be able to do anything with them or get anything out of them. We need in Berlin someone who can at least be civil to the Nazis and speaks German perfectly. . . ." Dodd spoke German, but he opposed a Franco-Nazi alliance, and was useless as a diplomat.

While Spain exploded, the First Couple's own family geography was unsettled. FDR returned home convinced that his son James was perfect to fill the empty spaces left by Louis Howe and Gus Gennerich. It was an impossible task for anyone, and ER was dismayed by her husband's blithe assumptions about his son's future. She wrote Anna that James had arranged for another New York State trooper for FDR "to try out," and James would begin his new post as secretary on 15 January. But: "I am saying nothing these days & Pa has no time to be talked to except on matters of business!"

After saying nothing for several weeks, evidently out of respect for FDR's state of mourning, ER finally "protested vehemently." She told FDR it was "selfish to bring James down"; and told them both that she was not only "unhappy" about their decision but "appalled."

ER had always opposed special privileges for her children, but she was virtually isolated in her opposition to many family decisions. The children were spoiled by their grandmother who was generally supported by FDR, and

ER's worries and sense of correctness were usually dismissed as overbearing and unnecessary. James wanted to work with his father. He enjoyed politics, and his father's company. He especially enjoyed his role as FDR's responsible eldest son, who served with distinction and protective intelligence.

Proudly, FDR detailed James's new chores as presidential secretary, at the rank of Stephen Early and Marvin McIntyre. He was to be liaison to the "little cabinet" and coordinate the activities of twenty agencies, including the Securities and Exchange Commission, the WPA, the Housing Authority, the Federal Reserve Board, the Social Security Board, the Maritime Commission, the Agricultural Adjustment Administration, the Federal Power Commission, the Federal Trade Commission, the National Labor Relations Board, the Veterans Administration, the Civil Service Commission, the Interstate Commerce Commission, the National Youth Administration, and the Civilian Conservation Corps.

It was a bit much, and he was called the "Crown Prince," and the "Assistant President." ER had only one ally in opposition, FDR's uncle, Frederic Delano.

Although his health failed and his marriage floundered, James considered it the happiest time of his life. It was the only time he and FDR had time to do "father-and-son things together." It was for ER a significant ordeal. That FDR returned too busy to speak with his wife about personal matters was one thing. That she increasingly learned about his political intentions from her son was another. On 16 December, she wrote Anna: "J told me & if true I think it diverting, they plan to make Harry Hopkins Sec of War to reorganize the Dept till Congress creates a Dept of Welfare or whatnot when Harry will go in there! A pacifist in the War Dept is funny, now isn't it?"

Embattled and distressed at home, ER sought comfort elsewhere. Shortly after FDR's return, she went to Val-Kill with Earl. She wanted to walk in the snow, take long vigorous horseback rides through the woods. The more difficult ER's family situation became, the more she turned to Earl, and again to Hick. Needed and wanted as she had not been for a long time, Hick responded with renewed warmth. Moreover, Hick was in a better mood. Her new job and time away with good friends had refortified her own sense of self. With new friends Hendrik van Loon and his son Willem, and Bill and Ella Dana, Hick was no longer dependent on ER and often seemed now practically carefree.

She was patient about ER's unexpected schedule changes. She accepted the primacy of ER's children's needs, especially when they were in extremis—as FDR, Jr., was all that season. She became almost gracious about all the people, old and new, in ER's life. Bernard Baruch, for example, entered ER's letters more and more frequently: "Such a joke. Mr. Baruch bought me a superlative vanity case for Xmas but the catch was broken so he took it back but you can think how much I need cigarettes, lip stick and powder in a light tortoise shell case!"

ER also turned to new allies, new organizations. Interested in share-croppers and the Southern Tenant Farmers Union, ER wanted Mary McLeod Bethune to be appointed to the new presidential study committee on farm tenancy. It was a thirty-eight-member committee, chaired by Henry Wallace, whose initial disinterest in race and the plight of the sharecropper changed after he made a fact-finding Southern tour. Surprised by the dire poverty he witnessed, Wallace was now eager to make amends for the damage done by AAA crop reduction programs. Florida's liberal senator Claude Pepper supported the First Lady, and Bethune was appointed.

Within the administration, and with ER's support, Bethune did more than any single individual to move the race agenda forward. Bethune invited ER to address a January conference, sponsored by the National Youth Administration's Division of Negro Affairs, which she now chaired. Planned with Aubrey Williams, the Conference on Government Policies and the Problems and Future of the Negro and Negro Youth was to be momentous. Bethune wrote ER: "Negroes all over the country so fully believe in you that it would mean much . . . to have your counsel."

ER attended and spoke at the three-day conference, which focused on economic security, educational opportunity, improved health and housing, and equal protection under the law. Grateful for her presence and "valuable contribution," Bethune wrote:

> You may well understand that this is the most significant conference ever held by a Negro group in connection with the Government. . . . It marks a new epoch and a very decided forward step. . . . A note of harmony and understanding was struck . . . that we have never before heard. . . . The recommendations present a unified voice of the twelve million Negroes of this country. Surely a new day has dawned.

On 21 December, ER hosted the annual Gridiron Widows party, working with Elinor Morgenthau and Betty Lindley on the entertainments. Held since 1933, ER's party for women journalists and public officials coincided with the men-only Gridiron party and tended to be just as much fun, and quite as silly. Over the years some spice was added to the parodies, but they were never scathing.

In 1934, ER participated in the first costume party. According to Bess Furman, it was "a night of sheer delight," and the First Lady stole the show when she appeared in complete disguise for her skit as Apple Mary, based on a film character. Her tattered rags were so dingy, her makeup so amazing, she was unrecognizable. In fact, the chief White House usher made a move to stop her.

As the lights went up, she sat under a large umbrella, rocked back and forth, muttered, and keened. Oh so cold; oh so hungry: "Oh, the divvil, the divvil!"

Thereupon a red devil in red leotards and tail leaped onto the stage. Anna looked hard at Apple Mary and recognized her mother: "So it has come to this! To keep yourself in the headlines you even disguise as an old Apple Woman!"

Apple Mary was apologetic: It had seemed "such a good way to see people."

But the devil was harsh and forced her to return to her role as First Lady and endure the ordeals of her position, for three scenes: In an effort to remain inconspicuous and knit on a train, she was mobbed by autograph hounds. At the airport she was laden with flowers in impossible profusion. In her own car she was hounded by an obnoxious motorist who sought to keep abreast of her. ER went faster and faster but the obnoxious motorist kept up with her, all the while hurling mean comments about her children. This was achieved by ER and Anna in a race astride rapidly moving chairs.

Finally, ER decided to return to the role of Apple Mary: "I like my miseries better this way."

After Howe died, for theatrical staging for the Gridiron Widows skits, ER relied on Elinor Morgenthau, and Gabrielle Forbush, a professional writer who worked in the Treasury department. According to *Time*, the 1936 Gridiron Widows party was "the most intimate show ever seen at the White House." There was a burlesque in which "a plump newshen did a striptease, another in red flannel underwear did a fan dance," and a scene in which the Roosevelts were honored because they liked people, "they marry so many of them."

"The big act" was "Romeo and Juliet, 1936" in three episodes: Juliet du Pont warned Romeo Roosevelt that if "my kinsmen see thee, they'll make thee join the Liberty League."

John Boettiger Juliet asked William Randolph Hearst Romeo: "Shall I deny my father-in-law and accept thy jack?"

Mrs. Simpson Juliet and Edward Romeo loved and lost "Pomp and Circumstance."

ER's act was off the record, but in song and square dance celebrated Tobacco Road's transformation into a model community.

Competitively, ER noted that her parties were more fun, and "lasted longer than the men's, so Franklin was usually home and in bed before I went upstairs after bidding my last guest good-night."

On 22 December, ER wrote Hick that she had decided to go to Boston to be with her ailing son FJr, and had to cancel all her plans including the special parties she had planned with Hick, and with Tommy and Henry: "Hick darling, I hate to write you this but you can't possibly feel lower about it than I do." She asked Hick to do her the favor of taking "Tommy's and Henry's things to them on Xmas eve and either take your own Xmas stocking there and open with them or here early in AM and I'll telephone you as soon as I get to the hotel on Xmas morning. . . ."

Instead, Hick went with ER to Boston, and they spent Christmas Eve and Christmas morning together. As she returned to New York, Hick wrote: "I love being with you more than with anyone else, of course, but I don't ever want to intrude or make you feel you've got to ask me to save my feelings. You don't need to worry about that, you know." Also Hick loved her gifts: the Val-Kill desk and chair—which she received earlier:

> And all the nice little things you remembered—like the black lace stockings—they mean so much—I may have had my bad times, dear, but they weren't your fault. And you've made me happier, too, than anyone else ever has. A happy Christmas and my love—all the best of it—

ER shared Hick's feelings about their unexpected journey together. After she left for New York, ER wrote her Christmas column, about loneliness. She recalled other lonely Christmas days, "one in Paris with a French family, and another in Rome, when I was at school." Then there was one "in bed with a baby two days old." But never before did she see "the children hang up their stockings in one city" only to arrive in another to be in a hospital "with one lone child. There were so many at home this year that I hated to leave, but we couldn't any of us bear to think of Franklin, Jr., alone by himself . . . so here I am in Boston."

While her son slept, she read, and noted with dismay that a newspaper announced "that $3,600 a year was really the minimum on which an average family could lead a satisfactory existence. Most of us know that a considerable percentage of our people see only from $200 to $600 . . . during the course of a year. Many other have incomes under $1,000. . . ."

This problem is so vast, ER wrote, the government needed help to solve it: "We, as a people, must solve it by deciding on the type of social and economic philosophy which we wish to see established in this country. . . ."

Unlike the New Deal's opponents, ER did not consider it communism, or near communism, to suggest that a certain amount of economic planning for social welfare was in order. Americans needed to think boldly or nothing really would get done: "When we know what changes we want, we can then set government machinery to work to accomplish them."

After Christmas, Ethel du Pont arrived, and ER wrote Anna that she was "a sweet child" with "much to learn. However, there is a practical streak there which may save many a situation!"

Weary and depressed, surrounded by journalists everywhere, ER wrote Hick from her hotel room:

> [One reporter] said I'd be saved a lot if I had the AP girl along who used to travel with me! I told them you came up with me but had returned to NY. I've become utterly unreasonable I know but I simply don't feel I can do anything but go in and out of the hospital and this hotel. I dread people's eyes and how stupid it is!
>
> Bless you dear for coming up with me . . . it was the nicest Xmas present you could have given me tho' I love all those others you did give me. The quilt, underclothes, raincoat, etc. are all a *great* joy. . . . You yourself were the grandest present. . . .

With her son's condition both painful and perilous, and press gossip about her family routinely unkind, ER was exhausted. But Hick admired the way ER handled the most fearsome situations:

> I think probably you are a lot more worried than you admit. Lord, I admire your courage and your calm. I know plenty of women—and so do you—who would be all in pieces if they were in the spot you are in right now. Madame, I salute you!

Hick urged ER to work on her book, and not think about her detractors: "Honey, don't let 'the eyes' get you! Just look right over their heads as you've always done and go about your business. You *mustn't* get that way, you know. . . ."

After several days, ER asked Tommy to join her and she agreed to move from her dreary hotel room to a friend's lovely home to work on the galleys of *This Is My Story* between hospital visits.

At last, FJr's nose stopped bleeding for forty-eight hours. His life had evidently been saved by an experimental antibiotic, and ER left immediately for New York. She wanted to surprise Hick with a visit on New Year's morning as soon as she arrived. But Hick's apartment was filled with her old friends, including Carolyn Marsh, and Hick was unprepared. ER wrote: "Dearest. It was good to see you today even if I did rout you out of bed! I hope Mrs. Marsh didn't mind!" Mrs. Marsh did mind a little. It was, after all, a curious way to meet Mrs. Roosevelt, and it was Carolyn Marsh's first trip to New York and away from her husband and children in decades—Hick chided.

ER concluded her New Year's letter with a reference to Hick's houseguests and social schedule, which kept her from her writing, with an uncharacteristic flourish: If Tommy and I "do as much on the train tomorrow as we did today it will be swell for I won't feel so guilty about 'my' book. I hope you feel guilty as Hell!"

From New York, ER raced to Washington for the diplomats' New Year dinner, the first big reception of 1937. The family took bets on whether Alice Longworth would appear after her nasty campaign against her cousins. ER noted the evening was a success, but "Alice came and FDR was rude, looked straight at [his aide Pa Watson] and said 'I won my bet'!"

Hick replied:

> I chuckled over your hoping I felt "guilty as Hell." . . . It always amuses me so when you get profane! And I also chuckled over the President's reception of Alice Longworth. He *was* bad, of course—but, oh, she so richly deserves it! Your indifference and your poise simply are more than human!

As Hick pulled away, and ER's family crises mounted, ER wrote a revealing New Year's column: "I have always thought the Japanese idea of keeping works of art put away and bringing them out one by one is a very good one, for you can always choose the ones which fit your mood," from light-hearted to gloomy. ER wondered if this was not also true about human relations. One could say in the morning:

> "This is the day I must look up Jane; she is just the person my mood requires." Or: "This is just the day for Alice." We never seem to take into consideration that there is an art in human relationships and that our appreciation of people may vary. . . .
>
> There are really very few things you want to look at every day in the year.

Still, ER countered Hick's withdrawal with suggestions for several exclusive trips together: In January they would tour Charleston, South Carolina, and New Orleans in April. Hick was agreeable: The dates "are *grand* dear"; "I'd love to go to Charleston"; "I don't care which car we take." But, "Will you let me drive yours?"

They would take ER's new convertible, "and you can drive all you want." Hick was thrilled about New Orleans: "We'd enjoy that place together."

Hick was not ER's primary worry as she contemplated her next four years. The political future, her children, and also her own health disturbed her: "I hear less and less. My voice gets worse and worse too. I'll probably be deaf and dumb in a few years more and perhaps that will make me really write—because I can't do anything else! Queer world!"

Because FDR insisted he required a groundswell of public activity in order to move toward real action on health security, ER invited Esther Lape and Elizabeth Read to Washington to attend the cabinet dinner and FDR's Annual Message to Congress on 6 January. They planned to introduce their new agenda to FDR during a relaxed moment.

Lape and Read had refocused the American Foundation's work on a national health care program for mandatory health insurance. The American Medical Association had blocked 1935 efforts to include health care in the Social Security Act. Now Lape and Read had assembled a distinguished roster of physicians and health educators to counter the AMA. Their team of 2,100 specialists in every branch of medicine worked to prepare a two-volume study, *American Medicine: Expert Testimony out of Court*, to arouse the nation to America's dismal health care realities, and with ER they planned a well-considered strategy to get their views before the nation and onto FDR's schedule of priorities.

In his 6 January message, FDR outlined his plans. First of all he sought an extension of the Neutrality Act to cover "the unfortunate civil strife in Spain," then he wanted to modernize and overhaul the executive structure to carry out the mandate for recovery.

Except for his words on Spain, FDR's speech echoed ER's interests and included new programs for slum clearance, the creation of healthful dwellings, and the end to "an un-American type of tenant farming." FDR proposed to end peonage and make tenant farmers "self-supporting on land which can eventually belong to them." As ER had demanded months earlier, he called for "the intelligent development of our social security system" through "frequent amendment of the original statute."

In conclusion, FDR devoted an undramatic paragraph to the Supreme Court: "The Judicial branch also is asked by the people to do its part in making democracy successful. . . . The process of our democracy must not be imperiled by the denial of essential powers of free government" acting "for the common good."

That paragraph heralded a secret plan that FDR had brooded over and developed for weeks. He consulted nobody except his attorney general, Homer Cummings; ER and his closest advisers were kept in the dark about this looming surprise—not to explode for another month.

Following his 6 January State of the Union message, ER had several conversations with her husband that resulted in what she considered an almost perfect second Inaugural Address. Although he again refused to mention lynching, ER's most urgent concerns were supported by FDR's powerful rhetoric on 20 January 1937:

> I see a great nation, upon a great continent, blessed with a great wealth of national resources. . . .
>
> But here is the challenge to our democracy: In this nation I see tens of millions of its citizens . . . who at this very moment are denied the greater part of what the very lowest standards of today call the necessities of life. . . .

I see millions of families trying to live on incomes so meager that the pall of family disaster hangs over them day by day. . . .

I see millions denied education, recreation, and the opportunity to better their lot and the lot of their children. . . .

I see one-third of a nation ill-housed, ill-clad, ill-nourished. . . .

We are determined to make every American citizen the subject of his country's concern. . . . The test of our progress is not whether we add more to the abundance of those who have much; it is whether we provide enough for those who have too little. . . .

FDR's speech was brilliantly delivered, despite dreadful weather, and ER marveled at her husband's dramatic skills. America's first winter inaugural occurred on a wet, springlike day. Grass was greening, forsythia was in bloom; an epidemic of flu and pneumonia raged. As FDR spoke, the rains came down in torrents on the presidential party, wearing lightweight formal attire.

In the lull between FDR's speech and the inaugural parade, ER wrote her column. Her impression so far was: "Umbrellas and more umbrellas!"

It was a day of mishaps and confusion. At nine in the morning, ER was presented with a profusion of her favorite flower, violets from Dutchess County, and "the entire family [left the White House] with bunches of violets." But en route to St. John's Church, the car with her grandchildren Sistie and Buzzie was stopped by policemen, who refused to let them in until the service was half over. Then she caused a delay at the Capitol while she arranged sheltered seating for her friends.

Edith Helm had forgotten to reserve seats for cabinet wives and other important guests. ER was furious. She actually spent almost thirty minutes looking for various notables to get them on the stand, including Dr. Peabody, Nan, Marion, Molly Dewson, and Laura Delano.

Hick reported that while ER scouted, holding up the ceremonies, radio announcers filled the air with rhapsodic praises of the First Lady: "Because of the delay, the announcers had to ad lib. . . . It was nice—they really said lovely things about you. You would undoubtedly have hated it."

ER confessed to Hick: "Yes, I gave Mrs. Helm a very bad time tho' I said nothing to her! She simply can't do that kind of work, and I should know it by this time."

ER's ability to give somebody a bad time, without saying a word, was one of her most unpleasant traits. But neither her irritation nor the weather spoiled the day: "Hardened as I am to official occasions, I could not hear the oath . . . without a catch in my throat." ER believed FDR's speech represented his sincere commitment to "the opening of the second stage in a long period of change."

FDR insisted they drive home with the top down. Bareheaded, they smiled and waved and became, wrote ER, "well soaked through." She had "a minute and a half" to change dresses before she greeted her luncheon guests. ER endured it all in appropriate style, and wrote her daughter, who was sorely missed that day:

> You would have been proud of Buzz taking off his cap whenever Pa did and standing by him all thro the parade. Sisty looked sweet too. . . .
>
> Well, another four years begins. I thought Pa's speech very good, what did you think? It is a new job & a hard one however. For me, some struggle for a personal life, an effort to do some good because of the position and a continuing effort to make Pa's life as far as the mechanics go easy so he can have what he wants materially and not think about it. I'm a bit weary as I think about it but I guess I'll live through it! I love you both a great deal.

ER wrote a more introspective letter to Hick:

> I went around and thanked everyone today for they were all wonderful and when you think that 710 ate lunch and 2700 had tea and everyone so far tells me things moved smoothly I think everyone deserves a pat on the back. I confess that arrangements and people bothered me beforehand but even more my sense of four years more beginning bothered me. . . .
>
> Why can't someone have this job who'd like it and do something worthwhile with it? I've always been content to hide behind someone else's willingness to take responsibility and work behind them and I'd rather be doing that now, instead I've got to use my opportunities and I am weary just thinking about it! Well, we'll live through it and worry along and see the irony of it and laugh at ourselves!

With Louis Howe gone, there was nobody to hide behind, or work behind. ER was on her own as never before.

22: 1937: To Build a New Movement

Two days after the inauguration, on 22 January 1937, ER embarked upon a more independent phase of her political life. She promoted Senator Robert Wagner's bill for federal aid to initiate a ten-year plan to rehouse low-income Americans in affordable decent housing, which FDR had not yet endorsed.

In her keynote address to the National Public Housing Conference, ER reaffirmed her conviction that decent affordable housing was the basic requirement for a better future. She read FDR's greetings, which celebrated PWA's housing efforts to date: fifty-one community projects were under way. The well-attended conference, chaired by pioneering housing advocate Mary Simkhovitch, seemed an auspicious way to begin the New Year, and the new administration.

January closed with FDR's annual birthday frolic. The first year without Louis Howe, it was also the first year Harry Hopkins attended. ER invited him:

> As you know, what we call the "Old Guard," who were in the 1920 campaign with Franklin, have for years had a dinner on his birthday. We used to have a stunt party, but none of us have the heart to do that now without Louis, who was always the moving spirit.
>
> We have decided that we would like to invite some guests, the gentlemen to sit in after dinner at a poker game. I hope very much that you will be among the guests this year. . . .

While the men drank and gambled, ER's "job" was to attend the fundraising "Birthday Balls" that raised thousands of dollars annually for polio research and other good causes.

ER's gift to her husband was a bound unfinished manuscript of her memoir, *This Is My Story,* accompanied by a handwritten note:

> This may not look it but it is,
> A book which will some day appear

> It promises to be a whiz
> So little else You'll get
> My dear!

Serialized in the *Ladies' Home Journal* before publication, it was immediately the subject of excitement. Fannie Hurst was ecstatic to hear the *Journal's* editors at a luncheon speak exuberantly about ER's book. Certain that "this will give you a thrill," she related their conversation: They especially "admired the 'fine clear prose' and the 'simplicity and forthrightness of the narrative.' . . ."

ER spent more time with Fannie Hurst, who sent her additional glasses to complete the vividly colored crystal set Howe had so awkwardly accepted the year before. ER wrote: "I can't tell you how sweet you are and . . . we will have a liqueur together for tender memory. . . ."

In some ways *This Is My Story* was ER's tribute to Louis Howe. Subsequently, ER noted that Howe was "more or less my agent" until the White House years, and then, "it was Howe who kept encouraging me to write, as he had from the beginning."

After he died, she wrote her memoirs to clear her mind, clarify her course, send a letter to her friend of friends. Her book was her major focus for the first six months of the second administration.

On 26 January 1937, ER brought a special guest to her press conference: Jane Hoey, director of public assistance for the Social Security Board. Hoey outlined the need for stronger social security measures and condemned states that attached punitive restrictions to aid for the needy, dependent children, the aged, and the blind. Based on Elizabethan poor laws, these state laws deprived the needy of all civil rights, including the right to vote, and recipients were obliged to "take a pauper's oath." The federal government opposed these requirements and wanted state legislatures to eliminate them immediately. Their elimination reflected only some of the changes ER had in mind, which included passage of a new health security package and a full-employment law.

Asked about FDR's comment that "federal hand-outs" were not his goal and represented no "permanent solution," ER said:

> Perhaps the President did not make himself clear. . . . He favors federal aid until economic conditions are raised. It has been misinterpreted into meaning that he opposes federal aid to communities too poor to care for their health and education.

That represented precisely, ER insisted, the "big job for the next decade." That big job was not only about social security but about prison reform. The first week of February, ER revisited the National Training School for Delinquent Girls, which had so offended her the year before that she protested and invited the girls (aged ten to twenty) to a White House garden party. The school was remodeled and modernized: "The change is so tremendous that I can hardly recognize the place. All the bars are gone, plenty of light and air, everything bright and new and clean. . . ."

ER agreed with Dostoevsky: "The degree of civilization in a society can be judged by entering its prisons." She urged all citizens to familiarize themselves with public institutions that, as taxpayers, they were responsible for: If one investigated, one might "find something really valuable" to be done. Personally, she wrote:

> The mere sight of the barred windows and doors, the thought of what nights must be with all that closely packed humanity thinking no very happy thoughts, makes me shiver as I go in, and breathe a prayer of gratitude as I come out again into the air and sun, free.

Also, the WPA was under assault, and ER stepped up her defense. She dismissed mean-minded accusations of "shovel leaning," and urged the critical to do hard manual labor, or shovel snow themselves, "and then see how you feel. I know because I've done it myself."

Speaking to a group of Junior Leaguers, ER acknowledged that some people were lazy, that there were employees everywhere who were "no good," but their children still deserved to eat, and everyone deserved jobs and training. ER repeatedly insisted that the only true anticrime bill was full employment.

She had never seen a WPA project she "was not really proud of." And she was particularly proud of WPA arts projects, which she hoped would create permanent institutions for leisure, recreation, and culture in every community:

> I hope also that we will continue to be able to look upon art and artists as one of the factors which can be used to draw nations together. . . . We need emotional outlets in this country and the more artistic people we develop the better it will be for us as a nation.

Closest to Hallie Flanagan's Federal Theatre Project, ER was credited for "saving" the murals project, which was under attack, and she campaigned for the Federal Music Project under Nikolai Sokoloff. Grateful, Sokoloff reported to the First Lady that by 1937 his unit employed almost sixteen thousand musicians in 163 symphony and concert orchestras, fifty-one bands, a composer's project, fifteen chamber music ensembles, sixty-nine dance orchestras, 146 teacher projects, grand opera and operetta companies, various library, copyist, and soloist projects, and a folk song project in the Kentucky hills.

After June Rhodes told Hick that ER looked unusually exhausted, Hick proposed an alternative to travel for their upcoming vacation. Hick wanted ER "to retire" with her for a week of peace in "the little house at the Danas."

Hick wanted ER to be with her in Long Island during her first spring vacation there. But the Danas planned to return to Nevada by April, and if they knew ER planned to visit, they might stay. Hick did not want to share their time together:

> They would pester us to death. Nor would I want Tommy or anyone else around. I'm very fond of Tommy—honestly—but I've decided that, while I can have a perfectly good time with either of you alone, I do not particularly enjoy being with you together. I suppose the reason is that when you are together you can never forget for more than fifteen minutes at a time your darned jobs. That shuts me out, and I get bored and miserable.

Also Hick worried that it might turn out as other times together in New York and Washington had, "when I was taking a vacation supposedly with you, but with you not actually taking one." In that case, she would "infinitely rather go on the trip."

The "little house" was little only by the baronial standards of the neighborhood. A bright, comfortable, sun-filled home, it was a two-story dwelling with several bedrooms, a small library, a sitting room, cozy fireplaces, and several rooms to spare. There was an upstairs deck and a downstairs porch. Part of a close community, it became Hick's home and refuge for almost twenty years. A short walk from the bay, nestled deep in the woods, surrounded by wildlife and nature, it was a serene space, and she felt at the moment content.

Hick's World's Fair boss, former state senator Joseph Baldwin, asked if she would work with him in the future. Baldwin intended to run for Congress "and would like to have me for his 'Mrs. Moskowitz.' . . . No, darling, I didn't laugh in his face." Actually, Hick was pleased: Belle Moskowitz, Al Smith's chief adviser and administrator, had been *one* powerful woman.

ER warned Hick: "Don't be anybody's Mrs. Moskowitz." The work was grueling, and anonymous, "and your temperament would find it hard!"

That week they spent an especially lovely evening together, and Hick wrote: "Darling, when one has one's emotions fairly well under control, life *can* be diverting, can't it?"

Politically, life was astir. ER had a long talk with Anna Louise Strong, who had just returned from Spain and Russia. ER had sent her a "warm welcome-home letter" and invited her for lunch. She wrote Hick that Strong had "told me interesting things" about the Spanish People's Front, the Soviet trials, "and who has softened towards us a bit!"

Strong's goal during their meeting was to convince ER that the United States should be supporting the Spanish Loyalists. She seemed to Strong "appreciative but noncommittal." ER brought their conversation to FDR, who remained adamantly committed to his policy of embargo and noninvolvement.

While the future of democracy, communism, and fascism exploded in Spain's civil war, America seemed in peril of taking the same path. Immediately after the inauguration, lawful strikes and innovative sit-down strikes were opposed by bloody strike-breaking episodes that challenged the future of democratic unionism promised by the Wagner Act and reinforced by FDR's oratory.

In February, ER received several letters demanding military action against strikers. She wrote Hick about a woman who wanted the sit-down strikers evicted "in the name of sacred private property rights—and if the militia can't do it the U.S. Army should be used! I ask you!"

ER supported the union movement and was revolted by the industrial violence resorted to each time unions tried to organize, beginning with the Southern and New England textile strikes of 1934. After 1920 when she joined the Women's Trade Union League, she remained convinced that nothing would change until workers organized for their own protection and economic needs.

ER's emphatic support for labor unions was demonstrated by her own membership in the American Newspaper Guild, which she joined when she became a United Features Syndicate columnist. In December 1936, the Newspaper Guild voted to leave the American Federation of Labor (AFL) and join the Congress of Industrial Organizations (CIO), a move ER publicly endorsed. Subsequently, she invited CIO leaders to a White House Conference on Youth, and pointed out that there were many more young people in the CIO than in the AFL.

Initiated by star reporter Heywood Broun in 1933, the Newspaper Guild was an aggressive union often damned as communist. ER was the first First Lady actually to join a labor union, although she told her press conference on 5 January 1937 that she would not join a picket line or strike, "at least in the immediate future." But she was proud to be a member of the Guild, which, she said, "had done perfectly splendid things." For ER the union "principle is sound and right."

Throughout the 1930s, ER was loyal to the Guild, and to Broun, who adored the First Lady. In 1937, he reported that the pecan workers of San Antonio wanted ER for president—a view he commended: "At the moment Eleanor Roosevelt has a deeper and closer understanding of the needs and aspirations of millions of Americans than any other person in public life."

ER always rejected such ideas: "Nothing on God's green earth would induce me to run for anything." But she demanded justice for all workers, including the embattled workers of General Motors in Flint, Michigan.

Although she initially deplored confrontations and sit-down strikes, ER condemned GM's Alfred P. Sloan for refusing to attend a conference Frances Perkins called with John L. Lewis in Washington. ER declared: "If we are going to settle things peaceably, we have to have a spirit of good will." Sloan's attitude of "fear and distrust" made it impossible to bargain collectively, which was labor's right, and to "reach reasonable conclusions."

In 1937 when the Supreme Court reversed its twenty-year stand and finally held the minimum-wage law for women and children constitutional, ER proceeded to battle for minimum-wage and maximum-hour laws for all workers. So long as employers could pay women less for the same work, all would be underpaid.

ER attended union meetings, participated in union socials, and personally helped mediate various strikes. She emphasized collective bargaining, and by 1938 hoped that unionism would promote "a yearly wage" to replace hourly wages, which, she said, were responsible for underemployment and workers' indignity. When unionism was fully accepted, there would be a new deal of full employment and a truly living wage.

For ER, democracy and workers' rights were synonymous. In May 1934 she gave a lecture to 2,700 delegates at a YWCA convention on peace and progress. There could not be progress for some unless there was "progress for everybody; and [that] must include cooperation between industry and labor; with labor organized in unions so as not to remain weak and unsubstantial." Industrial peace, as well as international peace, depended on justice for workers: "The old desire to gather profit for the few at the expense of the many" was what all religions and races must oppose today: Industrial peace depended on women's involvement and an awareness of labor conditions in every community.

ER made it clear that she did not limit her notion of community to white communities: We could not ostracize "some races" and pretend to be good Christians. We could not "follow the teachings of Jesus Christ and permit in this country some of the things we stand for today." It was the responsibility of the YWCA to "reach out to all countries and spread the belief that human beings can grow into a brotherhood the world over."

Although ER said nothing publicly about sit-down strikes, she honored picket lines. In 1939, she even refused to cross one to attend FDR's birthday ball at a Washington hotel where the waitresses were on strike for better daily wages.

ER continued to hope that unionism and collective bargaining might be achieved without strikes. In an address before the League of Women Shoppers, chaired by her friend Evelyn Preston (married to the ACLU's Roger Baldwin), ER said strikes "brought a great deal of harm" to both sides. Although she realized that in certain industries "there may be no other way," she preferred to see "all factions" bargain collectively "in a spirit of good feeling."

ER completely misjudged the labor situation in 1937. For John L. Lewis and the CIO it was the year to organize the unorganized. Lewis had rejuvenated the union movement, and was responsible for the successful slogan: "The President wants you to join a union." He had contributed heartily to FDR's 1936 campaign, and in exchange for the United Mine Workers' $500,000 cash contribution (the equivalent of $5 million in 1990s dollars), he expected presidential support for labor. Moreover, FDR's campaign oratory against "economic royalists" gave Lewis every reason to believe he had presidential support.

Sit-down strikes immobilized industry after industry and resulted in unionism's greatest triumphs and heartbreaks. From the Firestone rubber plant strike in Akron, Ohio, in 1936 to the famous General Motors autoworkers' triumph in 1937, there were almost seven thousand strikes. Mostly, the CIO achieved its goals: higher wages, shorter hours, better working conditions, paid vacations, dignity and respect for industrial workers. In fact, 60 percent of the strikes during the 1930s were for the right to unionize; union recognition meant respect. But everywhere the crusade was marked by contempt and organized cruelty.

ER's vision of an era of "good feeling" and amiable negotiation was mocked by industrial violence, company vigilantes, and local militias. Hundreds of workers were tear-gassed, wounded, shot. As the CIO organized to end industrial tyranny, antiunion terror intensified. In 1936, Ford, General Motors, U.S. Steel, and the du Ponts organized a "special conference committee" to crush the CIO with vigilante violence and charges of communism. These were the "economic Royalists" against whom FDR campaigned, and he was the target of their Red Scare tactics.

Now, Wisconsin's progressive Senator Robert La Follette held hearings on industrial violence, and his publicized findings stimulated a national debate about labor's democratic right to organize against repressive, even torturous, industrial tactics. According to the Senate's La Follette Committee on Civil Liberties, industry spent over $80 million to spy on and eliminate union efforts between 1934 and 1936. In addition to engaging in espionage, corporations stockpiled noxious gases, machine guns, and various projectiles. Between 1933 and 1937, Republic Steel, for example, purchased 552 revolvers, 64 rifles, 254 shotguns, 143 gas guns, 4,033 gas projectiles, 2,707 gas grenades, and many other weapons to use against its employees.

La Follette's committee deplored the climate of terror and intimidation, the armed brutality that curtailed "the exercise of constitutionally guaranteed rights of freedom of speech and of assembly," which now specifically protected unionists as a result of the Wagner Labor Relations Act. In contempt of procedures set up by the National Labor Relations Board, industrialists escalated their intimidation, and fortified their arsenals.

At the same time, strikes erupted nationwide: WPA artists, members of the Workers Alliance, held a "stay-in-strike" in New York City. College students picketed against food costs in Chicago. Newspaper reporters and workers struck from Seattle (the strike settled when Hearst hired the Boettigers) to Flushing, New York. Silver miners struck in Nevada; asbestos workers halted work in New Jersey's Johns Manville Company.

In January 1937, many Americans were disgusted to read in newspapers how Eleanor Roosevelt's name was used to discredit unionists. When the La Follette Committee held hearings on "Jack Barton" (a.k.a. Bart Logan), his story made headline news. His effort to organize the International Union of Mine, Mill and Smelter Workers, in Bessemer, Alabama, resulted in harassment and three arrests: once as a suspected communist (though the Communist Party was then legal in Alabama); once for being in possession of seditious literature (including *The Nation* and *The New Republic*); and once for vagrancy (although he had $35 cash in his pocket and was employed). When questioned about his "communist" activities, he was asked what his contacts were with Heywood Broun and Eleanor Roosevelt.

At his trial, the court refused him a lawyer or a jury, and he was sentenced to 180 days at hard labor and fined $100. When the International Labor Defense Committee provided bail, local authorities refused to accept it. He was forced into leg shackles on a chain gang. His legs became infected and his arrested case of tuberculosis flared. Within weeks he lost fifteen pounds, collapsed, and was sent to a sanatorium.

Although ER's connections to the many unionists who were asked about their alleged friendship with her were irrelevant, and usually nonexistent, she became personally close to one of the many heroes and victims of torture La Follette investigated, Joseph Gelders. The former physics professor at the University of Alabama, as Southern representative of the National Committee for the Defense of Political Prisoners, launched a campaign for Bart Logan's release. After a nighttime meeting in Bessemer, on 23 September 1936, Gelders was surrounded by four vigilantes and clubbed with a baseball bat. His nose was broken and he was beaten unconscious. When he awoke, he was stripped, flogged, kicked, and beaten again. Driven into the country and left for dead, Gelders survived and hitched a ride to a hospital in Clanton. Although he subsequently identified his assailants, the grand jury refused to indict them. The company controlled the town; unionists and their friends were unwelcome. Civil libertarians and Birmingham's labor community organized against terrrorism and class war, with support from Governor Bibb Graves, who offered a $200 reward for the capture of Gelders's attackers.

Ultimately, the La Follette Committee's revelations helped change the industrial climate of the country. Even though Southern senators opposed its investigations into local industrial habits and threatened to defund the committee, public opinion shifted in favor of the CIO. Logan and Gelders, the only Southern witnesses, dramatically improved the situation in Alabama, and their testimony influenced Myron Taylor, who announced that U.S. Steel would recognize the CIO.

By 1938, ER worked closely with Joseph Gelders and the CIO's Southern field representative Lucy Randolph Mason. Together they launched and organized the Southern Conference for Human Welfare. Gelders initially wanted a conference of liberals and labor leaders to focus on the economy and civil liberties. ER invited him to the White House to discuss his plans and arranged a meeting with FDR, who suggested the conference deal with all Southern controversies, including voting rights and the poll tax.

While the La Follette Committee broadcast the plight of unionists and encouraged workers' rights, the United Auto Workers organized General Motors plants in fifty-seven communities throughout the United States and Canada. ER subsequently became close to the Reuther brothers, who built the UAW, which in January and February changed labor history as thousands of strikers sat down in Detroit and Flint, Michigan. Unprecedented and dramatic, tense and dangerous, the six-week stand-off seemed like the dawn of Armageddon. Led by Roy, Victor, and Walter Reuther and supported by the wives, mothers, and grandmothers of the striking autoworkers, a grassroots movement democratized industrial America.

"With Babies and Banners," the Women's Emergency Brigade and the Women's Auxiliary, organized by twenty-three-year-old Genora Johnson, fed and protected their husbands and sons. With red armbands and red tams, they marched and sang, broke windows when their men were gassed, and put their bodies in front of threatening police. The strikers were family, creating a new social order. "A new type of woman was born in the strike." Union wives would never again, they vowed, be silent or uninvolved. "The home and the union are becoming fused. . . ."

The songs and rallies, the perseverance and courage, at Detroit and Flint changed industrial life and remained legendary: "We Shall Not Be Moved," "Union Maid," "Sit Down," "Write Me Out My Union Card," "Solidarity Forever."

CIO president John L. Lewis expected a sign of presidential support, at least a promise of relief for the strikers. The strikers assumed the president was "completely on their side." But FDR would say nothing to endorse the lawless occupation of private property.

Flint, Michigan, was the center of the vortex. Rubber workers and coal miners arrived to help out; "a revolutionary spirit surged through the town." Michigan's New Deal governor Frank Murphy, close to FDR, held frantic meetings with GM president Alfred P. Sloan, Frances Perkins, and John L. Lewis.

Charges of radicalism, of communism, abounded. But when Sloan refused Perkins's offer for government mediation, public opinion was with the strikers. Then, on 2 February, a Flint judge issued an injunction and ordered the strikers out. They refused, and sent a telegram to Governor Murphy:

> Unarmed as we are, the introduction of the militia, sheriffs or police . . . will mean a blood-bath of unarmed workers. . . . We have no illusions about the sacrifice this decision will entail. We fully expect that if a violent effort is made to oust us many of us will be killed and we take this means of making it known to our wives, to our children, to the people. . . . You are the one who must be held responsible for our deaths!

John L. Lewis headed for Detroit. Everything depended on Murphy's next move. He was with the union, but he was obliged to enforce the law of an injunction. When Lewis arrived, Murphy reported that FDR wanted sit-down strikes ended. Lewis was surprised. FDR had told him to "let them sit." Murphy called for clarification, with Lewis on an extension. They heard FDR together: "Disregard whatever Mr. Lewis tells you."

According to Saul Alinsky, those words started the unending and "deadly feud between Lewis and Roosevelt." Lewis later told Alinsky it was at that moment he "discovered the depths of deceit, the rank dishonesty and the doublecrossing character of Franklin Delano Roosevelt."

ER dreaded the implications of FDR's evenhanded silence, and grieved to see capital actually mobilized to crush labor in America on her husband's watch.

With a militia of thirteen hundred, reinforced by twelve hundred heavily armed cavalry and other military personnel, the strikers were surrounded. For a time a blockade threatened the workers with starvation. But Murphy called it off, and the CIO's auxiliary women's battalion got food to their men. Then Murphy replaced one National Guard unit with the 125th Infantry, from Detroit: Comprised of autoworkers and their sons, brothers, cousins, and friends, it was a heroic demonstration of support. Still the atmosphere crackled with trouble as unionists descended from every area, and street fights with armed vigilantes ensued.

Insurrection, even revolution, was in the air. GM turned off the heat, to drive the workers out. Workers opened the windows, which threatened to freeze everything inside, including the firefighting apparatus—which rendered GM's insurance policies void. In a frenzy, GM representatives at Murphy's insistence sat around a bargaining table with Lewis and Murphy, but refused to bargain. They dickered for a week, and settled nothing. On 9 February, Murphy alerted the National Guard. Death seemed imminent, as did the destruction of GM's plants. Flint was to become a battlefield, a cemetery. Murphy was about to give up; Lewis invoked the names of Murphy's Irish revolutionary forebears and urged the governor to remain steadfast. At 2:45 A.M. on 10 February, GM capitulated.

At noon on 11 February 1937, General Motors recognized the United Automobile Workers, CIO. Both sides of the strike now called for industrial peace. ER, like all friends of unionism, was relieved by the monumental victory.

In a February column, ER showed her support for organized labor—and workers' unity: She had been visited by six New York City unionists, five of them unemployed "probably because they belong to this union, which is not a very strong one as yet." Their demands seemed to her entirely reasonable: a wage to guarantee decent living, a forty-hour week, fair notice before layoffs. ER explained: "Many people do not believe in unions"; industrialists had competitive business needs; "unions and their leaders are not always wise and fair, any more than any other human beings." Nevertheless, she concluded, only unionization will protect workers; and she, like the "majority of the people," favored unions because they represented a democratic means to a necessary goal.

FDR's support for Murphy's arbitration helped avoid bloodshed and advanced union recognition. But his silence did not protect him. It invoked Lewis's bitter enmity and failed to stem charges of communism against the New Deal. The winds of the "little Red Scare" intensified as CIO victories mounted: Firestone, Goodyear, Studebaker, General Electric, Pittsburgh Plate Glass.

On 2 March 1937, Myron Taylor announced U.S. Steel's contract with Lewis. Without a strike, 60 percent of the steel industry was now CIO. But Walter Chrysler, considered a just and fair man by autoworkers, opted for a showdown with the strikers at Chrysler.

Ironically, Nicholas Kelley was Chrysler's general counsel. Florence Kelley's son was not spared Lewis's Shakespearean wrath: After a litany of his mother's pioneering support for workers and unionism, economic justice and democracy, Kelley shouted: "STOP IT, STOP IT, MR. LEWIS! . . . I—I—AM NOT AFRAID OF YOUR EYEBROWS." The stalled negotiations ended in laughter, and Chrysler signed the CIO contract. Walter Chrysler told Lewis: "I do not worry about dealing with you, it is the Communists . . . that worry me. . . ."

ER's steadfast friends and political allies Esther Lape, RIGHT, and Elizabeth Read, BELOW.

SDR's 80th birthday, 21 September 1934. Back row (*left to right*): FDR, Jr., Elliott, James, John; Middle row (*left to right*): ER, SDR, FDR. Front row (*left to right*): Ruth, Betsey, Sara, Eleanor (Sistie), Curtis (Buzzie), Anna.

ER with Ruth
Bryan Owen, the
U.S.'s first woman
ambassador,
4 October 1934.

With my devotion and deep
Roosevelt

The
"Cause and Cure
of War" dinner,
21 January 1936,
with Dr. Mary
Woolley and
Carrie Chapman
Catt.

Jane Addams, ABOVE, and
Lillian Wald, RIGHT, ER's
great mentors and models.

In Washington, ER met regularly
with the Four of Hearts, childhood friends Mary Harriman
Rumsey, Isabella Greenway…

…and Elizabeth, Lady Lindsay.
Frances Perkins regularly joined
their "air our minds" lunches.

Aubrey Williams, ER, Josephine Roche, and Harry Hopkins, National Youth Administration luncheon, 21 August 1935.

The first of ER's famous visits to coal mines, Bellaire, Ohio, 1935.

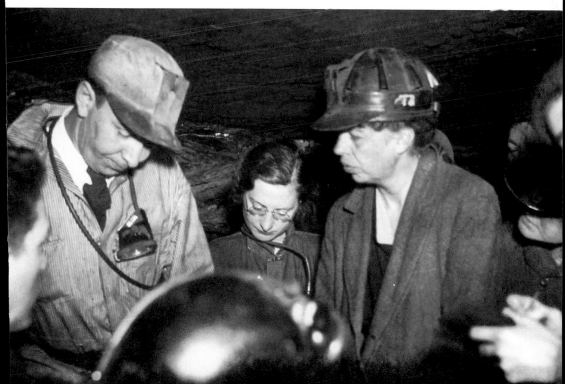

Louis Howe, the bridge between ER and FDR.

ER with her brother, Hall Roosevelt, at a ceremony for new PWA housing in Detroit, 1935.

First Lady Eleanor Roosevelt

In 1935, ER exchanged flowers with six-year-old Geraldine Walker in Detroit. *The Georgia Woman's World* ridiculed the tender moment in its hate campaign with the headline "BELIEVE IT OR NOT!" In 1998, the U.S. Post Office celebrated the same event with a commemorative stamp.

Bernard Baruch and ER at a
Metropolitan Opera benefit
for unemployed women,
2 April 1935.

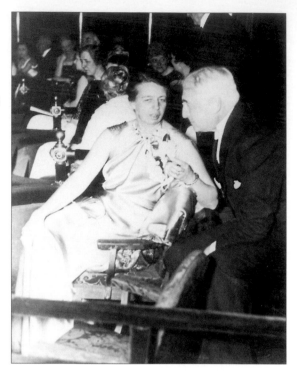

On the campaign train for the 1936 election.

Jim Farley, Molly Dewson, and ER launch the campaign in 1935.

ER and Tommy at Democratic National Headquarters, 1936.

There may be some as pretty,
And others just as witty,
But while my heart is beating
I'll ever keep repeating
It is you I want, my dearest,
only you.

May the world be full of
sunshine,
And our meetings frequent be,
Hours of joy & quiet
time,
Take us over life's rough
seas

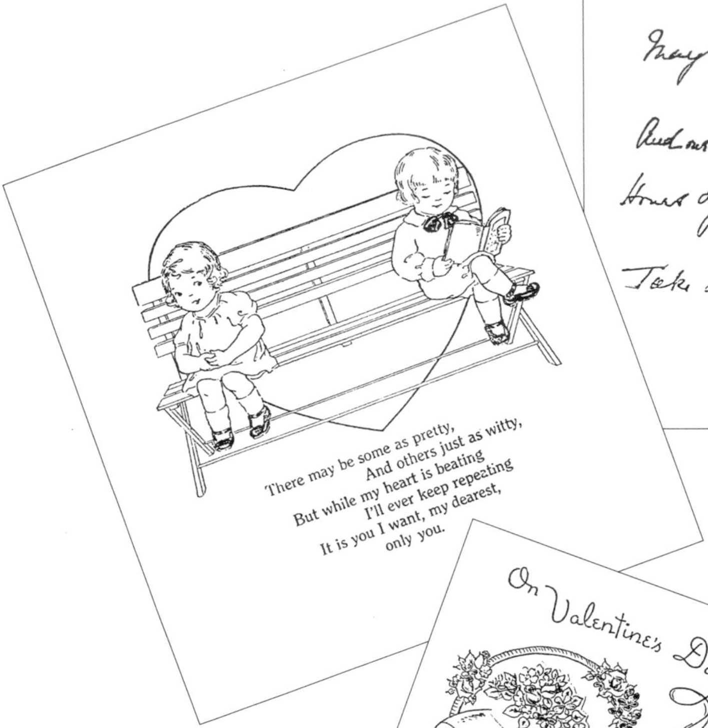

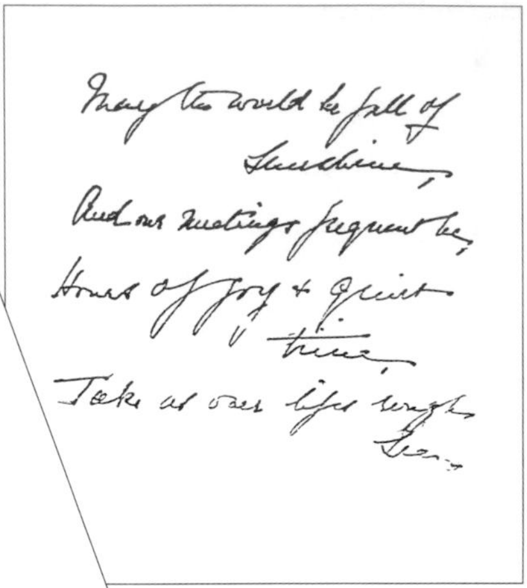

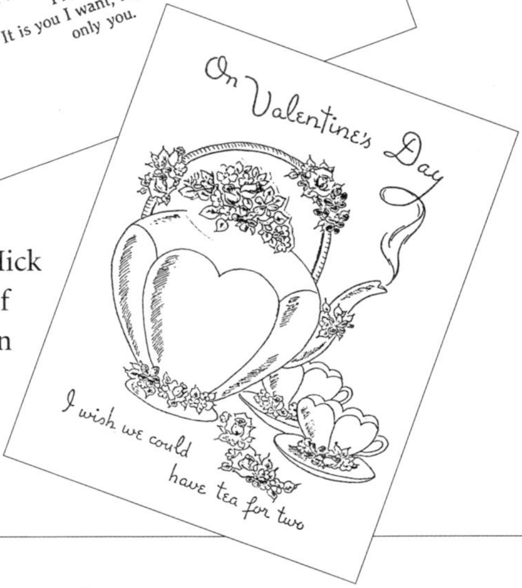

On Valentine's Day
I wish we could
have tea for two

ER's valentines to Hick illuminate the arc of their relationship. In 1934 there is romance, and "it is you I want, my dearest, only you." By 1935 "life's rough seas" have intruded. In 1937 even tea for two is difficult to arrange.

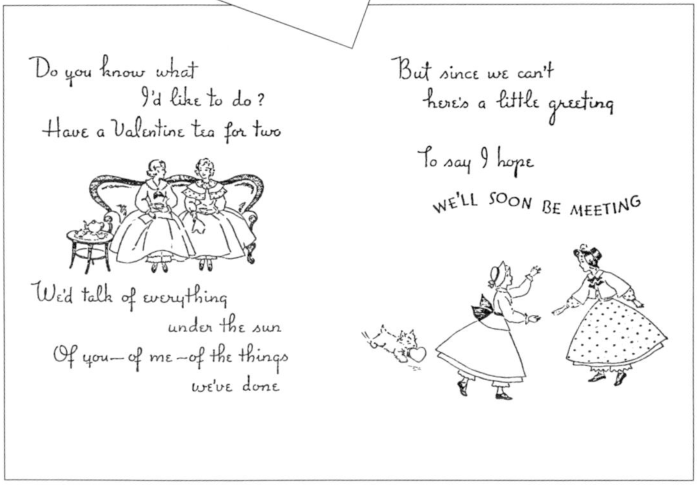

Do you know what
I'd like to do?
Have a Valentine tea for two
We'd talk of everything
under the sun
Of you—of me—of the things
we've done
But since we can't
here's a little greeting
To say I hope
WE'LL SOON BE MEETING

Weddings in the family: Franklin, Jr., marries Ethel Du Pont, June 1937.

And John Roosevelt marries Anne Clark, June 1938.

Mary McLeod Bethune, leader of the Black Cabinet.

Molly Dewson at a celebratory Democratic dinner, 1938.

Thanksgiving at Warm Springs, Ga., ER, FDR, and Robert Rosenbaum, 24 November 1938.

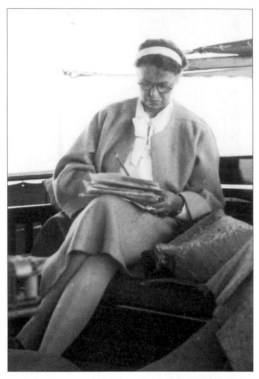

ER relaxing on the *Sequoia.*

Square dancing at Arthurdale.

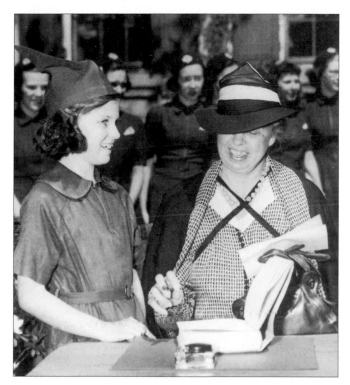

Signing a copy of
This Is My Story.

Listening and knitting
at the World Youth
Congress at Vassar,
1938.

OVERLEAF: ER at
Norris Dam.

The great CIO victories of February–March 1937 led to dignity for workers and the mobilization of a new American movement that united economic and racial justice.

On 5 February 1937, while the CIO dominated headlines, FDR eclipsed the news. The president held a startling news conference in which he announced that he wanted legislation enabling him to appoint a new Supreme Court justice for every justice over seventy who refused to retire. At the time six justices were over seventy. Though it was not an outrageous suggestion, given the Supreme Court's contempt for New Deal legislation, it exploded unexpectedly.

The plan he had referred to only obliquely on 6 January was now introduced without warning. He had alerted nobody, prepared no public support. The press went wild. Congress was frantic: "Power mad," FDR intended to "pack the court" and ruin the nation.

Never before had FDR acted without consulting his closest allies, or creating a congressional support base for his most controversial decisions. In part, he simply misjudged the political circumstances. After all, he was the first president since James Monroe, a century before, to enjoy a majority in both houses of Congress. After the election of 1936, there were 76 Democrats and 16 Republicans in the Senate and 332 Democrats and 89 Republicans in the House. Clearly he expected support from his co-partisans. But the landslide was a political illusion. Where real issues of liberal change were involved, Northern Democrats had little in common with Southern Democrats, and black and white Democrats remained embattled in every region.

FDR's secrecy was a misguided tactic. Fears of dictatorship, charges of a brutal violation against constitutional sanctity, emerged from unlikely quarters; a wide spectrum of friends and foes opposed his "court-packing" proposal.

ER was surprised and troubled by FDR's scheme. Although she agreed there was a need to transform the Court, she doubted the wisdom of his decision to increase the number of justices from nine to fifteen. She invited Esther Lape and Elizabeth Read to the White House to discuss what they considered FDR's threat to the nation's celebrated "balance of powers." Attorney and legal scholar, and ER's personal investment adviser, Elizabeth Read had actually sat and wept at her dining-room table when she first read of FDR's intentions. Nothing he had done, not even their differences over the World Court, had ever seemed to her so wrong and dangerous. She feared charges of dictatorship would create opposition to all his good works.

Bipartisan opposition to FDR's court-packing bill suspended all other issues for months. ER subsequently wrote that "he might have saved himself a good deal of trouble" had he had the patience to wait until several justices died or retired.

ER was mostly perplexed by her husband's priorities. Given his great election victory, he might have instead focused on positive solutions to the nation's ills. And she was always disturbed by FDR's secretiveness. She frequently lamented that everybody who left his office left convinced that he had been promised something specific, when he had been promised nothing at all. As ER contemplated FDR's Supreme Court proposal, she believed Howe would have prevented this boner, and she fully realized how far outside FDR's decision-making process she now stood.

Despite her private qualms, ER publicly defended her husband. Charges that he had become a dictator to grant favors to "a minority" were ludicrous. She wrote that all opposition to FDR's Court reform plan came from the very people who opposed the "social legislation of the present Administration, and the views of the people on this legislation were rather clearly expressed in November," by a vast majority. The people of America had voted for FDR; he represented them and was obliged to protect their needs and interests.

Although she initially told FDR that as she traveled across the country, she heard opposition to his plan across the political spectrum, she was persuasive in her defense. June Rhodes wrote: "I am reading everything you write about the Supreme Court each day, and . . . it seems in my humble opinion that [the President] is doing the right thing at the right time."

Esther Lape and Elizabeth Read remained bitterly opposed; Hick was in favor, but wavered; her circle was mostly opposed. ER's correspondence emphasized the subject for months as it absorbed the nation's business and dominated Congress.

In February, Hick spent several days at the White House to attend Democratic Party festivities and private events. On 15 February, "we all spent a very happy evening" celebrating Jim Farley. Hick enjoyed wearing her new black velvet gown, and for ER "the high point" occurred "when I suddenly saw my very dignified friend, Molly Dewson . . . turn and pin a rose on her chief, giving him a kiss at the same time."

ER made much of Molly Dewson's ceremonial kiss, and explained to the Democratic women of New York that tall, muscular Molly, Polly Porter's longtime partner, rarely if ever kissed men, and so this occasion "was not as spontaneous as it seemed for she is not accustomed to embracing gentlemen and I think she must have had some coaching—but it was profitable coaching for it went off very well."

That week ER had an "air our minds" luncheon with Elisabeth Lindsay and Isabella Greenway—who had decided not to run again for Congress, evidently because of her differences with FDR, and had moved to New York. Far less pleasant was tea with Alice Roosevelt Longworth. ER wrote her daughter that Alice had arrived "at her request, and she can't see why any of us should mind anything she has said."

Although Cousin Alice had been vicious during the campaign, and her "mollycoddle" column was unforgivable, ER nevertheless avoided a final break. Besides, she had for the moment won their lifelong competition. Alice's daily column, printed in some papers beside "My Day," was initially a spirited lark. ER wrote her old friend, now congresswoman, Nan Honeyman: "She certainly writes well. I wish I were as free as she, though I do not wish ever to be as bitter."

But Alice's columns were dull and soon canceled, and the final insult came when the *Ladies' Home Journal,* which had been losing money, was taken over by Bruce and Beatrice Gould. To get the serial rights to ER's memoir, they not only offered her $75,000, they offered Alice "a settlement of $2,000 to give up her column," so that ER would consider their bid more kindly.

On 16 February ER and Elinor Morgenthau drove off "in a young blizzard," heading north to Cornell, and Tommy wrote Anna that "your father was really upset. He told the usher that no matter what he was doing to bring him word from her at once that she had arrived safely somewhere for the night. He told your mother she was a little mad and she said she was glad— she got more fun out of life that way!"

At home, White House tensions bristled over the Supreme Court. ER wrote Hick: "FDR is tired and edgy and they are all working on a speech."

Elizabeth Read had a stroke that affected her memory and her ability to write and "to find the right words." ER rushed to be with Esther Lape: "Elizabeth is ill and must be absolutely quiet. . . . I rather hate leaving Esther she looks so worried. Theirs is a companionship of long standing with Elizabeth the more unselfish & understanding in the past."

ER's friends were in agony over FDR's Court scheme and also devastated that FDR had rejected the American Foundation's new health care plan, due out in April. Lape's committee of distinguished physicians, led by Dr. Hugh Cabot of the Mayo Clinic, concluded that America's health was unsatisfactory and in some regions entirely neglected. Their report provided brilliant testimony with incontrovertible evidence and made a splendid case. But FDR decided to postpone all consideration of the health security issue.

FDR wanted to fight only one big battle at a time, and he was absorbed by the Court fight. On 4 March he addressed a Democratic victory celebration dinner at the Mayflower. Ickes considered it "by all odds, the greatest [speech] he has ever made. . . . It was a fighting speech," with one clear point: There could not be "social justice and economic freedom" so long as the Supreme Court, "one of the three horses pulling the national plow," went off on its own and opposite direction.

We have only just begun to fight. . . .
Here are thousands upon thousands of men and women working for long hours in factories for inadequate pay—NOW!
Here are strikes more far-reaching than we have ever known, costing millions of dollars—NOW!
Here are spring floods threatening to roll again down our river valleys—NOW!
Here is the Dust Bowl beginning to blow again—NOW!
If we would keep faith with those who had faith in us, if we would make democracy succeed, I say we must act—NOW!"

Hick rhapsodized over FDR's speech: "God, it and he were magnificent! There MAY have been more powerful speeches than that, but I've never heard them or read them. And I had a year of Cicero when I was a kid."

In March, ER went south for her lecture tour. She sent Hick birthday greetings from New Orleans, "something small," and ordered "beautiful night-gowns," which she hoped had arrived. "You have my love every day dear . . . and may every year be happier than the last."

Tommy wrote Anna that New Orleans was fabulous, and ER liked it about as much as Santa Fe. All of ER's lectures went well, "your mother is quite professional." Tommy echoed ER's observations about Huey Long: Although Long "was a pain in the neck," he was not basically "very different in his interest in 'the people' than is your father." He introduced a gasoline tax "which pays for nearly everything which benefits the ordinary people—roads, schools, school books. . . . When you think of states like West Virginia which have been wrung dry . . . you realize how foresighted he was." But ER remained aloof from Huey Long's legacy, and whenever his name was mentioned "with much compliment, neither your mother nor I moved a muscle!"

23: A First Lady's Survival:
Work and Run

—◦◦◦—

On 9 March, FDR broadcast a Fireside Chat to defend his Court scheme: Economic recovery and all future legislative progress depended on Congress's ability to protect America from catastrophe, but the Supreme Court denied Congress's right to legislate and thwarted "the will of the people." We "must take action to save the Constitution from the Court and the Court from itself. . . . [We] want a government of laws and not of men."

FDR did not seek a bench of "spineless puppets." He wanted justices who would not override legislation demanded by the needs of the people. We "cannot yield our constitutional destiny to the personal judgment of a few men who, being fearful of the future, would deny us the necessary means of dealing with the present. . . ."

ER heard his address in Fort Worth, with Elliott, Ruth, and Tommy. She cabled their congratulations: It was a "grand talk." ER now fully supported FDR's plan. She could understand people's fears, but they minimized "the difficulties and obstacles" he faced.

While ER was in Oklahoma the first installment of her memoir appeared in the *Ladies' Home Journal*. It was a heady, exciting time. She was mobbed everywhere, and in some towns she was scheduled to do several lectures in a day, in addition to meetings, luncheons, teas, and dinners. Tommy blamed Colston Leigh's agency for being inconsiderate, and creating an itinerary without even a glance at a map. She wrote Anna from Oklahoma City: "We started off on this trek in a fairly peaceful frame of mind," but it had been altogether too hectic.

In Huntsville, Texas, Anna Pennybacker introduced ER for "exactly 29 minutes." Exhausted by her rhetorical bouquet, Tommy thought ER "should have lain down and let it serve as an obituary."

In Perry, Texas, ER "was actually mobbed by an enthusiastic crowd." Then they were driven a hundred miles to Alva, Oklahoma, where they were put up in a "dinky little place," with wretched food, and given a bill for $30—about

$300 in today's dollars. ER felt "in her 'position' she could not squawk, but I wanted to." Their last trek was by car through "miles of mud from Alva to Oklahoma City." Tommy vowed to go after Leigh's scalp. In the future, they would study a map, and insist on one lecture per day, without trappings, lunches, dinners, tours, meetings. "We could have done the whole thing in two weeks instead of three."

ER made no such complaints. But she was insulted by one encounter, and wrote Hick:

> Yesterday was the worst day I've had! The lady president of the college [Kate Zaners, State Teachers College, Durant, Oklahoma] told me that the people cared much more about seeing me and touching me than hearing me speak and if anything were canceled the speech would matter least! A point of view not calculated to make one do one's best but after both speeches I received between 2 and 3,000 people. . . .

In the Deep South, where ER was both hated and loved, the KKK had made death threats and she was surrounded by security:

> We've had some funny times as in Shreveport [Louisiana] where the police had me so on their minds that the five hours we were in the hotel they sat in our sitting room with us and so became our bosom friends!

In Birmingham, Alabama, ER was overwhelmed to be officially and enthusiastically welcomed: "My reception was horrible . . . and we went through the streets like FDR crawling behind a band and high school cadet corps and the flags." There was a heat wave, and ER was mobbed by thousands of people everywhere she went, including Negro and white PWA housing projects, and everywhere she spoke, including colleges, universities, and large public forums. There were casual events, formal events, and gatherings: "They love FDR but I'm a little weary playing prexy!" At no time did ER imagine the outpouring of affection and regard was for her. Tommy, on the other hand, wrote Anna: "There may be something in this rumour of running your mother in 1940!"

While ER toured, FDR was at Warm Springs with a party that included James's wife, Betsey, and William Bullitt. ER wrote her husband:

> I am glad to see that you got off and are now enjoying Warm Springs. . . . Newspapers in Oklahoma seem to be for you dear and in spite of [critical editorials] and Senators' speeches I think the people of such parts of Louisiana, Texas, and Oklahoma as I have seen are with you on the Supreme Court.

There was mostly amusing publicity about ER's toting a loaded pistol. She assured FDR that she carried it only when alone in her car. "I never carry it around at other times." Her schedule was "strenuous but one week is over and we are still intact and going strong. My love to Bets and Missy and I hope you all have a grand rest and much fun."

On 17 March, their wedding anniversary, ER reported that "a cunning little boy and girl appeared on the stage after my lecture," dressed as bride and groom. "They marched over and presented me with a bouquet of flowers, followed by someone bearing a wedding cake. It was a most amusing little ceremony and the children were very solemn about it."

ER returned to Washington on Good Friday, 26 March, "twenty-four hours ahead of the President." She needed the day to "pick up the threads and start the house at high speed again." On Easter Monday a record fifty-three thousand children enjoyed the White House annual egg-rolling festivities.

Home for less than two weeks, with spring in the air, ER's "Wanderlust" sent her with Hick on a ten-day trip to the Smoky Mountains. Enspirited by nature's bounty and gratified by the New Deal's efforts to preserve it, ER wrote about her holiday for the *Democratic Digest:* "I drove my own car with a friend," and saw "cedar trees about a thousand years old!" The ride was glorious, and in Gatlinberg, Tennessee, in the Great Smoky Mountain Park, the "Federal Government is preserving some virgin timber which is well worth seeing," as were the wonderful works achieved at various CCC camps.

ER wrote her daughter from Charleston, South Carolina:

> Darling, This trip has been really beautiful and I think Hick has enjoyed it except for a few rangers in the park! I hadn't planned on any hikes because I knew she was working in an office all winter but we did walk 4 miles to see some wonderful trees and she bore up nobly. The Great Smokies are lovely and would be wonderful for a week of climbing afoot or on horseback if ever I can find anyone who likes it!

ER wanted to return in June "when all the rhododendrons and azaleas and mountain laurel are out. . . ."

ER's need to find somebody she could hike and ride with, someone actually to enjoy the kind of vacations she craved, became a significant factor in the distance that grew between her and Hick. While they each wrote their time together was pleasant, Tommy wrote Anna:

> Your mother started off last Saturday with Hick on a week's motor drive. Each one separately told me she had no desire to go so I am wondering what kind of a time they are having. Naturally, I kept my own counsel and did not relay the messages. . . .

It seemed to ER rather a lonely spring. Her children were scattered, and Anna was unavailable for months. Isabella Greenway was in New York, and her Val-Kill companions were upset and upsetting.

Earlier in the year, Marion Dickerman had attempted to buy a school building without clear title. Tommy wrote Anna that "Dickie is having fits about the school," which was a business, and the building she wanted was in a residential zone.

> Her lawyer knew it but thought they could get away with it. When your mother turned her interests over to Harry Hooker, he discovered it at once and wouldn't let them ignore it because . . . if any suit was brought your mother's name would be the only one mentioned.

Dickie was furious, and the core of trust along the Val-Kill continued to erode.

ER was also in a cold rage about daughter-in-law Betsey. According to Tommy, "Betsey and Missy are still very thick and Missy spends most of her time with Betsey and Jimmy as far as I can see. Betsey's devotion to your father is something!"

With her household imbalanced by a daughter-in-law who usurped her place and increasingly took charge of details ER actually enjoyed presiding over, including seating arrangements and floral decorations, even when she was in residence, ER more frequently absented herself. She agreed to a series of radio programs, which Tommy thought would be easier than "lecturing and one night stands." But ER only added the radio programs to her lecture schedule.

ER herself added to household tensions when she wrote a column poking fun at FDR's mounting annoyance over bland White House food. FDR was unusually ruffled by his wife's words. ER wrote Anna:

> Pa is both nervous and tired. The court hue and cry has got under his skin. I thought stupidly his little outburst of boredom on meals was amusing and human and used it in my column and it was taken up by papers and radio and over the ticker and Steve [Early] and Jimmy got hate letters and were much upset and Pa was furious with me.
>
> James came and reproved me and said I must distinguish between things which were personal and should not be said or none of them would dare to talk to me and he thought I should apologize to Father. I did before McDuffie Monday night before leaving as I couldn't see him alone and Pa answered irritably that it had been very hard on him and he would certainly say nothing more to me on any subject! So it has become a very serious subject and I am grieved at my poor judgment and only hope it won't be remembered long. Will I be glad when we leave the WH and I can be on my own!

ER rarely allowed her anger to seep out so publicly. But her "misjudgment" reflected her rising bitterness over Betsey's interference, and White

House arrangements out of her control. FDR's ability to hurt ER with his attentions to women, even his flirtatious daughter-in-law, was surely in proportion to her ongoing love for him. Unable to forgive him, unable to have fun with him, she resented those who did. She felt aggrieved, but was unable to change her emotional patterns—except by more work, and longer trips away.

Before she left again for a Western tour, ER was steeped in controversy. After the second installment of her memoirs was published, she received a letter from a troubled reader, Esther S. Carey of Chicago: "My dear Mrs. Roosevelt: When it was announced . . . that you were going to write the story of your life, I was elated. . . . I couldn't wait to read the life story of the woman who seemed to be the paragon of American womanhood."

When it arrived, "I stopped work and literally devoured the First Installment." But then came the second installment:

> Alas as I was reading I came across two mentions of "darky." I couldn't believe my eyes. Surely no one of the Roosevelt blood could be guilty of using this hated term, and we do hate it, as much as the Jew hates "sheeny" and the Italian "dago" or "wop."
>
> I am a graduate of the Tuskegee Institute in Alabama and we looked upon your Uncle Theodore with reverence and thought that the blood of a Roosevelt could not hurt and humiliate Negroes who live and struggle under such dreadful handicaps.
>
> I am not given to writing letters of protest [and] this is the first I have ever written; but when the First Lady of the Land dubs us "darkies" it hurts—and I feel as Caesar felt when he had been stabbed by Brutus— I also ask "et tu Brute?"

ER replied: "My dear Mrs. Carey: 'Darky' was used by my great aunt as a term of affection and I have always considered it in that light. I am sorry if it hurt you. What do you prefer?"

The next week ER received a similar letter from a New York attorney, R. B. DeFrantz. Now DeFrantz noted that as one of her "millions of admirers" he was certain "it has never occurred to you that the word 'darky' . . . is offensive to many of your readers, and by many it is thought to do harm to the Negro as a race."

His letter pierced her defenses:

> I am terribly sorry if the use of the word "darky" offends and I will change it when my autobiography is published in book form. . . .

ER never used the term again, and forevermore excised words and stereotypes that lingered from her family traditions. She confronted the remnants of "race pride" in her own politics and within her own circle. She struggled against them privately and publicly. During a lecture at Barnard College, ER urged her audience of fifteen hundred women to consider their role in the future of democracy:

> Unless we can divest ourselves of that self-righteous feeling of superiority we are going to find it hard to understand how other people feel about their people, their history, their heroes and achievements.

ER considered it essential to know the truth "about our people and other peoples the world over." She received many letters from people affirming that their ancestors came over on the *Mayflower*. "How all the people who came to this country in the Mayflower were contained in the Mayflower I don't know." But she did know that it was that "sense of superiority because you think you are a little more native than somebody else [that] we have got to get over." After all, "every race and every nation has that feeling."

By 1938, ER had moved beyond insult and condescension and directly opposed white supremacy. She received a letter of regret from a white woman who was irate that Negro children were invited to Hyde Park events and had eaten with the family:

> The influence you are having on the Negroes may do great harm to this nation. You are making them feel they are equal to the white race. . . . You may not believe in amalgamation of the races, but they do not know that. . . .

ER replied:

> Eating with someone does not mean you believe in intermarriage. My grandmother was from Georgia and I was brought up in Southern traditions, but I have known colored people who are not only the equal of whites, but mentally superior. . . .

In April 1937, while ER was in Charleston, the Wagner antilynch bill was debated in Congress. In 1936, ER had urged her husband to take "even one step" toward recognition of this bill. When it failed, Walter White called the president's silence the bill's "greatest single handicap." Now, with FDR's monumental victory, White dared again to be optimistic.

After Costigan retired from Congress, Frederick Van Nuys of Indiana joined Wagner as cosponsor in the Senate, and Joseph Gavagan of New York City introduced a companion bill in the House. In April 1937, Walter White lobbied ER to support the Gavagan–Wagner–Van Nuys bill. He asked to meet with her during the House debate.

ER intended to support the bill, but was away for the entire week of the critical House debate, which featured important speeches by Caroline O'Day and Hamilton Fish—FDR's longtime enemy, the leading anti–New Dealer of Dutchess County.

More than a Republican effort to win back the black vote lost in 1936, Hamilton Fish's speech reflected a breach in conservative ranks in support of racial justice and labor's right to strike. He had commanded black troops during the war in Europe, and he declared:

> I would be derelict to those colored soldiers . . . who paid the supreme sacrifice on the battlefields . . . fighting to make the world safe for democracy. . . . The time has come to put an end to mob violence and the hideous plague of lynching. . . .

> Five thousand Americans have been lynched in the last 50 years in this great free country of ours, that is supposed to be the most civilized in the world. The rest of the world laughs at us every time we say we stand for justice and law and order. They bring up that stigma of lynching law and throw it back in our face. . . .

With fascist violence on the rise, Fish opposed his Republican colleague who asked: "If we cannot legislate on the greatest mob crime of the age, sit-down strikes, how in the world can we constitutionally legislate on this?" Fish replied: Sit-down strikes "involved the invasion of private property," not "the destruction of human lives. . . . I believe in placing human rights above property rights."

ER regretted that her husband lost a chance to challenge his longtime enemy on this important subject, and she particularly hailed Caroline O'Day's courageous political speech, given as a woman born and brought up in Georgia. Like ER, who in 1934 connected international and domestic race violence, O'Day declared that with Japan's atrocities in China and Hitler's repeated boast that he treated Jews in Germany better than Negroes were treated in the United States, worldwide floodlights were cast upon American lynchings.

O'Day had returned from a world tour, and everywhere she went she met people who believed that America was defined by a culture of bloodlust, sadism, and race hate. In her travels, she defended her country's honor and declared that only isolated incidents occurred, but she now addressed Congress with passionate urgency:

> This free country of ours, where our liberties are supposedly so fully guaranteed under the laws, is the only country in the world which tolerates lynching. . . .

> Enlightened Americans . . . are revolted at the thought of mob violence [and] . . . are now supporting the anti-lynching bill. . . .

In a recent poll, "7 out of 10, or 70 percent, of our citizens were in favor of a Federal anti-lynching bill; and to the honor of the South . . . a full 65 percent" favored it.

Unless it became law, O'Day declared, we stand before the world condemned as an outlaw nation. In India, for example, "I saw in many places for sale a book called *Uncle Sham*. This book held up our country as calling itself civilized, and then throughout the pages of the book was pointed out every dreadful thing that ever happened. . . . The chapter on lynching was particularly horrible." Not admitted into the United States, the book might be dismissed as communist propaganda; but it was written "by a Hindu . . . translated into 86 Hindu dialects and is one of the best sellers in India." It was also translated into Japanese, and she had similar experiences in China, Siam, and "in a far-away jungle in French Indochina. . . ." Even in South Africa, where race problems are "very much more acute . . . everywhere I went people . . . brought up this subject of lynching; and I assure you it is impossible to make people in other parts of the world believe that all of us here are not in favor of it. . . ."

Caroline O'Day was proud to be among many Southerners who wanted an end to the rule of states' rights, race discrimination, and lynching. The people of the world "cannot understand our philosophy of States' rights, for they look upon us as a unified nation under one federal government."

During the debate, a particularly grisly lynching witnessed by a mob of hundreds occurred in Mississippi. Two men were abducted as they were taken from the courtroom to jail in Winona; they were tortured with gasoline blowtorches and then burned on a pyre. Emmanuel Celler brought the outrage to the floor, noting a bitter irony: Governor Hugh White was giving an address in Jackson, proud that Mississippi "had not had a lynching in 15 months," when he was informed of the cruel facts. It was the third lynching of 1937. There had been eighty-three lynchings since 1933.

Another Southerner rose to support O'Day, and in a resounding speech, John Marshall Robison of Kentucky, who had supported the Dyer antilynch bill in 1922, challenged FDR personally. A Republican, he pointed out that Southern and border Democrats would block this bill unless FDR put it on his "must" list. "The Democrats have more than 3-to-1 majority in the House; and nearly 6-to-1 majority in the Senate;" 95 percent of Republicans supported the bill; Democrats opposed it. Robison argued that the bill could have been passed in the 73rd and 74th Congresses if FDR had spoken. There were sufficient "northern, western, and eastern Democrats . . . with the help of the Republicans . . . to put this . . . through, and even pass it over the president's veto. If it is not put through we know the administration is . . . deceiving the colored people of this country. . . ."

On 14 April 1937, the House passed the Gavagan–Wagner–Van Nuys bill, 277–120. ER promised Walter White every help in moving it through the Senate. As before, she personally appealed to FDR—who argued that his political capital was wrapped up in the Supreme Court fight. He refused to see White or Joel Spingarn and had no advice to offer the NAACP. With a heavy heart, ER wrote White:

The President says that he is not familiar enough with the proper procedure to give you really good advice. I think you had better trust to the people in charge of the bill. . . .

For months, ER appealed again and again to her husband for one public word. The legislation stalled in the Senate, and when it was brought up after the summer, it was confronted by a six-week filibuster. The South brought Congress to a standstill. Everything pending seemed doomed. Senator Wagner worried about his housing bill and his new wages and hours bill. Nothing would happen, ER and her allies believed, unless FDR spoke out. FDR disagreed with his wife's assessment of the defiant South and refused to risk the future of his other issues on lynching. Finally, in October 1937, Senator Wagner withdrew the Wagner–Gavagan–Van Nuys bill.*

Besides the Court, FDR's only legislative initiative during the dreary political months of the 75th Congress was to extend the Neutrality Act of 1935, which had been due to expire on 1 May 1937. The new law gave the administration more discretionary authority and allowed trade on a cash-and-carry basis. It extended embargoes to civil war situations, previously uncovered, which specifically legitimated FDR's embargo on Spain.

FDR left for a cruise on 27 April, to fish in the Gulf of Mexico for two weeks. He signed the Neutrality Act of 1937 aboard ship at 6:30 A.M. on 1 May. But it satisfied nobody, least of all his wife. ER considered it a hateful piece of legislation that made no distinction between aggressor and victim nations, and actually favored well-armed aggressors ready to attack. It also favored maritime nations, notably England, France, and Japan. In cash-poor Germany, the press condemned the cash-and-carry feature as "an Anglo-American alliance." Nevertheless, U.S. copper and steel companies continued to give Germany loans, since there was no embargo against Germany.

It appeased businessmen who resented limitations on export trade and ignored pacifist groups who wanted a full embargo of raw materials, especially those needed in war: petroleum, steel, copper, magnesium, phosphates, cotton. The new act placed an embargo on arms, ammunition, and travel, but specifically excluded raw materials.

ER was not alone in her bitter dismay over the embargo against Spain. It was a compromise neutrality that limited risks and preserved profits. It was a cold war neutrality that acknowledged Hitler and Mussolini as acceptable barriers to anarchists, communists, radical democrats.

---

*The bill came up again in 1938, but never passed. Hitler editorialized, on 28 January 1938, in the Nazi press that the United States treated black people less humanely than Germany treated Jews.

Howls of protest from both isolationists and internationalists emerged. World Court supporters, notably Henry Stimson (Hoover's secretary of state), deplored the abandonment of America's "self-respecting traditions, in order to avoid the hostility of reckless violators of international law."

Allen Dulles and Hamilton Fish Armstrong condemned the embargo as a reversal of America's traditional position on freedom of the seas and all Wilsonian principles and said it would serve as a terrible "instrument in the hands of the German and Italian totalitarian governments." Isolationist senator Gerald P. Nye agreed and condemned it as a terrible injustice.

Liberals then called for the embargo to cover Germany and Italy, since they were the aggressor parties to the "Civil War." But FDR refused to distinguish between aggressor and victim nations: That would not be "neutral."*

For ER, the Spanish Civil War was the moral equator. Furious over her husband's policy, which enabled trade to soar with Germany and Italy, trade which was then used to devastate Spain, she wrote of it regularly in her May columns.

On 26 April 1937, Guernica, a town of seven thousand people in the Basque province of Vizcaya, close to the sea and thirty kilometers from Bilbao, was the first open city to be bombed from the air, without warning or pity. On Monday, market day in Guernica, at 4:40 P.M., the central square, filled with farmers, florists, craftsfolk, and shoppers, was razed by Nazi Heinkel 111s. As the people ran for shelter and safety they were machine-gunned by diving planes. Incendiary bombs and high explosives were dropped every twenty minutes for four hours. The raid killed 1,654 and wounded 889.

Guernica was a Roman Catholic citadel, and Basque priests under the vicar-general of Bilbao, center of Basque nationalism, had voted to remain loyal to the democratic Spanish Republic, in defiance of the Catholic hierarchy. This bombardment was their punishment. It heralded the century's new wartime strategy of carpet bombing against civilian populations. Guernica also heralded a new psychological warfare technique of cover-up and denial. News of Guernica did not become public until 7 May 1937, when Britain's foreign minister, Anthony Eden, announced that Britain "had evidence Guernica was destroyed by airplanes" and called for a neutral inquiry. That same

---

*The United States "ranked first in value of exports to Germany in 1933, 1934, and 1938." Between 1934 and 1938, sales of American motor fuel and lubricating oil tripled in quantity and constituted 22 to 32 percent of German imports of petroleum. The United States supplied Germany with 20 to 28 percent of its imported copper and copper alloys and 67 to 73 percent of its imported uranium, vanadium, and molybdenum. In 1937 and 1938, U. S. exports of iron and scrap steel rose to 50 percent of Germany's imports. It was a curious neutrality.

day, *The New York Times* headlined that five thousand women and children had been taken from Bilbao to France for safety, guarded by British warships, and many other refugees were preparing to leave.

Franco claimed the Basques had destroyed their own town, and Germany denied all involvement.*

ER was haunted by Guernica: Every time she saw a newspaper photograph or read a new story about Spain, she was overcome with a "sense of horror." She called for relief measures, hoped that people would contribute to the English Quakers who rushed to aid the suffering children of Spain, and wondered "why people go on stupidly destroying" civilization.

One day, on a train up the Hudson, she could not work, could not knit, could do nothing but contemplate Spain. As she gazed at the rolling river she loved so well, she wondered: "If this were Spain would I be sitting so calmly and with such security . . . ?" Today, there were "no shells dropping on our cities and villages; no children in great number are being separated from their parents. . . ."

She hoped America's commitment to democracy would survive:

> If reforms do not come peacefully, they have to come through violent upheavals. As I looked out from the window of the train, I thought, "Thank God, this nation has had the courage to face the need of change before we reached the point where bloodshed was the only way to achieve a change. . . .

Spain and refugee issues would dominate the rest of ER's political life.

The day FDR left for his fishing vacation, ER left for a West Coast speaking tour that began in Seattle for a week with Anna and her grandchildren. Tommy wrote Anna that ER was "like a child starting out on her first outing. . . ."

On 5 May, ER and Anna launched her new broadcast series sponsored by Ponds Vanishing Cream. They discussed the education of a daughter for the twentieth century.

Anna asked her mother to explain her educational philosophy for her

---

*In 1946, Goering admitted that Guernica was Germany's testing ground. But not until April 1997 did Germany actually acknowledge "its guilt in the destruction" of Guernica. The raid, conducted by the German Condor Legion, was formally acknowledged in a ceremony to commemorate the victims. Germany's ambassador to Spain, Henning Wegener, read "a message of mourning and reconciliation." The German parliament rejected a motion to discuss the raid and include a formal statement of regret when Chancellor Helmut Kohl's coalition voted against debate.

only daughter. ER replied she wanted to end the restrictions she had grown up with, the notion that all women were to be "wives, mothers and adornments to society," and wanted to encourage "any aptitudes you showed."

Always disturbed by Anna's disinterest in school, which had represented her own liberation, ER asked her daughter to describe the "useful" aspects of her education. Anna replied: "It was the development of my bump of curiosity," encouraged by being with "you and father," which made up for her attitude in school. She revealed to her mother that she also "hated to play the piano," and hid "in the kitchen closet" when her music teacher arrived. Surprised, ER asked why Anna insisted that her daughter play the piano: "You'd better explain that a little. . . ."

They both agreed that access to books and uncensored reading were the best part of education. As a child, ER had run off into the woods of Tivoli with forbidden books, and she now believed in the absolute freedom to read and to know. She was certain that reading adult books never hurt children: If a child happened on an unsuitable book for her age, she probably "would not understand it, but it would do no harm."

Both ER and Anna discussed their emotional fears as girls, and ER acknowledged that she had battled "an inferiority complex" for years. Anna did as well, and blamed her mother: "I think that was your fault. . . . I never felt I could be as capable and interesting as you and father were. . . ."

ER: "If only our companionship could have developed as freely when you were little as it did later on, I would have probably understood a great deal more. You are doing a better job. . . ."

Anna: "That's nice of you, Mother. But how do I know how she'll feel about it when she grows up?"

ER: "Perhaps she'll feel as we do now. I don't think of you only as a daughter, but as my best friend."

ER asked Anna what she most wanted for her daughter, and Anna replied that she wanted freedom "from any sense of superiority or inferiority to any group of people, and . . . a sense of values that will help her to be tolerant, useful, and happy."

ER noted: "That's the 20th Century answer and I like it, and I think the girl will be well educated to live in our world. I think if my grandmother had been asked what she wanted for her daughter she *might* have answered simply: 'a good husband!' "

While ER was in Seattle, she worked on the revisions for her last installments of her memoir for the *Ladies' Home Journal.* Her publishers were displeased; they wanted ER to deal with the real issues of her early married days and FDR's polio. Hick suspected that "by this time you have come to the period where you can no longer be wholly truthful. And it shows in the story.

That's the trouble with autobiographies. Probably they should always be done anonymously."

ER sought, above all, to protect everybody she loved. Her manuscript was read by FDR, Tommy, Earl, Hick, and Anna, among others. Blue lines abounded, and some of them were surprising. FDR deleted a passage in which ER quoted Isabella Greenway's mother about Hall's first divorce: "If you love a person, you can forgive the big things. Infidelity under certain circumstances need not ruin a relationship."

Although convinced of the wisdom of that insight, ER agreed to take it out. But as she wrote, and rewrote, the days of her life during the tense spring of 1937, that observation concerning Franklin had a special meaning. Never had their political disagreements been so profound. Never had she had so much access to public forums. Her lectures were sold out; her broadcast series was hugely popular; her book was an immediate best-seller. But she could not persuade her husband to consider her views, reconsider his path. With little influence at home, she stayed far away. While FDR concentrated on the Supreme Court fight, all legislative initiatives were forestalled, and ER felt the 1936 electoral mandate was wasted.

The New York Times called ER "the most traveled First Lady in history." Away from the White House 60 percent of the time since 1933, she pointed out that she was there most of the time FDR was in residence.

ER's travels cheered her, and the success of her book encouraged her to do even more. Tommy wrote Anna that the "circulation of the *Ladies' Home Journal* has gone over three million per month, so they should be satisfied. George Bye says he will die regretting that he didn't hold out for twice what he got."*

Awash in controversy over the antilynch law and Spain, both celebrated and mocked by the partisan press, ER was happy to spend a quiet moment of affectionate domesticity with Earl. She had been intimately involved in all aspects of Earl's life, and her relationship with him was now a comforting blend of mother-and-son generosity, lady-and-squire protectiveness. On 8 May, ER wrote Hick from Earl's, who "has more things to do here than anyone I ever knew. I made curtains all morning but this afternoon we played ping pong and tonight we have to write scenes for the party tomorrow."

ER had fun at Earl's, was carefree and at ease with his show-business friends—and some, like Tiny, increasingly became her companions of choice.

FDR returned from his cruise in mid-May rested and restored. ER noted

---

*ER's earnings were significant that spring; the *Ladies' Home Journal* paid $75,000 for the serial rights, and her radio contract was for $3,000 per broadcast for a series of fifteen. In 1930s dollars that represented a major American fortune.

that "Franklin seems confident about everything!" Almost immediately after his return, ER flew to New York for "an orgy of theatre going."

ER loved the theater and attended openings whenever possible, usually escorted by Earl. Producer John Golden never refused ER's request for tickets for her theater parties, and he frequently presented lavish gifts to ER personally and to the White House, including a most extraordinary gold-leafed piano.

Nevertheless, ER chided her friend's male bias in a column:

> I noticed a little item in the paper the other day, and much as I like Mr. John Golden, I am going to differ with him. He says: "A writer of great plays must have lived, gone through most of the valleys, and over most of the hills of experience. Men can do that but women cannot. . . . There will never be any really great women writers in the theater, because women do not know as much as men."

ER dismissed that as "ludicrous." She considered it "funny" to think there would never be great women writers for the theater. They lacked only opportunity: "Because as a rule women know not only what men know, but much that men will never know. For how many men really know the heart and soul of a woman?"

Evidently stung by ER's column, Golden produced *Susan and God*, by playwright Rachel Crothers. Directed by Crothers and starring Gertrude Lawrence, it opened at New York's Plymouth Theatre on 7 October, and Golden invited ER to attend. She wrote:

> Many thanks for the flowers. Your note afforded me a great deal of amusement and you are magnanimous in producing a play by a woman which she "wrote alone." *Susan and God* certainly gives one an interesting evening. I felt a little let down by the last curtain but enjoyed all the rest more than I can say.*

ER and Golden also disagreed about WPA theater productions. He feared that Hallie Flanagan's productions did "not conform to professional standards" and might actually "harm" the theater. Although his opposition differed from the usual anticommunist bias that assailed WPA theater, ER vehemently disagreed. She considered WPA theater progressive and imaginative, the cutting edge of American culture. Because it dramatized labor issues, strikes, lynching, and other current events, an avalanche of opposition to its allegedly un-American procommunist sympathies resulted. The more controversial the Federal Theatre became, the more ER supported it. She called it excellent, and celebrated especially the theater's democratic outreach.

---

* Susan and God won the Theatre Club Award in 1938.

New and appreciative audiences were created throughout the country for both the classics and modern theater. Everybody thrilled to Orson Welles's African-American production of Macbeth, which went from Harlem to a four-thousand-mile tour. A WPA survey in New York revealed that only one high school student out of thirty had ever seen live theater; in many communities throughout America nobody had. Flanagan's stock companies, road companies, tent and truck shows, puppets, pageants, operas, revues, and theater in churches, schools, and community centers changed all that. By 1937, fifteen million Americans had attended a Federal Theatre production.

ER did a national broadcast to promote Flanagan's free Caravan Theatre, which played in parks throughout the country in summer. In 1937 "a really thrilling sequence of . . . Shakespeare, Shaw and Sinclair Lewis," beginning with a "beautifully staged and orchestrated" production of *A Midsummer Night's Dream*, brought a new level of culture to the long deprived.*

Newspapers filled with protest against ER and her support for WPA theater. It staged dangerous, immoral propaganda. One *New York Times* correspondent in May 1937 protested that all art and theater projects were dominated by "zealous" communists, and concluded: "I loathe fascists, but I cannot see how [fascism] can be avoided. . . . It is the only antidote for communism."

ER, however, was committed to freedom, experimentation, and Flanagan. When New York State passed the Dunnigan bill, which would give the New York license commissioner authority to close any "immoral" play, she urged Governor Herbert Lehman to veto it:

> The surest way to remove really undesirable plays from the stage is for the public to refuse to see them. Censorship by law has always seemed to me too difficult and complicated where art of any kind is concerned.

ER criticized only one play during the spring of 1937. In her monthly column for *Democratic Digest*, she wrote:

> I spent a few days in New York . . . going to the theatre. One of the plays was a very clever one called "The Women," but I cannot say that I enjoyed it for not only were the women rather dreadful creatures but you felt

---

*Playwrights especially welcomed Flanagan's vision. George Bernard Shaw donated all his plays for a token fee: "As long as you stick to your fifty-cent maximum admission . . . you can [stage] anything of mine you like." Eugene O'Neill did the same, and Sinclair Lewis spurned a commercial production of *It Can't Happen Here* to support the Federal Theatre. It opened to wild enthusiasm and controversy on 27 October 1936, in twenty-one theaters in seventeen states, and toured the country, appearing before millions of Americans for 260 weeks.

that the men who tolerated them must have been even more dreadful. Sad to say, those who were supposed to be bright spots in the way of virtue were so dull that you could not be thrilled by them! The play was clever and [about to be made] into a movie so you will probably become very well acquainted with these "Women."

Unable to be amused by Luce's comedy about a woman who has just learned that her husband has a mistress, ER wrote an even more fierce review in her *My Day* column. She considered the situation "a real tragedy" trivialized by women she would never want to know:

"I do not know the author, but I am very happy indeed that I do not very often have to associate with the women she gave us on the stage, nor, for that matter, the men. . . .

"They must have been such dull, stupid, little men to have cared at all at any time for such dull and cruel 'cats.' "

ER also deplored "the mother and her advice," as well as "the one woman who was supposed to be 'good' and was so stupid. . . ."

To compound her mean words, ER failed to name Clare Boothe Luce in both columns. She paid for her reviews almost immediately. *Time*'s previously benign coverage of the First Lady ended. She wrote Esther Lape:

I didn't see the article in *Time* to which you refer although I did see the one on my income tax evasion! You know the author of the play *The Women* is the wife of [Henry Luce] the owner and publisher of *Time*, so I am not surprised at anything he says about me. I was rather ruthless in what I said about the play.

Perhaps ER's overserious assault against Luce's catty comedy involved her resentment over Bernard Baruch's enthusiasm for his former lover's work. Struck by ER's words, Baruch encouraged her to see it again. She did, but Clare Booth Luce's characters annoyed her exceedingly: "I felt just as soiled by 'The Women' which I saw again last night as I did in the first instance. It is a beastly play and I hate to acknowledge its cleverness!"

Unlike ER, Hick rather enjoyed *The Women*: "Strange sort of play, isn't it? Queer, bitter, at times smart-alecky. At times, of course, very funny. Remember the scene between the cook and the maid? Pretty nasty, on the whole, and I can't say I really liked it much, although I found it very diverting. . . ."

The last days of May were so crowded with social obligations and official people that ER complained. Hick empathized:

I should think you *would* get sick of people! I get sick of them for you! God, how I loathe all that stuff! Bill [Dana] was describing to Ellie yesterday my manners at the White House. He said: "Most of the time Hick looks like a royal Bengal tiger that has been mussed up a bit!" Don't you love it? Well, cheer up, dear. It will be over pretty soon, and you can settle down at Hyde Park for the summer.

But, ER replied, there were "still some bad days ahead!" Among ER's bad days were 29 May, when she noted without comment that she "received the German Ambassador's wife." The next day, fifteen hundred steelworkers and their families were attacked in Chicago during a Memorial Day march and rally. While U.S. Steel had negotiated with the CIO, Republic and other "little steel" companies refused. They greeted strikers with tear gas and tanks in Ohio and elsewhere. But Chicago was a labor town with a labor Democrat for mayor, and the marchers were in a festive mood, with women at the head of the march. Then, without provocation or warning, 264 police officers attacked the crowd, first with tear gas. As they fled, police opened fire and 30 men, women, and children were shot; 60 were "sadistically beaten," and 10 died. The bloody violence was captured by Paramount newsreel journalists and given to the La Follette Committee.

That evening, ER drove Tommy, Harold Hooker and Roberta Jonay to Rock Creek Cemetery to contemplate *Grief*.

24: This Is My Story

O n 13 May 1937, three stories shared *New York Times* front-page head-lines: "HOUSEWIVES ENTITLED TO FIXED SALARIES, LIKE ANY WORKER, MRS. ROOSEVELT HOLDS." "GEORGE VI AND ELIZABETH CROWNED IN WESTMINSTER ABBEY." "BILBAO SUBURBS BOMBED. . . . MORE THAN 100 MISSILES WERE DROPPED—MADRID SHELLED. . . ." Fascist general Emilio Mola told Basque officials that since the world's attention would be on the coronation in London, it was a good day to "blast the capital to bits." The indignation aroused by a violent attack on civilians would be "thus lessened." Also, Franco's forces beat back government troops in Toledo and shelled Madrid.

Events in Spain and Japan's escalated warfare against China caused ER to reconsider her own pacifism: "I have just read Dorothy Thompson's 'The Dilemma of a Pacifist,' and I find that, by and large, she has reached the same conclusion I have." It was "dangerous" to let "the rest of the world stew in its own juice."

For ER, pacifism now meant that "you use every means in your power to prevent a fight, and this includes giving all the assistance you possibly can, short of military assistance. . . . But if war comes to your own country, then even pacifists . . . must stand up and fight for their beliefs."

Since war had come to Spain, ER was eager to give democracy in Spain "all the assistance" possible. The new facts of *Blitzkrieg*, "lightning war," from the sky by Nazi Heinkel 111s and Junker 52s clarified whatever confusion antifascists may have felt about the "neutrality" of FDR's desired blockade.

ER's understanding about events in Spain came firsthand from Martha Gellhorn, whose observations during her three-month tour of the war-torn areas were regularly reported to the First Lady. Now, Gellhorn was confused by the U.S. refusal to aid Bilbao refugees: "It seems that 500 kids . . . are wait-ing in Saint Jean de Luz to come to America. There is passage money for 100 of them, and countless offers of adoption." But every snag was set out to stop them. Gellhorn was outraged that the Labor Department decreed a "$500 bond per child" admission fee and "approval of the Catholic Charities." She found the Catholic lobby "incomprehensible," since "the children are all Catholics, Basque children . . . made homeless and orphaned by the people who wish to destroy the Godless Reds. That must be the root of it somewhere, but it is pretty terrible." Gellhorn noted that England and France welcomed the children and found it "amazing that only America should offer no sanctuary." It seemed to Gellhorn both "an injustice" and a retreat from America's tradition as a sanctuary. "What do you think about it?"

ER supported the Quakers' relief committee, sent a check to Allan Wardwell for his Spanish Children's Fund, and publicly defended her right to aid Spain against all critics who attacked her for abetting communism. But in 1937 she also felt that European children would be happier in Europe, as close as possible to their families and culture. In a June column she wrote:

> The U.S. should bear as much of the expense as we possibly can, but it is against all modern ideas of what is good for children to uproot them and bring them to this country, where they are definitely cut off from all that they know and that would make them feel secure. . . .

It was hard for her to imagine, in 1937, a world filled with refugees uprooted and cut off from their soil and their culture. For the moment she trusted that Allan Wardwell's AFSC efforts would create a national organization of various relief and rescue groups to coordinate all aid. She wrote Gellhorn: "Emotionally it is very easy to say that we should receive the children . . . but it requires a little more than emotion sometimes to do the right thing."

Gellhorn thought ER chastized her for being overemotional, she deplored emotional women, but:

> [It was] hard nowadays not to get emotionally terribly involved. . . . The attack on Bilbao is one of the nastiest things . . . when I think of those people in Bilbao strafed by low-flying airplanes with machine guns, and think of thirty shells a minute landing in the streets of Madrid, it makes me sick with anger. . . .
>
> I can't bear having the Spanish war turned into a Left and Right argument, because it is so much more than that, and increasingly it seems to me that the future of Europe is bound up in the outcome. . . . It also seems to me that the future of Europe is our future, no matter how much we want to be apart . . . our civilization is not divisible. . . .

ER encouraged Gellhorn: Her information was important, she had impressed many people, and a mutual friend had been "very deeply stirred by your perfectly remarkable address." So, ER concluded: "Remember when you

454   *Eleanor Roosevelt*

feel discouraged: We never know where we may have sowed the seeds of our own enthusiasm or of our own knowledge."

FDR's blockade against the legitimate government of Spain disturbed ER even decades later. He attributed his decision to "political realities," in particular the Roman Catholic vote.

> [But] this annoyed me very much. In the case of the Spanish Civil War . . . to justify his action, or lack of action, he explained to me, when I complained, that the League of Nations had asked us to remain neutral. By trying to convince me that our course was correct, though he knew I thought we were doing the wrong thing, he was simply trying to salve his own conscience. . . . It was one of the many times I felt akin to a hair shirt.

Since FDR had never before concerned himself with collective security or felt bound by any League of Nations decision and was entirely careless concerning supplies to Mussolini when he sacked Ethiopia, his excuses were bewildering, and ER never accepted them. Ardent about Spain, ER rejected the propaganda war that equated the democratic front or "Popular Front" with communism. Despite the State Department's emphasis on a war between fascism and communism, for many the primary enemy, ER was convinced the war was between democracy and fascism, for her the primary enemy.

ER studied the situation, understood Spain's history, and could not accept her husband's policy.

Spain had long been dominated by monarchy and feudal land ownership, but the new republic was voted into power by a vast majority in June 1931. King Alfonso had abdicated and fled in April, and the new democracy promised land reform, justice, and the participation of all classes and parties. A coalition government of trade unionists, liberal republicans, radical syndicalists, anarchists, socialists, and communists composed the Popular Front, while industrialists, landowners, military officers, monarchists, and Catholic fascists composed the National Front.

In Spain's February 1936 Popular Front election victory, the Communist Party represented only 4 percent of the government, and months of confusion, violence, mayhem followed. As Spain plunged into chaos, howls of rightist protest emerged from FDR's State Department. On 23 July 1936, six days after Franco's revolt, Cordell Hull wired FDR that the new Spanish government distributed arms and ammunition to "irresponsible members of left-wing political organizations." Assistant Secretary James Clement Dunn told a reporter that the State Department regarded "the Spanish Government as a lot of hoodlums."

Before the election of 1936, FDR wanted to do nothing to upset the Roman Catholic vote. A Catholic "Hands Off Spain" committee condemned the Loyalists as atheists and communists. Even John L. Lewis announced he could not publicly support Loyalists because there were too many Catholics in the CIO and "it's too dangerous for me."

Moreover, on 24 August 1936, FDR summoned J. Edgar Hoover to the White House to encourage a new FBI investigation policy of subversive groups. FDR wanted informants in every communist organization to collect general political intelligence. Throughout 1936 and 1937, FDR moved against communist influence in U.S. labor unions, with as surprising, though secretive, verve as he did against Spain.

In May 1937, the new government of Dr. Juan Negrin, physician, academic, former finance minister, and Socialist, was determined to be independent of communist domination. According to Hugh Thomas, Dr. Negrin had "no close relations" with Spain's communist leaders and "a strong dislike for La Pasionaria," Dolores Ibarruri, the leading Loyalist orator.

Franco's Falangists, or Catholic fascists, would have been quickly defeated had it not been for the military support of Hitler and Mussolini. "Beautiful, bleeding Spain" was torn apart not so much by civil war as by international fascist aggression. Most accounts agree the vast majority supporting the Popular Front would have ended the war quickly had they been able to get supplies to counter the might of Mussolini's invading army, and the new Nazi Wehrmacht.

According to Hamilton Fish Armstrong, longtime president of the Council on Foreign Relations, Spain "should have been a warning to civilized governments, but instead they adopted the strangling policy of nonintervention."

ER retained warm relations with the Popular Front Left, which supported Spain. During the 1937 Writers' Congress, Gellhorn and Anna Louise Strong, also returned from Spain, discussed the future of the International Brigades and the president's dismal policy. Gellhorn wrote:

> I saw Anna Louise Strong at the Writers' Congress, which was a wonderful show, Carnegie Hall jammed—3500 and many turned away at the door—only to hear writers. . . .
>
> [Anna Louise is] a great admirer of yours so I forgive her for being the messiest white woman alive and so overworked. . . . It seems I gave you an erroneous impression: she challenged me on my facts. Apparently you thought I said there were 12–14,000 *Russian* troops in Spain, but I said there were 12–14,000 International troops.

Gellhorn wanted ER to understand that despite all propaganda, neither she nor any other journalist ever saw Russian troops:

> I doubt if there are 500 Russians in Spain, not as many Russians as Americans. The Russians, like the Americans, come on private initiative as volunteers. . . . The ones whom I saw (I saw ten in all) are all technicians, engineers and aviators and munitions experts and writers. . . .

In July, ER invited Gellhorn, Ernest Hemingway, and Joris Ivens to Hyde Park so that the president could meet them and see their film. Both ER and FDR were riveted by *The Spanish Earth.* Gellhorn wrote:

> You did really like the film didn't you? Joris and Ernest were very happy about it. They were also impressed that you and Mr. Roosevelt said to make it stronger . . . by underlining the causes of the conflict. I think [Harry Hopkins] was very moved by it. You were heavenly to us and I hope you liked my two trench buddies, both of whom I adore. . . . It's awful hard to thank you adequately for all the good things you do. . . .

But for all the presidential enthusiasm for the film, the pain in the bombings of Madrid and the village of Morata, the agony of the attack at Jarama, FDR never considered changing his policy on Spain, which at the time prohibited the shipping of even medical equipment and ambulances.

Domestically, labor tensions continued. ER spent an afternoon with Frances Perkins, who was severely attacked for her support of the sit-down strikers, especially for her contributions to Governor Murphy's negotiations between the CIO and GM, which represented labor's most dramatic victory and stimulated unionism in every industry. During the summer of 1937, there were hundreds of strikes, and organizers at every workplace.

ER wrote Hick, in praise of Perkins: "How men hate a woman in a position of real power!"

But on 24 July 1937, ER celebrated a great congressional victory for women: The hated Section 213, which she had editorialized against since 1933, was abandoned. Federally employed women would not again be fired because they were married to federally employed men: "I am particularly happy today" because the "so-called Married Persons clause of the Economy Act" was finally repealed. Part of her husband's first act in office, it had caused "a great deal of hardship among government employees."

ER warned, however, the debate still raged. She had just received mail from an organization that vowed to remove any married woman from the workforce "whose husband earns enough to support her." ER was disgusted: "Who is to say when a man earns enough. . . . Who is to say whether a woman needs to work . . . for the good of her own soul?"

ER refused to see a conflict between "a woman's career and a woman's home." The reason for the ongoing conflict was that women's needs were never considered: "A woman, just like a man, may have a great gift for some particular thing. That does not mean that she must give up the joy of marrying and having a home and children." People had yet to consider how "women's lives must be adjusted and arranged for in just the same way that men's lives are."

On her 12 May radio program with Rose Schneiderman, they discussed not only women's right to work outside the home, but wages for housework. ER insisted: Wives and mothers needed at home "should receive a definite salary for their work." A woman or girl at home "has a job just as surely as anyone who operates a machine in a factory." And "if she is not needed at home, she loses out by not working."

ER predicted that wages for housework would someday seem ordinary, and current resentment over women working in industry would disappear. Schneiderman agreed: "Can you imagine what would happen if the 11 million working women in the U.S. suddenly quit their jobs and just waited for the men to support them?"

In her July column ER continued the argument: Some women worked for financial reasons, some for emotional reasons.

> This does not mean they are not good mothers and housekeepers, but they need some other stimulus in life. . . . It seems to me that the tradition of respect for work is so ingrained in this country . . . fathers have handed it down to their daughters as well as their sons.

ER predicted that the future guaranteed "respect for women who work."

The family's most significant 1937 milestone was Ethel du Pont and Franklin, Jr.'s, wedding. Surrounded by mean-spirited gossip, rumors of mergers between Liberty Leaguers and New Dealers, ER and FDR ignored it all. "Personally, I'm pretty immune!" ER worried only that the president did not steal the show, as her Uncle Theodore had at their wedding.

The 30 June wedding at Owl's Nest, the du Pont family home in Greenville, Delaware, was sumptuous and long. ER left the receiving line to broadcast. She wrote Hick: "The church was beautiful but the house, —well, for a variety of reasons I found it a bit hard to swallow. I ran away for about an hour. . . . Well, it's over and the future will be what it will be."

At her weekly broadcast, for which she drove to Wilmington, ER said: "I don't know whether to be happy or sad, but simply say prayers that fundamentally their lives may so develop that they may be useful lives and therefore happy ones."

Ambivalent, if not cynical, about the possibility of happiness in marriage, ER considered it "a very lovely wedding," but was always "torn" at such moments "between the realization of the adventure that two young things are starting on and its possibilities for good and bad."

ER had a tooth infection at the time of the wedding and wrote four letters to Hick that weekend in which she sounded "dreadfully uncomfortable." Hick noted that her pain "must have complicated an already burdensome situation. . . . Was there much drinking? I had an idea that there was."

ER replied: "The wedding reception was all you surmised but I was only sorry for the children."

According to James, FDR was particularly gay at Owl's Nest: He "relished infiltrating the du Pont nest, flanked by such staunch New Deal aides as Harry Hopkins, Frances Perkins, and Henry Morgenthau." Pa enjoyed the food and champagne, and "kissed all the bridesmaids." Even TR could not have taken up more space, nor had more fun. Surely his selection of companions— radical Hopkins, the controversial secretary of labor, and the Jewish treasury secretary—appealed to FDR's sense of mischief and merriment.

On the way home from Delaware, ER learned of Amelia Earhart's disappearance. ER wrote her daughter that she heard "about Amelia over the radio & felt even lower. I do like her and I'll miss seeing her if she's gone but perhaps she'd rather go that way. Life might not have held such a happy future for her."

The mystery of Amelia Earhart's Pacific disappearance during an around-the-world expedition, traveling with navigator Fred Noonan (an alcoholic who may or may not have been drinking), under risky weather conditions and unknown political conditions, has never been solved. ER's words are equally mysterious. Did she refer to Earhart's marital situation, or another reality we know as yet nothing about?*

The day she left, ER wrote:

> All day I have been thinking of Amelia Earhart somewhere over the Atlantic Ocean, and I hope she will make her flight safely. She is so utterly simple, which I suppose is an attribute of all great people. She never seems to think anything she does requires any courage. . . .

ER had long been impressed by the woman who said in June 1928 that it would have been "too inartistic" to refuse her first transatlantic flight. She inspired ER to fly, and they had become friends. She stayed at the White House, attended Gridiron Widows parties, and was a confidante.

When Earhart was insulted by Hearst columnist Arthur Brisbane after her

---

*A most curious exchange between ER and Henry Morgenthau, whose Treasury Department presided over FDR's Secret Service and Intelligence unit, heightens the puzzle. When ER asked him to release the *Itasca* file to Earhart's friends, aviators Paul Mantz, Jacqueline Cochran, and others, Morgenthau's office sent ER an unsigned memo: The secretary said he "cannot give out any more information than was given to the papers at the time of the search of Amelia Earhart. It seems they have confidential information which would completely ruin the reputation of Amelia and which he will tell you personally some time when you wish to hear it. He suggests writing [Paul Mantz] and telling him that the President is satisfied from his information, and you are too, that everything possible was done." ER followed that suggestion.

successful 1935 long-distance flight, which introduced two-way radio communications, ER joined the groundswell of protest. Bess Furman sent her the
details of Brisbane's attack, which climaxed in his insistence that Earhart quit
flying to have babies: " 'Six or seven children' was 'the real Earhart job' [since]
men and birds could fly."

ER had helped facilitate arrangements for her final flight. Earhart's husband
and chief promoter, publisher George Palmer Putnam, was deeply grateful:

> [After ER's intervention] everything is in splendid shape. The Navy
> has been most cordial and helpful. . . . Indeed so have all the Departments.
> Incidentally, the President was kind enough to make possible the construc-
> tion of an emergency landing field on a tiny pin-point of an island called
> Howland, just north of the Equator, half way between Honolulu and Aus-
> tralia. If all goes well, Amelia will be the first to use it. . . . That one feature
> of the flight is quite an adventure in itself.

After Earhart's disappearance, Putnam wrote several letters to thank ER
for her many kindnesses: "For you Amelia had a real devotion. Often I've
heard her call you 'the most intelligently civilized woman I know.' . . ."

On 7 July, ER wrote Hick that FDR was "not very hopeful that they will
find Amelia. It just makes me sick." Then on 20 July 1937, *The New York Times*
announced the search had ended, and the "disappearance of Amelia Earhart
and navigator Frederick J. Noonan [had been] officially declared one of aviation's mysteries." The aircraft carrier *Lexington* had sent planes thousands of
miles around Howland Island, and now returned to San Diego. The battleship
Colorado, the minesweeper *Swan*, and the Coast Guard cutter *Itasca* were also
ordered returned.

George Palmer Putnam still hoped for "a miracle," but had no plans to
charter a private yacht, since the Navy had been "so thorough." ER was certain
that Earhart's last words were "I have no regrets" when her plane disappeared
on 2 July 1937. The First Lady believed "to her it was worth the cost. . . . I only
hope she went quickly and that she was not subjected to great pain."

ER began her column with Amelia's own words, written in 1934:

> "Courage is the price that life exacts for granting peace,
> The soul that knows it not, knows no release
> From little things. . . ."

I am very sure that when she made the decision to go on this last trip,
she had every possible risk in mind. I don't suppose any of us ever really feel
we are about to die, even though our reason tells us death may be waiting
around the corner. I am quite sure she met death in the spirit of [her]
poem. . . . This attitude is one which we must never forget, for a nation is
poor indeed when it does not have men and women with this kind of spirit.

ER and others paid many tributes to the first woman of the air. Fannie Hurst saluted "her deathless spirit":

> We do not know where the corporeal Amelia Earhart of the slender boyish body, of the clear fearless eyes, of the tousled mane, may be at this moment. What I personally do feel, and think that the entire world feels . . . is that her bright transcendent spirit of valor, duty and idealism hovers over and blesses the century. . . .

Jacqueline Cochran said that Amelia did not lose, "for her last flight was endless."

July was a month of profound loss for the Roosevelts. Amelia Earhart's disappearance was followed by the sudden death of Joseph Robinson, who had served with distinction as Senate majority leader and was the man FDR had depended on to move his Court reform plan forward. In sweltering Washington, where air-conditioning was still uncommon, tempers frayed and spirits sagged as Congress contemplated FDR's "must" bill to enlarge the Supreme Court. Democrats were bitterly divided; Republicans were quiescent and enjoyed the disunity that rendered the 75th Congress a New Deal failure. Nothing had been achieved as FDR squandered his popularity on the Supreme Court business—even after the Supreme Court had responded to his pressure.

In a series of 5–4 decisions, with Justice Owen Roberts reversing himself, the Supreme Court finally upheld progressive and New Deal legislation. In March, Washington State's minimum-wage law, similar to New York's decreed unconstitutional the year before, was upheld. In April, Wagner's National Labor Relations Act was affirmed. On 24 May, the Social Security Act was allowed. Suddenly the Court acknowledged that Congress and state governments had the power to protect the interests of the people.

Then, on 18 May, seventy-eight-year-old Justice Willis Van Devanter announced his resignation. FDR's congressional team urged him to claim victory and withdraw his plan. But he refused. He had promised the first vacancy to his loyal floor manager Joe Robinson, who was a sixty-five-year-old conservative from Little Rock, known as a down-home diehard. It would be a defeat for the New Deal, FDR's image, and his entire political gamble if he replaced one aged conservative justice with another.

The NAACP was horrified by the prospect of Robinson. Walter White wrote ER that rumors about Senator Robinson's appointment stunned Negroes. He enclosed protesting editorials that "besieged" NAACP offices. ER sent them to her husband, who promised to call White.

Then suddenly, while action was pending on the Court bill, anguish erupted about racial discrimination that confronted Negroes at the PWA's most celebrated projects, at the Grand Coulee Dam in Washington and the Bonneville Dam near Portland, Oregon. NAACP field secretary William Pickens implored ER to address the situation, which had been ignored and left to fester for years: "The grossest and meanest discrimination" existed at Grand Coulee Dam, "against both colored American employees and visitors. The Negro workers cannot get their food at the common eating places . . . or by the concessionaires, unless they 'eat in the kitchen' or other insulting segregated corners." Also, workers were not permitted to live in Mason City, the official Grand Coulee Dam city, and "must tramp the weary miles to and from work."

Pickens was indignant that the U.S. government made no effort to change contractors and prevent further discrimination: Could not the U.S. government arrange its contracts "for which the money of the people is being spent, subject to the plain provisions of the 14th amendment . . . and the common laws of humanity?" Pickens suggested a clause to forbid federal contracts to discriminate in employment and accommodations against Americans regardless of "race, color, creed, or politics."

ER forwarded his letter to Ickes, with a query: "What should be done?" She was informed that Bonneville Dam was under the jurisdiction of the War Department, but that Interior would investigate the situation at the Grand Coulee Dam. Ultimately, Ickes removed the ranger responsible for insulting Pickens by sending his party to the back of a line and issued an order to contractors to end their discriminatory practices. That June 1937 decision was the beginning of a long and sustained crusade against federal discrimination.

Then on 14 June the Senate Judiciary Committee "damned" FDR's Court plan with a vehemence that shocked the press. Columnists Doris Fleeson and John O'Donnell were stunned that Democrats "would scourge themselves into an emotional frenzy to denounce" the most popular head of their party. To some it sounded like a call for impeachment.

The debate raged for weeks. Joe Robinson tried to manage the Senate floor. He made appeals, offered compromises, avoided a filibuster. After long brutal days, he left the Senate emotionally and physically drained. He was found dead of a heart attack on the morning of 14 July. By his bed were the pages of the previous day's blistering debate. Progressive senator Burton Wheeler thundered that FDR should now withdraw his plan, "lest he appear to be fighting against God."

On 15 July, ER left Hyde Park on the midnight train for Washington. Senator Robinson, she wrote, "was a loyal and devoted friend who fought under the party banner, sometimes subordinating his own preferences to those of the majority." The Senate funeral "was impressive," and many on both sides "truly mourned Joe Robinson, the man." Curiously, neither ER nor FDR went to Little Rock. That decision made FDR seem ungrateful, or careless.

As the congressional train returned from Little Rock, there were caucuses in every compartment. Vice President John Garner, who had unprecedentedly absented himself during the debate to protest both FDR's stubbornness on the Court and his silence on the sit-down strikes, went from car to car to assess the situation. The temper of Congress was clear; the game was over. FDR was defeated.

The president did not acknowledge defeat; he had lost the battle, but won the war. In fact, FDR had achieved a major constitutional transformation that promised economic justice and workers' rights. Under his threat, the Court reformed itself and for the first time legitimized national action for the common good. His great victory was to put the force of the national government, and the Supreme Court, behind the century-long struggle against discrimination, unbridled greed, and states' rights.

But it was a costly war. Democrats and liberal Republicans were in disarray and angry. In that overheated climate of discontent, FDR again called for a balanced budget and instituted new cuts in the most needed programs. He thereby derailed the drive toward a New Deal for poor and struggling Americans.

ER wrote another column to object to her husband's decision: While she, like all women, understood the need to pay one's bills each month, "I do hope that in this budget-balancing business we make our economies without making people suffer who are in need of help. There are wise and unwise economies. . . ."

FDR's summer 1937 budget cuts resulted in immediate deflation. By summer's end, the country was plunged into a deep recession. FDR's rhetorical concerns for significantly improved social security services and housing reform subsided. Economists disagree about how much FDR's policies contributed to the renewed recession, but there is no doubt his 1937 strategy curtailed the impact of the only two remaining New Deal bills still pending, which ER most championed: The Wagner-Steagall housing bill to build low-cost housing passed with its budget halved; and the Bankhead-Jones farm tenancy bill, to assist and encourage farm ownership among sharecroppers and tenant farmers through low-cost loans, was severely underfunded.

The bilious spirit surrounding the Court controversy spilled onto every issue. FDR believed the people were still with him, but the people were confused, and discouraged by his silence during the summer violence against strikers. He said nothing about the Memorial Day massacre, and then new blood was spilled in Youngstown. Tom Girdler, chosen by Republic Steel and the "little steel" companies to break the union, was eager to bludgeon the CIO's advance. With bullets and tear gas he succeeded.

On 30 June, FDR finally responded to John L. Lewis's appeals to speak out. He did, quoting Shakespeare's *Romeo and Juliet:* "A plague on both your houses." Hoping to forestall labor's rage, he later explained he meant to condemn the "extremists" of both houses. FDR wrote vice president Garner, whose antagonism was reserved exclusively for unionists, that he was "very confident" his strategy had created "the right psychology on the public as a whole. They are pretty sick of [both unionist and Girdler] extremists."

But the people were not equally divided, and FDR's rejection of unionists under siege threatened to separate him from his largest democratic base.

At the same time, ER publicly endorsed the CIO when she attended a picnic at the Heywood Brouns' for members of the Newspaper Guild. Then she hailed Hallie Flanagan's Living Newspaper on housing, "One Third of a Nation," as "truly excellent." With Ellen Woodward ER opposed cuts in both WPA arts and women's programs.

While FDR remained locked in budget battles in Washington, ER spent several weeks at Val-Kill. She read, gardened, ruminated; rode her horse Dot through an army of mosquitoes, until she gave it up when horse and rider returned covered by bites and blood. With Earl, she tried her hand at archery, which she found complicated but challenging.

For all their disagreements, ER was sympathetic to her husband's lonely struggle. Without keen advisers to protect him during his first year without Howe, he was vulnerable. She admired his resilience and buoyant spirits as he confronted implacable political enemies. One of the most remarkable columns she wrote that summer seemed a celebration of the man whose struggle she witnessed from crisis to crisis, sometimes from a distance, but always with an intimate perspective: "One of the qualities I admire most in the world is the courage which accepts whatever life may bring, and goes on with undiminished zest in life and apparent joy."

ER's column portrayed a woman physically handicapped and largely immobile, who nevertheless faced each day with "an eager spirit," forever curious, kindly, "gallant and gay." It was a perfect description of FDR, written during a trying time, and revealed the direction of her heart. However much they differed over strategy, tactics, even purpose, she sought in her writings to advance his efforts, even as privately she worked to change and redirect them.

But during the summer of 1937, FDR did not feel gallant or kindly; he felt peeved, and angry. He vowed again to "purge" his congressional enemies and defeat them in the 1938 elections. The idea spilled over even into ER's closest circle. While ER's personal friends were not "purged," a curiously partisan emphasis emerged that took everybody by surprise.

To avoid "misunderstanding," Esther Lape detailed the situation: "Dearest Eleanor, Three times in comparatively recent months, at the White House, retainers or friends (McIntyre, Dewson, Dickerman) have rather pointedly raised the question of the political affiliation of Lizzie and me." Marion Dickerman, "on the train the other day," actually asked Lape, "with what motive one can only guess—whether I had not been an 'organizer for the Republican Party.'"

Lape was indignant:

> For the record it is to be said that Lizzie and I are both enrolled Democrats. Lizzie always has been, I more recently. . . . I once enrolled in the Republican Party in order to be an officer of the Young Republican Club— which was to be a Liberal organization but . . . turned out to be as hidebound as the regular group. . . . I helped Leila Pinchot get out the vote. . . .
>
> That is the whole story. While we do reserve judgment on several policies of the present administration I think we are at least as "loyal" as if we accepted everything without qualifications. We are not alien, and we care.
>
> We know you would care about us just the same if we were communists or economic Royalists or whatever. The question of what we were has never even come up between you and us and would not now if we did not raise it. We do so because these questions put to us seem a bit purposeful and to call for a bit of plain speaking.

She ended: "Our dearest love," and "Lizzie says she wants to sign too."

ER was startled. Why would FDR send snoops after her dearest friends? Clearly, many of the board members of the Amerian Foundation were Republicans, including Helen Rogers Reid, but they were liberals. Perhaps it was their shift from the World Court to a national health care program, widely condemned as socialized medicine. Was it their views, their independence, or their closeness to ER that merited this sudden scrutiny?

ER replied:

> I have never cared what you and Lizzie were politically, but it turns out that you are exactly what I thought you were. I cannot imagine why McIntyre should inquire and certainly don't understand why Marion should ask you. Molly Dewson has [party loyalty] always on her mind, of course. It does not make the slightest difference unless either of you were trying for a Democratic Party job. I know that isn't even a remote possibility but if it ever happens, I will just simply have to beat them over the head. I will keep your letter for the record in case I am ever asked. . . .

ER and Hick saw each other only occasionally during the summer of 1937. Hick declined all invitations to Val-Kill. When they made dates, Hick canceled them. She currently preferred the life of a recluse: "I do so need to be alone— especially these days, when my temper and my state of mind are so uncertain. I'm getting so that I dread being with people. . . ."

Hick was now unhappy and discomforted at the World's Fair: "The truth is that I am absolutely unfit . . . to be an executive. All day I 'sit on myself' . . . to control my impatience, my natural irascibility, my loathing of friction and disorder. By night I'm exhausted." Her temper worsened with the heat, and she gave it free rein: "I guess my trouble is that, even at the ripe old age of 44, I still have not learned to live comfortably with people. I loathe them and despise them, mostly. Pigs!"

ER often enjoyed such fumings, which she never allowed herself. "Darling, what a pest conflicting personalities are. . . . If everyone liked everyone else it would be so simple and I suppose so dull!" But ER also worried: "Dearest, it was nice to see you last night but I was troubled at the way your hands shake. Your nerves must be pretty taut and I wonder if you don't need a real rest for a few days. Try to get here Thursday night next week."

Hick was busy but they planned a weekend away. They would travel together to Gloucester to visit Hick's theater friend Jean Dixon, then ER would motor on alone, incognito, to visit Cousin Susie at Newport. On the way home she would visit Esther Lape and Elizabeth Read in Connecticut. ER's plans, especially the risky part that involved traveling unnoticed, delighted her. After their visit ER wrote, "Dearest, I enjoyed every minute with you— and it was such fun seeing Jean and her family. . . ." But the big news was that she arrived in Newport without being recognized behind "large black goggles." Nobody called, there were no crises, and ER felt "that for once I was an acceptable guest!"

But their good time/bad time pattern was repeated almost immediately. No sooner had she returned home than ER realized she had messed up carefully crafted plans for another weekend with Hick: "Dearest, You are going to think me an unmitigated ass and I deserve it. I never looked in my engagement book." Now she had discovered that on the day of their date she was to lecture in Poughkeepsie, and FDR was due to arrive. "Dearest, I know how upsetting my uncertainties have been and this is the worst of all and I am so sorry, please try to forgive me. . . ."

In August, when FDR arrived at Hyde Park, ER moved into the Big House. To her relief, things went smoothly. With Uncle Fred Delano, often her ally, they had long discussions about the strikes—which restored ER's faith in her husband's good intentions about the labor situation: FDR believed "in the democratic process and [feels] everyone has been getting educated lately and perhaps he's right."

But FDR's cavalier Shakespearean plague on both houses created an irreparable rupture between the president and America's most effective union organizer. On Labor Day, John L. Lewis broadcast nationally over CBS, to attack the administration: Labor, he said, needed to identify its true friends and enemies.

[Labor's] cause is just and its friends should not view its struggle with neutral detachment. . . .

Those who chant their praises of democracy but who lost no chance to drive their knives into labor's defenseless back must feel the weight of labor's woe. . . .

Labor, like Israel, has many sorrows. Its women weep for their fallen, and they lament for the future of the children of the race. It ill behooves one who has supped at labor's table and who has been sheltered in labor's house to curse with equal fervor and fine impartiality both labor and its adversaries when they become locked in deadly embrace.

In addition to her concern over the labor struggles, ER was upset by the decision to close Camp Jane Addams at Bear Mountain, "for financial reasons." She had supported the camp with various gifts and more than $3,000 in contributions. As far as she was concerned it was a success, but it would close on 1 September. In a last-minute effort to save it, she toured the camp with Nan and Marion. Although all the 130 campers wanted it to continue, and despite all the classes and training projects, all the good work done, now under the direction of the National Youth Administration, it was doomed. ER was outraged: No similar cuts were made in CCC camps. To balance the budget it was condemned as a loss despite human gains, and she was powerless.

ER felt philosophical during the summer of 1937, and she read more than she had in years. For days, her columns were filled with quotations that moved her. Pericles inspired her to consider that not just "famous men" but all of us "can weave bitterness and hate and cruelty in other men's lives, or we can weave kindliness, love and joy." She wrote Hick there was "one thought I love and must pass on to you," from David Grayson's *The Countryman's Year:* "Long ago I made up my mind to let my friends have their peculiarities."

Surrounded by guests and controversy while at Val-Kill, ER sought to follow those precepts. Earl and three friends arrived, as did her brother Hall, with a "young lady," though not "*the* young lady."

ER wrote Anna about Hall's plans. Always her brother's champion, ER worried about Hall. But he had just become vice president of a New York investment firm at a "magnificent" salary and would be living partly in New York. Esther Lape agreed to lease him the apartment below ER's on 11th Street, and she was glad: Hall "sounds on the crest of the wave." His divorce would become final in three months, and he would then decide "whether he marries again at once or . . . [will] remain free to flit!"

Anna wanted to write an editorial about how rudely immigrants were treated. She had interviewed people on the West Coast and had been shocked by cruel displays of contempt and barriers of delay and hostility against all refugees. ER encouraged her daughter to write honestly:

I think it would be swell for you to do that. . . . When I used to go with people in New York [to the Immigration and Naturalization Bureau] for the Women's Trade Union League, I used to boil & a story such as you could write would do a lot of good & I don't see that it could do Pa or the administration any harm.

Despite guests, meetings, correspondence, and regular columns, ER wrote her daughter: "I've done so little work this summer that I'm ashamed." Nevertheless, she enjoyed most of her guests, including Harry Hooker, who arrived from Europe bearing many "amusing" stories "about Mama and Johnny."

Sara Delano Roosevelt's trip was highlighted by visits with European notables. She had tea with Mussolini, whom she considered a splendid leader of all the people, and wrote FDR: "The Duce sent me a grand bunch of flowers [and] all seems very flourishing and peaceful and the devotion to the 'Head of the Government' is general in all classes. . . ."

Concerning Spain, she spoke with exiled nobility and had it on royal authority that Franco's victory was essential. One Spanish countess assured her that Franco's forces "are the only hope for poor Spain."

SDR's blithe disregard for democracy was a subject of amusement in the White House. According to James, his father would read passages from his mother's "Assistant Secretary of State bulletins," which were "not always to Father's taste," and "wryly say: 'Well Ma-MA is having a grand time!' "

ER rarely commented on her mother-in-law's enthusiasm for dictators and royals. She wrote Hick: "Do you know Mama met the Duke and Duchess of Windsor at tea? I wonder how she will now feel about them!" But she hated "the papers these days with nothing but war and rumors of war."

FDR's holiday after his bruising Washington summer of delay and defeat was serene. ER marveled at her husband's spirit, and wrote of his time at Hyde Park in her column:

> [It] has been one of the most peaceful visits he has had in the last few years. . . . No one has been here to discuss any business or political problems. . . . We have almost forgotten we have a President among us.

ER contrasted his peaceful week with the "tension one usually feels in the Presidential atmosphere," even on vacation:

> The constant stream of visitors, the constant feeling that affairs of importance are going on, the rapid . . . adjustment that must be made in the household by the family, by the secretaries, to meet the requirements for as much peace and quiet as possible for the President himself, make for exhaustion. To understand this one has to experience it.

ER marveled at FDR's ability to unwind, concentrate, adjust to various personalities and subjects—and still retain an "inner calm. I have never seen my own husband ruffled, which must require a vast amount of self-control. . . ."

In September, ER and Hick made time for each other and discussed their hurt feelings and bruised friendship. Hick had tried to be on her own and happy with her friends all summer, rather than wait upon ER's infrequent availability. But now Hick veiled her anger at ER with a lament: she could not "give Alicent what she wants—which is a lot of affection and consideration. I can't seem to give those things to anyone any more. I'm all dried up inside, I guess. . . ."

Unable to explore such emotional turmoil, ER refused to feel guilty and replied with reassurance and advice: "Hick darling. I hate you to say you can't give affection and consideration. You can and do give both. . . ." ER blamed Hick's disagreeable feelings on her physical health and recommended rest, exercise, fewer foods to agitate Hick's diabetes.

After they spent a day together in ER's New York apartment, ER believed they had swept the air between them clean, and she felt refreshed: "It was very sweet to be with you even for so short a time and it was good for me. I am really better and I will try to be on an even keel!"

But Hick doubted that "we got anywhere much," and feared they were "drifting apart":

> I've tried hard to be perfectly acquiescent this summer. I think the feeling that I had to do most of the trying just got me down and completely discouraged. . . . And I've hated the thought so of seeing you—or trying to see you—when you didn't want to see me. . . . I may have been wrong. I don't know any of the answers.
>
> I guess the only thing I really do know is that I love you, with all my heart. And that it's a Hell of a lot harder to see you unhappy or listless than to be unhappy myself.

After a summer when her sincere efforts to get together were rejected, ER replied with crisp indignation. Considering her usual tone of empathic understanding, it was for her a cry of wounded fury:

> You don't realize that I have not been once to NY without trying to see you. There is no use in your coming here [Val-Kill] to be miserable. I could go to you, but there has been a good bit to do here and I didn't realize you felt we were drifting apart. I just take it for granted that can't happen!

But they had drifted apart. In the spring ER wrote, after a long separation while Hick was very social, "No, I don't much like your gypsy life!" Earlier, in an undated letter, ER had exploded with aggravation and wrote Hick while returning from New York to Washington on the train:

> I think you can scarcely realize how you made me feel tonight. I did not ask you and Ella to dine to be rude and yet you made me feel that I had been. You went right by me at the [radio] studio without speaking. You told me you would entertain yourselves in Washington before I had time to tell you whether I was busy or not. You barely spoke to Earl and Jane [Brett] at the play who were my guests and certainly did nothing rude to you and when I asked you to go in so you would sit by me you deliberately changed and sat as far away as possible.
>
> I am sorry if I've done something to offend, but I'm so deeply hurt tonight that I almost wish that I had no friends. Acquaintances at least preserve the social amenities and make life pleasant on the surface. I was happy to be seeing you but evidently you were not. For Saturday and Sunday at least let's try to be cheerful and polite and not make everyone around us uncomfortable!

Despite this unusually bitter undated later, their friendship survived and ER continued to depend upon Hick—who remained her emotional cornerstone. Hick made her feel good, and made her feel strong. ER believed their letters kept them together through all troubles and separations, and now wrote: "I'm really not unhappy and listless so don't worry. I think I just get annoyed with life as it is and my inability to change it for the moment! Bless you and I love you too."

After this exchange, Hick tried harder not to attack or hurt the First Lady. Although professionally she felt like a racehorse put out to pasture, her sense of pride demanded that she see new people, find new friends, keep herself occupied, and protect ER from her true state—which was often furious and depressed. There was now Dorothy Cruger, and her assistant at the World's Fair, Barbara—who lived in Greenwich Village and spent many weekends with Hick at the Little House.

Before ER left on a Western trip with FDR, followed by her lecture tour, she insisted that she and Hick see each other. Hick resisted; ER was adamant: "If you can't come for dinner come after dinner, for the night and breakfast at least."

Hick's elusiveness served almost as a magnet. After two weeks of such appeals, they finally spent a pleasant evening together in New York. Afterward, Hick wrote:

> I can't tell you how much I appreciate your having come down. I've missed you so terribly these last few months. I know we did see each other, but usually for only a few minutes at a time—and somehow we were rather

like strangers. But the last three or four times have been nice, and I feel happy about you and contented. You look so much better and seem much more like your old self.

Don't let that damned trip get you down, dear. And please send me the peace article if you want to. My love to you—always.

ER's peace article, which would become a book, grew out of a series of September meetings at Hyde Park filled with details about Germany's violence and Spain's tragedy. Bernard Baruch returned from his annual visit to a German spa with information, and two extravagant gifts for ER—and he told "me carefully why he thought I had given him permission to do so! He lunched alone with F and I had nine for a buffet on my porch."

ER was convinced that the United States could not remain aloof from the crises in Europe and Asia, and when her brother arrived with several friends, she had support. At dinner that night nobody believed the United States would be uninvolved if a general war occurred. Despite the depth of U.S. isolation, there were ways "to get our people into war," ER wrote Hick. "Hall thinks it can be done easily. What do you think?"

While ER focused on Spain and Europe, FDR was more concerned about the Pacific. He deplored Japan's invasion of northern China. Peking and Tientsin had fallen; Shanghai was surrounded. Japanese planes bombed cities, countless civilians were killed, and three thousand Americans were trapped in Shanghai. Hull issued "preachments" and counseled inaction.

FDR was so aggrieved that he reconsidered the need for collective security, which he had spurned since June 1933, when he doomed the London Economic Conference. When Ethiopia was invaded by Italy in October 1935 and when Germany reoccupied the Rhineland on 7 March 1936, FDR remained silent. No steps toward an embargo to limit Hitler's frightful rearmament program were undertaken, although for two years Dodd sent evidence that German factories belched out weapons of death day and night, every day, twenty-four hours a day, enhanced by the most vital raw materials from America.

By 1937, European internationalists no longer considered the United States a significant factor in diplomacy. Winston Churchill, England's leading anti-Nazi and only outspoken antifascist agitator, asked a profascist French acquaintance: "With Germany arming at breakneck speed, England lost in a pacifist dream, France corrupt and torn by dissension, America remote and indifferent—Madame, my dear lady, do you not tremble for your children?"

While the Roosevelts continued to remain silent about Nazi atrocities in 1937, Churchill railed at meetings of the Anti-Nazi Council and wrote articles about freedom's end, Nazi tyranny, concentration camps that now dotted

Germany's countryside, persecution of Jews: "It is a horrible thing that a race of people should be . . . blotted out of the society in which they have been born."

But while ER considered Spain the moral equator, even Churchill supported the embargo against Spain. That represented a fight between communism and fascism; if the embargo ensured fascism, England would benefit. ER was certain such convictions condemned democracy everywhere, and by summer's end both ER and FDR considered alternatives to America's international policy.

They both turned increasingly to Sumner Welles, an old family friend. His great-uncle was the abolitionist senator Charles Sumner; his mother (Frances Swan) and ER's mother had been close. Hall's Groton roommate, Sumner was the page who carried ER's wedding train in 1905, and he was loyal. ER relied upon him as refugees claimed more and more of her attention. However limited his interest in refugees, he was the only member of the State Department she trusted.

FDR had named him assistant secretary of state on 20 March 1937, and by autumn he upset the strict isolationists who dominated the State Department, a small brotherhood of 250 careerists and an occasional political appointee. Welles encouraged FDR to move beyond somnambulance on international issues.

FDR now hoped for an Anglo-American accord, at least to limit Japanese aggression. But it was too late. In May 1937, former minister of the exchequer Neville Chamberlain had become prime minister. He despised America, and never forgave FDR for his actions regarding the 1933 London Conference. He believed war might be forestalled by granting Hitler the territories he wanted for resources, and prestige. Churchill raged against his intentions: It would be "wrong for any nation to give up 'a scrap of territory to keep the Nazi kettle boiling.' " But in England, only Churchill called for collective security and rearmament.

In the United States, however, rearmament was under way during the summer of 1937. FDR bolstered the manufacture of U.S. warplanes, bombers, ships, and matériel; naval appropriations were increased by $1.3 billion. Clear about the need for U.S. defense measures, FDR refused to invoke the neutrality law and embargo for the Asian war, or to remove it against Spain. There were no discussions of economic reprisals against Germany, Italy, or Japan. An embargo, FDR argued, would only serve Japan.

Then, after Japan announced a blockade of the China coast on 25 August, a shipload of nineteen planes bound for China left Baltimore harbor. The isolationist press howled, and six peace societies, including the Women's International League for Peace and Freedom, demanded the arms embargo be invoked. Other peace activists, including Carrie Chapman Catt, supported FDR.

On 13 September, Joseph Kennedy, then head of the Maritime Commission, ordered the ship, the *Wichita*, detained in California and the nineteen planes off-loaded. FDR agreed: Government-owned ships would not carry munitions to either side. The Neutrality Act was still not invoked, on the legal ground that no state of war had been declared, but China was dismayed. America had forgotten "its moral obligations."

The liberal press noted that the United States was now aligned with the aggressors on two continents. Unlike the Spanish situation, however, American exporters were free to trade at their own risk—and the munitions trade with both Japan and China flourished.

ER considered America's policy unjust, inconsistent, and weak. While FDR worked on his own controversial foreign policy speech to be given in Chicago, she felt conscience-bound to speak her mind, but constrained from saying anything that would cause FDR additional difficulties. ER confided her dilemma to Hick, who encouraged her to be bold:

> This is a Hell of a time to be trying to write an article about peace! If you could only be absolutely honest, say exactly what you think, and rip things up generally, the article would be easy to write, wouldn't it? And fun. No wonder you get discouraged. . . .

ER's article turned into a major essay, published as *This Troubled World* in January 1938. Concerned that her views not disturb FDR, she asked him to read it. She wrote Hick: "FDR read the peace thing so he won't be surprised at any wallops that come."

ER's lead was vivid:

> The newspapers these days are becoming more and more painful. I was reading my morning papers on the train not so long ago, and looked up with a feeling of desperation. Up and down the car people were reading, yet no one seemed excited.
>
> To me the whole situation seems intolerable. We face today a world filled with suspicion and hatred. . . .

Only forty-seven pages long, *This Troubled World* was written with a sense of urgency and hope. Since it actually slammed FDR's policies, one can only wonder what he thought of their differences, or whether he read it carefully, and took it seriously. Perhaps, on the other hand, it influenced his decision to speak for the first time in his presidency as an internationalist.

In Chicago, on 5 October 1937, FDR, who had turned his back on the League of Nations and the World Court, on all their shared commitment to collective security, which ER adhered to throughout, now spoke as he had before 1932. He invoked the "high aspirations" of the 1928 Kellogg-Briand Pact, shattered by "a reign of terror and international lawlessness."

The very foundations of civilization were threatened; all progress toward "law, order, and justice are being wiped away," FDR said. "Innocent peoples, innocent nations, are being cruelly sacrificed to a greed for power and supremacy. . . ."

He called for all peace-loving nations to make "a concerted effort in opposition. . . . There must be a return to a belief in the pledged word, in the value of a signed treaty. . . ."

The world was at risk, 90 percent of humanity were jeopardized by 10 percent who had unleashed an "an epidemic of world lawlessness."

> When an epidemic of physical disease starts to spread, the community . . . joins in a quarantine in order to protect the health of the community against the spread of the disease. . . . War is a contagion whether it be declared or undeclared. . . .

An historic address, FDR's "quarantine" speech unleashed fierce opposition; his congressional allies reacted with fearful silence. Pacifists and isolationists condemned it as a major policy shift, a giant step toward involvement and war. Internationalists like ER and Ickes were encouraged. It reflected precisely her words in *This Troubled World*. Ickes considered it "a great speech" that would stiffen "the backbones" of Britain, France, the Spanish Republicans, and China and even "put a little courage into the League of Nations."

ER was not with FDR in Chicago, and hoped the press and congressional opposition would not cause him to back down. FDR's quarantine speech was the culmination of their Western trip taken to assess the New Deal's progress, and she had returned East. Although all the crowds were friendly from Seattle to the Yellowstone Park, ER was disturbed by a perceptible change in FDR's "attitude toward the press." Even on the presidential train filled with his favorite reporters, she noticed a difference. Her husband seemed curt:

> He is always looking for slams and wanting to get back at them. The old attitude of friendliness is gone and instead of indifference which I could understand there is this resentful feeling which I regret.

While FDR presented his Quarantine speech in Chicago, ER was at a *New York Herald Tribune* forum to pay tribute to Amelia Earhart. Mayor La Guardia introduced ER, and referred to her as one of the world's most significant pioneers, a woman who dared. He noted that Columbus had persuaded Isabella to imagine the unknown. She dared, and "a new era in history was started. It's a long time from Isabella to Eleanor," and people had now "discovered that the building of cheerful homes by the government for its people is a greater accomplishment than the conquest of new lands and the conquering of strange peoples."

ER's speech emphasized the need for individual courage:

> One of the greatest causes of trouble in the world today is the distrust we have for each other, which brings about fear, and fear is the basis of all our other evils. . . .
>
> A good deal of conscience and a certain amount of iron in the soul will be needed by the youth of this generation. It has come upon us so gradually that I think most of my generation hardly realizes how very soft we have become. . . .

To "escape chaos in the future we have got to recapture" the lost pioneering spirit of determination and strength.

That night, ER dined with her brother and they went to the pier to meet Mama, on her return from Europe. On the drive up to Hyde Park with her brother and SDR, ER heard many things that made her wish fervently FDR would have enough "iron in the soul" to withstand all opposition to his quarantine speech.

But the very next day, 6 October 1938, an excited press conference demanded his specific intentions. He had none. What did he mean by "quarantine"? Nothing.

> QUESTION. Is anything contemplated? Have you moved?
> FDR. No; just the speech itself.
> QUESTION. . . . [Is] it a repudiation of neutrality—
> FDR. Not for a minute. It may be an expansion.
> QUESTION. Doesn't it mean economic sanctions anyway?
> FDR. No . . . "sanctions" is a terrible word. . . . They are out the window. . . .

FDR parried and punted, finally concluding: "I can't give you any clue to it. You will have to invent one." The president trusted the conference was "off the record."

Distressed by FDR's waffling, ER still hoped his speech would influence public opinion toward collective security. In several columns, she called for diplomatic action against aggressors. Although she did not contradict her husband by name, she took issue with his failure to define a national policy, his refusal to state clear diplomatic "objectives." The world faced a perilous situation, while the great democratic nations floundered: "The real trouble is that we have no machinery which automatically deals with these difficulties."

Politically, it was the wrong time for FDR to have given a fighting international speech. Many of his former allies were still in active opposition, embittered by the Court-packing business. FDR was also bothered by reports that Jim Farley had resigned as postmaster general because he had been "slighted by the White House." And everybody was upset by the news that Supreme Court Justice designate Hugo Black had been a member of the Ku Klux Klan. A stalwart New Dealer who had supported FDR's Court plan, Alabama's senator was not perceived as a Klanner. FDR had sent his name to Congress on 13 August, without any congressional preparation or presidential inquiry, and the question had not come up during confirmation hearings. The newspaper exposé, however, was irrefutable. Black was traveling in Europe with his wife, Josephine Foster Black (Virginia Foster Durr's sister), and would say nothing until he returned.

ER's colleague Allie Freed, philanthropist and Arthurdale supporter, was incensed:

> The [Hugo] Black situation involves . . . the very fundamentals of Americanism, liberalism and tolerance.
>
> The horrors of the Klan can only be appreciated by those who cast their eyes on present day Germany. Surely the President has nothing in common with those who would carry America back. . . .

ER considered it "very bewildering":

> It certainly seems incredible that he should ever have belonged to the Klan. If he did belong . . . I cannot quite understand why he did not come out and say so . . . instead of allowing his friends to believe [otherwise].

On his return, Black—who became one of the Supreme Court's most consistent civil rights champions—admitted his former membership and disavowed Klan objectives.

ER spent the weekend before her birthday with Hick at the Little House. It was a "grand weekend" and ER was glad they had finally managed to pull it off, despite her schedule. Hick was in a good mood even though the Danas were in residence. They were lovely, ER wrote Anna, and "asked so much about you," and there was a "grand picnic on the beach."

Energized by their good time together, ER wanted Hick to reconsider her boycott of Val-Kill. Hick refused: There was no privacy, and altogether "too much friction up there. . . . At the WH one doesn't get so close to it, and your sitting room or Louis' old room will offer refuge. But at Hyde Park! . . ."

Their visit was shortened by tragedy. Barbara Duncan Hopkins, Harry Hopkins's wife, died of breast cancer, and ER returned to Washington for the funeral. Hick noted that "if anybody could ever be said to be indispensable, I think she could. I've thought a lot today about the time you went to see her in Washington and found her gazing sadly out the window at little Diana, playing."

Diana was not yet five, and Harry's inconsolable grief lasted for months. ER invited them to move into the White House.

After Barbara's somber funeral, with much "standing around with FDR and Mama both," ER escaped for a ride on her new horse, another gift from Earl. It was "glorious" and she "got a satisfaction out of finding I could manage a fairly spirited animal."

ER's fifty-third birthday was unusually festive. Since her September 1936 fever, FDR had begun a new tradition and planned merry celebrations for his wife.

ER wrote Hick:

> I wish you could have been here tonight. We had a gay party with Tommy Corcoran to play and sing. Everyone seemed to have a good time and Hall came from NY and was noisy as usual but very jolly. Franklin and Ethel drove up. . . .

The entire day was splendid. FDR gave his wife a fur lining for her raincoat:

> Dear Eleanor: One inside of a coat!
> I hope it keeps you warm, but it ain't much of a present!
> VERY much love

There was even politically good news that day: "Arthurdale seems to be progressing." She rode through Rock Creek Park at nine-thirty in the morning, swam at six-thirty in the evening, and enjoyed every minute of her day. "And now I am very sleepy and a year older! The nicest part was hearing your voice. You were a peach dear. A world of love."

The next day, FDR addressed the nation in a dramatic Fireside Chat. The economy had plunged into a recession, and FDR intended to compensate for the legislative time lost on the Court fight. He called Congress into special session, beginning 15 November. These were urgent times, which demanded urgent attention:

> Five years of fierce discussion and debate . . . have taken the whole nation to school in the nation's business. . . .
> Out of that process, we have learned to think as a nation. . . . As never before in our history, each section of America says to every other section, "Thy people shall be my people."

The people of America "do not look on government as an interloper in their affairs. On the contrary, they regard it as the most effective form of organized self-help."

FDR returned to the unfinished business of the New Deal:

Specifically, FDR sought legislation for a minimum-wage and maximum-hours law; an end to child labor, disallowed when NRA was declared unconstitutional; government reorganization, in the interests of efficiency; an expansion of the TVA for seven regions of the nation; and more vigorous antitrust activity, to curtail "private monopoly and financial oligarchies."

Permanent prosperity depended on long-range considerations—the need for reforestation to avoid desertification, the need for a permanent granary—food—available for all Americans at a cost base that guaranteed survival for farm families, with storage for years of scarcity. This involved an expansion of CCC and WPA efforts, tree plantings, dams and ponds and water tables.

FDR concluded on an internationalist note. Despite his disclaimer of 6 October he now said: "Nor can we view with indifference the destruction of civilized values throughout the world. We seek peace, not only for our generation but also for the generation of our children. . . ." Peace "must be affirmatively reached for." FDR again tilted toward collective security, the day after ER's joyous birthday. His speech, in part prepared that night, had contributed to her good mood.

Her husband seemed again on course. He was "satisfied with the State of the Nation and sounds as though he were enjoying himself." But her sense of well-being was short-lived. After two weeks of Harry Hopkins's residence in the White House, she was disturbed: "Gosh, he gives me a feeling of being hollow!"

When ER encouraged Hopkins to move into Louis Howe's room, she had not anticipated that he would abandon their alliance and move completely into FDR's court. All the issues that most concerned her, including the future of the NYA, were endangered as he lost interest. ER had lost not only a friend but her last powerful ally.

Immediately, ER turned to Aubrey Williams to save the National Youth Administration. Everything was threatened by the autumnal recession. With new resolve, ER campaigned with youth and student leaders to increase the NYA budget and fought for the long-delayed federal aid to education bill.

Her goals clear, ER left Washington for her autumn 1937 lecture rounds. She was glad to be removed from the White House as Congress's special session revealed a strident opposition to FDR's vision. While ER traveled, the special session gave him nothing he asked for.

Her schedule caused her to "criss-cross" the country, "going south as far as Memphis, Tennessee, and north as far as Fond du Lac, Wisconsin."

ER flourished on the road. Tommy thought she was so happy and never got depressed while traveling because she had no tensions "to tire her as she has at home or at Hyde Park."

ER had a remarkable capacity to see her audiences and relate personally to each individual. Her only complaint on tour was lack of exercise. Without her horse or an available swimming pool, she felt cooped up. Inactivity "upsets my digestion, and makes me sleepy."

In Indiana, ER visited a Negro housing project and laid a wreath on the tomb of the first soldier killed in World War I. She also visited friends of Hick's who were "very attractive and nice and so anxious to hear about you. People do remember you with warmth once they know you, don't they?"

In Illinois, ER wrote that her trip had been "more restful than any trip I've ever taken" and the audiences had been "bigger than ever before." She was pleased: "I'll probably always have to do a good deal of it till I retire and sit by the fire with my knitting!"

Despite the crowds, ER also found time to write several articles, including "My House" and "My Job." Her agent George Bye wanted more color and suggested that she allow an editor to rewrite. ER cabled him a resounding "NO" from Memphis and complained to Hick: "They will not believe that I'll write it myself or not at all!" But she wanted Hick's advice.

While ER traveled, wrote, and had the kind of exciting life Hick once had, the former reporter descended into a foul and angry mood. While Hick felt herself now no more than a glorified errand girl for the World's Fair, stuck in a stupid job she hated, ER sent her articles for editorial advice. Her own work was meaningless; she felt "bored with life," and wanted ER to appreciate her misery:

> I swore at other drivers all the way in, and I'm now about to go to the dressmaker and shall try not to bite her ear off. Yes—I'm thoroughly bad. And why do necessary people like Barbara Hopkins . . . have to die and leave me to live this fretful, innocuous existence of mine? Oh—I don't know the answers—none of them.
>
> On the whole, I like ["My Job"]. It's fresh, and I like the sincere tone of it. I do think, though, you might have put in more of your serious work and less of the White House social duties. They make me gag. I suppose that's what people want, though. Damned yokels.

Hick's frequent outbursts reflected another level of her private agony as she tried to steer a reasonable course through their complicated intimate and public friendship. She was desperate to express her feelings and was unable to contain them. Her desire to protect the most famous woman in America prevented her from confiding in anyone. Their relationship had to absorb her frustration and anger. ER was rarely willing to explore feelings, and instead offered advice, emotional platitudes:

You poor child! . . . You did have a bad day and react just as we all do. Everyone of us feels that way every so often and it certainly is hard. I do hope you get a chance to go on the road soon. You'll enjoy the change. . . . Stop worrying about why you should have to live and enjoy what you can.

And she defended her article:

I didn't put in anything but what is at present my job, the White House end. The rest is not my job just my preference and stolen from the time I can get away from "the job"! No one is interested in *my* [goals or ideas] they are only interested in a First Lady!

Curiously, ER suggested Hick spend social time with Tommy, who had told ER she missed Hick and hoped that they might go out together. But Tommy and Hick each resented the time ER spent with the other. More than ER's secretary, Tommy was devoted to ER. They spent every day together, and except for the few trips ER took with others, they traveled together everywhere. She typed all ER's columns, worked on her books, and arranged her business life. ER really could not function, write, or live without Tommy.

Tommy did not live in the White House, but with Henry Osthagen in Washington. They did, however, have an apartment in ER's new home at Val-Kill. Except for Henry, who occupied a corner of her time, Tommy's major concern was with ER and her work. And she was protective of her time and affections—which was, of course, why Hick never wanted Tommy included in her times with ER.

Moreover, Hick and Tommy were very similar: gruff and direct; drinking, smoking, high-life, hardworking women. ER enjoyed their company, and they enjoyed hers; but Tommy and Hick were no longer friends—although they were both willing to spend time together.

Hick wrote: "Tell Tommy I'd love to go on a bat with her sometime." But she was upset to hear that Tommy thought she had changed:

I *suppose* she means that I was never impressed by the WH and all that, and God knows I wasn't. I *would* be entirely occupied with a purely personal situation while right in the center of things, in a position where many, many people would have given their very eye teeth to be! And it would have been so much easier for you *had* I . . . enjoyed it instead of hating it, and had I been more preoccupied with that and less—much less—with you!

Anyway, Hick concluded, "I'm feeling better tonight," and her assistant Barbara was with her for dinner. "She is rather good for me, I think—fresh and humorous."

While on tour, ER received exciting news: The reviews of her autobiography in the *Times* and *Tribune* were ecstatic. The major newspapers agreed: Crisp, clear, profoundly moving, *This Is My Story* was "a portrait of a great lady in a democracy," who sorrowed and struggled, and found her own way. The book was a popular sensation. Joe Patterson of the *Daily News* wrote: "I think your book is splendid; and that it may become a classic."

Cousin Alice was overheard to ask at a party: "Have you read it? Did you realize Eleanor could *write* like that? It's perfect; its marvelous. . . ."

Dorothy Canfield Fisher wrote: "You see I think you are a kind of genius. Out of your personality and position you have certainly created something of first-rate and unique value . . . an example."

Isabella Greenway, her first and once closest confidante, wrote a long handwritten letter of gratitude. One of ER's bridesmaids, she knew many of the stories and all the players across the generations:

> Eleanor MY dearest—, &, for the moment NO one else's . . . You have in your own way (great in its kind honesty) found such a perfect [voice] for *narrative*. . . . You tiptoe, you run, you march & you stride. . . . your example of translating bitterness to triumph . . . will help many a person. . . .

ER was particularly touched by a scholar's essay in *The North American Review* and wrote to thank him for his "very interesting review." Lloyd Morris wrote that the enthusiastic praise for *This Is My Story* might initially have been because of curiosity about the First Lady, but actually it was "a tribute to genuine merit." Its "literary merits . . . spring from deeply personal sources. It is, in the best and literal sense, ingenuous," and "its warmth, candor, and simplicity" reflect "inherent qualities of mind, heart, and character."

After five effusive pages, Morris concluded that the book's "major significance and import . . . have to do with the future, and not the past." Without "vanity or ostentation, Mrs. Roosevelt opens up a vista for American women . . . of more complete individual function, of more thorough self-mastery, of more socially valuable activity. . . ." She pointed the way to full personhood "and a less superficial culture."

Despite her personal triumph, ER felt fettered by White House upset and her growing estrangement from FDR's court. Thanksgiving was a hard day. FDR recovered slowly from a dreadful infection that began with a painfully abscessed tooth. Untreated for too long, the infection spread throughout his body, causing fever and swelling. He canceled his plans for Warm Springs, and there was a small White House dinner for seven. ER wrote nothing of her husband's agony, and noted coldly: "Not much of a party, though two is enough if you really want to be together I suppose."

She understood that it was inconvenient to call Hick in the country, where the Danas had no easy-access phone. ER wished Hick a happy day, and hoped "you'll find something you can be thankful for."

Hall sailed for Europe. "It almost makes me want to go. How about you? . . ."

The next day, ER and FDR left Washington. FDR embarked on a cruise to the Florida Keys, and ER took Doris Duke Cromwell for a three-day trip through "the poor mining sections" and new homesteads of West Virginia and Pennsylvania.

Tommy wrote John Boettiger that Clarence Pickett had arranged it as "an intensive education for the little lady":

> I can't say it is very subtle—Clarence Pickett . . . inveigled Mrs. R into taking her with the hope that in such excellent company she will be so impressed that she will make a handsome contribution to the Friends. A hold-up without arms or ammunition!
>
> Clarence Pickett may be a saintly soul and a doer of good works, but he always inspires me with a desire to at least cut his throat. He asks Mrs. R to do so many things and is so persistent there is no getting out of them. Sweet and generous as Mrs. R is, I know she could easily think of many things she would rather do than tote Doris through the homesteads. . . .

Undoubtedly, Tommy's words reflected ER's reaction.

In December, ER juggled family and official life on an ever-faster carousel. She planned a special Christmas date with Hick: "Remember you are spending the night [at 11th Street] and what do you want for dinner? You are so much better at thinking up nice dinners than I am."

> If you just come on the 20th and have a happy evening that is enough present for me and please don't spend money on *things* for me. Love means so much more and Heaven knows you give me that 365 days in the year.

On 14 December 1937, ER had a literary lunch for *Washington Star* publisher Cissy Patterson, one of the most powerful women in Washington, and British writer Vera Brittain. Their luncheon coincided with the settlement of the *Panay* incident. Two days before Japan had bombed and sunk the U.S. gunboat *Panay* in Chinese waters, and Washington was in turmoil. Three public-spirited women brooded over the bitter possibilities for the future in Europe and Asia.

Vera Brittain wrote: "Eleanor Roosevelt's duchess-like dignity at first inspired me with an alarm which disappeared as I came to know her better and to understand with deep sincerity of her approach to human problems."

When ER took her in to meet FDR, he "interrupted a dispatch to Japan" to question Brittain closely about her travels through the Middle West and her opinion of isolationist sentiments. She sensed his struggle in his "pale, drawn countenance behind the mercurial smile," and concluded he was a "great man, with one of the most charming expressions I have seen on the face of any human person, and exquisite manners." Later that day, Japan apologized for its "mistake," and promised to pay for U.S. losses. U.S. neutrality continued, while bitter distrust escalated.

On 16 December, ER hosted the diplomatic dinner, usually the "gayest and most light-hearted" party of the year. This time ER sensed the grave "solemnity in all the [foreign dignitaries] that came past us." Everyone wore a somber expression, and there was no relief from the "tension in the air."

Throughout the week, there were also family tensions: Elliott was angry because after Hearst offered him all the radio stations (he already ran the "paying ones"), he canceled his entire broadcast contract—and explained: "The White House was the opposition." Evidently FDR had finally had enough of Hearst, and ER felt "no one is being entirely truthful with [Elliott]."

ER wrote Anna that Elliott thought "James did it, which I told him was not so."

ER was "so busy these two weeks in Washington that I was sick with inward rebellion and if I had not had a peaceful Friday in New York seeing Elliott and Ruth and Earl (who left . . . on a two weeks cruise with Roberta and Jane Brett), I think I would have blown up!" ER explained to her daughter that she found "the social racket increasingly distasteful and there is so much tension over internal and international affairs that one feels worn out for no real reason. . . . Well I suppose the world will run smoothly again. . . ."

On the 17th, ER went to New York to decorate the tree for the Women's Trade Union League children's party, and on the 20th she officiated at the opening of the Harlem Art Center, a WPA project. It was a gala event that included an exhibit of paintings and demonstrations of all the new opportunities available at the center. ER took great pride in this particular project, which offered courses in pottery, photography, drawing, painting, and sculpture.

Suddenly, on 22 December, ER abruptly changed her Washington Christmas plans to fly to Seattle and be with Anna, who was hemorrhaging. It was the second year in a row that FDR and ER were separated on Christmas. There were evidently various reasons for her decision, including her increased sense of exclusion from the happy social group that now surrounded FDR, intensified by her sense of loss over Harry Hopkins. Their "bridge-playing" and good cheer dotted ER's correspondence with Anna. Once again feeling "odd girl out" in her own home, she explained her decision in her column:

> Yesterday I decided very suddenly that with so many of the family together at the White House they would have a very jolly time. [And] I think mothers were meant to go where they are most useful. . . .

Before she left for Seattle she had her party with Hick, who was grateful:

> Darling, it was a lovely "Christmas" last night—one of the nicest I can remember. And I did mean it when I said that I would try all through the coming year to show you how happy your sweet thoughtfulness had made me. Gosh, it meant a lot! We were peaceful and contented and glad to be together. . . .
>
> Dearest one—still, and always, dearest one—you made me very, very happy, and I thank you. During the next few days there will be times when you feel tired and discouraged and low. Please try to remember at those times that there are several people who love you very very dearly, not because of your position, or because of being related to you, just because you are your own swell self—just *you*.

ER was relieved to be with Anna in Seattle. Although she looked "pale and thin . . . we are going to have a jolly time."

Anna wrote Tommy. "The five of us did indeed have a wonderful Christmas together. We were absolutely alone the entire time, except for Christmas dinner. . . . Ma pitched right in the day she arrived," and her presence caused Anna to feel cured: "All the transfusions, pills, and injections . . . have been nothing compared to the tonic of having her with us."

ER's time away cheered her up, and she returned to the White House in a festive mood for New Year's Eve: "Hall and a stream of wild youngsters came in. . . . Now a good dance is on and I've come up to send you just a line." ER was in an uncommonly good party mood: She loved to dance, and waltzed the night away with her brother, and others. Hall's loud ebullience and his wild circle of friends momentarily restored some balance to the war of the White House courts. She wrote Hick:

> I think our young people look very nice in a crowd! But Betsey has a dress I hate, it is so undressed! Darling I must get back but I love you and was so glad to hear your voice. A very Happy New Year.

On New Year's Day, ER and Hall "had a grand ride," which ER considered auspicious, and she hoped 1938 would be a year full of "peace and contentment," although peace appeared nowhere on the horizon.

25: This Troubled World, 1938

———◦◦◦———

This Troubled World was officially published on 3 January 1938 to good notices and brisk sales. Reviewed generously in the Sunday *New York Times* on 2 January, it was hailed as a valuable, tough-minded assessment of the world's grave problems. "Without sentimentality or undue optimism," ER discussed alternatives to disaster and concluded with a fervent appeal for a fundamental transformation "in human nature." A contribution to international understanding, this slim book's strength was "in its poise . . . its quiet forceful courage."

Within a month, Tommy wrote Anna, the "little book on peace has been very successful." It earned the book's advance "and a small amount besides." *This Is My Story* continued to do well, and "the year closed with 20,000 copies sold. The fan mail on both books has been very encouraging, and so has the press."

Suddenly it had become acceptable—even laudable—to be America's most ardent public citizen, and First Lady. ER had been elected the "outstanding woman of 1937" by a vast majority in "the mail poll" conducted by a popular NBC announcer, Howard Claney. She now inspired editorials of praise for all her work and her controversial positions.

In Ohio, *The Canton Repository* called her "the foremost individualist among all the First Ladies" and honored her because "she has lived her own life with a freedom that smashed precedent, traveling widely as she willed, speaking her own mind on every occasion and engaging in activities so diversified they are a little staggering."

A reporter for *The Denver Democrat* attended one of her lectures on youth and recommended it to "every boy and girl in our land." The apex of ER's lecture, he wrote, was her definition of success—which was a description of herself: to cultivate and express "one's talents and powers to the utmost," and to use "those powers for the welfare of the community." Then she spoke "of the hope of youth for peace and of America's mission to help bring peace to the world and at that the vast audience rose in tumultuous applause as a personal tribute to a great woman. . . ."

ER never referred to her public achievements, although she wrote her daughter about a personal achievement: "I'm getting really good on make up. You won't know me!"

Domestic life was untidy and strained as the New Year unfolded. Earl had been ill at her New York apartment for days, and ER was "really worried about him." "Hick has been ill with a very bad throat." Tommy has been "miserable ever since Christmas." "Missy also has been miserable." "Pa seems fine however!"—although he was still preoccupied with Betsey, and everybody was worried about Harry Hopkins. James told ER that Harry "sits & looks at his wife's picture for hours & can't be roused, & then is too gay. I'm sorry for little Diana." ER wrote her daughter, "I am the only healthy person I think in these parts!"

With her household laid low, ER was pleased to spend more time with her brother at 11th Street. He was just then in good spirits and, Tommy wrote, had become a dependable ally: "Hall has been particularly sweet to [your mother], always meets her when he knows she is coming to New York, etc., and I know that gives her a lot of pleasure."

Relations with Hick plunged to a new level of distress. At work Hick felt attacked by gossip and lies, fantasies and innuendos. The situation ate into her heart, and she felt powerless. She confessed to ER that it had been going on ever since she walked into the World's Fair headquarters, on 4 January 1937. Hick struggled to protect ER from the rumors, but they were the source of her anguish, and she could not keep it inside any longer: ER had gotten her the job, and she was miserable; actually angry. If only ER had encouraged her to resume her career. ER was fifty-three, in control of her life and destiny; Hick was forty-four, locked into the prison of a job she hated, when she could be in Madrid or Berlin or Moscow. ER had tried to control Hick, order her life, restore her health, protect her bank accounts. It was all a vast mistake, and she was very sorry.

Then Hick regretted the intensity of her outburst:

> I'm sorry I talked to you with such bitterness. . . . It wasn't fair, but— since I did say it—it's true. I've felt this way for nearly a year. . . . I'll try not to talk about it any more. You shouldn't be such a good listener.

Their anguished correspondence went on for a month. Initially ER tried to minimize the source of Hick's grief: "I doubt if the whisperings and side-long glances are all that you imagine but when one is sensitive one suffers doubly." Then she wrote: "Dearest, I hate all this you are going through and I know in some way it is connected with us." ER hoped Hick might find "another job soon and that it is so remote from our influence that you will be relieved from that blight!"

But Hick was not pleased by ER's response. ER replied to a lost letter:

> It seems so hard that life should be so little worth living to you when so many people love and depend on you but I have felt as you do and I keep hoping that someday things will change for you and seem more worthwhile.

While ER tried to soothe Hick, her own spirits were frayed: "I don't like the [social] 'season' nor the White House." But FDR's 7 January speech "was very good." The president reasserted leadership and seemed out of the doldrums. He opposed "predatory" monopolies and promised continued reforms. Ickes noticed that FDR's Democratic enemies did not applaud; they sat grim-faced throughout: The "war is on fiercer than ever between the reactionaries and the liberals" within the party.

On 16 January, ER wrote of Mrs. Baruch's death, "which must have been very sudden for I did not know she was ill. It was a curious relationship and yet he had affection for her and was always thoughtful so I imagine he will miss her." Although they traveled separately, Bernard Baruch was devoted to Annie Griffen Baruch, a mysterious figure John Golden remembered as a "laughing vibrant" former showgirl, and others found austere and reclusive. Her death was sudden, and Baruch was bereft. He told a friend no one could take her place: "My wife was the most wonderful woman in the world." But she was uninterested in public affairs, and Baruch turned his attention to women most involved with them—including and increasingly ER.

In mid-January, Hick's depression lifted after good conversations with Commander Flanagan about her excellent work, and her correspondence with ER became more expansive. When Hick finished reading *This Is My Story*, she wrote:

> I think it is probably a much better book than even I realized while you were writing it. I am so proud of you! And I think the last chapter, over which you had such a struggle last summer is the best chapter in the book. Somehow it brings back and very near the you that I love. A very big person. And yet—what a hellish state of mind you were in when you were writing that chapter, last summer!

In the same letter, she was contrite about her outbursts:

> I was hurt—yes. But you have also done a thousand things to make life easier and happier for me. And I'm deeply grateful. So don't, please, feel— as you seem to feel sometimes—that you have failed in your relationship with me. . . . As I look back over these last five years—I don't think anyone

ever tried harder to make another human being happy and contented than you have tried with me. . . .

ER replied with a determined finality that left little room for renewed fantasies:

> Your Tuesday night letter was a great pleasure and I'm glad you like This Is My Story—Of course dear, I never meant to hurt you in any way but that is no excuse for having done it. It won't help you any but I'll never do to anyone else what I did to you. I'm pulling myself back in all my contacts now. I've always done it with the children and why I didn't know I couldn't give you (or anyone else who wanted and needed what you did) any real food I can't now understand. Such cruelty and stupidity is unpardonable when you reach my age. Heaven knows I hope in some small and unimportant ways I have made life a little easier for you but that doesn't compensate. . . .

As their stormy month ended, ER devoted a column to emotional endurance. Someone had sent her a book of poetry by Patience Strong, *Quiet Corner*, which had encouraged her:

> Do not heed the world, its taunts and jeers—
> Lift your eyes and face the coming years—
> All great things are bought with human tears—
> So dream again.

ER concluded: "Eternal optimism makes it possible to dream," and "how thankful we can be that this power was given to us poor humans."

Energized by her honesty with Hick, ER planned FDR's fifty-sixth birthday festivities with gusto: Unlike the year before, when she could think of nothing interesting to do without Howe, ER now orchestrated a gala event, with costumes and reminders of "some special incident" in their lives. FDR was "to guess" the incident, "and we will all keep score." It was "a good dinner for Franklin . . . very jolly." Then ER made the rounds of all seven benefit dances in FDR's honor, and they were "very peppy this year."

She also planned more adventurous evenings with Hick at the opera and theater. *Lohengrin* was, ER wrote, "a real joy," and they attended WPA's *One Third of a Nation*, on Ash Wednesday. ER supposed "I can get away with it on Ash Wednesday if I don't write about it!" Hick wondered, "[D]oes one wear evening clothes on Ash Wednesday to the WPA theatre?"

These evenings were only partially successful, since Hick was still "bored with living." She wrote, however, that "you were dear, and I did enjoy it. The play was quite swell, wasn't it?" ER replied: "I know you are not feeling up to much but you were sweet. I love you."

Throughout January and February, ER studied the international news with dread. Daily the headlines were dire. Fueled by betrayal and violence, the storms of 1938 howled through Europe's statehouses like an evil nightmare with smoldering fumes. ER took solace in her work with the women's peace movement. She hosted 450 Cause and Cure of War ladies at tea and met with Elizabeth Read and Esther Lape before she spoke at the " 'Cause & Cure' conference," where Carrie Chapman Catt and Ruth Bryan Rohde "both made good speeches. . . ." ER sought to give publicity and legitimacy to the activist women of the peace movement.

At the last cabinet meeting of 1937, FDR had announced that "Romania had gone Fascist and Yugoslavia was on its way."* Romania followed Hitler's pattern and outlawed the Jews. Ickes wrote:

> There has always been a heavy proportion of Jews in Romania. . . . Apparently they are having a [dreadful] time . . . and it is reported that the rich Jews are already leaving. . . . Unfortunately the frontiers of many countries are now closed to Jews.

Then, at the first cabinet meeting in January 1938, FDR suggested "some representation or protest" to Romania "about its treatment of the Jews." But nothing was done.

Also at that first January cabinet meeting Vice President Garner reported that he had heard Joseph Goebbels announce that Germany "intended to pay no attention to treaties." He wondered what purpose negotiations or agreements now served. These were the dreadful conditions ER addressed in *This Troubled World*. She wrote it six months before, with the hope it might prompt her husband to end trade with aggressor nations. She demanded aggressor nations be named, and be confronted by collective action by the remaining democratic nations. Finally, FDR seemed to heed her advice, and he made a bold gesture toward collective security which she had urged for so long.

On 11 January 1938, Sumner Welles approached Sir Ronald Lindsay in Washington with a "secret and confidential message" from FDR to Chamberlain. The president proposed a Washington conference of world leaders to discuss "the deterioration of the international situation" and its "Underlying causes."

If England agreed, FDR would approach France, Italy, and Germany. Lindsay considered the plan "a genuine effort to relax" tensions. Churchill

---

*Romania's king appointed a fascist premier, although his party "won only nine percent of the vote . . . thus disregarding the popular will of his country." The Nazi press already had sixty newspapers there, and Romania received aid from Germany and Italy. It represented the end of France's alliance with the Little Entente.

considered it a splendid gesture, "formidable and measureless." But their ally Foreign Minister Anthony Eden was on holiday, and Chamberlain rejected the proposal. He preferred to recognize Italy's occupation of Abyssinia, and he cared nothing about U.S. influence.

FDR's effort was too late. Tom Lamont, who knew Chamberlain well, told Bullitt that if "any Englishman was anti-American, Chamberlain was that anti-American Englishman." Chamberlain considered Roosevelt a shifty scoundrel; and he trusted Hitler, a gentleman. Winston Churchill, however, recognized FDR's effort as the last hope: Its rejection ended the era of negotiation. Had FDR's intent become public, he risked isolationist outrage. His political courage to involve the United States in Europe's "darkening scene" endeared him to Churchill:

> To Britain it was a matter almost of life and death. No one can measure in retrospect its effect upon the course of events. . . . We must regard its rejection . . . as the loss of the last frail chance to save the world from tyranny otherwise than by war.

That Chamberlain, dull and inexperienced, dismissed "the proffered hand stretched out across the Atlantic" left Churchill "breathless with amazement."

Repelled by Chamberlain's action in his absence, Eden resigned. He too believed FDR's gesture represented the last possible collective effort to prevent Armageddon. His resignation, on 20 February 1938, was momentous. Britain was now entirely dominated by appeasers.

Churchill despaired. It was the worst day of his career. In his long life of success and failure, he never felt so alone and overcome. On that night solely, 20 February 1938, he tossed sleepless in his bed "consumed by emotions of sorrow and fear." Before his eyes marched the most painful visions, a long parade of death.

Hitler now had a free hand. Austrian by birth, Hitler had a vision of Germany as the mythical mystical lands of Siegfried and Thor. Every land upon which Germans ever lived was part of Greater Germany. Not just the territory lost at Versailles, such as the Rhineland, but all of it: the entire heart of Europe from the borders of the Holy Roman Empire through the Kingdom of Prussia (from Danzig to Königsberg; beyond the Polish Corridor from the Oder to the Vistula), and all the lands southward within the Hapsburg Empire, beginning with Austria, on to the lands of Sudeten Germans, Bohemia and Moravia, now "lost" to Czechoslovakia, and on through the Danubian Basin from Hungary to Romania.

In 1934, Mussolini opposed Hitler's moves toward Austria, mobilized 500,000 Italian troops to protect its borders and preserve its independence. But in 1935, Hitler supported Italy's occupation of Ethiopia; and in 1936 the military alliance to create fascist Spain terminated Mussolini's opposition to the Anschluss.

Hitler had intended to absorb Austria from the beginning. It was promised on the first page of *Mein Kampf:* Austria was German; union was inevitable. For years, Hitler had bombarded Austria with a relentless political warfare campaign, and he contributed vastly to Austria's Nazi Party. On 12 February 1938, with no organized centers of resistance left in Vienna, Hitler demanded an audience with Kurt von Schuschnigg to give him an ultimatum: the nazification of Austria, or invasion and military occupation— another Spain.

On 9 March, Schuschnigg resisted, and called for a plebiscite. But Hitler's troops mobilized to cross the border. On 13 March, Hitler canceled the plebiscite and Schuschnigg capitulated: There was no resistance, no bloodshed. As Hitler's army marched in, Austria's police and military donned Nazi insignia, to join frenzied crowds who pelted 100,000 German troops with flowers as they invaded. Goebbels called it the *Blumenkrieg,* flower war. Vienna seemed a pageant of swastika banners and unbridled enthusiasm, as Austrians shouted: *"Ein Volk, ein Reich, ein Führer!"* As Austrian citizens were transformed into Nazi subjects, there were also thousands of silent, grieving onlookers. For the moment, ignored and unphotographed, they had been rendered irrelevant: Austria's new wastepeople, democrats, Jews, anti-Nazi dissenters, in flight and despair. Seventy-five thousand were quickly rounded up, subject to the most sadistic public humiliations; there were more than two hundred suicides a day, and "many sickening incidents." When Churchill asked why the press failed to report that part of the story, London *Times* editor Geoffrey Dawson replied: "There is no doubt . . . the impression of jubilation was overwhelming."

Thousands of Austria's most esteemed citizens had been instantly transformed into German Jews, without rights, without respect. In a country where generations of assimilation obscured a tradition of seething Jew hatred, a *mischlinge* citizenry of high culture and affluence was transformed overnight into beggary by a circus of derision and contempt. Gleeful mobs taunted and brutalized aged Jews forced to scrub sidewalks with toothbrushes, toilets with bare hands, reminding them of the forgotten promise of another century: Austria would be *Judenrein*—Jew-free.

Now as Hitler ushered his homeland into his Reich, maniacal Jew-hatred became once again fashionable in cosmopolitan Vienna, the crossroads of European culture. From the diaspora through the medieval crusades to the various pogroms of modernizing Europe, Hitler's creed was familiar.

On 14 March, Churchill addressed the House of Commons: "The gravity" of the situation "cannot be exaggerated." Vienna was the geographic link of Central Europe: "This mastery of Vienna gives to Nazi Germany military and economic control of the whole of the communications of Southeastern Europe, by road, by river, and by rail."

In his vivid speech of doom and portent Churchill proposed a "Grand Alliance," a united front "for mutual defence against aggression." It "might even now arrest this approaching war." Although Churchill spoke only of a united front comprised of the Little Entente with France and England, Russia responded immediately.

Maxim Litvinov condemned the Anschluss as a dangerous act of aggression; it threatened all nations between the Soviet Union and the Reich. Russia was ready "to participate in collective actions" to check further aggression and eliminate the "danger of a new world massacre." On 18 March the USSR officially proposed a conference to discuss a pact to create a Grand Alliance. On 24 March Chamberlain rejected the idea. Harold Nicolson, among other members of Parliament, now joined Churchill in despair: "The Tories think only of the Red danger and let the Empire slide."

Wounded by Chamberlain's February rebuff, FDR said nothing about the Anschluss. ER read the papers in gloom; the "European situation" was cruel and incomprehensible. She used "Brotherhood Day," sponsored by the National Council of Jews and Christians, to address Austria's plight. The council had published "Ten Commandments of Good Will," and ER recommended three of them particularly: "I will honor all men and women regardless of their race or religion." "I will exemplify in my own life the spirit of good will and understanding." And, "I will do more than live and let live, I will live and help live."

She hoped that the new commandments would "sink into every heart and be remembered every day. . . ."

On 15 March 1938, ER wrote FDR: "I fear this European situation has you all worried pink and I fear work is pretty bad but hope you'll get away by the 20th. . . ."

By mid-March all the news was terrible. The cabinet understood that "matters in Spain are going badly," and Franco's troops had reached the Madrid side of the mountains. Heavily reinforced by additional Italian troops, Germany's "best" planes and most lethal "war machines" caused unlimited destruction. In China, Japanese forces had crossed the Yellow River, and in Russia the "terrible purges" continued. People were condemned for crimes of twenty years before. Ickes wrote that "it certainly looks as if Stalin had gone mad, and Russia is rapidly losing what sympathy she has had among liberals. . . ."

It was a grim time, and FDR's State Department, with few exceptions, was dominated by friends of fascism and appeasers. Rebuffed by England, his quarantine effort derided by isolationists and pacifists, FDR counseled continued silence. There was a sense of foreboding, but the rumbles were in the distance, and for the moment there was nothing to be done.

On 17 March, ER wrote again: "Evidently Europe is not giving you deep concern and you plan to get away. . . ."

Throughout March, ER was on a lecture tour to promote *This Troubled World*—which had forecast the headlines and demanded urgent attention. She had warned that "future wars will have no fronts." In Spain and China, war defied boundaries: "Gases and airplanes will not be directed only against armed forces." They will be "used for breaking the morale . . . shelling unfortified cities, towns and villages, and the killing of women and children." Modern war would involve "entire populations."

In Albuquerque, Santa Fe, El Paso, Phoenix, San Francisco, and Los Angeles, ER promoted collective security and urged Americans to reconsider isolationism. The future demanded a new level of concern and activism. She sought to create a groundswell of public opinion to move her husband's policy along. Everywhere she went, her message was the same, and she sold many copies of her book.

While nations everywhere readied their armies for war and plunder, she searched in vain for real leadership: "Few people are sitting down dispassionately to go over the whole situation in an attempt to determine what present conditions are, or how they should be met."

Since 1924 she had deplored apathy as a cause of war and called for a World Court that would condemn "war as murder." In 1934, she called for "an active crusade that women the world over must undertake . . . with the youth of our countries. We have got to face the fact that there are economic causes which bring about war."

These economic causes had remained unaddressed since the disastrous Treaty of Versailles. International trade had been rendered too costly, tariffs too high, competition too unequal. Unless changes occurred, war would triumph; education was essential, a slow, wearying process that might seem "futile." Nevertheless, ER insisted: "Faint heart, ne'er won fair lady, nor did it ever solve world problems!"

Not an absolute pacifist, ER rejected unilateral disarmament. She defended FDR's 1937 determination to reoutfit the U.S. Navy and dismissed Jeannette Rankin's plan to retire the Navy since we no longer intended to involve ourselves in overseas wars. That, ER said, was virtual suicide "in a world which is arming all around us."

Convinced that Hitler and Mussolini had unlimited ambitions, ER told her press conference on 14 February 1938 that it was "unfortunately true that we live in a world where force is the only voice which carries conviction and weight." She wished we lived instead "in a world where reason and patience prevailed," but until "the strong nations of the world can agree to disarm, we must maintain our own forces." She approved increased military spending and defended her husband's $1.2 billion military expansion bill, although she noted: "I have always felt that taking the profits out of war was a very salutary thing."

In March, she said a united front of democratic nations determined to stop aggression might still derail the rush to war and catastrophe. But now among world leaders only Maxim Litvinov voiced any hope for collective action.

With the League of Nations and World Court moribund, ER called, in her speeches and book, for some other negotiating body to resolve disputes and to be actually decisive: This was the heart of *This Troubled World:*

> We need to define what an aggressor nation is. We need to have a tri-bunal where the facts in any case may be discussed, and the decision made before the world. . . .

In total defiance of her husband's policy, ER called for trade embargoes exclusively against aggressor nations, and when economic sanctions failed to deter an aggressor, a world "police force could be called upon." This police force would not be an invading army, but a peacekeeping body, to prevent war, violence, mayhem.

ER even criticized FDR's limited Good Neighbor Policy. Although it ended "a bullying, patronizing attitude" toward Latin America, hemispheric progress was only a beginning: "We cannot be entirely satisfied with any-thing [that] does not include the world as a whole, for we are all so closely interdependent. . . ."

If we really wanted peace, ER insisted, we had to confront reality: The time to fight for peace was before war broke out. She counseled long-range goals that involved "a change in human nature." Women understood how each individual family fight needed to be personally negotiated. Imagination, understanding, respect were key: Nations too often spoke of religious free-dom, but "meant freedom only for their kind of religion."

ER considered the peace process akin to mountain climbing. There were no shortcuts from peak to peak. Humanity required patience, "vision and per-sistence," to make "peaceful quiet progress . . . laboriously up the side of the mountain."

Ultimately, she concluded, humanity must understand that "what serves the people as a whole serves them best as individuals." Unless we work to "change human nature . . . we are going to watch our civilization wipe itself off the face of the earth."

ER could not believe that anyone who had witnessed the last war, which had ended only twenty years earlier, could bear the thought of another: "I believe that anyone who thinks must think of the next war as they would think of suicide." Sometimes she felt despair about the "utter futility of human experience, feeling how deadly stupid we are." She wondered why our past experiences did not better inform our present policies:

> How can we study history, how can we live through the things that we have lived through and complacently go on allowing the same causes over and over again to put us through those same horrible experiences? I cannot believe that we are going to go on being as stupid as that. If we are, we deserve to commit suicide—and we will!

ER acknowledged the glamour and excitement of war. A friend had recently boasted to her that he could recruit young men anywhere to go to war in any part of the world. But, she countered, we needed to tell the truth about the ravages of war, the suffering and waste.

ER called herself a "practical pacifist." She toured the country speaking with peace societies, protesting war toys, calling for the elimination of profits in the munitions industry. She called for "government ownership" of munitions factories and wondered if the opponents to this idea were not self-interested investors "whose interests lie in this particular business."

Influenced by the Nye Committee and such books as *The Merchants of Death*, ER considered the arms trade and "private profit a great incentive" to war. In a democracy, she argued, freedom of the press and public accountability should combine with government ownership or "the strictest kind of government supervision" to control that profitability, "thus removing the incentive for constantly seeking and creating new markets" for war. Then we might consider world disarmament, with inspection procedures, but "very gradually I am sure."

ER ended her essay and lectures with a call for love as a principle in life, and in diplomacy:

> We can establish no real trust between nations until we acknowledge the power of love above all other powers. . . .
> We must reach a point where we can recognize the rights and needs of others, as well as our own rights and needs.

For ER this involved a great spiritual revival, a "new code of ethics" based on "an awakening sense of responsibility" for others. If our civilization merited preservation, "then our people must turn" to love, "not as a doctrine but as a way of living."

> You laugh, it seems fantastic, but this subject [love] will, I am sure, have to be discussed throughout the world for many years before it becomes an accepted rule. We will have to want peace, want it enough to pay for it, pay for it in our own behavior and in material ways. We will have to want it enough to overcome our lethargy and go out and find all those in other countries who want it as much as we do. . . .

Love was for ER the great driving principle of life, and politics. She did not consider it an endless battleground, but a continual arena for study, compromise, pleasure, fulfillment, and negotiation. While ER lectured about peace, she continued her negotiations with her loved ones.

When ER toured the Southwest, Hick spent time at the White House entertaining little Diana Hopkins, who moved her deeply. She wrote three pages about Diana's efforts to cope with her loneliness in that great house, concluding: "You know there are only three members of this household for whom I have any affection; they are you, Tommy and Mabel."

ER was particularly irked to have no communication from her husband: "I've not had a line from the WH. No letter, no wire, nothing since I left a week ago Sunday. I've wired & written twice and I am now going on strike!"

But on 17th March, FDR telephoned, and she also received his letter. She was relieved to hear; it was their thirty-third anniversary. But her reply was cool: Her lectures went well, and "the audiences are very good." She was sorry to hear his wisdom tooth had to be removed, and hoped "it gives you as little trouble as mine gave me." She sent FDR "best wishes for the 17th and much love."

Things were strained in their partnership. ER wrote her daughter that FDR had telephoned, "the first word from the WH since I left! All seems well. . . ."

Actually all was not well. ER was still angry about Betsey's role in the White House, which contributed to Betsey's marital difficulties. She and James were now estranged, which only seemed to intensify FDR's closeness to Betsey. ER was mystified to hear that he now planned to go to Warm Springs with Betsey at the end of March.

ER wrote Anna in confused and veiled tones:

> James is doing 2 weeks with the Marines. . . . there is a chance that Bets may go with Pa to Warm Springs. I don't understand it all but it seems very pleasant all around so I shouldn't worry I suppose!"

With Tiny in California on the 17th, ER visited NYA and WPA projects, including a crippled-children's hospital, "one of the best I ever saw. . . . This is a busy world!" It was also a successful tour.

In letters to her husband, ER downplayed the public significance of her lectures. But FDR's friend James Metcalf wrote the president with enthusiasm. He and his wife, Adelaide, who was vice president of the California Federation of Democratic Women's Study Clubs, had been dazzled by ER's address: "It's my opinion that your Wife is bringing *you* nearer to the People than you've ever been before—and during the past five years you've been closer to the Heart of the Nation than any of your predecessors."

FDR appreciated that ER's work benefited him in countless ways. He relied upon her ability to get out and meet the people, and he trusted her to introduce controversies and her own convictions, not only to test the political climate but to move public opinion. But their disagreements were often profound, and every program they both cared about was under siege by aggressive conservatives in Congress.

During the spring of 1938, ER's concerns focused on the "work projects" of the National Youth Administration and the WPA. She wanted them to meet "the needs of different racial groups." ER's priorities were not among FDR's priorities, and their gravest differences remained the world crises.

On the 18th, Hick wrote of her visit with FDR:

> My dear: I thought I told you I had seen the President last Sunday. . . . He was very cordial and asked me to stay to lunch. . . . He didn't seem to be particularly worried about the European situation. . . . But he was apparently very much concerned about the tax bill. . . .

ER left her West Coast tour to meet FDR and his party in Warm Springs, where Betsey's presence made her feel irrelevant. She wrote Hick that it seemed "too much trouble to go and swim alone," and besides she had to go to Fort Benning "to see FDR drive by the troops."

Everything about the visit annoyed ER. She felt trapped, and useless. Harry Hopkins was also there, recovering from cancer surgery. He was thin and weary, and ER worried about him, "but for Diana's sake I hope I am all wrong."

While ER was discontent in Warm Springs, Hick was in New York, with evenings at the opera and theater: *Tristan*, which was "lovely beyond description," and *Pins and Needles:* "Isn't it the freshest thing?" It "makes the average Broadway musical show look sick."

ER also loved *Pins and Needles* and was "so glad" Hick agreed. On the 30th, Hick told ER that Edna Gellhorn had written that Martha had returned to Spain: "The glorious little fool."

April began with Harry Hopkins and Aubrey Williams working all day to prepare their defense of WPA and NYA costs before Congress. "Quite an ordeal," ER noted, but worth it. FDR responded favorably.

During the winter, unemployment had soared, and New Deal programs seemed doomed by FDR's budget cuts. By April 1938, the U.S. economy had lost "two-thirds of the gains made since March 1933." FDR's romance with a balanced budget finally ended, and he called for emergency appropriations.

With an estimated twelve to fourteen million unemployed, FDR returned to his election promises. On 14 April, he asked Congress to increase relief expenditures by $3.7 billion: $1.25 billion for WPA, $150 million for the Farm Security Administration, $50 million each for CCC and NYA. He wanted the U.S. Housing Authority to have $300 million of additional slum clearance projects, and an additional $100 million federal aid to highways, and an additional $37 million for flood control, and more. These funds were to ensure the well-being of the majority of Americans and to guarantee the survival of American democracy: Around the world democracy disappeared, because people grew "tired of unemployment and insecurity."

> To abandon our purpose of building a greater, a more stable and a more tolerant America, would be to miss the tide and perhaps to miss the port. I propose to sail ahead. . . .

Henry Morgenthau disagreed, and threatened to resign. But Congress complied. ER was relieved. It had been a year of delays, a long period of inaction and loss. Now the fair labor standards bill, which promised minimum wages and maximum hours of work and outlawed child labor, stood a chance.

After the Anschluss, ER began to confront directly the rising tide of anti-Semitism at home and abroad. She wrote earnest letters of explanation to promote "tolerance" and supported countless Jewish organizations. Every letter sent to her received attention. She pursued visas, sought to reunite families, protested deportation proceedings, worked to find people jobs, housing, general support.

She endorsed the work of a small group of women in Irvington, New Jersey, representing the Daughters of Israel Malbish Arumim Society, who asked her to greet contributors of "clothing and other necessities" for the poor in a souvenir journal to be distributed at their annual concert and ball. On 11 April she sent greetings to the Glen Cove Jewish Ladies Aid Society, working to repair their temple. In May she hosted a tea for the ladies of B'nai B'rith at the White House. One of her guests that day, Doris Bernstein of Chicago, expressed the sentiments of many: "Your charm and your marvellous hospitality will remain with me for years. . . ."

Nazi victories in Europe had a dramatic impact on U.S. politics. Fascist groups were strong throughout the country, and anti-Semitism became more virulent. In the United States, no less than in Europe, a renewed Red Scare was under way. As in 1919–21, when the anticommunist reign of A. Mitchell

Palmer enabled agents to sweep through America's cities against Reds and suspected Reds, unionists and immigrants were once again rounded up, hounded, threatened with deportation.

In January 1938, the National Council of Jewish Women appealed to ER to consider "the tragic plight" of two endangered young people.

Born in Germany, Karl Ohm became a U.S. citizen in 1929. While he was Protestant, his wife was Jewish. In October 1932, Ohm was arrested during a demonstration called by the International Labor Defense to protest "an unusually severe sentence meted out to a Negro."

Upon his release, deportation charges were filed. He admitted being a member of the ILD, explaining that in Germany, "all of the great professors" were members, even Albert Einstein. He "did not think it a crime," and he had never been a communist.

The case went to the Labor Department for interpretation. Extensions were granted, but on 1 January 1938 they had expired, and he was ordered to sail back to Germany. Were he expelled from the United States as a communist, having also married "a Jewess, there is no question as to what his fate in Germany will be." The Labor Department granted him voluntary departure to any nation "not adjacent to the U.S." Both England and Belgium refused visas.

Lillian Strauss, headworker of the New York section of the National Council of Jewish Women, appealed to civil libertarian lawyers Morris Ernst, Carol King, and Arthur Garfield Hays; to labor activists Rose Schneiderman and Vito Marcantonio; and to others. All the old questions were again on America's political agenda. Did communists deserve free speech? Since the Communist Party was "a legal party," why was "it a crime for an alien to be interested"?

According to Strauss, Frances Perkins's Labor Department still enforced the law amended during the Red Scare in 1920, "making the deportation of aliens mandatory," if they were communists. Although Ohm had never been a communist, he was about to be stripped of his citizenship and deported.

Ohm was a popular masseur; his only crime had been to protest "an injustice." He had been brutalized by the police and required several stitches. Everything about the case stirred fear for the future. Would ER do something?

> We are assisting refugees to escape from abroad and to adjust to a newer and freer life in our country. Can we sit passively by and permit our government to send this young man . . . back to his certain fate into the welcoming arms of Mr. Hitler?

ER referred the case with a plea to Perkins; she sent it off to James Houghteling, commissioner of the Immigration and Naturalization Service. Because Ohm's membership in a subversive organization "appeared somewhat unconclusive," Houghteling canceled the deportation order. With profound gratitude, Strauss wrote that ER's interest and assistance had freed the couple "from a five year bondage of fear and spiritual suffering."

Other examples of random violence associated with the renewed Red Scare were sent to ER that spring. Upton Sinclair appealed to her to join civil libertarians dismayed when Socialist leader Norman Thomas was rudely pulled off a platform and arrested by New Jersey police while he attempted to address a rally for the Workers Defense League. When his wife tried to find out where they were taking him, she was punched in the face.

Arthur Vanderbilt, president of the American Bar Association, defended Thomas, and many prominent Americans spoke out against the outrage, including Alf Landon. Upton Sinclair asked ER to inform Mayor Frank Hague, an official of the National Democratic Committee, that it was impolite "in a democracy" to punch "a lady."

Throughout 1938, ER opposed the rising tide of violence and bigotry in America. She was distressed by Congress's assaults on the New Deal and the sweeping intentions of its new House committee to investigate un-American activities, launched in March under the chairmanship of Texas Democrat Martin Dies.

ER personally campaigned to allow German composer Hanns Eisler and his wife, Lou Eisler, into the country. A well-known radical who protested fascism everywhere, Hanns Eisler had condemned racism in America and wrote *The Ballad of Black Jim* with Bertolt Brecht in 1932. Its vivid depiction of the oppression of a Negro subway rider "In Manhattan/In Manhattan" was lambasted. But Eisler's supporters vowed he was no communist.

ER sent Sumner Welles the many papers brought to her by someone she considered "a perfectly honest person." He was "very much disturbed" because the State Department had "told the Cuban Consul that they do not wish to admit [the Eislers]." He was certain they would consider "our form of Government 'heaven.' " ER believed the Labor Department "did not examine the case carefully enough. Why not do it all over again and bring it out in the open and let the Eislers defend themselves?"

Throughout the spring, ER's attention returned to Europe. In one column she wrote:

> I have reached a point where I open the paper every morning with apprehension. . . . It seems incredible that human beings can risk another world upheaval when they realize what the last one meant to everyone.

Although ER never referred to specific nations in print, on 17 March she wrote privately to Elinor Morgenthau about the terrible and depressing situation in Austria and Spain.

In Europe, the Anschluss changed everything. The cruelty of Austria's Nazis emboldened fascists everywhere and became the new model of behavior: hard, immediate, personal, pitiless.

Only one syndicated woman columnist was more popular than Eleanor Roosevelt in 1938: Dorothy Thompson, who appeared in more than a hundred newspapers. Virtually alone among America's leading columnists, she was "On the Record" with outrage at FDR's silence. In Austria, "every gallant soul I have ever known—from the highest aristocracy to the last intelligent trade union leader—is dead, murdered or a suicide; or is in prison, in concentration camp, or in exile." The complacent west, the leaders of liberal democracy, she wrote, must confront critical choices: Take "a last stand against heavy odds" or go "under for generations."

Thompson earned her reputation as Cassandra by continually blasting the official policy of "ostrichism" and appeasement. She detailed both Hitler's excesses and the " 'cowardice' that sustained it."

The aftermath of Germany's victory and the agonies of Vienna's Jews were well known in Anglo-American circles. By the spring of 1938 Churchill was no longer alone in Parliament when he warned of unbridled Nazi ambitions, flaccid British defenses, coming world disaster.

Harold Nicolson, who had been partly responsible for Czechoslovakia and other geographic changes at Versailles, began to meet with Churchill in small groups of anguished concern. Indeed, by February, Nicolson felt he could no longer support appeasement, or represent his own National Labour Party—which "has behaved like worms and kissed the Chamberlain boot with a resounding smack." He offered to resign as vice-chairman of the Foreign Affairs Committee.

On 25 February he reported the extraordinary scene to his wife, Vita Sackville-West. After a singularly nasty event in a packed room, it was determined that his resignation would embarrass the government. At least Nicolson and his allies might wait until public "feeling had diminished." Then:

> Winston in all his majesty rose and said that they were being mean and petty . . . and he must insist on a vote, either Yes or No. They then voted. Those in favour of our not resigning were unanimous except for one little vicious hand against. That hand was the hand of Nancy Astor.
>
> We then adjourned in some excitement. In the corridor a friend of mine called Alan Graham [Conservative MP, 1935–45] came up to Nancy and said, "I do not think you behaved very well." She turned upon him and said, "Only a Jew like you would *dare* to be rude to me." He replied, "I should much like to smack your face." I think she is a little mad.

Coincidentally, that same day ER and Nancy Astor were together on an international hookup broadcasting to the world on the importance of women in world affairs. The broadcast was sponsored by the International Federation of Business and Professional Women, and neither ER nor her friend Lady Astor said anything very controversial. All seven women, including representatives from Italy, France, Norway, and Switzerland, emphasized the importance of peace.

Nancy Astor advised women to "help preserve freedom" and to protest against materialism and the concept that might makes right. ER spoke last and very briefly. She called upon women to work for peace and declared that neither men nor women should be deprived of educational opportunities or their full rights as citizens under law.

Although Nancy Astor had created a transatlantic stir in 1937, when she proclaimed that peace would be advanced by an Anglo-German accord, her views were then not very different from those expressed by FDR's personal envoys to Europe. Bill Bullitt struggled to arrange a French-German accord, and Joseph Kennedy—recently appointed ambassador to the Court of St. James's—became immediately identified with Lady Astor's Cliveden circle.

ER never understood FDR's diplomatic choices. She considered Bullitt untrustworthy and unpredictable, "clever" but mercurial. She ultimately came to despise Joe Kennedy, but in 1938 merely distrusted him. At a dinner in December, attended by Dorothy Schiff Backer, ER asked why FDR had appointed "that awful Joe Kennedy," who was by then not only a known enemy of the New Deal but a continual critic of FDR personally.

Although Henry Morgenthau had written in his diary that FDR "considered Kennedy a very dangerous man," when ER confronted her husband, he threw his head back and laughed: "Appointing an Irishman to the Court of St. James" was "a great joke, the greatest joke in the world." Evidently, nobody else laughed.

ER was also troubled by FDR's abrupt removal of William Dodd from his post in Germany just before Christmas. Dodd hated fascism, refused to attend Nazi ceremonies, boycotted the annual Nuremberg Party rallies, presented insulting lectures on Jeffersonian democracy, and stayed largely in his study writing his history of the South. At Bullitt's suggestion, Dodd was replaced by Hugh Wilson—considered much more acceptable in German circles.

Moreover, there had been no breach between the Roosevelts and the Astors. In 1937, Nancy Astor dined at the White House when she was in the United States on a private trip to visit her brother. And Nancy was known to be loyal to her old friends. It was, therefore, understandable that Felix Frankfurter turned to her for help when he learned that his most beloved eighty-two-year-old uncle, Dr. Solomon Frankfurter, an esteemed scholar and chief librarian at the University of Vienna, was among the 76,000 herded into concentration camps during the first days of the Anschluss.

All his earlier letters to FDR from England and Palestine in 1933 and 1934 concerning Hitler and Europe had been blithely ignored, simply lost in the blather of other business. Now the situation was urgent, deadly. Rather than risk the wobbles of State Department scrutiny, and a slow, careless, or devious response, Frankfurter turned to Lady Astor. Her reputation for audacity had in no way been tarnished by her newer reputation as a pro-German leader of the "Cliveden crowd."

Asked to intervene with her "German friends," she wrote Frankfurter in May:

> Dear Friend:
> The minute I received your wire I spoke to the German Ambassador in London, and gave him, in no uncertain terms, our views on arresting aged scholars. He promised to do what he could. Three days afterwards, having heard no more, I talked to him again and warned him that unless I received good news of Herr Frankfurter, I should go myself to Vienna! He assured me that it would be alright. As you know, your uncle was released on 28th March. The Ambassador [von Ribbentrop's successor, Herbert von Dirksen] tells me that he was only imprisoned a few days as a result of some unguarded remarks.

Deeply grateful, Frankfurter nevertheless used the occasion to inquire about Nancy Astor's views, and an extraordinary exchange on Cliveden and appeasement ensued. But in England, Nancy Astor's collaborationist views were challenged by the news, which worsened daily, and cracks in the wall of appeasement began to appear in London where Harold Nicolson dramatically reflected ER's views. On 6 June 1938, Nicolson confided in his diary:

> Our isolationists must see by now that isolation is not enough. . . .
> Chamberlain (who has the mind and manner of a clothes-brush) aims only at assuring temporary peace at the price of ultimate defeat. . . .
> People of the governing classes think only of their own fortunes, which means hatred for the Reds. This creates a perfectly artificial but at present most effective secret bond between ourselves and Hitler. Our class interests, on both sides, cut across our national interests. I go to bed in gloom.

Nicolson was even more distressed after he met an Austrian "who had just got away from Vienna, and what he said made me ill." He wrote Vita:

> [Nazi soldiers] rounded up the people walking in the Prater on Sunday last, and separated the Jews from the rest. They made the Jewish gentlemen

take off all their clothes and walk on all fours on the grass. They made the old Jewish ladies get up into the trees by ladders and sit there. They then told them to chirp like birds. The Russians never committed atrocities like that. You may take a man's life; but to destroy all his dignity is bestial. . . . The suicides have been appalling. . . .

England's official policy of unconcern was consecrated by widespread Hitler worship. Social conversation revealed British support for every atrocity. Nicolson noted that Unity Mitford adored but "does not hope to marry Hitler. . . . Hitler likes her because of her fanaticism. She wants the Jews to be made to eat grass."

Hitler counted on such approval. In the United States such views were represented by a wide range of congressional and diplomatic opinion, and during these critical days they were most dangerously expressed by Charles Lindbergh and Joseph Kennedy in England. According to Nicolson, Lindbergh's exaggerated report of Nazi airpower froze Britain's nerve.

ER was revolted when America's most celebrated hero became a major propaganda weapon for Hitler and accepted a Nazi medal for his services to the Reich. On 22 May, Lindbergh visited Sissinghurst and detailed the findings of his European tour. Nicolson recorded:

> He says that we cannot possibly fight since we should certainly be beaten. The German Air Force is ten times superior to that of Russia, France and Great Britain put together. Our defences are simply futile. . . . He thinks we should just . . . make an alliance with Germany.

Nicolson "discounted" Lindbergh's report: After all, "he believes in the Nazi theology." It was "all tied up with his hatred of degeneracy and his hatred of democracy as represented by the free Press and the American public." Nevertheless, Nicolson wrote in his diary, England was "outmastered in the air." Despite the evening news, which celebrated "a perfect summer day," Nicolson considered it "the most anxious and unhappy day that I can remember."

While the sun encouraged the azaleas and irises at Sissinghurst, ER too had moments of respite from the horror reported from Europe each day. In the country in May, she worked in her garden at Val-Kill; the violets were in bloom, and she pruned her exquisite apricot rose bushes. One morning as she watched the birds fly from tree to tree from her outside sleeping porch, she wondered "if they are getting their breakfast, or building their nests, or just working up an appetite with early morning exercise."

But when she saw a newsreel of the devastation in China and the bombardment of Barcelona, she felt "positively disgusted with human beings. How can we be such fools as to go senselessly taking human life in this way?

Why the women in every nation do not rise up and refuse to bring children into a world of this kind is beyond my understanding."

Since ER's *Lysistrata* solution of a women's strike for peace coincided with a major effort to persuade FDR to lift the embargo, we can only wonder what the words between them actually were. Several days after that newsreel, she "lunched with a friend high up in the Empire State Building. We sat at a window looking out over the city, which always takes my breath away." But as she gazed down at the city she so admired, a "horrible thought" intruded, and she wondered "what it would be like with planes flying over it dropping bombs. . . ."

News of stalemate, the bravery of the Loyalist army and underequipped International Brigades, and the suffering Spanish people captured her imagination. In 1938 she spent more time with the young activists of the American Youth Conference, who planned to go or had just returned from Spain. According to Joseph Lash, whom ER had first met in January 1936 at a White House tea attended by five members of the AYC National Council after a meeting to promote the American Youth Act, ER's sympathies were "passionately engaged upon the Loyalist side. She loved to hear the 'Six Songs of the International Brigade' and for many years kept on her desk a little bronze figure of a youthful Spanish militiaman in coveralls that was a symbol of the Republican cause."

FDR's continued insistence on a strictly enforced blockade against Loyalist Spain remained incomprehensible to her. Now, bipartisan liberal opposition was aroused. Even isolationist senators Borah and Nye, who had opposed it as unjust and unneutral, now promoted legislation to end the embargo. ER was hopeful. Ickes met with *Chicago Tribune* correspondent Jay Allen, who was fired because of his reports from the front: "Jay Allen came in to see me yesterday. . . . He is outraged over our embargo on munitions. . . . He thinks, and I agree with him, that this is a black page in our history."

Ickes blamed the president's policy on career State Department officials who "sit at the feet" of Britain's Foreign Office. Jay Allen called FDR's neutrality policy "an instrument of wanton destruction" with devastating long-term consequences.

On 12 May, Ickes met with FDR and asked about rumors he was "ready to lift the embargo." FDR replied that he was "opposed to doing anything about it." Ickes protested that "the embargo should never have been imposed." But FDR was adamant. He said Spain could not afford to buy munitions even if the embargo was lifted, and they could not pass through the now closed French frontier.

[FDR] said frankly that to raise the embargo would mean the loss of every Catholic vote next fall and that the Democratic Members of Congress were jittery about it and didn't want it done.

So, Ickes wrote with disgust, that ended the story:

> This was the cat that was actually in the bag, and it is the mangiest, scabbiest cat ever. This proves up to the hilt what so many people have been saying, namely, that the Catholic minorities in Great Britain and America have been dictating the international policy with respect to Spain.

But the story did not end for ER. She donated money for aid to private groups, especially the American Friends Service Committee, and continually fought propaganda that praised Franco's war against anti-Catholic communists.

Toward the end of May she listened to Ambassador Claude Bowers's broadcast from the U.S. embassy at St. Jean de Luz:

> I was very much impressed by the tragic things which he related as everyday occurrences in the lives of Spanish children. Probably a million children, undernourished, inadequately clothed, many dying from the slow torture of starvation, many sick and many wounded and many fatherless and motherless and homeless. . . .

She joined Bowers's plea for Americans to "live up to our past reputation . . . [and] care for the children of other nations, no matter what our attitude might be toward the government involved."

But aid for refugees and orphaned children was no longer enough. In June, ER sought to circumvent her husband's blockade and participated in a rather wild escapade with her brother Hall. On 21 June 1938, Bill Bullitt wrote a "Personal and Confidential" letter to FDR:

> This is a very private letter which requires no answer.
> Some days ago I received a telegram from Mrs. Roosevelt informing me that Hall was coming to Paris and asking me to do anything I could for him.

Then France's new foreign minister, Georges Bonnet, a peace-at-any-price appeaser, told Bullitt that the Spanish ambassador "informed him that the Spanish Government could buy more than one hundred planes in the United States at once for immediate delivery to Spain via France" and wanted the French frontier reopened to military shipments. Bullitt was astounded to hear that FDR personally "approved the sale of these planes to the Spanish Government and that you were arranging for the evasion of the Neutrality Act." Bullitt expressed his "skepticism to Bonnet and telegraphed the [State] Department for immediate instructions."

Then Hall telephoned Bullitt to announce that he was in Paris, with his son Daniel, who wanted to volunteer in Spain. Bullitt invited them to a ball, and Hall arrived for an urgent conversation:

When Hall came in at 4:15 this afternoon, he said that he, acting through Harold Talbott of Cleveland, had managed to gather for the Spanish Government approximately 150 new and second-hand planes of various makes—all of which he specified. He said that he had discussed this transaction with you and that it had your entire approval. He stated that you and he and Jimmy had discussed all the details and that you had agreed to wink at the evasion of the Neutrality Act involved, because of your interest in maintaining the resistance of the Spanish Government against Franco. . . .

Bullitt "expressed no opinion" to Hall, but informed him that U.S. policy "was to oppose absolutely the giving of licenses for shipments of planes to Spain via France." Hall "replied that you had thought of writing to me," but since "he would arrive in Paris as quickly as a letter you had preferred to have him explain the matter to me by word of mouth." The conversation continued:

I informed Hall also that the French Government had closed the frontier to Spain absolutely; that the French Government had a real hope that the volunteers might be withdrawn at last from both sides in Spain and that the British were pushing for an armistice pending the withdrawal of volunteers. I told him that I could not imagine a moment more unpropitious for an attempt to organize the shipment of planes to Spain in contravention of the wishes of the British and French Governments and our own Neutrality Act.

After Hall left, Bullitt received confirmation from the State Department and a telegram from Sumner Welles that U.S. policy was unchanged.

Bullitt concluded his query about this familial effort to bypass FDR's blockade:

I have not the slightest desire to know what lies behind this expedition of Hall's, and I am writing this letter for your own eye and no one else's, merely because I feel that since your name has been used by the Spanish Government in its conversations with the French Government, you ought to have a full account of the facts.

FDR would not have advised ER or her brother to contact Bullitt if he had wanted the planes to get through. Bullitt believed air travel rendered "Europe an absurdity." As he flew from Munich to Venice, he "crossed Austria in fifteen minutes." But instead of considering European amity and unity, these "dinky little European states" faced the future submerged in "national hatreds" and on the brink of "destroying themselves completely and handing Europe over to the Bolsheviks."

That, in the end, dictated all appeasement efforts, including FDR's committment to the blockade—which was ignored only to allow US supplies to reach Franco.*

ER never acccepted the abandonment of Spanish democracy, and she referred to it again and again. Even during her visit to London during the war, at a small dinner party hosted by the Churchills, attended by Tommy and Henry Morgenthau, among others, ER and Winston had "a slight difference of opinion," which she detailed: When the prime minister asked Henry Morgenthau if the United States was now sending sufficient supplies to Spain, ER interrupted to suggest "it was a little too late." The time to send supplies to Spain had been when it might have been possible "to help the Loyalists during their civil war":

> Mr. Churchill said he had been for the Franco government until Germany and Italy went into Spain to help Franco. I remarked that I could not see why the Loyalist government could not have been helped, and the prime minister replied that he and I would have been the first to lose our heads if the Loyalists had won. . . .
>
> I said that losing my head was unimportant, whereupon he said: "I don't want you to lose your head and neither do I want to lose mine."

At that moment Clementine Churchill "leaned across the table" to agree with ER: "I think perhaps Mrs. Roosevelt is right." Her remark evidently "annoyed" the prime minister who exploded: "I have held certain beliefs for sixty years and I'm not going to change now." It was not a congenial dinner: "Mrs. Churchill then got up as a signal that dinner was over."

With their effort to get planes through the blockade aborted, Hall and his son Danny went to Spain. Danny stayed for six weeks to interview members of the International Brigades. He described his efforts in letters home. He stayed for a time with the brigade that had just crossed the Ebro and was resting after a long battle. At night "as many as fifty or sixty bombers and pursuit

---

*If she knew of it, ER must have been particularly galled by the one-sided nature of the blockade that strangled democratic Spain: Franco's Insurgency was supplied by Standard Oil, the U.S.-owned Vacuum Oil Company in Tangier, and the Texas Oil Company (Texaco) from the beginning; and on credit, which was contrary to the neutrality legislation. According to Herbert Feis, Franco received 1,866,000 metric tons of oil and 12,800 trucks from the U.S. between 1936 and 1939—on credit. According to Herbert L. Matthews: "No oil was sold by American companies to the Republicans, ostensibly on the theory that Loyalist ports were unsafe whereas the Insurgent harbors were open and protected."

planes" were overhead. Ill-equipped, mostly in sandals, the men were nevertheless "in good spirits." Danny asked why they had come, "Frenchmen, Englishmen, Americans, Austrians, Poles, and expatriated Germans and Italians." He was surprised that most of their answers were the same: "to fight fascism." He asked if they were communists, and if they were fighting for communism. About 30 percent said they were communists, but "invariably" they said they were "fighting to give Spain a chance to work out her own government."

Danny interviewed Alvah Bessie, who had been fired from the *Brooklyn Eagle* because the Roman Catholic Church objected to his reportage. When he told Bessie he was writing down every word, Bessie said, "Please don't make it too silly." And tell them: "I'm more of a pacifist than ever, we all are; that's what we're fighting for mostly. The world doesn't realize what it's doing allowing fascism a free hand."

Her nephew's observations, along with those of everyone she spoke with during the spring and summer of 1938, confirmed ER's convictions.

For so long muffled about international events, ER was now in active opposition to her husband's policies. Although there is no record of her words with FDR over Hall's airplane expedition, which she supported, she was blunt about her support for Spain.

In recognition of her support for Loyalist Spain, she was given a gift of Goya's famous series *Los Proverbios*, eighteen etchings drawn from the original plates in Madrid and completed on 9 November 1937. According to Herbert Matthews, the *New York Times* columnist in Spain:

> The idea of this edition was primarily to raise foreign currency for the hard-pressed Loyalists, but also to prove that reverence for Spanish art was as great among the so-called "Reds" as among their critics abroad. So, the famous engraver Adolfo Ruperez was commissioned to make 150 sets of the four great Goya series.

The first five of these, on Antique Japan paper, were destined for very special presentation, and were accompanied by a map of Madrid to indicate "where bombs had dropped while the work was being done." Set Number Two went to Eleanor Roosevelt.

She insisted on her right to keep it, despite loud public protests that she was partisan, unneutral, anti-Catholic, procommunist. ER declared: "I am not neutral. . . . I believe in Democracy and the right of a people to choose their own government without having it imposed on them by Hitler and Mussolini."

26: Race Radicals, Youth and Hope

—⟨⟨◦⟩⟩—

*W*hile Europe was on a deathwatch, ER was encouraged by the vitality and vision of a burgeoning youth movement and felt increasingly drawn to their activities. Also in the spring and summer of 1938, some of ER's happiest days were spent with Aubrey Williams's extended circle of Southern liberals and race radicals who met regularly in the home of Alabama's Clifford and Virginia Durr. ER worked with them to create a liberal Southern movement, and fully confront race issues.

In April, she addressed the seventieth anniversary celebration of the founding of Hampton Institute, the historically black Virginia college opened by the Freedmen's Bureau after the Civil War. In a speech that emphasized leadership in "a very changing world," ER urged the students to prepare themselves for responsibility "not only for your race, but for all the people in this nation."

Since democracy required educated citizens and ignorance represented its "greatest danger," their most important challenge "is to see that in this nation there is no such thing as ignorance." ER appreciated that it was a daunting task, since America fell "far short" of its promise for "an equal opportunity for education."

ER said: "Know what you want" as public citizens; then campaign for it, "not for yourselves alone, but . . . so that the whole community may have the opportunity to live decently."

ER compared the plight of "minority groups" with the status of women before the suffrage. Only activism, organized pressure, would achieve influence and success. That was essential, ER concluded, because "democracy today is on trial as a form of government in the world. . . ."

The United States could no longer ignore its undemocratic practices: "We have to make our nation serve the needs of the whole people. We cannot have one section of the nation suffer and the rest of the nation prosper," and we cannot allow injustice and violence to continue.

ER's words might have been dismissed as mere platitudes had she not bolstered them by activities to change the social ills she protested. Throughout 1938 she worked with Lucy Randolph Mason, who reported on the difficulties of building unionism in the South. ER sent her checks for families in distress, passed on her reports to FDR, and sought to help end the scourge of Southern poverty and violence.

Mason's CIO campaign met intimidation, coercion, and fraud; industrial spies and detective agencies; vigilante violence and Red Scare activity. "One feels the sinister suppression of democracy by civil authorities" every day wherever the Textile Workers tried to organize. "It is hard to keep calm," Lucy Randolph Mason wrote ER. "Well, thank God Mr. Roosevelt is President and *you are you.*"

According to Mason:

> The only hope for progressive democracy in the South lies in the lower economic groups—particularly the wage earner. The power holding group, meaning the capitalists and manufacturers and business men, are distinctly reactionary and as a rule opposed to the present Administration. . . .
>
> Among the rank and file . . . both in the cities and on the land, the President is adored. Yet this is the group so largely disfranchised by the poll tax requirements of eight southern states. . . .

Mason's crusade was part of a radical effort to restore the region, end the nation's "most extreme" poverty, and enhance the political and purchasing power of its citizens. She sent the First Lady books to read, tasks to perform. Mason warned ER that her reports were not for quotation: "I can criticise the South as severely as I please when in it and talking or writing to southern people, but the unpardonable offence is to criticise it outside or to the rest of the nation!"

They met in Atlanta in March, when ER addressed the Georgia Rural-Urban Women, and again in New Orleans, and Mason lunched at the White House in April. FDR met with them, and after that meeting, he urged the poll tax be added to the agenda of the new committee they formed to launch the Southern Conference on Human Welfare (SCHW) at a South-wide meeting in Montgomery, Alabama.

The purpose of the SCHW was immodest. Mason and her allies Clark Foreman, Joe Gelders, Judge Louise Charlton, and Virginia Durr, among others, intended to transform the South. ER agreed to keynote their first meeting in November. They saw their effort as part of FDR's "concern for the economic rehabilitation of the South."

Everyone concerned about justice was encouraged when shortly after their April meeting, the president finally broke his silence about possible federal action whenever a lynching occurred. Since the Gavagan-Wagner bill seemed forever doomed in Congress, FDR suggested empowering Hoover's Justice Department agents (G-men) to investigate. Their findings might then be submitted to the attorney general for public prosecution, or to Congress to create "demand for prosecution." FDR's proposal was vague, and the NAACP made "no comment," still preferring an actual law, and the "arrest and prosecution of perpetrators."

Also in April, FDR called for a world conference to aid the desperate plight of Jewish refugees from Hitler to be held in July at Evian in France. The NAACP sent a telegram applauding his determination, but asked that the government "be equally indignant at the lynchings of American citizens on U.S. soil."

ER, Mason, and the conveners of the SCHW believed that FDR was now committed to action. After decades of neglect, the plight of the South was being addressed at every level, and she pressed for action on every front. She demanded oversight of WPA and PWA funding for women's prisons being built in Georgia and South Carolina. She learned that penologists were not consulted, and that there were underground rooms intended "for a punishment dungeon, which modern penologists abhor." Aubrey Williams promised to investigate.

She also protested discrimination "by private people" and WPA officials that resulted in the loss of many homes among Negro homeowners in Morgantown, West Virginia. ER wanted their loans extended, their homes refinanced. The local NAACP had turned to ER, and her protest initiated a thorough investigation. Lucy Randolph Mason considered ER "the most useful woman in America.

ER spent the summer of 1938 almost exclusively at Hyde Park. Her decision to stay put coincided with her new involvement with the student activists of the American Youth Congress, who were to host an historic second World Youth Congress at Vassar, which she agreed to address.

ER first met the radical leaders of the AYC in January 1936 when they arrived in Washington to protest the National Youth Administration, which they did not know was ER's idea. They condemned the NYA as a condescending sham. Rather, they argued, there should be a $3.5 billion youth unemployment relief bill. ER and Aubrey Williams believed there were no grounds for conflict, and sought an alliance.

After their first meeting, ER agreed to talk with them privately at their national council meeting. The militant students were impressed by ER's candor. According to Joseph Lash, then head of the American Student Union, ER had within an hour "transformed an adversary relationship into unabashed admiration."

ER told them firmly not to "make speeches to her." She fully appreciated NYA's limitations, and she appreciated their impatience. She invited them to tea at the White House, where the delegation was again confrontational. ER remained unrattled, and promised personal consideration for their urgent issues: unemployment, racial discrimination, union-busting, the militarization of youth. She intended to be "useful." But they needed to be more political, and more polite.

Williams was more impatient with the arrogance of AYC leaders and irately walked out of several meetings. ER enjoyed their fresh vitality and dismissed their arrogance as youthful determination. She observed their inner political battles with an expansive and maternal eye.

When NYA administrator Mark McCloskey wrote to tell the First Lady he was fascinated by her "patience and tact" during hours of questions and general badgering, she replied: "I have so much sympathy for those youngsters it is never hard to be patient." Besides, they reminded her of her own sons: brash, assertive, argumentative. Unsure, surrounded by unemployment and dreadful problems, they pursued a better world; she wanted to be helpful.

ER was fond of the optimistic, unfailingly cheerful AYC leaders; and the AYC's Declaration of Rights for American Youth resonated precisely with her own views:

> In song and legend America is exalted as a land of the free, a haven for the oppressed. Yet on every hand we see this freedom limited or destroyed. Progressive forces are persecuted. Minority nationalities are exposed to arbitrary deportation. The Negro people are subjected to constant abuse, discrimination and lynch law. Workers who strike for a living are met with increasing violence. . . .
>
> We are determined to realize the ideas of full democracy. We consider complete freedom for religious belief and practise an essential to this democracy. We demand not only the maintenance but the extension of our elementary rights of free speech, press and assemblage. We consider full academic freedom essential to progress and enlightenment.

The United States was one of the richest countries in the world; it was bountiful and resourceful. It could "more than provide a life of security and comfort for all." But today that was not the case: "We want work . . . but millions of us are forced to be idle. . . . *we refuse to be the lost generation.* . . . We oppose the use of labor spies, vigilantes, and private arsenals by industrialists. . . ." The AYC supported national planning for agriculture, government aid to farm workers, "equal wages for equal work," worker education, aid to education, and an end to discrimination for reasons of race or poverty.

In 1938, the AYC was led by young people ER found courageous, uncomplaining, and charming. Her own circle stalled and disordered, ER moved on—into this youthful community of determined activists. She considered them the best of America's united front agitators who supported a bold New Deal and worked for liberal unity against fascism everywhere. She knew that some were communists, but they did not rule, and they did not run away from urgent controversies.

No other group seemed to ER just then so vigorous. The women's movement of the 1920s, which had first raised many of the same issues the AYC now emphasized, seemed no longer a unified movement for social change. When she addressed the twenty-fifth anniversary of the Children's Bureau in 1937, she called for more determination and renewed organization.

When on 4 April 1938 she hosted Mary McLeod Bethune's White House conference on more equitable distribution of federal benefits to black women and the Negro community, she was dismayed by the slow progress reported throughout the nation. In a meeting coordinated by the National Council of Negro Women, representatives of over fifty organizations met with the women directors of government agencies to overcome discriminatory practices in the administration of public health services, social security benefits, and federal welfare programs.

ER was disturbed by how little had actually been done; she recommended that biracial women's committees be established in every community and black staff be added to each federal agency. But a new movement was needed to prevent Congress from destroying all New Deal efforts and to advance equitable goals. There was still discrimination in WPA and other major programs, and too many groups remained excluded from social security, including domestic and farm workers. In all federal agencies, state by state, countless injustices were tolerated.

Throughout 1938, ER worked to get women appointed to policy-making positions, insisted on equal opportunity, called for equal pay and equal treatment for women workers, and encouraged women to run for office. But she was increasingly critical of "the general apathy of women" and wondered why they were not more politically engaged. She noted the decline in the number of women legislators and scolded: "The trouble is women as a whole do not back [women] candidates." There were 149 women legislators in thirty-eight states in 1928, and only 130 women in twenty-eight states ten years later. Also there were nine women in Congress in 1928 and only five in 1938. ER wanted to see women make a difference, and believed that they would—when they reorganized. "It probably will take some major development to jolt women out of their apathy."

In 1938, ER felt that only the SCHW organizers and the leaders of AYC promised really multiracial movements for change. The leaders of the future, they were building grassroots democratic movements that challenged the moribund conservative anti–New Deal congressional opposition her husband had to work with. On domestic issues, ER and FDR seemed in the spring of 1938 entirely united. She worked to build a new movement, and he worked to purge his opposition. Every liberal step taken was greeted by shouts of communism, as the new Red Scare intensified. Every decent act toward racial justice, every union organized, every speech for equal rights, was again condemned as communist.

In March the AYC elected ER to its advisory board. Although she had accepted the nominal role in 1934, this time she declined the honor. Advised they were a suspect group, she could not accept: "I will consider it after I leave the White House, if the Council still wishes me. . . ."

The Roman Catholic lobby led the opposition against the AYC, and ER. Catholic groups opposed her support for Spain and condemned her as America's leading "Jezebel," because she referred in one column to lipstick and in another to divorce. In April, the League of Catholic Women assailed her for promoting a film called *Birth of a Baby*. She replied that divorce was a "recognized" aspect of life, and so was birthing a baby. The film "could not be harmful because it is honest."

The Boston Congress of Catholic Women joined the fray: It was "most unfortunate, unfair and dangerous for the wife of the President . . . to make pronouncements that give offense to a large part of our citizens." Radicals wondered how the Catholic Church could condemn birthing and not the bombing of Spain—including Catholic citadels.

Various church groups throughout the South held meetings to condemn ER as a Red leader. She received dozens of letters of inquiry from Democrats who attended Baptist and Catholic meetings, dismayed by reports of her alleged views. One woman wrote for information to refute the rumors presented in a talk on "what they are teaching our children in school." ER was "the neck" and FDR "the head" of "a gang of thousands of people called the reds." Aghast to hear "these lies," her correspondent wanted a useful answer to read at the next meeting of her church's study group.

ER replied that the charges were probably from Elizabeth Dilling's book "*The Red Network*, in which I am accused of being a Red, as is everyone in this country who is working for better living conditions." Dilling included Jane Addams, Carrie Chapman Catt, and Lillian Wald.

> Both my husband and I are frankly interested in seeing what can be done to help the masses of people in this country and we feel that those who have had special privileges are better equipped to take care of themselves for a while than are those who [are] underprivileged.

As war clouds gathered and the U.S. recession deepened, ER had less patience for diversions, and less interest in the relationships that had been for so long central to her life. Yet her understanding of the human condition remained generous and wise.

In May, rumors spread about Harry Hopkins's impending marriage to "some woman named Mrs. Hale, an actress." Hick was astonished: "It depresses me, profoundly," she wrote.

> It's not that I would wish him to deny himself any happiness, but how *could* he forget so quickly? It's only about six months! A year ago, in July, [Barbara] was still alive—a lovely, warm personality. . . . It says that Jimmy introduced them. Had you heard anything about it at all? Poor little Diana. . . .

ER replied:

> Hick darling, You don't know much about men do you? Harry was happy with Barbara and so he is lonelier than if he hadn't been. Women are sorry for him, they like to be seen with men whose names are in the paper and it helps him to forget.

ER did not think the rumors were serious. Harry "was disturbed [by them]; but I told him if he didn't let himself get bluffed into marrying someone he really didn't care for no permanent harm was done. I'm afraid Diana is more apt to be left alone than to have a step-mother tho' of course that may happen!"

ER and Hick did not see each other during April. When ER was free for lunch, Hick had a staff meeting; when Hick was free ER had a prior lunch date with Bernard Baruch. One evening ER called at 7 and again at 11, "but I realize you were out all evening." ER wanted to arrange at least a tea date. But there was no time.

At the end of April ER made a half-hearted gesture toward Hick. She invited her to the theater with her brother Hall and to lunch with Anna Louise Strong and Marie Morgan. There was no special time for Hick, who refused to join ER's cluttered calendar. She went instead to a concert of Beethoven and Wagner. But the performance was rather dull: "Barbirolli is too pedantic for me. I like lots of thunder in my Beethoven—and fire in my Wagner!"

In June, Congress passed the the Fair Labor Standards Act. Known as the wages and hours law, it was the kind of legislation ER, Florence Kelley, and the social reformers of the National Consumers League had advocated since 1912. Child labor was formally banned; the minimum wage was set at 25 cents an hour, scheduled to increase over time, and was finally pegged to inflation; and a forty-hour work week was affirmed. A signficant victory, it was the last liberal legislation to be gotten from Congress—and was limited by many loopholes. A much debated North-South wage differential was defeated, then furtively tucked into the legislation, and there were many exemptions.

Initially introduced by Alabama's Senator Hugo Black, later on the Supreme Court, the legislation passed with the vigorous support of New Jersey Congresswoman Mary Norton, Robert Wagner, and Florida's Claude Pepper.

The Labor Department's statistician Isadore Lubin considered it "the most vital social legislation" in U.S. history. And ER's circle toasted the memory of Florence Kelley and Jane Addams.

Also in June, Joseph Kennedy visited Hyde Park. ER was "amused" to hear Kennedy's impressions: "He says Rose is very close to the Queen, it is quite the talk of London and he finds the queen very nice." He evidently did not speak about his peace-at-any-price convictions, or his efforts to improve U.S. relations with Germany.

June's family highlight was John's marriage to Anne Lindsay Clark. Unlike FJr's wedding in Delaware, confined to the du Pont family compound, this turned into a crowded media event. The New York Times headlined, "Thousands Cheer at Nahant Church," as tourists blocked this small town to witness the "marriage of FDR's last bachelor son."

They arrived on buses and waited on camp chairs, an extraordinary testimony to a popular president so often now hobbled by a divided Congress. A crowd of thirty thousand lined the streets to cheer FDR's party from Salem's dock all along the ten-mile route to the reception at the Nahant Tennis Club. Not only was the town congested by sight-seers, police sirens competed with the church organ, drowning out a program of Bach and Brahms.

ER looked "cool and exceptionally tall in her gown of net and navy, combined with Eleanor blue." Under her large picture hat of "transparent navy straw," however, she "retained an unusual solemnity of face and manner until the bridal procession reached the head of the right aisle," then as Mendelssohn's "Bridal March" played, she smiled, "just as the bride, glancing at James Roosevelt, the head usher, winked broadly and also for the first time smiled."

After the wedding, FDR returned by yacht; the children scattered to different nearby country homes; ER returned by car to Hyde Park with grandchildren Sistie and Buzzie; and SDR, who stayed overnight to return by train, called the party "a fine shindig."

For several weeks at Val-Kill, ER relaxed: "I'm doing nothing but be lazy and it is fun!" She also wrote several articles, besides her column, and prepared the first two years of "My Day" for publication: "I think it may make a fairly interesting book. . . ."

While ER spent the summer at Hyde Park, FDR left on 7 July for a campaign journey to promote New Deal candidates for the bi-election of 1938. He toured Maryland, Georgia, Florida, Nevada, Texas, Oklahoma, and other states in what became known as his famous "purge" effort to be rid of conservative Democrats. FDR was particularly eager to unseat Georgia's senior senator, Walter George, and Maryland's Millard Tydings.

At the same time, the conference he called in response to the tragedy of the rising tide of refugees began. On 7 July 1938, delegates from thirty-two nations convened at Evian-les-Bains along the French shore of Lake Geneva to consider the future of Europe's desperate people. The Evian Conference established an Intergovernmental Committee on Refugees, but was in all other respects a disaster.

In his invitation, FDR had announced that the United States would not enlarge its own restrictive quota, which limited admission to 27,370 immigrants from Germany and Austria annually. The United States had never filled this quota, and now wanted to explore the intentions of other nations.

According to William Shirer, the U.S. delegation, headed by Myron Taylor, looked extremely unpromising. There was no leadership and no mandate for change:

> The British, French, and Americans seemed too anxious not to do anything to offend Hitler. It's an absurd situation. They want to appease the man who is responsible for the problem. The Nazis . . . will welcome the democracies' taking the Jews off their hands at their expense.

Hitler was pleased when the conference was called: "We are ready to put all these criminals at the disposal of these countries . . . even on luxury ships."

After Evian, Hitler had evidence of the world's prejudice and collusion. The conference actually resulted in more stringent restrictions adopted by Argentina, Chile, and Mexico. Nicaragua, Honduras, Costa Rica, and Panama issued a joint statement that they would accept no "traders or intellectuals." Australia, New Zealand, Canada, Colombia, Uruguay, and Venezuela wanted no immigrants at all.

While negotiations at Evian proceeded, FDR left the Southwest for Mexico, and an adventure in the Galápagos Islands accompanied by a Smithsonian scientist and crew led by Dr. Waldo Schmitt. FDR wrote ER they collected "many fine specimens of marine and plant life and birds." He thoroughly enjoyed the Galápagos—which remained as fascinating as they were to Charles Darwin. It was

> a very successful week in the Galapagos from every aspect . . . it is all interesting and colorful—especially remembering that the tortoises, iguanas, etc., are the oldest living form of the animals of 15,000,000 years ago! . . .

Aboard ship, FDR read Winston Churchill's prescient book *While England Slept*, a survey of Hitler's rise to power from 1932 to 1938, which his Uncle Fred Delano had sent him in June. Although he wrote nothing of it, it could only have firmed his resolve to do something to prevent the war that so clearly loomed when he returned on 5 August.

While FDR cruised, ER planned for her one week away that August, a visit with Hick at her Little House on Long Island's south shore. But she seemed to Hick oddly distracted, and perhaps had information about the conference at Evian that added to her discontent. She seemed so disgruntled before their visit that Hick worried.

ER replied:

> Hick dearest, Your sweet letter just came and I am *not* unhappy. Life may be somewhat negative with me, but that is nothing new. I think it was when I was a child and is now a habit! . . . Yes. I'll be with you till [5 August] whatever day I arrive! Any time you arrange for anything is alright with me—Much, much love.

Filled with anticipation over ER's first long holiday at her country place, Hick wrote: "If you like it one-tenth as much as I do, I'll be satisfied."

ER visited from 26 July to 5 August. Alone, without Tommy, she typed her daily column, and found it a tedious bore. She wrote several letters in longhand on Hick's stationery, and they contained a curious tone. On 2 August:

> Dearest Elizabeth and Esther:
>
> I'm here for a few days having promised Hick last winter I'd spend a few days with her during her vacation. She is a different person here because she is happy I imagine and I am glad to see her this way. . . .

Since Esther and Elizabeth understood ER's nuances, they asked her to explain her letter. Upon her return to Val-Kill, she replied frankly:

> You are quite right—I had a sense of real obligation to go down to Long Island but I am glad to say that I found Hick who has been very miserable both mentally and physically at times, quite happy and while I had promised this visit during her vacation six months ago, I did not want very much to leave when the time came. . . .
>
> I know just what you mean about gaiety departing from you. I am afraid it departs from us all as we grow older and encounter more and more of the difficulties of life, but if we keep even a few snatches of it, it is a great help to our friends as well as to ourselves. I feel that you and Lizzie have always had a kind of quiet gaiety which is more satisfactory than the very hilarious kind I sometimes have about me. . . .

In Hick's space, the full range of their different needs was revealed and gave ER a shock of recognition. She understood several things about herself after those ten days: She had very real preferences, likes and dislikes. And she abandoned certain fantasies—including the idea that she could ever be content to put her own interests, her own work on a back burner to accommodate the romance of a leisurely holiday.

ER realized how much she hated to be apart from Tommy; how much she resented time away from her own work, without staff and her usual conveniences. Although she gave Hick no hint that she was unhappy, nothing that gave Hick pleasure pleased ER at Mastic.

To Hick she wrote politely: "I miss you dear. I loved being with you. . . . I had a grand week tho I wish the mosquitoes had let us walk in the woods. . . . The chief thing however was my great pleasure in seeing you in the place where you are happy. . . ."

ER apologized for spending so much time on her articles and columns. She would have all her materials arranged, and perfect her typing, so the "next time we are together I won't take so long! . . . Much, much love and many thanks for a happy time."

To others, ER wrote letters of complaint. They were almost public notices of estrangement. She had never complained before, but now wrote Lape and Read, FDR, Anna, and even Elinor Morgenthau. Loyal to Hick, ER wrote nothing of her impatience each time she sat down to her column. Rather she complained that Long Island's heat was hotter and its humidity wetter; the endless sand was obnoxious, and the mosquitos were as big as bats.

To FDR, aboard the USS *Houston* somewhere between the Galápagos and the Canal Zone, ER wrote:

> Dearest Franklin, I wouldn't live on Long Island for all the world! Every thing sticks and I don't want to move! I've improved much in typing however having to do my own column every day here! Harry [Hooker] asked me over to the Piping Rock Club to spend another week with him and I said I was sorry I couldn't but I wasn't sorry at all!

ER wrote her daughter three letters about her putative holiday, and to Anna also acknowledged that emotional tensions were at a new high along the Val-Kill. She expected to be greeted on her return by Earl and three friends; Nan also had friends all summer, but nevertheless "looked mournful because she didn't see enough of me! I've had her for one meal every day I've been home but she seems so listless that I begin to wonder if she is ill. . . ."

ER returned from Mastic unwilling to keep up tired illusions. Determined to confront confusing and ambivalent relationships, she wanted to simplify her life. In another letter to Anna she revealed that her intimate world was in disarray:

> I've been a bit upset over Nan and her attitude here and after I got back a little thing precipitated a scene; so today I went over and had a calm

talk explaining why my feeling had changed toward them both and that we must have a business like arrangement. I added that we could have a friendly, agreeable relationship but my old trust and respect was gone and could not be recovered and I thought they probably felt the same way and were quite certainly as justified as I was. I told her to tell Marion of our talk and I now await the latter's return on the 18th. . . . I am glad to have been honest at last.

ER admitted to Anna that her summer had not actually been about any kind of holiday. She felt positively "driven" by "work and social obligations." Although at Val-Kill she spent time with Earl perfecting her dive and riding, deadlines neared for articles and speeches.

> [So] I think the exercise will have to go by the board for a while. . . .
> I hope the children are home and I long to hear how they are. Tell them I've learned to stand on my hands in the pool and get my legs up straight!
> Pa looks very well and had a grand trip. He's enjoying it here too though the stream of visitors never lets up. I'm running both this house and the cottage and I think all is going well. . . .

ER's conversation with Nancy Cook occurred just prior to the World Youth Congress held at Vassar, 15–25 August, while a dozen AYC leaders were at Val-Kill to prepare their presentations with ER.

Whatever else happened that summer, her attention was riveted on the World Youth Congress. It was the reason she refused to join FDR in Canada. From the Galápagos, FDR had sent ER two letters asking her to meet him in Canada on the 18th, where he would "get a degree, lunch, motor to the Thousand Islands, and dedicate the bridge." Mackenzie King would be along, it would be only a day, and then he would spend ten days at Hyde Park. "I do so hope you can come." Uncharacteristically, ER replied: "I don't want to go anywhere I don't have to go until my lecture trip which starts October 12th and takes me into the Middle West and south to Alabama. . . ."

FDR also failed to mention the reason for his equally uncharacteristic plea that she accompany him. He was finally to do what she had wanted him to do since 1933: On 18 August, at the dedication of the International Bridge between Canada and the United States, across the St. Lawrence River between New York State and Ontario Province, FDR extended the Good Neighbor Policy to Canada and made one of the most important international statements of his presidency.

FDR announced: "This bridge stands as an open door. There will be no challenge at the border and no guard to ask a countersign. Where the boundary is crossed the only word must be, 'Pass, friend.' " Then FDR went beyond his prepared speech to assure Canada "that the people of the United States will not stand idly by if domination of Canadian soil is threatened by any other Empire." It was the first internationalist commitment FDR made as Europe faced war over Czechoslovakia's impending demise.

ER's exchange with Nancy Cook, her refusal to go to Canada, even her dissatisfaction with her Long Island visit may be viewed through the filter of her preoccupation with the comings and goings of almost seven hundred young people from fifty-four nations, excluding Germany, who arrived for what ER considered a final chance for peace in our time.

From beginning to end, the World Youth Congress was a thrilling spectacle. Early arrivals stayed in New York at International House; they were treated to a baseball game and a gigantic outdoor pageant at Randalls Island in the East River, under the PWA's new Triborough Bridge, where 25,000 Americans cheered students, gymnasts, and performers from all over the world. Mayor La Guardia and Assistant Secretary of State A. A. Berle greeted them. Delegates arrived at Poughkeepsie aboard the Hudson River Dayliner, and the week of earnest talk and high hope evoked great enthusiasm—and great resentment by those who dismissed it all as communist, wicked, and dangerous.

When news of ER's enthusiasm hit the press, she was bombarded by protests. She wrote Hick on 15 August that virtually "every Catholic organization" in the United States deplored her association with the World Youth Congress and protested "my association with such a communistic organization! I don't think FDR will be able to go unless he is prepared to offend 'The Church'— . . . There is a horrible story on Nuremberg."

ER's reference to Hitler's Nuremberg rally, which William Dodd had refused to attend, but which the new U.S. ambassador, Hugh Wilson, did attend, was dedicated to territorial expansion for "Greater Germany." Opened on 5 September 1938, it was filled with harangues against Czechoslovakia, and pledged to its doom.

While State Department representatives attended the Nazi rally, Catholic protesters chided ER for attending the World Youth Congress at Vassar, which featured young people from Asia, Africa, Europe, and the Americas. Bishops of the National Catholic Welfare Conference protested: The World Youth Conference at Geneva was "practically controlled by the Communist Youth International, the Spanish Popular Front . . . and other groups [in] sympathy with Communistic principles." Now the First Lady endorsed this group that assured their associates, in "Russia and in Mexico, that American sympathy is with them." The bishops warned Catholic groups not to participate in the meeting, which, fostered "irreligion and the promotion of the class hatreds of Sovietism." The bishops condemned the meeting as anti-Catholic and un-

American and declared America would not survive "unless its people cherished religion and morality."

ER replied:

> I regret very much that I have to differ with the Bishops, though I hold them in great respect. . . .
>
> I do not doubt that there are many Communists among [the delegates], but they are not strong enough to rule the entire group.
>
> I have watched them and met with them over a period of four years and have seen them grow into more sensible and reasonable young people. I think it is a great mistake to simply condemn them. . . .

ER greeted the delegates "as the best agents for peace." Well covered in the press, the congress was supported by Tom Watson's donation of new IBM equipment that enabled every speech to be translated into the language of one's selection. ER and Vassar president Henry MacCracken greeted the delegates from fifty-five nations.*

The Congress was from first to last an extraordinary moment of hospitality and fellowship. Young people whose countries were at war spoke to each other with startling frankness. There were tragic, moving, ironic moments to witness: Chinese and Japanese delegates "exchanging experiences about their hometown YWCAs, each holding a copy of the *Times* with a big headline about a Japanese air raid on China."

AYC conveners, and especially Joe Cadden, who chaired the Arrangements Committee, impressed ER with their sensitive handling of every detail. She impressed them with her forthright manner:

> She didn't go around talking down to us. She came right in to every session, sat with earphones like everyone else. Ate ice cream cones and [conversed] with hundreds of delegates. Never forget the time she became so interested in the story of a Chinese student that she ruined an expensive summer dress by letting ice cream goo drip all over it.

That August 1938 meeting, which ironically coincided with the first public hearings of the House Un-American Activities Committee, chaired by Martin Dies, accelerated ER's commitment to individual AYC leaders and a politics of direct confrontation.† She spent an hour and a half at the session on economics and their effect on youth and peace, and wrote:

---

*The U.S. delegation elected Joseph Cadden, twenty-five-year-old Brown University graduate, chair; Myrtle Powell of the Business and Professional Women's Council, YWCA, and Carol Morris, chair of the Christian Youth Conference, vice-chairmen; and Dorothy Height of the youth division of National Negro Congress, secretary.

†The first Dies committee hearings began on 12 August 1938. During the week of

I felt what they *said* was young and impulsive, but their faces and their earnestness and the good manners and restraint of the audience was remarkable. Many groups heard their countries criticized without hissing or leaving, really a lesson to their elders.

ER "sat knitting" but "listened attentively" throughout the speeches. She heard a U.S. delegate condemn U.S. foreign policy as "basically imperialistic"; European delegates called for a reinvigorated League of Nations and condemned Britain for its "departure from League obligations to Ethiopia, Spain and the Far East."

After she endured tough questions for an hour and a half, she returned for the evening's pageant and was greeted with a standing and prolonged ovation. According to *The New York Times*, the master of ceremonies interrupted the program of songs and dances from around the world, introduced ER seated in the front row, and led the audience in "For She's a Jolly Good Fellow." The evening included dances by Czech, Indonesian, and U.S. Indian delegates, a comedy by Canadian delegates, Negro spirituals, and Chinese fireworks on the lawn.

The Congress ended with a "Vassar Pact," which pledged the delegates to work to "reverse the present ominous drift toward international anarchy and armed conflict." They sought "arms reduction, economic reconstruction, adherence to international law, abstention from the use of force and intervention, free intellectual exchange . . . , equality of all people and races through establishment of self-determination and democratic suffrage." They specifically condemned the bombing of "open towns and civilians" and "wars of aggression." They demanded "no aid for aggressors" and the establishment of "international machinery to settle differences between nations, and colonies."

ER left Vassar encouraged and involved. She wrote Hick that her dominant feeling was a mixture of respect and sadness for "all those young people so earnest and full of hope." She worried about their future and vowed to do everything possible on their behalf. Although some reporters considered their questions rude and their behavior pompous, ER admired their grit and honesty.

While youth leaders at Vassar dealt with the world's woes and aspirations, in Washington they were condemned as communist by J. B. Matthews, leading witness for Martin Dies's committee. A former communist organizer and pro-

---

the World Youth Congress, Hallie Flanagan and the Federal Theatre Project were under assault for days. Artists and writers were among HUAC's first targets: Committee member J. Parnell Thomas had announced in July that both the Theatre Project and the Writers' Project were infested with communists. "Practically every play presented . . . is sheer propaganda for Communism or the New Deal."

fessor of theology at Howard University, among other colleges, Matthews now led a vitriolic assault against all popular front organizations, including unions. He claimed that of the fifty U.S. delegates at Vassar, "35 are Communists." As a former communist leader, Matthews had personally persuaded American notables to sign on to various causes, and they had had no idea they supported "red-tinted" fronts. People like Eleanor Roosevelt were "innocent dupes."

Both ER and Vassar's president, Henry MacCracken, dismissed Matthews's testimony against all liberal causes that communists might in fact support and defended the World Youth Congress—especially its final declaration.

In a letter to disturbed citizens, worried by Matthews's charges, ER wrote: "I am rather surprised that you should consider Mr. Matthews a very good authority." She thought it "would be strange in any group of young people not to find some with these ideas. . . . I do not believe in Communism, nor in any other "ism," but I do believe in democracy. However, I do not think that refusing to allow people to talk about their ideas is the way to develop the ability to think clearly."

MacCracken denied that he and ER were "exploited" by communists:

> I think I have sufficient intelligence to know when I am being exploited. I am a Mayflower descendant. . . . [And] if I were to name the five most intelligent women in the world, Mrs. Roosevelt would be one of them. I don't think she is being exploited by any one.

ER returned to Val-Kill each evening of the Congress determined to relax and exercise. She spent many hours with Earl, who coached her to dive with excellence. Finally, on 21 August, she reported to Hick there was dispatch, spring, dash in her dive. Always protective of his "Lady" and suspicious of chiselers and users, of people generally and youth particularly, Earl may have cautioned ER about her new friends or the dangers of her commitment to them. If so, she wrote nothing about it. She emphasized rather her triumphant dive: The weather was "gorgeous" and "by dint of working *every* day" on her dive, there was progress: "I never worked so hard on any real work in my life!"

ER's enthusiasm for the AYC exacerbated her discontent with others—especially Nancy Cook and Marion Dickerman. In August 1938, ER saw her own mission clearly: The future depended on youth with vision, they needed her, and she needed new activist allies. Her new course required freedom from lingering dependencies—from people who no longer shared her goals.

Almost immediately after the Youth Congress departed, ER sent Hick the first in a series of letters that detailed the demise of one of the most important friendships of her life, her twenty-year partnership with her boon companions of Val-Kill. The immediate event concerned her brother, a car accident, and a sense of betrayal because she was not consulted. But the event merely reflected a long-simmering sense of betrayal, which had already seeped out in her 12 August conversation with Nan: "Dearest such a day and evening! Hall arrived about 5:30 got very tight, wrestled and threw [his son] Danny and put his shoulder out." Hall insisted on taking him to the hospital, driving himself, and "no one told me. Marion went with them, Hall met another car on our narrow road by the swamp and drove off" into the ditch at the end of the swamp. Danny's "collarbone was broken" and Hall was uncontrollably drunk, "so we had plenty excitement."

ER had been hosting "an enormous picnic" for one hundred people, including FDR, the La Guardias, Missy, Caroline O'Day, Herman Baruch, while Nan and Marion served Hall and a select few cocktails in their walled garden. Furious at her friends for refreshing his drinks, letting him drive, and not alerting her, also overwhelmed by her brother's behavior, ER exploded: "I'm fed up with life! Too much of it altogether. I'd like to be a fish in a back water."

Hall's behavior recalled their father's:

> [The next morning Hall] appeared at 7 a.m. at the cottage having had no sleep and waking Tommy and Henry. They had breakfast and at 9 he was at the big house. Last night is still rather a nightmare to me and it will take me a little while to recover. I wish I recovered more easily! These occurrences hang in the back of my mind for days! . . .

ER's fury was part of a deeply painful process that ended forever the Val-Kill partnership. Partly the friendship collapsed because ER embraced new people, many of whom Cook and Dickerman disliked.

Some were too radical, others too rambunctious. Some were crude, others unworthy. ER's social world had become more democratic. They had gotten used to Earl Miller and his endless parade of friends, including show-business people, but they never warmed to Hick and despised her unpolished, gruff ways. Now there were altogether too many new exuberant people about, children of sharecroppers and lumberjacks; children of immigrants, rude communist youth. What Hick had said about Cook and Dickerman for years was now undeniable: They were self-absorbed snobs.

While SDR had disapproved of their unconventional ways, their ties and knickerbockers, their cigarettes and bobbed hair, their assertive manners and family assumptions, Cook and Dickerman disapproved of all the new unconventionals swimming around ER's pool—their pool.

The peace and harmony of their private world was regularly invaded by an army of outsiders. They no longer controlled their own space, and felt discredited: The press gave ER, one-third a partner, total recognition; it was her school, her factory. At home, the gardens, tennis court, and pool were occupied continually by her children, her grandchildren, her friends, her constituents.

Political women, they were initially interested in new people. After all, they were the chosen insiders in a vast world of outsiders. But as ER's friendships expanded and deepened, they began to feel like onlookers.

ER had sensed earlier that scores of reporters and hundreds of guests trampling their gardens was not their idea of a charming summer day. She had offered to rent another space for public events: Their privacy would be restored, and tensions between them would subside. But they rejected the idea, and seemed insulted. When, during the summer of 1937, ER decided finally to move, at least into her own space in the renovated factory, they were disgruntled.

As in many separations, the emotional breach was initially translated into petty details, confusing financial arrangements. Dickerman was outraged when her plans to purchase a new building for the school were suspended during the 1937–38 recession. ER did not volunteer to pour more of her own money into Todhunter and bail out Dickerman's dreams, which had for so long been ER's as well.

Tommy sent Anna a running record of the situation as it intensified during the second inauguration:

> Everything from my point of view went well until the parade started. I sat between Mrs. Helm and Nancy Cook with Mary Dreier on Nan's other side. Mrs. Helm of course was very enthusiastic about the Navy and applauded, etc., when they went by. Nan made very disparaging remarks and Mary Dreier practically sat on her hands to keep from applauding. They are ardent pacifists (in their theories anyway) and for a moment I thought I should have to get the Marines or at least a few cops to keep the pacifists quiet. Finally I told Nan to shut up and later told her that she and Mary Dreier had no right to accept a seat at a parade which was well advertised as a military one. Gosh how I dislike these crusaders! . . .
>
> Anyway we lived through it and your mother and I have had some laughs over it. . . .
>
> Marion Dickerman wants to buy a building and Elizabeth Read [in her capacity as ER's financial adviser] is having a fit and wants the thing incorporated so you kids won't be left out. (Just between thee and me, don't tell your mother I said anything.) However, I think your mother has had a slight stiffening of the back bone, whether enough or not I can't tell at this writing. . . .
>
> Your mother seems very well and perhaps losing her temper did her good. She has been full of pep since.

Incidentally George Bye told me he could get your Ma a $25,000 a year job without any effort when she leaves here which spikes the chance of her going back to teach for $2,000. . . .

Tensions increased for over a year. In March 1938, Dickerman hired a professional firm to create a slick, glossy twenty-six-page fund-raising brochure that featured ER prominently. Titled "Our Daughters' Heritage," the frontispiece was comprised of a facsimile of ER's signature and a singularly innocuous quote:

I think a school, which has as its aim the preparation of pupils to know more about their environment and be better fitted to live in it, is entering the educational field with a new and more practical objective.

If Marion Dickerman resented the school's public connection with ER, she was certainly willing to exploit her for fund-raising purposes. And while ER agreed, with reluctance, to have her words and photo used, Dickerman was annoyed by her insipid quote. When asked "to strengthen it," ER refused:

I am terribly sorry, but as I do not intend to make the school one of my major interests, I feel it very much wiser to be absolutely honest. . . . I regret that I cannot change my statement.

After she learned that Dickerman whispered that ER's presence upset some of the school's Republican parents, ER turned Todhunter's annual senior class visit to the White House into a joint visit with Arthurdale High School seniors, writing Dickerman: "I thought they might be of value to your young people as a contact."

At Val-Kill there were displays of unusual pettiness over such details as who paid for lawn mowing, whose dredging caused silt in the pond, who might use the laundry on Tuesday at three o'clock. Tommy wrote Anna:

I think it is going to resolve itself into an endurance test. Those gals are not going to do anything to cause an open breach if they can help it, and at the same time they are going to grab all they can grab.

Also, Nan and Marion were rude to Tommy. She wrote Anna:

One day I inadvertently said something about "my house" and Nan turned on me with real fury and said it didn't belong to me, that she and Marion had much more money in this building than Mrs. R and Mrs. R could not give me any of it so that I could say "mine." I refused to get mad and simply said that henceforth I would refer to it as the place where I work and sleep! The unfortunate part of it was that your mother was sitting beside me and heard it all! . . .

I must tell you that Miss Dickerman has undertaken to complete my education—she tells me I talk too loud—I use certain phrases too often and I emphasize words when I shouldn't! I'm having a rare opportunity to polish off the rough corners!

Then came the bruising summer of 1938. Marion Dickerman was in Europe, sent by FDR at Bernard Baruch's request as one of a nine-member presidential commission to study industrial relations in England and Sweden. Tommy wrote Anna:

> I know you know all about Marion Dickerman getting herself appointed to the commission that went abroad to study labor conditions. . . . It was worked between Dr. [Herman] Baruch [whose daughter attended Todhunter] and Barney Baruch. I guess they believe in asking for what they want. It leaves Nan high and dry and very lonesome and rather forlorn looking.

When Baruch's transatlantic message about Dickerman's appointment arrived in Geneva, Frances Perkins was already at the ILO meeting and "thought I should drop." Perkins called FDR, who told her that he had agreed—since Baruch wanted the appointment and Baruch was a very important man. An amazing thing for FDR to say—since, despite Baruch's notable friendship with ER, the First Lady's efforts to get Baruch's suggestions before the president were rarely successful. It was mystifying. Perkins recalled:

> [I was] pretty well dumbfounded when I hung up. I thought that was about the poorest piece of business that I ever heard of. . . . I realize that she's the kind of person who had always been stuck in a corner. . . . After all, the husband of her great friend, Mrs. Roosevelt, was now President and . . . she would like to have something conspicuous fall on her. It would boost her stock in her school, her standing in New York. . . .

Perkins considered Dickerman's appointment a wild and silly idea. Nevertheless, Dickerman sailed on 28 June, and ER sent a bon voyage greeting with flowers and a check to her cabin.*

---

*ER had once before tried to get Marion Dickerman a job. In a remarkable letter to Harry Hopkins on 14 June 1935, she sent him a list of three people she wanted to help and thought might be useful, including FDR's Groton mentor George Marvin, whom ER felt protective of for familial reasons. He was alcoholic, and ER hoped Harry might find "some writing" project for him to "do at home," when he was sober. "He is a writer of experience and a very old friend of ours . . . a perfectly uncertain quantity," but would perform assigned tasks well. He might be disappointing, "but black sheep have to eat too! He can write if he will stay straight. . . ." As for Marion Dickerman, ER wrote candidly: She "wants to work for a month this summer . . . to go out anywhere or do anything at all. I thought she might be helpful to Aubrey Williams on account of her interest in and knowledge of young people, and he could get rid of

Dickerman's 1938 sojourn was, according to Frances Perkins, a disaster. In an extraordinarily nasty passage, Perkins wanted history to know that Dickerman and Anna Rosenberg, the only women on the commission, did nothing but party. They went to nightclubs and dances every night. It was the talk of the town. Anna Rosenberg took Dickerman "to a very swell dressmaker . . . one of the great fashionable dressmakers of London," and they bought an extraordinarily "handsome dress." Then "took her to a hairdresser and had her hair all curled, waved, and jazzed up. She looked like a different person." Then got "a partner for her and they had a good time" every night. "Then they went to Sweden . . . [where] it was just the same and a little more startling because the Swedish people were so astonished. . . . This was supposed to be a serious delegation and serious delegations don't go for fun and flirtation ordinarily." Perkins concluded: "All this" really had "nothing to do with the [commission], except that Marion Dickerman had the time of her life."

There is no evidence that ER agreed with Frances Perkins, and even after their estrangement she wrote in the *Women's Democratic Digest* that when Dickerman returned from her trip to England and Sweden, she "told us much of interest." Dickerman returned filled with rage over Joe Kennedy's attitude. He saw nothing particularly terrible about the persecution of the Jews and thought the future of European Jews depended entirely on whatever financial arrangements U.S. Jews might make toward their settlement in Africa and the Americas.

Marion Dickerman observed Kennedy's sympathies personally when the industrial commission was en route home. Their train was stopped outside of Hamburg and the passengers were searched by Nazi officials. It was a menacing and ugly scene, especially because the commission's chair, Gerard Swope of General Electric, was Jewish. Dickerman had never seen Swope so "absolutely harassed." He was "undone."

The experience did not prepare Swope for their subsequent lunch at the U.S. embassy in London, where Kennedy expressed "great sympathy and admiration for Adolf Hitler, great antipathy and contempt for certain features of English and American life, and he said so forcefully, crudely." In reaction, "Swope's face hardened in cold fury." He handed Dickerman a note: "In five minutes you and I are leaving this table." Dickerman thought it would be too rude to leave: To make "a scene," she felt, would be "a disservice to the government." They remained, "but it was an unhappy time and left a very unpleasant feeling in my mind in regard to Mr. Kennedy."

------

her at the end of the month. Her great desire is to get a feeling of being in something that is being done . . . because she feels that running a school is rather narrowing. She would have to have her expenses if she were sent away and a small salary."

It was while Dickerman was away that ER's bitter conversation with Nan occurred and relations between them permanently soured. Tommy wrote Anna:

> The Cook-Dickerman situation seems to get worse. . . . I am glad Harry Hooker is going to draw up a legal agreement about what belongs to who around here. I am terribly sorry about the whole thing because I think it makes your mother very nervous.

When Marion Dickerman returned on the 18th, Nancy Cook met her at the dock. Dickerman "was flabbergasted at the way she looked." Drawn and pale, Nancy Cook's eyes were red and raw from a week of tears. She was agitated and mostly incoherent. Dickerman could extract only two facts: Nancy Cook had "a long and tragic talk" with ER and they each had said things "that ought not to have been said." And "Eleanor had hurt her beyond anything."

According to Dickerman, Nancy Cook never told her the full story of their conversation. She neither repeated the cruel words she hurled at ER nor the final words ER spoke to her. But from that moment on, ER was as ice to them. "Eleanor never forgot a hurt, never. There was a forgiveness in Franklin in many instances but I never found it in Eleanor."

Nancy Cook's words were like acid on her heart. According to Nancy, she and Marion actually felt they were responsible for ER's political and public achievements. They seriously believed, and Nancy had the gall to tell her, that they had created one of America's most vital leaders. Nancy Cook actually told ER that she and Dickerman did everything they did "to build" her up. Because one of ER's lifelong difficulties involved her inability really to take credit, to claim authority, to feel secure in her own good work, that pronouncement seemed to ER's other friends more than calumny—actually hateful.

Indeed, Tommy had written Anna the year before:

> I agree with you that your mother never takes any credit to herself, but in the next part of the book, she comes to the establishment of the cottage, school, shop, etc., and I will try a little insidious propaganda to make her speak up for herself. However, I guess you and I are alone in thinking that she ever did anything for any one—they the "helped" all seem to think they would have been just as well off.

Cook and Dickerman always referred to the demise of their friendship exclusively in terms of their own pain. But it devastated ER. For an entire week, ER simply took to her bed. Esther Lape vividly recalled that most unusual time: Tommy telephoned, frantic with worry, to report that ER had been ill for days, refused to see anybody, and showed no signs of improvement. "Never before" had Tommy seen ER silent, brooding, closed to company, politics, diversion. She had simply turned "her face to the wall."

The finality with which one of the most important friendships of her life ended was wrenching for ER. Not since her confrontation with FDR over Lucy Mercer had she felt so fundamentally disregarded and misunderstood by her loved and trusted family of choice.

It was unlike ER to end a relationship, to cut it off entirely, to be permanently unforgiving. Her lifelong criticism of her mother's cold emotional abandonment of her father in his alcoholic troubles, despite his outside families, caused her to embrace people similarly in need. Whatever her criticisms or private pain, she sought changes, and persevered—as with her Uncle Vallie and her brother Hall.

Even in the midst of her greatest misery as a young matron, hurt and betrayed by Franklin's affair, she worked to create an abiding partnership, and a profound respect and friendship endured. Although she lived, perhaps always, with pain in her heart, she was satisfied when her efforts pleased FDR. At the end of August, despite the World Youth Congress and other tensions, she was happy to write Anna: "Pa's ten days here were very pleasant for him I think—everything went smoothly."

Whatever the elements of her friendship with Earl Miller, and his ever-changing young women, he was a continually loyal and protective companion, by her side whenever she needed him. Her deep and easy friendship with Esther Lape and Elizabeth Read seemed never emotionally troubled, as they worked together from issue to issue. Although she and Hick pulled away from each other and ER became impatient with her grumblings, Hick remained a loved and trusted confidante.

But with her partners of the Val-Kill the break was total. Even if Nancy Cook had been drinking, as she had been that lonely summer in Dickie's absence, ER could not excuse her words. She felt she had never known her friends until that dreadful fight when Nancy Cook revealed their substance, and their real interests. Their entire relationship, she now believed, had been built on a lie. It all seemed to her now a bitter hoax.

One can only imagine what images appeared as she contemplated the end of a friendship so cherished, so filled with excitement and travel, freedom, good works, seemingly infinite trust, and love. Only fifteen years before they had planned their lives together, and initialed their towels and various household adornments "EMN." They had toured Europe with the children, enjoyed countless Campobello picnics, longed for each other's company when apart. They worked together on every major project, and had been one another's most intimate companions. During the 1920s, ER and Nan had matching knickerbocker suits; ER called Marion "Dickie," they called her "Muddie," which sounded like what the children called her; and they shared convictions, as well as hilarious, important, and wonderful times. Their friendship had seemed devoted, and forever.

During the White House years, ER included Nancy Cook in her Arthurdale work, put her in charge of major woodworking projects for the settlement communities, and lavished gifts and money on her—more than $30,000 for one year's work at Arthurdale. In an undated Easter letter at the time she decided to move into her own space, ER wanted it understood that despite their need for separateness and occasional solitude, "on the whole what is mine is thine."

Now it was over, and ER was bereft. Esther Lape wrote that ER's behavior "drove us to despair." Both Lape and Elizabeth Read felt Tommy's call "was incredibly dashing," and they worried for days. Finally, at her 11th Street apartment, ER snapped out of it, went down to see Lape, and explained:

> I know it is your dinner time and I have guests waiting, but there is something I must tell you. I know you think that I have been very ill. I have not. You know I have always been aware that people anxious to gain my interest were really hoping thereby for a link with Franklin. I have known this but there was one person of whom this did not seem to me to be true. Don't ask how I could make such a fundamental error. I simply did. I have recovered from my disappointment. That, after all, is based on my own weakness. . . . I simply had to let you know that all is now well. I am unable to lead a life based on an illusion.

Cook and Dickerman made several efforts to involve FDR in the settlement arrangements, which dragged out for months. He was not overtly involved, but meddled in a way that only finalized the breach, and deepened the wounds: Evidently he transmitted to ER every petty nasty piece of business that he overheard.

The legal dissolution of the partnership dragged on, because Cook and Dickerman refused a simple, and generous, cash settlement that ER offered in order to get clear title to the shop building that was now her cottage. On 29 October, ER wrote:

> I thought I had made it very clear to both of you that I did not care to accept the shop building unless I made financial arrangements which would equalize whatever money you claim to have in the building. . . .
>
> If you will look back, I think you will realize that in all of our relationship I have never before wanted anything, nor suggested anything about the cottage or the school, and therefore it is entirely natural that we have had no difficulties in previous years. This was quite easy for me because I had no objection to acceding to your wishes.
>
> In this matter I have a distinct preference and as you do not care to handle it in the way I wish, I have decided to turn over to you now, instead

of at my death, my entire interest in the cottage, the shop building and the other buildings, exclusive of the stable which was built entirely with my money.

I shall, of course, take everything out of the building which I have paid for and store it until I build somewhere else. If I had had any idea of how you both felt when I planned the remodelling of the building, I would never have spent the many thousands of dollars which I have spent. This has been a very costly lesson both financially and spiritually, but it is good for me to know that one can never know how any other person reasons or what motivates them. . . .

In view of what has happened I feel that I wish also to withdraw entirely from the school. I will give you both with great pleasure my share of the school fund which has been held in my name and on which I have paid income tax every year. I do not expect you to take my name off the letter head this year if that will cause you any embarrassment. I am sure however, that you will prosper better without any connection with the name. . . .

I shall only come to Hyde Park when the President is at the big house and I will stay at the big house. . . .

Her total withdrawal pleased nobody, and negotiations continued. Dickerman sent a telegram: "Can not our years of close association help us at such a time? . . ."

ER replied: "Very sorry every minute today is filled. . . . Leaving everything in Harry's hands."

ER's refusal to negotiate was understandable. Tommy sent the details to Esther Lape and Elizabeth Read:

Nancy is to submit a statement of their "assets" and claims $21,000 as salary for managing the shop. Mrs. R's money contribution, her name and her work count for exactly zero. . . .

In essence, what they are worrying about is not the present but what will happen when ER dies. They said plainly and distinctly that they wished always to be able to control the place and they know they could not control it if one of the children had a claim. . . .

I felt so sorry for ER I could have wept and I don't think tears were very far away from her. I can't for the life of me understand why such a fine person as she is has so many chiselers around her. I know the money means nothing whatsoever to her, but it must be a blow to realize that she has been only a money-making opportunity and not a person to them and she can't help knowing that.

She said she would jog along until we leave Washington and in the meantime look around for a place which she could own and control. She gave me permission to tell Henry [Osthagen] and of course he wanted to start ripping out the plumbing fixtures, tiles, sinks, etc., in order to leave the building the way ER found it. I told her what he said, fully expecting her to be shocked and to my utter amazement she said that is what she intended to do if she found a place where she wanted to build! . . .

On 9 November, ER wrote a long letter that served finally as the basis of their separation agreement and in which she told Dickerman much of what had been said during that dreadful 12 August conversation with Nancy Cook:

> She told me, for instance, that while we were working in the [Women's Democratic] committee, in the school, and in the industries together, you had both always felt that whatever was done was done for the sole purpose of building me up. My whole conception was entirely different. I went into the industries because I felt that Nan was fulfilling something which she had long wanted to do. I would never have done it alone. I had neither the knowledge nor the background nor the interest.
>
> I went into the school because I had an interest in education and in young people and being fond of you I was anxious to help you in what you wanted to do. It gave me an opportunity for regular work which I was anxious to have. I went into the political work because Louis was anxious to have me do something to keep up Franklin's interest in a field which he eventually hoped Franklin would return to. I had no personal ambitions of any kind and I have none today. . . .
>
> [To accommodate my] firm decision that I do not care to live in the shop building unless I pay you and Nancy for the money you have involved there, therefore I make the proposition of a payment of a thousand dollars a year over the next ten years to be paid jointly to you and Nancy or separately as you desire.

The letter continued for many paragraphs of financial and household details. Every step was agonizing, and ER left nothing to chance.

The agreement was more than generous in anybody's language, and Cook and Dickerman finally signed it on 12 November.

They evidently got some aid, or at least comfort, from FDR, and Nancy Cook sent a handwritten letter of gratitude on New York State Democratic Committee Women's Activities stationery:

> Franklin dear:
> You were a dear to bother with us and I did hate to worry you with it all. As a peace negotiator you are Number One! We should have had your help before emotions ran so high.
> Bless you dear and a world of thanks and love.

For a time, Dickerman tried to hold on to a semblance of the Todhunter partnership. She also tried to get ER to make a distinction between Nancy Cook's role and her own in the breach between them. But ER rejected her efforts.

In May 1939, Dickerman asked ER if she wanted her name removed entirely from Todhunter literature, and she used the opportunity to rehash their estrangement. Marion felt innocent, and unjustly treated:

> The only instance in which I am conscious of having displeased you was on the night I went to the hospital with Danny. My judgment in that instance may not have been wise. My motive however was a kindly one. I have never understood why you spoke to me that night as you did. . . . Three times I asked to see you . . . [and] you refused. I know nothing of what has brought this on my head save the incident [with Danny] . . . and that, unless far more was implicated than I know of, seems rather out of proportion to all that went before.

ER's answer to this letter represented her interpretation of the entire situation, and was her final personal communication with Dickerman except for formal invitations and courteous notes. In the end, ER's decision was influenced by FDR: "One real factor was that certain things came back to me through Franklin which made me realize many things which I had never realized before." Whatever FDR's words, they convinced her to terminate the friendship entirely.

Dickerman rejected ER's explanation and disclaimed all responsibility:

> First I was no part of your talk & Nan's last summer and feel that I should be allowed to speak for myself. I do not know where this 'building up' idea came from. . . . I have never used the expression nor entertained the idea. . . .
>
> I know nothing of what came back to you from Franklin. . . .
>
> Unless you wish to refer to this matter again I shall consider it closed for I have found nothing in it but disillusionment and unhappiness.

The partnership of the Val-Kill was devoured. The place—the gardens and pool, the tennis court and picnic area—once filled with so much joy and spontaneous gaiety was now marked by a cold, emotionally empty divide. Cook and Dickerman held on to the illusion of friendship with Franklin. Whatever FDR's role, in the final breach between "the three graces of Val-Kill," his words were key, and among the most hurtful.

For years, Cook and Dickerman lingered beyond ER's emotional scope. They neither moved away nor distanced themselves from the social whirl of official life. They were invited to major events and family gatherings, but ER now felt to them cold and severe, however correct and courteous.

Without the warmth and intimacy that had so fully marked their friendship, every event turned into an agony of neglect. What had seemed an enchanted era ended in everlasting pain.

Tommy reported the final agreement to Anna and observed: "I think it is an empty victory for your mother. But her life is so completely changed she does not need to depend on them for any companionship."

Tommy was now closer to ER than anybody else. They were together most of the time, and she took dictation for books, articles, and lectures on trains, in cars, waiting at airports, and while ER was in her bath. Except when ER exercised, she hardly allowed herself an unused moment. Tommy was by her side, and fun to be with.

Unlike Hick, who had no use for crowds or strangers and barely managed to be polite in public, Tommy was unfailingly amiable. She never complained and seemed rarely to tire. Devoted to her job, she was available whenever ER needed her.

When Tommy took a moment off for some minor surgery in June, Lucy Randolph Mason wrote a letter of concern to ER:

> I have resisted the impulse to write either of you to say how sorry I was about it. She is a grand person for your partner and since I met her I realized more than ever what her good sense, good judgment and good feeling mean to you. May she soon be well again—God bless her.

ER replied with relief that Tommy was "much better and is home again." After her surgery, ER was glad for the opportunity to do something useful for Tommy, who asked Anna:

> Did [your mother] tell you that Dr. Steele prescribed hypos for me and showed her how to do it and once each week she gives me a jab in my posterior? She is really expert, it never hurts a bit. Wouldn't that make a good story, especially to these people who chant: "I don't see how you do *all* the things you do."

Tommy, like all ER's closest friends, understood ER's pain over the demise of the Val-Kill friendship: "I do however feel that a complete disillusionment and disappointment such as this hurts deeply, especially as she defended them all these years against all criticism."

ER and Hick dined together after it was over, and Hick wrote:

> I hate to see you disillusioned that way. I cannot understand how they could be such damned fools! . . . You are one of the kindest, most thought-

ful humans I've ever known. I think I've said that to you before, haven't I? Well—it's all settled now for you, anyway, and I hope you'll enjoy your place up there for many, many years. Please do try to get some fun out of it. For yourself.

Negotiations with Cook and Dickerman went on from August to November, while ER became increasingly preoccupied by national and international emergencies.

27: Storms on Every Front

In September, war clouds gathered at a furious pace and New Dealers struggled to avert political ruin, after the collapse of congressional support for social reform. FDR resumed his purge campaign to end the conservative domination of Congress by condemning the South's reliance on peonage and poverty. In a series of stunning speeches, he compared fascism in Europe and feudalism in the South, "both controlled by oligarchy" which allowed people no rights or freedoms.

During the summer, his startling words infuriated antiunion, states' rights conservatives and thrilled ER's allies as they organized the Southern Conference on Human Welfare. But FDR's opponents won their primaries by large margins, and now the campaign turned ugly. New Deal issues of economic security were replaced by tirades for white supremacy—and tirades against communism, foreigners, foreign ideas. For both ER and FDR it was a harrowing campaign season.

All political activity suddenly stopped, however, as they dealt with son James's emergency surgery. On 9 September, ER flew with James to the Mayo Clinic in Rochester, Minnesota. Because of Harry Hopkins's recent surgery, ER feared the worst and felt that nobody was giving her accurate information. "Betsey arrived this morning and the situation is most confusing to me. I've come to the conclusion that I like facing facts and I hate living unrealities!"

To everybody's relief, James's bleeding ulcers were not life-threatening. Although both parents were by his side at the Mayo Clinic and ER had flown up with him and stayed for the duration, James did not mention his mother's presence:

> Father came to Rochester to see me before I went under the knife, and remained there several days until I was out of danger. He was in my room, squeezing my hand, soon after I came out of the anesthetic. . . .

ER also described the hospital vigil:

Franklin, with his usual necessary entourage, arrived the morning of the operation. He was very calm, as he usually was in a crisis, and chatted as though nothing were on his mind. I can be calm and quiet, but it takes all the discipline I have acquired in life to keep on talking and smiling and to concentrate on the conversation addressed to me. I want to be left alone while I store up fortitude for what I fear may be a blow of fate. . . . I still remember waiting through the operation that morning and then waiting some more until the doctors came with the laboratory report that said nothing malignant had been found. They told James the nervous strain was bad for him, and he accepted their advice not to return to his duties at the White House.

His marriage in shambles, and his health diminished, James resented ER's unwanted advice and excised her presence from his life. For ER, it was only the first ordeal of a turbulent autumn.

On 12 September, in the presidential railroad car on a siding near the Mayo Clinic, ER and FDR listened to Hitler's violent rhetoric—threats against Czechoslovakia and grotesque lies about Czech persecution of Germans living in the Sudetenland. On 15 September, ER wrote with disgust: "Hitler patting himself on the back because Chamberlain is going to see him makes me sick. Just the same if war can be averted by flattering him why it is worth doing."

For weeks, war seemed imminent. France vowed to mobilize if Hitler marched into Czechoslovakia; Britain vowed to follow France if France mobilized. At first, Hitler only demanded the Sudetenland, a mostly German-populated area of Czechoslovakia carved out of the heart of the former Hapsburg Empire. A rich industrial nation that extended from the Elbe to the Moldau, Czechoslovakia contained areas that Germany, Hungary, and Poland considered their rightful territory. To legitimize his claims, Hitler railed against imaginary offenses against birthright Germans by Czechs, Slovaks, and Slovenes, who were less than human.

France and England intended to prevent war by compromise and capitulation. With James out of danger, ER and FDR rushed directly back to the White House. ER wrote Anna that FDR and the State Department were in continual communication to see if the United States might prepare a useful statement to forestall war "and the tension in the house is great."

ER had long believed Hitler would never be satisfied, as she had said when he absorbed Austria. Europe's disunity, England's appeasement, and America's isolationism encouraged Hitler's ambitions. ER joined those among FDR's advisers who urged him at least to signal his moral commitment to England and France and his opposition to the demise of democratic Czechoslovakia.

The crisis peaked after the Nuremberg Rally when the the nineteenth meeting of the League of Nations Assembly opened at Geneva—and Czechoslovakia was not even on the agenda. Only Maxim Litvinov at Geneva, on 21 September, reaffirmed his country's treaty with Czechoslovakia.*

Someone told journalist William Shirer, as they walked around Lake Geneva, to look at the "beautiful granite sepulchre! Let us admire its beauty." As they paused to contemplate the League's contours, he said: "There, my friend, are buried the dead hopes of peace for our generation."

In Czechoslovakia everyone expected Hitler's bombers; the Czechs declared martial law in the five Sudeten districts and prepared to fight. American journalists reported what they could over one working phone at a Prague hotel as they witnessed "Jews excitedly trying to book on the last plane or train" out of their homeland.

On 14 September, Japan and Italy announced their commitment to Germany. Russia mobilized its fleet, and Chamberlain announced he would fly to Berchtesgaden to meet with Hitler.

On 15 September, Chamberlain agreed to the secession of the "German-speaking areas." According to Shirer, the Czechs were "dumbfounded" by Chamberlain's "sell-out." In London, on 18 September, Daladier and Bonnet drew up an Anglo-French plan by which all areas of Czechoslovakia with majority German populations should be transferred to Hitler without a plebiscite—a total betrayal. Some imagined the Czechs would fight alone.

On 22 September, Chamberlain returned to Germany, only to be told even the Anglo-French capitulation was no longer sufficient. Shirer observed the meeting place at Godesberg: "The Swastika and the British Union Jack flying side by side in this lovely Rhine town—very appropriate, I find." It was after all a Wagnerian town, filled with myths of frolic among "Wotan, Thor, and the other gods of the early Teutons."

France refused to accept Hitler's new terms; Britain again threatened to support France; both countries mobilized, as did Czechoslovakia. War seemed imminent.

Virginia Woolf wrote her sister, Vanessa Bell, that everyone in London "took war for granted. They were digging trenches in the parks, loud speakers were telling one to go and be fitted for gas masks. . . . Not much gossip, only eternal war talk." All one's friends, she wrote, believed London was to be bombed every twenty minutes with gas and explosives.

*Nicolson lunched with Litvinov on 22 August and asked for his views on the looming crisis. Litvinov replied that the "old pan-Slav feeling is dead, Russia has no sympathy for the semi-fascist systems established in the Balkans, and . . . is profoundly disillusioned with the western democracies." If Britain and France defended the Czechs, "then Russia would help. But if the western powers abandon Czechoslovakia, then Russia will become isolationist."

One of ER's Allenswood chums cabled urgently: "Dear Eleanor, one word from America will save Europe. Your school fellow, Marguerite Few, Once Baxter."

At one in the morning, 26 September, FDR sent a message to Chamberlain, Daladier, Czech President Edvard Beneš, and Hitler urging continued negotiations: "Should hostilities break out the lives of millions of men, women and children in every country involved will most certainly be lost under circumstances of unspeakable horror." Europe's economic systems would be shattered; its social structures would be wrecked:

> On behalf of the 130 millions of people of the United States of America and for the sake of humanity everywhere I most earnestly appeal to you not to break off negotiations. . . . Once they are broken off reason is banished. . . .

The three democracies assured FDR they wanted peace, but Hitler was bellicose: Versailles's injustices and the League's failure "to carry out its obligations" doomed peace. It all depended entirely on Czechoslovakia's decision.

FDR sent a personal appeal to Mussolini and another to Hitler to suggest a wider conference.

On 27 September the French army and British fleet partially mobilized; more than two million Czech soldiers fortified the German border. Mussolini proposed another conference, at Germany's request. On 29 September, the Munich Conference convened. Nicolson was convinced that Hitler sought time after Britain and France mobilized their navies, and Britain reaffirmed its alliance not only with France but with Russia.

Chamberlain, Daladier, Hitler, and Mussolini met without Czech, Russian, or U.S. representatives. At 1:00 A.M. on 30 September, Hitler obtained everything he asked for. "Daladier and Chamberlain never pressed for a single concession from Hitler." Czechoslovakia, "asked to make all the sacrifices" for Europe's peace, "was not consulted here at any stage of the talks."

Chamberlain returned to London triumphant, claiming "peace with honour," delighted to report that Britain and Germany had pledged "never to go to war with one another again."

Winston Churchill spoke of "total and unmitigated defeat." Leonard Woolf called it "peace without honour" and imagined it would last perhaps six months. Parliament, by an overwhelming majority, upheld the betrayal of Czechoslovakia.

ER wrote her husband: "The poor Czechs! I don't somehow like the role of England and France do you? We can say nothing however for we wouldn't go to war for someone else—"

FDR agreed with his wife, and at a cabinet meeting compared the "outrage" committed at Munich by Britain and France to Judas Iscariot's. He believed British public opinion opposed Chamberlain's peace-at-any-price diplomacy, and he anticipated a long and tragic air war, with England, France, and Russia united and the United States neutral, though economically supportive of the Allies.

Furious and humiliated to have been excluded from the negotiations, Russia abandoned Litvinov's quest for collective security and declared a policy of complete isolation.

On 4 September, at a ceremony in Bordeaux for Americans who had fought during World War I, William Bullitt said if war broke out in Europe "no one can say or predict whether the U.S. would be drawn into such a war." That statement might have given Hitler pause. But in mid-September, FDR rejected Bullitt's warning:

> Ambassador Bullitt's speech does not constitute a moral engagement on the part of the U.S. toward the democracies. . . . To include the U.S. in an alliance [with] France and Great Britain against Hitler is an interpretation by the political analysts one hundred percent false.

From Hitler's perspective, his victory at Munich was total: The United States was out of the picture; Europe was in disarray and opposed to a Soviet alliance. During the postwar Nuremberg Trials, Marshal Wilhelm Keitel, Hitler's chief of staff, was asked by the Czech counsel: "Would the Reich have attacked Czechoslovakia in 1938 if the Western Powers had stood by Prague?" Keitel answered: "Certainly not. We were not strong enough militarily. The object of Munich was to get Russia out of Europe, to gain time, and to complete the German armaments."

Also, the United States had sent mixed signals to the Allies about supplies. According to French Foreign Minister Georges Bonnet: "At the moment of the Munich crisis, Ambassador Bullitt told me that the U.S. could not sell us the airplanes which we had asked them for."

Internationalism was dead; the Soviets were bitter; the Poles and Hungarians marched to Berlin for their new territories to be carved out of Czech borderlands; and Hitler planned his next move.

Churchill, still the loudest voice for resistance against Hitler in Britain, assessed the damage of Munich and foretold tragedy:

> All is over. Silent, mournful, abandoned, broken, Czechoslovakia recedes into the darkness.
> I find unendurable the sense of our country falling into the power, into the orbit and influence of Nazi Germany. . . .

[We] have sustained a defeat without a war, the consequences of which will travel far . . . the whole equilibrium of Europe has been deranged. . . . This is only the beginning. . . .

The cruel personal humiliations of Jews instituted in Austria were repeated in Czechoslovakia and intensified everywhere throughout the greater Reich. During the spring and summer of 1938, there was widespread panic and flight. As the Czech crisis mounted, ER received an urgent letter from Gertrude Ely.

One of ER's least known but most interesting friends, a philanthropist and pillar of Bryn Mawr society, Ely had spent part of the summer in Germany and Austria, and since her return she had received letters of anguish and hope from both Christians and Jews. She sent "one of many" to ER from "a well known archaeologist in Berlin." Ely was impressed especially by his "unselfishness." "He is not a Jew himself," and Ely thought his letter would move ER as she had been moved: "It is almost impossible for us to realize over here the utter despair of most of those people."

Ely's correspondent, Dr. Emil Forrer, had been one of countless guests at her Bryn Mawr place, Wyndham Barn, known for sparkling conversation and evenings of music. His purpose was to introduce her to the needs of "a neighborly Jewish family with son and daughter of 16 and 17 years." The father had lost his business and was cut off from all work by a new law to take effect 1 October. Survival depended on their leaving Germany. For this they needed an affidavit that they would not become "a burden to the state," and they knew no one. "They are all extremely industrious and assiduous," all clever, able, good at everything.

[The] daughter takes care of the big garden, the chickens and rabbits which they have; she could go as housemaid. The mother could sew or do tailoring for other people. . . . They wish to remain together and they would prefer some position out in the country. . . .

He therefore begged Ely for affidavits for these four people, the Fritz Putziger family: "I am the only hope for them, and you the only hope for me."

ER wrote Gertrude Ely of her interest, but said she had at the moment nothing really to offer, beyond her recommendations about the humanitarian work of Clarence Pickett's American Friends Service Committee.

Although FDR wanted to help find compatible spaces for refugees, he did nothing to ease the rigid refugee rules. The United States was locked into a particularly vicious anti-Semitic, frankly racist campaign. Moreover, members of his State Department were unsympathetic to refugees.

In London, Joseph Kennedy counseled complete uninvolvement. London's radical newsletter published by left investigative journalist Claude Cockburn, *The Week,* quoted Kennedy as assuring his Cliveden friends that U.S. policy was "a Jewish production" and FDR would "fall in 1940." Kennedy was ecstatic over Munich: "Isn't it wonderful?" he crooned to an astounded Jan Masaryk, then Czechoslovakia's minister to London. "Now I can get to Palm Beach after all!"

While more flamboyant than most, Kennedy's views were shared on every level of FDR's State Department. Even Cordell Hull, who had a Jewish wife, wanted to do nothing, to say nothing, to upset Hitler or Mussolini. William Bullitt's repeated anti-Semitic outbursts horrified more sensitive ears. As ambassador to Russia, Bullitt had described Soviet Foreign Minister Maxim Litvinov's press secretary and later ambassador to the United States, Constantine Oumansky, as "a wretched little kike. . . . It is perhaps only natural that we should find the members of that race more difficult to deal with than the Russians themselves." From Paris, Bullitt's correspondence with his colleagues continued to be sprinkled with curious details about Jews, often unsubstantiated, generally in "poisonous" tones.

Bullitt's State Department colleagues shared his views, and they had more immediate authority over the future of "that race." Jay Pierrepont Moffat, assistant secretary of state and division chief for European affairs (1933–40), consistently opposed sanctions against Germany and argued for increased business and trade with Hitler. Educated at Groton and Harvard, Moffat was incensed when Harvard's president, James Conant, withdrew an invitation for Hitler's primary publicist, Ernst Hanfstaengl, to be honored at Harvard's 1934 commencement. Good Cambridge fellows ought to resist the pressure of "all the Jews in Christendom [who] arose in protest." Moffat was consistent. While posted to Warsaw he advised a colleague to be wary of Litvinov: He had "the malevolent look of an untidy Jew."

In Dublin, Ambassador John Cudahy originally worried little about Nazi violence and had earlier compared Hitler's brownshirts to college boys, not unlike a "fraternal order." Later more repelled by atrocities, he nevertheless intended to see the situation "realistically":

> [The] handling of the Jews, [while] shocking and revolting, is from any realistic or logical approach a purely domestic matter and none of our business. It is not stretching the analogy too far to say that Germany would have just as much warrant to criticize our handling of the Negro minority if a race war between blacks and whites occurred in the United States.

In a climate of rapidly escalating hatred, ER and her friends at the AFSC were rudely treated when they demanded official changes in U.S. refugee policies. After November 1938, it became one of ER's most abiding issues.

Even before the European tragedies and the refugee crisis were added to ER's agenda, Hick wrote with wonder:

> How do you manage to do all you do, anyway? There is one thing, though, that makes life easier for you. That is that you always have servants. You don't have to cook or wash dishes or make beds or fix the laundry. All those things take so much time—and so much energy. Just keeping people fed, and the house in order. Seeing that the fire in the fireplace doesn't go out. . . .

ER replied that all busy women needed staff: "I think I should give you as a Xmas present an efficient maid to move from city to country with you and take care of you. It would be more useful than money towards your car, wouldn't it?"

No matter how difficult or elusive Hick became, ER trusted her, needed and enjoyed her company. She relied on her for honest advice as she had on Louis Howe. She offered various dates and persisted despite Hick's repeated refusals. "Your work sounds hectic and so does your social life!" "I am anxious for a glimpse of you and sometime before long I'd like an evening!"

On the 21st they finally lunched together after weeks apart; ER wrote:

> It was good to see you today. I do love to talk to you for you are stimulating. . . . I went back and did two columns and Hall made me look at some movies of the German plane and then I picked up Cousin Henry [Parrish] and drove out here [to the Parrishes' country place, Llewellyn Park, in Orange, New Jersey] in quite a storm and wondered if you were having more rain and wind. It seemed to be clear tonight. . . .

ER had driven through the preliminary head winds of the ferocious hurricane of 1938, which coincided with the Munich crisis. She wrote Hick the next day: "I do hope you found the Danas, Ross, and the 'little house' safe. I fear all the Beach people suffered and Fire Island and West Hampton sounded horrible. Doesn't one feel helpless when nature gets going?"*

*The savage hurricane of 1938 blasted into the east coast without warning on 21 September in the middle of the afternoon. The *New York Times* headlined Czechoslovakia's demise, and gave the forecast for the Northeast as overcast, a chance of rain, a mild September day. By three o'clock winds exceeded 100 miles per hour and the ocean rushed five miles from the shore in mighty waves on the East End of Long Island. Just east of Hick's Little House, towns from Westhampton to Montauk were rendered rubble. In Westhampton, where 179 houses stood, 153 completely vanished. In Rhode Island, 380 people were dead. Up and down the coast 63,000 people were rendered homeless; 275 million trees were uprooted, including half of New Hampshire's white pines and most of Vermont's maples.

For weeks, everybody around ER focused on the great eastern storm of 1938. It only moderately wrecked the Hudson River Valley: "Our cellars here are flooded and no furnace but it isn't very cold!" It had, however, bashed Long Island, Connecticut, and the coast. Neither Hick nor Esther Lape could write or think of anything else. From Coram to Mastic it looked like the ravages of a typhoon combined with a biblical flood. It seemed to Hick "that there could hardly be a tree left standing in the woods." She arrived at the entrance to the Dana place just as dark was falling:

> I started in on our road, drove about a block, with branches of fallen trees sweeping the top of the car, and found myself blocked. A huge pine lying right across the road. I can hardly describe to you my sensations. It was dark now. Not a sound—not even any katydids. And that tree lying there, the branches so green and fresh. It was like looking at a person who had just died.

With one feeble flashlight, Hick and a young neighbor set out on foot; they "climbed and crawled over what seemed like a solid mass of fallen trees" for over a mile.

> I shall not soon forget that night, my dear. The further we went, the more hopeless it seemed to me. I did not see how any living thing could have survived. . . .
> Finally, after about an hour and a half, we came to a tractor. We were almost up to the Dana house by this time, and they had managed to clear the road that far. They had literally sawed their way through the thick trunks of big trees!
> From that point on, we ran. . . . Then I saw a light. And I heard a motor running—the Danas' Delco [generator].
> Well—I found them all alive, even Prinz, who had had a narrow escape. All camped in the Dana house, which wasn't hurt at all. . . .
> But the trees, dear—not a single one of those beautiful old locusts around the Little House is left. And practically every tree around the Dana house, including that beautiful old apple tree in the courtyard. The houses stick up now, wholly bare. Ella says the place looks like a brand new real estate development. . . .

Although no one perished, Hick and her friends were plunged in gloom:

> For the time being, at least, all that I loved so much down there is gone—the peace and the beauty of it. Maybe it will come back some day. . . . I pray that it will. That place down there and what it gave me—they were about the only things left in the world that I cared about. . . .
> Why is it that as soon as I get to care about or depend on any one or anything it must always be taken away from me? . . .

ER mourned the devastation, but at the White House "the hurricane is eclipsed by the world situation which keeps FDR on edge all the time." "No one can think of much else these days." ER was philosophic: FDR had decided because of Europe's uncertainty not to go "to HP tomorrow and of course he is right but if we are in for a long pull, we'll have to do many of these normal things or everyone will go under."

The ferocity of nature's storm, which destroyed so much everyone close to ER valued, only highlighted the madness of war, which would destroy everything. ER sent Hick her autumn itinerary through the Northeast, which had not been canceled by the storm. She planned to visit Esther and Elizabeth en route. Their place in Connecticut "suffered much as yours did. . . . In case you have forgotten, my love again, Madame."

The hurricane of 1938 was the most vicious storm since the great hurricane of 1815. For ER's friends the international news made the storm of the century both metaphor and portent.

On the 27th, two days before Munich, when war still seemed certain, Hick apologized for having written "so feverishly yesterday about my troubles."

> After all, with another world war imminent, little things like a house in the country and trees, with the peace they contributed to one individual, aren't so very important, are they? . . .
>
> I wonder if you feel as depressed about the whole thing as I do. . . . I do think the President's message [urging continued negotiations] was swell. . . .

ER replied: "F said he's done the last thing he can do and we can all pray something moves Hitler tomorrow. What a mad man!"

As she proceeded through the Northeast, ER observed the wreckage philosophically:

> I don't know that it will cheer you, but nature does cover up her ravages quickly as I realized in France after the war and next spring you will find new beauties which it is impossible to imagine now.

She felt more foreboding about Europe. After the Munich agreement, FDR cabled Chamberlain: "Good man." But ER doubted the pact served any significant purpose. She wrote Anna:

> Pa's second message was grand and so well timed. I feel of course that Hitler having acquired all he wanted this time will begin again to get the next thing he wants when he is ready to do so. Therefore we have only postponed a war unless we are prepared to let Hitler and his ideas domi-

nate Europe. It does not seem to be our business really and yet I wonder if we can remain uninfluenced by the growth of those ideas.

ER dreaded the idea of a fascist peace, and she spent part of her days during the Munich crisis reading Thomas Mann's book *The Coming Victory of Democracy*. She sent it on to Anna and John:

> I'd like to know what you both think about it. I would like to get an opportunity to talk to [Thomas Mann] in the light of recent events, for he stirred many questions in my mind.

On 23 September, ER devoted a column to the profound shift she felt in her own thinking after she read Mann's book. He had toured the United States in the hope that Americans would respond to the tragedies that now blanketed Europe. Thomas Mann no longer believed that democracy anywhere would survive unless it responded with vigor to the vile circumstances imposed by the fascists: "Force must be met with force."

ER wrote that that was "what we had been doing from generation to generation." She had believed that military violence in itself settled nothing, and was its own evil: an evil that always intensified the "bitterness that we built up before." Now she felt that the alternative was to permit those nations that believed "exclusively in force, to have everything their own way." The pacifist's dilemma was troublesome:

> If we decide again that force must be met with force, then is it the moral right for any group of people who believe that certain ideas must triumph, to hold back from the conflict?

ER rapidly moved toward a commitment to what was subsequently derided in the United States as "premature antifascism." Before 1941 it was deemed un-American, practically treasonous, certainly radical or communist, really to oppose Hitler and fascism sufficiently to contemplate war as a lesser evil. It was the dilemma answered by thousands of Europeans who joined the International Brigades, by thousands of Americans who marched off to Spain in the Lincoln and Washington Brigades. ER was sympathetic to their decision and agreed with their purpose. But she hated war; it only spawned further war. There were no final victories. There had to be another way to settle conflicts. But Hitler was an aggressive madman, and Munich inflamed his ambitions.

Like other antifascists who opposed war, ER was torn about the sacrifice of Czechoslovakia. "Czechoslovakia was set up in an arbitrary way" at Versailles, she wrote, "and my whole feeling is that the question should have been discussed in a calm atmosphere and not at the point of a pistol." Her heart divided, she wrote an Allenswood chum, Helen Gifford, in Britain:

I feel with you that things are not definitely settled and I can well imagine that Mlle Souvestre with her feelings about minorities might be very unhappy. However, I cannot help being glad that the countries involved did not send thousands of young people to be killed over this particular question.

The "deathwatch" of the summer and autumn of 1938 was informed by widespread knowledge of new munitions of destruction introduced since 1933. In 1929, Churchill had published *The Aftermath*, an amazing book of prescience: When the 1914–18 war ended, scientists and workers in a hundred laboratories, a thousand arsenals, and countless factories suspended their projects. "But their knowledge was preserved," and they were poised to deliver weapons ever more "formidable and fatal." From 1933 to 1938, they had created a new reality—already displayed in Ethiopia and Spain. Modern technology rendered military destruction "wholesale, unlimited, and perhaps, once launched uncontrollable."

Mankind has never been in this position before. Without having improved appreciably in virtue . . . it has got into its hands for the first time the tools by which it can unfailingly accomplish its own extermination. . . . Death stands at attention, obedient, expectant, ready to serve . . . ready, if called on, to pulverise . . . what is left of civilization.

As ER read the newspapers, she was convinced that if peace failed, unspeakable tragedy would follow. But to grant Hitler all he demanded was not peace. Horrified by fascist military triumphs in Asia and Europe, she wrote Elizabeth Baker, an absolute pacifist:

I have never believed that war settled anything satisfactorily, but I am not entirely sure that some times there are certain situations in the world such as we have in actuality, when a country is worse off when it does not go to war for its principles than if it went to war. . . . I am afraid conditions in the rest of the world are going to decide that for us.

In a world filled with propaganda, political warfare, lies, and deceit, America's press was increasingly the only source of real news:

Everywhere people listened as I did to their radios and I think read the papers with the same avidity. Since then taxi-drivers, hair dressers, sales girls . . . have talked to me about the situation with intelligence and a knowledge which shows their deep interest.

Never before in history . . . have nations been armed for war and so close to war and yet not taken the first step, and I lay it largely to the awareness of the people and the force of public opinion on the leaders. . . . But as long as we have peace and an aroused public opinion, I shall hope that we may tackle our international problems with the same fervor which we are putting into the solution of some of our national problems.

After her lecture tour through New England, ER went south to Kentucky and Tennessee, returned to Washington for her birthday week, and spent a day in Charlottesville with her youngest grandson, FDR III, who was a delight:

A more placid, healthier baby I have rarely seen and even at three months old, he smiles back at you and, while you might object to a double chin in a year or so, it is really quite engaging in a baby!

That evening, 9 October, she dined with Aubrey and Anita Williams, Ellen Woodward, Josephine Roche, and others. There was much discussion about the state of the world. They agreed about many issues, and ER seemed relieved that both "Aubrey and Josephine Roche have a good deal of sympathy with Mexico in her present position in retaking her [oil] lands if she will pay in the future."

Tensions over Mexico's nationalization of its oil properties had simmered since April. FDR's policy was to keep the region united against fascist penetration. His old Navy boss, Ambassador to Mexico Josephus Daniels, warned that Pan-American solidarity was needed to "save democracy. Oil ought not to smear it." Despite Cordell Hull's opposition to "communists" who disrespected and nationalized private property, and to agitation by oil interests, notably "Standard Oil," which had "heavy investments in Mexico," FDR supported President Lázaro Cárdenas's right of eminent domain.

The economic implications of good neighborliness and America's response to nationalism and anti-imperialist activities changed as Europe readied for war—and fascists turned for military commerce to resource-rich Latin America. Indeed, in August the State Department created two new bureaus to improve relations with Latin America—a Division of Cultural Relations and a Division of International Communications. The goal was to exchange teachers and students, cooperate in music, art, and literature, and initiate "international radio broadcasts." Sumner Welles said it was a modest beginning, and "not a propaganda agency." But the goal was to enhance Cordell Hull's reciprocal trade agreements and culturally improve hemispheric relations, since there was known "penetration, economic and intellectual, of the German and Italian dictatorships in Latin America."

On her birthday, 11 October 1938, ER received a poem from Harry Hopkins:

MY DAY

My Day is a dignified
column

It tells you right from
wrong

In the morning I'm dressing
in Frisco

At noon I lunch in
Hong Kong.

I fly way over Spain
Because Franco is a pain
And Hitler's a terrible
mug

I tea with the Queen
And Kennedy's spleen
The while I knit me a
rug.

I curtsy my best
And hop over Brest
And land at the White
House door.

My day's hard on the legs
But I scramble the eggs
Bless you my children
once more.

Though ER thought she was inured to jokes about herself, she wrote to correct Harry:

> I enjoyed your poetic effort, but I must take issue with you. I never could tell anyone the difference between right and wrong. There are too many shades for me to ever be sure! I only wish I could cover all the lands you suggest!

ER's White House birthday celebration, without Nancy Cook and Marion Dickerman, even without Hick or Earl, was grand. FDR had arranged a splendid evening and gave her a birthday check with a jolly note: "Many Happy Returns! This is TOWARD the new 'Lake Eleanor' at ValKill. I will take you cruising on it."

The check was to help defray the costs of the controversial dredging that ER had done, which had so annoyed Cook and Dickerman. It was a considerate gift.

Actually, ER's fifty-fourth birthday seemed rather a state occasion. The *New York Times* ran two editorials celebrating her life and work. On 13 October, the paper surveyed her riding and sporting habits and noted that she "talks a great deal too." But the previously critical tone reserved for such observations was now gone:

> This is not in the tradition of the wives of former Presidents. But she is so patently sincere and unpretentious in all she says and does, so ebulliently a part of every activity she undertakes, so good-humored even in the face of criticism, that she remains today one of the most popular women who ever lived in the White House. At 54 she could command a landslide of votes as Mrs. America.

Other observers thought far beyond that. A poll taken by the New York League of Business and Professional Women nominated ER for governor of New York State, and at least one newspaper editorialized that ER should be nominated for president. Her nomination would avoid a third-term conflict for FDR, and in addition to "the prestige she may have won as wife of President Roosevelt, she merits the Presidency on the basis of her own personality and her performance." Citing the careers of Catherine in Russia, Victoria in Britain, Isabella in Spain, and Wilhelmina in the Netherlands, the paper asked: "What sound reasons can be advanced against a woman for President of the U.S.?"

ER's birthday also coincided with the Women's National Press Club party honoring "Good Queen Eleanor." According to the *New York Times*, "the most noteworthy observation" made during the evening was the "total subsidence of the criticism to which she was subjected in her first two years or so because she did not 'stay home and tend to her knittin.' . . . One does not hear that any more."

ER's birthday was not even dampened by family concerns. She minimized her mother-in-law's meddlings and seemed now almost sympathetic to her intrusions. ER wrote Anna:

> I hope Granny is feeling well and that she can refrain . . . from trying to plan your lives! She seems to me to be aging fast but she still takes so much interest in us all that she would be glad to direct our actions even in the future!

SDR, at eighty-four, worried about everything. She worried about the grandchildren, their children, and everybody's future. She particularly worried about Hyde Park. She wanted some assurance that the estate would be retained by the family after her death. ER now felt protective of her mother-in-law and wished "she would not worry about my friends for I think she has reached an age when she should not bother about any one she does not like."

Publicly, ER praised SDR. She had summered in Campobello, and then gone off to Seattle:

> At eighty-four, this seems to me quite an achievement and I only hope that many of us will learn from this older generation how to preserve our interest in life and our desire to participate in the interests of the young. Certainly my husband's mother is younger in spirit than many people whose years are far fewer than hers.

ER seemed to put petty family annoyances in perspective that October:

> Too bad Curt had to tell Sis that he never liked me but after all in the end children have to make up their own minds as to whom they like and dislike.

James, who possibly never forgave her opposition to his White House job or her contribution to the tensions with Betsey, was barely speaking to his mother:

> James has not said one word to me about his plans since I left him. He telephoned me once, and wired the day after my birthday and that is all I've heard. . . .

But ER was rarely in one place long enough to brood. The day after her birthday she lectured at Hollins College in Roanoke, Virginia, where she found the students "particularly happy and healthy and ready to absorb all the education available." She returned that night just long enough to see films from Africa made "by our cousin Leila Roosevelt Dennis and her husband." ER heartily recommended *Dark Rapture;* it "is really very beautiful and interesting." She and Tommy left on the midnight train for the Midwest, for Missouri, Wisconsin, and Ohio. Then they headed south to Alabama, and to Columbia, South Carolina.

At some point on her tour, ER spent a day in Atlanta, drove to "my grandmother's old home in Roswell," and inspected the new building going on at Warm Springs, "so I could tell my husband all that was being done." Also she finally had a chance to see the Eleanor Roosevelt School. After FDR built a new brick school for the white children of Warm Springs, ER helped raise the money to build a modern brick school for the area's black children. To put some meaning behind "separate but equal" in her husband's adopted town seemed a little enough thing, but it inflamed white supremacists. Sixty years later some residents still complained about ER's "interference." She was proud of her achievement and grateful for FDR's speech at the school's dedication, in December 1937. They both understood that her school and his speech contributed to Georgia's violent racialist campaign in 1938.

On the road, ER wondered when she and Hick would "take our evening together before Xmas? We ought to plan it next time we meet!" ER wondered how they would "manage an occasional glimpse" of each other; but Hick indulged in her old fantasy of touring with ER through the Midwest:

> If you only weren't the President's wife—with all the fuss and pushing and hauling that goes with it—how I should love to travel with you to those places! But if you weren't the President's wife, the chances are you wouldn't be going. . . . It would be a lot of fun if some day we could just go off bumming, looking at things, visiting all sorts of funny little towns. But that sort of traveling is expensive, isn't it, when one is not on a job or a lecture trip. And I don't think you are so keen about motor trips as you used to be. I'd still rather drive a car than do almost anything else I can think of!

For the first time, ER rejected Hick's fantasy and discouraged further musings about long trips:

> I doubt dear, if I'll ever have the money to travel except on a money-making basis such as lecturing or writing and I cannot imagine that you would enjoy it even if I were not the President's wife for one does of necessity so much one does not want to do. We can take short motor trips when I have more time someday and those, when I am no longer recognized wherever I go you will enjoy again.

When ER returned she proposed a week together in Washington, and promised "to have time free part of [each] day and you might not mind it so much now. . . ." Hick agreed, to ER's surprise: "I'm delighted that you are considering my December invitation. I thought you had put the White House aside forever!"

ER returned to a Washington poised for the midterm elections and faced painful dinner conversations about renewed labor strikes; the resurgence "of the KKK, vigilantes, etc."

After one weekend in Washington, and another in New York for Christmas shopping, ER left on 2 November alone, for an "entirely personal" visit to Seattle, where she was present at the delivery of Anna's third child, John Boettiger, Jr. Anna wrote Tommy:

> You would have got a tremendous kick out of seeing mother selling my Seattle physician on the idea that she must be allowed to don a nurse's mask and uniform to watch the actual arrival. This doctor is, unfortu-

nately, a strong and very reactionary Republican, so that sometimes I am sure he would like to punch my nose, and I sure have felt like punching his. . . . But after all, I'm producing a baby and not a political machine. . . .

Delayed by a blizzard, ER reached Hyde Park just in time "to join the President and his mother at the polls."

The midterm elections of 1938 were disastrous. Except for the reelections of New York's Senator Robert Wagner and Governor Herbert Lehman (vigorously challenged by Thomas Dewey), which were of great personal concern to both ER and FDR and were markedly narrow victories, the results nationally were a triumph for anti–New Deal forces. Michigan's Governor Frank Murphy was defeated by Dies Committee accusations that he was a Red communist anti-industry unionist. In the South, every anti–New Deal candidate FDR opposed in his "purge" campaign was reelected. New conservative leaders appeared, including Senator Robert Taft of Ohio—son of President Howard Taft, and a fervent isolationist.

Republicans in the House doubled, from 88 to 170, and increased in the Senate by eight. Although Democrats nominally controlled Congress, it was now overwhelmingly dominated by Southern Democrats and conservative Republicans who despised labor unions, New Deal liberals, and ER particularly.

Amazingly buoyant, FDR wrote Josephus Daniels in Mexico that he was "wholly reconciled" to the results, which he felt "on the whole helpful." The election cleaned out "some bad local situations," and FDR predicted the next Congress would be "less trouble" than the last. At least he had sent a clear message: "I am sufficiently honest to decline to support any conservative Democrat."

ER admired FDR's courage in battle and under attack. After all, he often said, "once you've spent two years trying to wiggle one toe, everything is in proportion!"

But the election results quickly changed the national mood. A month earlier, Hallie Flanagan warned ER about "libelous misinformation" being circulated to destroy the Federal Arts Projects, initiated by Martin Dies's House Un-American Activities Committee. Flanagan sent ER a report which refuted every charge, so she would not be "inconvenienced."

ER had replied, casually: "I never worry about the hearings, but I will ask you if I ever want to know a specific thing." After the elections, the Dies Committee became far more worrisome, and ER condemned its tactics as "Gestapo-like." But in November 1938, ER was more concerned with Gestapo violence throughout Nazi-controlled countries.

Between 9 and 15 November, Jewish homes, schools, hospitals, synagogues, businesses, and cemeteries were invaded, plundered, burned. Kristallnacht, the night of broken glass, was a week of contempt, abuse, destruction.

If anybody doubted the intent of Hitler's words, so clearly revealed in his writings, speeches, and previous outrages, those November days in Germany, Austria, and the Sudetenland shattered any illusion. The violence coincided with Armistice Day, 11 November, when the Allies ended World War I. The defeat of that war was for Hitler to be avenged with new blood, and unlimited terror.

The violence began on 28 October, when Germany expelled thousands of Polish Jews who had lived for decades within the historically changing borders of Germany. Nazis rounded up children and old people on the streets, emptied houses and apartment buildings, allowed people to take nothing with them except 10 marks ($4) and the clothes they wore, shoved them into waiting trucks and trains, and dumped them across the border onto the desolate flats of Poland's borderlands. More than ten thousand Jews were deported in this manner.

Among the deportees was the family of Zindel Grynszpan, whose seventeen-year-old son, Heschel, had previously fled the family home in Hanover to Paris. When he received a letter from his father recounting his family's ordeal, Heschel Grynszpan bought a gun and on 7 November walked to the German embassy in Paris to assassinate the ambassador. Ironically, he was detained by a minor official, Ernst vom Rath, who was himself under investigation by the Gestapo for his opposition to the increasing anti-Semitic violence, and shot him. This murder was the immediate excuse used to launch the well-orchestrated burnings, lootings, and round-ups known as Kristallnacht.

Then on 12 November, German Jews were fined a billion marks—$400 million—as penalty for the murder. This "money atonement" was astronomical and rendered it virtually impossible for most Jews to retain sufficient savings to emigrate. Yet another decree ordered the victims to pay for the repair and restoration of their former shops, buildings, and homes—from which they were permanently banished.

These fines had another, more sinister purpose. Hitler had announced: "If there is any country that believes it has not enough Jews, I shall gladly turn over to it all our Jews." Now, if they left, they left penniless. Moreover, most countries had closed their doors, and those who would accept Jews would not accept paupers.

It was a major challenge for FDR, whose policy was to do nothing to involve the United States in European affairs, but who wanted to respond somehow to the thousands of refugees who stood for hours before the U.S. embassy seeking asylum, only to be routinely turned away.

Within days, Jews were stripped of their remaining human rights. They were no longer permitted to drive cars, travel on public transportation, walk in parks, go to museums, attend theaters, or concerts. Passports and visas were canceled. They were stateless and impoverished. Charged for the violence and fined for the damage, the Jewish community now owed the Reich, collectively, one billion Reichsmarks. For a time, they were not molested in their homes. But there was nothing to do, no work to be had; no place to pray; no recourse from agony. Many committed suicide; most tried to leave.

ER wrote:

> This German-Jewish business makes me sick and when FDR called tonight I was glad to know [U.S. Ambassador to Germany Hugh] Wilson was being recalled and we were protesting. How could Lindbergh take that Hitler decoration!

ER's formerly private protests against bigotry were increasingly for public attribution. Although she had resigned in silence from the Colony Club for its discrimination against Elinor Morgenthau, she now canceled a speaking engagement at a country club in Lancaster, Pennsylvania, with a statement of distress that it excluded Jews.

While she counseled complete assimilation and urged Jews to "wipe out in their own consciousness any feeling of difference by joining in all that is being done by Americans" for justice and democracy, she also spoke on behalf of support for refugees in Palestine. In 1937 she helped spearhead a drive for a home for immigrant girls in Jerusalem, and was perceived as so supportive that an Eleanor Roosevelt Vocational Training Classroom in the new home was dedicated in her honor.

On 6 December 1938, ER appealed to fifteen hundred people assembled at the Hotel Astor under the auspices of a national committee for refugees chaired by William Green, president of the American Federation of Labor, to help promote the Léon Blum colony in Palestine for the settlement of one thousand Jewish refugee families. ER urged all Americans to celebrate the democratic vision of the nation's founders and by "thought and example" to help restore "kindness, good-will and liberty" to the world.

While ER called for demonstrations of "thought and example," little was done, or said, by FDR's administration to indicate official outrage at Hitler's violence. No message of protest warning of boycott or economic reprisal was sent. Yet history abounds in such protests on behalf of victimized peoples. In 1903 and 1906, Theodore Roosevelt protested against Jewish pogroms in Russia, after Jacob Schiff lobbied for an official U.S. condemnation of the massacre of Jews in Odessa. In 1902, TR ordered his secretary of state, John Hay, to send an official U.S. protest to Romania:

> The political disabilities of the Jews in Romania, their exclusion from the public service and the learned professions, the limitations of their civil rights and the imposition upon them of exceptional taxes . . . [are] repugnant to the moral sense of liberal modern peoples. . . . This government cannot be a tacit party to such an international wrong. It is constrained to protest against the treatment to which the Jews of Romania are subjected . . . in the name of humanity.

FDR sent no similar message to Germany.

FDR did respond to the pitiless carnage and massacre in China. In December 1937, Japan destroyed Nanking in a vicious episode of rape, horror, and death. Half the population, an estimated 300,000 people, were tortured and killed. Whether the details were immediately known to FDR, even of Japan's 12 December sinking of the U.S. gunboat *Panay*, remains controversial. But on 11 January 1938, FDR sent a memo to Cordell Hull and Admiral Cary T. Grayson, head of the American Red Cross. He called for additional relief funds for the "destitute Chinese civilians" and for medical aid. "I think we could raise $1,000,000 without any trouble at all." On 17 January, the U.S. Red Cross launched an appeal for aid to the Chinese people, initiated by FDR's formal request for such a drive.

No similar appeal was made by FDR to the Red Cross on behalf of Europe's Jews.*

Since he was considered by many the best friend American Jews ever had, FDR's reactions to the European events of 1938 are unexplainable. He wrote nothing to Mussolini after he issued his summer 1938 decrees expelling Jews who had settled in Italy after 1919 and removing all Jews from schools, universities, businesses, and the professions. On 15 September 1938, however, FDR sent a crass note to William Phillips, the U.S. ambassador to Rome: "What a plight the unfortunate Jews are in. It gives them little comfort to remind them that they have been 'on the run' for about four thousand years."

Subsequently, FDR told Phillips to confer personally with Mussolini on "the Jewish exile question." According to Ickes:

> [FDR wanted to cultivate Mussolini and] drive a wedge between him and Hitler and at the same time use his good offices to prevail upon Hitler to ameliorate the economic condition of the Jews who are being driven

*During the 1940s, the International Red Cross deflected complaints about its neglect of Jewish needs, given the magnitude of the mounting tragedy, with the explanation that the Red Cross "could not interfere in the internal affairs of a belligerent nation."

into exile. Mussolini agrees that it is not fair to the rest of the world for Germany to strip her Jews bare and then exclude them. They ought at least be allowed to convert enough of their property into money to take them to other lands and establish themselves there.

For all moral and political purposes, Kristallnacht was the terminal event. Civility in the heart of western Europe lay in ruins, surrounded by broken glass, bloodied streets, desecrated temples, burned Torahs, ripped books of prayer to the one shared God. Hitler's intentions were flagrant, and the whole world was invited to witness. Twenty thousand Jews were removed to concentration camps, which the Anglo-American press named: Dachau near Munich, Oranienburg-Sachsenhausen north of Berlin, Buchenwald near Weimar.

These great centers of learning and high culture had been transformed into locations of unspeakable humiliation and agony.

Except for Father Charles E. Coughlin, who hailed the violence against "Jewish-sponsored Communism," the press was unanimous in its condemnation. Sir George Ogilvie-Forbes, British counselor in Berlin, wired Foreign Secretary Lord Halifax: "The Jews of Germany are, indeed, not a national but a world problem, which, if neglected, contains the seeds of a terrible vengeance."

FDR told his 15 November press conference: "The news of the past few days from Germany has deeply shocked public opinion in the U.S. . . . I myself could scarcely believe that such things could occur in a 20th century civilization." FDR agreed to allow all German aliens on visitor visas to remain in the United States for six months "and for other like periods so long as necessary." At the time there were between twelve thousand and fifteen thousand political refugees covered by his order, and "not all Jews, by any means," the president assured the press. "All shades of liberal political thought and many religions are represented."

Anti-Semitism in FDR's State Department increased after Hitler's November atrocities. Breckenridge Long now dedicated himself to keeping refugees out of America. Curiously, FDR continually promoted Breckenridge Long, who had life-and-death control over visas and passports. Nevertheless, in 1938, for the first time, the United States filled its refugee quota.

ER and her asylum-seeking circle faced the urgent refugee crisis in a lonely political environment. Thousands of the earliest refugees who left in 1933 were still wandering Europe seeking safety and political asylum. After 31 January 1933, over 30 percent of Germany's 500,000 Jews had become refugees. After the March 1938 Anschluss, Germany's annexation of Austria, when the Nazis began to expel Austria's 190,000 Jews, the situation became critical. The flight of Czech Jews compounded the problem, and Kristallnacht ignited refugee panic.

FDR expanded his search for underpopulated and suitable lands upon which to place the world's unwanted Jews. He ordered Myron Taylor, the U.S. representative on the Intergovernmental Committee on Political Refugees, to return to London for further discussions with George Rublee, director of the committee. But again FDR told his press conference that he had no intention of asking Congress to alter existing immigration quotas. He acknowledged Hitler's determination to send Jews out of his territories, on luxury ships if necessary, by searching the world's waste spaces for possible places of sanctuary.

During her own press conference, ER called for temporary emergency measures to do whatever was possible "to deal with the refugee problem, and at home, for renewed devotion to . . . the American way of life." Wary of her husband's strategies, she hesitated to criticize him directly and said: "Of the international issues involved, or existing conditions abroad, [she] would not speak." But this was "a special situation" which required "special and speedy relief methods . . . of an emergent and transitory nature. For ourselves, I hope we will do, as individuals, all we can to preserve what is a traditional right in this country—freedom for different races and different religions."

FDR appealed for special emergency asylum in the United States for temporary residents. He urged Congress not to introduce "new legislation, to force the deportation of the unfortunates who have sought temporary asylum here, any more than it sought to force the deportation of white Russians to face certain death at the hands of the Soviet Union."

But antirefugee feelings were virulent, and Congress wanted no part of any refugee liberalization schemes. New York Congressman William Sirovich planned to introduce one, and also a resolution to call for the United States to break off diplomatic relations with Germany. Martin Dies said any such proposal would receive fewer than a hundred votes.

FDR cast about for some alternative to carnage. After Kristallnacht, FDR appointed geographer Isaiah Bowman, president of The Johns Hopkins University and formerly territorial adviser to the U.S. delegation at Versailles, to scout the globe for potential areas for settlement. Given the failure of the Evian Conference, FDR was particularly interested in undeveloped lands or weak colonial centers. Bowman's mandate included a study of resource-rich areas for future investment and development. From 1938 to 1940, Bowman and a State Department team explored possibilities in underpopulated areas of Central and South America, the Caribbean, and Central Africa. This amazing investigation revealed FDR's early interest in British and French colonial territories as well as nominally independent and sovereign nations.

On 21 November 1938, Henry Morgenthau reported his conversation with Dr. Bowman "on colonies" to FDR: The "only country in Central America which offers possibilities for colonization is Costa Rica." But Morgenthau wanted "to remind" FDR that the president of the United Fruit Company "informed you" that Costa Rica required "$5,000,000 to put them on their feet financially."

Costa Rica was particularly suited for refugees because of its "excellent" climate and the fact that it was "democratic and sympathetic toward immigration." Perhaps 100,000 refugees could be accommodated.

Honduras had a sparse population. There were good mining possibilities in gold and silver, but the "attitude of government toward immigration doubtful."

Nicaragua was "sparsely inhabited but capable of sustaining two or three 10,000 groups by subsistence agriculture. . . ."

Guatemala offered "good prospects in certain areas." But these areas were already inhabited by "some influential English and American Farm Owners," and there were many German plantations. "Government likely to favor immigrants, but some foreign [especially German] land owners likely to oppose."

British Honduras (Belize) was unsuitable, since additional settlers "would strengthen Britain's hold on the territory."

Panama was a possibility for "several 10,000 groups." Salvador was impossible, "due to dense population and intensive development."

South America varied widely: The underpopulated areas of Venezuela failed from every point of view. Brazil had geographic possibilites but political drawbacks. Paraguay, while not a "paradise," did have space. But politically the entire region was disastrous.

Bowman cautioned FDR against the whole idea. He objected to the impact of "a large foreign immigrant group" upon these countries, and particularly worried that FDR's interest in their presence would "seriously" involve the United States in "European quarrels."

> Why not keep the European elements within the framework of the Old World? Even if we do not favor migration to Latin America, but allow it, difficulties will arise. . . .

FDR evidently agreed. In any case, no further steps were taken by the United States—except subsequently for economic investment. Sumner Welles briefed FDR on the resettlement situation worldwide. It was grim.

Australia would admit five thousand a year, but wanted no publicity. South Africa had refused to participate in Evian and was not interested: There was "strong and increasing anti-Semitism in the Union." Canada would not discuss the subject.*

Welles had one bold idea: Appropriate Lower California (Baja) for a Jew-

---

*Between 1933 and 1945, Canada admitted only five thousand refugees. Early in 1945 a senior Canadian official was asked during a press conference how many Jews would be admitted after the war. "None," he answered, "is too many."

ish homeland in partial settlement of the U.S.–Mexican oil controversy over the nationalization of PEMEX. But the State Department thought Mexico would be averse to any further "alienation of its national domain."

Britain admitted refugees from Germany at the rate of seventy-five a day, but wanted "to avoid any publicity concerning it." Britain also planned to settle two hundred refugees in Tanganyika and considered settlements in other African territories. Regarding Palestine, Britain's policies became more restrictive. Jewish immigration into Palestine from 1933 to 1936 varied from 30,327 in 1933 to 61,854 in 1935. But in 1937, Britain restricted immigration to 10,536, although emergency provisions were made after Kristallnacht.

No other government represented on the Intergovernmental Committee on Refugees created at Evian indicated a willingness to consider colonization. France rejected a community in Madagascar or French New Caledonia, and neither Belgium nor the Netherlands would discuss the subject. Most countries in Latin America agreed to accept refugees, although some introduced greater restrictions after Evian.

ER was staggered by the contempt for human suffering expressed at Evian and revealed in the Welles and Bowman reports. In the bitter time before the burning time there was hope for rescue country by country. But there was no official objection to Hitler's intention to remove Jews from Germany and all his new territories. ER increasingly bypassed State Department restrictions; she worked, often covertly, with private groups and individuals. She campaigned for a less restrictive refugee policy, pursued visas for individuals, and answered and passed on to government officials every appeal sent to her.

Revolted by world events, ER called for entirely new levels of action. Her speeches became more pointed and vigorous, and she spent more time in the company of radical activists, especially members of the American Youth Congress whose ardent views now coincided most completely with her own.

For ER, AYC leaders represented hope for the best of liberal America. Christian theology students, Jewish children of immigrants, black and white activists from the rural South and urban North imagined a nation united for progressive antifascist action.

A week after Kristallnacht, ER contemplated her future and her new allies. On 18 November, she defended the AYC at the annual luncheon of New York's branch of the American Association of University Women and spoke of the need for courage and fearlessness in perilous times.

Helen Rogers Reid, vice president of the *New York Herald Tribune*, introduced ER as a woman who had "the qualities of mind of the great scholars—'flexibility and complete free-mindedness.' " ER's speech was bold: She rejected the current Red Scare tactics which branded the AYC communist and her a dupe or fool: Such name-calling had destroyed democracy in Europe, and she wanted democracy to survive here.

"People whose opinions I respect" had warned her not to attend the AYC convention.

> [But] I didn't think that those youngsters could turn me into a Communist, so I went just the same. . . .
>
> I listened to speeches which you and I could easily have torn to shreds. The Chinese listened while the Japanese spoke; the boy from India spoke with the British delegates. . . . Nobody hissed or left the room. I have been in lots of gatherings of adults who did not show that kind of respect. . . .

She spoke with many delegates, asked what they thought of the Soviet Union; she left convinced that there was interest in communism, but not domination by communists: "We who have training, and have minds that we know how to use must not be swept away" by fear and propaganda. The urgent problems before the United States and the world required scrutiny, debate, honest disagreement, democratic participation, not a wild and fearful flight from controversy.

After the luncheon, anticipating future events with her new young friends and co-conspirators, ER went on a shopping spree and decided to change her public image. She had already altered her hairstyle to a more free-fashioned "modified upswing coiffure," and she now refurbished her wardrobe. According to the press, ER selected unusually glamorous and dramatic styles for both day and evening wear. Among her eight new costumes was a floor-length "evening gown of glacier satin in an ashes-of-roses shade"; a dinner gown "of Bagheera velvet in Lanvin red"; a "black crepe gown cut with V-neck, back and front, worn with a gold cloth jacket." For daytime, ER selected "a grape-wine ensemble with tuxedo reveres of skunk, and a teal-blue frock adorned with fourteen strands of pearls. . . ."

On 22 November 1938, ER embarked on a dangerous mission when she keynoted the radical biracial Southern Conference on Human Welfare, in Birmingham, Alabama. For the first time since the Civil War, Southern liberals were determined to face the race issue embedded within the region's struggling economy. Since 1890 there had been talk of a "New South," but always before, racial cruelties at the heart of peonage and poverty had been ignored in the interest of white supremacy. For decades, New South proponents echoed Henry Grady's insistence on Negro degradation "because the white race is the superior race. This is the declaration of no new truth. It has abided forever in the marrow of our bones, and shall run forever with the blood that feeds Anglo-Saxon hearts."

Race defined the limits of change for all programs ER cared about, including Arthurdale and the efforts to build decent housing to replace Washington's alley slums. Until race issues could be addressed frankly, nothing would really change.

In the aftermath of Kristallnacht, there was a new level of commitment and urgency at the Birmingham meeting. Regional race and antiunion violence was behind the call for the SCHW, first conceived as a civil liberties conference by Joseph Gelders and Lucy Randolph Mason. According to Virginia Durr, they wanted to deal with the "terrible things happening" to CIO organizers in Mississippi. Many people were beaten; crosses were burned; the Wagner Labor Relations Act was held in contempt. In Tupelo, Ida Sledge, kin to the Bankheads of Alabama, sent by the International Ladies Garment Workers Union, was run out of town. John Rankin represented Tupelo in Congress, and "he was anti-Semitic and anti-black and very much against unions." He called everyone in the CIO a communist, and it was time for a meeting.

The entire venture was fortified by FDR's National Emergency Council's study of the South, by Lowell Mellet, Arthur Raper, Lucy Randolph Mason, Frank Graham (president of the University of North Carolina), and Clark Foreman, with input from leading Southerners for the New Deal, including Virginia and Clifford Durr, Lister Hill, Senator John Sparkman, Tex Goldschmidt, and Abe Fortas. The Council's *Report on Economic Conditions of the South* announced that the South was America's economic problem number one.

While the South "led the world" in cotton, tobacco, paper, and other products, it was a disaster area. The average per capita income was half the nation's; the poll tax limited voting rights to 12 percent of the population in eight Southern states, including Virginia; the region's children were being undereducated. The South was hampered by backward and colonial customs; and its entrenched leaders wanted no changes.

The Southern Conference on Human Welfare determined to change the South and challenge segregation. Fifteen hundred delegates, black and white, sat anywhere they wanted Sunday night, 21 November 1938, in the city auditorium of downtown Birmingham. According to Virginia Durr: "Oh, it was a love feast. . . . Southern meetings always include a lot of preaching and praying and hymn singing. . . . The whole meeting was just full of love and hope. It was thrilling." Frank Graham was elected chair, set a beautiful tone, "and we all went away . . . that night just full of love and gratitude. The whole South was coming together to make a new day."

Somebody reported the integrated seating at the opening-night gala, and the next morning the auditorium was surrounded by black Marias. Every police van in the city and county was there. Policemen were everywhere, inside and out. And there was Eugene "Bull" Connor "saying anybody who broke the segregation law of Alabama would be arrested." Tensions escalated; violence was in the air. The delegates complied and arranged themselves into separate sections.

ER, Mary McLeod Bethune, and Aubrey Williams arrived late that day, out of breath. ER "was ushered in with great applause," looked at the segregated audience—and took her seat on the black side. One of Bull Connor's police officers tapped ER on the shoulder and told her to move. ER noted in her memoirs: "At once the police appeared to remind us of the rules and regulations on segregation."

As if to announce fascism would not triumph here, ER refused to "give in" and placed her chair between the white and black sections. Pauli Murray recalled that ER's demonstration of defiance and courage meant everything to the young people of the South, who now knew they were not alone. Although the national press did not report ER's brave action, the weekly *Afro-American* editorialized: "If the people of the South do not grasp this gesture, we must. Sometimes actions speak louder than words."

ER was given a little folding chair and sat in the middle of whatever meeting hall or church she attended for the rest of the four-day meeting. She said she refused to be segregated, and carried the folding chair with her wherever she went. According to Durr: "Policemen followed us everywhere to make sure the segregation laws were observed, but they didn't arrest Mrs. Roosevelt."

ER's address to the SCHW stirred the packed auditorium:

> We are the leading democracy of the world and as such must prove to the world that democracy is possible and capable of living up to the principles upon which it was founded. The eyes of the world are upon us, and often we find they are not too friendly eyes.

ER emphasized "universal education" in which "every one of our citizens, regardless of nationality, or race," might be allowed to flourish.

The next day, she participated in a workshop on youth problems, which organized a SCHW youth council to work directly with NYA and CCC. The workshop included former theology student turned radical Arkansas activist Howard Lee, Birmingham attorney Helen Fuller, and Myles Horton. ER was particularly impressed by Lee, who became chair of the new Council of Young Southerners—which ER personally supported—and then executive secretary of the SCHW.

A dramatic moment occurred when Aubrey Williams joked about revolution. He was "a very jolly, funny fellow, always cracking jokes." It was a throwaway line about the usefulness of "class warfare," but it received endless radio coverage. The press milked it for days: Marxist WPA leader shows New Deal's true content. FDR called Aubrey: "What are you and my wife doing down there? What do you mean by . . . saying you are for the revolution?"

Aubrey, "heartsick," went to ER and offered to resign. But she said, "You will do no such thing," and immediately called her husband. FDR did not want Aubrey's resignation; he wanted him "to quit making speeches."

Williams's career was not over, but FDR refused to appoint him head of WPA to replace Hopkins, the job he actually did for two years, throughout Hopkins's long illness and convalescence. ER felt personally betrayed when FDR instead appointed conservative Army engineer Colonel F. C. Harrington. Nevertheless, NYA was given significant authority and made a permanent agency, and ER felt fortified and encouraged by the burgeoning grassroots movements represented by the AYC and the SCHW. She believed that their determined activity would move the New Deal forward.

The 1938 SCHW adopted thirty-six resolutions, all of which involved the plight of African-Americans, and eight of which directly concerned racial issues, including freedom for the four Scottsboro boys who remained in prison; availability of medical services by African-American physicians in all public health facilities; more funding for public housing and recreation facilities for African-Americans; equal funding for graduate education in state-supported colleges; and—inspired by ER's demonstration—a resolution to support fully integrated SCHW meetings.

Perceived as "one of the gravest sins that a white southerner could commit," that direct assault against tradition created a furor. The antisegregation resolution divided the delegates, some of whom withdrew, and was branded communist, subversive, and un-American. On the other hand, it transformed national assumptions about the unspeakable: White supremacy, and its primary bulwark segregation, were forevermore on the nation's agenda—put there by an integrated conference, led by Southern New Dealers.

Traditional "race etiquette" was also challenged when Louise Charlton called on Mary McLeod Bethune to speak. According to Virginia Durr:

> She said, "Mary, do you wish to come to the platform?" Mrs. Bethune rose. She looked like an African queen. . . . "My name is Mrs. Bethune." So Louise had to say, "Mrs. Bethune, will you come to the platform?" That sounds like a small thing now, but that was a big dividing line. A Negro woman in Birmingham, Alabama, was called Mrs. at a public meeting. . . .

Virginia Durr, wife of Clifford Durr, the assistant general counsel of the Reconstruction Finance Corporation, and sister-in-law of Justice Hugo Black, addressed the meeting to denounce the South's refusal to educate its people and the prevailing ignorance so general throughout the country. The reasons for an uninformed public, she declared, were propaganda and a controlled press dominated by Wall Street. She accused the National Manufacturers Association of being a "huge propaganda machine" intent on the "liquidation of organized labor."

From ER to Aubrey Williams to Virginia Durr, the sentiments expressed at the SCHW represented the outer borders of the New Deal. The SCHW was viciously attacked by conservatives, the KKK, and white citizens' groups. SCHW delegates were accused of eating together, partying together, all the same "old dirt . . . it was disgusting. . . ." But Virginia Durr and others were surprised by the attacks from their putative allies on the liberal left.

ER and Durr knew that there were communists in attendance, and in every radical movement for decency and social change. Although not particularly interested in communists, ER insisted on her right to work with every ally for change she could find. Like ER, Durr wanted to see an alliance of all Southern radicals opposed to fascism, and she dismissed as ideological imprisonment "the intricate distinctions" between various communists, socialists, anarchists, and Trotskyites:

> All the different groups and isms used to bore me to death. I always felt it was exactly like the distinctions in religions—are you going to get to heaven by dipping or sprinkling or total immersion. . . .

In November 1938, FDR evidently felt the same way, and in his supportive message to the liberal leaders of the South he noted:

> It is heartening to see the strength of Southern social leadership mustered to face these human problems, not locally or individually, but in a United Front from Fort Raleigh to the Alamo.

The SCHW represented an assemblage of the South's best talents, dedicated to the hardest long-range issues.* The last night of the conference was

---

* In addition to the conveners, Louise Charlton, the Durrs, Joe Gelder, and Lucy Randolph Mason, there were journalists and scholars; administration representatives, including Aubrey Williams and Mary McLeod Bethune; industrialists, lawyers, clergymen; socialists and communists, including Jane and Dolly Speed, who ran a Communist Party bookstore in Birmingham, and Rob Hall, party secretary for Alabama; AYC activist James Jackson, there as Gunnar Myrdal's assistant; politicians, including Governor Bibb Graves and Florida senator Claude Pepper; historians C. Vann Woodward, Horace Mann Bond, and Arthur Raper; sociologist Charles S. Johnson of Fisk University; Tuskegee University president F. D. Patterson; representatives of the National Urban League and the NAACP; John Davis of the National Negro Congress; Myles Horton and James Dombrowski, who ran the Highlander Folk School in Monteagle, Ten-

like "a revival meeting. All of a sudden you felt that you were not by yourself," lonely Southerners for change. Rather, ER and Justice Hugo Black, CIO leader John L. Lewis, Negro leaders from Mary McLeod Bethune to John Davis were prominent. It was "marvelous."

"It was the New Deal come south. . . . We had the feeling of having the power of the government on our side." Bull Connor had the police but he wouldn't arrest ER, and he wouldn't arrest Hugo Black. And at the end, the auditorium packed to the roof, ER and all the leaders, white and black, stood "at the center of the stage" and sang for tomorrow. After four days in downtown Birmingham, everything seemed possible.

Tommy had feared for ER's life, but the *New York Times* failed to notice ER's movable chair protest against segregation, and emphasized the economic changes called for. The SCHW had set new goals for the nation: a Federal Rural Housing Authority empowered to build one million Southern homes for $500 each, at one-tenth the cost of the new national defense program; more federal credit for farmers; federal aid for education; repeal of poll-tax laws; and a Wagner antilynching law in every state.

ER left Birmingham filled with energy and plans for the future. With Tommy, she went to Georgia to join FDR for Thanksgiving. Hick, in New York, wondered: "How did you finally get away with the trip to Birmingham? Have they torn you limb from limb yet?"

ER was unscathed, and rather excited. She wrote Hick: In addition to her speech, followed by questions for over an hour, she had long talks with Aubrey Williams and Lucy Randolph Mason, held a press conference, and presented her views in a panel on youth and another on women's labor conditions. At one lunch she "argued at length with Gov Bibb Graves [about] the poll tax and the right of the Negro to vote."

But, she confided:

> Tommy doesn't feel well on this trip. I think she was worried all day yesterday for fear I would get myself in trouble!
>
> We are going to get our hair washed and combed and our nails done before we drive down to Warm Springs this morning.

As she toured the South, between Atlanta and Birmingham, ER had an idea that would reunite Hick to politics and bring her closer into ER's own newly expanded orbit. Without preparation or discussion, ER asked Hick to

---

nessee, which ER supported and which trained union organizers; H. L. Mitchell and representatives of the Southern Tenant Farmers Union; mine workers, steelworkers, and grassroots activists.

consider taking over Molly Dewson's job as head of the Women's Democratic Committee. Surprised, Hick thought about ER's offer overnight, and replied the next morning with unqualified enthusiasm:

> I've been thinking about that Democratic National committee business. If you want to ask Jim [Farley] about me, I think it might be a good idea. I'm not particularly anxious to leave the Fair at this time, but . . . if I should do it, I'd like to do a good, thorough job, and it might not be a bad idea to start even earlier than January, 1940. . . . I think I ought to make a swing around the country to contact my women's editors, etc., and I might work them in together some way. It would be fun, wouldn't it?

Fun, and supremely important. FDR had lost many liberal battles since his overwhelming 1936 victory. Every New Deal agency was under attack, threatened with cuts, denounced as communist and dangerous. FDR promised to fight the reactionaries, and he rejected those advisers—including Farley—who urged him to move with his party to the right.

ER talked with FDR about her plan:

> He's much interested but doubts if Jim [Farley] wants a liberal Democratic party. I'll talk to Jim soon and let you know how things develop. I'd rather see you in [the newspaper] business and yet this cries to be done and is most interesting. . . .
>
> I don't suppose I can reach you on Thanksgiving . . . so here is my love dear and may you have much to be thankful for.

Hick agreed that Jim Farley was not much interested in a liberal party.

> But let's hope he has the political acumen to keep it more liberal than the Republican party. . . .
>
> Yes, my dear, I have much to be Thankful for—a great deal of that "much" being YOU.

While ER was at Warm Springs, the Nazi press announced that Germany had embarked upon "the final and unalterably uncompromising solution" to the Jewish question. In the Gestapo's official paper, *Das Schwarze Korps*, on 24 November, the front-page feature announced that it should have been done immediately, brutally, and completely in 1933. But "it had to remain theory" for lack of the "military power we possess today."

> Because it is necessary, because we no longer hear the world's screeching and because, after all, no power on earth can hinder us, we will now bring the Jewish question to its totalitarian solution.

Two weeks after Kristallnacht, accepted without notable "screeching" from any government, Hitler felt sufficiently unrestrained to publish his intentions for all Jews caught in his widening web. First would come pauperization, isolation, ghettoization. They would all be marked for positive identification. Nobody would escape. Then, the starving, bedraggled remnant would become a scrounging, begging scourge. They would be forced to crime, would be an "underworld" of "politico-criminal subhumans," breeders of Bolshevism. At that stage "we should therefore face the hard necessity of exterminating the Jewish underworld. . . . The result will be the actual and definite end of Jewry . . . and its complete extermination."

While the announcement was made two years and eight months before it was actually implemented, the time to protest and resist was at hand. After it was reprinted in the U.S. and European press, many understood the implications of such crude words given the reality of the cruelties under way in Germany, Austria, and Czechoslovakia. Since Kristallnacht, race hatred had triumphed completely and Jews had been removed from all German institutions, doomed to a pariah existence in complete segregation. Jews could no longer dine with Gentiles—not in restaurants, not anywhere; nor could they buy food in the same stores. Nazis established separate stores where Jews were restricted in the purchase of life's staples—milk, bread.

Such laws cast a torchlight on American traditions. ER made the connections: brown shirts, white sheets; the twisted cross, the burning cross. Yet the internal affairs of a nation were deemed sacrosanct, nobody else's business. ER and other citizens no longer agreed with that diplomatic principle.

Citizens of conscience petitioned FDR. Thirty-six prominent writers sent an urgent telegram, including Pearl Buck, Marc Connelly, Edna Ferber, John Gunther, Lillian Hellman, George S. Kaufman, Clifford Odets, Van Wyck Brooks, Dorothy Thompson, and Thornton Wilder:

> We feel we no longer have any right to remain silent, we feel that the American people and the American government have no right to remain silent. Thirty-five years ago a horrified America rose to its feet to protest against the Kishinev pogroms in Tsarist Russia. God help us if we have grown so indifferent to human suffering that we cannot rise now in protest against pogroms in Nazi Germany. We feel that it is deeply immoral for the American people to continue having economic relations with a country that avowedly uses mass murder to solve its economic problems.

FDR remained virtually silent about human rights abuses, and did not end trade with Germany, but he began a vigorous rearmament program, emphasizing military planes and naval construction. Immediately after Kristallnacht, on 14 November, he reported to Josephus Daniels, his Wilson-era boss, that he was working on "national defense—especially mass production of planes." By December, he ordered the navy yards to run full-time, "two shifts or even three" wherever possible. It "is time to get action."

While ER approved of all defense programs, she also called for a world-wide educational crusade to address prejudice. In November, at Warm Springs after the SCHW meetings, ER wrote her first articles specifically about Jews and race hatred. One, initially called "Tolerance," was for the *Virginia Quarterly* and attacked the kind of anticommunist hysteria that had resulted in fascist triumph and appeasement throughout so much of Europe. The other, which addressed the mounting hatred against Jews, was dated 25 November 1938.

She sent them both to Hick, who considered the article on tolerance "the best thing you've done in ages. It satisfies me completely. I gather that the President okayed it. What did he say about it?" Evidently FDR "read it" with no particular reaction, and "just said it was OK with him to send it."

FDR also read her article on Jews, which she wrote for *Liberty* magazine, without comment: "FDR read it and it is the way I feel so I hope no one whom I care about will have their feelings hurt."

Untitled, ER's "Jewish article" called for a campaign of understanding to confront "the present catastrophe for Jew and Gentile alike. . . . In books . . . schools, newspapers, plays, assemblies we want incessant truth telling about these old legends that divide and antagonize and waste us."

As she struggled to understand "the kind of racial and religious intolerance which is sweeping the world today," ER rejected her former emphasis on assimilation. On 19 November 1938, ER replied to a correspondent who had written asking how to end "the ever-increasing tide of anti-Semitism": "I think it is important in this country that the Jews as Jews remain unaggressive and stress the fact that they are Americans first and above everything else."

Now ER assessed the historic hatred of Jews, their isolation, and forced ghettoization in the Middle Ages, and the ongoing contempt for Jews: Even where restrictive laws had been eased, assimilation had been "a slow process, particularly where a proud people is concerned and today we are seeing . . . a return to the attitude of the Middle Ages."

ER now pointed out that even when Jews attempted to assimilate they were condemned for "being too ostentatiously patriotic and of pushing themselves forward as nationals," as in Austria and Germany.

ER was also sensitive to the difficulties assimilated Jews faced among their coreligionists, who resented those who strayed from tradition. Never quite accepted into the majority culture, they were everywhere marginalized. She asked: How had these difficult and emotional problems been so quickly transformed into a raging epidemic of bigotry and official policies of persecution that now threatened doom.

Opposition to Jews as a race and a religion was complicated, and began with Christianity. The "blame it seems to me can not be entirely shrugged off the shoulders of the Gentiles." ER rejected ghettoization and deplored signs that appeared in many American neighborhoods that read "No Dogs or Jews Allowed."

She reviewed the cavils against Jews, their "mannerisms or traits of character which rub us the wrong way," but none of that was enough to explain this hateful, bewildering moment. There were other stereotypes used for "other nationals and we have no desire to wipe out any of them." Nobody suggested "we go forth and slay the foreign citizens" from France, Spain, Germany, Italy, or countries in Asia.

ER believed that the missing element was fear:

> It is the secret fear that the Jewish people are stronger or more able than those who still wield superior physical power over them, which brings about oppression. I believe that those nations which do not persecute are saved only by confidence in themselves and a feeling that they can still defend themselves and their own place in the world. Therefore, I am forced to the conclusion that the Jewish people though they may be in part responsible for the present situation are not as responsible as the other races who need to examine themselves and grapple with their own fears.
>
> I think we, and by we I mean the people of Europe as well as the people of the U.S., have pushed the Jewish races into Zionism and Palestine, and into their nationalistic attitude. Having that great responsibility upon us, I think it lies with us to free ourselves of our fears. . . .

Written from within the veil of her own stereotypes, ER concluded that the future was not up to the Jews.

> The Jew is almost powerless today. It depends almost entirely on the course of the Gentiles what the future holds. It can be cooperative, mutual assistance, gradual slow assimilation with justice and fair-mindedness towards all racial groups living together in different countries or it can be injustice, hatred and death.
>
> It looks to me as though the future of the Jews were tied up as it has always been with the future of all the races of the world. If they perish, we perish sooner or later. . . .

ER's first article on Jew-hatred assumed Jews were the other. It was written in language that reflected stereotypes of the 1930s. She now intended to combat those attitudes; Hick also confronted her feelings:

> I like it very much. Of course my feeling personally is that Gentiles are more afraid of the everlasting energy of the Jews than of their ability. I sus-

pect that energy, the energy of a people who have always had to go twice as far to get anywhere as people of other races, is what gives them the traits that some of us gentiles dislike so much. That's probably why they push and shove in crowds, elbow their way in ahead of you at ticket windows, and try to "put things over" on you in business deals. Thousands of years of conditioning in an unfriendly world that doesn't want them has made them that way. The result is that, given a Jew and a gentile, with equal ability, the Jew will nearly always outdistance the Gentile! Am I right or wrong?

If ER winced at her friend's words, she knew that anti-Jewish feelings were as pervasive throughout Anglo-American society as they were within the Reich. In self-protection, many prominent Jews clung to a steadfast silence, which ER regretted. Her November article on tolerance, subsequently published as *Keepers of Democracy*, was among her most forthright.

> If you are in the South someone tells you solemnly that all the members of the Committee of Industrial Organization (CIO) are Communists, or that the Negroes are all Communists. . . . In another part of the country someone tells you solemnly that the schools . . . are menaced because they are all under the influence of Jewish teachers and that the Jews, forsooth, are all Communists. And so it goes, until finally you realize that people have reached a point where anything which will save them from Communism is a godsend; and if Fascism or Nazism promises more security than our own democracy we may even turn to them.

She recalled that as a child her uncle Theodore Roosevelt once said "that when you are afraid to do a thing, that was the time to go and do it. Every time we shirk making up our minds or standing up for a cause in which we believe, we weaken our character and our ability to be fearless."

To fight intolerance, we must fight fear. Fascism depended on fear and intolerance; on lies and twisted words; on force and violence. ER rejected easy solutions, and defended especially the new movements the AYC and the SCHW represented.

ER was also convinced that this moment presented a particular challenge to women "to foster democracy" and reignite their movement.

> Only our young people still seem to have some strength and hope, and apparently we are afraid to give them a helping hand. . . .
>
> I think we need a rude awakening, to make us exert all the strength we have to face facts as they exist in our country and in the world, and to make us willing to sacrifice all that we have from the material standpoint in order that freedom and democracy may not perish from this earth.

ER challenged Americans to think and act politically, to engage in activist citizenship, to become their best selves. A sense of personal unimportance was encouraged by dictators. Democracy depended on "freedom from prejudice, and public awareness." It required education, economic security, and personal devotion, "a real devotion to freedom. . . . Freedom is something to guard jealously," but it can never be "freedom for me and not for you."

The bolder ER became, the tougher and more adamant her statements, the higher her public approval rating soared. On 16 January 1939, the *New York Times* published a poll taken by George Gallup regarding America's feelings about ER during 1938. The results were astounding. Two voters in every three voted in her favor (67 percent approved of her conduct, 33 percent disapproved). The poll was accompanied by such comments as "She lives a useful life and keeps busy." "She sets a good example by encouraging worthwhile things."

According to the poll she had a greater approval rating than FDR. Over 30 million favored ER, while the president polled 27.5 million. Also unlike FDR, ER had the approval of a majority of voters even in the upper income group: upper income, 54 percent; middle income, 65 percent; lower income, 76 percent.

Given the nature of the controversies ER engaged in and her challenge to work for the transformation of customs and traditions that subjected so many to poverty and powerlessness, America's response indicated a commitment to the very democracy she spoke about so earnestly. ER touched a nerve center in America, and the country would never be the same.

On 20 December, ER and Hick shared their annual pre-Christmas party. Free of the tensions that had soured their friendship on occasion, the evening was warm, tender, perfect. Hick wrote:

> Dearest, I did have a grand time last night. I can't really find words to tell you about it. It isn't the *things* you give people . . . but the thought and care that you put into it all that means so much. All the little details, like the artichokes for supper, the candles and Christmas tree, the warmth and coziness of it all, the expression on your face when one is opening the presents and is pleased—oh, darling, you are swell! It's a kind of generosity of the soul that you have. . . .
>
> You will gather, Mrs. Doaks (Joseph V., of Oelwein, Iowa) that I had a thoroughly good time last night and this morning. . . .

ER returned to Washington on the 23rd, where she was greeted by a "house full of people and so far all is well! FDR has a slight cold but not bad."

She reported: "I've worked all day on mail and Xmas things and done nothing official but have Lady Lindsay bring some English ladies to tea. . . ."

But her private fears were revealed in her reply to Hick's lost Christmas greeting. Although she wanted Hick close by, and more routinely in Washington, as her new job as Molly Dewson's replacement would assure, she did not want Hick to entertain illusions about long and exclusive times together:

> Your day letter came today and I wish you a quiet heart and a sense of serenity. —Few of us know what our heart's desire is dear and if we had what we fancied was our desire it would probably turn to dust and ashes so serenity and peace are safer wishes dear! . . .

On 28 December, all thoughts of gloom were suspended entirely for a night of carefree festivity to honor ER's niece Eleanor Roosevelt II, Hall's daughter. It was the first debutante dance in the White House since William Howard Taft's 1910 party for his daughter Helen. ER hosted a splendid affair and looked dazzling in "bright red chiffon sparkling with rhinestones and jeweled embroidery." ER II was radiant in an "all white ruffled frock of French organdy," and led the dancing with her father in a Virginia reel. The First Lady and her brother waltzed through the night, surrounded by friends and family, mostly cousins, including TR's family, and SDR was regal in "black satin and old lace." The evening was highlighted by Mayris (Tiny) Chaney's new dance, the Eleanor Glide.

As 1938 drew to a close, ER emphasized action, a politics of example. She had joined the fray with her first April 1934 speech to black educators, when she said that we all "go ahead together, or we go down together." In a 1937 address in Harlem, to "an enthusiastic, cheering crowd of 2500" at the Mother A.M.E. Zion Church, she called for "equal rights" for all Americans:

> In this country we should all have, certainly, equal rights, and minorities should certainly have those exactly as majorities have them.

On 10 February 1938, ER commemorated the seventy-fifth anniversary of the Emancipation Proclamation by asserting that while Abraham Lincoln took the "first step toward the abolition of slavery . . . we still do tolerate slavery in several ways." Her words, addressed to nine thousand people at a meeting sponsored by the National Negro Congress, were electrifying:

> There are still slaves of many different kinds, and today we are facing another era in which we have to make certain things become facts rather than beliefs.

As Europe fell to fascism, ER and her new network of youth and race radicals heralded the greatest changes in America since the betrayal of Reconstruction.

In her 8 December 1938 column, ER criticized liberals, smug partisans, and patriots for celebrating incomplete victories. The speeches given the night before at a dinner for the Léon Blum colony for European refugees in Palestine had annoyed her profoundly. She supported the refugee sanctuary founded to honor France's first socialist and Jewish prime minister. His popular front government collapsed after the left withdrew because he failed to support democratic Spain, and the right campaigned with the slogan "Better Hitler than Blum." In the bitter context of that meeting, ER was dismayed by the unwarranted pride and complacency of the speakers:

"As I listened . . . I could not help thinking how much all human beings like to fool themselves. . . . [They] made us feel that . . . we were more virtuous and fortunate than any other people in the world. Of course, I concede this, and I feel for me it is true, for I have been free and fortunate all my life. While I listened, however, I could not help thinking of some of the letters which pass through my hands.

"Are you free if you cannot vote, if you cannot be sure that the same justice will be meted out to you as to your neighbor, . . . if you are barred from certain places and from certain opportunities? . . .

"Are you free when you can't earn enough, no matter how hard you work, to feed and clothe and house your children properly? Are you free when your employer can turn you out of a company house and deny you work because you belong to a union?"

Her thoughts turned to refugees in this country, "of the little girl who wrote me not long ago: 'Why do other children call me names and laugh at my talk? I just don't live in this country very long yet.'" ER concluded:

"There are lots and lots of things which make me wonder whether we ever look ourselves straight in the face and really mean what we say when we are busy patting ourselves on the back. . . ."

With grit, determination, and a very high heart, ER helped launch America's crusade for freedom in the fascist era. She was fortified every day by her new allies, her abiding partnership with FDR, love for the people in her life, and love of the world.

NOTES

1: Becoming First Lady

10 For Elisabeth Marbury see *Notable American Women.* See also Kim Marra, "A Lesbian Marriage of Cultural Consequence: Elisabeth Marbury and Elsie de Wolfe, 1886–1933," in Kim Mara and Robert Schanke, eds., *Passing Performances: Queer Readings of Leading Players in American Theater History* (University of Michigan, 1998). In the *Women's Democratic News,* ER celebrated Marbury's "ease of expression and witty and fertile mind. She was always interesting even though we did not always agree with her. . . ."

11 For Malvina Thompson Scheider, first called Tommy by the children, I am grateful for information from her niece, Eleanor Lund Zartman.

12 *"We may have . . . a new social and economic order":* ER's broadcast quoted in *NYT,* 29 Nov. 1932.

12 *Prohibition:* The national ban on the "manufacture, sale, or transportation of intoxicating liquors," called the Volstead Act, was the 18th amendment to the Constitution ratified in 1919. A year after ER's broadcast, the 21st Amendment to repeal the 18th passed on 5 Dec. 1933, by over 70 percent. Norman Vincent Peale and the WCTU condemned ER's broadcasts; *NYT,* 10 Dec. 1932; 15 Jan. 1933.

12 *ER's last broadcast, in the pre–White House series:* Quoted in *NYT,* 5 Mar. 1933.

13 *ER's initial traveling intentions: NYT,* 25 Feb. 1933; Raymond Moley, quoted in Frank Freidel, *Launching the New Deal* (Little, Brown 1973), p. 291. At *Grief:* Hickok, *Reluctant First Lady,* pp. 91–92.

13–14 *ER's new wardrobe: NYT,* 25 Feb. 1933; complimented, *NYT,* 5 Mar. 1933.

13–14 *shopping spree and Morgenthau:* ER to FDR, nd, Feb. 1933, Roosevelt Family Papers, Children, Box 16.

15 *"ER was disappointed":* Morgenthau was at first appointed to the Farm Credit Administration. For Howe's reaction, see Alfred B. Rollins, *Roosevelt and Howe* (Knopf, 1962), p. 392; see also Henry Morgenthau III, *Mostly Morgenthaus: A Family History* (Ticknor & Fields, 1991), p. 267.

15 *Old school chums rallied:* Helen Cutting Wilmerding to ER, 14 June 1933; ER to HCW, 23 June; Joseph Lash, *Eleanor and Franklin* (W. W. Norton, 1971), p. 365; ER in Junior League journal, 1933.

16 *Alice Roosevelt Longworth on FDR:* Quoted in Bess Furman, *Washington*

By-Line (Knopf, 1949), p. 203; cf. Carol Felsenthal, *Alice Roosevelt Longworth* (G. P. Putnam's Sons, 1988).

16 *FDR's Fiftieth birthday:* Ted Morgan, *F.D.R.: A Biography* (Simon & Schuster, 1985), p. 336.

16–17 *Ida Saxton McKinley:* Betty Boyd Caroli, *First Ladies* (Oxford University Press, 1987), pp. 57, 109–12; Carl S. Anthony, *First Ladies, 1789–1961* (William Morrow, 1990), p. 284.

17 *Ellen Axson Wilson:* see esp. *Ellen Axson Wilson: First Lady/Artist,* by Frank J. Aucella, Patricia A. Piorkowski Hobbs, with Frances Wright Saunders (Woodrow Wilson House National Trust); the Florence Griswold Museum, Old Lyme, Connecticut; and Frances Wright Saunders, *Ellen Axson Wilson: First Lady Between Two Worlds* (University of North Carolina Press, 1985); and Joy Gordon and Jeffrey Andersen, *En Plein Air: The Art Colonies at East Hampton and Old Lyme, 1880–1930* (Florence Griswold and Guild Hall Museums, 1989).

18 *Ellen Wilson on "exactions of life":* Anthony, p. 349. Ellen Wilson's death in *NYT,* quoted in Caroli, p. 142.

18 ER was moved by the second Mrs. Wilson, especially Edith Wilson's gracious manner when they visited the American Hospital: "She left a few flowers at each boy's bed, and I was lost in admiration because she found something to say to each one."

ER, *Autobiography,* p. 99; Jonathan Daniels, *The End of Innocence* (Lippincott, 1954), p. 280; Anthony, p. 359.

18 *Mary Peck:* See Daniels, p. 190; Anthony, pp. 359, 370. Bernard Baruch allegedly contributed $75,000 to prevent publication of the letters, and in 1915 Mrs. Peck evidently acknowledged a much smaller "loan."

18 *Calvin Coolidge:* See ER, *Autobiography,* p. 102; at the sink, Anthony, pp. 401, 400, 453.

18–19 *Lou Henry Hoover and Oscar DePriest:* I am grateful to Alan Teller for his work on the Herbert Hoover and Lou Henry Hoover installations at the Hoover Library and Museum in Iowa. See also Joan Hoff-Wilson, *Herbert Hoover: Forgotten Progressive* (Little, Brown, 1975); Anthony, pp. 440–446.

19 *Edith Roosevelt and ER:* See Anthony, pp. 305–6; adulterers shunned, pp. 299–300; tusks and grin, Sylvia Jukes Morris, *Edith Kermit Roosevelt* (Coward McCann Geoghagan, 1980), p. 126; beloved shackles, Caroli, p. 124.

20 In 1924 ER campaigned for Al Smith, in a car with a giant teapot, which implicitly connected her cousin Ted to the Republicans' Teapot Dome naval oil land scandal; see Blanche Wiesen Cook, *Eleanor Roosevelt, Vol. I: 1884–1933* (Viking, 1992) (hereafter, BWC, vol. 1); and Morris, p. 479.

20 ER to Aunt Edith, ibid, p. 483; 17 Nov. 1933, ER Derby Papers, Houghton Library.

20 *"My poor cousin":* Carol Felsenthal, *Alice Roosevelt Longworth* (G. P. Putnam's Sons, 1988), p. 171.

21 Nicholas Longworth died of pneumonia on 10 Apr. 1931 while visiting Laura Curtis, his "poker pal" and former lover in Aiken, South Carolina. Called when his condition became dire, Alice was present but refused to be by his side during his final hours. She relinquished that place to his current mistress, the beautiful

Alice Dows. She hated her husband so thoroughly by the time of his death that she burned his papers and most precious possessions, including his Stradivarius violin. Felsenthal, pp. 166, 168.

21 *Alice Roosevelt's attacks:* Teague, p. 161; Felsenthal, pp. 171–73.

21 *ER on gossip:* "Curiosity," *Saturday Evening Post*, 24 Aug. 1935, p. 9.

22 *breast-feeding: Babies*, Apr. 1933.

22 ER's most egregious advice regarding regularity and thumb-sucking is in the Apr. and May issues of *Babies*; 1950s quoted in Paul M. Dennis, "Between Watson and Spock: ER's Advice on Child-Rearing from 1928 to 1952," *Journal of American Culture* (Spring 1995), pp. 44–45.

22 In 1933, ER wrote: "I believe very strongly that it is better to allow children too much freedom than too little." Mothers should not "nag their children about little things." *It's Up to the Women*, pp. 130–31. To protect the younger boys, ER to Isabella Greenway, nd, Greenway Papers, Tucson, Spring, 1932; ER to Greenway with gratitude, 6 Sept. 1932.

23 *ER on TR and Elliott: Hunting Big Game in the 'Eighties* (Scribner's Sons, 1933), p. 33.

24 *"You can't rent your grandfather":* ER, *This I Remember* (hereafter *TIR*), p. 81.

24 *ER to Metropolitan Opera audience: NYT*, 11 Dec. 1932. *Simon Boccanegra*, program 10 Dec. 1932, Saturday matinee, 2 pm, Maria Mueller as Maria Boccanegra; with thanks to John Pennino, assistant archivist, Metropolitan Opera Association, libretto translated by Lionel Salter, 1977, Deutsche Grammophon.

25 *ER invited 72 relatives: NYT*, 5 Mar. 1933.

25 *Emma Bugbee: NY Herald-Tribune*, 5 Mar. 1933.

26 *Germany: NYT*, 5 Mar. 1933.

27 O'Day, "The Inaugural Festivities," *Women's Democratic News*, Mar. 1933.

27 *Cermak:* Lorena Hickok, *Eleanor Roosevelt: Reluctant First Lady* (Dodd, Mead, 1980 [1962]), p. 82; on Cermak's death, *NY Herald-Tribune*, 27 Feb. 1933; *NYT*, 6 Mar. 1933; *Tribune*, 7 Mar. 1933; Freidel, pp. 169–74.

28 *On Walsh: NY Herald-Tribune*, 3 Mar. 1933; ER pp. 69, 78–79.

28 *Pleas for ball:* See esp. *NY Herald-Tribune*, 4 Mar. 1933.

28 *On balls:* See esp. *Washington Evening Star*, 2 Mar. 1933; also *Tribune* and *NYT*, 5 Mar. 1933.

29 *ER's party: Washington Star*, 5 Mar. 1933.

29 *ER on FDR: Autobiography*, p. 159.

29 *his mind: TIR*, p. 117.

29 ER to FDR, Swedish diplomat, Apr. 1936, nd, Roosevelt Family, Children, Box 16.

29–30 Felix Frankfurter, memo of visit, 8 Mar. 1933, in Max Freedman, ed., *Roosevelt and Frankfurter: Their Correspondence, 1928–1945* (Little, Brown, 1967), p. 113. Frankfurter declined even though FDR said it would be easier to appoint him to the Supreme Court from a Federal post; there was not only the question of Frankfurter's politics and his support of Sacco and Vanzetti, but his "race."

2: Public and Private Domains

32 *Democratic and simple:* Inaugural articles, especially Associated Press's Lorena Hickok, *NY Herald-Tribune,* 5 Mar. 1933; Apr. unsigned AP articles on ER by Hick, Hickok Papers.

32 *Bess Furman wrote:* Furman, p. 151; Hickok, *Reluctant First Lady,* pp. 106–7.

32 *Reorganized the household:* ER to Hick, 8, 9, 19, 20 Mar. 1933.

32 *My first act:* ER, *TIR,* pp. 80–81; Lincoln's bedroom, ibid.

33 *Details of rooms:* See White House histories, esp. Frank Freidel and William Pencak, eds., *The White House* (Northeastern University Press, 1994); Wendell Garrett, ed., *Our Changing White House* (Northeastern University Press, 1995); White House Historical Association Publications, Washington, DC 20503.

35 *Pool time: TIR,* pp. 117–18.

35 *George Fox:* ER was particularly grateful to Lieutenant Commander George Fox, who was FDR's physical therapist in residence, *TIR,* pp. 116, 118; on water polo, Hickok, p. 149; and Henry Goddard Leach, *My Last 70 Years.* (Bookman Associates, 1956), p. 213. I am grateful to Dorothy Warren for this reference.

35 Henrietta Nesbitt, *White House Diary* (Doubleday, 1948), p. 131.

35 *ER often impatient: TIR,* pp. 80–81; Hickok, p. 113.

35–36 On Crim and J. B. West, in J. B. West, *Upstairs at The White House* (Warner, 1947), pp. 30–31, 51.

36 *Emma Bugbee recalled:* Bugbee in *Reader's Digest,* Oct. 1963, p. 95; *TIR,* p. 4.

37 *Once, only once:* Hickok, *Reluctant First Lady,* p. 148.

37 *Missy LeHand: TIR,* p. 114; excluded, p. 108.

38 *Tommy seemed gruff:* Lillian Rogers Parks and Frances Leighton, *The Roosevelts: A Family in Turmoil* (Prentice Hall, 1981), pp. 67–69. Tommy, long separated from her husband, lived with her new companion, Henry Osthagan, who worked for the Treasury Department.

38 *Edith Helm: TIR,* p. 83.

39 *Louise Hackmeister: TIR,* p. 115; *NYT,* 3 Mar. 1933; Nesbitt, p. 39; Parks, p. 46.

39 *Mary Eben: TIR,* p. 115; Rogers, pp. 253–54.

39–40 For FDR's staff, see esp. Charles Hurd, *When the New Deal Was Young and Gay* (Harper, 1965), pp. 85, 88–89.

40 *Gus and Earl Miller: TIR,* pp. 28, 70; Hurd, pp. 85–86.

40–41 *ER's press conferences:* Hickok, pp. 108–9; Maurine Beasley, ed., *The White House Press Conferences of Eleanor Roosevelt* (Garland, 1983); cf. Furman.

41 On 8 Mar. Bess Furman interrupted ER's contemplative walk home from Justice Oliver Wendell Holmes's birthday tea with the good news that Hick would attend. ER to Hick, 8 Mar. 1933.

42–43 *Nobody else:* ER to Hick, 11 Mar. 1933; hilarious details, 10 Mar. 1933.

43 On Monday, 13 Mar., ER's first visit to New York as First Lady was filled with private business. According to Hick's report, she went to her physician and dentist, hosted fifteen Todhunterites for tea on 65th Street, addressed a Todhunter assembly, attended a student's wedding; shopped for clothes, and "had a private appointment for dinner."

44 The WTUL temporary shelters committee included ER's daughter Anna, Fannie Hurst, Nancy Cook, Pauline Emmet, Mary Dreier, and Rose Schneiderman. WTUL meeting, and ER's activities, *NYT*, 15, 16 Mar. 1933.

44 *The Roosevelts' 28th anniversary:* Nesbitt, pp. 43–44; FDR marked the occasion with a note and a check to his wife: "Dearest Babs: After a fruitless week of thinking and lying awake to find whether you need or want undies, dresses, hats, shoes, sheets, towels, rouge, soup plates, candy, flowers, lamps, laxative pills, whisky, beer, etchings or caviar / I GIVE IT UP!

"And yet I know you lack some necessity of life—so go to it with my love and many happy returns of the day! F.D.R." *FDR's Letters*, III, p. 339. There is no record of ER's gift to her husband.

44–45 *Bonus Marchers:* Roger Daniels, *The Bonus March: An Episode of The Great Depression* (Greenwood, 1971), esp. pp. 167–81; Joan Hoff-Wilson, *Herbert Hoover*, pp. 161–62; ER was stunned. *TIR*, p. 112.

46 *An hour with the veterans: TIR*, pp. 111–13; *NYT*, 16, 17 May 1933; Furman, p. 171; Beasley, p. 9.

46–47 *Women's Press Club frolic: NYT*, 21 Mar. 33; Furman, pp. 160–61. Hick's unpublished fifteen-page article on this visit, Hick's papers.

48 *Blue sky & sun:* ER to Hick, 13 Apr. 1933.

48 *On 12 Apr.* ER to Hick; on Ramsay MacDonald and U.S. peace leaders in World War I, see Blanche Wiesen Cook, "Democracy in Wartime: Antimilitarism in England and the U.S., 1914–1918," in Charles Chatfield, ed., *Peace Movements in America* (Schocken Books, 1973). See also Charles Chatfield, "Alternative Anti-War Strategies of the Thirties," ibid.

49 Lillian Wald to Mary Rozet Smith, with FDR-MacDonald correspondence references, 12 Apr. 1933, *JA Papers Project*, 24–1074.

50 *20 Apr., Traveler's Aid and Amelia Earhart: NYT*, 20, 21 Apr. 1933; Emma Bugbee, *NY Herald-Tribune*, 21 Apr. 1933.

50 *ER rejoiced in the modern adventure: NYT*, 10 Dec. 1932.

51 *"Do you shake and think": TIR*, pp. 91–92.

3: ER's Revenge

52 *ER was actually fussy:* Parks, p. 19.

52 *fresh-cut flowers: TIR*, p. 78.

52 *Flowers pleased ER:* During her second week in Washington, ER attended an amaryllis show. She considered it "a good color show," but the amaryllis was "not a flower I would enjoy." ER to Hick, 21 Mar. 1933.

52–53 *Harold Ickes was discreet: The Secret Diary of Harold Ickes: The First Thousand Days, 1933–1936* (Simon and Schuster, 1954), pp. 248–49.

53 Ickes, 19 Dec. 1934, pp. 248–49.

53 *subject of derision:* Catherine Mackenzie, *NYT*, 9 Dec. 1934, "Simple Fare for the White House" sect. 6; *NYT*, 13 Apr. 1935; Ickes Diary, 19 Dec. 1934, pp. 248–49; FDR joked, Ickes Diary, pp. 250–51.

54 *The home economics movement:* See esp. Martha Van Rensselaer and Flora Rose to ER, beginning Nov. 1930, Home Economic Records, Cornell University,

23/2/749; Flora Rose Interview, New York State College of Home Economics Records, c 1953.

54 *balanced meals:* Bugbee, *NY Herald-Tribune,* 21 Mar. 1933. See also "MRS R for Home Science," *NYT,* 27 Mar. 1933; *Time,* 27 Nov. 1933.

55 *even ER was mystified:* Henrietta Nesbitt, *White House Diary* (Doubleday, 1948), pp. 14–15; peas, p. 192; Schrafft's, p. 64; watery, p. 186; headlines, pp. 185–87. ER's poem to FDR, 29 Jan. 1938/PSF, box 177.

55 *ER had persuaded herself that FDR had no serious gourmet interests:* Even Nesbitt knew better than that, and tried to consider some "fancy" dishes on occasion. See Nesbitt, pp. 66, 68–70, for ER's list of FDR's favorite foods.

55 *ER on bacon and eggs:* S. J. Woolf, "Mrs. R of the Strenuous Life," *NYT Magazine,* 11 Oct. 1932.

56 *Major bit: TIR,* p. 118. Rosamond Pinchot, Gifford Pinchot's niece who had worked at ER's campaign headquarters and was a young reporter and actress, visited ER on 28 Apr. 1933, and observed Major's attack on Richard Bennett, Canada's prime minister: As ER walked down the stairs to say goodbye, Major "flew at him making angry sounds. Then he bit the Premier in the thigh. Bennett was rather taken aback but said, 'It's all right, he didn't draw blood.' I made the tactless remark, 'An ideal dog for the White House.' " Pinchot's diaries, 28 Apr. 1933, Nancy Pinchot Pitman collection; see also Bess Furman's account, pp. 165, 188.

57 *Upset by those who burned cigarette holes in the tablecloths:* Nesbitt, p. 276.

57 *ER's guests made demands:* Nesbitt, p. 195.

57 Katherine Buckley to Farley, 30 Jan. 1933; Farley to Katherine Buckley, 15 Feb. 1933; ER to Miss Buckley, 17 Feb. 1933, box 1256/100.

58 *Worker's rights to the White House:* Nesbitt, p. 211.

58 *SDR:* Nesbitt, pp. 212–13.

58 *Lillian Rogers Parks on Mrs. Nesbitt:* 30–31; p. 266 (n); pp. 69–70.

59 Bess Truman, J. B. West (with Mary Lynn Kotz), *Upstairs at the White House: My Life with the First Ladies* (Warner, 1974), p. 78.

4: Mobilizing the Women's Network

60 FDR's first hundred days of legislation and executive orders resulted in the Banking Act; the Economy Act which cut veterans benefits and government salaries; the Agricultural Adjustment Act (AAA); the Glass-Steagall Act, which created the Federal Deposit Insurance Corporation (FDIC); the National Industrial Recovery Act (NIRA)—the centerpiece of the first New Deal, which launched both the National Recovery Administration (NRA) and the Public Works Administration (PWA), and also contained a provision (Article 7A) to promote independent unionism; the Federal Emergency Relief Administration (FERA); the Securities and Exchange Commission (SEC); the Tennessee Valley Authority (TVA); and the Civilian Conservation Corps (CCC).

60 Frederic Howe's memoir, *Confessions of a Reformer,* detailed his work with antiwar activists and radicals.

62 *During the 1920s, ER's feminist articles:* See esp., "Women Must Learn to Play the Game as Men Do," *Redbook,* 1928; see BWC, vol. I, pp. 365–71; reprinted in

Allida Black, *What I Hope to Leave Behind: The Essential Essays of Eleanor Roosevelt* (Carlson, 1995).

62 Florence Kelley was an independent socialist who translated Friedrich Engels and was active in many causes. One of the original 1909 organizers of the National Association for the Advancement of Colored People (NAACP), like ER, her radicalism emerged out of the conditions of her own childhood. Kathryn Kish Sklar, ed., *Notes on 60 Years: The Autobiography of Florence Kelley* (Charles Kerr, 1986), pp. 30–31; see also Sklar, *Florence Kelley and the Nation's Work: The Rise of Women's Political Culture, 1830–1900* (Yale University Press, 1995).

62 *the mother of us all:* Frances Perkins decided on a career in social reform after Kelley addressed her graduating class at Mount Holyoke in 1902. Susan Ware, *Beyond Suffrage: Women in the New Deal* (Harvard University Press, 1981), pp. 35–37.

62 *ER on Sheppard-Towner:* Congressional Record, 6 Jan. 1927, p. 1154; see also Sklar's introduction to Florence Kelley *Autobiography,* pp. 30–31, 112. A revision of the Sheppard Towner law, defunded in 1927, was included in the Social Security Act of 1935. But WIC was so limited most African-Americans were denied care. Subsequently extended, it became an accepted part of American life until it was again attacked and defunded during the 1990s. Cf. Mimi Abramovitz, Linda Gordon, and Alice Kessler-Harris.

63 *ER was attacked: Woman Patriot,* 1, 15 Feb., 1928. I am grateful to Christie Balka for this reference.

63–64 *ER–Robert Bingham exchange on child labor:* ER to Bingham, 8 Jan. 1934, 100/ Box 1286; ER to Frances Perkins, 3 Feb. 1934, Perkins Papers, Columbia; Bingham to ER, 14 Jan. 1934; ER to Bingham, 27 Jan. 1934, FDRL.

64 *child labor amendment an entering wedge:* ER in *NYT,* 20 May 1934; May 1934 column in *Woman's Home Companion.*

64–65 *Kelley and white labels:* See Kathryn Kish Sklar, in Linda Kerber, et al., eds., *US History as Women's History* (University of North Carolina Press, 1995).

65 *ER and Nancy Astor at 30th anniversary NCL:* Lady Astor championed working women and social reform, including minimum wages and fair labor practices. A longtime friend of the NCL, she was later associated with anti-communism and fascist "appeasement." Kelley and ER quoted in *NYT,* 14 Dec. 1932; *Accredited "newsgirls":* Margaret Chase Smith to BWC, in Skowhegan, Maine, June 1992.

65 *ER's press conferences:* See esp. Maurine Beasley, pp. 42–46, 103–4 passim. Emma Bugbee, Oral History, Columbia.

66 *No gossip, no leaks:* Emma Bugbee, *NY Herald-Tribune,* 4 Mar. 1933; also Oral History.

66 *thrown into the mud: NYT,* 14 Apr. 33.

66 ER intended to manage the news, and refused to speak publicly about certain subjects, notably birth control—although she "always belonged" to the birth control league: ER to Agnes Brown Leach, 21 June 1935, 100, Box 1346. In 1931 spoke at an event to honor Margaret Sanger. See Ellen Chesler, *Woman of Valor: Margaret Sanger* (Simon & Schuster 1992), p. 339.

66 *rejected ghostwriters:* White House press office announcement, 15 Aug. 1933, ppf Box 1.

67 Anna Ickes's book, *Mesa Land: The History and Romance of the American*

Southwest, was published by Houghton Mifflin in November 1933, the same month as ER's book *It's Up to the Women*—and their reviews appeared side by side in major newspapers; *their difficult marriage:* See T. H. Watkins, *Righteous Pilgrim: The Life and Times of Harold L. Ickes, 1874–1952* (Henry Holt, 1990), pp. 147–51, 168–71, 219–20, passim. See also Jeanne Clarke.

67 *ER on Farley: TIR,* p. 66.

68 *like Kipling's cat:* Dewson quoted in Furman, p. 228.

68 *patronage letters:* ER to Jim Farley, 20 Sept. 1933, 100, Box 1261; on McAdoo, see Douglas Craig, *After Wilson,* (Univ. of North Carolina Press, 1993), p. 32.

68 *Amy Beach:* See Adrienne Fried Block, "Amy Beach: From Song to Opera," Alice Tully Hall, 13 May 1995, program; and Block's *Amy Beach* (Oxford University Press, 1998). ER particularly enjoyed her "Silver Birches." *Musical Leader,* 9 May 1936.

68 Amy Beach was also a family friend, particularly close to ER's Aunt Corinne. Amy Beach to ER, 27 Apr. 1934; I am grateful to Adrienne Fried Block.

68 *Ruth Bryan Owen hoped for Interior:* Owen to Fannie Hurst, 3 July 1932; Hurst Papers, Austin, Texas.

69 *RBO named ambassador:* When FDR offered a State Department appointment, she wrote Fannie Hurst: "Please burn all the candles you have in front of your shrines and icons." RBO to FH, 21 Mar. 1933. See Harold Ickes's snide version of his meeting with RBO, 13 Mar. 1933; for FDR's curious role, see Ickes diary, p. 6: "She believes [FDR said] she sold herself to me."

69 *ER honored RBO:* Toasts in *NYT,* 10 May 1933; see *Notable American Women.*

69 ER named several pioneers as the great harbingers of a new day: Katharine Lenroot, chief of the Children's Bureau; her Children's Bureau associate, Dr. Martha Eliot; Dr. Louise Stanley, chief of the Bureau of Home Economics in the Department of Agriculture; Mary Anderson, since 1920 head of the Women's Bureau of the Department of Labor; and Mary McLeod Bethune, president of the National Association of Colored Women, founder of the Bethune-Cookman College in Ocala, Florida, subsequently appointed to the National Youth Administration (NYA), and chair of the Negro Division. See esp. *It's Up to the Women,* pp. 200; 193–204; *TIR,* p. 174; *NYT,* 17 Feb. 1935.

69 *seventeen-page letter:* Dewson to ER, 27 Apr. 1933; also Dewson to ER, 29 June, 2 July, 1933; see Ware, *Beyond Suffrage,* p. 49; ER to Dewson, 3 Aug. 1933, 100, Box 1259.

5: ER's New Deal for Women

70 *Initial spirit of cooperation: TIR,* p. 107.

70 *"a states' rights, limited government":* Freidel, *Launching,* p. 238.

71 *Bishop Manning on schools: NYT,* 25 Mar. 1933; ER on schools, *It's Up to the Women,* pp. 15–17, 21.

71 *ER and FDR disagreed on the Economy Act:* See especially *Women's Democratic News,* Feb. 1933; and *It's Up to the Women,* pp. 110, 120–21.

72 *Healthy family life:* pp. 85, 86–89.

72 FDR thought the teachers of America were making too much money. If they all took a 15 percent cut, he opined, "they would still be getting relatively more than in 1914!" FDR to Josephus Daniels, 27 Mar. 1933; cf. Freidel, p. 254.

72 *Schools closed or closing:* Bernard Asbell, *The FDR Memoirs* (Doubleday, 1973), p. 67; James Macgregor Burns, *The Lion and the Fox* (Harcourt, Brace, 1956), p. 172; Joyce Kornbluh, *A New Deal for Workers' Education, 1933–1942* (University of Illinois Press, 1987), p. 25.

72 *An amazing document: New Dealers,* pp. 124–28.

72–73 *Lew Douglas:* Quoted in Ted Morgan, *FDR: A Biography* (Simon & Schuster, 1985), p. 382.

73 *Isabella Greenway:* See Hope Chamberlin, *A Minority of Members: Women in the U.S. Congress* (New American Library, 1973), pp. 108 ff., and Greenway mss., congressional files, Tucson.

73 *"air our minds" luncheons:* Jack Greenway to BWC; ER to Isabella, 12 Apr. 1936; ER on Lady Lindsay, *TIR,* p. 185.

73 *Greenway on the plane within 30 minutes:* ER in *Women's Democratic News.*

73 *Their first collaboration:* Greenway, in Chamberlin; Huey Long, in Freidel, p. 244; department cuts, pp. 250–52. The hated 213 clause to fire married women, first introduced by Herbert Hoover, enraged feminists across the political spectrum. See esp. Alice Kessler-Harris and Sara Evans, *Born for Liberty* (Free Press, 1989), pp. 201–3.

74 *ER rejected FDR's idea, government workers earning more: NYT,* 11 Apr. 1933.

74 *FDR's returned 15%:* Freidel, p. 254.

74 *A bitter rule:* See esp. *My Day,* 24 July 1937; and Genevieve Parkhurst, "Is Feminism Dead?" *Harper's Magazine,* May 1935, pp. 742 ff.

74 *ER specifically rejected: It's Up to the Women,* esp. pp. 143–45, and 142–52 passim.

74 *Women and workplace:* Ibid., pp. 166–67.

75 *Mary Ritter Beard on ER: NY Herald-Tribune,* 5 Nov. 1933.

76 7 Apr. 1933, for ER's sentiments on "the evils of Prohibition," "the power of the brewery," and "the bootlegger," ER to Isabella Greenway, 23 Jan. 1932, Tucson.

77 *FDR asked for $3.3 billion:* Rex Tugwell, *The Democratic Roosevelt,* (Doubleday, 1957), p. 286.

77–78 *"Joker" clause and wage discrimination:* see *Harper's,* p. 743; Ware, pp. 91–92.

78 *"square deal for women," and "some special reason": NYT,* 12 Aug.; ER to Hick, 11, 12 Aug. 1933.

78 *Rose Schneiderman's efforts:* Annelise Orleck, *Common Sense and a Little Fire: Women and Working Class Politics in the US, 1900–1965* (University of North Carolina Press, 1995), pp. 151–54.

79 *ER on women's vigilance and boycotts: NYT,* 20 June 1933; 10 Oct. 1933; and *It's Up to the Women,* pp. 46–47.

79 After her husband, artist Charles Cary Rumsey, died in a car accident in

Sept. 1922, Mary Harriman Rumsey turned more fully to politics. In 1929 she initiated a "block aid" campaign in New York City to mobilize communities, block by block, door to door, to assist people in need. An ardent New Dealer, she encouraged her younger brother Averell to join her in Washington. Jack Greenway to BWC; see esp. S. J. Woolf, "Champion of the Consumer Speaks Out," 6 Aug. 1933; *NYT* magazine profile, *Notable American Women*; and Marjory Potts, "Averell Harriman Remembers Mary," *Junior League Review*, 1983; Caroline Ware, Radcliffe Oral History, pp. 46 ff., and Frances Perkins, Columbia Oral History Project.

79 *ER supported NRA Blue Eagle: NYT*, Oct. 1933; 8 Feb. 1934; her own shop, and professionalization of housework, *NYT*, 20 Sept. 1933; *Woman's Home Companion* (Sept. 1933).

80 *NRA fatally flawed: TIR*, p. 136. While the Supreme Court doomed NRA because it gave the president too much power, Bernard Bellush explains that industry was given most of the power: Bellush, *The Failure of the NRA* (W. W. Norton, 1975).

80–81 *TVA was the first:* During World War I, the federal government had built a great dam and hydroelectric power plant at Muscle Shoals, in northern Alabama. The electricity generated was to run nitrate plants to make gunpowder. But at war's end all work stopped. Neither Coolidge nor Hoover wanted the government to maintain a public power facility, however useful or valuable.

Senator George Norris, progressive Republican of Nebraska, fought to prevent the dam and its future hydroelectric benefits from becoming privatized. FDR considered George Norris "one of the major prophets of America." See esp. T. H. Watkins, *Righteous Pilgrim: The Life and Times of Harold Ickes, 1874–1952* (Henry Holt, 1990), pp. 379–81. For TVA, see Freidel, pp. 304, 351 ff; *TIR*, pp. 136–37; *New Dealers*, pp. 190–93; and Leuchtenberg, "Roosevelt, Norris, and the Seven Little TVAs," in *The FDR Years* (Columbia University Press, 1995).

81 *"neither fish nor fowl"*: Burns, *Roosevelt: The Lion and the Fox,* p. 179.

81 *ER visited TVA: TIR*, p. 137.

81 The TVA's most enduring and challenging innovation was the sale of electricity developed by public facilities. Within ten years the Tennessee Valley experienced a "renaissance." *New Dealers*, pp. 193–96.

82 *On pigs:* Ken Davis, *FDR: The New Deal Years* (Random House, 1986), pp. 271, 274, 270–81; see also Edward and Frederick Schapssmeier, *Henry A. Wallace of Iowa, vol. I: 1910–1940* (The Iowa State University Press, 1968).

82 *ER not credited:* Ruby Black, p. 199, Lash, *Eleanor and Franklin,* p. 384.

83 *Tugwell's "Chamber of Horrors":* Arthur Schlesinger, *The Age of Roosevelt, Vol. II: The Coming of the New Deal* (Houghton Mifflin, 1959), p. 356; see esp. Bernard Sternsher, *Rexford Tugwell and the New Deal* (Rutgers University Press, 1964). Press assaults against Tugwell, George Seldes, in Sternsher, p. 231; Davis, pp. 472–73, 486.

83 *Publishers refused to print ER's support:* Sternsher, p. 234.

83–84 *pure food and drug efforts:* See esp. Rexford Guy Tugwell, *The Democratic Roosevelt* (Doubleday, 1957), p. 464; Ruth deForst Lamb, *American Chamber of Horrors* (Farrar Straus, 1936); Sternsher, p. 247–50; See excerpts from Consumers Advisory Board Hearings, *NRA*, 8–9 Feb. 1934, before deputy administrator Walter White; Emily Newell Blair, 22 Feb. 34 to Malvina for ER, 70, Box 712.

84 *Harry Lloyd Hopkins:* See esp. George McJimsey, *Harry Hopkins: Ally of the Poor and Defender of Democracy* (Harvard University Press, 1987); Alden Whitman, ed., *American Reformers* (H. W. Wilson, 1985), pp. 443–45. See June Hopkins, *The First & Final Task: Harry Hopkins and the Development of the American Welfare System*, Ph.D. dissertation Georgetown University, 1997).

86 *Meridel Le Sueur:* See Harvey Swados, ed. *The American Writer and The Great Depression*, pp. 181–90; Meridel LeSueur, *Ripening: Selected Works* (Feminist Press, 1982); *Women on the Breadlines* (West End Books, 1977), Introduction.

86 *Ellen Woodward:* See esp. Martha Swain, *Ellen Woodward: New Deal Advocate for Women* (University of Mississippi Press, 1995), Preface, pp. 1–5 passim, 39–42; for Woodward and ER, see Ware, pp. 109–10.

87 *Light work:* Swain, pp. 45–47; and Ware, pp. 109–10.

88 *FERA librarians:* Swain, pp. 50–51.

88 For CCC, I am grateful to Barbara Kraft, "The CCC: A job stimulus that worked," *Progressive Review*, July 1993, pp. 4–7; and Kraft's additional CCC interview notes. During a hike down the Grand Canyon, a park ranger told of the many people who believed the site a CCC project, to BWC and CMC.

88 *"She She She" camps:* Kornbluh, esp, p, 83.

09 *ER was angry: NYT,* 19 June 1933.

89 *curriculum for adult education program:* Kornbluh, pp. 29–31.

89 During the 1920s Bryn Mawr's program inspired other residential summer schools, including the Southern School for Women Workers, a similar program at Barnard College, and the Wisconsin School for Workers. See Dagmar Schultz's dissertation on Hilda Smith. Helen Lefkowitz Horowitz, *The Power and Passion of M. Carey Thomas* (Knopf, 1994); and Kornbluh, pp. 34–35; 16–17.

90 *By 1936:* Ware, pp. 112–14.

90 *The educational camps:* Kornbluh, p. 87; also *NYT,* 20 June 1933; 16 June 1934.

90 Pauli Murray's "idyllic existence" ended because she'd gotten too friendly with a counselor. Pauli Murray, *Song in a Weary Throat* (Harper, 1987), pp. 95–96.

91 *"Peace time can be as exhilarating":* ER in *NYT,* 29 Dec. 1933.

6: Family Discord and the London Economic Conference

92 *Great Excitement: Women's Democratic News,* Apr. 1933. Lew Douglas quoted in Ted Morgan, *FDR: A Biography* (Simon & Schuster, 1985), p. 382.

93 *Chazy Lake plans:* ER to Hick, 3–9 May 1933.

93 *Al Kresse story:* Ruby Black, *Eleanor Roosevelt: A Biography* (Duell, Sloan and Pearce, 1940), pp. 208–9.

94 *"Dull dinner":* ER to Hick, 23 May 1933.

94 *"feel soiled":* ER to Hick, 27 May 1933.

94 *"No misunderstandings between us":* ER to Hick, 4 Apr. 1933.

94 *"ate into my soul":* ER to Hick, 8 Apr. 1933.

94 *Right about Elliott:* ER to Hick, 26 Apr. 1933; wise about emotional issues, ER to Hick, 9, 11, 23 May 1933.

95 *"I'm planning our trip":* ER to Hick, 20 Apr.; 4 May 1933.

95 *"Heart ached for Betty":* ER to Hick, 14–15 Apr. 1933.

95 Hamilton Fish Armstrong, *Peace and Counterpeace: From Wilson to Hitler* (Harper & Row, 1971), p. 517.

95 *SDR's taunts:* ER to Hick, 31 May 1933.

96 *ER's meeting with Elliott arranged by Isabella Greenway:* ER to Greenway, 1 June 1933; various telegrams that week, Greenway collection, Tucson.

96 *During trip:* ER to Hick; Anna to ER, quoted in Ted Morgan, p. 461; upon return, ER to Hick, 14 June 1933. ER to FDR, 18 July 1933, Roosevelt Family Papers, Children, Box 16.

97 *World Court:* See BWC, vol. I, the Bok peace prize, charges of propaganda and "un-Americanism," the Congressional Hearing of 1924, and the creation of ER's first FBI file. Also, ER's articles, "The American Peace Award," *The Ladies' Home Journal,* Oct. 1923, p. 54; "The Bok Peace Prize," *NY League of Women Voters Weekly News,* 12 Oct. 1923.

97 Elizabeth Read's text went into a second 1927 edition, and emphasized the pioneering work of the World Court; its treaties and multilateral conventions concerning trade in arms and ammunition, opium and other drugs; mandate problems involving colonial administration and control; and "minorities conventions," which sought to protect "racial, religious and linguistic minorities, living in nations where other races, creeds and tongues prevail."

97 Lape to Helen Rogers Reid, 22 Apr. 1927; for work of the World Court, see esp *Foreign Relations Bulletin,* 10 Aug. 1927; Reid Papers, LC.

97 ER first met Helen Rogers through her beloved Aunt Bye, Anna Roosevelt Cowles. Anna Roosevelt Cowles to HRR, 29 Apr. 1931, Reid Papers, LC.

98 *Hearst, the American Foundation's enemy:* Lape to Helen Reid, 18 Mar. 1924; HRR to Lape, 22 Mar. 1924, Reid Collection, LC.

99 Hearst to former wife, Millicent Hearst, 5 July 1932. I am grateful to David Nasaw for this letter, Box 12, W. R. Hearst Mss.

99 *bipartisan world court delay:* See esp. Lape to HRR, Oct. 1930; 11 Nov. 1930; Reid Collection, LC.

In 1932 the Republican platform urged adherence. But at the Democratic convention, the World Court plank was "in and out again." The most unexpected opposition came from Wilson's own son-in-law, William Gibbs McAdoo, who, wrote Lape, tried "to pull Hearst's chestnuts out of the fire." Lape, confidential report to members, HRR, 1–30 June 1932, D197/LC.

99 Actually, Hoover preferred Japan's actions to increased Soviet influence in Asia. But he wanted to make it clear that the United States did not approve of this first breach of the Treaty of Versailles and the famous 1928 Kellogg-Briand Pact, which fifty-four nations signed, including the United States—because it demanded nothing binding while it rhetorically outlawed belligerence, aggression, war.

100–1 Stanley Hornbeck, in Freidel, *Rendezvous,* p. 110. According to State Department advisers, Japan at this time did not want war but rather wanted the west to recognize its sphere of influence in Asia; see Waldo Heinrichs, *American Ambassador: Joseph Grew and the Development of the US Diplomatic Tradition* (Little, Brown, 1966), pp. 191–201.

101 *In response to FDR's 16 May speech:* Davis, pp. 121–27.

101 *within days FDR renounced:* Ibid., pp. 128–29.

101 *filled with pious nothings:* Burns, p. 177.

102–3 *ER's editorials: Women's Democratic News,* Apr. 1933, Feb. 1935, p. 6.

103 *FDR to Tumulty, 19 May 1933, FDR's Collected Letters, III,* p. 346.

103 *FDR telephoned Dodd:* William Dodd Diaries, Preface, p. 3.

103 *Hull embarked for London:* FDR's May correspondence in Moley, p. 217.

103 Ramsay MacDonald, "We Must Not Fail," in Oswald Garrison Villard, "The Damage to America in London" (2 Aug. 1933), in *Villard: The Dilemma of the Absolute Pacifist in Two World Wars,* ed. by Anthony Gronowicz (Garland, 1983), p. 424.

103 *ER urged all women:* 15 June press conference in Maurine Beasley, ed., p. 11.

104 FDR's London delegation represented a wide range of political wrangling: James Cox, former governor of Ohio and FDR's 1920 running mate, was a Wilsonian allied with Hull. Their chief opponent was Nevada's Senator Key Pittman, chair of the Foreign Relations Committee. Dedicated to cheap money and high tariffs, Pittman's personal interest was the expanded use of silver. A wild man when drunk, he was best remembered for shooting out streetlights as he sauntered about London by night, and chasing Herbert Feis through Claridge's corridors with a bowie knife.

See esp. Davis, pp. 129–31; see also Jeanette Nichols, "Roosevelt's Monetary Diplomacy in 1933," *American Historical Review* (Jan. 1951); and Herbert Feis, *1933: Characters in Crisis* (Little Brown, 1966).

104 *Hull was devastated:* Arthur Schlesinger, p. 210. Others were even more horrified by FDR's Executive Order No. 6174, issued on 16 June 1933, which distributed Public Works Administration and FERA funds, and allocated $238 million for the construction of naval vessels, including 31 aircraft carriers "sixteen to be built in private yards and fifteen in navy yards." This was the beginning of a sustained rearmament that continued throughout the first administration, and contributed to the renewed arms race. FDR's timing for this EO is curious, if he had any serious international goals in London. EO in Samuel I. Rosenman, *The Public Papers and Addresses of Franklin D. Roosevelt,* with notes by President Roosevelt (Random House, 1938), vol. II, pp. 29–251; for its impact see William Neumann, *America Encounters Japan* (Johns Hopkins Press, 1963), pp. 203 ff.

104 *Bullitt on Hull:* Bullitt to FDR, 13 June 1933, Bullitt, pp. 34–35; see also Davis, p. 131. On 15 June 1933, Warren Delano Robbins wrote to his cousins, "Dear Franklin and Dear Eleanor," Cordell Hull was "very temperamental and was on the verge of resigning." Edgar Nixon, ed., *FDR and Foreign Affairs* (Harvard University Press, 1969), p. 237.

104 *Groton graduation: NYT,* 17 June 1933.

105 *The schooner was accompanied:* Davis, pp. 158–60; Charles Hurd, *When the New Deal Was Young and Gay* (Harper, 1965) pp. 157, 150, 153.

105 FDR to Herbert Bayard Swope, telegram, 16 June 1933, in *Letters, III,* p. 353.

105–6 James Warburg considered it urgent for FDR to accept dollar-pound stabilization. Unless he did, the U.S. could not "assume a leading role" in the effort to achieve "lasting economic peace." But FDR rejected his advice. Schlesinger, pp. 215–16; Davis, pp. 155–57.

106 *ER distracted and agitated:* ER to Hick, 17 June, 20 June 1933.

106 *In sour mood:* ER to Hick, 23 June 1933.

106 *"FDR and the whole fleet":* Davis, *FDR*, pp. 164–65; Davis, *Invincible Summer*, pp. 115–16.

106–7 *"I hope we have good weather":* ER to Hick, 24–25 June 1933.

107 *ER went sailing:* ER to Hick, 27 June 1933.

108 *"I was amazed":* Moley, pp. 245–49.

109 *Moley's cable:* 29 June 1933, Moley, pp. 252–55.

109 *FDR lifted anchor:* Davis, *Invincible Summer*, p. 116; Davis, *FDR: The New Deal Years*, p. 185.

109 Hurd, *When the New Deal Was Young and Gay*, pp. 165–71.

110 *"Mama would cancel all the debts":* FDR to Waldorf Astor, Apr. 1933, *FDR's Letters, III*, p. 341.

110 *"kings cannot err":* Moley, pp. 255–57. Hull ordered minutes burned, Herbert Feis, "Some Notes on Historical Record Keeping," Frances Lowenstein, ed., *The Historian and the Diplomat* (Harper, 1967), p. 97.

111 *blamed his wife:* For example, Davis, *FDR*, pp. 187–88; Freidel, *Rendezvous*, p. 117; but see also Freidel, *Launching*, pp. 478–79.

111 *learned one very important lesson:* See ER, "The Importance of Background Knowledge in Building for the Future" (July 1946), in Allida Black, ed., p. 545.

111 *"recaptured a little serenity":* ER to Hick, 27–29 June 1933.

112 *FDR's bombshell:* Moley, pp. 259–61.

112 *MacDonald, "I don't understand":* Moley, p. 263.

112 "Roosevelt Praised in German Press," *NYT*, 4 July 1933.

112–13 FDR was supported by an odd assortment of boosters, including Felix Frankfurter, who dismissed the London "formula, with all its mischievous ambiguities," as a "literary shell-game." FF to FDR, 6 July 1933, Freedman, ed., pp. 147–48; and Moley was satisfied, p. 267.

113 *Supported in the new Germany:* For Schact, Selig Adler, *The Isolationist Impulse* (Collier, 1961), p. 153; John Garratty, *The Great Depression* (Doubleday, Anchor, 1987), p. 201. See also, John Weitz, *Hjalmar Horace Greeley Schact* (Little, Brown, 1997); *felt hopeless:* 2 Aug. 1933, *Villard* in Gronowicz, ed., p. 424.

113 *Litvinov worked the room:* Villard, p. 427.

114 *Esther Lape's "Committee of Inquiry":* Lape to HR Reid, 14 June 1933; on Monday, 3 July 1933. Reid collection, LC.

7: Private Times and Reports from Germany

115 *Woman's Home Companion.* ER's two-year contract, *NYT*, 18 Feb., 8 July, 20 July 1933; *TIR*, p. 99; The last issue of *Babies—Just Babies* was published in June. See Robert Ernst, *Weakness Is a Crime: The Life of Bernarr Macfadden* (Syracuse University Press, 1991), pp. 86, 127. There is no evidence, however, that ER resigned because the venture was "widely ridiculed."

116 *Hick's pay slashed:* Lowitt and Beasley, p. xxix.

116 *Easier for both of them:* ER to Hick, 6 Apr., 20 Apr. 1933.

116 *ER failed to appreciate:* ER to Hick, 20 Apr.; 4 May 1933.

116 *"you won't be spoiled":* ER to Hick, 15 June 1933.

116 *"Some day":* ER to Hick, 24 June 1933.

117 *"Where would they hide us":* Hickok, p. 120.

117 *"You take the first bath":* Hickok, p. 122.

118 *"All Republicans here":* Ibid., p. 123.

118 *The trip around the Gaspé:* ER in *Women's Democratic News,* July 1933, p. 6.

118 *After Quebec:* Ibid., p. 133.

118 *From Campobello:* ER to FDR, 8 July 1933 Family, Box 16.

119 *Catt worried that Austria:* Carrie Chapman Catt to Rosa Manus, in Mineke Bosch, with Annemarie Kloosterman, eds., *Politics and Friendship: Letters from the International Woman Suffrage Alliance, 1902–1942* (Ohio State University Press, 1990), pp. 227–28.

118–19 The Christian Women's protest was not sent directly to Germany for fear of reprisals against their remaining allies. It was intended to pressure Germany by an aroused public opinion. Jacqueline Van Voris, *Carrie Chapman Catt* (Feminist Press, 1987), p. 214. Rosa Manus was moved by Catt's efforts "more than I can tell you . . . and the Jews of the world can never be grateful enough to you for having done this masterly piece of work." Manus to Catt, 31 Aug. 1933, p. 229.

119 *ER spoke dramatically: NYT,* 26 July 1933; ER to Anna Pennybacker, 11 May 1933, Pennybacker collection, Austin, Texas.

119–20 Pennybacker to ER, "please remember me to Miss Hickok who impressed me deeply," 9 Aug. 1933; cf. 9 Sept. 1933, Texas; cf. Stacey Rozek, "Anna Pennybacker and ER: Feminism Between the Wars," unpublished paper, c. 1986, University of Texas at Austin, to author.

119 In Washington, the Hulls visited and Mrs. Hull confided to ER that the London conference was "a great strain." On the Hulls' visit, ER to Hick, 4–5 Aug. 1933; see Irwin Gellman *Secret Affairs: FDR, Cordell Hull, and Sumner Welles* (Johns Hopkins University Press, 1995), p. 40.

120 *Hick loved her new car, Bluette:* Hick to ER, 7 Aug. 1933.

120–21 ER described her trip to Abingdon in the *Women's Democratic News,* Aug. 1933, p. 6; See David Wishnaut, *All That Is Native and Fine,* pp. 186–93. I am grateful to Chris Brown for this reference. ER told her story, Furman, pp. 178–79.

121 *"Newport depresses me":* ER to Hick, 1 Sept. 1933.

121 *Mayris Chaney performed at White House:* ER in *Women's Democratic News,* Apr. 1933, June 1933, p. 6.

121 *Nan through test of friendship:* ER to Hick, 20 Sept. 1933.

121 *Earl under par:* ER to Hick, 15 Sept. 1933.

121 ER's summer idyll was disrupted by the sudden death of head White House usher, Ike Hoover, who had devoted "42 years of faithful and loving service." She left immediately that evening to attend Ike Hoover's funeral, and returned to Chazy Lake the next day. ER to Hick, 15 Sept.; ER in *Women's Democratic News,* Sept. 1933, p. 6.

122 Alice Hamilton reported to Jane Addams on shipboard, returning to New

York, 1 July 1933; Barbara Sicherman, ed., *Alice Hamilton: A Life in Letters* (Harvard University Press 1984); also Alice Hamilton, "Woman's Place in Germany," *Survey Graphic,* Jan. 1934, pp. 26–47. I am grateful to Barbara Sicherman for Hamilton's articles.

123 *"How could anyone refuse?":* Charlotte Perkins Gilman to Catt, 9 Aug. 1933, Catt Papers, Box 1, NYPL. Others doubted, Evelyn Riley Nicholson to CCC, 1 July 1933, ibid. Catt shocked by FDR's battleships, to Nicholson, 2 Aug. 1933, ibid. Catt believed 30 new naval vessels were "snuck" into the public works bills in April and May, and only radical peace veterans such as Oswald Garrison Villard in *The Nation* had bothered to protest. In "The President and a Big Navy," Villard pointed out that FDR would "yield to the demand" to waste another $230 million on "munitions manufacturers and shipbuilders," because he had always been a "big navy" partisan. Hearst supported a big navy, and there was little public discussion about this development, which so bewildered Catt and Villard, who wondered how the United States could criticize Hitler's demands for rearmament, "if we go piling up our own armaments? Certainly, if we engage in a naval race with . . . England and Japan, there will be only one outcome—another terrible conflict." OGV, 19 Apr. 1933, Gronowicz, ed., p. 423.

124 Catt refused to lunch with ER and FDR at Hyde Park, "unless I am overcome with a desire to make a plea for something." Catt to ER, 15 Aug. 1933, ER, Box 1257/sh100.

124–25 Details of Alice Hamilton's visit from Barbara Sicherman's collection, Hamilton's date books.

125–27 Alice Hamilton, "His Book Reveals the Man," *Atlantic Monthly,* Oct. 1933.

127 Alice Hamilton to Jane Addams, 1 July 1933, in Sicherman, p. 345.

Initially, Catt resisted calls for a German boycott. Catt to Samuel Untermeyer, 12 Sept. 1933, Catt papers NYPL.

128 *Germany walked out:* Schlesinger, p. 232; Arnold Offner, p. 40. *NYT,* 15 July 1933, quoted Hitler's *Volkischer Beobachter,* and ACLU effort, Arthur Morse, *While Six Million Died: A Chronicle of American Apathy* (Random House, 1968), p. 122.

129 *ER's first letter to appeal for racial justice:* ER to W. H. Matthews, 18 Aug. 1933; Matthews to ER, nd; ER to Matthews, 31 Aug. 1933; Box 1270, 100.

129 ER did not publicly write of the crises Jews faced in Germany. In her monthly article for the *Women's Democratic News,* she bypassed her meetings with Wald, Addams, and Hamilton; ignored her conversations and correspondence with Catt; and wrote only of her 18 Aug. visit to West Virginia.

8: Creating a New Community

130 *Arthurdale:* See Stephen Edward Haid, "Arthurdale: An Experiment in Community Planning, 1933–1947," Ph.D. dissertation, University of West Virginia, 1975, pp. 11–12; 19–21; and Clarence Pickett, *For More Than Bread* (Little, Brown, 1953), pp. 19–40.

130–31 *Hick's report:* Beasley and Lowitt 16–26 Aug. 1933, pp. 114–24; Pickett, p. 20; Ronald Lewis, "Scott's Run: America's Symbol of the Great Depression in the Coal Fields," in Bryan Ward, ed., *A New Deal for America* (Arthurdale Heritage, 1995), pp. 1–23.

131 *Hick's reports inspired ER:* ER to Hick, 25 Aug. 1933.

131 *ER wrote a searing column: Women's Democratic News,* Sept. 1933, p. 6; Cf. report of Arthurdale visit by AFSC worker, ibid.

132 *white rabbit: TIR,* p. 127. Bullitt, named America's first ambassador to the Soviet Union, was attending a White House dinner to honor Maxim Litvinov. Coincidentally, FDR recognized the USSR the same day the first twenty-five families moved from Scott's Run to begin work on their new homes, 7 Nov. 1933. See chapt,/ Silence; "Experiment & Error," *Time,* 4 Feb. 1935.

132–33 *Scott's Run and Alice Davis: TIR,* pp. 128–30. Subsequently, Alice Davis was named to the County Welfare Board to administer all federal relief funds allotted by the state for the area.

134 *ER first discussed Arthurdale at press conference: NYT,* 4 Nov. 1933.

134 The other mining communities were Norvelt, just over the mountains from Arthurdale in Westmoreland County, Pennsylvania, and named for ER; the Tygart Valley Homesteads, also in West Virginia, and the Cumberland Homesteads near Crossville, Tennessee. For back-to-the-land visions, and the legislative history of Section 208, see Haid, pp. 34–58; see also Paul Keith Conkin, "Tomorrow a New World: The New Deal Community Program," Cornell University Press, 1959 (University Microfilms, 1970).

134 Ickes subsequently criticized Wilson as a poor administrator. Pickett also thought him slow and ponderous, but considered M. L. Wilson a philosophic visionary. See Pickett, pp. 44–53; and "Promised Land," *Time,* 18 June 1934.

135 *"Louis don't be absurd":* Meeting and ER quoted in Haid, pp. 70–74.

135 *Cost overruns:* Haid, pp. 87–88. According to *Time* (4 Feb. 1935), of the $25 million funded for Subsistence Homesteads, the Interior Department spent "$437,645, not including c. $140,000 worth of work by CWA, CCC and FERA employees" on Arthurdale. In January 1935, Interior added another $900,000 to the project.

136 *Arthurdale expenses indefensible:* Ickes diary, 10 Mar. 1934, p. 152. But Ickes also resented ER's "poking her nose" around his bailiwick. FDR, "My missus," Ickes, 4 Nov. 1934, pp. 218–19; and "I am very fond . . ." Ickes, 19 Nov. 1934, pp. 227–28.

137 *Houses furnished with:* Haid, pp. 90–91; and Mountaineer Craft Cooperative, see Haid, pp. 23–26.

137 *Arthurdale identified with ER:* See esp. ER, "Reedsville" mss. for three articles, 70, Box 662.

138 *First families to be restricted:* ER's report, sent to Hick, 26 Mar. 1934, Box 1.

138 *Interviewers were to ask:* Haid, pp. 75–79; Questions quoted from "Record of Interview to determine eligibility . . . , Monongalia Rehabilitation Association, prepared and conducted by representatives of West Virginia University," in Arthurdale Archives. For Jew Hill, see Sandra Barney, "You Get About What You Pay For," in Bryan Ward, ed., *A New Deal for America* (Arthurdale Heritage, 1995), p. 32. I am grateful to Arthurdale's Bryan Ward for these materials.

140 The community in Monmouth County, New Jersey, also benefited from

Eleanor Roosevelt's enthusiasm. The thriving community is best known as Ben Shahn's home. Claude Hitchcock to ER, 16 Feb., 1934, 70, Box 628; Pickett to ER, 1 Mar. 1934.

140 *"I want you to succeed":* Haid, pp. 93–94; "My husband adores onions," *Time*, 18 June 1934. See esp. ER's article, "Subsistence Farmsteads," *Forum*, 1 Apr. 1934, pp. 199–201.

140–42 ER depended on her friends to support Arthurdale. Among those who gave generously were Elinor Morgenthau, the Allie Freeds, Henry Hooker, Gertrude Ely, Doris Duke, Agnes Brown Leach, and Dorothy Payne Whitney Straight Elmhirst. Their correspondence, and Baruch's in ER's Arthurdale files, 70. ER wrote Hick about Baruch, 27 June 1934.

141 On 15 Feb. 1935, ER began a ten-week series of broadcasts sponsored by the Selby Shoe Company, earmarked exclusively for her work at Arthurdale; see *Time*, 4 Feb. 1935.

141 *ER spent:* ER to Pickett, 27 May 1935; Pickett to ER, 24 May 1935, with Bernard Baruch balance sheet; ER Transit Funds of AFSC, 14 May 1934–31 Dec. 1934, George Schectman, CPA, to Pickett, 31 Jan. 1935, 70, Box 661.

141 Doris Duke in Betty Hovatter Carpenter, "Homesteader's Corner," (Arthurdale newsletter), Summer 1993.

142 ER to Oscar Chapman, 17 Nov. 1934, 70, Box 605.

143 *Ickes was relieved:* Ickes, 19 Nov. 1934, pp. 227–28.

143 *ER never doubted: Forum* article, 1934.

144 Arthurdale was mostly attacked as Red, but it was also attacked by Communists. See esp. Harold Ware and Webster Powell, "Planning for Permanent Poverty: What Subsistence Farming Really Stands For," *Harper's*, Apr. 1935; and T. R. Carskadon, "Hull House in the Hills," *The New Republic*, 1 Aug. 1934.

144 *Arthurdale's abiding value:* "Is Reedsville Communistic? Mrs. Roosevelt Says 'No,' " *The Literary Digest*, 21 Apr. 1934, p. 45; press conference, 11 Apr. 1933; Beasley, pp. 20, 23; ER's press conference 23 Apr. 1934.

In the House, Isabella Greenway made an impassioned speech implying that the death of the factory would be the death of Arthurdale. Arthurdale's representative, Jennings Randolph, argued that the Keyless Lock Company was one of America's "worst antiunion plants," and paid the lowest wages. The company's president opposed the child labor bill, the women's nine-hour bill, and workers' compensation: "Should Mrs. Roosevelt's plan to let a little sunlight into the lives of coal miners be wrecked in order that this kind of a concern may be preserved?' " Haid, pp. 125–28.

144 Upton Sinclair to ER, 31 Jan. 1934, 70, Box 632.

144 *"Man is vile . . .":* ER to Hick, 2 July 1934. As she drove, 4 July 1934.

144–45 *Upton Sinclair:* See esp. Greg Mitchell, *The Campaign of the Century: Upton Sinclair's Race for Governor of California and the Birth of Media Politics* (Random House, 1992), pp. 6–7, 208. See also Leon Harris, *Upton Sinclair: American Rebel* (Crowell, 1975), pp. 298–99. ER to Sinclair, "I have read your books," quoted in Harris, p. 302. Wallace and Hopkins supported Sinclair, Mitchell, pp. 7, 11, 27. If EPIC communism, Mitchell, pp. 21–23.

146 *Hick's report:* Beasley and Lowitt, pp. 305–8. A $10 million campaign of minsinformation, Leon Harris; see also Hick to ER, 3 July; ER to Hick 7, 8 July 1934. ER defended Arthurdale's cooperative fiercely.

ER's answer to Dr. Wirt, and Senator Schall, + clip, nd, Schall's charge, 23 Apr. 1934, 100/ copy with Baruch's correspondence, 24 Oct. 1935, 70, Box 662; cf. Beasley.

147 *All handicrafts continually ridiculed:* See esp. Thomas Coode and Dennis Fabbri, "The New Deal's Arthurdale Project in West Virginia," *West Virginia History*, July 1975, pp. 291–308; and Haid, chapters 5 and 6.

148 M. L. Wilson prepared a study, in "compliance with your request," on industrial research, see: Wilson to ER 24 Sept. 1934/70, Box 628; see Scheider to Wilson, 5 Sept. 1934, 100 re Wilson's visit to Hyde Park to report in further detail.

148 *ER and Baruch agreed with the homesteaders:* Baruch to ER, 24 Oct. 1935, with enclosures, esp. p. 4; 70, Box 662. Consider also, Homesteaders Club to ER, 7 June 1934/ 70, Box 629. Baruch quoted by ER in Educational Committee Meeting, WH, 31 Oct. 1935; attached Elsie Clapp to ER, ibid.

149 *Sherman Mittell:* Mittell to Peterson, 25 Oct. 1935, 70, box 662. The "scraps" distressed Elsie Clapp, see Clapp to ER, 18 Oct. 1935; Peterson to Dr. E. E. Agger, director of the Management Division, 28 Oct. 1935.

149 *"They expect them to fail":* Clapp to ER, 2 Nov. 1935, 70/662; Clapp to ER, 8 Nov. 1935; also Clapp to ER, 31 Oct., with attachments, including Meeting of Educational Committee, WH, 31 Oct.: present Clapp, Lucy Sprague Mitchell, Dr. Agger, Pickett, Dr. Rainey, ER, etc.; and Pickett to Clapp, 5 Nov. 35: FDR planned to journey from Warm Springs to Arthurdale on 10 Dec., with ER. *NYT*, 27 Jan. 1934; Haid, pp. 124–30; See also, Wesley Stout, "The New Homesteaders," a particularly nasty article, *The Saturday Evening Post* (4 Aug. 1934), pp. 6–7, 61.

149 Bernard Baruch, "I do not think you ought," to ER, 22 Mar. 1937; 70, Box 722. On the Phillips Jones Corporation, see J. O. Walker to ER, 3 Apr. 1937, ibid. ER re Margaret Innes, to Baruch, 22 Sept. 1937, 100, Box 1414.

150 *On the schools and Elsie Clapp:* See Charles Pynchon, "School as Social Centre: Life in a Subsistence Homestead Turns About an Experiment in Education," *NYT*, 5 May 1935, 70/662; Sam Stack, "Elsie Ripley Clapp & Progressive Education," pp. 115–34.

151 See also Frazier Hunt, "Listening to America," *NY World Telegram*, 23 July 1935.

On 27 June Baruch telegrammed ER: "Hope you understand that despite Franklin's expressed opinions will stand with you." BB to ER, telegram, 27 June 1936; telegram, 3 July 1936: "Delighted to contribute ten as requested." ER's five-page letter to BB, 12 July 1936, 100. See also, ER to Tugwell, 3 Dec. 1936, 70/700. Significantly, Tugwell had resigned by Dec., and Will Alexander replied.

151 *ER moved by a visit at Christmas: NYT*, 29 Jan. 1935; *TIR*, pp. 132–33. Also, Ickes, pp. 207, 218; Hickok, pp. 135–42; Lash, *Eleanor and Franklin*, pp. 393 ff. We are grateful to Bryan Ward for the sweatshirts.

152 *"Nothing we learn in this world is ever wasted": TIR*, pp. 131–32.

152 *plea to end discrimination:* Haid, pp. 81–82.

9: The Quest for Racial Justice

153 *Clarence Pickett recalled:* Pickett, *For More Than Bread* (Little, Brown, 1953), p. 49.

154 *ER asked Hopkins:* ER to Harry Hopkins, Nov. 1934, quoted in Lash, *Eleanor and Franklin,* p. 514; for Aubrey Williams, Columbia Oral History Project, John Salmond, *A Southern Rebel: The Life and Times of Aubrey Williams, 1890–1959* (University of North Carolina Press, 1983); Harvard Sitkoff, *A New Deal for Blacks: The Emergence of Civil Rights as a National Issue* (Oxford University Press, 1978), pp. 65, 59.

154 *The week before:* ER to Hick, 16 Jan. 1934; a lovely weekend, Hick to ER, 22 Jan. 1934.

155 *Even sixty years later:* Residents and descendants to author. For FDR's Warm Springs, see esp. Geoffrey Ward, *A First-Class Temperament: The Emergence of Franklin Roosevelt* (Harper & Row, 1989), p. 766; Hugh Galagher, *FDR's Splendid Deception* (Dodd, Mead, 1985).

155 *Before white conquest:* "The Spirit of Warm Springs," FDR's Thanksgiving weekend address, 29 Nov. 1934; I am grateful to Beverly Bulloch (Director of Development) for this and other Warm Springs brochures and materials; and for the detailed tour she and Diane Blanks conducted for us in Feb. 1994.

156 *Roswell:* Clarece Martin, *The History of Bulloch Hall and Roswell Georgia* (Lake Publications, 1987).

156 27 Jan. 1934, National Public Housing Conference, *NYT,* 28 Jan. 1934; Mary Simkhovitch, president of the conference, Harold Ickes, and Herbert Bayard Swope also spoke.

156 *Washington alley slums:* John Ihlder, "What Can You Do to Help Rid Washington of Its Inhabited Alleys," to ER with attachments, 1 May 1934, 70.

156 For Ellen Axson Wilson's alliance with Charlotte Everett Hopkins, see Edith Elmer Wood, "Four Washington Alleys," *The Survey,* 6 Dec. 1913, pp. 250–52; Anthony, pp. 344–50; details of her last day, see "Mrs. Wilson's Death and Washington's Alleys," *The Survey,* 6 Dec. 1914; Mrs. Ernest Bicknell, "The Home-Maker of the White House," *The Survey;* 3 Oct. 1914.

157 *"We drove":* New York Tribune, 21 Mar. 1933; see also Charlotte Hopkins's *NYT* obituary, 8 Sept. 1935; Robert Cruise McManus, "District's Grand Old Lady Wins Struggle to End Squalor."

157 Martha Strayer, "Mrs. Archibald Hopkins . . . Lives to Witness Alley Clearance Victory," *Washington Daily News,* June 1934; other clippings in Charlotte E. Hopkins Papers, Schlesinger.

158 Melvin Chisum to ER, 16 Jan. 1934; ER to Chisum, 24 Feb. 1934; Chisum to ER, 20 Mar.; ER to Frances Perkins, 4 Apr., 100, Box 1314.

158 *During the first years:* Hazel W. Harrison, "The Status of the American Negro in the New Deal," *The Crisis* (Nov. 1933).

159 In 1933 Will Alexander, a former Methodist minister, and leader of the 1920s Atlanta-based Commission for Interracial Cooperation (CIC), and Edwin Embree, director of the Rosenwald Fund, lobbied the White House and several government agencies to accept a "Special Adviser on the Economic Status of Negroes," subsidized by the Rosenwald Fund. Ickes accepted the challenge, and in

July appointed Clark Foreman. Foreman, who had spent years studying southern schools with Black educator Horace Mann Bond, fully understood the "cult of the south," which Dr. Bond had analyzed as a "psychological entity" where southerner meant white man, and the "Negro—well, a Negro." He agreed with the protestors, and advised Ickes to appoint Robert Weaver his assistant. Weaver, a recent Harvard Ph.D., was appointed in Nov. 1933, and quickly took charge of housing for PWA.

By 1936 Weaver, with William Hastie, as assistant solicitor, created a housing program which became the "the most racially inclusive New Deal initiative, securing black participation in all phases of the slum-clearance and low-rent housing programs," in twenty-nine cities, north and south, including Birmingham, Atlanta, and Memphis. See esp. Patricia Sullivan, *Days of Hope: Race and Democracy in the New Deal Era* (University of North Carolina, 1996) pp. 46–49, 52–56; see also Kirby; T. H. Watkins, pp. 646–47. See Sullivan, *Days of Hope,* for Embree's telegram to Foreman (p. 40); Alexander's caution on Foreman to Ickes, (pp. 24–25); Horace Mann Bond, (p. 12).

159 *Mary McLeod Bethune:* See "My Secret Talks with FDR," *Ebony* (Apr. 1949), in Bernard Steucher, ed., *The Negro in Depression and War, 1930–1945* (Quadrangle, 1969).

159 *"That grand old lady took my arm":* Bethune, *Ebony* (Apr. 1949); Nancy Weiss, pp. 143, 167–68.

162–64 *Hick's reports from Savannah and Atlanta:* Beasley and Lowitt; Harry Hopkins and CWA in Sherwood, pp. 52–62.

163 *"It spoils them":* Hick to Harry Hopkins, 16 Jan. 1934.

164 *Simon Legree:* Hick to Hopkins, 23 Jan. 1934.

165 *ER's response:* ER to Hick, 7–10 Jan. 1934; 24–29 Jan. 1934; see also Lash, *Love Eleanor,* p. 181.

165 *Hick reached Florida:* Beasley, pp. 164–65.

165 *"I might like it with you":* ER to Hick, 27 Jan. 1934; Hick to ER, 26 Jan. 1934. See also ER to Hick, 28 Jan. 34: "I love you dear so much. Three weeks and two days more and you will be home. . . ."; 29 Jan. 1934: "I would like to be with you all the time. I love you deeply, tenderly."

166 *ER's days were full:* ER to Hick, 5–10, 13 Feb. 1934; FDR's birthday party, ER to Hick, 30 Jan. 1934.

166 *"I have wanted you all day":* ER to Hick, 2, 3 Feb. 1934; "I often feel rebellious, it will all work out," 4, 5 Feb.

167 *By 14 February:* Hick to Hopkins, Beasley, pp. 186–87. Hick now defended CWA: many local administrators did important work. One, Verde Peterson, assigned over four hundred CWA teachers to educate adults in the rural areas of South Carolina. They worked directly with the people and taught them to repair their homes, "delouse their chickens, build toilets, raise gardens."

Hick to Hopkins, 5 Feb. 1934, Beasley, pp. 170–74; Robert Sherwood, *Roosevelt and Hopkins* (Harper, 1948), p. 57; Hick to Hopkins, 14 Feb. 1934, pp. 186–87.

168 Hick to Kathryn Godwin, 18 Feb. 1934, in Beasley, pp. 191–92.

168 *ER tried to console:* 8 Feb. 1934; ER's "heart was light," 9 Feb.

168 *ER was alarmed by Hick's accidents:* "I should have known Monday night when you sounded so queer but I hoped you were just sleepy." ER encouraged her to cancel her planned trip to Arthurdale, she had seen enough to "write the stories" Hopkins wanted: "a rest just with me in Washington is absolutely essential." 17 Feb. 1934.

169 *On the train to Florida: NY Herald,* 6 Mar. 1934; landed in Haiti, protected from unrest in Cuba, Furman, p. 197.

170 ER to FDR, 10 Mar. 1934, Family, Children, Box 16. On her return, ER reported to Secretary of the Interior Ickes that she "felt encouraged" by what Governor Pearson was trying to do. Ickes, pp. 156–57, 298.

170 In ER's honor, Pearson had "cut across the color line" and poll tax. Furman, p. 199.

170 See esp. ER's reports in the *Women's Democratic News* (Apr. 1934), where she protested a policy "of exploitation with very little understanding," a policy of "cruelty and greed."

170 *In Puerto Rico: NY Tribune,* 9–12 Mar.; Furman, p. 200.

171 *ER saw no reason, last day: NY Tribune,* 14–15 Mar.

172 *"Dearest Babs":* FDR to ER, 5–12 July 1935.

173 *For new housing:* Ruby Black, *Eleanor Roosevelt: A Biography* (Duell, Sloan and Pearce, 1940), pp. 296–98; Hick's report to Hopkins in Beasley, pp. 196–203.

173 ER met with Oscar Chapman, to discuss the political situation in the Virgin Islands, to defend Governor Pearson, and to promote suffrage. She also endorsed tourism and reduced taxation

While "Governor Pearson was not a genius," ER wrote Chapman, he "had the interest of the people at heart." See, Black, pp. 296–97; ER to Oscar Chapman, 30 Mar. 1934; communication from Ella Gifft, Suffragist League of St. Thomas, to Chapman, Chapman to ER, 26 Apr. 1934, 70, Box 605.

He initiated a summer institute for teacher training, scholarships for study abroad, the first senior high school, and adult education. See esp.: William Boyer, *America's Virgin Islands: A History of Human Rights and Wrongs* (Durham: Carolina Academic Press, 1983), pp. 147–61.

Walter White "followed with very great interest" ER's trip, and Governor Pearson wrote him of "the magnificent effect of your contacts with the people of the Virgin Islands." White to ER, 2 Apr. 1934; Chapman to ER, 4 Apr. 1934, and 26 Apr. 1934; cf. Ickes, pp. 156–157, 298; ER's report in WDN, Apr. 19, 1934, where she protested a policy of "exploitation . . . cruelty, and greed."

174 *It was all sparsely funded, neocolonial:* Years later ER observed: The islands remained "a difficult problem and one which the US is far from having solved satisfactorily." TIR, pp. 138–140.

174 Cuba's new dictatorship disturbed ER's friends. Within a year, Lillian Wald sent ER Helen Hall's correspondence on Cuba, where she served on an investigative commission in June 1934. Hall, who had succeeded Wald as director of Henry Street was convinced the United States was "partly responsible for the present military control. While the President has been so farsighted in his treatment of Cuba . . . the American Ambassador played an interfering role. . . ." Hall's friends worried about Caffrey's "growing intimacy with Batista." The Cubans felt that again their government was being manipulated by outsiders.

By Mar. 1935 civil liberties disappeared. There were "mass arrests and repressions," all identified with "the army and with Batista, leaning on support from the American Embassy." There was an effort to get this information to FDR, but "these efforts failed." If ER passed this correspondence on to Sumner Welles or FDR, she never referred to the Cuban troubles in her writings. See anon. correspondent to Hall, 15 Mar. 1935; Helen Hall to Wald, 26 Mar. 1935. 100, Box 1361; Helen Hall, + Paul Kellogg's commentary in *Survey, Christian Science Monitor,* Mar. 1935.

Sandino's assassination in the *NYT*, 12 Mar. 1934.

174 *"I believe it gets harder":* ER to Hick, 26 Mar. 1934.

174 *"These Roosevelts are born":* William Allen White in *Emporia Gazette,* 27 Mar. 1934; ER to Hick, 27, 28 Mar. 1934.

175 *ER counseled Hick to discount:* 4, 5 Apr. 1934. Hick from the Monteleone, 9 Apr. 1934.

175 *"Someday we'll lead":* ER to Hick, 9 Apr. 1934.

175 ER and Earl were together at Val-Kill after Nancy Cook's father's funeral. The next day, 10 Apr., ER's cousin Teddy Robinson, the son of Aunt Corinne, died from pneumonia and alcoholism.

10: The Crusade to End Lynching

178 *The Wagner-Costigan bill:* Robert Zangrando, *The NAACP Crusade Against Lynching, 1909–1950* (Temple University Press, 1980), pp. 111, 114–15.

178 *During the 1920s:* See esp. Jacquelyn Dowd Hall, *Revolt Against Chivalry: Jessie Daniel Ames and the Women's Campaign Against Lynching* (Columbia University Press, 1974), pp. 159–67. For Will Alexander, see his Columbia Oral History interview; and Wilma Dykeman and James Stokely, *Seeds of Southern Change: The Life of Will Alexander* (University of Chicago Press, 1962).

178 *Jessie Daniel Ames:* Hall, *Revolt Against Chivalry,* esp. pp. 159–67.; Harvard Sitkoff, *A New Deal for Blacks: The Emergence of Civil Rights as a National Issue* (Oxford University Press, 1978), pp. 270–75; cf. Jessie Daniel Ames, "Whither Leads the Mob?" (Commission on Interracial Cooperation, Atlanta, Jan. 1932), in Ames to ER, Apr. 1934, 100, Box 1284.

179 *White puzzled by Ames:* White to ER, 14 Apr. 1934, 70; the real urgency, White to ER, 20 Apr. 1934, 100, Box 1325.

179 ER to Jessie Daniel Ames, 20 Apr. 1934, 100/1284; also Ames to ER, 16 Apr. with pamphlets, esp. "Wither Leads the Mob?"; cf. Hall, pp. 24–241; Ames to ER, 29 Jan. 1935.

180 *"wildest lynching orgy":* NYT, 19 Oct. 1934; cf. Ralph Ginzburg, *100 Years of Lynching* (N.Y.: Lancer Books, 1969), pp. 200–201.

180 *FDR's first reference to "lynch law," 6 December 1933,* see Zangrando, p. 104; Nancy Weiss, p. 101.

181 *White's meeting at the White House:* Walter White, *A Man Called White,* (Viking, 1948), pp. 168–69 (misdated as 1935).

181 White to ER, 14 May 1934, 100/1325.

181 *"I did not choose":* FDR quoted in Nancy Weiss, pp. 105–106, and White, p. 169.

181 *CWA discarded:* FDR had created CWA by executive order on 9 Nov. 1933. Suddenly he ordered it liquidated; it simply ceased to exist on 1 Apr. 1934. Although many of its job programs were "folded back into the FERA," in the four months of its existence CWA had been the largest employer of non-relief white-collar, single, and professional women engaged as teachers, recreation leaders, nutritionists, stenographers, writers, public health nurses, and librarians. Ellen Woodward sent ER a state-by-state report of thousands of women's projects discontinued.

182 *Hick wrote from North Carolina:* 18 Feb. 1934; Beasley, p. 195.

182–83 For NRA abuses and rampant job discrimination, cf. Nancy Weiss, pp. 56–57; John Kirby, *Black Americans in the Roosevelt Era* (University of Tennessee Press, 1980), pp. 134, 160n; and Raymond Wolters, *Negroes and the Great Depression* (Greenwood, 1970), pp. 140–42.

183 *"If we have to have a dictator":* Beasley, pp. 216–19; *Hick had two suggestions:* Hick to ER, 13 Apr. 1934; Beasley, pp. 219–22, 204–8; *Hick from New Mexico:* 25 Apr. 1934, Beasley, pp. 231–34.

183 ER to Hick, 15 Apr. 1934; *"depressed":* 19 Apr. 1934.

184 *"No, I am always glad":* ER to Hick, 16 Apr. 1934.

184 *"deeply moved":* Crystal Bird Fauset to ER, 24 Apr. 1934, 100, Box 1314; cf. Fauset to ER 27 May 1934. Peabody sent ER's letter to L. Hollingsworth Wood, a "great hearted" Quaker and wrote ER: "I have a great desire to talk with you respecting the relation of our Southland with its 25% of our population."

185 ER to Peabody, 4 May 34; Peabody to ER, 26 May 1934; ER to Peabody, 2 June, "interested to hear what you have to tell me about the South"; thank you re Fauset, 100, Box 1314.

184 ER to Vincent Astor, 22 May 1934, 100, Box 1284; ER to Henry Morgenthau, Sr., 21 June 1934, 100, Box 1311.

185 L. Hollingsworth Wood, "greatly complimented" to be approached, was particularly grateful to ER for her "very generous support of our Quaker relief work in the coal-mining districts," which earned her both "a great deal of criticism and a great deal of affection and appreciation." L. Hollingsworth Wood, to Peabody, 5 June; Peabody to ER, 8 June; ER to Peabody, 18 June 1934/100, Box 1314; The Institute conference, with seminars led by Charles Johnson, Fisk; Robert Park, Chicago; Otto Klineberg, Columbia; Helen Bryan and Crystal Bird Fauset, AFSC, was held in Phila. 1–28 July 1934; Howard Odum considered it "one of the most perfect units of work I have ever seen."

185 *ER's 11 May 1934 speech: Journal of Negro Education,* Oct. 1934; reprinted in Allida Black, ed., pp. 141 ff. Harvard Sitkoff, p. 201. Sitkoff on ER, pp. 65, 69.

186 See ER's correspondence with John Studebaker, 1935–1936, 70/ esp. boxes 666, 699; on the much-embattled efforts toward federal aid to education, see Studebaker's 12-page report to the NEA, "New Federal Expenditures for Certain Phases of Education," 1933–1935, (1 Jan. 1936), Studebaker to ER, 10 Jan. 1936; cf. ER to Studebaker, 3 Dec. 1936; Studebaker to ER via Scheider, 10 Dec; and Studebaker to Charles A. Lee, Washington University, 4 Dec. 1936, Box 699.

186 Initially education grants were made through FERA and CWA, and after 1935 through WPA and NYA, when the situation improved and college aid expanded to $14 million by 1936, and served 104,658 students. Studebaker's report, pp. 4–5.

186 *Williams assured ER:* Aubrey Williams to State Relief Administrators and State Chief School Officers, 2 Nov. 34; Klinefelter to Scheider, 6 Nov. 1934; 70/616.

187 *"my foolish temperament":* ER to Hick, 24 May 1934.

187 *ER relieved:* ER to Hick, 25–27 May 1934; *"mind of a man",* ER to Hick, 30 May 1934.

187 *Alderson Prison, FDR, what for: TIR,* pp. 170–72.

188 *White was desperate:* Walter White to FDR, copy to ER, 13, 14, June 1934/ 100, 1325; Helen Boardman, *Crisis,* "Grand Jury Adjourns, Lauren County Fails to Indict Dendy Lynchers," re 4 July 1933 lynching of Norris Dendy: despite witnesses, and five named suspects, the case ended typically: "Another insufferable crime has been committed and the perpetrators are being shielded by the silence and passivity of the 'better element.' "

188 *ER told her press conference: NYT,* 7 June, 23 June 1934; Strayer, newspaper clips, C. Hopkins Papers.

ER lobbied to secure Ihlder's appointment; and FDR urged Charlotte Hopkins to arrange a meeting between Ickes, Harry Hopkins, and Ihlder to "work out a comprehensive program." Hopkins to ER, 15 June; ER to Hopkins, 28 June 1934; FDR to Hopkins 15 Jan. 1935; Hopkins Papers, Schlesinger Library.

188 *Ickes asked ER:* Ickes to ER, 8 Mar. 1935; ER to Ickes, 12 Mar. 1935; committee membership as of 25 Feb. 1935, 70, Box 654.

Charlotte Everett Hopkins died on 6 Sept. 1935, just as the real work to dismantle the alleys began.

11: Private Friendship, Public Time

190 *As her train ran alongside the Hudson:* ER to Hick, 23 Apr. 1934; *conference on aging:* 20 Apr. 1934.

190 *"I've been wondering":* ER to Hick, 30 May 1934.

191 *ER felt protective of FDR, and SDR:* ER to Hick, 1 June 1934.

191 *ER II on SDR:* to author in San Francisco, 1997.

192 *Emma Bugbee asked:* ER to Hick 14 Nov. 1933.

192 *Russia was recognized:* ER to Hick, 18 Nov. 1933. During the autumn of 1933, ER's letters of longing were interspersed with letters of stern advice: Buy a coat; see a dentist; watch your diet. See esp. ER to Hick, 25–26 Sept. 1933. ER to Hick, 6 Nov. 1933.

193 *"Mama to FDR":* ER to Hick, 7 Nov. 1933.

193 *ER's checkbooks:* Bess Furman, p. 196; *ER bragged:* 9 Nov. 1933; 12–13 Nov.; 22 Nov. 1933.

194 *"How lucky you are not a man":* ER to Hick, 23 Nov. 1933.

194 *"only I wished it was you":* ER to Hick, 25 Nov. 1933; *"so you think they gossip":* ER to Hick, 27 Nov. 1933; *ER confided:* 29 Nov. 1933; *"I'll be back in obscurity again,"* ER to Hick, 1 Dec. 1933.

195 *"I'm selfish enough":* ER to Hick, 3 Dec. 1933.

195 Hick to ER from Minnesota, 6 Dec. 1933.

196–97 *ER's ardent letters:* "I'm going to think of nothing else," 6 Dec. 1933; "Funny everything I do my thoughts fly to you, never are you out of them dear. . . ." 7 Dec. 1933; "I can remember just how you look I shall want to look long and very lovingly at you."

197 *Drinking and "felt as a child":* ER to Hick, 9 Dec. 1933.

198 *The ardor of their winter correspondence:* "Gee what wouldnt I give . . . to hear your voice now." "It is all the little things . . . the feel of your hair, your gestures . . ."

199 ER to Hick, 27 Jan. 1934; cf. 24, 25, 28 Jan. "I would like to be with you all the time. I love you deeply, tenderly." 29 Jan. 1934.

199 *"We must be careful":* ER to Hick, 16 Apr. 1934.

199 *dream to marry Earl:* Hick to ER, 20 Apr. 1934.

199 *"Love is a queer thing":* ER to Hick, 4–5 Feb. 1934.

200 *"you can tell her how to snap out of it":* ER to Hick, 6 June 1934.

200 *"even disagreeable things come to an end!":* ER to Anna, 19 June 1934, in Asbell, p. 59.

200 *Cousin Susie "made a scene":* ER to Hick, 16 June 1934; *"I could spank you":* ER to Hick, 25 June 1934.

200 *"Yes, dear, . . . happy with a man":* ER to Hick, 28 June 1934; cf. 29 June.

201 *"Things happen often enough," "pick up where we left off," "neither of us is going to be upset":* ER to Hick, 8, 9, 10 July 1934.

201 *Broadcasts picked up:* ER to Hick, 19 Apr. 1934.

201 *ER criticized: Time,* 4 June 1934, p. 33.

202 *After Chicago:* ER to John Boettiger, in Lash, *Love Eleanor,* p. 197.

202 *Hick recorded the entire drama: Reluctant First Lady,* pp. 157–61.

204 *At the Danas':* Hick, pp. 162–64; ER, *TIR,* p. 142; and *Women's Democratic News,* Aug. 1934.

204 ER did not respond to Clarence Pickett until 7 Aug. 1934. She thanked him for the Arthurdale information, suggested that Ickes visit in Sept., and noted: "I have had a grand time, a good rest, and have enjoyed the summer immensely."

205 *Mono Lake:* ER's implication that nothing lived in Mono Lake, an inland sea twice the size of San Francisco, and her blithe comment about the lake's future development, reveals a remarkable lack of information. Mono Lake was then and remains one of the greatest environmental controversies since the drowning and damming of the magnificent Hetch Hetchy Valley. The struggle to use not ruin nature's great bounty in the high Sierra continues—as ER in other writings predicted it would. See esp. John Hart, *Storm Over Mono: The Mono Lake Battle and the California Water Future* (University of California Press, 1996); Mono Lake Committee P.O. Box 29, Lee Vining, CA 93541.

205 *Yosemite camp details: TIR; Reluctant First Lady;* Shirley Sargent, *Yosemite's Famous Guests* (Flying Spur Press, 1970), pp. 33–35; and interviews with Carl Sharsmith and Elizabeth Stone O'Neill.

206 *"Climbing mountains": Reluctant First Lady,* p. 166.

206 According to Shirley Sargent, Chief Ranger Forrest Townsley died of a heart attack in the high country on 11 Aug. 1943.

206 Peter Browning credits park naturalist Douglass Hubbard for naming Lake Roosevelt to commemorate ER's July 1934 visit. Others had suggested "My Day Lake;" cf. Peter Browning's *Yosemite Place Names* (Lafayette, Calif.: Great West Books, 1988), p. 121. Curiously, one scours the well kept Yosemite archives in vain for one single picture of Hick, although there is a reference to the presence of ER's "secretary" in John Bingaman, *Guardians of the Yosemite: A Story of the First Rangers* (Desert Printers, 1961), p. 40.

206 *ER's interest in the sites TR visited with John Muir:* The boy so eager to kill birds and buffalo came to understand fully how endangered wildlife and wilderness had become, and sought as president to protect them. The battle between Muir's concept of wilderness conservation and TR's divided legacy of conservation and national lands for use (grazing rights, water power, forestry) intensified during FDR's administration.

207 *Hick's horse in the river: Reluctant First Lady*, pp. 166–67; ER to Anna, "The Yosemite was grand. I loved it and the rangers are a grand bunch. Hick ended by having her horse. . . . ," "She's going to try to get herself in better condition for she suffered from the altitude."

207 *Years later:* 29 July 1935, box 56. *TIR*, p. 142.

207–208 *Ickes at dinner; and chipmunks: Reluctant First Lady*, pp. 169–70. Ickes Diary, 31 July 1934, p. 177.

209 *FDR had written regularly:* FDR to "Dearest Babs," 5 July–12 July 1934, *Letters*, pp. 404–9.

209–11 *San Francisco and Oregon: Reluctant First Lady; corpse to mourn: TIR,* p. 143.

211 *ER joined FDR: NYT,* 5 Aug. 1934; itenerary, *NYT* 3 Aug. 1934, included several other dam-sites along the upper Mississippi; Ickes, pp. 183–84.

212 *Ickes considered the evening:* Ickes, p. 184; cf. Kenneth Davis, p. 383; *But ER worried: TIR,* p. 144.

212 *ER's correspondence resumed:* ER to Hick, 3 Aug. 1934; *Hick felt forlorn;* Hick to ER, 10 Aug. 1934.

212 *Blackfoot tribe: NYT,* 6 Aug. 1934; ER to Hick, 6 Aug. 1934; *"What fools these mortals be": TIR* 144.

212 On 18 June 1934, the Wheeler-Howard bill, to incorporate Indian communities, and achieve "Indian self-government," the Indian Reorganization Act passed. Much amended, with endless compromises and trimmings, it was a flawed and limited first step. See esp. T. H. Watkins, pp. 361–62; 530–48; and Alison Bernstein, "A Mixed Record: The Political Enfranchisement of American Indian Women During the Indian New Deal," *Journal of the West* (July 1984).

12: Negotiating the Political Rapids

214 *"For heaven sake":* ER to Hick, 27 Aug. 1934.

215 *Gertrude Ely:* Feminist, pacifist, social worker, musician, brilliant raconteur, a "personality with charisma," Gertrude Sumner Ely was known for her hospitality on the Bryn Mawr campus—first in her family home, Wyndham Manor inherited from her father a vice president of the Pennsylvania Railroad, then in Wyndham Barn refurbished in 1940. Devoted to music and the arts, a member of the AFSC, Ely headed Pennsylvania's women's committee of the WPA after 1935, and joined ER on many projects. There is no biography of Gertrude Ely. A memorabilia collection is in the Bryn Mawr College Archives.

215 I am grateful to Lorett Treese, Bryn Mawr archivist, for Ely articles; to anonymous of Fowler's beach; and especially Rodney Hart Clurman, for information about Ely and her friendship with ER. Also, Margaret Edwards, "Gertrude Ely Owned This House," from Bryn Mawr archives; "Maverick from the Main Line," 3 Oct. 1965, obits, esp. *Phila. Bulletin*, 27 Oct. 1970.

216 *Their turbulent vacation:* ER to Hick, 9, 11 Aug. 1934; *Tiny "as good as Earl":* ER to Hick, 19 Aug.; *ER to Bess Furman on bull's-eye:* Furman, *Washington By-Line.* ER's pistol permit was renewed annually throughout her life; *"your sweater":* ER to Hick, 17 Aug. 1934; *ER sat unrecognized:* ibid. *"Yes, I am happy here":* ER to Hick, 13 Aug. 1934.

217 ER to Elinor Morgenthau, 19 Aug. 1934; Morgenthau to ER, Elinor Morgenthau collection, FDRL.

217 *"Yes, dear, . . . can't unlock":* ER to Hick, 21 Aug. 1934; cf. ER to Hick on Elinor Morgenthau's upset, 19 Aug. 1934.

218 *"Made headlines, aground in a motorboat":* NYT, 16 Aug. 1934; *F was amused:* ER to Hick, 30 Aug. 1934; *"you and Earl need me":* 31 Aug. 1934.

218 At the 1934 Nuremberg rally, Hitler also addressed 2,000 women members of the Nazi Party to condemn women's rights as a " 'product of Jewish intellectualism.' " " 'The Nazi program for women has but one point: the child.' " See editorial, "Adolf Hitler," 26 Sept. 1934, *New Republic;* see also William Shirer, *Berlin Diary: The Journal of a Foreign Correspondent, 1934–1941.*

218 *Europe's social insurance:* See esp. June Hopkins, *The First and Final Task: Harry Hopkins and the Development of the American Welfare System,* Ph.D. dissertation, Georgetown University, 1997, pp. 273–75.

219 ER was delighted to tell Hick that Hopkins "said today that your reports would be the best history of the depression in future years." ER to Hick, 30–31 Aug. 1934.

219 *FDR in a "militant" mood:* ER to Hick, 1, 2 Sept. 1934; *At the party:* Ken Davis, pp. 407–8; *Tone of tenderness, "lie down beside you":* ER to Hick, 1 Sept. 1934; *"papers don't worry me":* ER to Hick, 2, 3 Sept.; *Hick busy:* Hick to ER, 5 Sept.; *"I would die":* ER to Hick, 8 Sept. 1934.

219 *All the boats:* ER to Hick, Lash, *Love Eleanor,* p. 203.

220 *FDR appointed Winant:* see Bernard Bellush, *He Walked Alone: A Biography of John Gilbert Winant* (The Hague: Mouton, 1968), pp. 104–6; cf. Davis, pp. 409–13.

221 *Provincetown:* ER to Hick, 14 Sept. 1934; *at Cousin Maude's:* ER to Hick, 16 Sept.

221 *ER and Hick arranged reunion:* ER to Hick, 21 Sept. 1934; *but interrupted:* ER to Hick, 2 Oct. 1934.

222 *"I like being in a campaign":* ER quoted in *NYT,* 12 Oct. 1934.

222–23 *ER's long friendship, and speech: NYT,* 16 Oct. 1934; *Buffalo: NYT,*

26 Oct. 1934; *"I am acting as an individual"*: *NYT*, 26 Oct.; *To charges, "As a citizen"*: John Henry Lambert to ER, 30 Oct. 1934; ER to JHL, 12 Nov. 1934/100.

223 *"We have short memories"*: *NYT*, 27 Oct. 1934; *Dorothy Frooks*: *NYT*, 29 Oct. 1934; *refused to debate*: *NYT*, 1 Nov. 1934.

223 *"I am sorry you were hurt"*: ER to Hick, 31 Oct. 1934.

224 *Frooks crashed*: *NYT*, 2 Nov. 1934.

224 *"Damn the newspapers"*: Hick to ER, 2 Nov.; *velvet dresses*: ER to Hick, 7 Nov. 1934.

225 Eager to help O'Day staff a creative, politically alert congressional office, Hick suggested young FERA investigator Martha Gellhorn, whose journalistic and punchy style had impressed her, to serve as secretary to the new member of Congress.

225 *O'Day protested*: *NYT*, 7 Nov. 1934.

225 *"Franklin wants to know"*: ER to Greenway, nd, with 15 Nov., ibid; Greenway replied, 27 Nov. 1934, Tucson.

226 In September White became optimistic when the *Miami Daily News* endorsed the antilynch legislation: "Isnt this great coming from Florida? If you deem wise, I wish you would show it to the President and warn him that he is going to hear a great deal more about the Costigan-Wagner bill between now and next spring." White to ER 5 Oct. 34; ER to Pickett 5 Oct., 15 Oct., 11 Dec. 34; Pickett to ER, 25 Oct. 34, with housing enclosure by John Murchison to Pickett to ER, 70/ 628.

226 ER on Villard to Dorothy Canfield Fisher, see Fisher to ER, 9 Apr. 1934; ER to Fisher, 13 Apr., 1934/ 100. Fisher agreed: "yes, of course you're quite right about Mr. Villard!" DCF to ER, 23 Apr. 34/100, Box 1297; ER to DCF, 25 Ap 34; DCF to ER, 26 May 43; ER to DCF 13 June/100; Scheduled to speak at the Adult Education Association Convention, DCF stayed at the White House on 23 May.

227–228 *Dewson and fears of radicalism*: Radical youth materials enclosed with Dewson to ER, 30 Nov. 1934 100, Box 1293.

229–230 *"Dearest, I don't wish you were here"*: ER to Hick, 10 Nov. 1934; *"I behaved very badly . . ."*: ER to Hick, 19 Nov. 1934; also 20 Nov.; ER to Anna, 19 Nov.; *She credited Hick*: 21 Nov. 1934. Hick received three letters from Warm Springs in one day, and she concluded: "God knows *I'd* love it if you came home, but—it's only nine more days. . . . And sometime later, maybe, you and I might be able to go down there alone and have fun, as we did before. I'll never go down there with the mob." Hick to ER, 21, 22 Nov. 1934.

231 *"wouldn't you, like every one else, spoil me"*: ER to Hick, 23 Nov. 1934. Rexford G. Tugwell joined the party at Warm Springs on his return from a tour of Europe and at lunch ER was dismayed to hear that Tugwell and the others seemed "to accept the possibility that what may be needed to get us there is more wars, whereas I rebel at the thought!"

231 At Mary Harriman Rumsey's bedside were her daughter, Mary Averell Harriman Rumsey (21), her sons, Bronson Harriman Rumsey (17), student at St Paul's, and Charles Cary Rumsey, Jr. (22 and recently married).

232 *A great personal loss in ER's network*: Isabella Greenway to Molly Dewson, 26 Dec. 1934, Tucson.

232 As chair of NRA's Consumer Advisory Board, Mary Harriman Rumsey vigorously opposed increased prices, which only passed the cost of industrial recovery on to the consumer. She organized consumer councils, fought for retail codes, and hired many of the New Deal's most advanced and "aggressive" liberals, including: Robert Lynd, Frederic Howe, Paul H. Douglas, journalist Dexter Keezer, Gardner Jackson, and historian Caroline Ware. In 1933, with Vincent Astor and her brother Averell, she bought *Today*, which Ray Moley edited, and which became *Newsweek* in 1937. According to Raymod Moley: "The idea of a new magazine originated in the fertile mind of Mary Harriman Rumsey." Moley, *After Seven Years*, pp. 278–81. For the drama of her bid to buy the *Washington Post*, see Ralph Martin, *Cissy*, pp. 328–30.

232 See esp. Mary Harriman Rumsey, "Champion of the Consumer Speaks Out," S. J. Woolf, *New York Times Magazine*, 6 Aug. 1933; *NY Times* "Mrs. Roosevelt at Rumsey Rites," 20 Dec. 1934; *NY Herald Tribune*, 19 Dec. 1934; cf. Rudy Abramson, *Spanning the Century: The Life of W. Averell Harriman, 1891–1986* (William Morrow, 1992), 253–259; BW Cook, ER, v. I; Persia Campbell [who N.Y. Governor Averell Harriman appointed first state consumer affairs adviser in 1959] *MHR, Notable American Women, III*, pp. 208–9; I am grateful to Marjory Potts of Vineyard Video Productions, for her correspondence, her interview with Averell Harriman, and her work on France Perkins and MHR.

13:1935

233 *FDR's plans to achieve a proper security: NYT* 22 May 1935.
234 Lillian Wald to Jane Addams, 19 Dec. 1934; Swarthmore College Peace Collection; Jane Addams Papers Project.
234 FDR wanted social security to be universal, simple, nondiscriminatory. FDR quoted by Frances Perkins, *The Roosevelt I Knew*, pp. 282–83. For the complexities of Social Security's labyrinthian history see esp. Davis, pp. 437–62; Linda Gordon, *Pitied But Not Entitled* (Free Press, 1994); Alice Kessler-Harris, *Out To Work* (Oxford University Press, 1982); and Alice Kessler-Harris, forthcoming book on Social Security; also AKH, "Designing Women and Old Fools: The Construction of the 1939 Social Security Amendments," in Linda Kerber, et al, eds., *U.S. History As Women's History* (University of North Carolina Press, 1995); Mimi Abramowitz, *Regulating the Lives of Women* (South End Press, 1996).

FDR's 4 Jan, 17 Jan. 1935 speeches quoted from John Gabriel Hunt, ed., *The Essential FDR* (Gramercy Books, 1995), pp. 82–93.
235 ER to John Boettiger, and "Lovely Lady," 4 Jan. 1935, in Asbell, pp. 68–69.
236 In *1902, TR and World Court*: Jane Addams, "The World Court," in Allen F. Davis, ed., *Jane Addams on Peace, War, and International Understanding* (1976), pp. 188–94; Garland, cf. Howard N. Meyer, "A Global Look at Law and Order: The 'World Court' at the UN's 50th," *Social Education* (Nov/Dec. 1994), pp. 417–19; David Patterson, "The U.S. and the Origins of the World Court," *Political Science Quarterly* (Summer 1976).
236 *December 1933, FDR to Lape, "politically speaking . . . it would be unwise to do anything about the World Court."* See Robert Dallek, *FDR and American Foreign Policy* (Oxford University Press, 1979), p. 71.

237 *"On this hope we rest":* Lape to Helen Rogers Reid, 13, 16 Jan. 1934, Reid Papers, LC. Senator Roscoe Patterson told Lape: "no legislation will be considered during this session which does not meet with the approval of the President." Patterson to Lape, 22 Feb. 1934, in ER box 1306.

238 ER, "Because the War Idea Is Obsolete," in Carrie Chapman Catt et al., Rose Young, ed., *Why Wars Must Cease* (Macmillan, 1935), pp. 21–29.

239 *"Private profit":* Identified with the Women's International League for Peace and Freedom, whose executive secretary Dorothy Detzer was most responsible for persuading Senator Gerald P. Nye of North Dakota to investigate the Munitions Industry, ER agreed with the conclusions of the Nye Committee that industrial profits needed to be removed from the business of national defense. See Wayne S. Cole, *Senator Gerald P. Nye and American Foreign Relations* (University of Minnesota Press, 1962), pp. 66–76.

239 *Throughout the two-week debate:* See: "Up Senate, Down Court," *Time,* 11 Feb. 1935, pp. 13–15; cf. esp. Gilbert Kahn, "Presidential Passivity on a Non-salient Issue: FDR and the 1935 World Court Fight," *Diplomatic History* (Spring 1980), p. 137 ff. Privately, FDR to Joe Robinson, *FDR Letters,* pp. 449–50; Kenneth Davis, pp. 495–96.

241 *Lape was bitter:* transcript, Lape interview with Joseph Lash, 17 Feb. 1970; 24 Feb. 1970; Lash Papers, FDRL. *nevertheless defended her husband:* ER to Mrs. Kendall Emerson, 12 Feb. 1935, 100, Box 1336.

242 *Unknown to ER:* William Dodd to to A. Walton Moore for FDR, 24 Feb. 1935, FDR PSF; Dodd Collection.

242 *Ickes censured ER's involvement:* Ickes, pp. 284–85.

242 *A shocking aftermath:* On tax threat, Lape to Nellie Bok, 22 Jan. 1964, Lape Papers, Box 2, FDRL; *FDR's hardball against Huey Long, a precedent:* FDR had Henry Morgenthau initiate a tax investigation of Huey Long as one of his "first acts as treasury secretary" in January 1934. Leuchtenberg, *The FDR Years* (Columbia, 1995), pp. 93–94; Davis, pp. 493–95; Alan Brinkley, *Voices of Protest: Huey Long, Father Coughlin and the Great Depression* (Knopf, 1982); and William Ivy Hair *The Kingfish and His Realm: The Life and Times of Huey Long* (Louisiana State University Press, 1991).

242 *Health seemed the most urgent issue:* Lape to Nellie Lee Bok, 22 Jan. 1964, Lape Papers, FDRL; *ER "worked up some things" for FDR's birthday:* ER to Hick, 30 Jan. 1935.

243 *Claude Neal lynching:* FDR, "I have forgotten," quoted in Nancy Weiss, pp. 108–9. White to ER 24 Jan. 1935: your letter of 22 Jan. "has done a great deal to revive my somewhat flagging spirit" re bill; "I shall look forward eagerly to the letter" FDR said he will write." White to ER, 24 Jan. 1935/100/Box 1362.

243 *Marianna lynching horrible:* ER to White, 20 Nov. 1934; White to ER, 8 Nov. 1934; White to ER, enclosure to FDR, 27 Dec. 1934; ER to White, n.d., Dec. 1934/100, Box 1362; *"I wonder if you could advise me":* White to ER, 10 Jan. 1935; *"I talked to the Pres":* n.d., Jan. 1935; cf. White to FDR, 12 Jan. 35/ re the brazen shooting of Jerome Wilson, 28, by a mob yesterday in Louisiana. His father, John Wilson, was a prosperous farmer, and the cause was envy: In 1934, he purchased 80 acres to add to his already large farm: "Mr. Wilson's prosperity . . . aroused the enmity and jealousy of some of the whites. . . ."

244 *looked forward to visiting a controversial art exhibit:* White to ER, 17 Jan. 1935; ER to White, 21 Jan. 1935; *NYT called it "macabre":* Sitkoff, p. 288.

244 *safer if ER did not attend:* ER to White on the exhibit, 13 Feb, n.d., Mar. 1935, 100/Box 1362. White to ER, 12 Feb. 1935; 18 Feb. 1935.

245 *Triplet controversy:* Wiley Hall, chair of the Theban Beneficial Club, Richmond, 14 Jan. 1935; ER to Hall 22 Jan. 1935/100; ER to Woodward, 20 Dec. 1934; Woodward to Scheider, 18 Dec. 1934; Ella Agnew to Woodward, 14 Dec. 1935; Woodward to Scheider, 23 Jan. 35 ("we all regret"); Agnew to Woodward, 22 Jan. 1935; Agnew to every member of the staff, "these files are confidential; any violater will be summarily dismissed," 22 Jan. 1935/70/672.

245 Leonidas Dyer to White, 28 Jan. 35; White to ER 1 Feb. 35, "I, however, still cling to my belief that you and the president. . . ." Also, WW to Dyer, 2 Feb. 1935, sent to ER.

245 *ER had penciled on White's letter:* 14 Mar. 1935, Box 1362.

246 *White resigned in protest:* White to ER, with enclosures, 3 May 1935, including "last week's Afro-American which pays you so well-merited a tribute"; White to FDR, 6 May 1935; 1362; cf. Nancy Weiss, pp. 113–14; *"I am so sorry":* ER to White, 8 May 1935; White to ER, 9 May 1935 with copy of his resignation letter; and 23 May, with letter NAACP sent to senators, including the *Des Moines* (Iowa) *Register* editorial of 4 May/100, Box 1362.

246 *Wilkins invitation:* Roy Wilkins to ER, 20 May 1935; FDR memo to Scheider, 28 May 1935; ER acquiesced, letter of regret, ER to White, 15 June 1935. Ultimately Josephine Roche attended, and made a "great speech." White to ER 3 July.

248 *Morgenthau's testimony:* "Statement of the Secretary of the Treasury on the Economic Security Bill," 5 Feb. 1935, in ER, Box 665; with "Summary of Social Security Bill as it is at present before the House (HR 7260), n.d., May 1935, Box 665; *Europe's social security precedents:* in Mimi Abramovitz, p. 230. Frances Perkins, p. 293; 297–98.

249 *ER contradicted Morgenthau's proposals:* ER, "Mobilization for Human Needs, *Democratic Digest* (Nov. 1933), pl; see esp. ER's response to Dr. Townsend's movement for old-age security in citizen letters, for example, ER to Janie Ballard, 5 Dec. 1934; ER to C. H. Bartels, 1 Nov. 1934; 70. On 5 Jan. 1934, to D.C. branch of American Association for Social Security.

249 "First Lady Pleads for Old Age Pensions," herein she called for "universal old age insurance," *Social Security* (Feb. 1934), pp. 3–4.

250 *ER's 27 Feb. 1935 press conference:* Beasley, pp. 28–29; *NYT,* "Wife Acclaims Roosevelt's Deeds . . . ," 3 Mar. 1935, p. 1.

250 *"Here I hardly count anything":* ER to Hick, 22, 23 Jan. 1935; *glad for their talk:* ER to Hick, 25 Jan. 1935.

251 *"Would you like to write it":* ER to Hick; *"I know how you feel":* 26 Jan. 1935.

251 *WPA a compromise for work security:* June Hopkins to BWC, July 1997.

252 *"a gray and gloomy day":* ER to Hick, 29 Jan. 1935. The height of the social season was under way, there were congressional receptions, endless events, FDR's birthday balls: "Hick darling, I want you but you would be more unhappy, as you were, hanging around here while I went through this deadly round. At least in New York you've got people you like and a city you enjoy." 31 Jan. 1935.

253 *"Of course you should have had a husband":* ER to Hick, 1 Feb. 1935.

253 *"I'd have to be chloroformed first!":* ER to Hick, 7 Feb. 1935.

253 *February songs of duality:* 14 Feb. from Elmira; 15 Feb. in Ithaca; with Earl 16 Feb. 1935.

254 *snowbound Hyde Park weekend:* ER to Hick, 24 Feb. 1935.

254 *"Dearest Babs":* FDR to ER, 31 Mar. 1935; *Letters,* pp. 469–70.

254 "You have been constantly in my thoughts through Howe's illness—the strain must be unbearable. . . ." Greenway to ER, 4 Apr. 1935, 100/Box 1340; Hope Chamberlin on Greenway, p. 111.

254 *particularly mindful of NAACP opposition:* Haynes, "Lily-White Social Security," *The Crisis,* Mar. 1935, pp. 85–86.

255 *ER distributed articles from* The Crisis*:* Roy Wilkins to ER, 27 Oct. 1934; Oct. 1934 issue of *Crisis;* ER to Richberg, 10 Oct., 1 Nov.; Richberg to ER 9 Nov. 1934, with Gustav Peck's answer in *The Crisis,* and Suzanne La Follette's 5 Sept. 1934 *Nation* article, "A Message to Uncle Tom;" and Peck to Richberg, 6 Nov. 1934.

255 *ER to Richberg, 20 Nov.; 22 Nov. 1934; "I sincerely hope. . ."* 100, Box 1316; *ER hated ceremony:* ER to Hick, 25 Apr. 1935; *"Every president and his family go through it":* ER to Hick, 26 Apr. 1935; *exchange with SDR:* 26 Apr. 1935.

256 *Harlem exploded:* Thomas Kessner, *Fiorello La Guardia and the Making of Modern New York* (Penguin, 1989), pp. 368–77.

257 Dewson to Agnes Brown Leach, 26 Feb. 1935; Dewson to Greenway, 20 Dec. 1934; Dewson to Leach, 11 Mar. 1935, Women's Division Papers, Box 118; cf. BWC on Leach in Crystal Eastman; cf. vol. I. Leach on Perkins, quoted in Ware, p. 100; Dewson to ER, and Lucy R. Mason, quoted in Ware, p. 100; on social security, Dewson to ER, 10 Apr. 1935.

In 1964, Frances Perkins taught at Cornell and was surprised to be confronted by student questions about race. Bewildered by her disinterest, one student asked if the "Negro question were not the litmus test of liberalism?" Perkins answered: "Many people never gave it a thought," and in FDR's administration the Negro question "came very late." It was "really not" an issue "until the war." Perkins lectures, Cornell University Archives, 22 Sept. 1964, pp. 49–52. On lily white Social Security, Perkins said nothing.

257 *ER in a rare state:* ER to Hick, 27, 28 Apr. 1935.

258 28 Apr. 1935, FDR's Fireside Chats, pp. 63–72.

258 *ER supported Wagner:* Richard Lieberman to BWC.

259 *"My calm":* ER to Hick, 29 Apr.; 1 May 1935. Lash, *Love Eleanor,* p. 222; *never blow off to F:* ER to Hick, 2 May 1935.

259 *Jane Addams considered it a "wild" idea:* Hannah Clothier Hull to Jane Addams, 31 Jan. 1935, SCPC/JA Project; Jane Addams to Hull, declining a congressional resolution, though pleased ER and Edna St. Vincent Millay planned to speak, "it is lovely and thrilling," 13 Mar. 1935; Mary Moss Wellborn to JA, 13 Mar. 1935; Hull to JA, 14 Mar. 1935.

259 *Silenced by the State Department:* Mary Moss Welborn to Edith Helm, 27 Apr. 1935, with State Department Memo; international broadcast and dinner lists of speakers, 2 May 1935.

260 *"Touch the floor!":* ER to Hick, 8–9 May 1935; *new pool lovely:* 10 May 1935.

260 ER wished Hick "could be happy"at Val-Kill, "but you and I will have to build a cabin together somewhere else sometime!" 11 May 1935.

260 *poem:* Elizabeth Barrett Browning, "A Woman's Shortcomings," see vol. I.; *ER on love:* 13 May 1935.

261 ER to Hick, 15 May 1935. But above all, 15, 16, 17, 19 May.

262 See ER's FBI files on "Eleanor Clubs"; Sandy Vanocour to BWC on "pushing" days in his childhood.

262 *tours coal mines: NYT,* 22 May 1935; *ER's press conference:* Beasley, p. 32.

263 ER telegram to Jane Addams, 20 Jan. 1935, Jane Addams Project; Louise deKoven Bowen, *Open Windows* (Chicago: Fletcher Seymour, 1946), p. 271.

Elizabeth Dillings, *The Red Network* (1934), quoted in Allen F. Davis, *American Heroine: The Life and Legend of Jane Addams* (Oxford University Press, 1973), pp. 268–69; cf. Elizabeth Dilling, *The Roosevelt Red Record and Its Background* (published by the author in Chicago, 1936).

263 *Jane Addams's obituary and Hitler's Reichstag speech: NYT,* 22 May 1935.

14: The Victories of Summer, 1935

264 In 1936, when the Veterans' Bonus came up again, it finally passed over FDR's veto; and in that election year veterans received their bonus.

264 Ken Davis, pp. 513–14; cf. Hope Chamberlin on Greenway, p. 111; Caroline O'Day voted to uphold his veto. FDR was pleased to have her "slant on things," and "I am grateful to you for voting 'No.' " O'Day to FDR, 23 May 1935; FDR to O'Day, 29 May 1935, PPF.

265 *ER regretted: TIR,* 136; Ken Davis, 516.

266 *ER and WTUL:* See esp. Annelise Orleck, *Common Sense and a Little Fire: Women and Working Class Politics in the U.S., 1900–1965* (University of North Carolina, 1995, pp. 159, 166.

266–67 *women's labor movement refortified:* See especially Anne Firor Scott, "After Suffrage: Southern Women in the Twenties," in Cott, ed., *History of Women in the U.S.,* vol. 17, part 2, pp. 586–606; Lucy Randolph Mason, *To Win These Rights: A Personal Story of the CIO in the South* (1952); John Salmond, *Miss Lucy of the CIO: The Life and Times of Lucy Randolph Mason* (University of Georgia, 1988); *"the men instinctively got to their feet":* Virginia Durr on Miss Lucy, quoted in Pat Sullivan, p. 96.

267 *Harry Hopkins escorted Flanagan:* Hallie Flanagan, *Arena: The Story of the Federal Theatre* (Limelight Editions, 1985 [1940]), pp. 3–4.

268 *Soon the Federal Theatre:* Flanagan to ER, Report, 23 Dec. 1935; Hallie Flanagan, *Arena,* pp. 9–12; 24–28; Flanagan to ER, 8 Jan. 1936/ 70 Box 681; cf. Jacob Baker to Vassar president H. H. MacCracken, 28 May 1935, cc Scheider, 70/ Hopkins, Box 653; Jane DeHart Matthews, *The Federal Theatre, 1935–1939: Plays, Relief, Politics* (Princeton University Press, 1967), pp. 20–21, 28–29.

268 *ER relished:* Flanagan to ER, 8 Jan. 1936, with enclosure "Men at Work," L.A.'s Federal Theatre Bulletin, with Flanagan quote.

269 *"stranded generation," and "wandering women":* Ruby Black, pp. 210–11; *She agitated for a youth conference:* ER to Studebaker, 8 Mar. 1935; with Studebaker's speech, Box 666.

269–70 *"I waited":* TIR, p. 163.

270 *NYA was inclusive:* In May, FDR also issued EO 7046, which prohibited discrimination on WPA projects. On 22 July, Hopkins assured ER: "The work program does not permit any discrimination against Negro workers." White to ER, 13 June 1935, with attachments; ER to White, with Hopkins 22 July statement, 1 Aug. 1935/100. *NYA "politically popular":* TIR, p. 163; see also Sitkoff, p. 73; Anthony Badger, pp. 207–9; Ruby Black, p. 215.

271 The 28–30 Mar. 1935 conference on "Women's Work and Women's Stake in Public Affairs" honored ER; Robert Wagner keynoted; sponsored by Connecticut College's Institute of Women's Professional Relations; copy of program attached, ER to Studebaker, 8 Mar. 1935, Box 666.

271–72 *ER and NYA details, correspondence:* Margaret Ordway to ER, 12 Apr. 1937; Aubrey Williams, Box 4; ER to Williams, 30 Nov. 1935; Williams to ER, 22 Nov. 1935; Williams to ER, 20 Aug. 1935, Box 671; 16 Jan. 1936, with summary of NYA program and results to date; Williams to ER, NYA Activities with Special Reference to Negro Youth, 12 Feb. 1936; re Flora Rose's idea of a survey: ER to Williams, 3 June 1936; Williams to ER, 10 June 1936; Pickett to ER, 14 Nov. 1935.

272 Robert Sherwood quoted in Sitkoff, p. 61.

272 *FDR's "soak the rich" Revenue Act:* See Anthony Badger, *The New Deal* (Hill & Wang, 1988), pp. 102–4; Mark Leff, "Taxing the 'Forgotten Man': The Politics of Social Security Finance in the New Deal," *Journal of American History* (Sept. 1983), pp. 359–81; Eliot Janeway, *The Economics of Crisis: War, Politics, & the Dollar* (Weybright and Talley, 1968).

273 *ER at Campobello:* ER to Hick, 9, 10 July, 15 July 1935.

273–74 *"quite a household":* ER to Hick, 26 July 1935; *Characteristically:* 28 July; *"I realize":* 29 July; *time to read:* 31 July 1935; *Rebel Saints:* 6 Aug.; *and tennis:* 9 Aug. 1935. Hick replied, 31 July; *"ER had to laugh":* 2 Aug. 1935.

274–75 *Hick to ER on Herzog:* 31 July 1935; *Woodward to ER:* 16 July 1935; *telegram to Welchpool:* n.d., July 1935.

275 *Leslie County, Kentucky:* Woodward to ER, 2 Feb. 1935, FERA Library Service Work Projects for Women, report; Goodwin to ER, 24 Jan. 1935; Scheider to Kathryn Goodwin, 5 Feb. 1935, with photographs of the riders, which ER appreciated, led by Elizabeth Fullerton, Dir. Women's Work, Ky.; Woodward to ER, 26 Oct. 1935, "This shows that as fast as General McCarl releases funds, women are being put to work along with the men."

275–76 *practice houses; sewing rooms:* Woodward to ER, 7 Mar. 1936; 31 Oct. 1935; Woodward to ER, 6 Feb. 1935; 7 Feb. 1935; Woodward to ER, 3 Sept. 1935, with enclosures, on sewing rooms, which employed over 200,000 women, and purchased 150 million yards of cotton textiles—a boon to the cotton industry; Box 672; *"For the first time in history," WPA:* ER to Woodward, 16 Nov. 1935, recommending June Hamilton Rhodes and Mary Dillon for her national advisory committee; Woodward to ER, 21 Dec. 1935; 7 Mar. 1936.

275–76 *Woodward to ER:* 25 May 1936; ER to Woodward, re glowing defense of NY's sewing project, "I think it is grand!" 3 June 1936.

276–77 *ER's article, "Can a Woman":* ER to Hick, 30 July 1935; *negative publicity:* cf. *Times Dispatch,* 17 June 1935, in Hick, Box 2.

278 *displeased by the first meeting of the AYC:* ER wrongly understood it to be influenced by AYC organizer Viola Ilma's visits with German and Italian youth groups.

278 For the AYC's origins, and Detroit meeting, see Leslie Gould, *American Youth Today* (Random House, 1940), with foreword by Eleanor Roosevelt. I am grateful to Vivian Cadden for this book. 1935 meeting, pp. 63–66; for Viola Ilma's 1934 beginnings at NYU, pp. 54–62.

278–79 *NYA's first conference on black youth:* Aubrey Williams to ER, 13 July 1935; George Peabody to ER, "I am glad to think of the conference of Negro Leaders he is to call," 23 July; 70. Williams to ER, 16 Aug., with report, 70, Box 671. ER to Williams, 28 Aug. 1935; Williams to ER, 22 Aug., with *Pittsburgh Crusader* article of the meeting, 16 Aug. 1935; 100.

279 *Throughout the summer:* Walter White to ER, 13 June 1935; White to Hopkins, 12 June; ER to White, 1 Aug. 35, with Hopkins's 22 July wage schedules; 100.

279–80 *Early was irate:* Steve Early to Malvina Scheider, 5 Aug. 1935; 100; "I realize perfectly": ER to Early, 8 Aug. 1935, PPF, 1336.

280 *As ER prepared to leave:* ER to Hick, 3 Aug. 1935; "After all dear": 12 Aug. 1935; cf. 6, 8 Aug. 1935.

280–81 "Not one damned thing": Hick to ER, 7 Aug. 1935; *In Buffalo:* 9 Aug. 1935. Ishbell Ross, another pioneering woman reporter, was working on the first major history of women in journalism, *Ladies of the Press,* and had written Hick. Relieved to know that she was not alone in her feelings, she sent Ross's letter to ER:

"Yesterday I heard from Winifred Black who, at 72, says she still cannot bear to stay away from a newspaper office and has no patience with her only daughter because she chose marriage instead of a newspaper career. Beyond a doubt, it's *got* something, Lorena. We cant all be crazy. . . ."

281 *14 August 1935:* a generation of feminist scholars led by Alice Kessler-Harris, Linda Gordon, and Mimi Abramowitz have fully explained the connections between the 1935 Social Security law and America's acceptance of permanent poverty.

282 *Social Security Act a first step:* See esp. ER, "Are We Overlooking the Pursuit of happiness?" *Parent's Magazine* (Sept. 1936), 21ff.

282 Hilda Worthington Smith to ER, with book *Frontiers,* n.d., 1935, Box 655.

15: Mobilizing for New Action

283 ER to Elinor Morgenthau, 26 Aug. 1935; "In Defense of Curiousity," *The Saturday Evening Post*, 24 Aug., 1935, reprinted in Allida Black, 17–25. Upon her return from Campobello, ER and Hick settled Louis Howe into the naval hospital and then drove north to Chautauqua. ER presented a rousing speech on community responsibility for America's neediest and still neglected people."

284–85 *Initial U.S. response to Mussolini:* in Breckenridge Long, *The War Diary of Breckenridge Long*, ed. by Fred L. Israel (University of Nebraska Press, 1966), pp. xviii, xix; Long to FDR 1, 27 June 1933; *"at war within two years":* Long to FDR, 21 Feb. 1935; *By September:* Long to FDR, 6 Sept. 1935; Long to Joseph Davies, 16 Sept. 1933; *FDR at cabinet, 27 August 1935:* Ickes, pp. 422–23.

286 George Padmore, "Abyssinia Betrayed by the League of Nations," *The Crisis*, June 1937, 166ff.

286 *Winston Churchill:* quoted in Manchester, 160–61.

287 *Haile Selassie:* quoted in Padmore, p. 188.

287 *"May I draw your attention";* E. Benson to ER, 23 Nov. 1936, from 1 Swiss Cottage Rd., London SE/100.

288 *"When the League failed Ethiopia":* David Bradford, "The Failure of Geneva," *The Crisis*, Sept. 1936, p. 270; Dorothy Detzer, "Ethiopia at Geneva," *The Crisis*, Dec. 1935, 361 ff.

288 Walter White to ER, 12 Sept. 1935; ER to White, 16 Sept. 1935.

288–89 On Anna and Harold's courtship and marriage, see Jeanne Nienaber Clarke, *Roosevelt's Warrior: Harold Ickes and the New Deal* (The Johns Hopkins University Press, 1996), pp. 13–14, 30–32, 50–52; T. H. Watkins, p. 307. On the demise of their marriage, T. H. Watkins, pp. 148–51; Clarke, pp. 90–91.

289 *Anna Ickes's death: NYT*, 1 Sept. 1935; *on funeral, 4 September 1935:* T. H. Watkins, pp. 408–10.

289 *"It's funny what sex can do to a man":* Jeanne Clarke, pp. 52–54.

289 When Genno Herrick returned to Washington, ER, Tommy, and their friends (Martha Strayer, Emma Bugbee, Ruby Black, and Bess Furman) surprised her with a "swell party right around her bed," where she remained for several months. Beasley, *ER and the Media*, pp. 61, 105.

290 *"I'm glad you like Jane Ickes":* ER to Anna, 12 Aug. 1938; 30 Aug.; Anna Halsted, Box 57.

290 *"Will I ever have any leisure":* ER to Hick, 5 Sept. 1935; *"Mama is furious":* 6 Sept. 1935.

290 *ER's daily column; Hick edited:* ER to Hick, 8 Sept; *"structure":* 10 Sept. 1935; *"tough as you like, . . . don't mind at all":* 14 Sept. 1935.

290–91 *Huey Long was shot:* William Ivy Hair, *The Kingfish and His Realm: The Life and Times of Huey Long* (Baton Rouge: Louisiana State University Press), pp. 320–26; see also Jeansonne and T. Harry Williams.

291 *ER in Detroit: Detroit Evening Times*, 10 Sept. 1935, "Better Homes Visioned by First Lady," Vera Brown; 10 Sept. 35, *Detroit Free Press*, "A fluttering handkerchief fells a house," Helen Bower; in Hall Roosevelt's scrapbook, thanks to Diana Jaicks and ER II.

292 Felix Frankfurter to ER, 30 Apr. 1936, in Lash, *Eleanor and Franklin,* p. 520.

293 White to ER, with W.E.B. Du Bois's book, 3 Sept; ER to White, 10 Sept. 1935.

293 *black woman journalist:* Lash, p. 519; Early to ER, 11 Sept. 1935.

293 *"Just nothing":* Hall to ER, 7 Apr. 1937; ER to Ickes, 9 Apr.; Burlew to ER 14 Apr., with enclosure/ 70.

293 *Dec. 1935 housing meeting:* After that meeting, ER worked closely with individual members of the NYC Housing Authority, Langdon Post, chair, Mary Simkovitch, Rev. E. Roberts Moore, Louis Pink, and B. Charney Vladek; *NYT,* 4 Dec. 1935.

294–95 *"Ma is really getting a kick":* Lash, *Love Eleanor,* p. 231.

295 *"I could shake you":* ER to Hick, 21 Sept. 1935; *"I don't quite deserve":* Hick to ER, 23 Sept.

295 *"Missy tried it":* ER to Elinor Morgenthau, Nov. 1934, Elinor Morgenthau Papers, FDRL.

295 Esther Lape on Elinor Morgenthau: interview with Lash, 17 Feb. 1970, Lash MSS.

295–96 Hick from Cleveland, 25 Sept. 1935; ER from California, 19 Sept. 1935. Ickes on shipmates, p. 449–50; on Pa Watson and Harry Hopkins, p. 461.

297 Hick certainly would have enjoyed the country's enchanting beauty, at least. 28, 29 Sept; 1, 2 Oct. 1935.

298 ER spent her birthday at Val-Kill with Tommy, Henry Osthagen, Earl Miller, and others including Molly Dewson, with whom she played good tennis. ER received a gold chain, among other presents from Hick.

298 *"If FDR could get out this year!":* ER to Hick, 23 Oct. 1935.

298–99 *Hick's report from West Virginia:* Hick to ER, 16 Oct. 1935. Red House, in Putnam County, West Virginia, was renamed "Eleanor." It was populated by unemployed chemical and munitions workers, stranded after World War I.

299–300 Hick's 19 Oct. 1935 nine-page single-spaced report from Red House; *"You confirmed":* ER to Hick, 24 Nov. 1935; see also ER to Hick 14 Oct.

301–2 ER to Urban League, 12 Dec. 1935, published as "The Negro and Social Change," *Opportunity Magazine,* Jan. 1936, pp. 14–15.

301–2 *"damn this women's work":* Hick to ER, 10 Dec. 1935.

302 *"ER outraged about the maids":* 13 Dec.

302 *"don't let anyone hold memorials":* ER to Hick, 19 Dec. 1935.

302–3 Lillian Smith in Cliff, ed., p. 206; cf. Rose Gladney, *How Am I to Be Heard? Letters of Lillian Smith* (University of North Carolina, 1993).

303 *FDR on Dodd:* in Ickes, p. 494; only Dodd refused to attend the Nazi Nuremberg rally. Michael Berenbaum, *The World Must Know* (Little, Brown, 1993), pp. 33–34.

16: A Silence Beyond Repair

304–5 Maria Meyer Wachman to ER, 5 Jan. 1934/100/1324. When I first referred to Wachman's letter in Marjorie Lightman, Joan Hoff, eds., several historians wrote to me to express doubt about its early date. Since the fall of the Berlin Wall, a monument has been erected to one of Hitler's most abusive centers of detention and torture. It opened in April 1933, and is commemorated now where it originally stood in history's triangle between the Bauhaus Museum and the Reichstag, just beyond the Wall's rubble.

306 On Hoover's willingness for Japan to serve as an anticommunist barrier, see William A. Williams, *American-Russian Relations* (Rinehart, 1952), p. 226.

306 *Ivy Low Litvinoff an "ER type":* George Fischer to author.

306 One segment of the business community, led by Raymond Robins and Senator Borah, had called for recognition and trade from the beginning. *Russia agreed to pay:* Bullitt, pp. 29, 49. *Debts after 1934,* Feis, 1933, p. 266.

307 *"Well, now Max":* in Ted Morgan pp. 397–98; ER, *TIR,* pp. 134–35; Ickes, p. 124; Perkins, p. 143; Dallek, p. 81.

307 *Perkins on Nazi propaganda:* Ickes, p. 111–12.

308 ER to Hick, 13 Nov. 1933.

308 See Lape papers; Lamont quoted in Lash, *Eleanor and Franklin,* p. 590.

308 *telephone conversation,* and *"My husband told me":* TIR, p. 134.

308 Dickerman and Mary Simkhovitch promoted the idea of John Dewey for the U.S.'s first ambassador, MD to ER, n.d., Nov. 1933.

308–9 Bullitt's mission to Russia released to Senate Foreign Relations Committee Sept. 1919; Bullitt in Justin Kaplan, *Lincoln Steffens,* pp. 246–49; to Bernard Baruch, p. 250; *"at least eleven wars":* pp. 253–4; *"lie on the sand":* Steffens, p. 303.

309 *to Moscow, 11 Dec. 1933:* Orville Bullitt, p. 18.

309 Bullitt denied Jewish roots, but his detractors referred to his mother, Louisa Gross Horwitz, a descendant of Berlin scholars and physicians, including eminent surgeon Samuel Gross. Although she was Episcopalian, her heritage raised questions of Jewish ancestry.

309–10 *Spring 1934, "to explore":* Clarence Pickett, *For More Than Bread,* p. 93; "confidential report to our friends," Pickett to ER, May 1934, 70, Box 628.

310 During his first weeks in Vienna, Franz von Papen boasted: "Southeastern Europe to the borders of Turkey was Germany's natural hinterland." Papen's mission was to achieve "German economic and political control over the whole of this region." Austria was to be the "first step." Quoted in Winston Churchill, pp. 103–4. cf. *For More Than Bread,* pp. 98–100.

312 *State Department memo to ER, opposing international radio broadcast:* Gertrude Bussey, Margaret Tims, *Women's International League for Peace and Freedom, 1915–1965* (London: Allen & Unwin, 1965), p. 151.

312 *"a new tulip" mistake:* 13 May 1935, Steve Early to Malvina Scheider/70/660; Scheider to William Phillips, 15 May 1935; Phillips to Scheider, 16 May 1935, etc.

313–14 TR also protested, in 1902 and 1905, against violent pogroms. Correspondence over Tydings resolution in Greenway Papers, Tucson.

313–14 Herman Lewkowitz to Isabella Greenway, 25 Jan. 1934; Greenway to Lewkowitz, 7 Apr. 934; Greenway Mss 31, Box 55, "Jews," Tucson; on the Tydings Resolution see also Arnold Offner, *American Appeasement*, pp. 81–83.

313–14 *"Four of us":* ER, *My Day*, Jan. 1936; pp. 15–16.

314 *Mock trial:* cf. Offner, pp. 82–83.

314 *Hitler and Dodd:* Offner, p. 68; Dodd Diary, 16 June 1933, pp. 4–6.

315 Sarah Gertrude Millin, *The Night Is Long* (London: Faber & Faber, 1941), pp. 249–55. I am grateful to Merle and Martin Rubin for this reference.

317 *Henry Morgenthau III:* In 1978, Oral History, FDRL, p. 74.

317 *Brains Trust on Baruch:* Margaret Coit, *Mr. Baruch*, pp. 429–30.

317 *"Jew party":* ER to SDR, 14 Jan. 1918; 16 Jan. 1918; see BWC, I.

317 *On Frankfurter:* ER to SDR, 12 May 1918.

318 *ER and Baruch, during the Smith campaign:* Coit, p. 374.

318 *"One of the wisest":* TIR, p. 256; *"There are few":* ER to Baruch, 16 May 1936; cf. Coit, p. 451.

318 *Baruch, and Churchill the gambler:* William Manchester, *The Last Lion: Winston Spencer Churchill/ Alone, 1932–1940* (Little, Brown, 1988, pp. 13–15; see also Martin Gilbert, *Churchill: A Life*, p. 379; Coit, pp. 190–93, 272–273.

318 *Baruch esoteric womanizer:* Helen Lawrenson, *Stranger at the Party: A Memoir*, pp. 107; 136–37; *Hobcaw and biographical details:* Coit pp. 13, 27, 317–18; Laurenson, p. 148; and Patricia Spain Ward, *Simon Baruch: Rebel in the Ranks of Medicine, 1840–1921* (University of Alabama, 1994), pp. 83, 92, 316n43.

320 *For Ford's "paper pogrom":* See Lewis Carlson and George Colburn, *In Their Place: White America Defines Her Minorities* (Wiley, 1972) pp. 259–61; Leonard Dinnerstein, *Anti-Semitism in America* (Oxford University Press, 1994), pp. 81–84 and passim. *Ford's apology* to Samuel Livingston, 7 Jan. 1942, ADL papers, with thanks to Ernest Nives.

320 *Baruch reviled:* Coit, 35–37; 359; 361; 469.

320 Felix Frankfurter once remarked to Baruch's great friend Herbert Bayard Swope that he thought Baruch was "kidding himself" to think he was in a different category from other Jews. Frankfurter and Walter Lippmann both worked in Newton Baker's Office of War Information, then criticized for employing too many Jews. Lippmann asked Frankfurter: " 'What is a Jew anyhow?' " Frankfurter offered, "as a working definition": Anybody " 'whom non-Jews regard as a Jew.' " Jordan Schwarz, *The Speculator: Bernard Baruch in Washington* (University of North Carolina Press, 1981), p. 560.

320–21 *Henry Morgenthau, Sr., on Palestine:* Peter Grose, *Israel in the Mind of America* (Knopf, 1983), p. 72.

321 *Henry Morgenthau, Jr., "drive for total Americanization":* Mostly *Morgenthaus*, pp. 80–81; 274; *Elinor Morgenthau blackballed by the Colony Club:* ER to *NYT*, 1937. Bill Preston's friend John Marquand said his mother (Christina Sedgwick) also resigned in protest when ER did: He was certain, since she spoke about it subsequently, and often. Henry III described his own sense of brooding adolescent loneliness at school the year his parents moved to Washington, and Hitler came to power. His grandfather visited him at Deerfield in the spring of 1933, and gave him Edgar Ansel Mowrer's *Germany Puts the Clock Back:* "It was as though my concept of Jewish alienation had permeated my sensibilities. . . ." Mowrer's book "chilled me to the marrow of my bones."

Mowrer, *The Chicago Daily News's* Berlin correspondent, was accused of exaggeration when he wrote in March 1933 that Germany had become an "insane asylum." When the State Department's Allen Dulles visited Berlin, he told Mowrer he was "taking the German situation too seriously." As president of the Foreign Press Association, he retained significant support among journalists, and the State Department did nothing when Hitler demanded his resignation. But on 20 Aug. 1933, his publisher Frank Knox transferred him to Tokyo. Mowrer left behind his prescient words: The goal of Hitler's "barbarous campaign was the extermination, permanent subjection or voluntary departure of the Jews from Germany."

See *Mostly Morgenthaus*, pp. 269–70; on Mowrer, Lipstadt, *Beyond Belief*, p. 25ff; Offner, p. 69.

321 Louise Wise to ER, 27 Oct. 1933/100, Box 1282.

321–22 ER to Mrs. Stephen S. Wise, American Jewish Congress, 14 Nov. 1933/100/1282; Louise Wise to ER, 22 Nov. 1933. On 23 Nov. 1933 ER presented the American Hebrew Medal to Carrie Chapman Catt at City College. Henry Morgenthau, Sr., presided; Rabbi Isaac Landman and Einstein celebrated Cott's work.

322 *ER at the Hotel Commodore: NYT*, 29 Feb. 1934; "Mrs. Catt to Receive the Hebrew Medal," *NYT*, 17 Nov. 1933; "Mrs. Catt Honored," Praised by ER, *NYT*, 24 Nov. 1933; "Catt, Women Ask Haven for Nazi Victims," *NYT*, 19 Mar. 1934.

322 *NYT*, 1 Mar. 1934; Florence Rothschild, "The Mistress of the White House," *The Wisconsin Jewish Chronicle*, 9 Mar. 1934; FDR/PPF, Box 1.

323 ER received hate mail, and letters of polite protest: As a "ninth generation" American, "of the same stock as you and your husband," and also an officer of "The Netherlands Society of Philadelphia," one correspondent wanted ER to know that she would only hurt her husband's future if she persisted complimenting Jews. H.S.J. Sickel to ER, 5 May 1934; ER to Sickel, 16 May 1934/100,1320.

323 *On Ruth Liberman:* ER to Dr. J. Edgar Park, President, Wheaton College, 4 June 1936/ 100 1397; cf. ER to Armand May, Hebrew Orphanage of Atlanta, 13 Jan. 1934/ 100/1309; ER to Rabbi Louis L. Mann, to speak at his Temple, Chicago Sinai Congregation, 16 Sept. 1936; ER to Ruth Oppenheimer, 30 Sept. 1934/ 100/1313.

323–24 Felix Frankfurter to FDR, and James McDonald's letter to Frankfurter, 20 Nov. 1933, in Freeman, ed., p. 173ff; 20 February 1934 telegram, pp. 194–95; FF to FDR, 22 Mar. 1934, p. 209.

324 *answered paragraph by paragraph:* FDR to FF, 24 Mar. 34.

325 *"It glittered and it glared":* Churchill, *The Gathering Storm*, 101–2ff.

326 Madison Square Garden rally, *NYT*, 7 Oct. 1934; *Jewish Examiner,* 12 Oct. 1934; in Mrs. S. Miller to ER, 18 Oct. 1934; ER to Mrs. Miller, 12 Nov. 1934; 100, Box 1310.

327 In honor of ER's address and her 50th birthday, she received a "tree certificate" which announced that fifty trees would be planted in the Hadassah Forest at Kiryath Anavim, near Jerusalem. "Zionism held hope of Jew in Europe . . . Mrs. Roosevelt honored . . . ," *NYT*, 17 Oct. 1934.

328 Alice Youngbar to ER, with article on Dachau, 20 Nov. 1934/100/ 1326; ER to Miss Youngbar, Oswego, Oregon, 11 Dec. 1934.

329–30 For information relating to the Brodsky family, I am grateful to Dr. Michael Brody for his family's correspondence and memorabilia. See, *NYT* 8 Feb. 1934; Florence Rothschild's 9 Mar. 1934 article also referred to Bertha Brodsky, and to ER's frequent gifts to the residents of Washington's Jewish Old People's Home, *The Wisconsin Jewish Chronicle*, 9 Mar. 1934. ER to Bertha Brodsky, 28 Feb. 1934/ Henrietta Nesbitt to Bertha re cherries, 22 June 1934; monthly notes, Feb. 1934 to Apr. 1935, Brody collection.

330 See also ER to Bertha Brodsky, 2 Apr. 1935; Milgrim to ER 22 Apr. 1935/100, Box 1349; ER to Rex Tugwell, 8 May 1935/100 668; Frank Brodsky to ER, 10 June 1935/ Brody coll; ER to Rex, 19 June 1935/ 70 Box 668; ER to Bertha 3 July 1936, Brody coll. ER left bonds to Brodsky grandchildren; and remained close to Frank, who had monthly breakfasts with ER until her death.

330 Dec. 1933 *Woman's Home Companion*; and cf. *NYT* 19 Dec. 1933.

330–31 On 10 December, ER said to the National Student Federation: "Peacetime can be as exhilarating to the daredevil as wartime. There is nothing more exciting than building a new social order."

331 *"We can't go on that way"*: ER in *NYT*, "Students March to White House," 22 Dec. 1933.

331 Hick's report from Ajo, May 1934; Dodd to R. Walton Moore, PSF Dodd, 5 Nov. 1934.

331 Hick to ER 4 May 1934; 8 May to Hopkins, in Beasley, p. 250.

331 On Ethiopia's resistance, see esp. *NYT* "Ethiopia woman to lead 15,000 men," 10 Oct. 1935 and *The Crisis* on Ethiopia.

332 George Biddle, "Artists' Boycott of Berlin Olympics Art Exhibition," in Matthew Baigell & Julia Williams, eds., *Artists Against War and Fascism: Papers of the First American Artists' Congress* (Rutgers University Press, 1986), pp. 90–91.

332 "Stay Out of the Olympics," *The Crisis*, Sept. 1935, p. 273.

332 *"Fair Play in Sports"*: *NYT*, 15 July 1936; "Mahoney Declares Boycott is Reason for Olympic Deficit," *NYT*, 7 July 1936.

333 *Not everyone fooled: NYT*, 12 Jan. 1936; *feast of Nazi pageantry: NYT*, 6 July 1936.

333 Also, N.Y.'s Emmanuel Celler and Rhode Island's Senator Peter Gerry raised the issue of a boycott to oppose persecutions of Jews and Catholics; *NYT*, 14 Aug. 1935; "Buffalo Jews in Protest," against "the savagery and barbarism of the Hitler regime," and call for a boycott of the 1936 games: *NYT*, 14 Aug. 1935.

333 *The Crisis* editorialized: "America's track ace, Jesse Owens," put Hitler "on the spot. He has been telling the Germans . . . that they are the chosen people . . . and all others, especially Jews and Black people, are the low scum of the earth. . . . Yet here before the amazed German nation were black and brown boys winning honors. Hitler could have greeted all winners impartially. . . . But Hitler is a small man."

333 *The Crisis*, Sept. 1936, p. 273.

17: Red Scare and Campaign Strategies, 1936

335–36 Ethiopia, *the Living Newspaper:* Hallie Flanagan to ER, with Baker to Flanagan, 18 Jan. 1936/70; ER to Flanagan, 21 Jan.; Baker to Flanagan, 23 Jan.; Flanagan, *Arena,* pp. 64–66; Jane DeHart Matthews, *The Federal Theatre,* pp. 65–73.

336–37 *ER censored Chicago revue:* Flanagan to ER; ER to F, 13 Feb. 1936; Flanagan to ER, telegram with script, 9 Dec. 1936.

338 *"When in New York":* ER to Jacob Baker, 19 Feb. 1936; Report and History of Federal Art Project, n.d., to ER, as of 15 Feb. 1936, ibid. /70, Box 675.

339 *women and work:* "First Lady Outstanding Forum Leader," *School Life* (Mar. 1936), p. 177ff; Studebaker to ER 19 Mar. 1936; ER to Studebaker, 21 Mar. *Protest mail:* see esp. Jesse Gordon, with address, to ER, 22 Aug. 1935; ER to JG, "I am afraid your attitude," 29 Aug. 1935, 100, Box 1339.

339 *General Federation of Women's Clubs:* ER to Clara Kelley, 29 Feb. 1936/ 100; tea and dinner for Federation, 15, 17 Jan., *Democratic Digest,* Mar. 1936.

339 *ER on Mary Breckenridge: Democratic Digest,* Mar. 1936; ER's press conference, 4 Feb. 1936.

339 *ER and Charl Williams, "Microphone Duet": Independent Woman* (May 1936), pp 145–46; cf. ER's Dec. 1937 article for *Good Housekeeping:* "Should Wives Work?"

340 *but they did create a jolly atmosphere:* ER to Hick, 4 Jan. 1936.

340 *"you were low":* ER to Hick, 14 Jan. 1936; *"we'll forget I'm in N.Y.":* ER to Hick, 17 Jan. 1936.

340 *"being leisurely with Newky," "You have in the savings $255.43":* ER to Hick, 19 Jan. 1936;

340–41 ER's answers to Hick's lost letters sounded hurt and angry. After some earnest negotiation, she gave up: "I'm not making *any* plans ahead but I will keep your dates in mind and be here as much as possible! There, is that indefinite enough?" One of Hick's letters seemed to ER incredible: "What a fool letter that was! I could hardly believe it." ER to Hick, cf. esp. 26, 28 Jan. 1936.

341 *Al Smith and Liberty League: NYT,* pp. 25, 26, Jan; *Cousin Corinne:* ER to Hick, 24–26 Jan. 1936.

341–42 ER to press conference: "Preserving Civilization," in *NYT,* 29 Sept. 1935; ER to Jeannette Rankin, 25 Jan. 1936, NCPW, Box 74, SCPC; *NYT* 22 Jan., Catt, Mary Woolley, ER, Britain's Kathleen Courtney, at Cause and Cure of War; also, *Dem. Digest,* March To Youth Congress: *NYT,* 2 Feb. 1936; Pickett arranged ER's peace tour, and subsequent broadcasts scheduled for Apr.: 4/15 broadcast after dinner; ER's Mar. lecture tour "for charity," was billed as "Ways to Peace," *NYT* 4 Mar. 1936.

342 *a scintillating evening:* ER to Hick, 5 Feb. 1936.

342–43 *Anna Louise Strong:* Wald to ER, 17 Jan. 35; ER to Wald, 21 Jan. 100; on Buro Bidgin, see Robert Weinberg, with Bradley Berman photographs, *Stalin's Forgotten Zion: Birobidzhan and the Making of a Soviet Jewish Homeland, 1928–1996* (University of California Press, 1998). Unfortunately, this book fails to deal with refugees and the settlement's role as a temporary sanctuary.

343 *Anna Louise Strong:* see Cedric Belfrage and James Aronson, *Something* *to Guard: The Stormy Life of the National Guardian, 1948–1967* (Columbia, 1978), p. 87; Ella Winter, *And Not to Yield: An Autobiography* (Harcourt, 1963), p. 118. Tracy Strong and Helene Keyssar, *Right in Her Soul: The Life of Anna Louise Strong* (Random House, 1983); ER to Hick, [12] Feb. 1936; Strong to ER, 13 Feb. 1936.

343 *"so very, very sorry":* ER to Hick, 18 Feb. 1936.

344 ER's friends argued for a more liberal immigration policy. During her visit in May 1935 Jane Addams pointed out to FDR that the low price of wheat would be adjusted by new immigration. According to Perkins she said: "I figured it out the other day, Mr. President. It is just about what a million new immigrants a year would have eaten up. I think it is active population that is needed." Perkins, *The Roosevelt I Knew*, p. 348.

344 *Individual cases:* Jurkowitz to Scheider, 28 Aug. 1935; Commissioner Mac-Cormack to Perkins, 6 May 1935. Charles Milgram to ER re. two rabbis; ER to FP, 13 Oct. 1936; FP to ER, 20 Oct. 1936; ER, 70.

344 ER and Hick spent some part of Hick's birthday week together, and then ER began a new series of well-paid lectures arranged and managed by the Colston Leigh Agency. Her first stop was Grand Rapids, Michigan, where ER finally met Alicent (Alix) Holt, "a charming person with a lovely face and I was so glad to see her."

345 *3,500 Southern Democrats met in Macon: NYT*, 30 Jan. 1936. In April, the Senate Lobby Committee, chaired by Senator Hugo Black, which investigated the Macon "grassroots" convention, announced that it was supported primarily by the Liberty League: John J. Raskob, former chair of the Democratic National Committee, and Pierre du Pont were the principal backers of the 29 Jan. meeting, and donated $5,000 each. *NYT*, 17 Apr. 1936; *Crisis* editorial, Mar. 1936, p. 81.

While the South rallied against ER, she was pleased to note: "I do like Ishbell Ross": ER to Hick, 18 Apr. 1936;

345 Walter White on Talmadge to ER, n.d., 1934, 100, box 1325.

345–46 *Democratic women irate:* Dewson to ER, 5 Nov. 1935, 100. ER to James Farley, 18 Apr. 1936.

346 Campaign details, ER to Farley, 18 Apr. 1936; Dewson to Farley, 15 Apr., with Leah Pollock's offending letter; cf. ER to Tugwell, 18 Apr. 1936, 70, Box 700.

346 *on Omlie and Vidal:* ER to Farley; and cf. Amelia Earhart to ER, 15 Sept. 1936; and Vidal to Dewson, in Sue Butler, pp. 348–52.

346 *Farley assured ER:* ER to Farley, n.d., May 1936; Farley to ER, 9 May 1936, 70, Box 680.

347 *WTUL:* Rose Schneiderman to ER, 16 Apr. 1936, 100; RS reported that Max Zaritsky was to join David Dubinsky in his "courageous" resignation from the Socialist Party to be free to work for FDR; see also Pauline Newman to ER, 27 May 1936, Box 5, Schlesinger; Pauline Newman quoted in Orlick, pp. 158–59; cf. ER, *Democratic Digest*, July 1936.

347 *ER and country women: NYT*, 2, 3 June 1936.

370 Ishbel Ross, on ER and Hick, *Ladies of the Press* (Harper Brothers, 1936), pp. 311–22.

348–49 The April 1936 conference "On Better Housing Among Negroes" afternoon sessions featured noted black architect Hilyard Robinson; Nannie Burroughs, chair of the National Committee on Negro Housing; white activists John Ihlder and Anson Phelps Stokes; and Ethel Roberson Stephens, Department of Home Economics, Howard University. There were also panels on housing and health, the family, recreation, and education. Conference Schedule, 18 Apr. 1936, at Miner Teachers' College, box 701; Florence Stewart to Scheider, 20 Apr. 1936, Box 698; Scheider to Stewart, 22 Apr.; Campbell Johnson, chair Conference Committee, to ER, 23 Apr. 1936, box 701: statistics on attendance and "the cttee on reports and records" will send your statement / to make revisions / since proceedings to be printed. But ER's remarks seem to have disappeared, and were nowhere quoted. Minutes/ 29 May 1936.

349 *As if in direct retaliation:* Minutes of Emergency Meeting, 8 May 1936/Box 701.

349 *Langston Project saved for African-Americans:* Minutes, 29 May 1936.

349 FDR to Mac, 12 May 1936; Ihlder to ER, 9 May; 70, Box 687; the Wagner-Ellenbogen Housing Bill was delayed until after the election.

350 *ER stunned by Howe's death:* ER to Hick, 19 Apr. 1936.

350 *Howe's funeral and burial: NYT,* 20, 21, 22, 23 Apr. 1936.

350 On the train to Howe's burial at Fall River, Massachusetts, ER wrote: "Death should be calm and serene when work is done and well done. There is nothing to regret, either for those who go, or for those who stay behind. . . ." *My Day,* pp. 32–35.

350 *ate at table, and Louis Howe Rasputin:* Lella Styles, p. 224; *Fannie Hurst's colored glasses:* Styles, pp. 169–71.

350–51 *ER on Howe:* TIR, 144–45; Autobiography, pp. 195–96; *"Rabbit is the one":* ER to Hick, 20 Apr. 1936.

351 *"He always wanted to 'make' me President when FDR was through, and insisted he could do it":* ER to Hick, 15 Nov. 1940. Louis Howe's essay in Dewson, FDRL, Box 2.

18: The Roosevelt Hearth, After Howe

353 *ER "loved him":* Frances Perkins, Columbia Oral History, vol. 2, p. 553.

354 *Betsey Cushing Roosevelt awakened at 3:30 A.M.:* Ted Morgan, p. 209. For Betsey Cushing as "rough," "imperious," "rivalrous with anybody," see Sally Bedell Smith, *In All His Glory: The Life of William S. Paley* (Simon & Schuster, 1990) p. 248. *ER liked "to lead:"* Betsey to Ted Morgan, p. 448.

354 James Roosevelt, *My Parents,* pp. 106, 223–24, passim; "Staffing My Father's Presidency: A Personal Reminiscence," reprinted in "In Memoriam: James Roosevelt: 23 Dec. 1907–13 Aug. 1991," *Presidential Studies Quarterly* (Fall 1991), pp. 845–46.

355 *Tugwell and Barbara Hopkins:* ER to Hick, 20 Apr. 1936.

356 *Jeannette Bryce and "these men are naive!":* ER to Hick, 2, 5 May 1936.

356 *Vineyard Shore School:* See Hilda Smith to ER, 6 Feb. 1936; ER to Smith, 12 Feb. 1936.

357 *"Reds Rule FERA Schools": Washington Herald,* 24 Feb. 1935; other clips, including a *NY Post,* 11 May 1935, criticizing the NYC School for Workers at the Henry Street Settlement; ER defended Smith.

357–58 *"landscaping":* ER to Lieut. Francis A. Maloney, 2 Mar. 1936; Maloney to ER, 26 Feb. 1936, 100; *"we have you . . . to thank":* Smith to ER, 21 Apr. 1936; see esp. Smith, Box 18, Schlesinger. Despite the 1934–35 Red Scare Hilda Smith had ER's endorsement, and Hopkins agreed. See Scheider to Smith, 5 June 1935; Smith to ER, 2 Aug. 1935: "You will be glad to know . . . that the plan for educational camps for women has been approved," and will be under the NYA. Aubrey Williams authorized 100 camps. ER to Smith, 25 Sept. 1935/ 70. Smith to ER, 23 May 1936; cf. correspondence re camp for delinquent girls, Knoxville, Tenn., Apr.–May 1936. Advisory Committee Meeting, 13 Apr. 1936, including Louise Stanley, Elizabeth Wickenden, Josephine Brown, others, Smith, chair. Smith to ER, plans for summer camps, 4 May 1936; summer 1936 statistics: Smith to ER, 23 Sept. 1936.

358 *"Camp Jane Addams assailed as Red":* NYT, 3 July 1936; *NYA camp not Red:* ER, 9 July 1936; cf. ER's correspondence with Mark McCloskey, and via Scheider, n.d., July 1936; re Sarah Rosenberg's 25 June 1936 letter on Workers' Alliance letterhead.

McCloskey to ER re new camp director, Mills removed, replaced by Bernice Miller, 4 Feb. 1936; cf. in March there was a meeting of the advisory committee to register "Negro girls," and it was agreed that Cecilia Saunders of Harlem's YWCA would be brought in to advise regarding "the right kind of Negro girl." As for stipends: "It was decided that they should be given 50 cents a week." McCloskey to ER, with minutes, 11 Mar. 1936.

358–59 *garden party for National Training School for Girls:* NYT, 16 May 1936, *My Day,* 8 May 1936.

359 *unemployment "throbbing with human pain":* My Day, Apr. 1936, p. 37.

359–60 Hick's report was immediately assailed by industrialists, and ER defended it. In June FDR sent a memo to ER that he had received statistics "to show that the figures which interested you and me so much were almost wholly incorrect." ER replied that the facts came from "the Chamber of Commerce of Youngstown. . . . I wonder if any figures are accurate; everyone colors to please themselves. . . ." ER to FDR, 16 June 1936, family, Box 594; the next year Hick's report was entirely vindicated. Hick to ER, 17 Mar. 1937.

360 *If you mind:* ER to Hick, 6, 7 May 1936.

360 *ER on SDR: My Day,* May 1936, p. 41.

361 *Dickerman lamented:* Davis, *Invincible Summer,* p. 145.

361 *FDR "upset":* ER to Hick, 28 May 1936; FDR to Robert Bingham, 4 May 1936, *Letters,* p. 587.

362 *Val-Kill, and "I wonder where you are":* ER to Hick, 30–31 May 1936.

19: The Election of 1936

363 *ER told press conference: NYT,* 5 Feb. 1936.

364 Various deaths contributed to ER's gloom in early June. ER to Hick, 1–6 June 1936. Her cousin Bobby Delano committed suicide, and then Joseph Byrns, the Speaker of the House died suddenly.

364 *wearied "of cheering crowds":* ER to Hick, 10, 11 June 1936.

364 *ER's spirits, 10–16 June 1936.*

364–65 *Dionne quintuplets:* ER to Hick, 13 June 1936.

365–66 *ER at Val-Kill:* ER to Hick, 19–21 June 1936.

366 *Alice Hamilton and Alderson:* ER to Hick, 24 June 1936.

366 *listened on the radio, and future dates:* ER to Hick, 25 June 1936.

366 *Molly Dewson's breakfasts:* Furman, p. 241.

366–67 *"I might get myself into trouble!":* ER to Dewson, 22 June; Dewson to ER, 20 May 1936.

367 *"undignified and meaningless":* ER to Hick, 27 June 1936.

367 *Perkins's speech on ER: NYT,* 25 June 1936; cf. Bess Furman. The next day Fannie Hurst also presented a praisesong for ER, who "is more than a pioneer.".

367 *women in Philadelphia "made history":* Furman, pp. 240, 227.

368 *Daisy Harriman and Alice Longworth:* Furman, p. 240.

368–69 *KKK violence and Red Scare again on agenda:* In 1935 Dewson, who sought to protect FDR, was not prepared to tackle the race issue directly. Dewson, Women's Division, Box 118.

369 Emma Guffey Miller championed ER in her speech on 16 June. See *NYT* 17 June 1936; On their split, see Dewson to Alice Disbrow, 11 June, Box 118; Furman, pp. 242–45.

369–71 *largest political rally:* Furman, pp. 245–46; speech quoted in *The Essential FDR,* pp. 113–19.

369–70 Arthur Schlesinger, *The Politics of Upheaval,* pp. 582–85.

371 *ER on FDR's speech: My Day,* 28 June 1936; Ickes, pp. 626–27; *ER wanted rhetoric transformed: Democratic Digest,* Aug. 1936, p. 3; *ER's advice to women in political life: Democratic Digest,* July 1936, p. 3.

372 *"Hate myself":* ER to Hick, 27 June, 28 June 1936.

373 *coordinated activities:* ER and Dewson, 15 July 1936, list and plans, Women's Committee, Box 117; meetings: see Ruby Black, p. 138.

373 *Kathleen McLaughlin:* "Mrs. R. Goes Her Way. . . ," *NYT,* 5 July 1936.

373–74 *"I'm an idiot":* ER to Hick, 8 July 1936.

374 *from Lake Superior:* Hick to ER, 27, 28 June 1936.

374 *no plans to see each other:* ER to Hick, 8, 9 July 1936.

374–75 *in Chicago with Kruger:* Hick to ER, 11 July 1936.

375 *aboard the* Potomac: Ickes, p. 629.

375 That weekend, ER and Esther rode together, but "Esther couldn't hold Pal, so we had an exciting ride." ER to Hick, 11–12 July 1936.

375–76 *Ickes's party:* Ickes, pp. 634–35.

377 *"While FDR smiles and fishes":* Ickes, pp. 639–40, 18 July 1936.

377 *Ickes despaired: Ickes,* pp. 643–46.

377 *the women were organized:* See Ickes, Agnes Leach to Virginia Rishel, 14 May, Women's Division, 118; Molly Dewson to Ruth Bryan Owen, 31 Mar. 1936.

377 Owen to Dewson on Phoebe Omlie, 28 Apr. 1936, Dewson, Box 3.

378 *Owen/Rohde wedding:* Bess Furman: pp. 247–48.

378–79 *ER's memo, 16 July 1936:* FDR Letters pp. 598–601. In addition, ER sent Farley a more specific letter about "zealous" fund-raising practices. Also, she wanted Farley to give Ed Flynn "some definite responsibility."

Jim Farley replied with a ten page single-spaced point-by-point answer. Zealous solicitations would be watched by Forbes Morgan. Ed Flynn would be brought into headquarters. In addition to Will Alexander and Sidney Hillman, Sam Rayburn would run the speakers' bureau; Leon Henderson would be in charge of research. Sol Rosenblatt was named chair of the Motion Picture Division. He promised to send her all significant reports, throughout "the entire campaign," as well as "all letters which in my judgment carry information that you should have. . . ." ER to Farley, 16 July; Farley to ER, 25 July 1936, 70. Farley's upset over FDR's purge efforts, and Walter George, in James Farley, *Jim Farley's Story* (McGraw-Hill, 1948), p. 128. See Mary White Ovington to ER, 28 May 1924, NAACP Papers, LC, Box C-70. I am grateful to Clare Coss for this reference.

380 *"Cotton Ed" Smith:* William Leuchtenberg, *The FDR Years* (Columbia University Press, 1995), p. 130.

380 *"for the purpose of permissive ravishment":* Arthur Schlesinger, p. 522; for the ditty see Leonard Dinnerstien, p. 109.

381 *Almost nonchalantly:* ER to Hick re *TIMS*, 22 July 1936.

382 *" 'Where's his hat?' ":* Wald's ice story was later used by FDR in a momentous speech, against Liberty Leaguers and businessmen who lost his top hat, with great effect. Lillian Wald, "Why I Am for Roosevelt," *Women's Democratic News*, Aug. 1936, pp. 2, 4, 13.

382 *ER on Wald: My Day*, 21 Aug. 1936. Wald told ER she was convinced that college students had achieved a new interest in world affairs because of her activities. It was, she wrote ER, "largely due to you" that the situation turned around. Constance Cummer for LDW to ER, 12 Mar. 1935; 100, Box 1361; Wald to ER, 7 Aug. 1936.

382 *FDR rushed to her bedside: NYT,* 19 Sept. 1936.

383 Frances Perkins to ER, n.d.; Scheider's note of thanks, 19 Sept. 1936; 70.

383 Wald to ER, 21 Sept. 1936; ER to LDW, 23 Sept. 1936.

383 Aubrey Williams to ER, 22 Sept. 1936, with 23 Sept. 1936 speech; ER to Williams, 25 Sept., 70; Hilda Smith to ER, 18 Sept. 1936; ER to Smith, 23 Sept. 1936. See also *My Day*, 18 Sept., 21 Sept. 1936.

383 *"Terrifying reading": My Day*, 25 Sept. 1936.

384 *"We read daily": My Day*, 9 Dec. 1936.

384 *"victory rode the rails":* Bess Furman, p. 249; also birthday, p. 251.

384 *In 1920, "glad for my husband": TIMS*, p. 311.

385 *ER on Howe: TIMS*, pp. 314–19; see *ER*, vol. I.

385 *ER's stereotypic words on race:* for example, *TIMS*, pp. 295–96.

385 *"wrung his neck":* ER to Anna, 12 Oct. 1936, Box 56; Mark McCloskey to ER, 19 Oct. 1936.

385 *"Mollycoddle": My Day*, 5 Oct. 1936.

386 *ER in Providence: Providence Journal*, 22 Oct. 1936.

387 *Providence Journal:* FDR shared headlines with "Russia Prepares to Help Madrid with Warplanes:" Stalin convinced Europe at war's brink, plans to end neutrality pact so that Spain will not become "another Rightist dictatorship similar . . . to Italy and Germany."

387 *"I have not sought" FDR in Syracuse:* Burns, pp. 279–80.

387 *FDR's Madison Square Garden speech:* Burns, pp. 282–83; Davis, pp. 644–45.

387 *Ended an era:* Moley, p. 352.

388 *ER quoted: NYT,* 1 Nov. 36.

388 *The family voted: NYT,* 4 Nov. 1936.

388 *Election results:* Davis, p. 647.

388 *ER told reporters: NYT,* 8 Nov. 1936.

388 *ER at Temple University: NYT,* 9 Nov. 1936.

20: Postelection Missions

389 *"Just written Pa":* ER to Anna, 14 Nov. 1936.

389 *"catarrh . . . a pest":* ER to Hick, 10 Nov. 1936; cf. *NYT,* 10 Nov.

389 *speech went "well but very hectically":* ER to FDR, 11 Nov. 1936; and ER to Hick, 12 Nov. 1936.

390 *N.Y. Fair job:* ER to Hick, 10 Sept. 36; Hick to ER 11 Nov. 1936.

390 *"For my sake?":* Hick to ER, 8 Nov. 1936.

391 *"love Milwaukee":* Hick to ER, 9 Nov.; ER to Hick, 12 Nov. 1936.

391 *in Milwaukee, no audience because communist:* ER to Hick, 11 Nov.; Hick to ER 12 Nov. 1936.

392 *ER enjoyed meeting Hick's friends:* particularly Tom and Clarissa Dillon. ER to Hick, 21 Nov. 1936.

392–93 *visits with friends:* 11, 12 Nov.; Hick to ER, 10 Nov., re her interview; ER to Hick 10, 11, 13 Nov. 1936.

393 *Bye and Leigh ecstatic:* Hick to ER, 13 Nov.; ER to Hick, 14 Nov. 1936.

393 *Hall and Buick:* ER to Hick, 17 Nov. 1936.

393–94 *Ernestine Schumann-Heink, "happy in Valhalla!":* Hick to ER, 18 Nov. 1936.

394 *wear her ring:* ER to Hick, 20 Nov. 1936. This exchange has been misinterpreted as a "careless blow" representing a cruel reflection of their diminished friendship, Faber, p. 227; also Rodger Streitmatter, p. 198.

394 *"She grouses":* ER to Gellhorn, 30 Nov. 1936, 100, Box 1380.

394 *correspondence over World's Fair publicity job:* ER to Hick, 14, 16, 18 Nov.; Hick to ER, 17 Nov. 1936.

394 *"I don't approve":* ER to Hick, 20 Nov. 1936.

394 *Anna and John to Seattle:* Curiously, in 1936, ER wrote that Phoebe Hearst, Hearst's mother whom she admired (and who died in 1919) traveled across country from Kansas City by stagecoach, with her six children. ER had six children, but Phoebe Hearst had only one, William Randolph—then in the process of absorbing the lives of several of her children. *TIMS,* pp. 221–22.

395 *"John and Anna are blissful":* ER to Hick, 19 Nov. 36; ER to FDR, 22 Nov.; 27 Nov. 1936.

395 *Hearst "slobbered":* Ickes, pp. 704–5.

396 *Budget cuts:* Davis, p. 663; *ER agonized, to Anna:* 10 Dec. 1936, Halstead, Box 56.

396 *Hick's reaction mixed:* to ER, 20 Nov. 1936.

396 *ER "an ogre":* ER to Anna, 16 Nov. 1936.

397 *"You sound very jolly":* ER to FDR from Massachusetts General Hospital, 27 Nov. 1936.

397 *"Survive all that gossip":* ER to FDR, 22 Nov. 1936; ER to Hick, 26 Nov. 1936.

397 *confided her divided heart:* ER to Elinor Morgenthau, 26 Nov. 1936, E. Morgenthau Papers, FDRL.

397 *ER seen to "munch" and game: NYT,* 29 Nov. 1936; to Elinor Morgenthau; ER to FDR, 27 Nov. 1936.

397 *ER kept worst news:* ER to FDR, 22 Nov. 1936.

397 FDR to "Dearest Mama": 17 Nov. 1936, *Letters,* pp. 630–31.

398 FDR to "Dearest Babs," a "happy ship": 26 Nov. 1936, ibid., p. 632. For a description of this event, see William Poundstone, "Queens for a Day: An Inside Look at the Navy's Most Perverse Ritual," *Spy* (Mar. 1993), pp. 50–53, ff.

398 *"felt like an impostor":* James Roosevelt, *Affectionately FDR: A Son's Story of a Lonely Man* (Harcourt Brace, 1959), p. 284; James was ultimately sufficiently embarrassed to retire his rank; although he never forgave his mother's disapproval.

398 *ER and Hick drove to Arthurdale:* ER to Anna, 4–6 Dec. 1936.

398–99 *from Rio:* FDR to ER, 30 Nov. 1936; also to SDR, *Letters,* p. 634.

399 *in Brazil:* see Ken Davis, pp. 656–57.

399 *in Montevideo, "don't blow":* James Roosevelt, *Affectionately,* p. 288.

399 *1 December, first Inter-American Conference address:* FDR's Selected Addresses, pp. 73–79.

400 *many achievements, no mutual accord:* Ickes, p. 15; Robert Dallek pp. 126–36.

401–2 *Gus Gennerich's death, FDR devastated:* See Ted Morgan, p. 547, for examples of Gennerich and liquid revelries. FDR to ER, 2 Dec. 1936; ER to FDR 3 Dec. 1936, children, Box 16. Although FDR believed that Gennerich died of a heart attack, James subsequently suggested that his death was an aftermath of the equator crossing party when Gus hit his head with great force. He complained of headaches thereafter and, James believed, died of a cerebral hemorrhage. James Roosevelt, *My Parents,* pp. 237–38; *"Gus was an amazing person":* Hick to ER, 6 Dec. 1936; FDR to ER, pp. 635–36; *TIR,* p. 149; Ken Davis, p. 660.

403 *King Edward abdicated, toast:* FDR to ER, 10 Dec. 1936.

403 *FDR "disgusted":* Ickes, pp. 16–17.

403 *"Poor little King":* Hick to ER, 5 Dec. 1936.

403 *"Poor fellow":* Hick to ER, 10 Dec. 1936; 11 Dec. 1936.

403 *ER, "his love too!":* ER to Hick, 10 Dec.; also, 7 Dec. 1936.

404 *Marshall Haley's funeral:* ER to Hick, 9 Dec.; ER to Anna 10 Dec. 1936.

405 *Earl Miller's nerves "about like yours":* ER to Hick, 5 Dec. 1936.

405 *"frying pan into the fire":* Hick to ER, 8 Dec. 1936.

405 *dined with Baruch:* ER to Anna, 7 Dec. 1936.

405 *"my work cut out":* ER to Hick, 7, 8 Dec.; ER to Anna, 10 Dec., Halsted, Box 56.

405 *"stumbled into a lot of the early letters":* Hick to ER, 6 Dec. 1936.

406 *"now and always":* Hick to ER, 6 Dec. 1936.

21: Second Chance for the New Deal

407 *"It takes a hungry man"*: Hilda Smith to ER, 7 Dec. 1936; ER to Smith 16 Dec. 1936: "The President was very much interested in the story. . . ."

407 *Crystal Bird Fauset:* ER to Farley, 14 Jan. 1937, 70, Box 710; see also Aubrey Williams to ER, with memo by Alfred Edgar Smith, in charge of Negro Activities for WPA, 20 Oct. 1936; *The Crisis,* Oct. 1936; *on black vote: The Crisis,* Dec. 1936, p. 396.

407 *ER believed Walter White:* See *The Crisis,* editorials, Jan. and Feb. 1937.

408 18 December 1936 cabinet meeting, in Ickes, vol. II, p. 20.

408 *"rather dread the future"*: ER to Elinor Morgenthau, 17 Nov. 1936.

409 FDR nominated Hull for a Nobel Peace Prize annually, presumably for his reciprocal trade agreements. Hull was awarded the prize in 1945. FDR, *Letters,* pp. 642–43; FDR to R. Walton Moore, 28 Dec. 1936.

409 Claude Bowers to FDR, 26 Aug. 1936, Davis, p. 665; Bowers quoted, p. 653. See Supreme Court, "this vast external realm," *Time,* 4 Jan. 1936.

409 *"terrible catastrophe"*: FDR to Bowers, 16 Sept. 1936, *Letters,* 614–15.

410 *Dodd:* Bullitt to FDR, 7 Dec. 1936; Bullitt, ed., p. 196.

410 *"saying nothing"*: ER to Anna, 6 Dec. 1936; *"protested vehemently"*: ER to Anna, 16 Dec. 1936.

411 *happiest time of his life:* James Roosevelt, *Affectionately,* pp. 290–94, 308.

411 *Hick patient:* Hick to ER, 7, 9, 10 Dec. 1936.

412 *Bethune to study committee:* Mack Roth to Pepper to McIntyre, to Wallace, 4 Dec. 1936; Will Alexander, RA, 9 Dec. 1936; PPF 9079.

412 Mary McLeod Bethune to ER re conference, 1 Dec. 1936; ER to Bethune 3 Dec.; re SDR's tea, and Jan. conference, 8 Dec. 1936; 4 Jan. 1937, 100, Box 1366.

412 *"new day has dawned"*: Bethune to ER, 11 Jan. 1937, re Clara Bruce and "the wonderful conference"; quoted from 13 Jan. 1937, 100, Box 1415.

412 *Gridiron Widows party:* ER to Elinor Morgenthau, 13 Nov. 1936, E. Morgenthau Papers.

412–3 *Gridiron Widows parties: NYT,* 10 Dec. 1933; 9 Dec. 1934; *Bess Furman on 1934:* Apple Mary, pp. 224–26; In *TIR,* ER credited Louis Howe for her makeover; Furman, pp. 224–26; 1936, Tobacco Road, Bess Furman, p. 237; *Time,* 4 Jan. 1937; *NYT,* 22 Dec. 1936, Romeo and Juliet; four hundred women cavorted at ER's party, capped by a midnight supper in the State Dining Room.

440 *Competitively: TIR,* pp. 93–94.

414 *lonely Christmas column: My Day,* p. 98.

441 *This problem is so vast: My Day,* Dec. 1936, p. 99.

414 *Ethel du Pont:* ER to Anna, 1 Jan. 1937.

415 *"Madame I salute you"*: Hick to ER, 27 Dec. 1936.

415 *"Don't let 'the eyes' get you"*: Hick to ER, 28 Dec. 1936.

415 With Tommy, ER moved into Peter Filene's lovely home on 12 Otis Place: "What a sensible man to live like this, all you need for comfort, much charm and no fuss and feathers. . . . I think I could enjoy Boston. We should come here sometime!" ER to Hick, 29 Dec. 1936.

415 *Carolyn Marsh:* ER to Hick, 1 Jan. 1937; *FDR rude to Alice:* ER to Hick, 2 Jan. 1937.

416 *"your poise more than human":* Hick to ER, 4 Jan. 1937.

442 Hick very social and not guilty about her book. Hick to ER, 18 Jan. 1937.

416 *revealing column: My Day,* Jan. 1937, p. 105.

416 *plans for Charleston and New Orleans:* Hick to ER, 16, 18 Jan. 1937; ER to Hick, 17 Jan. 1937.

416 *"I hear less and less":* ER to Hick, 7 Jan. 1937.

443 In early January Hick was dazzled by ER's bold words to the Junior League: "My dear, it was simply corking! Give it to 'em baby—straight from the shoulder! I like your speeches so much when you get very straight forward and say what you really think." 8 Jan. 1937.

416–17 *American Medicine,* published in April 1937. The *NY Times* considered the American Foundation report incontrovertible. The *AMA* no long spoke for "organized medicine." Lape's team demanded "far-reaching, socially-conceived reforms in medical education and practice." The Foundation's report "refutes a Bourbonism which holds that all's well." The future required fundamental changes to serve community needs. Lape and Read embarked on a long crusade that FDR never did join. Patricia Spain Ward, "U.S. v. *AMA* et al.: The Medical Anti-Trust Case of 1938–1943," *American Studies* (Fall 1989), and John Kingsbury, *Health in Handcuffs,* 1939.

417 FDR's 6 Jan. speech did not reflect several areas that dominated ER's correspondence, including federal aid to education, full employment, and renewed work on behalf of the Wagner-Costigan antilynch bill. Both the National Education Association and NAACP endorsed a Harrison-Fletcher bill for federal aid to education, which ER promised to support. White to ER, 5 Jan., 13 Jan. 1937; Virginius Dabney to White (to ER), 17 Jan., predicting the antilynch bill's passage; ER to White, 25 Jan.; White to ER, 3 Feb., with *DC Post* article on poll, 30 Jan. 1937; ER's penned reply atop page.

418 *"Umbrellas and more umbrellas":* My Day, 21 Jan. 1937; *announcers "said lovely things":* Hick to ER, 20 Jan. 1937; *"gave Mrs. Helm a bad time":* ER to Hick, 22 Jan. 1937.

419 *"Well, another four years":* ER to Anna, 20 Jan. 1937.

419 *more introspective:* ER to Hick, 21 Jan. 1937.

22: 1937

420 *fourth annual National Public Housing Conference: NYT,* 23 Jan. 1937; FDR to Mary Simkhovitch, 14 Jan. 37.

420 *invited Harry Hopkins:* ER to Harry Hopkins, 7 Jan. 1937, 70.

421 Fannie Hurst to ER, 13 Feb. 1937, Hurst Papers, Texas.

421 ER to FH, 16 Feb. 1937; "we are looking forward to your visit the 26th," Texas.

421 *"a liqueur for tender memory":* ER to FH, 5 Mar. 1937, Texas.

421 TIMS *as tribute to Howe: TIR,* p. 177.

421 *Jane Hoey on social security restrictions:* Ruby Black, pp. 170–71.

421–22 *revisited National Training School for Girls: NYT,* "Remodeled After Her Protests," 4 Feb. 1937; *"the mere sight": My Day,* Jan. 1937, p. 108.

422 *to Junior Leaguers: NYT,* 4 Feb., 55 WPA women from Atlantic City sewing project tour White House; ER urged Junior Leaguers to visit WPA projects themselves, and try "shoveling snow," *NYT,* 8 Jan. 1937; Hopkins and ER campaigned for work not dole, 5 May 1936.

422 *WPA art projects: My Day,* 22 Jan. 1937.

422 *Nikolai Sokoloff's Federal Music Project report to ER:* n.d., 1936, Box 681/70; cf. a letter of gratitude to ER "for saving" the Treasury Relief Art Project, PWA: We "are most happy to have received word that it is to be left intact." Edward Bruce, also on behalf of Olin Dows, to ER, 12 May 1936, Box 676/70; re appropriations for 1935–1937 artists to decorate [2500] federal buildings, at going WPA rate, via EO 7046.

423 *vacation plans at the Little House:* Hick to ER, 22, 23 Jan. 1937. Hick loved everything about her new home, and planned to have stationery made up to read: *The Little House/On the Dana Place/Moriches, Long Island.* As for their vacation plans, ER was glad that Hick had been "blunt," and would do whatever she enjoyed most; although ER still preferred the drive. ER to Hick, 25 Jan. 1937.

423 *"Don't be anybody's Mrs. Moskowitz":* ER to Hick, 10 Feb. 1937.

423 *"life can be diverting":* Hick to ER, 8 Feb. 1937.

423–24 Although U.S. ambassador Joseph Davies attended many of the trial sessions, there was little mention of the purges at this time. Indeed, Marjorie Merriweather Post Davies wrote ER long letters from Moscow about the changes under way for women, and the ongoing suffering of the people due to years of famine and natural disasters, despite great material bounty and huge factories.

Marjorie Davies to ER, 3 Mar. 1937, PSF, Russia. See also Joseph Davies, *Mission to Moscow* (Simon & Schuster, 1941); Nancy Rubin, *American Express: The Life and Times of Marjorie Merriweather Post* (Villard Books, 1995). Subsequently, ER wrote about the "horrors" of dictatorship which distorted "the real communist theory." ER to Mrs. Maloney, 28 Nov. 1938, in Lash, *Eleanor and Franklin,* pp. 594–95.

423–24 *Anna Louise Strong's visit:* ER to Hick, 2 Feb. 1937; Strong's goal in Tracy B. Strong and Helene Keyssar, *Right in Her Soul: The Life of Anna Louise Strong* (Random House, 1983), p. 171.

424 *"the U.S. Army should be used! I ask you!":* ER to Hick, 10 Feb. 1937.

424 *more young people in the CIO than in the AFL:* ER in Ruby Black, p. 177.

424 Broun quoted in Ruby Black, p. 141; *ER to press conf.:* Beasley, p. 167; on Guild, p. 185; for Broun see Heywood Hale Broun's *Collected Edition of Heywood Broun* (1941); and Alden Whitman, ed., pp. 124–25. *ER condemned Sloan:* Black, p. 172; *moved to yearly wage:* Black, pp. 182–83.

425 *ER to YWCA:* in *NYT,* 5 May 1934.

425 *said nothing about sit-down strikes:* Ruby Black, p. 178. However completely ER supported unionism, even the right of WPA workers to join the Workers' Alliance, she opposed "the strike" as an inappropriate weapon for WPA and other federal workers "against the government," in Ruby Black, p. 185.

426 ER with Evelyn Preston, to audience of over 1000, at League of Women Shoppers, N.Y., Ethical Culture Society, *NYT,* 9 Dec. 1937.

426–27 *John L. Lewis and La Follette hearings:* Saul Alinskey, *John L. Lewis: An Unauthorized Biography* (Vintage, 1970 [1949]), pp. 89–94; Jerold S. Auerbach, *La-*

bor and Liberty: The La Follette Committee and the New Deal (Bobbs-Merrill, 1966), pp. 100–2 and passim; Alinskey on Lewis's contribution to 7A, pp. 66–70; on La Follette; Alinskey, pp. 105–6.

427–28 Jack Barton (pseudonym for Bart Logan) and Gelders in Auerbach, pp. 94–5; 108; Robin Kelley, *Hammer and Hoe: Alabama Communists During the Great Depression* (University of North Carolina Press, 1990), pp. 130–31, 184–85. I am grateful to Marge Frantz, Joe Gelders's daughter, for background.

428 "Babies and Banners," the film; Mary Heaton Vorse, "Women Stand By Their Men," re Genora Johnson, mother of two and wife of strike leader Kermit Johnson, home and union fused, pp. 175–78; Vorse, "Soldiers Everywhere in Flint: Unionists Hold the Fort," pp. 179–80; "The Emergency Brigade in Flint," pp. 181–85, in Dee Garrison, ed., *Rebel Pen: The Writings of Mary Heaton Vorse* (New Feminist Library, Monthly Review, 1985); Sidney Fine, *Sit-Down: The General Motors Strike of 1936–1937* (University of Michigan Press, 1970), pp. 200–1, 279–80, passim; Philip Foner, *Women and the American Labor Movement* (Free Press, 1982), pp. 327–37.

428–29 *strikers assumed;* "*Unarmed as we are*"; *Lewis to Detroit:* Alinskey, pp. 127–30.

429 "*deadly feud;*" *militia of 1300:* Alinskey, pp. 144–47.

430 *Majority favor unions:* Feb. 1937, *My Day*, pp. 114–16.

430 "Nicholas Kelley, I am not afraid of your eyebrows": Alinskey, p. 152.

432 *ER defended her husband: My Day*, 10 Feb. 1937; *persuasive in Supreme Court columns:* June Rhodes to ER, 15 Feb. 1937; *Lape to Lash about Democratic opposition, and public confusion:* Lape interview, Lash Papers; "*might have saved himself a good deal of trouble*": TIR. For Supreme Court controversy, see especially Leuchtenberg.

432 *Molly kissed Farley:* ER in *Democratic Digest*, Apr. 1937.

432 Hick to ER, re Washington festivities, 12, 16 Feb. 1937.

433 *Alice to tea:* ER to Anna, 10 Jan. 1937, Box 57.

433 ER to Nan Honeyman, Jan. 1936: Lash, *Eleanor and Franklin*, p. 427.

433 *Alice lost the competition:* see Felsenthal, pp. 178–79; ER wrote Hick that she would divide the $75,000—spend half, and give the other half to causes, mostly Arthurdale.

433 *On 16 February, drove off* "*in a young blizzard*": Tommy to "Dear Gorgeous," n.d., Feb. 1937, ARH, Box 75; ER's Apr. *Democratic Digest* column tells the story of 16 Feb.

433 On 24 Feb., ER and Frances Perkins attended Maud O'Farrell Swartz's funeral. ER was close to the WTUL activist, Rose Schneiderman's partner of 23 years, then secretary of N.Y. State's Department of Labor. Maud Swartz had initiated a WTUL campaign to unionize laundry workers, and end the domestic workers' "slave markets," whereby housewives hired day workers at dreadful wages from street corners. ER supported the WTUL's campaign for standardized salaries and minimum wages for domestic workers. N.Y. Governor Herbert Lehman appointed Schneiderman to succeed Swartz as New York's secretary of labor. In 1938, Sidney Hillman's CIO-affiliated Amalgamated Clothing Workers admitted laundry workers; within a year a union of 27,000 laundry workers won "contracts that guaranteed decent wages, reduced hours, sick leave with pay, and paid vacations." That success was followed by the unionization of hotel workers and cleaning staff. See ER, *Democratic Digest*, Apr. 1937; Anilise Orlick, pp. 163–65.

433 *"FDR is tired and edgy"*: ER to Hick, 27 Feb. 1937.

433 *Elizabeth Read had a stroke:* ER to Hick, 2, 3, Mar. 1937.

433 *Lape devastated by FDR's rejection of their program:* See Patricia Spain Ward, U.S. v. AMA, et al.: The Medical Anti-trust Case of 1938–1943," *American Studies* (Fall 1989); Ward, "Medical Maverick, Hugh Cabot's Crusade for Universal Health Care," *Humanities* (*NEH Journal*, Mar., Apr. 1994). Lape's two-volume American Foundation Report, *American Medicine: Expert Testimony Out of Court*, published in April 1937, created a sensation, and a movement, but little official response. ER to Lape, "better meeting next time": Mar. 1937.

433–34 *FDR's 4 March speech:* Ickes, pp. 88–89. ER was amused to be with the women of the Liberty League as she listened to her husband's speech. With FJ's fiancé Ethel du Pont and her mother to plan the June wedding festivities, ER noted: "I couldn't help thinking over my company!" as FDR declared: "We have only just begun to fight. . . ." ER to Hick, 4 Mar. 1937; "*Cicero when I was a kid*": Hick to ER, 4 Mar. 1937.

434 From Louisiana, ER wrote Hick, "Huey did some good things for them!" 6, 7 Mar.

23: A First Lady's Survival

435 *a "grand talk":* ER to FDR, telegram from Fort Worth, 9 Mar. 37; fam/chldn, Box 16; *ER now supported:* ER to Hick, 20 Mar. 1937.

435 *from Oklahoma to Pennybacker in Texas:* Tommy to Anna, 14 Mar. 1937; ARH 75.

436 *"Yesterday was the worst":* ER to Hick, 19 Mar. 1937; Hick to ER: "you are with president Kate Zaners. . . . I hope it isnt too awful and that you are not too tired," 17 Mar. 1937.

436 *from Oklahoma to Shreveport:* ER to Elinor Morgenthau, 16 Mar. 1937.

436 *"My reception was horrible":* ER to Hick, 24 Mar.; "*your mother in 1940*": Tommy to Anna, 17 Mar. 1937.

436–37 *ER to FDR at Warm Springs:* 12 Mar. 1937, fam/chldn, Box 16.

437 *On 17 March, "cunning little":* ER in *Democratic Digest*, May 1937.

437 *In Washington, ER to Hick:* 28 Mar. 1937, Hick and the Danas visited for the Easter weekend.

437 *Smoky Mountains:* ER and Hick also drove through a Cherokee reservation, spent a night in Asheville, North Carolina, and visited a Friends (AFSC) crafts school "for young mountaineers"; then went on to Charleston, South Carolina. "There is a rather sweet melancholy about this city. . . ." *Democratic Digest*, June 1937.

437 *"wonderful for a week of climbing":* ER to Anna, 14 Apr. 1937.

437 *"Your mother":* Tommy to Anna, 14 Apr. 1937, ARH Box 75.

438 *"Dickie is having fits":* Tommy to "Dear Gorgeous," n.d., Feb. 1937, ARH, Box 75. Nancy Cook also *"gave your mother a bad time":* Tommy to Anna, 14 Apr. 1937.

438 *"Betsey's devotion to your father":* Tommy to Anna, 14 Apr. 1937.

438 *"Pa is both nervous and tired; outburst on meals":* ER to Anna, 3 Mar. 1937.

439–40 *use of "darky":* Esther S. Carry to ER, 13 Apr. 1937, 100, Box 1417; ER to Esther Carey, 20 Apr. 1937. ER wrote more fully to a NY attorney, who "had the pleasure of being at the dedication of the Eleanor Roosevelt School for colored pupils in Warm Springs . . . dedicated by the President last month." Although ER was responsible for the brick school, she did not attend its dedication in April because she was lecturing in Oklahoma. She had earlier written Hick that a speech she had made in 1935 had resulted in the building of a fully equipped modern brick school: "It salved my conscience a bit for I feel a skunk not to do more on the lynching thing openly." ER to Hick, Mar. 1936; ER to R. B. DeFrantz, 22 Apr. 1937, 100, Box 1420.

440 *ER at Barnard College: NYT,* 23 Oct. 1935.

440 *By 1938, eating, and amalgamation:* Augusta Conrad to ER, 31 Aug. 1938, ER to Augusta Conrad, 7 Sept. 1938, 100, Box 1453.

440 *Lynching, ER to FDR, "even one step":* 19 Mar. 1936; White to ER, 9 Apr. 37; Scheider to White, 12 Apr., 100, box 1446. ER's East Coast travels took her through New York, Connecticut, and Pennsylvania. She visited her cousins Corinne and Joseph Alsop at Avon, and spoke at Hartford and Scranton, *Democratic Digest,* June 1937.

440–43 *Wagner-Gavagan debate: Congressional Record* on HR 1507, beginning p. 3423; Fish, 13 Apr. 1937, pp. 3430–32; *Caroline O'Day: CR,* 13 Apr. 1937, v 81, pt 3, p. 3448; *Emmanuel Celler, on Winona lynching: CR,* p. 3434; John Marshall Robison: *CR,* pp. 3439–43.

443 *President "not familiar enough":* ER to White, 22 May 1937, 100, Box 1446; see also, Zangrando, pp. 142–46.

443 *FDR's neutrality:* See "The Cash and Carry Compromise of 1937," in Robert Divine, *The Illusion of Neutrality: FDR and the Struggle Over the Arms Embargo* (Quadrangle Books, 1962), pp. 190–99.

443 *Only legislative initiative, renewal of Neutrality Act of 1935:* See FDR to Hull, to study possible copper and steel embargo, 21 Apr. 1937, pp. 674–75. The study never materialized.

443–44 *Henry Stimson, Allen Dulles, and Hamilton Fish Armstrong:* Allen Guttmann, *The Wound in the Heart: America and the Spanish Civil War* (Free Press, 1962), pp. 88–93; Wayne Cole, *Senator Gerald P. Nye and American Foreign Relations* (University of Minnesota Press, 1962).

444 *Guernica bombed, 26 April:* headline, *NYT,* 7 May 1937.

444 *U.S. "ranked first in value of exports":* Arnold Offner, "Appeasement Revisited: U.S., Britain, Germany, 1933–1940," *JAH* (Sept. 1977), pp. 373ff; stats, p. 374; Watson, p. 376. Standard Oil, General Motors, and Du Pont maintained secret and illegal agreements with German firms, on restricted items of chemicals, rubber, aviation fuel; and enabled stockpiling of strategic materials. Despite the embargo against Spain, Franco's forces received U.S. oil. On 18 July 1936 Texaco's Thorkild

Rieber diverted 5 oil tankers to Franco-controlled ports in Spain, in violation of Texaco's long-term contract to supply the Spanish government's oil monopoly, CAMPSA. "Texaco supplied Franco fuel on credit until the civil war's end. . . ." See Ed Doerr in *The Nation*, January 1997; Arthur Landis, *Spain! The Unfinished Revolution*, pp. 206–8; and Herbert Feis, *The Spanish Story*, pp. 269–71.

445   *ER haunted by Guernica: My Day*, May 1937, p. 141; on Basque children, June columns, 145–149.

445   *"like a child":* Tommy to Anna, 14 Apr. 1937, ARH, 75.

445   "Germany Admits Guilt Over Guernica," *NYT*, 28 Apr. 1997. See Hugh Thomas, *The Spanish Civil War* (Harper Colophon, 1961), pp. 419–23.

445–46   *ER and Anna broadcast transcript:* Halsted, Box 62, 5 May 1937.

446–47   *autobiographies should be done "anonymously":* Hick to ER, 5 May 1937.

447   *"Infidelity need not ruin":* Lash, *Eleanor and Franklin*, p. 432.

447   *most traveled first lady in history: NYT*, 16 May 1937.

447   Tommy to Anna, n.d., May 1937, ARH, 75; fees in Beasley, *ER and the Media*, p. 113.

447   ER liked Earl's current companion, and encouraged Roberta Jonay to study with Irene Lewisohn at the Neighborhood Playhouse; and subsequently tried to get her a job with the WPA.

448   *ER on John Golden: My Day*, Mar. 1937, pp. 124–25.

448   ER to Golden, 2 Nov. 1937; original letter in author's collection, a gift from Elizabeth Harlan, 20 Apr. 1991.

448   *disagreed about WPA theater:* Golden, quoted by Flanagan in *Arena*, p. 40.

448–49   *Federal Theatre part of a great democratic movement:* Flanagan to ER, 21 May 1937, ER's office to Flanagan, 25 May; with attachment for ER, including Wilson Whitman, "Job for Jumbo," reprinted from *Stage*, Mar. 1937, a celebration of WPA theatre projects, with NY audience and national facts. 70, Box 710; ER's 1 June 1937 broadcast quoted in *Arena*, p. 206.

449   *"zealous" communists:* Frank Banks, *NYT*, 16 May 1937.

449   *ER opposed to Dunnigan bill: My Day*, May 1937, pp. 140–41.

449   *criticized only one play:* ER in *Democratic Digest*, July 1937; *My Day*, 13 May 1937.

449   *Playwrights especially:* in Edward Robb Ellis, *A Nation in Torment: The Great Depression, 1929–1939* (Capricorn Books, 1971), pp. 518–19.

450   *"rather ruthless" about* The Women: ER to Esther Lape, 21 June 1937, Arizona collection.

450–51   *"royal Bengal tiger":* Hick to ER, 24 May 1937. Hick also reported that Martha Gellhorn returned from Spain, parked herself at the Lewisohns' apartment on Park Avenue to write about all the terrible things she witnessed.

451   On 27 May, ER invited Gellhorn to Washington for lunch with Elinor Morgenthau and others so they could hear about Spain. ER was impressed by her new maturity and arranged a day with Gellhorn and her companeros, Ernest Hemingway and filmmaker Joris Ivens at Hyde Park so FDR could see their documentary, *The Spanish Earth*, ER to Hick, 27 May 1937.

451   *"Some bad days ahead":* Also a gratifying visit with Bernard Baruch, and they "settled many things," ER to Hick, 25 May 1937.

451 *Memorial Day massacre:* Philip Foner, *Women and the American Labor Movement* (Free Press, 1979), pp. 330–31; Art Preis, *Labor's Giant Step: Twenty Years of the CIO* (Pathfinder Press, 1972), pp. 67–70; see also Mary Heaton Vorse in Dee Garrison. To *Grief,* ER to Hick, 30 May 1937.

24: This Is My Story

452 *"Dorothy Thompson's 'The Dilemma of a Pacifist' ":* My Day, June 1937, pp. 147–48.

452 *"500 kids are waiting":* Martha Gellhorn to ER, n.d., June 1937.

453 *ER supported:* Malvina Scheider to Clarence Pickett, 24 June 1937, 70, box 718; see also Luis Galvan, 13 Aug. 1937, re ER's support published in *NYT;* he opposed ER's aid to communism; 70, box 711.

453–54 *"Emotionally":* ER to Gellhorn, 14 June 1937; *Martha Gellhorn to ER, "not divisible":* "I can never forget about the other people, . . . in Madrid or the unemployed or the dead strikers in Chicago or the woman who sells pencils in the subway. . . ." June 1937; *ER encouraged Gellhorn:* 24 June 1937.

454 *"annoyed me . . . hair shirt": This I Remember,* pp. 161–62.

454 Cordell Hull and James Clement Dunn quoted in Ted Morgan, p. 439.

455 FDR's 24 Aug. 1936 agreement with J. Edgar Hoover to investigate subversives was between the two of them, and it was allegedly confirmed by a written memo placed in the White House safe. Ted Morgan, p. 439.

That memo authorizing Hoover's domestic surveillance has yet to be found. The only source is J. Edgar Hoover's 24 Aug. 1936 confidential memo of his White House meeting with FDR, concerning communist activities within the U.S. Hoover told the president that Harry Bridges's Longshoremen's Union, John L. Lewis's United Mine Workers (CIO), and Heywood Broun's Newspaper Guild were all communist-involved, and "the Communists had planned to get control of these three groups . . . so they would be able at any time to paralyze the country." They could "stop all shipping in and out . . . ; stop the operation of industry . . . ; and stop publication of any newspapers. . . ." Also, the Communist Internationale in Moscow "issued instructions for all Communists in the U.S. to vote for President Roosevelt . . ."

FDR replied that he was "considerably concerned about the movements of Communists and of Fascism . . . and the Secret Service of the Treasury Department had assured him that they had informants in every Communist group." But FDR believed they were limited to plots on his life, and he was now "interested in obtaining a broad picture of the general movement." An agreement to obtain "general intelligence information" was thereupon made, with State Department support. They met next day with Cordell Hull, so that all would be coordinated with Military and Naval Intelligence services. Confidential Memo, Hoover, 25 Aug. 1935, in Athan Theoharis, ed., *From the Secret Files of J. Edgar Hoover* (Ivan Dee, 1993), pp. 180–82. See also Frank Donner, *Age of Surveillance* (Knopf, 1980), p. 53; Kenneth O'Reilly, "A New Deal for the FBI: The Roosevelt Administration, Crime Control and National Security," *Journal of American History* (Dec. 1982); Richard

Gid Powers, *Secrecy and Power: The Life of J. Edgar Hoover* (Free Press, 1987), pp. 228–31.

On 28 Aug., Hoover's aide Ed Tamm submitted a tentative outline of procedure, which included surveillance of the "maritime, steel, coal, clothing, garment and fur industries; the newspaper field; government affairs; the armed forces; educational institutions; communist and affiliated organizations; Fascist and anti-Fascist movements." Hoover considered it a "good beginning." See also Curt Gentry, *J. Edgar Hoover: The Man and the Secrets* (Norton, 1991), pp. 207–8.

455 *government of Juan Negrin:* Hugh Thomas, *The Spanish Civil War* (Harper Colophon, 1961), pp. 443–56.

455 *"should have been a warning":* Armstrong, pp. 475–76.

455 *"saw Anna Louise Strong at the Writers' Congress":* Gellhorn to ER, n.d., June, 1937.

455–56 On 29 May 1937, ER wrote a *My Day* column on Gellhorn, who was convinced that "the Spanish people are a glorious people and something is happening in Spain which may mean much to the rest of the world."

456 *"You really did like," The Spanish Earth:* Martha Gellhorn to ER, 18 July 1937.

456 *FDR never considered changing his policy:* After 4 Mar. 1937, all U.S. passports were stamped "NOT VALID for Travel in Spain." This resulted in treks across the Pyrenees for many of the 3,000 U.S. volunteers in the International Brigades. Over time, there were 35,000 volunteers from 50 nations. See Robin D. G. Kelley, "This Ain't Ethiopia, But It'll Do: African-Americans and the Spanish Civil War," in *Race Rebels: Culture, Politics, and the Black Working Class* (Free Press, 1996); and William Loren Katz and Marc Crawford, *The Lincoln Brigade* (Atheneum, 1989).

456 *"How men hate a woman in a position of real power":* ER to Hick, 28 June 1937; for Perkins and the CIO, see esp. Sidney Fine, *Sit-Down: The General Motors Strike of 1936–1937* (University of Michigan Press, 1970).

456–57 *"I am particularly happy today":* My Day, 24 July 1937; *women and work: It's Up to the Women*, pp. 142–52; *ER's broadcast with Rose Schneiderman: NYT*, 13 May 1937.

457 While all New Deal efforts remained suspended by the Court controversy, FDR compounded congressional bitterness by declaring war on tax dodgers. He promised to publish the names of cheaters, and pursue them. As surprised as anyone, ER wrote Hick, 1 June 1937: "What do you think of the new tax thing? I'm more troubled over Europe, tho the tax excitement does take people's mind off the court." Ironically, ER was plunged into the fray, accused of being a "tax dodger." She told her press conference: "On every penny of income I have ever received, I've paid my full tax." But the accusations caused her to pay her taxes first, and make her AFSC contributions with whatever remained. *NYT*, 15 June 1937.

457–58 *du Pont wedding, "I'm immune":* ER to Hick, 24 June 1937.

457 *"Well, it's over":* ER to Hick, 1 July 1937; *broadcast: NYT*, 1 July 1937, p. 22; see also *Democratic Digest*, Aug. 1937.

457–58 *"was there much drinking?":* Hick to ER, 6 July 1937; *"all you surmised":* ER to Hick, 7 July; *FDR particularly gay:* James Roosevelt, with Sidney Shalett, *Affectionately, FDR* (Harcourt Brace, 1959), pp. 304–5.

458–59 *Amelia Earhart:* ER to Anna, 3 July 1937; *day she left: My Day,* 8 June 1937; cf. 9 June and 22 June 1937, when AE in Java, and told monsoons would ground her for three months in India.

459 *Brisbane's attack:* Bess Furman to ER Jan. 1935; ER to "Dear Bess", 17 Jan. 1935, 100, Box 1338. According to Susan Butler, Eugene Vidal, Gore Vidal's father, was AE's lover. Butler suggests that because Gene Vidal was "no longer at the Bureau of Air Commerce" when Earhart disappeared there was no one to ask the right questions about radio frequencies, time, weather, location. See Earhart to ER, 15 Sept. 1936, 17 Sept. 1936; Butler, pp. 350–51; 397.

459 *grateful, Howland:* George Putnam to ER 19 Jan. 1937, 100, Box 1437; *after disappearance:* Putnam to ER, 5 Aug. 1937, in hand, 100, 1437; also Missy's attachment of ER's words about Amelia, sent to Putnam and returned to ER.

459 *"Courage is the price":* My Day, 23 July 1937; see also *My Day* on Amelia Earhart, 7, 8, 14 July 1937.

459 A year later, Amelia's mother wanted to reopen the search. Amy Earhart to ER, 16 Mar. 1938; ER from Warm Springs, Ga., 30 Mar. 1938, 100, Box 1457 to Amy Earhart. ER wrote Paul Mantz on 14 May 1938: "I have made inquiries about the search which was made for Amelia Earhart and both the President and I are satisfied from the information which we have received that everything possible was done. We are sure that a very thorough search was made."

460 *paid many tributes:* Hurst and Cochran, at Floyd Bennett Field, where 200 gathered to praise Earhart's dauntless courage. *NYT,* 22 Nov. 1937.

460 *NAACP was horrified by the prospect of Robinson:* White to ER, 10 June 1937; White had toured America with Gavagan, and was gratified by the public enthusiasm for the antilynching bill. ER was "glad your trip was successful," and FDR would call, 16 June 1937. On 24 June 1937 the Judiciary Committee of the Senate reported the Gavagan-Wagner-Van Nuys bill (1507) out, 13–3 (Connally, Borah, Pittman against). Connally at first said there would be no filibuster; than changed his mind. White to ER, 24 June 1937.

461 *"grossest and meanest discrimination":* William Pickens to ER, 12 June 1937, with Pickens to Ickes, 6 June; 12 June 1937; Charles West to ER, 25 June 1937, 70, Box 718; for Ickes's actions, see T. H. Watkins, p. 647.

461 *Fleeson and O'Donnell:* "Capitol Stuff," *NY Daily News,* 15 June 1937.

461 *Burton Wheeler:* quoted in Davis, p. 93.

461 *ER on Robinson and funeral: Democratic Digest;* see also ER to Elinor Morgenthau, July 1937. On the Supreme Court fight, see especially William Leuchtenberg, "FDR's Supreme Court Packing Plan," in Melvyn Dubofsky, ed., *The New Deal: Conflicting Interpretations and Shifting Perspectives* (Garland, 1992), pp. 271–304.

462 *ER disapproved, "wise and unwise economies": My Day,* 17 Aug., 1937.

462 The Wagner-Steagall Act resulted in a power struggle between John Ihlder and Nathan Straus, New York's Housing Commissioner. ER was deeply involved in the controversy and, ultimately, supported Straus who had a more expansive vision of modern planned neighborhoods than Ihlder and wanted to see comfortable dwellings enforced by new building codes and zoning laws. See Kessner, *La Guardia,* pp. 333–35; Ihlder to ER 2 June 1937, with Anson Phelps Stokes to Robert Wagner, 17 May 1937.

462–63 See Alinskey, pp. 156–59; *"right psychology"*: FDR to Jack Garner, who left on a fishing trip peeved by FDR's silence about the strikers, urging him to return to Washington, 7 July 1937, III, pp. 692–93.

463 *ER at the Brouns', hailed Flanagan's Living Newspaper, at Val-Kill:* June and July detailed in *Democratic Digest*, Sept. and Oct. 1937.

463 *"zest in life"*: *My Day*, 10 Aug. 1937.

463–64 *not purged, but:* Lape to ER 4 July 1937; ER to Lape, 8 July, 100, Box 1430.

464–65 *"need to be alone"*: Hick to ER, 16 June; 7 July 1937; *"unfit"*: 16 July; *"Pigs!"*: 20 July 1937.

465 *"so simple, so dull"*: ER to Hick, 3 July; 8 July 1937.

465 *ER also worried:* 15, 19 July 1937; *"enjoyed every minute, black goggles"*: ER to Hick, 22, 25 July; ER was so pleased with her caper in her open car, she also wrote Anna, 30 July 1937.

465 *"unmitigated ass"*: ER to Hick, 27 July 1937; *"perhaps he's right"*: ER to Hick, 8 Aug. 1937.

466 *"Labor's cause is just"*: Lewis in Alinskey, pp. 159–60.

466 *close Camp Jane Addams:* NYT, 16 Aug. 1937; ER's contribution, $3,300, in 11 checks of $300 each. Hers was the only name on the column of private contributions, 14 July 1937; *NYT,* 17 Aug. 1937.

466 ER to Hick, quotations, 22 July, 30 July; *Hall "free to flit"*: ER to Anna, 5 Aug. 1937.

466–67 *"swell" to write honestly about immigrants:* ER to Anna, 5 Aug. 1937.

467 *"so little work"*: ER to Anna, 12 Aug.; re SDR, *"amusing stories,"* 17 Aug. 1937.

467 *According to James:* James R., *Affectionately, FDR,* p. 302; Tea with Duke and Duchess, ER to Hick, 27 July 1937; *hated papers:* ER to Hick, 25 Aug. 1937.

468 *ER marveled at FDR's spirits: My Day*, Aug. 1937, pp. 171–73.

468 *"all dried up"*: Hick to ER, 27 Aug. 1937; *letters of advice:* ER to Hick, 27–30 Aug. 1937; *feared "drifting apart"*: Hick to ER, 8 Sept. 1937.

468–69 *"can't happen"*: ER to Hick 9, Sept. 1937; *"don't much like your gypsy life"*: 20 Mar. 1937; *but had drifted apart, "you can scarcely realize"*: floating letter, no date, Wednesday, on the train. Streitmatter, without evidence, dates this 20 Feb. 1935.

469 *"I'm really not unhappy"*: ER to Hick, 9 Sept. 1937.

469–70 *"for the night and breakfast at least"*: ER to Hick, 12 Sept. 1937; *"send me the peace article . . . My love to you—always"*: Hick to ER, 21 Sept. 1937.

470 *Baruch returned:* ER to Hick, 11 Sept. 1937; *"Hall thinks"*: ER to Hick 8 Sept. 1937.

470 For the devastation in China in 1937, see esp. Dorothy Borg, *The U.S. and the Far Eastern Crisis of 1933–1938* (Harvard University Press, 1964); Winston Churchill, *"do you not tremble"*; Gilbert, p. 545.

471 *"It is a horrible thing"*: Churchill, 21 Dec. 1937, in Gilbert, p. 585.

471 *turned to Sumner Welles:* See Irwin Gellman, *Secret Affairs: FDR, Hull, and Sumner Welles* (Johns Hopkins University, 1995), p. 59; Benjamin Welles, *Sumner*

Welles: FDR's Global Strategist, A Biography by His Son (St. Martin's Press, 1997), pp. 196–200.

471 *rearmament, arms trade:* Divine, *The Illusion of Neutrality,* 205–9.

472 *"say exactly what you think":* Hick to ER, 9 Sept. 1937.

472 FDR read it, and ER hoped Hick "wont find it worthless," ER to Hick, 18 Sept; Hick found it tremendous, and sent a letter and a telegram: "the best article you've ever written on any subject. Gosh, it packs some good hefty wallops, and I wonder how the President liked it. . . ." Hick to ER, 28 Sept. 1937.

472 ER dedicated what she always called her "little book on peace" to Carrie Chapmann Catt, "who has led so many of us in the struggle for peace."

473 *"a great speech":* Ickes, p. 222; see Dorothy Borg, "Notes on FDR's Quarantine Speech," *Political Science Quarterly* (Sept. 1957).

473 FDR *"always looking for slams":* ER to Hick, 18 Sept. 1937.

473–74 For ER it was an arduous ten days, and she was "glad to get on plane alone": ER to Hick, 29 Sept. 1937.

473 ER at *Tribune* forum: *NYT,* 6 Oct. 1937.

474 *"iron in the soul":* ER to Hick, 5 Oct. 1937.

474–75 In her 7 Oct. 1937 column ER referred specifically to FDR's press conference: "They want to know so many things I would like to know also. . . ."; *her calls for diplomatic action: My Day,* Sept., p. 186; Oct., pp. 192–93.

475 Hick to ER, 25 Sept. 1937, about the *Herald Tribune* "dope story" re Farley; on Hugo Black see Durr, *Outside the Magic Circle;* Allie Freed to ER, 19 Sept. 1937; ER to Freed, 22 Sept., 100, Box 1423.

475 *at Little House:* ER to Anna, 8 Oct. 1937, next day to Barbara Hopkins's funeral, Halsted, Box 57.

475 *Hick refused to visit Hyde Park:* 2 Nov.; *Barbara Hopkins indispensable:* Hick to ER, 7 Oct. 1937; *NYT* obit, 10 Oct. 1937.

476 *"gay party":* ER to Hick, 11 Oct. 1937; FDR to ER, *Letters,* p. 716.

477 *"feeling of being hollow":* ER to Hick, 30 Oct. 1937.

477 *Fight for NYA and federal aid to education:* ER to Hick, 18 Oct., 30 Oct. 1937.

477 *nothing "to tire her":* Tommy to Anna, 26 Nov. 1937.

478 *ER's November activities: Democratic Digest,* Jan. 1938; *no exercise "makes me sleepy":* ER to Hick, 10 Nov. 1937.

478 *In Indiana:* ER to Hick, 13 Nov.; *in Illinois:* ER to Hick, 14–15 Nov. 1937.

478 *"write it myself or not at all":* ER to Hick, 16 Nov.; *"swore at drivers":* Hick to ER, 15 Nov. 1937.

479 *"only interested in a First Lady!":* ER to Hick, 18 Nov. 1937.

479 *on Tommy:* Hick to ER, 14, 16, 17 Nov. 1937.

480 *Reviews of* TIMS: ER to Hick, 16 Nov. 1937; Katherine Woods, *NYTBR,* 21 Nov. 1937; Mary Ross, *NY Herald Tribune,* 21 Nov. 1937; Cousin Alice and Dorothy Canfield Fisher quoted in Lash, *Eleanor and Franklin,* p. 433.

480 Isabella Greenway, 19 Dec. 1937, Tuscon; ER to Isabella, 30 Dec. 1937: "A world of thanks for your letter. . . ." ER missed Isabella, who left Congress, many assumed, because of her differences with FDR. She had actually sent a copy of a notarized affidavit that testified Isabella Greenway was not in fact a member of the anti-Roosevelt group "Americans, Inc." Isabella Greenway to ER, 7 June 1935: "Dearest E. I just thought this would amuse & interest you . . ."; affidavit, J. W. Haverty, 21 May 1935, 100, Box 1340. Nevertheless, their personal relationship endured.

480 ER to Morris, 13 May 1938; *North American Review*, "An Education for Life," pp. 202–6, 100, Box 1470. Most newspaper reviews appeared Sunday, Thanksgiving weekend, spent at the White House in 1937. Hick was thrilled. They were "marvelous, . . . at last you are coming into your own . . ." Hick to ER, 21 Nov. 1937.

480–81 *Thanksgiving a hard day:* ER to Hick, 23–24 Nov. 1937.

481 *Doris Duke to the homesteads:* Tommy to John Boettiger, 26 Nov. 1937, Halsted, box 75; *ER on Duke in Arthurdale and Penncraft: Democratic Digest,* Jan. 1938.

481 Special Christmas Dinner, ER to Hick, 7 Dec. 1937; *"Love means so much more":* ER to Hick, 11 Dec. 1937. On 11 Dec. ER hosted the Gridiron Widows party, which "far surpassed all previous parties." Guests included Agnes Brown Leach, Fannie Hurst, Mary Dreier, Nancy Cook, Tiny Chaney, June Rhodes, and Dorothy Schiff Backer of the *NY Post. Dem. Digest*, Jan. 1938.

481–82 ER's lunch with Vera Brittain and Cissy Patterson in *Democratic Digest; "duchess-like dignity":* Vera Brittain, *Testament of Experience* (Macmillan, 1957), p. 183. For the *Panay,* and the Dec. 1937 events, see Iris Chang, *The Rape of Nanking* (Penguin, 1997); Waldo Heinrichs, *American Ambassador: Joseph C. Grew and the Development of the U.S. Diplomatic Tradition* (Little, Brown, 1966), pp. 255–59; and Herbert Feis, *The Road to Pearl Harbor* (Atheneum, 1964), pp. 6–7. Before Pearl Harbor, Japan was regarded as an "effective opponent of Communism in Asia."

482 *on diplomatic dinner, and family tensions:* ER to Hick, 14, 17 Dec. 1937; also, ER to Anna 19 Dec., Halsted, Box 57; *diplomatic dinner: My Day*, 18 Dec. 1937; *abruptly changed her plans: My Day*, for Dec., 209–12.

483 "—*just you":* Hick to ER, 22 Dec. 1937. Hick was "darned glad" ER decided to go to Seattle. "I think you'll be much happier out there. Oh, do have a happy, contented Christmas, without feeling low or discouraged or under a nervous strain": 23 Dec. 1937; also 24–25 Dec. letters of relief that ER away, and happy.

483 Anna to Tommy, 31 Dec. 1937, ARH, 75; for details of ER's stormy winter trip, *Democratic Digest*, Feb. 1938.

25: This Troubled World, 1938

484 *"little book on peace has been very successful":* Tommy to Anna, 18 Jan. 1938, ARH, Box 56.

484–85 *ER is celebrated:* "Speaking of Mrs R," *Canton Repository* and *Denver Democrat*, reprinted, Mar. 1938, clippings, ER Papers.

485 *"really good on make up"; Hick ill:* ER to Anna, n.d., Jan.–Feb. 1938; 13 Feb. 1938; in Asbell, pp. 97–98.

485 *anguished correspondence:* Hick to ER, 6, 8, 9 Jan. 1938.

486 *"It seems so hard":* ER to Hick, 8 Jan 1938; Ickes on FDR's speech, and on his own "It Is Happening Here," a war between democracy and fascism—if the unbridled tycoons Ford, du Pont, Girdler, and Rand were allowed to continue, pp. 282–83, 287–88.

486 *Annie Griffen Baruch's death:* ER to Hick, 16 Jan. 1938; see Coit, pp. 456–57 passim.

486 *"I was hurt":* Hick to ER, 18 Jan. 1938.

487 Hick, 17, 18 Jan.; *"I never meant to hurt you":* ER to Hick, 19 Jan. 1938. This exchange included praise for Erskine Caldwell's *Have You Seen Their Faces,* illustrated by Margaret Bourke-White. Hick offered to send the "magnificent" book about tenant farmers and sharecroppers to ER. But Caroline O'Day had given it to her for Christmas. Then on 22 January Hick wrote: "The AP called me today wanting to know where you were. Where are you, by the way, I wonder. I told them I had no idea!"

487 *Patience Strong column: My Day,* Jan. 1937, p. 219.

487 *Plans for FDR's birthday, and peppy birthday balls:* ER to Hick, 29, 30 Jan.; on arrangements, invitation ER to Colonel Edwin Watson, 13 Jan. 1938, 100, box 1481.

487 Lohengrin *"a real joy,"* One Third of Nation: ER and Hick, 20, 22, 26 Feb.; 3, 4 Mar. 1938.

488 *Cause and Cure luncheon:* ER to Hick, 19 Jan. 1938.

488 *Romania gone Fascist:* On 23 Dec. 1937 meeting, Ickes, p. 287; 8 Jan. entry, p. 291.

489 *Chamberlain anti-American:* Bullitt to FDR, 5 May 1937, p. 213.

489 *Churchill "breathless with amazement": The Gathering Storm,* pp. 251–55.

489 *long parade of death:* Churchill, pp. 257–58.

489 For an eyewitness account of 11–14 Mar. events see William Shirer, *Berlin Diary,* pp. 96–108; *Blumenkrieg:* Davis, p. 184.

490 *Churchill asked, Dawson:* William Manchester, *The Last Lion: Winston Spencer Churchill, Alone, 1932–1940* (Little, Brown, 1988), p. 283.

490–91 *Hitler ushered his homeland into his Reich:* See Alan Bullock, *Hitler: A Study in Tyranny* (Harper Torchbooks, 1962); and Peter G. J. Pulzer, *The Rise of Political Anti-Semitism in Germany and Austria* (John Wiley, 1964).

491 *Churchill to House, 14 March:* "The Rape of Austria," *Gathering Storm,* pp. 272–75; Manchester, pp. 287–88; *"think only of the Red danger":* Harold Nicolson, *Diaries and Letters,* Feb.–Mar. 1938.

491 *"Ten Commandments of Good Will": My Day,* Feb. 1938, p. 230.

491 *all news terrible:* Ickes, 12 Mar. 1938, p. 335.

491 Joe Davies, U.S. ambassador to Russia, worried about a "Fascist peace." He believed the purge trials proved a massive plot between anti-Soviet traitors within the government and Nazi and Japanese forces. Joe Davies, *Mission to Moscow,* letters and journal, pp. 261ff.

492 ER letters to FDR, 15–17 Mar. 1938; *"future wars will have no fronts": This Troubled World* (H. C. Kinsey, 1938), pp. 41ff.

492 *"war as murder," ER 1924:* quoted in Jacqueline Van Voris, *Carrie Chapman Catt* (Feminist Press, 1987), p. 200; *In 1934, she called for:* Delegate's Worksheet, Conference on the Cause and Cure of War, 16–19 Jan. 1934; ER's address, p. 9; copy, Hick, Box 1.

492–93 In her speeches, ER defended new naval spending, and attacked Jeannette Rankin's proposal without naming her, *My Day*, 29 June 1937. ER to Katherine Devereaux Blake, 31 July 1937, 100, Box 1415; Iola Kay Eastburn, Middlebury College, to ER, 18 July 1937, 100, Box 1422; ER to Eastburn, 31 July 1937.

493 "More Arms Needed Mrs R Says," *NYT*, 15 Feb. 1938; press conference notes, 14 Feb. 1938, Beasley, p. 48.

493 *From* This Troubled World: need to define aggressor nation, trade embargoes, p. 15; *Good Neighbor Policy*, pp. 10–12; *religious freedom*, p. 19; *mountain climbing*, p. 23; *"change in human nature,"* p. 25–26, 28; *"commit suicide—and we will!"* 1934 speech, Cause and Cure of War conference.

494 *glamour of war, Troubled*, pp. 29–32.

494 *influenced by Nye, profits out: Troubled*, pp. 34–37.

494 *"power of love": Troubled*, pp. 45–46; see also *NYTBR*, 2 Jan. 1938; and news item, 2 Jan. 1938.

495 *Diana Hopkins:* Hick to ER from White House, 12 Mar. 1938.

495 *no word from FDR:* ER to Hick, 16 March 1938. In the White House, Hick enjoyed several guests, including Betty Lindley, who was "fun but a great slob with ashes all over and nothing put away." Hick to ER, 14 March; ER replied: "I smiled over Betty as a guest. You and I are old fuss cats!" ER to Hick, 16, 17 Mar.

495 *first word:* ER to Anna, 17 Mar. 1938; *Betsey to Warm Springs:* ER to Anna, 5 Mar. 1938; *"This is a busy world":* ER to Hick, 17 Mar. 1938.

496 *"your Wife is bringing you nearer to the People":* James Metcalf to FDR, 21 Mar. 1938, ppf, 2.

496 *felt irrelevant at Warm Springs:* ER to Hick, 30 Mar. 1938.

496 *felt trapped and worried about Harry Hopkins:* ER to Hick, 31 Mar. 1938.

496 Hick loved *Pins and Needles*, 27, 28 Mar.; ER also wrote a column to celebrate the ILGWU's "theatrical venture," which was a "delight." Nobody "could be disappointed by this entertainment." ER went to the musical with Esther Lape, and hoped "We've Just Begun" was "prophetic." *My Day*, 15 Feb. 1938.

496 *ER and Hick did not see each other:* Hick to ER, 11, 13, 14 Apr. 1938.

Hick was, however, inspired by FDR's 14 April address on economic conditions: It "aroused the first spark of interest" she felt in a long, long time. . . . Please tell the President, for me, 'More power to you!' Oh, he is alright, but, my God, some of the people around him!" Hick to ER, 15 Apr. 1938.

497 *to defend WPA and NYA costs:* ER to Hick, 1 Apr. 1938; *by April, the economy had lost "two-thirds of the gains made since March 1933":* Davis, p. 205.

497 *After the Anschluss; Irvington, New Jersey:* Frieda Elias to ER, 8 Feb. 1938; ER to Elias, 10 Feb. 1938, 100, Box 1457; Ruth Bessell to ER, 30 Mar. 1938; ER to RB, 11 Apr. 1938; 100, Box 1449; Doris Bernstein to ER, 19 May 1938; ER to DB, 24 May 1938, 100, Box 1449.

498–99 *Karl Ohm deportation case:* Lillian Strauss to ER, 28 Jan. 1938; James Houghteling to Malvina Thompson, 10 Feb. 1938; Thompson to Lillian Strauss, 11 Feb. 1938; Strauss to Thompson, 14 Feb. 1938, 70, Box 738.

499 *Upton Sinclair to ER, Norman Thomas rudely arrested:* see *NYT*, 3 May 1938.

499 *campaigned for Hanns Eisler:* ER to Sumner Welles, 11 Jan. 1939; 7 Feb. 1939, 70, Box 766.

499 *"every morning with apprehension":* My Day, Mar. 1938, p. 234; ER to EM, 17 Mar. 1938, Elinor Morgenthau Papers.

500 *"every gallant soul":* Dorothy Thompson, quoted in Peter Kurth, *American Cassandra: Biography of Dorothy Thompson* (Little Brown, 1990), p. 241; *Thompson detailed both Hitler's excesses and the " 'cowardice' that sustained it":* Kurth, p. 280.

500 *"behaved like worms"; Nancy Astor "a little mad":* Harold Nicolson to Vita Sackville-West, 25 Feb. 1938, in Nicolson, pp. 325–27; *Coincidentally, ER and Nancy Astor:* NYT, 26 Feb. 1938.

501 *appointment of Joe Kennedy "a great joke":* Michael Beschloss, *Kennedy and Roosevelt: The Uneasy Alliance* (Norton, 1980), p. 157.

501 *Hugh Wilson—considered much more acceptable in German circles:* See Joseph Lash on ER and Bullitt, *A Friend's Memoir*, pp. 86, 154; also William Shirer on the Nuremberg rallies. See esp. *The Diplomats*, for the astonishing record of Anglo-American appeasement; cf. Britain's pro-Nazi ambassador to Germany, Neville Henderson, who told his friend Göring that Hitler could have Austria, "so far as he is concerned," 5 July 1937, p. 76; Vienna, Mar. 1938; pp. 110–11.

502–3 *Deeply grateful for Nancy Astor's assistance, Frankfurter nevertheless used the occasion to inquire about her and the alleged Cliveden crowd:* Nancy Astor rejected the propaganda which began in Claude Cockburn's "communist sheet," *The Week*. It was all a plot "to create suspicion and class war" and bring down the government. She was not a fascist, "and I am very much surprised that you, knowing me and having visited Cliveden, should have swallowed this propaganda against us! . . ."

Frankfurter replied, on 2 June 1938, that he did not refer to "the silly chatter regarding plots and conspiracies," but rather to Cliveden's "political philosophy. I had in mind the views expressed in the summer of 1935 by Montagu Norman [governor of the Bank of England] when he said that Hitler saved Europe from Bolshevism, a point of view that I often encountered during my year in England and again in the summer of 1936; the point of view of 'appeasement' by acquiescence in the series of violent measures taken by Hitler and the general undermining of international law and order and the decencies of civilization. . . ."

To demonstrate his alternative views, Frankfurter enclosed two articles—by Norman Angell and Dorothy Thompson. "And since we are talking with the candor of friendship let me suggest to you that you must not be too surprised if you are widely misunderstood regarding the anti-Semitic aspect—an essential aspect—of Nazism. . . . I wish we could talk all this out." But that was the last letter between them, Frankfurter/Astor exchange in Freedman, ed., pp. 473–75; see Christopher Sykes, *Nancy: The Life of Lady Astor*, pp. 382–89; re Lady Astor's remarks, NYT, 30 June 1937. Although FDR appointed Frankfurter to the Supreme Court in 1939, he never told the president of his uncle's difficulties, and they evidently never discussed the death of Austria. See Freedman.

502 *"Our isolationists must see":* Nicolson Diary, 6 June 1938, pp. 345–46; *"The suicides have been appalling. . . .":* Nicolson to Vita Sackville-West, 17 June 1938, p. 347.

502–3 *"Jews to be made to eat grass":* Nicolson Diary, 30 June 1938, p. 348.

503 Nicolson contemplated "the Decline and Fall of the British Empire," while Lindbergh circulated his reports of German military superiority. On 18 May Nicolson heard "three young peers" declare they preferred "to see Hitler in London than a Socialist administration." Nicolson Diary, 18 May 1938, p. 342; Lindbergh visit to Sissinghurst, 22 May 1938, p. 343.

503 *ER at Val-Kill, birds fly:* May 1938, *My Day*, pp. 249–50.

503–4 *China and Barcelona: My Day*, Apr. 1938, p. 238.

504 *ER at Empire State Building, thought intruded: My Day*, Apr. 1938, p. 241.

504 *ER loved to hear the songs of the International Brigade:* Joseph Lash, *A Friend's Memoir* (Doubleday, 1964), pp. 198–99; see also Leslie Gould, *American Youth Today* (Random House, 1940), p. 71; ER wrote the foreword for this AYC celebration.

504 *FDR and Spain:* FDR had discussed Spain with congressional leaders, Speaker Bankhead and Majority Leader Sam Rayburn. Ickes Diary, 7 May 1938, 12 May, pp. 388–90.

505 *ER joined Bowers's plea: My Day*, May 1938, p. 253.

505–6 *Hall and Daniel in Paris:* Bullitt to FDR, telegram #970, 21 June 1938. Bullitt, pp ?74–76. Freidel argues that FDR was part of this effort. Perhaps he was; but it is unlikely that he would have encouraged Hall or ER to communicate with Bullitt if he wanted it to succeed. Bullitt's views were well known: On 24 November 1936, Bullitt wrote FDR: "The war in Spain, as you know, has become an incognito war between the Soviet Union and Italy. . . . My own impression is that Mussolini has decided to put through Franco whatever the cost may be. I think that the cost will be very high." Bullitt, pp. 186–87. See Herbert L. Matthews, *Half of Spain Died* (Charles Scribner's Sons, 1973), p. 179.

507 *Too late to help Spain, ER and Churchill: TIR*, p. 275.

507–8 *Danny in Spain for six weeks, confirmed ER's convictions:* Daniel Stewart Roosevelt, "Wings Over Spain," in Hall Roosevelt with Samuel Duff McCoy, *Odyssey of an American Family: An Account of the Roosevelts and Their Kin As Travelers, 1613–1938* (Harper & Brothers, 1939), pp. 328–35. With gratitude to Diana Roosevelt Jaicks.

508 *ER received set number two of Goya's* Los Proverbios: Matthews, *NYT*, 8 Sept. 1954; see Armstrong, p. 477, cf. 470–78; *ER, "I am not neutral":* Lash, *Eleanor and Franklin*, p. 569.

26: Race Radicals, Youth and Hope

509–10 *ER's address at Hampton Institute:* 21 Apr. 1938; *The Southern Workman*, July 1938, pp. 164–77.

510–11 *Lucy Randolph Mason:* Lucy Randolph Mason to ER, 1 Feb. 1938; 11 Feb. 1938; re SCHW, 28 July 1938; Mason to Frances Perkins and ER, 24 Mar. 1930; ER to Mason, 7 Feb., 18 Apr. 1938. ER sent Mason's reports to FDR via Missy LeHand: "FDR should read. She is a level-headed person and an old hand." He returned her letters, with a memo: "The President has seen." On FDR's FBI proposal on lynching, and Evian, see editorials, *The Crisis*, Apr. 1938, esp. p. 119.

511 *Oversight for women's prisons:* Mason to ER, 7 Apr.; Mason to ER,

9 May 1938; ER to Aubrey Williams, to protest WPA and PWA funding for armories and new women's prisons in Georgia and South Carolina. Gay Shepperson protested; and Dr. Jean Davis of Wells College and Bedford Reformatory; on West Virginia discrimination, ER to John Fahey, 25 May 1938; John Hager to ER, 28 May, 70.

511 *Mason considered ER "the most useful woman in America":* Mason was particularly grateful to ER for her appointment to the National Emergency Council, which FDR convened to address the South's regional problems. Southern leaders would meet in July, and Mason hoped to see ER there. But ER intended to be exclusively at Hyde Park. *Masterful,* Mason to ER, 1 July 1938; ER to Mason, 3 July 1938.

511 *World Youth Congress:* ER to Elizabeth Shields-Collins, secretary, World Youth Congress Movement, Geneva, 13 Jan. 1938, 100, Box 1477: "I will be glad to attend . . . 15 August." Originally, ER tried to persuade FDR to accept the World Youth Congress as an official government-sponsored conference, and finance it. ER to FDR, 7 Jan. 1938; FDR memo to ER, 10 Jan. 1938, rejecting idea. There were altogether too many groups to support.

511–12 *Aubrey Williams and AYC:* Gould, p. 86; McCloskey to ER, in Lash, *Eleanor and Franklin,* p. 545. ER was particularly fond of Joseph Cadden, then editor of the *National Student Mirror* and associated with the National Student Federation; William Porter of Kentucky, president of the AYC's Southern branch; and especially William Hinckley, AYC chairman. Born in South Dakota, Hinckley was "big and bouncing." An award-winning scholar and athlete, he graduated from Rollins College, and had a master's in social science from Columbia. Unfailingly cheerful, he and his widowed mother worked hard for every educational opportunity he achieved. He had great respect for struggling people, a profound commitment to democratic activism, and unbounded admiration for ER. I am grateful to Vivian Cadden for information and AYC memorabilia.

512 *AYC's Declaration of Rights:* Hinckley to ER, 23 Mar. 1938; Leslie Gould, *American Youth Today* (Random House, 1940).

513 *ER moved on:* ER became close to several AYC leaders, notably Hinckley, Joseph Cadden (executive secretary), Abbot Simon (legislative secretary), Joseph Lash (AYC vice president and president, American Student Union), Molly Yard (a vigorous organizer, and vice president of the American Student Union), and Jack McMichael (a student orator from Quitman, Georgia, who went to China for the YMCA; he succeeded Hinckley as AYC president, then attended Union Theological Seminary and became a progressive rural Methodist minister). In 1938 the AYC executive board included Louise Meyerovitz of Young Judea; unionist James Carey (UERMWA, United Electrical Workers, CIO), Hipolito Marcano (Puerto Rican Youth Congress), Lael Moon (American Country Life Association), Edward Strong (National Negro Congress), and Myrtle Powell (YWCA).

513 *"to jolt women out of their apathy":* ER quoted in *NYT,* 28 Dec. 1938.

514 *ER elected to AYC advisory board:* Hinckley to ER, 23 Mar. 1938; ER to Hinckley, 16 April, with attachments on congressional investigation of the AYC, 100, Box 1462; on Hinckley, Gould; Abbott Simon and Vivian Cadden to BWC.

514 *Catholic lobby, divorce and birthing: NYT,* 27 April 1938; Lash, *Eleanor and Franklin,* p. 568.

514 *ER a Red leader:* ER to Mrs. Jack Trautman, 1 July 1936; Trautman to ER,

13 June 1936 (Columbus, Ohio), 100, Box 1408. See also Elizabeth Dilling's *The Red Network*; and Jeansonne, *Women of the Radical Right.*

515 *Rumors of Hopkins's impending marriage:* Hick to ER, 19 May; ER to Hick, 21 May 1938.

515 *no special time, Barbirolli "too pedantic":* ER to Hick, 29 Apr. 1938.

515–16 *Wages and hours law, and Lubin:* in Davis, pp. 240–41.

516 *ER amused by Kennedy's impressions:* ER to Hick, 22 June 1938.

516 *Anne Lindsay Clark marries John Roosevelt: Sun. NYT,* 19 June 1938.

516 *At Val-Kill:* ER to Hick, 6 July; 23 June 1938.

517 *Evian Conference:* Morse, pp. 170–76; Hitler quoted in Davis, p. 197; Evian resulted from a suggestion made by Sumner Welles on 25 Mar. 1938; Shirer, *Berlin Diary,* 7 July 1938, pp. 119–20.

517 *Galápagos:* FDR to ER aboard USS *Houston,* 24 July 1938, 31 July, 1 Aug., 2 Aug., pp. 799–800.

517–18 *Winston Churchill's book:* FDR to Uncle Fred, 25 June 1938, "Ever so many thanks. . . . It will make great reading on the trip . . . ," p. 793. Upon his return, jolly and satisfied, ER noted: "F seems to have had a perfect holiday." ER to Hick, 12 Aug 1938. Although she never wanted to join him on his fishing adventures, ER envied FDR's trip to the Galápagos and vowed one day to go there herself, which she did during the war.

518 *"life may be somewhat negative":* ER to Hick, 21 July 1938.

518 *"If you like it one-tenth":* Hick to ER; *curious tone:* ER to Elizabeth and Esther, 2 Aug. 1938.

518 *ER replied frankly:* ER to Esther, 11 Aug. 1938.

518 *In Hick's space:* Hick had once written ER about her hilarious moments with Bill Dana, the two of them together through the woods hunting, with music and brandy, in his Rolls-Royce town car. "That's the sort of thing that would happen only out here!" It was not, however, something that might thrill ER. Hick to ER, 30 Oct. 1937, LH, Box 4; I am grateful for Doris Dana's memories of her father and Hick on the place; *politely:* ER to Hick, 5 Aug. 1938.

519 *Letters of complaint:* ER to FDR, 4 Aug.; to Elinor Morgenthau, 6 Aug. 1938.

519 *three letters to Anna:* ER to Anna, 4 Aug. 1938; Halsted, Box 57; ER to Anna, 12 Aug. 1938; *driven by work:* ER to Anna, 22 Aug. 1938.

520 *A dozen AYC leaders:* William Hinckley to ER, 5 August 1938, 100, Box 1462; *NYT,* 10 Aug. 1938.

520 FDR to ER, 2 Aug.; n.d., Aug., from Balboa, pp. 800–801; *"I don't want to go anywhere":* ER to FDR, 4 Aug. 1938.

520–21 *FDR speech, 18 August 1938:* Selected speeches, pp. 158ff.; Dallek, p. 163. Germany dismissed his words as "moral preachment."

521 *World Youth Congress, from beginning: NYT,* 10 Aug. 1938; Gould, passim.

521 *On U.S. attendance at Nuremberg rally:* See FDR to Sumner Welles, 3 June 1938, pp. 790–91; see also Offner.

522 *ER differs with the bishops:* "Radicals at Vassar," in *America,* 6 Aug. 1938; sent to ER by Reverend J. Murphy; ER to Father Murphy, 16 Aug. 1938, 100, Box 1470.

522 *ER greeted the delegates: NYT,* 17 Aug. 1938.

522–23 Details of the Youth Congress in Gould, pp. 90–94.

523 *"a lesson to their elders":* ER to Hick, 27 Aug. 1938; see also Lash, *Friends,* pp. 1–6.

523 *Hallie Flanagan and first Dies committee hearing:* See Eric Bentley, *30 Years of Treason* (Viking, 1971), pp. 3–55.

523 *endured tough questions:* NYT, 21 Aug. 1938.

523 *ER left Vassar:* ER to Hick, 16 Aug. 1938; 27 Aug. 1938.

523 *ER defended the Congress:* NYT, 21 Aug. 1938. Matthews also explained the origin of the ASU in the autumn of 1935: The National Student League and the Student League for Industrial Democracy, associated with Norman Thomas, merged and the ASU became the united front's student movement. ER initially ignored the Dies hearings that August, and defended the Youth Congress as "an outstanding event," in her *Democratic Digest* column, Oct. 1938.

524 *letter to disturbed citizens, "I do not believe in Communism":* ER to Ellinor Heiser, Md., 6 Sept. 1938, 100, Box 1461.

524 *triumphant dive:* ER to Hick, 21 Aug. 1938.

525 *"fish in a back water":* ER to Hick, 27 Aug. 1938.

525 *Hall appeared:* ER to Hick, 28 Aug. 1938; *additional details:* 31 Aug. 1938.

526–27 *Inauguration letters:* Tommy to Anna, Jan. 1937; *"George Bye told me . . . $25,000 job":* n.d., Jan. 1938, Halsted, Box 75.

527 *"Our Daughters' Heritage":* Marion Dickerman Papers, Box 4.

527 *"I am terribly sorry":* ER to MD, quoted in Davis, *Summer,* pp. 148–49. Still, ER was not ready simply to abandon Todhunter. On 30 Mar. Tommy wrote "Dear Gorgeous" that "Todhunter hogs a lot of time." Still it was an "affliction to be born with so much generosity and kindness as your mother has." Then, in April, Tommy wrote with glee: "Your mother will probably tell you about Myron Taylor's dinner. [He] told them in no uncertain terms that your mother was the one and only drawing card. . . . He frankly admitted that he would have no interest whatsoever unless it were for your mother. . . ." Tommy to Anna, 15 Apr. 38.

527 *"as a contact":* ER to Dickerman, with details of the meeting with Hooker, Bernard Baruch, and Judge Gerard, 26 Apr. 1938.

527 *"endurance test":* Tommy to Anna, n.d., 30 Mar. 1937; *"my house":* 10 Sept. 1937.

528 *Dickerman appointed to commission:* Tommy to Anna, 11 July 1938.

528 *ER once before tried to get Dickerman a job:* ER to Hopkins, 14 June 1935, 70, Box 653.

529 *Dickerman's sojourn a disaster:* Frances Perkins, Columbia Oral History, vol. 5, pp. 415–40.

529 *ER in* Democratic Digest: Oct. 1938; *Dickerman observed Kennedy, and Swope:* Davis, *Summer,* pp. 149–50.

530 *"it makes your mother very nervous":* Tommy to Anna, 6 Aug. 1938.

530 *at dock:* Davis, p. 150; *"Eleanor hurt her":* Dickerman, Columbia Oral History Project, p. 352.

530 *"Eleanor never forgot a hurt":* Dickerman, Oral, p. 352.

530 *"your mother never takes any credit":* Tommy to Anna, May 1937, Halsted, Box 75.

531 *"Pa's ten days"*: ER to Anna, 30 Aug. 1938, Halsted, Box 57.

532 For the significant Arthurdale sums in Nancy Cook's account, see Pickett to ER, 1934–37.

532 *Tommy's call "incredibly dashing"*: Lape, *Memories of Saltmeadow*, in Lape Papers, FDRL, pp. 25–26. ER confided her deepest feelings to Lape, "I am overcome now and then by the shameless way in which I tell you all the little things of life but then they do make up the major part of our existence, dont they?" ER to Lape, 5 Oct. 1938.

532–33 *"I thought I had made it very clear"*: ER to Nan and Marion, 29 Oct. 1938, MD, Box 4, p. 577; *the final separation agreement*: ER to MD, 9 Nov. 1938, ibid.

533 *Dickerman–ER telegrams*: Davis, p. 153.

533–34 Tommy to Lape and Read, Nov. 1938.

534 *"Franklin dear"*: Nancy Cook to FDR, 14 Nov. 1938, ppf, 1256.

535 *"The only instance"*: Dickerman to ER, 16 May, in Davis, p. 155.

535 *"I know nothing," Dickerman's final letters*: in Davis, pp. 155–57.

536 *"an empty victory"*: Tommy to Anna, 12 Nov. 1938.

536 *Tommy had minor surgery*: Lucy Randolph Mason to ER, 24 June 1938; ER to Mason, 5 July.

536 *Dr. Steele, "complete disillusionment"*: Tommy to Anna, 12 Nov. 1938, Halsted, box 75.

536 *"I hate to see you disillusioned"*: Hick to ER, 17 Nov. 1938.

Chapter 27: Storms on Every Front

538 *FDR's words thrilled ER's allies*: See Linda Reed, *Simple Decency and Common Sense: The Southern Conference Movement, 1938–1963* (Indiana University Press, 1991), intro; Virginia Durr, *Outside the Magic Circle: The Autobiography of Virginia Durr* (University of Alabama Press, 1985), pp. 116–18.

538–39 *"I like facing facts"*: ER to Hick; *"Father came to Rochester"*: James Roosevelt, p. 309; *ER described her lonely hospital vigil, and their flight*: TIR, p. 166; *Democratic Digest*, Nov. 1938.

539 *to avert war by "flattering him why it is worth doing"*: ER to Hick, 15 Sept. 1938.

539 "tension in the house is great": ER to Anna, 15 Sept. 1938.

540 *Lake Geneva, 14–22 Sept.*: Shirer, *Diary*, pp. 124–37.

540 *Nicolson lunched with Litvinov*: Nicolson, p. 356.

540 *No gossip, only war talk*: Virginia Woolf to Vanessa Bell, 28 Sept., 1 Oct., 3 Oct. 1938, *Letters*, VI, pp. 273–79.

541 *Marguerite Few, Once Baxter, to ER*: Lash, *Eleanor and Franklin*, p. 573.

541 *FDR's 26 Sept. 1938 message, and responses*: Sumner Welles, *The Time for Decision* (Harper, 1940), pp. 69–71.

541 *Munich Conference*: Shirer, *Diary*; A.J.P. Taylor noted that Hitler wanted an Anglo-Saxon alliance, but U.S. isolation prevented that. For a recent and important discussion of appeasement and historians, see Clement Leibovitz and Alvin

Finkel, *In Our Time: The Chamberlain-Hitler Collusion* (Monthly Review Press, 1998).

541 The most dramatic description of the weeks that led to Munich, and beyond, is Harold Nicolson, pp. 350–76.

541 *"The poor Czechs!":* ER to FDR, 21, 27 Sept. 1938, fam/childn, box 16.

541–42 *FDR to cabinet:* Ickes, p. 468.

542 FDR quoted in Bullitt, p. 285; Keitel quoted in Churchill, p. 319; Bonnet in Bullitt, p. 284; Daladier in Bullitt, p. 287.

542 *"All is over":* Churchill, pp. 327–28.

543 *"He is not a Jew himself":* Gertrude Ely to ER, 13 Sept. 1938, 100, Box 1457; ER to Ely, 19 Sept. 1938, 100, Box 1457.

543–44 *Joseph Kennedy:* Beschloss, pp. 159ff.; 177, 172, 187; see also Ickes Diary, Nov. 1938.

544 *Bullitt, Moffat, Cudahy:* Ted Morgan, pp. 498–99, passim; see also Dallek.

545 *"How do you manage":* Hick to ER, 19 Sept. 1938.

545 *"an efficient maid":* ER to Hick, 20 Sept. 1938; *"anxious for a glimpse":* ER to Hick, 19 Sept.

545 *"Doesn't one feel helpless when nature gets going?":* She also wrote, "Of course you are glad to have no one on your mind—You are too busy to be bothered!" ER to Hick, 22 Sept. 1938.

546 *"Our cellars here are flooded":* ER to Hick, 23 Sept. 1938. I am grateful to David Rattray for "The Hurricane of '38," written and produced by Thomas Lennon and Michael Epstein for the American Experience.

546–47 *"I shall not soon forget that night":* Hick to ER, 26 Sept. 1938; *at the White House, "eclipsed by the world situation":* ER to Hick, 27 Sept. 1938; *Esther Lape rushed to be with Elizabeth Read:* see Lape, *Saltmeadow*, pp. 36–41.

547 *"What a mad man!":* ER to Hick, 28 Sept. 1938.

547–48 *"nature does cover up":* ER to Hick, 29 Sept. 1938; *Pa's speech and Thomas Mann:* ER to Anna, 3 Oct. 1938; *Mann and "Czechoslovakia set up in an arbitrary way":* My Day, 23 Sept. 1938.

548–49 ER to Helen Gifford, 14 Oct. 1938; Lash, *Eleanor and Franklin*, p. 574.

549 *"Mankind has never been in this position before":* Churchill in *Gathering*, pp. 38–41.

549 *"I have never believed":* ER to Elizabeth Baker, National Committee on the Cause and Cure of War, 20 Jan. 1938, SCPC.

549 *"everywhere people listened," speeches on tour, and youngest grandson:* Democratic Digest, Nov. 1938.

550 *dined with Aubrey Williams, Josephine Roche, others, sympathy with Mexico's oil lands:* ER to Hick, 9 Oct. 1938; Dallek, pp. 175–76; Ickes, pp. 352, 521–22; see also *Time*, 8 Aug. 1938.

551 ER to HH, 13 Oct. 1938, with poem, 70, Box 731.

552 *ER's birthday a state occasion:* NYT, 13 Oct. 1938; also, 10 Sept.; *New York State women's poll; and Women's National Press Club honored "Good Queen Eleanor":* NYT, 16 Oct. 1938, sect. 4.

552 *Granny "aging fast":* ER to Anna, 3 Oct. 1938; *worried about everything:* ER to Anna, 23 Oct. 1938; *publicly, "younger in spirit":* Democratic Digest, Nov. 1938.

553–54 *"Too bad Curt," and James:* ER to Anna, 23 Oct. 1938; *on the road:* ER to Hick, 12 Oct.; *"If only you weren't the President's wife":* Hick to ER, 12 Oct. 1938; *"I doubt dear":* ER to Hick, 15 Oct. 1938.

554 *proposed a week in Washington:* ER to Hick, 21 Oct.; *"thought you had put the White House aside forever!":* ER to Hick, 25 Oct. 1938; Hick to ER, 27 Oct. 1938; *KKK, labor strikes:* ER to Hick, 28, 29 Oct. 1938.

554–55 *birth of John Boettiger, Jr.:* Anna to Tommy, 7 Nov. 1938, Halsted, box 75.

555 *Returned in time to join FDR and SDR at the polls: Democratic Digest,* Dec. 1938.

555 *1938 elections disastrous:* Davis, pp. 362–64.

555 *"wholly reconciled":* FDR to Josephus Daniels, 14 Nov. 1938, *Letters,* IV, p. 827.

555 *"libelous misinformation":* Flanagan to ER, 22 Sept. 1938; ER to Flanagan, 28 Sept. 1938, 70.

557 *"This German-Jewish business makes me sick":* ER to Hick, 14 Nov. 1938.

557 *canceled engagement because it excluded Jews:* E. Digby Baltzell, *The Protestant Establishment* (Vintage, 1966), p. 237.

557 *drive for home for immigrant girls in Jerusalem":* NYT, 19 Oct. 1937; *spoke for Léon Blum colony in Palestine:* NYT, 7 Dec. 1938.

558 *TR's 1902 message to Romania:* Arthur D. Morse, *While Six Million Died,* p. 107.

558 *For aid to China:* FDR to Hull, 11 Jan. 1938, *Letters,* IV, pp. 744–45; see esp. Iris Chang, *The Rape of Nanking: The Forgotten Holocaust of World War II* (Penguin, 1997).

558 *Jews on the run for 4,000 years:* FDR to William Phillips, 15 Sept. 1938, *Letters,* IV, p. 811.

558 *to drive wedge between Hitler and Mussolini:* Ickes, 7 Jan. 1939, p. 548.

558 *Red Cross:* Morse, p. 262.

559 *FDR appealed for emergency asylum:* NYT, 19 Nov. 1938.

560–61 *Bowman's report:* 21 Nov. 1938; 25 Nov. 1938; psf, 177, refugees.

561–62 *Appropriate Baja, California:* Sumner Welles to FDR, 28 Nov. 1938, with 12-page memo: The Dominican Republic agreed to accept 10,000; and at the subsequent London Conference raised that to 100,000. But of 2,000 refugees who applied for Dominican visas, only 20 had been granted in the preceding four months. Nicaragua admitted "a fair number of refugees." El Salvador did not attend Evian, and refused to accept refugees. Colombia had admitted 10,000 refugees, and "believes that it is unwise to admit more." Ecuador admitted "substantial numbers" as agriculturalists, but they all settled in cities. Ecuador then began deportation proceedings, which it rescinded "due to the efforts of the local Jewish community." Brazil and Paraguay were willing to admit additional refugees. Argentina had a population of 350,000 Jews, "more than in the rest of Latin America combined." "New and more restrictive immigration regulations went into effect October 1st. It is nevertheless probable that the government will continue to admit a not inconsiderable number of refugees." Chile and Uruguay adopted greater restrictions after Evian. Bolivia had limited settlement potential. Peru was cooperative and wanted agriculturalists and people "with capital to establish many non-existing industries which the country seriously needs." Cuba "has been relatively hospitable to refugees," but made no commitment as to the future. Within six months of Welles's discouraging assessment, additional barriers were raised everywhere. Welles, 28 Nov., psf, 177.

562 for Canada, see esp. Abella and Troper, *None Is Too Many* (Random House, 1982).

562 *ER defended the AYC at AAUW luncheon at Hotel Astor: NYT,* 20 Nov. 1938; Marion Dickerman spoke as president of N.Y.'s AAUW, on her ILO mission; Virginia Gildersleeve spoke about the need to find havens for Europe's university women, now deprived of all research opportunities.

563 *ER's shopping spree at Arnold Constable:* On 21 Oct., *NYT* printed a photo of ER's new hairstyle; *NYT,* 20 Nov. 1938.; Henry Grady quoted in Linda Reed, *Simple Decency and Common Sense,* p. 2.

564 *SCHW meeting:* See Reed, pp. 15–16, and passim; Virginia Durr, *Outside the Magic Circle,* and Durr to BWC.

565 *"Sometimes actions speak louder than words": Afro-American,* quoted in Pauli Murray, *Song in a Weary Throat: An American Pilgrimage* (Harper & Row, 1987), p. 113.

565 *ER's 22 November 1938 speech at the SCHW:* Allida Black, ed., *Courage in a Dangerous World: The Political Writings of Eleanor Roosevelt* (Columbia University Press, 1999).

566 Aubrey Williams, in Virginia Durr; also, John Williams, *A Southern Rebel: The Life and Times of Aubrey Williams* (University of North Carolina, 1983), pp. 101–3.

566 *resolutions, "one of the gravest sins":* Linda Reed, pp. 46–48.

566 *Louise Charlton called on Mrs. Bethune:* Virginia Durr, p. 121.

567 *propaganda and a controlled press:* Virginia Durr in *NYT,* 23 Nov. 1938.

567 *"by dipping or sprinkling or total immersion. . . .":* Durr, *Outside,* pp. 124–25.

568 *"the New Deal come South," and at the end:* Durr, pp. 127–28.

568 *"Have they torn you limb from limb yet?":* Hick to ER, 28 Nov. 1938.

568 *"Tommy doesn't feel well": NYT,* 23 Nov. 1938. ER also wrote that Birmingham "invoked an old ordinance and required segregation at all meetings even in churches and it caused most vigorous protest. I felt very uncomfortable and some of the questions I longed to answer as I really felt. . . ." ER to Hick, 23 Nov. 1938.

568–69 *Women's Democratic Committee, to reunite Hick to politics:* ER to Hick, 18 Nov. 1938; *FDR "much interested," doubts Farley:* ER to Hick, 21 Nov.; "more liberal than the Republican party": 22 Nov. 1938.

569 *24 Nov. 1938, "the final and unalterably uncompromising solution":* Morse, p. 196; Michael Berenbaum, *The World Must Know* (Holocaust Museum, Little, Brown, 1993), p. 35.

570 *Citizens of conscience petitioned FDR:* in Morse, p. 190.

570 *rearmament, especially mass production of airplanes:* FDR to "Dear Chief," 14 Nov. 1938, *Letters,* IV, p. 827; FDR to Swanson, Edison, Leahy, 28 Dec. 1938, IV, p. 843; to General John J. Pershing, 3 Dec. 1938, IV, p. 838, re a study of military stores and requirements.

571 *article on tolerance, "I gather that the President okayed it":* Hick to ER, 22 Nov. 1938; *FDR read both, "just said . . . OK . . . to send":* ER to Hick, 25 Nov. 1938.

571 *untitled manuscript on Jews:* sent to Fulton Oursler, 25 Nov. 1938, in Hick, box 6; "Mrs. Roosevelt Answers Mr. Wells on 'The Future of the Jews,' " *Liberty,* 31 Dec. 1938; reprinted in Allida Black.

571 *important for Jews to remain unaggressive:* Lash, *Eleanor and Franklin,* p. 750.

573 *"I like it very much":* Hick to ER, 30 Nov. 1938.

573 *Keepers of Democracy,* written in Nov. 1938, published in *The Virginia Quarterly Review* (Winter 1939); also in Allida Black.

574 *freedom can never be "freedom for me and not for you":* ER at Brooklyn Academy, in *NYT,* 13 Dec. 1938; *"democracy is going forward":* NYT, 22 Jan. 1939.

574–75 *"grand time":* Hick to ER, 21 Dec. 1938; *"dust and ashes," serenity safer:* ER to Hick, 23 Dec. 1938.

575 For press coverage of ER II's debutante party, I am grateful to ER II and Diana Roosevelt Jaicks.

575 *equal rights for minorities as well as majorities:* ER in *NYT,* 23 Oct. 1937.

575 *"There are still slaves of many kinds":* ER to National Negro Congress, *NYT,* 11 Feb. 1938.

576 *"As I listened," ER's response to speeches for Léon Blum colony: My Day,* 8 Dec. 1938. While ER spoke on behalf of the settlement for 1,000 Jewish refugee families in Palestine named to honor France's first Jewish and socialist prime minister, France was on the verge of civil war. Even as Blum's government fell in April 1938, left pacifist Simone Weil wrote deputy Gaston Bergery that she preferred German hegemony to war, although it would mean "laws of exclusion against Communists and Jew"; quoted in Michael Marrus and Robert Paxton, *Vichy France and the Jews* (Basic Books, 1981), p. 39.

NOTE ON SOURCES
AND SELECTED BIBLIOGRAPHY

The Eleanor Roosevelt Papers at the Franklin Delano Roosevelt Library (FDRL) at Hyde Park are in several collections, as cited in the notes. Series 70 largely includes correspondence with public officials and citizens; series 100 includes more personal correspondence and papers of the Roosevelt family, donated by the children. Of additional significance for this volume are individual collections, including the Molly Dewson, Marion Dickerman, Lorena Hickok, Esther Lape, Elinor Morgenthau, Aubrey Williams, and FDR papers.

ER's correspondence with Jane Addams is at the FDRL and at the Swarthmore College Peace Collection (SCPC). I am grateful to Mary Lynn McCree Bryan for documents from the Jane Addams Papers Project. See Mary Lynn McCree Bryan, *The Jane Addams Papers Guide* (Ann Arbor, University Microfilms, 1985).

Carrie Chapman Catt's papers are at the New York Public Library, including the file on the Christian Women's Protest Against Germany's Treatment of the Jews. Her letters to ER are at the FDRL.

Gertrude Ely's papers have not yet been located. Although there is correspondence with ER at the FDRL, her life story has yet to be told. I am grateful to Lorett Treese for biographical memorabilia on Ely in the Bryn Mawr College Archives, to Anonymous of Fowler's Beach for letters and memories of Ely, and to Rodney H. Clurman.

Isabella Greenway's Papers are in the Arizona Historical Society, Tucson.

Alice Hamilton's correspondence with ER is at the FDRL and in the Jane Addams Papers Project. I am grateful to Barbara Sicherman for excerpts from Hamilton's daybook and Hamilton's articles on Germany: "An Inquiry into the Nazi Mind," *NY Times Sunday Magazine*, 6 August 1933; "The Youth Who Are Hitler's Strength," *NY Times Sunday Magazine*, 8 October 1933; "Hitler Speaks," *Atlantic*, October 1933; "Below the Surface," *Survey Graphic*, September 1933; "Sound and Fury in Germany," *Survey Graphic*, November 1933; "The Plight of the German Intellectuals," *Harper's*, January 1934; "German Intellectuals," *NY Times*, 7 January 1934.

ER's correspondence with Fannie Hurst is mostly in the Fannie Hurst Papers, in the Harry Ransom Collection, Humanities Research Center, University of Texas at Austin. Hurst's correspondence with Ruth Bryan Owen in this collection is significant.

The Helen Rogers Reid, Harold Ickes, and NAACP Papers are at the Library of

Congress. ER's correspondence with Molly Dewson, Hilda Worthington Smith, and Charlotte Everett Hopkins is at FDRL and the Schlesinger Library. Other collections used for this book at the Schlesinger Library include Pauli Murray, Pauline Newman, and Charl Ormond Williams. Flora Rose and Martha van Rensselaer Papers and Frances Perkins's lecture notes are at Cornell. Frances Perkins's papers and oral history are at Columbia University. The Lillian Wald Papers are at the New York Public Library and at Columbia University.

ER's monthly columns in New York State's *Women's Democratic News* were folded into the national *Democratic Digest* in 1936. In 1938, ER selected her favorite daily columns and published them in *My Days*. These are undated except by month and year; I refer to them by page. Rochelle Chadakoff edited *ER's My Day: Her Acclaimed Columns, 1936–1945* (Pharos Books, 1989); these are cited by date. In addition to the daily *New York Times*, the NAACP's *Crisis Magazine*, which ER routinely sent to New Deal officials, were basic to this study. Columns and articles are in the notes.

BY ELEANOR ROOSEVELT

It's Up to the Women (Frederick A. Stokes, 1933).
Hunting Big Game in the 'Eighties: The Letters of Elliott Roosevelt, Sportsman. Edited by His Daughter (Charles Scribner's Sons, 1933).
This Is My Story (Harper & Brothers, 1937).
This Troubled World (H. C. Kinsey & Co., 1938).
My Days (Dodge Publishing, 1938).
This I Remember (Harper & Brothers, 1949).
You Learn by Living (New York: Harper & Brothers, 1960)
The Autobiography of Eleanor Roosevelt (Harper & Brothers, 1960).

ABOUT ELEANOR ROOSEVELT

Asbell, Bernard, ed. *Mother and Daughter: The Letters of Eleanor and Anna Roosevelt* (Coward, McCann, Geoghegan, 1981).
Beasley, Maurine. *Eleanor Roosevelt and the Media: A Public Quest for Self-Fulfillment* (University of Illinois Press, 1987).
———, ed. *The White House Press Conferences of Eleanor Roosevelt* (Garland, 1983).
———, and Richard Lowitt, eds. *One Third of a Nation: Lorena Hickok Reports on the Great Depression* (University of Illinois Press, 1983).
Bethune, Mary McLeod. "My Secret Talks with FDR," *Ebony* (April 1949); reprinted in Bernard Sternsher, *The Negro in Depression and War, 1930–1945* (Quadrangle, 1969).
Black, Allida M. *Casting Her Own Shadow: Eleanor Roosevelt and the Shaping of Postwar Liberalism* (Columbia University Press, 1996).
———, ed. *What I Hope to Leave Behind: The Essential Essays of Eleanor Roosevelt* (Ralph Carlson, 1995).
———, ed. *Courage in a Dangerous World: The Political Writings of Eleanor Roosevelt* (Columbia University Press, 1999).
Black, Ruby. *Eleanor Roosevelt: A Biography* (Duell, Sloan and Pearce, 1940).
Chadakoff, Rochelle, ed. *ER's My Day: Her Acclaimed Columns, 1936–1945* (Pharos Books, 1989).

Cook, Blanche Wiesen. *Eleanor Roosevelt,* Vol. I: *1884–1933* (Viking, 1992).

———. "Eleanor Roosevelt and Human Rights." In Edward Crapol, ed., *Women and American Foreign Policy* (Greenwood, 1987).

———. "Eleanor Roosevelt and the South," *Atlanta History: A Journal of Georgia and the South* (Winter 1995).

———. "Turn Toward Peace: ER and Foreign Affairs." In Joan Hoff-Wilson and Marjorie Lightman, eds., *Without Precedent* (University of Indiana Press, 1984).

Davis, Kenneth S. *Invincible Summer: An Intimate Portrait of the Roosevelts Based on the Recollections of Marion Dickerman* (Atheneum, 1974).

Faber, Doris. *The Life of Lorena Hickok: ER's Friend* (Morrow, 1980).

Flemion, Jess, and Colleen M. O'Connor, eds. *Eleanor Roosevelt: An American Journey* (San Diego State University Press, 1987).

Furman, Bess. *Washington By-Line: The Personal History of a Newspaperwoman* (Knopf, 1949).

Haraven, Tamara. *Eleanor Roosevelt: An American Conscience* (Quadrangle Books, 1968).

Hickok, Lorena A. *Eleanor Roosevelt: Reluctant First Lady* (Dodd, Mead, 1980 [1962]); Introduction by Allen Klots.

Hoff-Wilson, Joan, and Marjorie Lightman, eds. *Without Precedent: The Life and Career of Eleanor Roosevelt* (University of Indiana Press, 1984).

Jeffreys-Jones, Rhodri. *Changing Differences: Women and the Shaping of American Foreign Policy, 1917–1994* (Rutgers University Press, 1995).

Kearney, James. *Anna Eleanor Roosevelt: The Evolution of a Reformer* (Houghton Mifflin, 1968).

Lash, Joseph P. *Eleanor Roosevelt: A Friend's Memoir* (Doubleday, 1964).

———. *Eleanor and Franklin* (W. W. Norton, 1971).

———. *Dealers & Dreamers: A New Look at the New Deal* (Doubleday, 1988).

———. *Love, Eleanor: Eleanor Roosevelt and Her Friends* (Doubleday, 1982).

Nesbitt, Henrietta. *White House Diary by Henrietta Nesbitt: FDR's Housekeeper* (Doubleday, 1948).

Parks, Lillian Rogers, and Frances S. Leighton. *The Roosevelts: A Family in Turmoil* (Prentice Hall, 1981).

Roosevelt, Elliott. *Mother R: Eleanor Roosevelt's Untold Story* (Putnam's, 1977).

Roosevelt, James, and Sidney Shalett. *Affectionately FDR: A Son's Story of a Lonely Man* (Harcourt Brace, 1959).

———, with Bill Libby. *My Parents: A Differing View* (Playboy Press, 1976).

Scharf, Lois. *Eleanor Roosevelt: First Lady of American Liberalism* (Twayne, 1987).

Streitmatter, Rodger. *Empty Without You: The Intimate Letters of Eleanor Roosevelt and Lorena Hickok* (Free Press, 1998).

West, J. B., with Mary Ann Klotz. *Upstairs at the White House: My Life with the First Ladies* (Warner Paperback, 1974).

Young, Rose, ed. *Why Wars Must Cease* (Macmillan, 1935), with ER's "Because the War Idea Is Obsolete."

Youngs, William J. *Eleanor Roosevelt: A Personal and Public Life* (Little, Brown, 1985).

ABOUT FRANKLIN DELANO ROOSEVELT

FDR: His Personal Letters, 1928–1945, Vols. III and IV (Kraus Reprint, 1970 [1950]), edited by Elliott Roosevelt and Joseph P. Lash; foreword by Eleanor Roosevelt.

Rosenman, Samuel I., ed. *The Public Papers and Addresses of FDR,* 13 vols. (Macmillan, 1938–1950).

Asbell, Bernard. *The FDR Memoirs* (Doubleday, 1973).

Beschloss, Michael R. *Kennedy and Roosevelt: The Uneasy Alliance* (Norton, 1980).

Blum, John Morton. *Roosevelt & Morgenthau: From the Morgenthau Diaries* (Houghton Mifflin, 1970).

Bullitt, Orville, ed. *For the President, Personal and Secret: Correspondence Between FDR and William C. Bullitt* (Houghton Mifflin, 1972).

Burns, James MacGregor. *Roosevelt: The Lion and the Fox* (Harcourt, Brace, 1956).

Davis, Kenneth S. *FDR: The New Deal Years, 1933–1937* (Random House, 1986).

———. *FDR: Into the Storm, 1937–1940* (Random House, 1993).

Farley, James. *Jim Farley's Story* (McGraw-Hill, 1948).

Freedman, Max, ed. *Roosevelt & Frankfurter: Their Correspondence, 1928–1945* (Little, Brown, 1967).

Freidel, Frank. *Franklin D. Roosevelt: Launching the New Deal* (Little, Brown, 1973).

———. *Franklin D. Roosevelt: A Rendezvous with Destiny* (Little, Brown, 1990).

———. *FDR and the South* (Louisiana University Press, 1965).

Gallagher, Hugh. *FDR's Splendid Deception* (Dodd, Mead, 1985).

Goodwin, Doris Kearns. *No Ordinary Time: Franklin and Eleanor Roosevelt and the Home Front in World War II* (Simon & Schuster, 1994).

Hurd, Charles. *When the New Deal Was Young and Gay* (Harper, 1965).

Leuchtenburg, William. *FDR and the New Deal: 1932–1940* (Harper Torchbooks, 1963).

———. *The FDR Years: On Roosevelt & His Legacy* (Columbia University Press, 1995).

———. *The Supreme Court Reborn: The Constitutional Revolution in the Age of Roosevelt* (Oxford University Press, 1995).

Lindley, Ernest K. *Half Way with Roosevelt* (Viking, 1937).

Moley, Raymond. *After Seven Years* (Harper & Brothers, 1939).

Morgan, Ted. *FDR: A Biography* (Simon & Schuster, 1985).

Perkins, Frances. *The Roosevelt I Knew* (Viking, 1946).

Rollins, Alfred B. *Roosevelt and Howe* (Knopf, 1962).

Rosenman, Samuel I. *Working with Roosevelt* (Harper & Brothers, 1952).

Schlesinger, Arthur M. *The Age of Roosevelt,* Vol. II: *The Coming of the New Deal* (Houghton Mifflin, 1959).

———. *The Age of Roosevelt,* Vol. III: *The Politics of Upheaval* (Houghton Mifflin, 1960).

Sherwood, Robert E. *Roosevelt and Hopkins: An Intimate History* (Harper, 1948).

Steward, William J., ed. *The Era of Franklin D. Roosevelt: A Selected Bibliography, 1945–1971* (FDR Library, GSA, 1974).

Stiles, Lela. *Louis Howe: The Man Behind Roosevelt* (World Publishing, 1954).

Tugwell, Rexford Guy. *The Democratic Roosevelt: A Biography of FDR* (Doubleday, 1957).

Ward, Geoffrey C. *A First-Class Temperament: The Emergence of Franklin Roosevelt* (Harper & Row, 1989).

Winfield, Betty Houchin. *FDR and the News Media* (University of Illinois Press, 1990).

FRIENDS, NEW DEALERS, RACE RADICALS: DOMESTIC ISSUES

Abramovitz, Mimi. *Regulating the Lives of Women: Social Welfare Policy from Colonial Times to the Present* (South End Press, 1996).

Abramson, Rudy. *Spanning the Century: The Life of W. Averell Harriman, 1891–1986* (William Morrow, 1992).

Addams, Jane. "The World Court." In Allen F. Davis, ed., *Jane Addams on Peace, War and International Understanding* (Garland, 1976).

Alinsky, Saul. *John L. Lewis: An Unauthorized Biography* (Vintage, 1970 [1949]).

Anthony, Carl Sferrazza. *First Ladies* (William Morrow, 1990).

Auerbach, Jerold. *Labor and Liberty: The LaFollette Committee and the New Deal* (Bobbs-Merrill, 1966).

Badger, Anthony. *The New Deal* (Hill & Wang, 1988).

Bain, George. "How Negro Editors Viewed the New Deal," *Journalism Quarterly* (Autumn 1967).

Baker, Leonard. *Back to Back: The Duel Between FDR and the Supreme Court* (Macmillan, 1967).

———. *Brandeis and Frankfurter: A Dual Biography* (Harper & Row, 1984).

Baltzell, E. Digby. *The Protestant Establishment: Aristocracy and Caste in America* (Vintage, 1966).

Belfrage, Cedric, and James Aronson. *Something to Guard* (Columbia University Press, 1978).

Bellush, Bernard. *The Failure of the NRA* (Norton, 1975).

———. *He Walked Alone: A Biography of John Gilbert Winant* (Mouton, 1968).

Bentley, Eric, ed. *Thirty Years of Treason: Excerpts from the Hearings Before the House Committee on Un-American Activities, 1933–1968* (Viking, 1971).

Bernstein, Alison. "A Mixed Record: The Political Enfranchisement of American Indian Women During the Indian New Deal," *Journal of the West* (July 1984).

Berry, Mary Frances. *Black Resistance/White Law: A History of Constitutional Racism in America* (Appleton-Century-Crofts, 1971).

Biles, Roger. *A New Deal for the American People* (Northern Illinois University Press, 1991).

Block, Adrienne Fried. *Amy Beach: Passionate Victorian* (Oxford University Press, 1998).

Bosch, Mineke, with Annemarie Kloosterman, eds. *Politics and Friendship: Letters from the International Woman Suffrage Alliance, 1902–1942* (Ohio State University Press, 1990); includes Catt's correspondence with Rosa Manus.

Bremer, William. "Along the 'American Way': The New Deal's Work Relief Programs for the Unemployed," *Journal of American History* (December 1975).

Brinkley, Alan. *Voices of Protest: Huey Long, Father Coughlin & the Great Depression* (Vintage, 1982).

Brittain, Vera. *Testament of Experience, 1925–1950* (Macmillan, 1957).

Browning, Peter. *Yosemite Place Names* (Great West Books, 1988).

Butler, Susan. *East to the Dawn: The Life of Amelia Earhart* (Addison Wesley, 1997).

Caroli, Betty Boyd. *First Ladies* (Oxford University Press, 1987).

———. *The Roosevelt Women* (Basic Books, 1998).

Chamberlin, Hope. *A Minority of Members: Women in the U.S. Congress* (New American Library, 1973).

Chesler, Ellen. *Margaret Sanger: Woman of Valor and the Birth Control Movement in America* (Simon & Schuster, 1992).

Clarke, Jeanne Nienaber. *Roosevelt's Warrior: Harold L. Ickes and the New Deal* (Johns Hopkins University Press, 1996).

Cliff, Michelle, ed. *The Winner Names the Age: A Collection of Writings by Lillian Smith* (Norton, 1987).

Coit, Margaret L. *Mr. Baruch* (Houghton Mifflin, 1957).

Conkin, Paul. *FDR and the Origins of the Welfare State* (Crowell, 1967).

———. *Tomorrow a New World: The New Deal Community Program* (Cornell University Press, 1959)

Conn, Peter. *Pearl S. Buck: A Cultural Biography* (Cambridge University Press, 1996)

Coss, Clare. *Lillian D. Wald: Progressive Activist* (Feminist Press, 1989).

Daniels, Doris Groshen. *Always a Sister: The Feminism of Lillian Wald* (Feminist Press, 1989).

Daniels, Jonathan. *The End of Innocence* (Lippincott, 1954).

———. *The Washington Quadrille: The Dance Beside the Documents* (Doubleday, 1968).

Daniels, Roger. *The Bonus March* (Greenwood, 1971).

Davis, Allen F. *American Heroine: The Life and Legend of Jane Addams* (Oxford University Press, 1973).

Dinnerstein, Leonard. *Anti-Semitism in America* (Oxford University Press, 1994).

Dubofsky, Melvyn, ed. *The New Deal: Conflicting Interpretations and Shifting Perspectives* (Garland, 1992).

———, ed. *American Labor Since the New Deal* (Quadrangle Books, 1969)

Durr, Virginia. *Outside the Magic Circle: The Autobiography of Virginia Durr* (University of Alabama Press, 1985).

Dykeman, Wilma, and James Stokely. *Seeds of Southern Change: The Life of Will Alexander* (University of Chicago Press, 1962).

———. *Neither Black nor White* (Rinehart, 1957).

Egerton, John. *Speak Now Against the Day: The Generation Before the Civil Rights Movement in the South* (Knopf, 1994).

Embree, Edwin, and Julia Waxman. *Investment in People: The Story of the Julius Rosenwald Fund* (Harper Brothers, 1949).

Evans, Sara M. *Born for Liberty: A History of Women in America* (Free Press, 1989).

Fant, Barbara G. H. "Slum Reclamation and Housing Reform in the Nation's Capital, 1890–1940." (Ph.D. dissertation, George Washington University, 1982).

Farrell, John C. *Beloved Lady: A History of Jane Addams' Ideas on Reform and Peace* (Johns Hopkins University Press, 1967).

Felsenthal, Carol. *Alice Roosevelt Longworth* (G. P. Putnam's Sons, 1988).

Fine, Sidney. *Sit-down: The General Motors Strike of 1936–1937* (University of Michigan Press, 1969).

Flanagan, Hallie. *Arena: The Story of the Federal Theatre* (Limelight Editions, 1985 [1940]).

Foner, Philip. *Women and the American Labor Movement* (Free Press, 1979).

Garrison, Dee. *Mary Heaton Vorse: The Life of an American Insurgent* (Temple University Press, 1989).

———, ed. *Rebel Pen: The Writings of Mary Heaton Vorse* (Monthly Review, 1985).

Ginzburg, Ralph. *100 Years of Lynching* (Lancer Books, 1969).

Gladney, Margaret Rose, ed. *How Am I to Be Heard? Letters of Lillian Smith* (University of North Carolina Press, 1993).

Gordon, Linda. *Pitied but Not Entitled: Single Mothers and the History of Welfare, 1890–1935* (Free Press, 1994).

———. "Putting Children First: Women, Maternalism and Welfare in the Early 20th Century." In Kerber et al., eds., *U.S. History as Women's History: New Feminist Essays* (University of North Carolina Press, 1995).

Grafton, David. *The Sisters: The Lives and Times of the Fabulous Cushing Sisters* (Villard Books, 1992).

Greenbaum, Fred. *Fighting Progressive: A Biography of Edward P. Costigan* (Public Affairs Press, 1971).

Grubbs, Donald. *Cry from the Cotton: The Southern Tenant Farmers Union* (University of North Carolina Press, 1971).

Haid, Stephen Edward. "Arthurdale: An Experiment in Community Planning, 1933–1947" (Ph.D. dissertation, West Virginia University, 1975).

Hair, William Ivy. *The Kingfish & His Realm: The Life and Times of Huey P. Long* (Louisiana State University Press, 1991).

Halasa, Malu. *Mary McLeod Bethune* (Chelsea House, 1989).

Hall, Jacquelyn Dowd. "Women & Lynching," *Southern Exposure* (Winter 1977).

———. *Revolt Against Chivalry: Jessie Daniel Ames and the Women's Campaign Against Lynching* (Columbia University Press, 1979).

Harris, Leon. *Upton Sinclair: American Rebel* (Crowell, 1975).

Hart, John. *Storm over Mono: The Mono Lake Battle and the California Water Future* (University of California Press, 1996).

Heilbrun, Carolyn. *Writing a Woman's Life* (Norton, 1998).

Hoagland, Alison, and Margaret Mulrooney. *Norvelt and Penn-Craft, Pennsylvania: Subsistence Homestead Communities of the 1930s* (National Park Service, U.S. Department of Interior, 1991).

Holt, Rackham. *Mary McLeod Bethune: A Biography* (Doubleday, 1964).

Hopkins, June. "The First and Final Task: Harry Hopkins and the Development of the American Welfare System" (Ph.D. dissertation, Georgetown University, 1997).

Horowitz, Helen Lefkowitz. *The Power and Passion of M. Carey Thomas* (Knopf, 1994).

Hutchmacher, Joseph J. *Senator Robert F. Wagner and the Rise of Urban Liberalism* (Atheneum, 1968).

Ickes, Harold. *The Secret Diary of Harold L. Ickes: The First Thousand Days, 1933–1936* (Simon & Schuster, 1954).

———. *The Secret Diary of Harold L. Ickes, Vol. II: The Inside Struggle, 1936–1939* (Simon & Schuster, 1954).

James, Edward, and Janet James et al., eds. *Notable American Women*, 3 vols. (Harvard University Press, 1971).

Janeway, Eliot. *The Economics of Crisis* (Weybright & Talley, 1968).

Jeansonne, Glen. *Messiah of the Masses: Huey Long and the Great Depression* (HarperCollins, 1983).

———. *Women of the Far Right: The Mothers' Movement and World War II* (University of Chicago Press, 1996).

Johnson, Charles S., Edwin Embree, and W. W. Alexander. *The Collapse of Cotton Tenancy* (University of North Carolina Press, 1935).

Kaplan, Justin. *Lincoln Steffens: A Biography* (Simon & Schuster, 1974).

Kelley, Robin. *Hammer and Hoe: Alabama Communists During the Great Depression* (University of North Carolina Press, 1990).

Kerber, Linda, Alice Kessler-Harris, and Kathryn Kish Sklar, eds. *U.S. History as Women's History: New Feminist Essays* (University of North Carolina Press, 1995).

Kert, Bernice. *The Hemingway Women* (Norton, 1983).

Kessler-Harris, Alice. "Designing Women and Old Fools: The Construction of the Social Security Amendments of 1939." In Kerber et al., eds.

———. *Out to Work: A History of Wage-Earning Women in the United States* (Oxford University Press, 1982).

———. *What's Fair/What Discriminates: Women and Economic Citizenship in the 20th Century.* (Forthcoming).

Kessner, Thomas. *Fiorello H. La Guardia and the Making of Modern New York* (Penguin, 1989).

Kester, Howard. *Revolt Among the Sharecroppers* (Arno Reprint, 1969 [1936]).

Kirby, John B. "The Roosevelt Administration and Blacks: An Ambivalent Legacy." In Barton Bernstein and Allen Matusow, eds., *20th Century America* (Harcourt Brace Jovanovich, 1972).

———. *Black Americans in the Roosevelt Era: Liberalism and Race* (University of Tennessee Press, 1980).

Kornbluh, Joyce L. *A New Deal for Workers' Education: The Workers' Service Program, 1933–1942* (University of Illinois Press, 1987).

Kraft, Barbara S. "The CCC: A Job Stimulus That Worked," *The Progressive Review*, July 1993.

Krueger, Thomas. *And Promises to Keep: The Southern Conference for Human Welfare, 1938–1948* (Vanderbilt University Press, 1967).

Kurth, Peter. *American Cassandra: The Life of Dorothy Thompson* (Little, Brown, 1990).

Lawrenson, Helen. *Stranger at the Party: A Memoir* (Random House, 1975). Particularly useful for Bernard Baruch.

Lerner, Gerda, ed. *Black Women in White America* (Pantheon, 1972).

LeSueur, Meridel. *Ripening: Selected Works* (Feminist Press, 1982).

———. *Women on the Breadlines* (West End Books, 1977).

Lieberman, Richard. *Senator Robert F. Wagner: A Biography.* (Forthcoming).

Lindley, Betty, and Ernest K. Lindley. *A New Deal for Youth: The Story of the National Youth Administration* (DaCapo Press, 1972 [1938]).

Louchheim, Katie, ed. *The Making of the New Deal: The Insiders Speak* (Harvard University Press, 1983).

McJimsey, George. *Harry Hopkins: Ally of the Poor and Defender of Democracy* (Harvard University Press, 1987).

Mangione, Jerre. *The Dream and the Deal: The Federal Writers' Project, 1935–1943* (Avon Books, 1972).

Markowitz, Gerald, and Marlene Park. *Democratic Vistas: Post Offices and Public Art in the New Deal* (Temple University Press, 1984).

———, and David Rosner. *Deadly Dust: Silicosis and the Politics of Occupational Disease in 20th Century America* (Princeton University Press, 1991).

———. *Children, Race and Power: Kenneth and Mamie Clark's Northside Center* (University of Virginia Press, 1996).

———, eds. *Dying for Work: Essays on Workers' Safety and Health in 20th Century America* (Indiana University Press, 1987).

———, eds. *Slaves of the Depression: Workers' Letters About Life on the Job* (Cornell University Press, 1987).

Martin, Clarece. *The History of Bulloch Hall and Roswell Georgia* (Lake Publications, 1987).

Martin, George. *Madame Secretary: Frances Perkins* (Houghton Mifflin, 1976).

Martin, Ralph G. *Cissy: The Extraordinary Life of Eleanor Medill Patterson* (Simon & Schuster, 1979).

Mason, Lucy Randolph. *To Win These Rights: A Personal Story of the CIO in the South* (Harper & Brothers, 1952).

Matthews, Jane DeHart. *The Federal Theatre, 1935–1939* (Princeton University Press, 1967).

Millin, Sarah Gertrude. *The Night Is Long* (London: Faber & Faber, 1941).

Mitchell, Greg. *The Campaign of the Century: Upton Sinclair's Race for Governor of California and the Birth of Media Politics* (Random House, 1992).

Morgenthau, Henry III. *Mostly Morgenthaus: A Family History* (Ticknor & Fields, 1991).

Morris, Sylvia Jukes. *Edith Kermit Roosevelt: Portrait of a First Lady* (Coward, McCann & Geoghegan, 1980).

Murray, Pauli. *Song in a Weary Throat* (HarperCollins, 1987).

O'Neill, Elizabeth Stone. *Meadow in the Sky: A History of Yosemite's Tuolumne Meadows Region* (Albicaulis Press, 1984).

Orleck, Annelise. *Common Sense and a Little Fire: Women and Working Class Politics in the United States, 1900–1965* (University of North Carolina Press, 1995).

Paige, Jerome, and Margaret Reuss. "Safe, Decent and Affordable: Citizen Struggles to Improve Housing in the District of Columbia, 1890–1982." In Steven Diner and Helen Young, eds., *Housing Washington's People* (DC History and Public Policy Project, 1983).

Peck, Mary G. *Carrie Chapman Catt: A Biography* (H. W. Wilson, 1944).

Pickett, Clarence. *For More Than Bread* (Little, Brown, 1953).

Potts, Marjory. "Averell Harriman Remembers Mary," *Junior League Review* (1983).

Preis, Art. *Labor's Giant Step: 20 Years of the CIO* (Pathfinder, 1972).

Reed, Linda. *Simple Decency and Common Sense: The Southern Conference Movement, 1938–1963* (Indiana University Press, 1991).

Richmond, Al. *A Long View from the Left* (Houghton Mifflin, 1973).

Rosenberg, Rosalind. *Divided Lives: American Women in the Twentieth Century* (Hill & Wang, 1992).

Ross, B. Joyce. "Mary McLeod Bethune and the National Youth Administration: A Case Study." In Darlene Clark Hine et al., eds., *Black Women in US History*, Vol. IV (Carlson Publishing, 1991).

Ross, Ishbell. *Ladies of the Press* (Harper, 1936).

Rubin, Nancy. *American Empress: The Life and Times of Marjorie Meriweather Post* (Villard Books, 1995).

Rubinstein, Annette. "The Radical American Theatre of the Thirties," *Science & Society* (Fall 1986).

Rupp, Leila. *Worlds of Women: The Making of an International Women's Movement* (Princeton University Press, 1997).

St. Johns, Adela Rogers. *The Honeycomb: An Autobiography* (Doubleday, 1969).

Salmond, John. *Miss Lucy of the CIO: The Life and Times of Lucy Randolph Mason, 1882–1959* (University of Georgia Press, 1988).

———. *A Southern Rebel: The Life and Times of Aubrey Williams, 1890–1959* (University of North Carolina Press, 1983).

Sargent, Shirley. *Yosemite's Famous Guests* (Flying Spur, 1970).

Schapsmeier, Edward, and Frederic Schapsmeier. *Henry Wallace of Iowa: The Agrarian Years, 1910–1940* (University of Iowa Press, 1968).

Schulz, Constance B. "Samuel Dickstein: Congressional Investigator, 1934–1939" (Master's thesis, the College of Wooster, 1964).

Schwarz, Jordan A. *The Speculator: Bernard M. Baruch in Washington, 1917–1965* (University of North Carolina Press, 1981).

Sicherman, Barbara, ed. *Alice Hamilton: A Life in Letters* (Harvard University Press, 1984).

——— et al., eds. *Notable American Women* (Harvard University Press, 1980).

Sitkoff, Harvard. *A New Deal for Blacks: The Emergence of Civil Rights as a National Issue* (Oxford University Press, 1978).

Sklar, Kathryn Kish, ed. *The Autobiography of Florence Kelley: Notes of Sixty Years* (Charles H. Kerr, 1986).

———. *Florence Kelley and the Nation's Work* (Yale University Press, 1995).

Smith, Elaine. "Mary McLeod Bethune and the National Youth Administration." In Darlene Clark Hine et al., eds., *Black Women in U.S. History*, Vol. IV (Carlson Publishing, 1991).

Smith, Sally Bedell. *In All His Glory: The Life of William S. Paley* (Simon & Schuster, 1990).

Sternsher, Bernard. *Rexford Tugwell and the New Deal* (Rutgers University Press, 1964).

———, ed. *The Negro in Depression and War: Prelude to Revolution, 1930–1945* (Quadrangle Books, 1969).

———, and Judith Sealander, eds. *Women of Valor: The Struggle Against the Depression as Told in Their Own Life Stories* (Ivan R. Dee, 1990).

Strong, Tracy B., and Helene Keyssar. *Right in Her Soul: The Life of Anna Louise Strong* (Random House, 1983).

Suggs, Henry Lewis, ed. *The Black Press in the South, 1865–1979* (Greenwood, 1983).

Sullivan, Patricia. *Days of Hope: Race and Democracy in the New Deal Era* (University of North Carolina Press, 1996).

Swain, Martha H. *Ellen S. Woodward: New Deal Advocate for Women* (University of Mississippi Press, 1995).

Swanberg, W. A. *Whitney Father: Whitney Heiress* (Scribner's Sons, 1980).

Teague, Michael. *Mrs L: Conversations with Alice Roosevelt Longworth* (Doubleday, 1981).

Unofficial Observer [John Franklin Carter, aka Jay Franklin]. *The New Dealers* (Literary Guild, 1934).

Van Voris, Jacqueline. *Carrie Chapman Catt: A Public Life* (Feminist Press, 1987).

Ward, Bryan, ed. *A New Deal for America: Proceedings from a National Conference on New Deal Communities* (Arthurdale Heritage, 1995).

Ward, Patricia Spain. *Simon Baruch: Rebel in the Ranks of Medicine, 1840–1921* (University of Alabama Press, 1994).

———. "In Recognition of Esther Everett Lape," *Women and Health* (Summer 1980).

———. "United States v. American Medical Association, et al.: The Medical Anti-Trust Case of 1938–1943," *American Studies* (Fall 1989).

———. "Hugh Cabot: Medical Maverick," *Humanities: Magazine of the National Endowment of the Humanities* (March/April 1994).

Ware, Susan. *Beyond Suffrage: Women in the New Deal* (Harvard University Press, 1981).

———. *Holding Their Own: American Women in the 1930s* (Twayne, 1982).

———. *Partner and I: Molly Dewson, Feminism, and New Deal Politics* (Yale University Press, 1987).

———. *Still Missing: Amelia Earhart and the Search for Modern Feminism* (Norton, 1993).

Watkins, T. H. *The Great Depression: America in the 1930s* (Little, Brown, 1993).

———. *Righteous Pilgrim: The Life and Times of Harold Ickes, 1874–1952* (Henry Holt, 1990).

Weiss, Nancy. *Farewell to the Party of Lincoln: Black Politics in the Age of FDR* (Princeton University Press, 1983).

Whisnant, David. *All That Is Native and Fine: The Politics of Culture in an American Region* (University of North Carolina Press, 1986).

White, Walter. *A Man Called White* (Viking, 1948).

Whitman, Alden, ed. *American Reformers* (H. W. Wilson, 1985).

Williams, T. Harry. *Huey Long* (Louisiana State University Press, 1969).

Wilson, Joan Hoff. *Herbert Hoover: Forgotten Progressive* (Little, Brown, 1975).

Winter, Ella. *And Not to Yield: An Autobiography* (Harcourt, 1963).

Wolters, Raymond. *Negroes and the Great Depression* (Greenwood, 1970).

Zangrando, Robert L. *The NAACP Crusade Against Lynching, 1909–1950* (Temple University Press, 1980).

Zinn, Howard, ed. *New Deal Thought* (Bobbs-Merrill, 1966).

COLLECTIVE SECURITY OR ISOLATION:
THE INTERNATIONAL DIMENSIONS OF 1933–1938

Abella, Irving, and Harold Troper. *None Is Too Many: Canada and the Jews of Europe, 1933–1948* (Random House, 1982).

Accinelli, Robert. "The Roosevelt Administration and the World Court Defeat, 1935," *The Historian* (May 1978).

Adler, Selig. *The Isolationist Impulse* (Collier, 1961).

———. *The Uncertain Giant: American Foreign Policy Between the Wars, 1921–1941* (Macmillan, 1965).

Armstrong, Hamilton Fish. *Peace and Counter-Peace: From Wilson to Hitler, Memoirs* (Harper & Row, 1971).

Bacon, Margaret Hope. *One Woman's Passion for Peace and Freedom: The Life of Mildred Scott Olmstead* (Syracuse University Press, 1993).

Baigell, Matthew, and Julia Williams, eds. *Artists Against War and Fascism: Papers of the First American Artists' Congress* (Rutgers University Press, 1986).

Berenbaum, Richard. *The World Must Know: The History of the Holocaust as Told in the US Holocaust Memorial Museum* (Little, Brown, 1993).

Berry, Paul, and Alan Bishop, eds. *Testament of a Generation: The Journalism of Vera Brittain and Winifred Holtby* (Virago, 1985).

Borg, Dorothy. *The US and the Far Eastern Crisis of 1933–1938* (Harvard University Press, 1964).

———. "Notes on FDR's Quarantine Speech," *Political Science Quarterly* (Sept. 1957).

Bridenthal, Renate, Atina Grossmann, and Marion Kaplan, eds. *When Biology Becomes Destiny: Women in Weimar and Nazi Germany* (Monthly Review Press, 1984).

Bullitt, Orville H., ed. *For the President: Personal and Secret, the Letters of William Bullitt* (Houghton Mifflin, 1972).

Bullock, Alan. *Hitler: A Study in Tyranny* (Harper Torchbooks, 1962).

Bussey, Gertrude, and Margaret Tims. *Women's International League for Peace and Freedom, 1915–1965* (London: George Allen & Unwin, 1965).

Chang, Iris. *The Rape of Nanking* (Penguin, 1997).

Chase, James. *Acheson: The Secretary of State Who Created the American World* (Simon & Schuster, 1998).

Chatfield, Charles. *For Peace and Justice: Pacifism in America, 1914–1941* (University of Tennessee Press, 1971).

———, ed. *Peace Movements in America* (Schocken Books, 1973).

Churchill, Winston S. *The Gathering Storm* (Houghton Mifflin, 1948).

Cole, Wayne S. *Senator Gerald P. Nye and American Foreign Relations* (University of Minnesota Press, 1962).

Cooper, Sandi E. "Pacifism, Feminism, and Fascism in Inter-War France," *International History Review* (February 1997).

———. "Women in War and Peace, 1914–1945." In Renate Bridenthal, Susan Mosher Stuard, Merry Wiesner, eds., *Becoming Visible: Women in European History* (Houghton Mifflin, 1998).

Craig, Gordon, and Felix Gilbert. *The Diplomats: The Thirties*, vol. II (Atheneum, 1963).

Dallek, Robert. *Franklin D. Roosevelt and American Foreign Policy* (Oxford University Press, 1979).

Davies, Joseph. *Mission to Moscow* (Simon & Schuster, 1941).

Divine, Robert A. *The Illusion of Neutrality: Franklin D. Roosevelt and the Struggle over the Arms Embargo* (Quadrangle Paperbacks, 1962).

Dodd, William, Jr., and Martha Dodd, eds. *Ambassador Dodd's Diary, 1933–1938* (Harcourt, Brace, 1940).

Dulles, Foster Rhea. *America's Rise to World Power, 1898–1954* (Harper Torchbooks, 1954).

Feis, Herbert. *1933: Characters in Crisis* (Little, Brown, 1966).

———. *The Road to Pearl Harbor* (Atheneum, 1964).

———. *The Spanish Story: Franco and the Nations at War* (Norton, 1966).

Fink, Carole. *Marc Bloch: A Life in History* (Cambridge University Press, 1989).

Foster, Carrie A. *The Women and the Warriors: The US Section of the Women's International League for Peace and Freedom, 1915–1946* (Syracuse University Press, 1995).

Gellman, Irwin. *Secret Affairs: Franklin Roosevelt, Cordell Hull, and Sumner Welles* (Johns Hopkins University Press, 1995).

Gilbert, Martin. *Churchill: A Life* (Henry Holt, 1991). The official biographer's one-volume essential life derived from his eight-volume masterpiece.

Gronowicz, Anthony, ed. *Oswald Garrison Villard: The Dilemmas of the Absolute Pacifist in Two World Wars* (Garland, 1983).

Grose, Peter. *Israel in the Mind of America* (Knopf, 1983).

Guttmann, Allen. *The Wound in the Heart: The U.S. and the Spanish Civil War* (Free Press, 1962).

Heinrichs, Waldo. *American Ambassador: Joseph Grew and the Development of the U.S. Diplomatic Tradition* (Little, Brown, 1966).

Hoff-Wilson, Joan. *American Business and Foreign Policy, 1920–1933* (Beacon, 1971).

Israel, Fred L., ed. *The War Diary of Breckinridge Long* (University of Nebraska Press, 1966).

Jonas, Manfred. *Isolationism in America, 1935–1941* (Cornell University Press, 1966).

Jordan, Nicole. *The Popular Front and Central Europe: The Dilemmas of French Impotence, 1918–1940* (Cambridge University Press, 1992).

Kahn, Gilbert N. "Presidential Passivity on a Nonsalient Issue: President Franklin D. Roosevelt and the 1935 World Court Fight," *Diplomatic History* (Spring 1980).

Katz, William Loren, and Marc Crawford: *The Lincoln Brigade: A Picture History* (Atheneum, 1989).

Kelley, Robin D. G. " 'This Ain't Ethiopia, But It'll Do': African-Americans and the Spanish Civil War." In Kelley, *Race Rebels: Culture, Politics, and the Black Working Class* (Free Press, 1996).

Koonz, Claudia. *Mothers in the Fatherland: Women, the Family, and Nazi Ideology, 1919–1945* (St. Martins, 1987).

Landis, Arthur H. *Spain! The Unfinished Revolution* (Camelot, 1972).

Leibovitz, Clement, and Alvin Finkel. *In Our Time: The Chamberlain-Hitler Collusion* (Monthly Review Press, 1998).

Liggio, Leonard, and James J. Martin, eds. *Watershed of Empire: Essays on New Deal Foreign Policy* (Ralph Myles, 1976).

Lipstadt, Deborah E. *Beyond Belief: The American Press and the Coming of the Holocaust, 1933–1945* (Free Press, 1986).

Maddox, Robert James. *William E. Borah and American Foreign Policy* (Louisiana State University Press, 1969).

Manchester, William. *The Last Lion: Winston Spencer Churchill, Alone, 1932–1940* (Little, Brown, 1988).

Mandell, Richard. *The Nazi Olympics* (University of Illinois Press, 1987).

Marrus, Michael, and Robert Paxton. *Vichy France and the Jews* (Basic Books, 1981).

Matthews, Herbert L. *Half of Spain Died: A Reappraisal of the Spanish Civil War* (Scribner's, 1973).

Meyer, Howard N. "A Global Look at Law and Order: The World Court at the UN's 50th Anniversary," *Social Education* (November/December 1994).

Morse, Arthur D. *While Six Million Died: A Chronicle of American Apathy* (Random House, 1968).

Neumann, William L. "FDR and Japan, 1913–1933," *Pacific Historical Review* (May 1953).

―――. *America Encounters Japan. From Perry to MacArthur* (Johns Hopkins University Press, 1963).

Nichols, Jeannette P. "Roosevelt's Monetary Diplomacy in 1933," *American Historical Review* (January 1951).

Nicolson, Harold. *Diaries and Letters, 1930–1939*, ed. Nigel Nicolson (Atheneum, 1966).

Nicolson, Nigel, ed. *Vita and Harold: The Letters of Vita Sackville-West and Harold Nicolson* (Putnam's Sons, 1992).

Nixon, Edgar B., ed. *FDR and Foreign Affairs*, 3 vols. (Harvard University Press, 1969).

Offner, Arnold A. *American Appeasement: United States Foreign Policy and Germany, 1933–1938* (Harvard University Press, 1969).

―――. "Appeasement Revisited: The U.S., Great Britain and Germany, 1933–1940," *Journal of American History* (September 1977).

Patterson, David S. "The United States and the Origins of the World Court," *Political Science Quarterly* (Summer 1976).

Pois, Anne-Marie. "The Process and Politics of Organizing for Peace: The U.S. Section of the WILPF, 1919–1939" (Ph.D. dissertation, University of Colorado, 1988).

Pulzer, Peter. *The Rise of Political Anti-Semitism in Germany and Austria* (Wiley, 1964).

Roosevelt, Daniel Stewart. "Wings over Spain." In Hall Roosevelt with Samuel McCoy, *Odyssey of an American Family: An Account of the Roosevelts as Travelers* (Harper, 1939).

Rosenberg, Emily. *Spreading the American Dream: American Economic and Cultural Expansion, 1890–1945* (Hill & Wang, 1982).

Rosenstone, Robert. *Crusade of the Left: The Lincoln Batallion in the Spanish Civil War* (Pegasus, 1969).

Shirer, William L. *Berlin Diary: The Journal of a Foreign Correspondent, 1934–1941* (Galahad Books, 1995 [1941]).

Stansky, Peter, and William Abrahams. *Journey to the Frontier: Two Roads to the Spanish Civil War* (Norton, 1966).

Sternsher, Bernard. "The Stimson Doctrine: FDR vs Moley and Tugwell," *Pacific Historical Review* (August 1962).

Sykes, Christopher. *Nancy: The Life of Lady Astor* (Harper & Row, 1972).

Thomas, Gordon, and Max Morgan Witts. *Guernica: The Crucible of World War II* (Stein and Day, 1975).

Thomas, Hugh. *The Spanish Civil War* (Harper, 1961).

Weinberg, Robert. *Stalin's Forgotten Zion: Birobidzhan and the Making of a Soviet Jewish Homeland, an Illustrated History, 1928–1996* (University of California Press, 1998).

Weitz, John. *Hjalmar Horace Greeley Schacht: Hitler's Banker* (Little, Brown, 1997).

Welles, Benjamin. *Sumner Welles: FDR's Global Strategist, a Biography* (St. Martin's, 1997).

Welles, Sumner. *The Time for Decision* (Harper & Brothers, 1944).

Williams, William Appleman. *American-Russian Relations, 1781–1947* (Rinehart, 1952).

Wittner, Larry. *Rebels Against War: The American Peace Movement, 1933–1983* (Temple University Press, 1984).

Wyman, David. *Paper Walls: America and the Refugee Crisis, 1938–1941* (Pantheon, 1985 [1968]).

INDEX

Abbott, Grace, 130
Acheson, Dean, 107, 109
Adams, Henry, 13, 73
Addams, Jane, 3, 49, 61, 67, 78, 123, 127,
    128, 135, 236, 259, 263, 304, 322n,
    514, 516; in peace movement, 5, 49,
    111, 113, 122, 239; social security
    and, 234, 235, 247
Advisory Committee on Economic
    Security, 218, 234, 248–49
African-Americans, 57–58, 152–89,
    254–57, 333, 566; Arthurdale and,
    138–40, 153; in Congress, 19, 88;
    election of 1936 and, 335, 345–46,
    379–80, 408; ER's alliances with, 4,
    153–54, 160–61, 176–81, 183, 188,
    226, 243–47, 288, 314; New Deal
    and, 75–76, 78, 88, 90, 129, 138–40,
    153, 226, 247, 248, 254–55, 268, 270,
    278–80, 282, 288, 291–93, 345–46,
    407–8, 460–61; see also antilynching
    legislation; civil rights movement
Afro-American, 565
Aftermath, The (Churchill), 549
Agnew, Ella, 244–45
Agricultural Adjustment Act (AAA),
    81–82, 247, 336–37, 412
Agriculture Department, U.S., 14–15, 60,
    81–83
Albert, King of Belgium, 205–6
Alexander, Will, 154, 178, 282, 379, 380
Alfonso XIII, King of Spain, 454
Alinsky, Saul, 429
Allen, Florence E., 68, 239
Allen, Jay, 504
Allenswood, 2, 3, 20, 41
Alley Dwelling Authority (ADA), 189, 349

alley dwelling bill, 157–58, 166, 167, 176,
    188
Alsberg, Henry, 267
Alsop, Corinne Robinson, 16, 341
Amateur Air Pilots Association, 50
America First, 225–26
American Association of University
    Women, 562–63
American Civil Liberties Union (ACLU),
    128, 180
American Federation of Labor, 150, 314,
    424, 557
American Foundation, 11, 97, 114, 236,
    242, 433, 464
American Friends Service Committee
    (AFSC), 129, 133, 137–41, 184, 202,
    309, 453, 505, 543, 544
American Jewish Congress, 314, 321–22
American Medical Association (AMA),
    62, 417
American Red Cross, 558
American Student Union, 280, 511
American Union Against Militarism, 49
American Youth Act, 504
American Youth Congress (AYC), 4, 6,
    278, 280, 341, 504, 511–14, 520, 522,
    562, 566, 573
Ames, Jessie Daniel, 178–79
anticommunism, 6, 60, 81, 259, 281;
    Arthurdale and, 138, 143–46; Bonus
    Marchers and, 45, 46; labor unrest
    and, 131, 209–10n, 220, 426, 427,
    430; women's network and, 61, 62
antilynching legislation, 160, 176–81, 188,
    226, 243–47, 256, 279, 346, 391,
    408–9, 440–43, 510–11, 568
anti-Semitism, 240, 295, 309–18, 319–21,

anti-Semitism (*cont.*)
    323–25, 376, 497; in Austria, 490,
    500, 502–3; in Nazi Germany, 5–6,
    118–19, 122–24, 125–26, 162, 303–5,
    307, 309–13, 320–25, 328–29, 561; in
    State Department, 543–44, 559
"Appeal to the Nations" (F. D. Roosevelt),
    100
Argentina, 399, 400, 517
Armstrong, Hamilton Fish, 95, 444, 455
Armwood, George, 180
Army, U.S., 45, 91, 210*n*
Arthur, Richard, 134
Arthurdale project, 129, 133–52, 157, 164,
    166, 173, 188, 189, 201, 204–5,
    215–16, 255, 299, 300, 351, 476, 527,
    532, 563
Associated Press (AP), 12, 39, 43, 65, 95,
    116, 169
Association of Southern Women for the
    Prevention of Lynching, 178–79
Astor, Nancy Langhorne, 65, 95, 216,
    500–502
Astor, Vincent, 95, 184–85, 254
Astor, Waldorf, 110
Augsburg, Anita, 122
Australia, 517, 561
Austria, 26, 119, 126, 134, 248*n*, 310,
    324–25, 499, 517, 570; German
    Anschluss of, 490–91, 559; Jews of,
    490, 500, 502–3, 543

Babies—Just Babies, 21–22
Bach, Mme. Kraemer, 118
Backer, Dorothy Schiff, 373, 501
Baeck, Leo, 311
Baer, Gertrude, 122
Baker, Elizabeth, 549–50
Baker, Joseph, 336–38
Baker, Mary, 350
Baker, Ray Stannard, 103
Baldwin, Joseph Clark, 394, 423
Baldwin, Roger, 128, 426
Baldwin, Stanley, 287*n*, 401
Ballad of Black Jim, The (Eisler and
    Brecht), 499
Bankhead-Jones bill, 462
Banking Act (1933), 70
Barber, Philip, 336
Barton, Bruce, 364–65
"Barton, Jack," hearings on, 427
Baruch, Annie Griffen, 318, 319, 320, 486

Baruch, Belle Wolfe, 319
Baruch, Bernard, 77, 140–42, 148–51, 300,
    308, 317–20, 356, 405, 411–12, 450,
    470, 486, 515, 528; Jewish question
    and, 305, 312, 320; London
    Conference and, 105, 106, 107, 109
Baruch, Herman, 525, 528
Baruch, Simon, 319
Batista, Fulgencio, 173, 400
Beale, Howard K., 186
Beard, Mary Ritter, 75
Beatty, Bessie, 373
"Because the War Idea Is Obsolete"
    (Eleanor Roosevelt), 238–39
Beer and Wine Act (1933), 76
Belgium, 107, 205–6, 498, 562
Bell, Vanessa, 540
Beneš, Edvard, 541
Benét, Stephen Vincent, 117
Berge, Otto, 361
Berle, A. A., 15, 521
Bernstein, Doris, 497
Bessie, Alvah, 508
Bethune, Albert, 159–60
Bethune, Mary McLeod, 4, 159–61, 280,
    379, 380, 412, 513, 565, 566, 567*n*,
    568; National Youth Administration
    and, 270, 278
Beyer, Clara, 62
Biddle, George, 332
Bingham, Robert, 36, 63, 361
Birth of a Baby, 514
Black, Hugo, 475, 568
Black, Josephine Foster, 475
Black, Ruby, 82, 169, 173, 195
Black Cabinet, 160
Black Reconstruction (Du Bois), 293
Blum, León, 401, 557, 576
Boettiger, Anna Roosevelt Dall, 13–14, 47,
    79, 166, 174, 221; employment of,
    21, 115, 394, 395, 427; ER's
    correspondence with, 203, 230, 288,
    290, 379, 385, 389, 396, 405, 411,
    414, 419, 433, 437, 438, 458, 466–67,
    475, 485, 495, 519–20, 531, 547–48,
    552; ER's relationship with, 394,
    445–46, 482–83; Hick's
    correspondence with, 198, 294–95;
    John Boettiger's relationship with,
    31, 194, 202, 216, 221, 235; marital
    problems of, 31, 116, 192, 194, 199,
    200; Tommy's correspondence with,

672   Index

election of 1934, 146, 147, 211, 218, 221–25, 345, 380; World Court and, 237
election of 1936, 255–56, 257, 281, 291, 292, 334–53, 363–88, 407, 408, 426, 441, 447, 454, 569; Democratic convention in, 346, 361, 366–72; Hearst and, 387, 394–95
election of 1938, 463, 538, 554, 555
election of 1940, 16
Elmhirst, Dorothy Payne Whitney Straight, 141
Ely, Gertrude, 215–16, 543
Emergency Relief Act (1933), 84
Emergency Unemployment Relief Committee, 24
End Poverty in California (EPIC), 145–47, 292
England, 2, 20, 113, 134, 248n, 403, 443, 453, 470, 471, 473, 489, 491, 498, 506, 562; Ethiopian crisis and, 286–87, 331; financial problems of, 26, 92, 101–2, 306; London Conference and, 48, 49, 101–3, 107–8, 112, 113, 127; Nazi Germany, appeasement and, 6, 49, 100, 286–87, 303, 305, 320, 331, 502, 517, 539, 540, 542; Spanish Civil War and, 401; U.S. relations with, 48–49, 92, 101–2, 103, 112, 113, 127, 306
Enright, Adel, 364
environmental issues, 7, 64, 69, 83
Epstein, Szmul Elia, 344
Equal Rights Amendment, 77, 78
Ethiopia crisis, 283–88, 331, 335–36, 341, 454, 470, 489, 549
Evian Conference, 511, 517, 560, 561

Factory Investigating Commission (FIC), 77
Fairfax, John, 134
Fair Labor Standards Act (1938), 266, 515–16
Farley, Elizabeth Ann, 53
Farley, James A., 57–58, 67, 68, 69, 407–8, 432, 474, 569; election of 1936 and, 291, 346, 367–69, 370, 375, 377, 378, 379
Farm Credit Administration, 81
Farm Resettlement Administration, 82
Farm Security Administration, 497
fascism, 4, 5, 6, 9, 10, 81, 113, 449, 548–50,

573; in U.S., 183, 240, 307, 376; see also Germany, Nazi
Fauset, Crystal Bird, 184–85, 407
Federal Bureau of Investigation (FBI), 455
Federal Council of Churches of Christ, 180, 196n
Federal Emergency Relief Administration (FERA), 82, 84, 89, 247; Hick's job at, 116, 119–20, 129, 130–31, 145, 146, 161–68, 172–76, 181–84, 187, 207–8, 215, 231, 393; racial justice and, 154, 159, 186; Women's Division of, 86–88
Federal Rural Housing Authority, 568
Federal Surplus Commodities Corporation, 82
Federal Theater, 267–68, 448–49, 523n
Federation of Jewish Women's Organizations, 321–22
Feuchtwanger, Lion, 97–98
Few, Marguerite Baxter, 541
Finland, 102, 110, 248n, 306n
Finney, Ruth, 82
Fish, Hamilton, 440–41
Fisher, Dorothy Canfield, 227, 239, 480
Flanagan, Hallie, 267–68, 335–36, 422, 448, 449, 463, 523n, 555
Fleeson, Doris, 461
Forbush, Gabrielle, 413
Ford, Henry, 320
Foreign Policy Association, 118
Foreman, Clark, 510, 564
Forrer, Emil, 543
Forster, Rudolph, 279
Fox, Eddie, 121–22, 216, 255
Fox, George, 35
France, 17, 49, 113, 134, 248n, 310, 318, 443, 453, 470, 473, 488, 491, 505–6, 517, 539, 540, 542, 562, 576; Ethiopian crisis and, 286–87; financial problems of, 26, 92, 101–2, 306; Germany and, 100, 303, 309, 410; London Conference and, 107–8; Spanish Civil War and, 401; U.S. relations with, 306, 309
Frances, Bar, 204
Franco, Francisco, 331–32, 401, 409, 410, 445, 452, 454, 455, 467, 491, 507
Frankfurter, Felix, 29–30, 128, 149, 292, 304, 317, 323–25, 354, 501–2
Frankfurter, Solomon, 501–2

and, *see specific elections;* emotional life of, 2, 5, 41, 52, 56, 58, 94–97, 184, 190–213, 214–21, 252–54, 260–61, 384; evolving racial views of, 161, 244–45, 439–40; family background of, 3–4, 23, 25, 155–56, 197, 230; family tensions of, 13, 16, 20–21, 31–32, 41, 55–56, 94–97, 116, 191–92, 197, 200, 246–47, 255–56, 260–61, 269, 353–54, 410–11, 438–39; feminist activism of, 3, 60–91, 118–19, 170, 173, 187, 338–39, 456–57, 513; foreign policy views of, 5–6, 11, 48, 49, 97, 102–3, 114, 192–93, 283–88, 303–5, 309–12, 330–32; gift giving of, 120, 141–42, 200, 414, 421; gifts received by, 34, 56, 79, 140, 318, 319, 393, 411–12, 448, 476, 508, 551–52; as grandmother, 22, 56, 193, 340; Greenwich Village hideaway of, 2, 294–95, 298, 362; horseback riding of, 34, 36, 37, 66, 96, 121, 195, 204, 207, 215, 476, 519, 552; internationalism of, 11, 97, 103, 114, 235–42, 283–84, 305–6, 341–42; jealousy of, 199–200, 356; labor unrest and, 424–25, 463, 465–66; lecturing of, 3, 168, 341–42, 388–93, 434, 435–37, 438, 447, 484, 492, 494–96, 550, 553; loneliness of, 3, 9, 38, 42, 144–45, 165, 192, 251–52, 356, 364; love as viewed by, 5, 22, 38, 229, 260–61; mentors of, 2, 3, 53, 61, 118–19, 231; as mother, 1, 3, 5, 21–23, 31–32, 41, 66, 94–97, 192, 235; nominated for governor of New York, 552; passive-aggressive behavior of, 2–3, 55–57; peace movement and, 5, 45–46, 60, 111, 118–19, 238–39, 330–31, 341–42, 452, 488, 492–95, 501; presidential ambitions and, 351; pro-Jewish activities of, 314, 321–23, 328, 329–30, 344; radio broadcasts of, 10, 12, 21, 201–2, 238, 240, 250–51, 301, 339, 356, 445, 457; reading of, 117, 203, 238, 274, 293; refugee efforts of, 5, 128, 344, 445, 452–53, 471, 543, 544, 562; self-awareness of, 518–19, 563; as silent about German Jews, 303–5, 309–12, 327–29; speeches of,

5–6, 24, 47, 50, 65, 118–19, 156, 170, 185–87, 222, 224, 225, 238–39, 249–50, 259, 262, 291, 301, 321–23, 327–28, 339, 348–49, 388, 391–92, 420, 425, 493, 494, 509–10, 513, 562–63, 565; swimming of, 34–35, 204, 206, 212–13, 215; teas and receptions of, 32, 34, 35, 51, 54, 96, 145, 432–33; theater interest of, 447–50; vacations of, 1, 93, 106–7, 115–18, 120–22, 154–56, 202–13, 216, 273–74, 301, 423; wardrobe of, 13–14, 28, 79, 224–25, 291, 386, 563; in Warm Springs, 154–55, 195, 229–31; White House conferences organized by, 86, 90, 156; women-only press conferences of, 1, 24, 40–41, 46, 56, 65–66, 96, 103, 112, 142, 188, 241, 250, 261–62, 292, 348, 363, 421, 424; women's network and, 43–44, 60–69, 234; Women's Trade Union League and, 43–44, 62, 65, 77, 86, 220, 347, 424; youth movement and, 509, 511–14, 520, 564

Roosevelt, Archibald (cousin), 25
Roosevelt, Betsey Cushing (daughter-in-law), 13, 55, 219, 354, 436, 483, 538, 553; ER's resentment of, 438–39, 539; FDR's relationship with, 439, 495, 496
Roosevelt, Betty Donner (daughter-in-law), 13, 32, 94, 95, 200
Roosevelt, Daniel (nephew), 505–8, 525, 535
Roosevelt, Edith (aunt), 19–20
Roosevelt, Eleanor, II (niece), 575
Roosevelt, Elliott (father), 2, 4, 21, 120, 197, 199, 207, 230, 435, 482; death of, 4, 23, 217; ER's correspondence with, 2, 41; ER's tributes to, 23–25
Roosevelt, Elliott (son), 13, 116, 435, 482; family abandoned by, 31–32, 94–97; second marriage of, 175
Roosevelt, Franklin Delano (husband): anniversary of, 44; anticommunism and, 81, 143, 387, 426; antilynching legislation and, 440–43; Arthurdale and, 133, 135–36, 140, 142–43, 157; assassination attempt against, 27–28; as assistant secretary of Navy, 39; birthdays of, 16, 47, 166, 242, 420–21, 425; Caribbean issues and,